Fodor's

AUSTRIA
11TH EDITION

Where to Stay and Eat
for All Budgets

Must-See Sights
and Local Secrets

Ratings You Can Trust

Fodor's Travel Publications   New York, Toronto, London, Sydney, Auckland
www.fodors.com

FODOR'S AUSTRIA

Editor: Robert I. C. Fisher, Amy Wang

Editorial Production: Jacinta O'Halloran

Editorial Contributors: Bonnie Dodson, Gary Dodson, Diane Naar-Elphee, Horst Ernst Reisenböck

Maps: David Lindroth, *cartographer;* Rebecca Baer and Bob Blake, *map editors*

Design: Fabrizio La Rocca, *creative director;* Guido Caroti, *art director;* Moon Sun Kim, *cover designer;* Melanie Marin, *senior picture editor*

Production/Manufacturing: Colleen Ziemba

Cover Photo:(Abtenau, Lammertal Valley, Tennengau, Salzburg region): Schmid Reinhard/Fototeca 9x12

COPYRIGHT

SPECIAL SALES

This book is available for special discounts for bulk purchases for sales promotions or premiums. Special editions, including personalized covers, excerpts of existing books, and corporate imprints, can be created in large quantities for special needs. For more information, write to Special Markets/Premium Sales, 1745 Broadway, MD 6-2, New York, New York 10019, or e-mail specialmarkets@randomhouse.com.

AN IMPORTANT TIP & AN INVITATION

Although all prices, opening times, and other details in this book are based on information supplied to us at press time, changes occur all the time in the travel world, and Fodor's cannot accept responsibility for facts that become outdated or for inadvertent errors or omissions. So **always confirm information when it matters,** especially if you're making a detour to visit a specific place. Your experiences—positive and negative—matter to us. If we have missed or misstated something, **please write to us.** We follow up on all suggestions. Contact the Austria editor at editors@fodors.com or c/o Fodor's at 1745 Broadway, New York, New York 10019.

DESTINATION: AUSTRIA

Think of Austria and you think of operettas and psychoanalysis, Apfelstrudel and marble staircases, Strauss waltzes and Schubert melodies. Baroque and imperial, this is a white-gloved country where Lipizzaner horses still prance to a string minuet and whose headwaiters still bow as though addressing a Habsburg prince. With a heart that beats in three-quarters time, Vienna is a capital filled with grandiose cupolas, stage-set plazas, and time-burnished coffeehouses where you can enjoy the chocolate and whipped cream fantasies of Austrian sugar bakers. Or you can savor the champagne-splashed whirl of Salzburg, which is pulling out all the stops in 2006 to honor the 250th birthday of its most famous home boy, Mozart. If you prefer Rodgers & Hammerstein, just head to the nearby Lake District, immortalized in all its Hollywoodian splendor in *The Sound of Music*—this region is still filled with plenty of villages just too adorable to be taken very seriously. Wherever you journey, you'll soon discover that Austria's *gemütlichkeit* is more *gemütlich* than anyone else's.

Tim Jarrell, Publisher

CONTENTS

On the Road with Fodor's *F7*
About This Book *F10*
What's Where *F12*
Great Itineraries *F18*
When to Go *F22*

On the Calendar *F23*
Pleasures & Pastimes *F25*
Fodor's Choice *F30*
Smart Travel Tips *F34*

1 Vienna   1

Exploring Vienna *5*
The Inner City: Historic Heart
  of Vienna *11*
Bittersweet Vienna: Baroque
  Gems & Cozy Cafés *21*
Vienna's Shop Window: From
  Michaelerplatz to the
  Graben *29*
An Imperial City:
  The Hofburg *33*
The Ringstrasse: Gems
  of the "Ring" *40*
Monarchs & Mozart: From
  St. Stephan's to the
  Opera House *51*

Pomp & Circumstance:
  South of the Ring to the
  Belvedere *55*
Splendors of the Habsburgs:
  A Visit to Schönbrunn
  Palace *62*
Where to Eat *67*
Where to Stay *91*
Nightlife & the Arts *104*
Sports & Outdoor
  Activities *113*
Shopping *114*
Vienna A to Z *122*

2 Side Trips from Vienna   130

On the Road to Baden &
  Mayerling *136*
The Weinviertel *141*

Side Trips from Vienna
  A to Z *147*

3 Eastern Austria   149

Land of Castles *155*
Graz and Its Environs *169*

Through Styria to Vienna *183*
Eastern Austria A to Z *192*

4 The Danube Valley   196

The Wachau: Along the North
  Bank of the Danube *200*
Linz *214*
Excursions from Linz *226*

The Wachau: Along the South
  Bank of the Danube *230*
Danube Valley A to Z *237*

5 Salzburg   240

Exploring Salzburg *244*
Where to Eat *270*
Where to Stay *277*

Nightlife & the Arts *285*
Shopping *288*
Salzburg A to Z *289*

6 Salzkammergut 294

On the Road to
St. Wolfgang &
Bad Ischl *300*

Gosau, Hallstatt, &
Bad Aussee *316*
Salzkammergut A to Z *324*

7 Carinthia 328

Klagenfurt & the Southern
Lakes *332*

The Gurktal Region *345*
Carinthia A to Z *353*

8 Eastern Alps 355

To Lienz, Up the Defereggental,
& Back *359*
Across the Grossglockner
Pass *367*

Mountain Spas & Alpine
Rambles *376*
Eastern Alps A to Z *386*

9 Innsbruck and Tirol 389

Innsbruck *397*
Around the Lower Inn
Valley *411*
On the Road to Kitzbühel *416*

West from Innsbruck *424*
Landeck, Upper Inn Valley,
& St. Anton *429*
Innsbruck & Tirol A to Z *433*

10 Vorarlberg 438

Bregenz *444*
Through the Bregenzerwald to
Bludenz & Feldkirch *449*

The Arlberg & Montafon
Resorts *454*
Vorarlberg A to Z *460*

Understanding Austria 463

Do I Hear a Waltz? *464*
Powder-Perfect Skiing *467*
Austria at a Glance *474*
Books & Movies *476*

Chronology *477*
Words and Phrases *481*
Menu Guide *485*

Index 488

Maps

Austria *F9*
Exploring Vienna *14–15*
The Hofburg (Imperial
    Palace) *36*
Schönbrunn Palace & Park *64*
Where to Eat in Vienna *68–69*
Where to Stay in Vienna *92–93*
Vienna Shopping *116–117*
Vienna Subways *127*
Baden & Environs *134*
The Weinviertel *142*
Burgenland *154*
Graz *172*
Eastern Styria & Lower
    Austria *184*
Lower Danube Valley *201*

Upper Danube Valley *202*
Linz *216*
Salzburg *230*
Where to Stay & Eat in
    Salzburg *272–273*
Salzkammergut/The Lake
    District *299*
Carinthia *335*
Eastern Alps *360–361*
Eastern Tirol *394*
Western Tirol *396*
Innsbruck *399*
Where to Stay & Eat in
    Innsbruck *404*
Voralberg *440*
Ski Areas *470–471*

Close-Up Boxes

Mozart, Mozart, Mozart! *19*
Tracking Down the Third
    Man *28*
The "Neue" City *45*
A Hop through Hip Vienna *49*
Wine-Wien-Wein-Vienna *85*
Vienna's Sweetest Vice *90*
Just Like Taking Candy from
    Mozart! *109*
A Glittering Trove *119*

The Castle Road *166*
Grape Expectations *207*
On a Clear Day You Can Flee
    Forever *221*
"Oh, The Hills are
    Alive . . ." *260*
Mozart: Marvel & Mystery *255*
Happy Birthday, Wolferl! *266*
Hannibal on Ice *427*

A trip takes you out of yourself. Concerns of life at home completely disappear, driven away by more immediate thoughts—about, say, what marvels will beguile the next day, or where you'll have dinner. That's where Fodor's comes in. We make sure that you know all your options, so that you don't miss something that's around the next bend just because you didn't know it was there. Because the best memories of your trip might well have nothing to do with what you came to Ireland to see, we guide you to sights large and small all over the region. You might set out to savor the sublime paintings by Pieter Brueghel in Vienna's Kunsthistoriches Museum but back at home you find yourself unable to forget experiencing high noon at the city's Clock Museum, when more than 3,000 cuckoo-clocks, wall-pieces, and watches peal forth with full cacophony. With Fodor's at your side, such serendipitous discoveries are never far away.

Our success in showing you the most fascinating corners of Austria is a credit to our extraordinary writers. Although there's no substitute for travel advice from a good friend who knows your style, our contributors are the next best thing—the kind of people you would poll for travel advice if you knew them.

Just when Bonnie Dodson thinks she's seen everything Austria has to offer, she makes another discovery. That's one of the happy end results of her work on several editions of this book (for this edition, she updated the Exploring and Where to Stay sections of the Vienna chapter, along with our Smart Travel Tips chapter and the regional chapters of Side Trips from Vienna, Eastern Austria, the Danube Valley, and Carinthia). A native of Minneapolis with a graduate degree in writing, Bonnie moved to Vienna eight years ago with her husband and still gets a thrill every time she walks around the cobblestone streets of the historic First District. Like a true Viennese, she believes that coffee-drinking is a life's work. Updating our section on Vienna's cafés, she rarely could resist stopping into her favorite coffeehouses for a *Mazagran*—a melange with a dollop of whipped cream—and, of course, for the latest city news and gossip. Doing research for this edition also involved lots of driving, making the best of snowy mountain roads, and lots of good eating. Bonnie's husband, Gary Dodson, has worked around the globe and speaks five languages. His passions are travel, wine, movies, and Mozart, and he enjoys partaking of all four in Austria.

Diane Naar-Elphee adores her "adopted" Vienna, having lived in the imperial city since she left her native Yorkshire in the early 1970s. As a guide-lecturer, she has shared her passion with many travelers (including Mary Tyler Moore and Dick Cavett) on her private, bespoke tours through historic Vienna. Nowadays, Diane has broadened her horizons—sheparding travelers through the Balkans, for instance—and now finds as much pleasure extolling the beauty of Alt Wien on paper rather than over the microphone. "Vienna is a village—*everyone* is familiar," she laughs. "That particular feeling of intimacy is what makes it so special." So much so that she's been able to rub shoulders with José Carreras, Dame Joan Sutherland, and, only very recently, Thomas Quasthoff, since she considers the fabled Vienna State Opera house her home-away-from-home. But then there's always that cozy coffeehouse waiting just around the corner, and if you look long enough, you'll probably find Diane there, editing or updating one of the many guide books her husband Walter has written. For this edition, she has updated our Where to Eat, Nightlife & the Arts, and Shopping sections of the Vienna chapter.

It was the siren song of the mountains that drew Lee Hogan to the Austrian Alps. An amateur bicycle racer since the early

1970s, Lee was spellbound by scenes of professional cyclists challenging the high Alpine passes in Europe. Since arriving in Innsbruck four years ago, he has been busy discovering the mountain roads in Austria, northern Italy, and Bavaria. "Seeing things from the seat of a bicycle has always been my favorite way to travel," says Lee. "The pace is slow enough that you can really see where you are, and it is always fun to stop for coffee and strudel and talk with the locals." Talking comes easy for Lee, who stateside was a radio broadcaster since getting a graduate degree in journalism two decades ago. In addition to his work on this edition (he updated our chapters on the Eastern Alps, Innsbruck and Tirol, and Vorarlberg, and section on "Powder-Perfect Skiing," plus wrote our smashing Great Itineraries section for Chapter 1), he writes for the Innsbruck Tourist Office, Tirol Werbung, and the Austrian National Tourist Office. Having done voice-overs for some major companies, he continues to work in the studio, doing voice-overs for clients including Swarovski Crystal and other Tirolean-based companies, and has recently moved with his wife and two children to the scenic province of Carinthia.

"To the age, its art; to art, its freedom" was the motto of the famous Vienna Secession group, and George Sullivan firmly believes in this maxim, as any reader of our magisterial Vienna Exploring texts can vouch. The history, art, and architecture of European cities have been his favorite subjects since he spent a college summer in London many years ago. A native of Virginia, he gets to Europe as often as he can (he's also written about Florence for Fodor's) and is currently working on an architectural guide to Rome. Austria—the country that gave us *Silent Night, Holy Night*—is never too far from his thoughts: in addition to his writing assignments, he helps run his family's Christmas tree farm.

At the height of 6 feet 5½ inches, Horst Erwin Reischenböck is considered by some to be a significant landmark himself in his home base of Salzburg (the city's steeples and castellated peaks offering a lot of competition). His family has been living there since the 19th century and, like all children growing up in Mozart's home town, he was already humming tunes from *The Marriage of Figaro* barely out of the nursery. A music critic for various newspapers for three decades and author of two books in German (their English titles are *The Mozarts in Salzburg* and *1,200 Years of Music in Salzburg*), Horst can't begin to count the number of Mozart concerts he's attended but can only agree with Robert Schumann's famous observation— "Does it not seem that Mozart's works become fresher and fresher the oftener we hear them?" Today, Horst is known as one of the best personal guides for English-speaking visitors to Salzburg and the Salzkammergut. For this edition, he updated our chapters on Salzburg and the Salzkammergut.

Author of our section on "Powder-Perfect Skiing," Lito Tejada-Flores has shared his passion for mountain adventure in a series of books, films, and most recently his *Breakthrough on Skis* instructional videos. As a contributing editor to *Skiing* magazine, Lito has skied around the world. He is in love with the Alps and visits Austria every chance he gets.

ABOUT THIS BOOK

SELECTION	Our goal is to cover the best properties, sights, and activities in their category, as well as the most interesting communities to visit. We make a point of including local food-lovers' hot spots as well as neighborhood options, and we avoid all that's touristy unless it's really worth your time. It goes without saying that no property mentioned in the book has paid to be included.
RATINGS	Orange stars ★ denote sights and properties that our editors and writers consider Fodor's Choice, the very best in the area covered by the entire book. These, the best of the best, are listed in the Fodor's Choice section in the front of the book. Black stars ★ highlight the sights and properties we deem Highly Recommended, the don't-miss sights within any region. Use the index to find complete descriptions. In cities, sights pinpointed with numbered map bullets ❶ in the margins tend to be more important than those without bullets.
SPECIAL SPOTS	Pleasures & Pastimes focuses on types of experiences that reveal the spirit of the destination. Watch for Off the Beaten Path sights. If the munchies hit while you're exploring, look for Need a Break? suggestions.
TIME IT RIGHT	Check On the Calendar up front and chapters' Timing sections for weather and crowd overviews and best days and times to visit.
SEE IT ALL	Use Fodor's exclusive Great Itineraries as a model for your trip. In cities, Good Walks guide you to important sights in each neighborhood; ▶ indicates the starting points of walks and itineraries in the text and on the map.
BUDGET WELL	Hotel and restaurant price categories from ¢ to $$$$ are defined in the opening pages of each chapter. For attractions, we always give standard adult admission fees; reductions are usually available for children, students, and senior citizens. AE, DC, MC, V following restaurant and hotel listings indicate whether American Express, Diners Club, MasterCard, or Visa are accepted.
BASIC INFO	Smart Travel Tips lists travel essentials for the entire area covered by the book; city- and region-specific basics end each chapter. To find the best way to get around, see individual modes of travel (car, bus, train, etc.).
ON THE MAPS	Maps throughout the book show you what's where and help you find your way around. Black and orange numbered bullets ❶ ❶ in the text correlate to bullets on maps.
BACKGROUND	In general, we give background information within the chapters in the course of explaining sights as well as in Close-Up boxes and in Understanding Austria at the end of the book.

FIND IT FAST

The Vienna and Salzburg chapters begin with Exploring information, with a section for each neighborhood (each recommending a walking tour and listing sights alphabetically). All regional chapters are then divided geographically; within each area, towns are covered in logical geographical order. To help you decide what you'll have time to visit in the days available, all chapters begin with our writers' favorite itineraries. The A to Z section that ends every chapter covers getting there and getting around and provides more helpful contacts and resources.

DON'T FORGET

Restaurants are open for lunch and dinner daily unless we state otherwise; we mention dress only when there's a specific requirement and reservations only when they're essential or not accepted—it's always best to book ahead. If not noted otherwise, hotels have private baths, phone, TVs, and air-conditioning and operate on the European Plan (a.k.a. EP, meaning without meals), unless otherwise indicated (all-inclusive, with meals and beverages included; BP, breakfast plan with full breakfast; CP, Continental plan with Continental breakfast; FAP, full American plan with all meals; MAP, modified American plan with breakfast and dinner). We always list facilities but not whether you'll be charged extra to use them, so when pricing accommodations, find out what's included.

SYMBOLS

Many Listings

★ Fodor's Choice
★ Highly recommended
⊠ Physical address
✛ Directions
🕮 Mailing address
☎ Telephone
🖷 Fax
⊕ On the Web
✉ E-mail
🎫 Admission fee
☉ Open/closed times
► Start of walk/itinerary
Ⓜ Metro stations
▭ Credit cards

Outdoors

⛳ Golf
⛺ Camping

Hotels & Restaurants

🏨 Hotel
🛏 Number of rooms
♨ Facilities
🍴 Meal plans
✕ Restaurant
🍽 Reservations
👔 Dress code
🚭 Smoking
🍺 BYOB
✕🏨 Hotel with restaurant that warrants a visit

Other

🅲 Family-friendly
🛈 Contact information
⇨ See also
⊠ Branch address
☞ Take note

Vienna & Environs

If you go to Vienna today expecting to hear *Tales of the Vienna Woods,* airs from Lehár's *Merry Widow,* or *The Land of Smiles,* you won't be disappointed. The city's Kursalon, the Prater, and the Volksoper are still echoing with this light-hearted, beloved music. It goes without saying that Vienna has an Old World charm—a fact that the natives are both ready to acknowledge and yet hate being reminded of. It remains a white-gloved yet modern metropolis, a place where Andrew Lloyd Webber's *Phantom of the Opera* plays in the same theater that premiered Mozart's *Magic Flute.* A walk through the city's neighborhoods—many dotted with masterpieces of Gothic, Baroque, and Secessionist architecture—offers a fascinating journey thick with history and peopled by the spirits of Empress Maria Theresa, Haydn, Beethoven, Metternich, Mozart, and Klimt.

Most visitors start along the **Ringstrasse,** the grand boulevard that surrounds the inner city, whose broad sweep grandly evokes the imperial era of Strauss, Metternich, and emperor Franz Josef during the cultural heyday of the Austro-Hungarian empire. Here you'll find great art treasures in great museums and magnificent spectacles at Austria's finest opera house. Even within the shadow of the city's spiritual heart—the great **Stephansdom** cathedral (which leads off the massive roll call of dazzling Gothic and Baroque churches in the city), Vienna comes alive during the "Merry Season"—the first two months of the year—when raised trumpets and opera capes adorn its great Fasching balls; then more than ever, Vienna moves in three-quarter time. **Café Hawelka** and the city's other famous coffeehouses—of which Vienna is said to have more than Switzerland has banks—are havens in which to share gossip, read, and conduct a little business, but most of all to engage in the age old coffee-drinking ritual that every dutiful Viennese observes daily.

Pomp, circumstance, and no small amount of innovation hold sway in Vienna's 90 museums and its hundreds of houses of worship and other landmarks. The city's vast holdings range from the Brueghels, Rembrandts, Vermeers, and other treasures in the **Kunsthistorisches Museum** to the magnificent **National Library,** where rare manuscripts are as lovingly showcased as the rooms' splendid frescoes. Travelers in search of Imperial Vienna will find no dearth of Habsburgian opulence throughout the city: there's **Schönbrunn Palace,** in whose Grand Salon the Congress of Vienna celebrated the defeat of Napoléon; there's the Imperial Palace known as the **Hofburg,** where the Lipizzaner horses of **Spanish Riding School** fame still prance to a measured cadence, just as they did when pulling emperor Franz Josef's royal carriage; and then there's the **Karlskirche.** This Baroquely ornate church looks, especially when illuminated at night, like a magical vision, although, to the architectural purists who first denounced its Trajan columns, it seemed a bad dream. This uncharacteristic, over-the-top embellishment nevertheless set the stage for the emergence of the city's visionary art and artists, among whom the most famous is Gustav Klimt. This Jugenstil artist was among the first to shock turn-of-the-century Vienna with his luxuriously nontraditional paintings, such as *The Kiss*—housed in truly regal splendor in the **Belvedere Palace** museum—and his artistic bravado was soon emulated by legions of other painters and architects. In our own age, that honor has been bestowed on Friedensreich Hundertwasser, whose **Hundertwasserhaus** has, until recently, been the city's most outrageous, anti-traditional structure. Today, the modernist laurels have been bestowed instead on the gigantic new **MuseumsQuartier** complex, home to several fabled modern-art collections, and itself a Baroque landmark now fitted out with strikingly contemporary architectural additions.

Thanks to the great musicians and composers who, at times, made Vienna their own, travelers are quite likely to approach the city with a song in their heart. The Vienna of the past has inspired some of the world's most beautiful music, from Beethoven's *Pastoral Symphony* to Johann Strauss the Younger's "Blue Danube Waltz." As a traveler soon discovers, these and other ineffable strains are heard nonstop in the Vienna of the present as well. In fact, monuments commemorating many of the musical geniuses who have lived here are to be found throughout the city in various forms. Check out the bust of Mozart in the **Figarohaus**, one of the composer's many residences in the city, where he wrote some of his most famous works and which are holding celebrations in honor of his 250th birthday in 2006; pay your respects at the **Pasqualatihaus**, which was Beethoven's address when he composed *Fidelio*, his only opera; and tip your hat to the merrily gilded statue of Johann Strauss II in the Stadtpark. Chances are that somewhere nearby an orchestra or an opera company or a church organist will be performing the works of these great men; the city is, after all, home to two of the world's greatest symphony orchestras (the Vienna Philharmonic and the Vienna Symphony) and is graced with a top opera house (the Staatsoper) as well as a world-renowned concert hall (the Musikverein). Head for the Theater an der Wien to hear beloved operettas (*Die Fledermaus* and *The Merry Widow* both premiered here) or to the Volksoper. Amble into the Gothic interior of the Augustinerkirche any Sunday morning and you may have the pleasure of hearing its mighty organ accompany a high mass oratorio by Mozart or Haydn. Unfortunately, a seat at the Philharmonic's famous New Year's Eve concert is harder to come by—much harder. Equally prized is a ticket to the annual Opernball at the Staatsoper; if you do manage to snag one, and if you are one of those romantic souls for whom the mere mention of Vienna conjures up images of hand kissing, deep bows, and white-tied men twirling white gloved women across the floor, you may think you've died and ascended into heaven—to the accompaniment of a waltz, of course.

Vienna Environs

The Viennese take their leisure seriously. Fortunately, there is a plethora of opportunities for them to indulge their pleasure-seeking natures, for they live in a city surrounded with enticing places to hike, plunge into natural thermal baths, and, perhaps best of all, sip a glass of Riesling wine. The Vienna Woods—the **Wienerwald**—march right from the city's outskirts south to the Alps and across rolling hills sprinkled with dense woods, vineyards, and the occasional palace. The only dark patch in this otherwise blessed terrain is **Mayerling**, where emperor Franz Josef built a Carmelite convent on the site where Rudolf, his only son, and Marie Vetsera met an untimely end (lovers' pact or political intrigue—to this day, no one really knows). Of more interest to the Viennese out for an idyllic getaway is **Gumpoldskirchen,** the tiny village with the big reputation for producing one of Europe's most famous white wines. Tempting as it may be to linger over a glass or two at one of its vintners' houses, press on into the romantic countryside north and west of Vienna where the vines are even thicker in the **Weinviertel** (the Wine District).

Eastern Austria

A great white stork glides to a landing on the chimney of the hooded roof of a house—a timeless image as far from the bustle of civilization as you can imagine, and one common in Austria's easternmost province. For those familiar with other parts of Austria, this region's far-awayness offers the contrast of simple, homely, exceptionally charming pleasures: whitewashed Magyar-style houses, vast stretches of *puszta* (steppe), evenings filled with the haunting sounds of Gypsy music—legacies attesting to the fact that much of eastern Austria belonged to Hungary before World War I.

A region of castle-capped hills, fields of grain, and vineyards (some of the best Austrian wines, including the regal Trockenbeerenauslesen, are produced here), **Burgenland** has major sights, including **Lake Neusiedl**—so gigantic it's called the "Viennese Sea"—and the Old World town of **Eisenstadt,** site of the exquisite Esterházy Palace where famed composer Josef Haydn worked for many years (don't miss a concert in the palace's Haydn Hall). **Graz,** the capital of Styria—Austria's southeastern province—is the country's second-largest city and boasts a historic city center that is as strikingly preserved as any other.

The Danube Valley

The famously blue Danube courses through Austria on its way from the Black Forest to the Black Sea, past medieval abbeys, fanciful Baroque monasteries, verdant pastures, and compact riverside villages. Though the river's hue is now somewhat less than pristine, this is still one of Europe's most important waterways, and to traverse its scenic length is to immerse yourself with a heady dose of history and culture, and, of course, to enjoy some pleasant scenery while doing so. Hereabouts, legends and myths stoke the imagination. In enchantingly picturesque **Dürnstein,** Richard the Lion-Hearted spent a spell locked in a dungeon. Not far away, the Nibelungs—immortalized by Wagner—caroused at the top of their lungs in battlemented forts. The Danube is liquid history, and you can enjoy drifting eight hours downriver in a steamer or—even better—traveling 18 hours upriver against the current.

Along the way you discover the the storybook Gothic market town of **Steyr,** where Anton Bruckner composed his Sixth Symphony. For ten years he was the organist at the neighboring Abbey of St. Florian, where he is buried; his organ still fills the high-ceilinged church with its rich, sorrowful notes. **Krems,** founded just over 1,000 years ago, is another delightful spot, where wine is the main business of the day. For nonpareil splendor, head to nearby **Melk Abbey,** best appreciated in the late afternoon when the setting sun lights the twin towers cradling its Baroque dome. Inside, its magnificent library was the real-life setting of Umberto Eco's novel *The Name of the Rose.* In addition to Melk, the **Wachau** valley—"crown jewel of the Austrian landscape"—includes the robber castles of **Studen** and **Werfen-**

stein. A convenient base point is **Linz,** Austria's third-largest city (and its most underrated): its Old Town is filled with architectural treasures, glockenspiel chimes, and pastry shops that offer the best Linzertortes around. The town is right on the Danube, which, if you catch it on a bright summer day, takes on the proper shade of Johann Strauss "blau."

Salzburg

Depending on who is describing this elegant city filled with gilded salons, palatial mansions, and Italianate churches, Salzburg is alternately known as the "Golden City of the High Baroque," the "Austrian Rome," or, thanks to its position astride the River Salzach, the "Florence of the North." What you choose to call this beloved city will depend on what brings you here. It may well be music, of course, as Mozart was born here in 1756 on the third floor of a house now cherished as **Mozarts Geburtshaus.** His operas and symphonies ripple through the city constantly, most particularly during its acclaimed, celebrity-packed, summer music festival, most fervently during the year-long celebration the city is hosting to honor the 2006 Mozart Year. Art lovers, on the other hand, will pounce on the city's heritage of Baroque churches, cloistered abbeys, and Rococo palaces, such as **Schloss Leopoldskron,** and, inevitably, climb the hill to **Hohensalzburg,** the brooding medieval fortress towering over the city, whose lavish state rooms are belied by its grim exterior. Many come here to follow in the footsteps of the von Trapp family, or, at least, their Hollywood counterparts, as many of the city's most celebrated sights, such as the **Mirab ell Gardens,** were used as ageless backdrops for that beloved Oscar-winner, *The Sound of Music.* Those in search of drama—as if the setting here amid Alpine peaks and glacial lakes doesn't provide enough—will want to attend the annual performances of *Jedermann* (*Everyman*) on the cathedral square, or take in a show at the famed **Marionettentheater.** Of course, you need not come to Salzburg with a goal any more ambitious than relaxing over a meal of Neue Küche cuisine, which is a little lighter than traditional Austrian fare, at nearby Hotel Schloss Fuschl (while trying not to peek at the opera diva across the room). Music may top the bill for some, but everyone will enjoy the stupendous panoply of churches and museums, old-fashioned cafés, narrow medieval streets, and glorious fountains. Indeed, the playful water gardens of **Hellbrunn Castle** remind us that not all archbishops were stern and unpleasant.

Salzkammergut

The Salzkammergut, the country's "salt shaker" if you will, stretches across three states—from Salzburg through Styria to Upper Austria. The German word *Salz* is frequently encountered here; indeed, the entire economy has been based on salt mining for millennia. The region's name means "Salt Estates," but this unappealing moniker doesn't begin to do justice to the gorgeous scenery in Austria's Lake District. Think of *The Sound of Music,* filmed here on the home turf of the musically inclined von Trapp family, and you will easily envision the region's scenic pleasures. It's little wonder why **Hallstatt,** nestled between the dark waters of the Hallstätter See and the granite needles of the Dachstein range, is touted as one of the world's prettiest lakeside villages. More difficult, by far, is to choose the region's prettiest lake. The clear blue Wolfgangsee, with the popular vacation village of **St. Wolfgang** on its shores, is the choice of many travelers, while the

Traunsee, reflecting **Schloss Orth** in its breeze-rippled surface, is the favorite of as many others. At **Bad Aussee,** the only spectacle likely to divert your attention from the ever-present vista of lake and mountains is that of the unusually costumed citizenry getting into the swing of a summer festival. For natural beauty, however, **Gosau** takes best in show, for here the great Dachstein massif is mirrored in a fjord-like lake—a panorama so magical it inspired Wagner when he composed *Parsifal.* Hidden within these mountain peaks you'll discover the eerily lit **Dachstein Ice Caves,** while deep below ground you can also explore caverns that have for centuries been mined for, yes, salt. For a heaping spoonful of sugar, however, repair to **Bad Ischl,** famed for its pastries. This charming turn-of-the-20th-century resort was where Emperor Franz Josef kept a villa (his birthday is still celebrated on August 18) and where Franz Lehár wrote *The Merry Widow.*

Carinthia

Carinthia—or Kärnten in German—is the country's sunniest (and southernmost) province. Here you'll find **the Austrian Riviera,** a happy blend of mountains, valleys, and placid blue-green lakes that rest serenely between the shoulders of low forested hills and reflect the golden-white light of the rocky faces of the Karawanken and Carnic Alps. Around the shores of the largest lake, the Wörther See, waterside gaiety emanates from lovely resorts. Everyone adores the jaunty town of **Velden,** where few can resist a stroll along the famous lakeside promenade, lined with 19th-century mansions, and illuminated by gas lamps casting a soft glow over the glimmering waters of the Worther See. Another favorite spot for holidaymakers is **Maria Wörth,** a quaint place set on a peninsula, where the waterside gaiety of beaches and pleasure boaters is backdropped by Baroque churches and crooked alleys.

Nature's glories are only part of Carinthia's allure, for many of its Alpine towns contain artistic treasures of the highest order. A great Romanesque basilica broods over tiny **Gurk** and don't forget **St. Veit an der Glan**'s town square—probably the most beautiful in the country, alive with sidewalk cafés in summer. And when you see the 9th-century **Hochosterwitz Castle** from afar, high atop a hill, you almost expect a dragon to appear in a puff of smoke or to hear troubadours warbling (the castle was the model for the one in Walt Disney's *Snow White*). **Klagenfurt** is the official capital of Carinthia, but **Villach** has emerged as the "secret" capital, no more so than when the town hosts the most riotous Carnival celebration in Austria.

Eastern Alps

If you want a region that conveniently packages the panoramic, the most gemütlich little towns in Austria, and an all-out array of sports, head for the Eastern Alps, magnificently sited within the regions of East Tirol, Salzburg Province, and West Styria. Most towns and villages in this region have not been scarred by bland, quick-fix architecture, while deep valleys are carpeted with wheat fields and the rare white edelweiss that allegedly moved crusty Baron von Trapp to sentimental song (don't worry if you pick a few flowers for souvenirs—they are cultivated here precisely for this purpose). No road in Europe matches the 48-km (30-mi) **Grossglockner High**

Alpine Highway, which crosses this section of the Tauern mountains and is the most spectacular pass through the Alps. A ride here produces a thrill a minute, or at least a breathtaking glimpse of a fearsome glacier or a swath of dozens of mountain peaks every few hundred yards. A word of caution: if you approach the pass from the south, you may never get any farther than **Heiligenblut,** a town cowering in an amphitheater of ragged peaks— a sublimely picturesque setting. Mountain climbers flock to this small town to conquer the neighboring peaks, but skiers head instead to the nearby resorts of **Schladming, Filzmoos,** and **St. Johann im Pongau.** After a bracing day on the Kitzsteinhorn slopes you'll feel like checking into **Badgastein** to thaw out in one of the town's luxurious hotel spas. **Lienz,** a sunny town with a very Italianate flair, lies just south of this scenic mountainscape.

Innsbruck & Tirol

The Tirol is a region richly graced with cosmopolitan cities, historic monuments, and the soothing balm of age-old faith. But, not surprising given the region, with the glorious Alps playing the stellar role, Nature steals every scene. Nevertheless, the proofs of human endeavors in ample evidence in these environs are far from second fiddle, as you can see by traveling to historic **Innsbruck.** The city's famous tower, the **Stadtturm,** was built in the 15th century, when Innsbruck was the regal and magnificent seat of the Holy Roman Empire in the reign of Maximilian I. The emperor's marble tomb in the **Hofkirche** is one of the city's many marvels, as is the **Goldenes Dachl,** the legendary "Golden Roof" mansion, topped off by a roof of gilded tiles ordered by Duke Friedrich (who soon, not surprisingly, was nicknamed Friedl the Penniless). Maximilian's rule signified an era of peace and prosperity for the Tirol, a heritage still evidenced in tidy, little mountain villages and religious traditions like Schemenlaufen, the Shrove Tuesday procession. When the mountains call, you can do no better than find your way to the peaks of the Ötztal Alps near **Obergurgl,** Austria's highest village, surrounded nearly all year by glittering glaciers. Skiers may also choose to make the trip up to **St. Christoph,** founded as an inn for stranded travelers in the 15th century and still a welcoming refuge for enthusiasts in search of pristine snow and uncrowded runs on which to test their mettle. For more suave skiing pleasures, head to **Kitzbühel,** one of the world's oldest ski resorts; for more rustic ones, aim for the resorts in the Ziller and Ötz valleys.

Vorarlberg

"What God has put asunder by a mountain, let no man join by a tunnel"— so said the Vorarlbergers of old. Once the Arlberg Tunnel linked Austria's westernmost province to the rest of the country, the secret was out. Vorarlberg—nicknamed the *Ländle,* the "Little Province"—was really Austria's Switzerland: cheaper in some ways, perhaps less efficient in others.

Tops on all visitors' lists are the fresh air and aria-making of the **Bregenz Music Festival** on Lake Constance; the **Bregenzerwald**—forests of Wagnerian romanticism; the **Schubert Festival in Hohenems;** and the endless, powdery snows of its skiing regions. **Lech** is for the wealthy, but try the Brandner Valley east of Bludenz for remoteness or the **Lüner Lake** for its icy waters, or spend a night in the Hotel Traube in Schruns, where Ernest Hemingway played cards in the winter of 1926.

GREAT ITINERARIES

Vienna to Vorarlberg

So, you want to taste Vienna, gaze at its beauty, and inhale its special brand of gemütlich—all in a one-week to 10-day trip. This itinerary allows you to travel the country end-to-end within two weeks, feeling a bit like a Habsburg emperor as you tour the top sights.

Duration: 14 Days.

VIENNA **3 days.** Austria's glorious past is evident everywhere, but especially where this tour begins, in Vienna. Get to know the city by trolley with a sightseeing tour of the Ringstrasse. Take in the Kunsthistoriches Museum (the incredible detail of the famous Brueghel paintings could keep you fascinated for hours, even if you're not an art aficionado), walk along Kärntnerstrasse to magnificent St. Stephen's Cathedral, and spend an afternoon in one of the city's cozy coffeehouses. Devote a half day to Schönbrunn Palace, and set aside an evening for a visit to a jovial Heuriger wine tavern. *Chapter 1: Exploring Vienna.*

DANUBE RIVER FROM VIENNA TO LINZ **1 day.** To zoom from Vienna to Linz by autobahn would be to miss out on one of Austria's most treasured sights, the blue Danube. To tour some quaint wine villages, follow the "Austrian Romantic Road" (Rte. 3), along the north bank of the river, instead of the speedier A1 autobahn. Cross to the south side of the Danube to the breathtaking Baroque abbey at Melk and along the way visit the 1,000-year-old town of Krems and picture-perfect Dürnstein, in the heart of the Wachau wine region. *Chapter 4: The Danube Valley.*

LINZ **2 days.** Fast-forward into Austria's future with a stop in progressive Linz, the country's third largest city. Linz is a busy port on the Danube and an important center for trade and business. Techno geeks will enjoy the recently opened Ars Electronica Center; other visitors will enjoy the beautifully restored medieval courtyards of the Altstadt (Old Town). For great views, ride the city's Pöstlingbergbahn, the world's steepest mountain railway, or opt for a Danube steamer cruise to Enns. *Chapter 4: The Danube Valley.*

SALZKAMMERGUT **2 days.** For Austria in all its Hollywood splendor, head to the idyllic Salzkammergut, better known as the Lake District, where *The Sound of Music* was filmed. The town of Bad Ischl—famous for its operetta festival and pastries—makes a good base. Travel south to Ebensee on Rte. 145 toward Hallstatt, one of Austria's most photographed lakeside villages. Return to Bad Ischl, then head west to St. Wolfgang and St. Gilgen for swimming and sailing. More adventurous souls will follow A1/E55 to the Hallein salt mines and then to Europe's largest ice cave, in Werfen. *Chapter 6: Salzkammergut.*

SALZBURG **2 days.** This is a city made for pedestrians, with an abundance of churches, palaces, mansions, and—as befits the birthplace of Mozart—music festivals. Stroll through the old city center, with its wrought-iron shop signs, tour the medieval Fortress Hohensalzburg, and relax in the Mirabell Gardens (where the von Trapp children "Do-Re-Mi"-ed). Children of all ages will adore the famed Marionettentheater. *Chapter 6: Salzburg.*

INNSBRUCK & TIROL 2 days. Tour Innsbruck's treasures—including the famous Golden Roof mansion and the Hofburg—but do as the Tiroleans do and spend time reveling in the high mountain majesty. After all, Innsbruck is the only major city in the Alps. For a splendid panorama, take the Hungerburgbahn (cable railway) to the Hafelekar, high above the Inn Valley. For a trip through the quaint villages around Innsbruck, ride the Stubaitalbahn, a charming old-time train, to Neustift, or head by bus to the Stubai Glacier for year-round skiing. *Chapter 9: Innsbruck.*

BREGENZ 2 days. Taking the Arlberg Pass (or the much more scenic Silvretta High Alpine Highway), head to the city of Bregenz, capital of Vorarlberg. Bregenz owes as much of its character to neighboring Switzerland and Germany as to Austria, and is most appealing in summer, when sun-worshipers crowd the shores of Lake Constance to enjoy an opera festival set on the world's largest outdoor floating stage. Take a lake excursion and explore Bregenz's medieval Oberstadt (upper town). Trains can easily connect you to Zürich or Munich, or you can head south to Italy via the Brenner Pass from Innsbruck. *Chapter 10: Voralberg.*

By Public Transportation There is frequent train service between the major cities. Side trips into the countryside are possible by bus or train. Trains leave every half hour from the Westbahnhof in Vienna, arriving in Linz in about 2 hours. From Linz, it is 2½ hours to the Salzburg Hauptbahnhof, and another 2 hours to the Innsbruck terminal, then another 2½ hours to Bregenz. For a more romantic kickoff, travel by a DDSG/Blue Danube Schiffahrt riverboat from Vienna to Linz (departs Vienna daily at 7 AM).

Mountain Magic

This is a tour for romantic dreamers—a trip where Alpine glory is all around you: meadows and forests set against a backdrop of towering craggy peaks, and gentle wooded rambles that lead to clear mountain lakes and storybook castles. The emphasis here is on letting go of your worries and allowing the natural beauty of the countryside to work its magic.

Duration: 9 Days.

BAD ISCHL/ST. WOLFGANG 2 days. The villages and lakes of the Salzkammergut region extend south from Salzburg like a string of pearls. Base yourself in Bad Ischl, a first-class spa in the heart of the Lake District. From there, head 16 km (10 mi) west to St. Wolfgang, one of the most photofriendly villages in Austria. For the most scenic surroundings, park in nearby Strobl and hop one of the lake ferries to the pedestrian-only village, where you can relax with a coffee on the terrace of the famous Weisses Rössl (White Horse Inn), marvel at the 16th-century Michael Pacher altarpiece in the parish church, and take the railway up the 5,800-foot Schaftberg peak for gasp-inducing vistas. *Chapter 6: Salzkammergut.*

HALLSTATT 1 day. Set on fjord-like Hallstätter See, this jewel is an optical illusion perched between water and mountain—a tight grouping of terraced fishermen's cottages and churches, offering, at first glance, no apparent reason why it doesn't tumble into the lake. On a sunny day the views of the lake and village, considered the oldest settlement in Austria, are spectacular, and on a misty morning they are even more so. Consider a canoe outing, or tour the Hallstatt salt mine, the oldest in the world. *Chapter 6: Salzkammergut.*

WERFEN 1 day. Take in the birds-of-prey show at the formidable Burg Hohenwerfen castle, built in the 11th century, tour the Eisriesenwelt ("World of the Ice Giants")—the largest collection of ice caves in Europe—and cap the day with dinner at Obauer, one of Austria's finest restaurants. *Chapter 8: Eastern Alps.*

ZELL AM ZEE 1 day. Some 50 km (30 mi) from Werfen, the charming lake resort of Zell am See is nestled under the 6,000-foot Schmittenhöhe mountain. Ride the cable car from the center of town for a bird's-eye view, then take the narrow-gauge Pinzgauer railroad through the Salzach river valley to famous Krimmler Falls. *Chapter 8: Eastern Alps.*

HEILIGENBLUT 1 day. Head skyward over the dizzying Hochglockner High Alpine Highway (open May–October) to one of Austria's loveliest villages, Heiligenblut, which fans out across the upper Möll Valley with fabulous views of the Grossglockner; at 12,470 feet the highest mountain in Austria. *Chapter 8: Eastern Alps.*

KITZBÜHEL/GOING 1 day. Travel to the glamorous resort town of Kitzbühel for a bit of window shopping and celebrity spotting, then continue to Going, Ellmau, and Söll along Route 312. These villages have superb restaurants and hotels, but the real reason to overnight here is to admire the view of the rugged "Wild Emperor," one of the most beautiful mountains in the Alps. *Chapter 9: Innsbruck and Tirol.*

RATTENBERG/ALPBACH 2 days. In these two charming villages, you might think you've been transported back in time, if it weren't for all the tourists roaming the ancient streets. Rattenberg has colorful medieval facades, famous glassware, and a delightful Inn River promenade, and the narrow, flower-bedecked streets of tiny Alpbach are set within one of Tirol's most bucolic valleys. Take the Wiedersbergerhorn gondola to the top of the mountain for a panorama, then hike back to town. End your trip in Innsbruck, 32 km (20 mi) west. *Chapter 9: Innsbruck & Tirol.*

By Public Transportation Although it is much simpler to travel this route by car, it can also be undertaken using public transportation (note that many trains do not run on Sunday). Trains link Salzburg, Bad Ischl, and Hallstatt; travel to St. Wolfgang by post bus. From Hallstatt, hop the train to Bad Aussee and on to Irdning, where you may have to change trains to Bischofshofen before reaching Zell am See. Travel to and from Heiligenblut by bus. Trains will take you to Kitzbühel but not to Going, so bus it from Kitz, and then continue by bus to the train station in Wörgl, which is on the main line to Innsbruck. This line includes a stop in Rattenberg, but the bus is the only way to get to Alpbach.

The Lake Districts

Although separated by only a few hours' drive, the two most famous lake districts of Austria have distinctly different personalities. The

Salzkammergut is the Alps at their most brilliant, an area rich in Habsburg history, first as the source of wealth in the form of "white gold," or salt, and later as the imperial playground, after Emperor Franz Josef I made his official summer residence here in 1854. Today the region is still the playground of the wealthy, who come to luxuriate in royal-class spas. In contrast, the lake district of sunny Carinthia, known as Austria's Riviera, is all about summer fun: swimming, fishing, boating, and soaking up rays along the shores of the country's warmest lakes.

Duration: 7 days.

MONDSEE **1 day.** Mondsee (Moon Lake) makes a good starting point in the Salzkammergut thanks to easy access from the A1 autobahn. You'll want to see St. Michael's parish church, made famous as the wedding chapel in *The Sound of Music.* Even if the thought of icy-cold lake water makes your toes turn blue, give swimming here a try, as the Mondsee is one of the warmest lakes in the region. *Chapter 6: Salzkammergut.*

GOSAU AM DACHSTEIN **1 day.** Today leave your bathing suit packed, but lace up your hiking boots. Richard Wagner was inspired by the spectacular view of the Dachstein massif, reflected in a sparkling, fjord-like mountain lake of the Vorderer Gosausee. Two more (less dramatically situated) lakes can be reached on foot in two hours. Take the gondola up to the Gablonzer Hütte for a refreshment, then hike back to Gosau. *Chapter 6: Salzkammergut.*

BAD AUSSEE **2 days.** A year-round favorite, Bad Aussee is girded by steep mountains that keep the village cool in midsummer and snowy all winter. Only card-carrying polar bears will want to swim here in the icy, spring-fed lakes. Others will take to the heated pools of the spa complex and explore the charming village of Altaussee. *Chapter 6: Salzkammergut.*

VILLACH **1 day.** 184 km (110 mi) from Bad Aussee, Villach is one of the main gateway hubs of the Carinthia lakes region. Austrians flock to the city to savor its Renaissance square, charming Old City south of the Drau River, and cruise on the MS Landskron to the ruined castle of Landskron. *Chapter 6: Carinthia.*

KLAGENFURT **2 days.** After nosing around this lakeside resort, head north on Rte. 83 to Schloss Hochosterwitz, the model for Walt Disney's Snow White castle. Return to Klagenfurt, then follow the north bank of the Wörther See to elegant Pörtschach, beloved for its promenade, beach, and some of the warmest waters in Austria. Nearby are chic, lively Velden, known for its upscale shopping and casino, and the relentlessly picturesque village of Maria Wörth. Both can be reached on a boat tour. *Chapter 7: Carinthia.*

By Public Transportation With the notable exception of one town, Gosau am Dachstein, it is possible to make this trip using a combination of train and bus. Bus service is regularly offered throughout the Salzkammergut. From Bad Aussee you will have to backtrack to Salzburg for trains to Carinthia. Trains connect Salzburg and Klagenfurt, but it is more convenient to make short hops by bus.

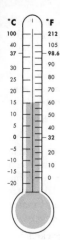

Austria has two main tourist seasons. The weather usually turns glorious around Easter to mark the start of the summer season and holds until about mid-October, sometimes later. Because much of the country remains "undiscovered," you will usually find crowds only in the major cities and resorts. May and early June, September, and October are the most pleasant months for travel; there is less demand for restaurant tables, and hotel prices tend to be lower. A foreign invasion takes place between Christmas and New Year's Day, and over the long Easter weekend, and hotel rooms in Vienna are then at a premium.

Climate

Austria has four distinct seasons, all fairly mild. But because of altitudes and the Alpine divide, temperatures and dampness vary considerably from one part of the country to another; for example, northern Austria's winter is often overcast and dreary, while the southern half of the country basks in sunshine. The eastern part of the country, especially Vienna and the areas near the Czech border, can become bitterly cold in winter. The *Föhn* is a wind that makes the country as a whole go haywire. It comes from the south, is warm, and announces itself by very clear air, blue skies, and long wisps of cloud. Whatever the reason, the Alpine people (all the way to Vienna) begin acting up; some become obnoxiously aggressive, others depressive, many people have headaches, and (allegedly) accident rates rise. The Föhn breaks with clouds and rain. The following are average monthly maximum and minimum temperatures for three cities in Austria.

Forecasts **Weather Channel Connection** ☎ 900/932–8437 95¢ a minute from a Touch-Tone phone ⊕ www.weather.com.

VIENNA

Jan.	34F	1C	May	66F	19C	Sept.	68F	20C
	25	– 4		50	10		52	11
Feb.	37F	3C	June	73F	23C	Oct.	57F	14C
	27	– 3		57	14		45	7
Mar.	46F	8C	July	77F	25C	Nov.	45F	7C
	34	1		59	15		37	3
Apr.	59F	15C	Aug.	75F	24C	Dec.	37F	3C
	43	6		59	15		30	– 1

SALZBURG

Jan.	36F	2C	May	66F	19C	Sept.	68F	20C
	21	– 6		46	8		50	10
Feb.	39F	4C	June	72F	22C	Oct.	57F	14C
	23	– 5		52	11		41	5
Mar.	48F	9C	July	75F	24C	Nov.	46F	8C
	30	– 1		55	13		32	0
Apr.	57F	14C	Aug.	73F	23C	Dec.	37F	3C
	39	4		55	13		25	– 4

Hundreds of festivals and events are held annually in Austria. Here are some of the better known and better attended in and around Vienna and Salzburg. If you plan to visit during one of them, book well in advance.

WINTER

December

The world-famous Christkindlmärte set up shop in various locales in major cities in Austria. In Vienna, the biggest Christmas Market goes up in late November in the plaza in front of the city's Rathaus town hall; there are smaller ones in the Spittelberg Quarter and on the Freyung square, as well famous markets that open during the Advent season in both Salzburg and Graz. The Christmas Eve service in the tiny memorial chapel at Oberndorf, north of Salzburg, features the singing of *Silent Night,* which Franz Gruber wrote when he was an organist here in the early 19th century. The New Year opens in Vienna with the world-famous concert by the Wiener Philharmoniker Orchestra; write a year—or more—in advance (⊠ Wiener Philharmoniker, Musikverein, Bösendorferstrasse 12, A-1010 Vienna ☎ 01/505–6525 ⊕ www.musikverein.at). Those who can't get into the Philharmonic concert can try for one of the performances of the Johann Strauss operetta *Die Fledermaus* or another light delight in the Volksoper (⊠ Währinger Strasse 78, A-1090 Vienna ☎ 01/513–1513 ⊕ www.volksoper.at) or at the intimate Kammeroper (⊠ Fleischmarkt 24, A-1010 Vienna ☎ 01/513–1513). The New Year is marked by an array of balls, such as the Kaiserball, held in the elegant rooms of the Hofburg (⊠ WKV, Hofburg, Heldenplatz, A-1014 Vienna ☎ 01/587–3666–14).

January

On January 6th, children disguised as the Magi walk the streets, especially out in the country, knock at doors, sing a song and recite poems about coming from afar, and ask for a small donation. They then chalk a "C+M+B" and the year on entrance door frames to bless the house for a year. Also special at this time is the ancient pre-Christian custom of the *Perchtenlauf,* masked figures that go on a rampage, mostly found in Salzburg Province, in Bad Gastein, for example.

Week of Jan. 27

Mozart's Birthday is always celebrated in Salzburg with the Mozart Week, a festival organized by the city's Mozarteum (⊠ Mozarteum, Schwarzstrasse 26, A-5020 Salzburg ☎ 0622/872996 ⊕ www.mozart2006.net), featuring operas, recitals, and theme concerts. In 2006, however, the great composer will see a year-long, 24/7 celebration throughout Austria to honor his 250th birthday. The initial champagne corks will be popped in Salzburg, but Vienna and the entire country will soon follow with a full slate of special concerts, galas, and exhibitions. See the various Close-Up boxes on Mozart in Chapters 1 and 7 for more details.

Feb.	Fasching (or Fasnacht, as its called in the western part of the country), the carnival period before Lent, can become very wild with huge processions of disguised figures, occasional unwilling participation by spectators, who may even suffer (light) blows. The entire country starts going to dances—and the ball season begins. In Vienna, which is comparatively quiet at this time, the ball season opens on the Thursday before Fasching and lasts through Shrove Tuesday (Mardi Gras). The biggest gala is the Opernball (Opera Ball), held at the Staatsoper (☎ 01/514–44–2606 ⊕ www.staatsoper.at).

SPRING

Late Mar.–early Apr.	Easter Festival, Salzburg's "other" major music festival, offers opera and concerts of the highest quality, with ticket prices to match (✉ Hofstallgasse 1, A-5020 Salzburg ☎ 0662/8045–361).
Mid-May–mid-June	The Wiener Festwochen takes place in Vienna—a festival of theater, music, films, and exhibitions (✉ Lehargasse 11, A-1060 Vienna ☎ 0222/582–2222 ⊕ www.festwochen.at).
Late May–early June	The religious holiday Corpus Christi is celebrated—on the second Thursday after Pentecost, falling in either late May or early—throughout Austria with colorful processions and parades. In the Lungau region of Land Salzburg, villagers dress up in local costumes. Equally colorful are the processions of gaily decorated boats and barges on the Traun and Hallstätter lakes.

SUMMER

June 21	Midsummer Night is ablaze with bonfires throughout the country, with the liveliest celebrations taking place in the Wachau region along the Danube in Lower Austria.
July–Aug.	Musical Summer/KlangBogen in Vienna has nightly recitals in one of the city's many palaces or orchestral concerts in the courtyard of the city hall (✉ KlangBogen Wien, Stadiongasse 29, A-1010 Vienna ☎ 01/4000–8410 🖷 01/4000–99–8410).
Last week of July–Aug.	The Salzburger Festspiele brings together the world's greatest musical artists for a citywide celebration, with many events and performances revolving around the town's most famous native son, Mozart. Write several months in advance, especially for the festival events scheduled for the Mozart Year of 2006, when the city (and the world) will go Mozart-mad celebrating the composer's 250th birthday (✉ Salzburger Festspiele, Postfach 140, A-5010 Salzburg ☎ 0662/8045–322 ⊕ www.salzburgfestival.at). For complete information, see Chapter 5.

FALL

September 1	This date marks the start of the theater and music season in Vienna.

PLEASURES & PASTIMES

Mozart Mania Somewhere, at almost any hour, an orchestra will be playing his music; somewhere, shoulders will be swaying, fingers tapping. It may be at a gala evening concert, an outdoor festival, or an Easter Mass. But chances are the music of Johannes Chrysostomus Theophilus Wolfgang Amadeus Mozart will be traveling through the air when you visit Austria. The most purely inspired of any composer crammed a prodigious amount of composing into his short 35-year life. Today—thanks to Tom Hulce's characterization in the film *Amadeus*—this youthful genius and native son of Salzburg wears the crown of "rock star of the 18th century."

And confirmation of his continuing popularity is renewed each year at the annual Salzburg Music Festival, perhaps the world's most polished and prestigious musical gathering. What Wagner is to Bayreuth, Mozart is to Salzburg. Well, not absolutely—many performances at Salzburg are devoted to other composers—but the true spirit, soul, and style of the magical city are best captured when "Wolfi" takes center stage at the Grosses Festspielhaus. On such nights, platoons of the rich and famous may take in a new production of *Don Giovanni* in one theater, hear the hottest conductor take on the "Linz" Symphony in another, then head over to the Goldener Hirsch for extravagant after-opera meals and diva-watching.

But anywhere in Austria you can be walking along thinking of nothing special, and you are suddenly hearing a concert, a recital, an orchestra rehearsing, a soprano going through her scales. You can sit in the Mirabellgarten in Salzburg enjoying coffee and cake, and listen to the opera singers rehearsing. As for Vienna itself, no city can boast such a roster of concerts of fine composers and performers. From the huge empire and beyond, the great composers poured in in droves (assuming they were not born there)—the better-known being Mozart (naturally), Beethoven, Schubert, Haydn, Johannes Brahms, Mahler, Richard Strauss, Johann Strauss the Younger (no relation), and Arnold Schönberg. Clearly, it's music in general that seems to be the spiritual fuel of the country—no time more so than during the big 2006 Mozart Year. For information about the special events planned to honor his 250th birthday, see the performing arts sections and Close-Up boxes on Mozart in Chapters 1 and 5.

Schnitzels, Strudels & Sachertortes These days, food in Austria is undergoing a revolution as New Vienna Cuisine—*Neue Vienna Küche*—is making headlines (read all about it in Chapter 1). But the mainstays of yore are still to be savored. All the gastronomic traditions of the old empire have left their mark here, so be prepared for genuine Hungarian *pörkölt* (what we call goulash) and *lecsó* (red pepper and tomato stew), and for divine Bohemian desserts. The *Palatschinken* are originally Hungarian as well, thin pancakes that can be stuffed around chocolate, marmalade, or a farmer's-cheese stuffing (*Topfen*). Serb *cevapcici* (kebabs) and *rasnici* also appear on menus with fair frequency, even in Austrian establishments, as does *Serbische Bohnensuppe*, a mighty Serb bean soup.

The national gastronomy itself includes lean spareribs and heavy-caliber bread or potato dumplings (also a Bohemian legacy) mixed with bacon or liver or stuffed with anything from cracklings (*Grammel*) to apricots (*Marillen*). In Carinthia (and to an extent in Burgenland), you should try *Sterz* (also called polenta), filling and healthy cornmeal dishes that have roots in Italy and Slovenia as well. From western Austria comes *Kaiserschmarrn*, the "emperor's nonsense" eaten with cranberry jam. The Styrians have their salads, goat's and sheep's cheeses, their various soups, garlic soup, pumpkin soup (*Kürbiskremsuppe*), and a basic soup of meat and root vegetables (*Wurzelfleisch*). In some friendly country *Heuriger* in Lower Austria you can try blood sausage; *Blunz'n*, with mashed potatoes; or the standard *Schweinsbraten*, pork roast. And there is more: the famous *Wiener Schnitzel* (veal scallop, breaded, deep-fried in fresh oil); *Schinkenfleckerl* (broad flat noodles with ham—a Bohemian recipe), and the cheap but delicious *Beuschl* (lung and heart of beef in a thick sauce always served with a giant Knödel). *Tafelspitz mit Kren* is boiled beef fillet with horseradish.

Venison (*Wild*) is a specialty that crosses restaurant class boundaries. A nice *Rehrücken mit Serviettenknödel* (saddle of deer with a bread dumpling cooked wrapped in cloth) at a four-star establishment is something to write home about. By the same token, you may find a robust *Gamsgulasch* (chamois goulash) in a rustic little hut near the summit of a Styrian mountain, or excellent smoked sausages and hams being offered by a Carinthian *Almbauer* at a few tables outside his summer farm in the mountains.

You need not go thirsty either on your travels. Austria has excellent water, which can be drunk from the tap or straight from the spring at times, and that, good brewers will tell you, makes for excellent beer. Murau in Styria has a top brewery, with a fine restaurant attached. Some swear by Vienna's own Ottakringer. All the orchards in the country also make for terrific fruit juices. The new kid on the block for the past few years is elderberry (*Hollunder*), which comes in dry reds or whites and which—like wine—can be *gespritzt*, mixed with either tap water (*stilles Wasser*) or mineral water (*Mineral*). The *Sommergespritzter* is one-third wine, two-thirds water. As for wines, Austria has many fine choices—see below.

Hiking Heaven

Austria is one of the most participant-sports-minded countries in the world. Babies barely out of diapers practically learn to walk on skis. At a snowflake's notice, half the population takes to the slopes; in summer they all head for the lakes and rivers—even to the Danube at Vienna—or to go canoeing, rafting, canyoning, rock-climbing, mountain biking, or spelunking.

Tennis is a standard fixture in the Austrian sports world, and golf is on the rise. But one of the great sports, again thanks to the mountains, is hiking, known as *das Wandern.* This can mean anything from a leisurely stroll along the shores of Lake Fuschl to a major hike through the Karawanken in Carinthia lasting several days. Tourist offices inevitably have a *Wanderkarte,* a walking map, to help guide you on your way up, across, around, and down mountains. In fact, there are walking paths that crisscross the Alps, and if you are really a hot hiker, you can stay at refuges on the way and hardly ever come in contact with the "civilized" world of the valleys. Even Vienna is surrounded and traversed by hiking paths: you can bring a special pad along distributed by the tourist office, and at specific sights you'll find a stamp. Bring enough stamps back to the tourist office, and you will receive a pin.

Do not underestimate the mountains. Either have someone along who knows them or have your Wanderkarte and keep your eyes peeled for the telltale markings on the trees and rocks indicating where the road is going. Getting caught in the dark somewhere in the Rax mountains of Lower Austria or around Kühtai in Tirol will suddenly make little Austria feel like the wilds of Washington State. Bring good hiking boots that go over your ankles, thick socks, water-resistant clothing, good sunglasses, headgear, and sunblock. A compass can also be of assistance.

A final note on hiking: there are very stringent rules for hikers. First, try to avoid disturbing wildlife (that's why mountain biking is often forbidden). Further, leave no garbage behind, including cigarette butts. Do not set fires. If you have a dog along, keep it on a leash or walking close to you—foresters have the right to shoot any roaming dogs, and they are sometimes very trigger-happy and rude. Finally, large posters usually near ski lifts or at rest stations in the mountains indicate what plants are protected (the edelweiss, for example, and several types of gentian as well), and the law is enforced.

Singular Wines

Every Viennese knows the joys of *Heurige* wine—"this year's wine," usually served *gespritzt* (mixed with seltzer water) and imbibed in one of those rustic, picturesque *Heuriger* wine taverns that dot the suburbs of Grinzing, Nussdorf, and the gentle slopes of the Vienna Woods. Savoring these vintages in lantern-lit gardens to the tune of *Schrammel* folk music proves the favorite occupation of Saturday afternoon or Sunday evening for thousands of Viennese who long for simpler times. But Austrian vintners have gone a long way toward changing the outdated image of the simple, undemanding white of the *Heurige* and the world is taking note of Austria's many and varied regional wines. Don't hesitate to ask waiters for advice, even in the simpler restaurants, and as with the food, go for the local wine, if possible. For a light, dry white wine, try the Grüner Veltliner. The Welschriesling is a slightly heavier, fruitier wine. In some areas, the wines have their own special names, for example, Styrians are particularly proud of their Schilcher, a generally dry rosé. The reds, too, are well represented, especially in Burgenland. Blauer Portugieser, Traminer, and Zweigelt tend to be on the lighter side. For a slightly heavier red, select a Blaufränkisch or Blauer Burgunder. A novelty, if you happen to be traveling around Heiligenbrunn in Burgenland, is the powerful Uhudler, made of ungrafted vines that originally came from the United States to make European vines resistant to devastating phylloxera. The Austrian government prohibited making it because of its high alcohol content, but after Austria joined the EU in 1995, the prohibition was lifted for fear other European nations would catch on and turn a good penny making this quintessential Austrian wine. The majority of grapes grown in Austria are still traditional varieties, with 80% of these used for white wines like Grüner Veltliner and Welschriesling. Of the reds, Zweigelt is the most widely grown; Blaufränkisch is capable of greater complexity; and Blauer Portugieser produces pleasant, softer wines. But wine growers are becoming more venturesome and are experimenting with chardonnay, Riesling, pinot noir, and cabernet sauvignon.

There are five major wine-growing regions: the Wachau, which encompasses the lush Danube Valley west of Vienna; the Weinviertel (Wine Quarter), extending from the area north of Vienna to the Czech border; Burgenland, the province east of Vienna that was formerly part of Hungary; and southern Styria, bordering on Slovenia and reminiscent of Tuscany with its sweetly rolling hills. Within the city limits of Vienna itself are a number of family-owned vineyards that maintain their own Heurige.

Each wine region has its own character. Burgenland and southern Styria have warmer climates, which make for full-bodied red wines, while the Wachau's cool climate is tempered by the Danube River and produces more Germanic, Rhine-style whites. The Weinviertel boasts of having the least rainfall and most sunny days of all the wine-growing regions in Austria, and it has been producing wine since the Middle Ages. Burgenland consists of two different territories: the hilly, wooded southern area and the flatlands around the vast Neusiedlersee (Lake Neusiedl), including Carnuntum, where vineyards were established as early as Celtic and Roman times. This is red wine country, famous for its Zweigelt and Blaufränkisch, and it also produces some very good dessert wines. Though southern Styria is also blessed with a warm climate, it produces a great number of white wines as well as red. Chardonnay is rich and full-bodied here, and you will also find the spicy, fragrant Traminer and Welchriesling, the most common varietal in Styria. But Styrians swear by their Schilcher, a tart, peach-colored rosé that is unique to the region. The Wachau produces light, fruity white wines, most notably Grüner Veltliner and Riesling, as well as some of the country's best Sekt (sparkling wine); the Kamptal, set back from the river, makes the area's best reds. The

Weinviertel is also known principally for light, fresh whites, but interesting things are being done with chardonnay and Weiss Grau Burgunder (Pinot Gris). Austrian wines have been steadily improving for the last decade, so this is a perfect time to start sampling their charms.

Souvenirs, Austrian-Style

Not so long ago, almost any store on Vienna's Kärntnerstrasse could boast that it once created its exquisite jewelry, fine leather goods, or petit-point handbags (as Viennese as St. Stephen's Cathedral) for the imperial Habsburgs. The court has vanished, but a few of the *Hoflieferanten* (court suppliers) still maintain their name and at times the old-fashioned grace, slightly fawning touch, and lots of *Gnä Frau* and *der Herr* thrown in for good measure. There are various types of "gifts that say Austria" to take home and enjoy, of course: fine glassware from Riedel's in Kufstein (founded 1756); Swarovski crystal; ceramics from a variety of manufacturers, including Gmunden (from Traun near Salzburg); and Augarten porcelain, Europe's oldest china after Meissen. These wares are distributed throughout the country in large and loud shops in the pedestrian zones of Vienna, Salzburg, Graz, Innsbruck, Klagenfurt, and so on. The same applies to traditional clothing: *Trachten, Lederhosen, Dirndls,* and the like can be purchased at such places as Lanz (Vienna and Salzburg), Geiger (in Salzburg), Giesswein (in Vienna) or by keeping a sharp eye out for the magic word *Trachten* while driving about. You may accidentally stumble over some treasures in small towns such as Tamsweg or Feldkirchen in Carinthia, or run across a farmer's market where honest-to-goodness handmade traditional clothing and ornamentations are being sold alongside sheep, boar, or deer skins, leatherwear of all sorts, the best plum schnapps, and elderberry and wild raspberry syrups. As for pottery and crockery, you may prefer to take home some of the cottage-industry ware from Stoob in Burgenland. Of course, sipping a cooled Schilcher on a warm summer evening on your porch at home may be the best way of remembering a terrific trip to Austria.

The Great Outdoors

Into Ecotourism? Austria is a popular vacation spot for those who want to experience nature—many rural hotels offer idyllic bases for hiking in the mountains or lake areas. There are an increasing number of *Urlaub am Bauernhof* (farm vacations) offered throughout Austria, where families can stay on a working farm and children can help take care of farm animals. There are numerous associations that can give you information on these increasingly popular accommodation options, as well as outfitters for specialty farms, such as organic farms or farms for children, for the disabled, or for horseback riders. Here are some top contacts. **Landidyll-Hotels in Österreich** (⊕ www.landidyll.at). **Farmhouse Holidays in Austria** (⊠ Gabelsbergerstrasse 19, A-5020 Salzburg ☎ 0662/880202 ⊕ www.farmholidays.com). **Kärnten/Landesverband Urlaub auf dem Bauernhof** (⊠ Viktringer Ring 5, A-9020 Klagenfurt ☎ 0463/330099 ⊕ www.urlaubambauernhof.com).

FODOR'S CHOICE

The sights, restaurants, hotels, and other travel experiences on these pages are our editors' top picks—our Fodor's Choices. They're the best of their type in the area covered by the book—not to be missed and always worth your time. In the destination chapters that follow, you will find all the details.

QUINTESSENTIAL AUSTRIA

New Year's Day concert in Vienna's Musikverein. You've seen it on television, but now you're *here* in the Golden Hall—its gilt bare-breasted ladies supporting the balconies, the walls festooned with floral displays—sharing in the excitement of a Vienna Philharmonic concert seen and heard by millions around the world.

Waltzing around the clock at a Fasching ball. Whether you go to the Opera Ball or the Zuckerbäckerball (sponsored by pastry cooks), remember that gala etiquette states a gentleman can kiss only a lady's hand.

Taking a boat to Melk Abbey on the Danube. The vineyards are glowing in all fall colors or the apricot and cherry trees are in bloom. Spring or fall or warm breezy summer, this is heaven on earth. The setting sun always makes the villages radiate, and the great Baroque monastery of Melk seems like poured gold.

A summer evening in the Weinviertel The hills of the Southern Wine Road (südliche Weinstrasse) are dotted with little family-run Heurige, where the wine is excellent, the food simple and good, the people hospitable. Often, the house's garden serves as a guest garden (*Gastgarten*); you can stay as long as the place stays open, meet other people, and make friends.

The Lipizzaner stallions at the Spanish Riding School. Where else can you see horses dance to a Mozart minuet? For sheer elegance, the combination of the chestnut-colored riding habits of the trainers and the pure white of the horses' coats can't be beat.

A hike up Salzburg's Untersberg mountain. Pack a bag with water, bread, cheese, cold cuts, and fresh fruit, and spend a day roaming the mountain, crossing icy streams, traversing cool forests, meeting cows and sheep—maybe the odd deer or fox, or kindred walker, or farmer. What's good for the body is good for the soul!

Vienna from the Leopoldsberg. The metropolis sprawls on a plain embraced on the one side by hills, traversed on the other by the flows and canals of the Danube, its barges like toys. Every detail of the city is visible on a clear day, the great Ferris wheel of the Prater, St. Stephen's Cathedral, the refinery of Schwechat. You can see way into the distance almost all the way to Bratislava.

Salzburg from the Kapuzinerberg after the first snow. A blanket of white softens the somber gray of the city and brings buildings and squares to life; you'll see features you've overlooked before, with the solid Festung watching patiently over the Christmas-card scene.

The Wachau when its apricot trees are in blossom. In spring, the narrow Danube Valley becomes a riot of fruit trees in delicate pastel blossom sweeping up hillsides from the very riverbanks.

LODGING

$$$$ **Imperial, Vienna.** Where else would Elizabeth Taylor stay when in Vienna? A dream in whipped-cream neo-rococo, this is the greatest hotel along the grand Ringstrasse boulevard. Suites may come with their own butler but few can resist the Biedermier-style attic aeries.

$$$$ **Palais Schwarzenberg, Vienna.** It's hard to believe you're in the heart of the city at this secluded hotel, set in its own vast, formal park. Built in the early 1700s, this palace is still owned by the Schwarzenberg princely family but the welcome makes you feel this is *your* home.

$$$$ **Sacher Salzburg, Salzburg.** From its vantage point along the banks of the Salzach with a staggering view of the Old City and looming fortress, this grande dame of Salzburg hotels offers rooms so exquisitely decorated, the danger is that you won't want to leave the hotel to explore the sights.

$$$$ **Schloss Dürnstein, Wachau Valley.** With an impressively Danubian ambience, this early-Baroque castle-manor has grand guestrooms, a grand river terrace, and a utterly charming restaurant.

$$$$ **Schloss Fuschl, Fuschl, Salzkammergut.** Once the retreat for Salzburg's prince-archbishops, this dramatic 15th-century tower-like castle is now a favorite for music festival celebs. The restaurant's lakeside stone terrace is pure magic.

$$$ **König von Ungarn, Vienna.** Once the home-away-from-home for 19th-century court nobility in 1815, this favorite rubs elbows with Mozart's Figarohaus. Wolfie would certainly cotton to its glowing Mozartstuberl restaurant, beautifully aglow in Schönbrunn yellow.

$$–$$$ **Cortisen am See, St. Wolfgang, Salzkammergut.** A Lake District xanadu, "At the Court" is replete with gemütlichkeit nouvelle—chintz fabrics, tin-wrought lanterns, Swedish woods, and sash windows, but updated with chic.

$$–$$$ **Römischer Kaiser, Vienna.** A pastel-pink confection of a hotel, the Roman Emperor once hosted Liszt, Wagner, and Grieg. Lots of burnished wood trim and crystal chandeliers make this place staidly, wonderfully Viennese.

$$-$$$	**Schloss Leonstain, Pörtschach, Carinthia** Brahms was inspired to write his Second Symphony at this magisterially charming retreat, which comes adorned with a Bohemian cupola, Tyrolean red-and-white doors, and an enchanting Renaissance courtyard.
$$	**Altstadt, Vienna.** Located in the charming Spittelberg quarter, set with high-style, design-y interiors, and blessed with gentle prices, the Altstadt is always in the winner's circle.

RESTAURANTS

$$$$	**Steirereck, Vienna.** A true culinary temple, Austria's most raved-about restaurant is now housed in a Jugendstil-vintage Milkhaus-pavilion. The menu is nouvelle Styrian and just one bite of the warm artichoke "cocktail" with caviar promises a meal with great flair.
$$$$	**Obauer, Werfen, Eastern Alps.** Salzburgers make the trek here to dine on the newer-than-now creations of the brothers Karl and Rudolf—stuffed duck with mugwort, anyone?
$$$-$$$$	**Ruben's Palais, Vienna.** Once you've feasted your eyes on the Prince of Liechtenstein's fabled Old Master paintings, head to his garden palace's restaurant for a true feast for the tastebuds.
$$$-$$$$	**Taubenkobel, Eisenstadt, Eastern Austria.** Alpine luxe is the keynote here, with wooden beams, cathedral ceilings, and a kitchen that is haute farmhouse. Save room for the liquid chocolate cake.
$$-$$$$	**Stiftskeller St. Peter, Salzburg.** Europe's oldest Gasthaus—Mephistopheles supposedly met Faust here—this abbey landmark offers everything from candlelit Mozart dinners to fingerlickingly good schnitzels.
$$-$$$$	**Villa Schratt, Bad Ischl.** Fabled retreat of the actress Katharina Schratt—Franz Josef's beloved amour—this enchanting villa now attracts discerning diners, not European royalty. Who can resist the emperor's favorite, warm-from-the-oven Guglhupf cake?
$$-$$$	**Zum Eulenspiegel, Salzburg.** This little cottage looks as if it's straight out of a fairy tale, and happily the food matches the unique setting. Nooks, crannies, odd staircases: Forget kitsch, this is genuine Old World authentic.
$$-$$$	**Griechenbeisl, Vienna.** Head to the Zitherstüberl room to tap your toes to the zither at this time-stained tavern, once graced by the likes of Beethoven, Mozart, Schubert, and Gina Lollabrigida, and set on the most charming square.
$	**Café Central, Vienna.** Nothing embodies the spirit of Viennese café society than this grand, plush coffeehouse. Trotsky supposedly plotted the Russian Revolution here under portraits of the Austrian imperial family.

HISTORIC TOWNS & PICTURESQUE SQUARES

Hauptplatz, Linz. The spacious main square of the Upper Austrian capital has been handsomely restored; church spires rather than skyscrapers shape the skyline. The square is the site for local markets just as it was centuries ago, with many of the same buildings gracing the scene.

Old City, Graz. Narrow winding streets tucked below the city's "mountain" invite exploration. The old quarter exudes charm and has attracted a host of boutiques and tiny restaurants, all wedged willy-nilly into odd corners. This is one of Austria's better-kept secrets.

Steyr, Upper Austria. Wonderfully colorful decorative facades address the main square, brooded over by the castle above. Tiny, half-concealed stairways lead upward to the castle area, while other stone steps take you down the opposite side to the riverbank. The setting is an ensemble worthy of Hollywood; in this case, it's all charmingly real.

CHURCHES & ABBEYS

Melk, Lower Austria. Probably the most impressive of Europe's abbeys, Melk perches like a magnificent yellow-frosted wedding cake overlooking the Danube, its ornate library holding rows of priceless treasures. If you can visit only one abbey in all of Europe, Melk should be among the top contenders.

St. Florian, Upper Austria. This abbey, where composer Anton Bruckner was organist, is impressive for its sheer size alone. Add to the symmetrical structure the glorious church and the representational rooms, and you have one of Austria's religious highlights.

St. Stephan's Cathedral, Vienna. The country's Catholic life centers on St. Stephen's, rebuilt after burning during the last days of World War II. It is one of Europe's finest Gothic structures, with two different towers, one of which can be climbed on foot; the other has an elevator and holds the *Pummerin,* Austria's largest bell. Like the exterior, the interior of the cathedral is a masterpiece, especially of stone carving.

PARKS & GARDENS

Mirabell Gardens, Salzburg. For an idyllic view, look up through the formal garden to the castle (Festung) dominating the city, but don't miss the droll Baroque side garden with its amusing stone dwarfs.

Schönbrunn, Vienna. Was the palace an excuse for the gardens, or vice versa? The manicured trees, the symmetrical walkways, the discoveries at various intersections—all add to the pleasure of exploration here. Climb to the Gloriette, which is now a moderately good café, for a sweeping perspective of the gardens and the city beyond.

SMART TRAVEL TIPS

Addresses
Air Travel
Airports
Bike Travel
Boat & Ferry Travel
Bus Travel
Business Hours
Cameras & Photography
Car Rental
Car Travel
Children in Austria
Computers on the Road
Consumer Protection
Customs & Duties
Dining
Disabilities & Accessibility
Electricity
Embassies
Emergencies
English- & Local Language Media
Etiquette & Behavior
Gay & Lesbian Travel
Health
Holidays
Language
Lodging
Mail & Shipping
Money Matters
Packing
Passports & Visas
Safety
Senior-Citizen Travel
Sports & Outdoor Activities
Students in Austria
Taxes
Telephones
Time
Tipping
Tours & Packages
Train Travel
Travel Agencies
Visitor Information
Web Sites

Half the fun of traveling is looking forward to your trip—but when you look forward, don't just daydream. There are plans to be made, things to learn about, serious work to be done. The following chapter will give you helpful pointers on many of the questions that arise when planning your trip and also when you are on the road. Finding out about your destination before you leave home means you won't squander time organizing everyday minutiae once you've arrived. You'll be more streetwise when you hit the ground as well, better prepared to explore the aspects of Austria that drew you here in the first place. The organizations in this section can provide information to supplement this guide; contact them for up-to-the-minute details. Many trips begin by first contacting the Austrian tourist bureau: consult the Austrian National Tourist Offices listed under Visitor Information, below. Happy landings!

ADDRESSES

Willkommen in Österreich—welcome to Austria! Now that you are about to hit the ground running, here's a quick rundown on the basic geographical terms you'll want to be familiar with. The word for city is *Stadt*—prominently used when referring to Vienna's big First District, the *Inner Stadt*, or the historic center of Salzburg, the *Alt Stadt* (or Old City). The most frequently used term is *Strasse*, or street, and it is sometimes merged with the actual name of the street, as in Mahlerstasse 9 (note that the number of the street address comes after the name), or not, as in Ottakringer-Strasse. Next up is the word for square, or plaza: *Platz*, as in Mozartplatz or Südtirolerplatz. Many cities and towns have their marketplace squares, and this word translates into *Markt*, as in Neumarkt. Other words to know are *Brückenpfeiler* for pier, and *Bastei*, which means bastion. Another term is *Weg*, which means way or path, as in the street name of Rennweg. The words for castle is *Burg*, while *Schloss* usually means palace. If lost, try the following German phrase: *Entschuldigen Sie, kön-*

nen Sie mir sagen wo ist der Rennweg oder wo ist die Kärntnerstrasse—"Please, can you show me where is Rennweg or Kärnter Street." Or you can use the simpler *Kennen Sie den Rennweg?* which means "Do you know Rennweg?" Every Austrian will know you mean you need directions to this street.

AIR TRAVEL

CARRIERS & CONSOLIDATORS

When flying internationally, you must usually choose between a domestic carrier, the national flag carrier of the country you are visiting, and a foreign carrier from a third country. You may, for example, choose to fly **Austrian Airlines** to Austria. National flag carriers have the greatest number of nonstops. Domestic carriers may have better connections to your home town and serve a greater number of gateway cities. Third-party carriers may have a price advantage.

Austrian Airlines is the only air carrier that flies nonstop to Vienna from various points in the United States. There are no longer any American or Canadian carriers who fly directly to Vienna. Many major American carriers—such as American, Northwest, and United—instead fly passengers to major European hubs, such as London, Amsterdam, or Frankfurt, for transfers to flights with other airlines. Austrian Airlines is currently in partnership with United Airlines. Austrian Airlines also has many routes connecting Vienna with every major European destination.

Travelers from North America should note that many international carriers do service Vienna after stopovers at major European airports. For instance, Lufthansa flies from the U.S. to Frankfurt, Düsseldorf, and Munich, then can offer you connections to Vienna. British Airways (which has 15 gateways from the U.S. alone) offers many direct flights to Vienna from London's Heathrow and Gatwick airports. Note, too, that the western sector of Austria—including Innsbruck, the Tirol, and Vorarlberg—are actually closer by air to Munich than Vienna, so you might consider the option of using an international carrier to Mu-

nich, then traveling by train or connecting by air to Innsbruck or even Salzburg. Also, Ryanair flies from London Stansted to major destinations in Austria—except Vienna—for rock bottom prices, if you book early.

Within Austria, Austrian Airlines and its subsidiary, **Austrian Arrows,** offer service from Vienna to Linz and Innsbruck; they also provide routes to and from points outside Austria. In addition, **Welcome** is now providing some nice air links between Innsbruck, Graz, and other European cities. Winter schedules on all domestic lines depend on snow conditions.

Other than the main carriers, consolidators are another good source. They buy tickets for scheduled international flights at reduced rates from the airlines, then sell them at prices that beat the best fare available directly from the airlines, usually without restrictions. Sometimes you can even get your money back if you need to return the ticket. Carefully read the fine print detailing penalties for changes and cancellations, and **confirm your consolidator reservation with the airline.**

✈ Major Airlines Austrian Airlines ☎ 800/843-0002. **British Airways** ☎ 800/247-9297, 020/8897-4000 London, 0345/222-111 outside London. **Lufthansa** ☎ 800/645-3880.

✈ From the U.K. Austrian Airlines ☎ 020/7434-7300. **Ryanair** ⊕ www.ryanair.com. **British Airways** ☎ 020/8897-4000, 0345/222-111 outside London.

✈ Within Austria Austrian Airlines ✉ main Austrian office, Kärntner Ring 18, A-1010 Vienna ☎ 05/1789 from all over Austria. **Welcome** ☎ 0512/295-296 in Innsbruck ⊕ www.welcomeair.at.

✈ Consolidators Cheap Tickets ☎ 800/377-1000. **Discount Airline Ticket Service** ☎ 800/576-1600. **Unitravel** ☎ 800/325-2222. **Up & Away Travel** ☎ 212/889-2345 ⊕ www.upandaway.com. **World Travel Network** ☎ 800/409-6753.

CHECK-IN & BOARDING

Assuming that not everyone with a ticket will show up, airlines routinely overbook planes. When everyone does, airlines ask for volunteers to give up their seats. In return, these volunteers usually get a certificate for a free flight and are rebooked on the next flight out. If there are not enough volunteers, the airline must choose who will be denied boarding. The first to get bumped are passengers who checked in late and those flying on discounted tickets, so **get to the gate and check in as early as possible,** especially during peak periods. Although the trend on international flights is to drop reconfirmation requirements, many airlines still ask you to reconfirm each leg of your international itinerary. Failure to do so may result in your reservation's being canceled. Always **bring a government-issued photo ID to the airport.** You will be asked to show it before you are allowed to check in.

FLYING TIMES

Flying time is 8 hours to Vienna from New York, 9 hours from Washington, and 90 minutes from London.

AIRPORTS

The major airport is Vienna's **Schwechat Airport,** about 12 mi southeast of the city. Just south of Graz, in Thalerhof, is the **Graz Airport. Salzburg Airport** is Austria's second largest airport, located about 2½ mi west of the center.

🛪 Airport Information **Graz Airport** ☎ 0316/2902–0; **Schwechat Airport (Vienna)** ☎ 01/7007–0. **Salzburg Airport** ☎ 0662/8580.

AIRPORT TRANSFERS

The fastest way into Vienna from Schwechat Airport is the sleek, double-decker **City Train.** The journey from the airport to Wien–Mitte (the center of the city) takes only 16 minutes and operates daily every 30 minutes between 5:30 AM and midnight. The cost is €8 one-way and €15 round-trip.

The cheapest way to get to Vienna from the airport is the **S7 train,** called the *Schnellbahn,* which shuttles twice an hour between the airport basement and the Landstrasse/Wien–Mitte (city center) and Wien–Nord (north Vienna) stations; the fare is €3 and it takes about 35 minutes (19 minutes longer than the City Train). Your ticket is also good for an immediate transfer to your destination within the city on the streetcar, bus, or U-Bahn. Another cheap option is the **bus,** which has two separate lines. One line goes to the City

Air Terminal at the Hilton Hotel (near the city's 1st District) every 20 minutes between 6:30 AM and 11 PM, and every 30 minutes after that; traveling time is 20 minutes. The other line goes to the South and West train stations (Südbahnhof and Westbahnhof) in 20 and 35 minutes, respectively. Departure times are every 30 minutes from 8:10 AM to 7:10 PM, hourly thereafter, and not at all 12:10–3:30 AM. Fare is €5.80 one-way, €10.90 for a round-trip. Prices may be higher in 2005 and beyond. Another possibility is via taxi with **C&K Airport Service** (☎ 01/44444 🖶 01/689–6969), charging a set price of €25 (don't forget to tip). C+K will also meet your plane at no extra charge if you let them know your flight information in advance.

If you land in **Salzburg,** the bus line No. 77 shuttles every 15 minutes from the airport to the train station, otherwise take a taxi. If you land in **Munich,** the cheapest way of getting to town is with the S8 train, which takes about 45 minutes to the main train station (Hauptbahnhof) with stops along the way and connecting rides.

BIKE TRAVEL

Biking is a popular sport in Austria. In central Vienna, special bike lanes make transportation fast, easy, and safe. Throughout Austria there are several cycling trails, including the well-known Passau (Germany) to Vienna route, which follows the Danube across the country, passing through the spectacular Danube Valley. There are other cycling trails in the Alps and around lakes in Carinthia and the Salzkammergut (*see* Sports & Outdoor Activities, *below*). Mountain biking is increasingly popular, with "mountain bike hotels" welcoming enthusiasts, along with rigorous guided tours.

🚲 **Mountain Bike Hotels** ✉ Margaretenstrasse 1, A-1010 Vienna ☎ 0810/101818 🖶 0810/101819 ⊕ www.austria.info.

BIKES IN FLIGHT

Most airlines accommodate bikes as luggage, provided they are dismantled and boxed. For bike boxes, often free at bike shops, you'll pay about $5 from airlines (at least $100 for bike bags). International travelers can sometimes substitute a bike for a piece of checked luggage at no charge; otherwise, the cost is about $100. Domestic and Canadian airlines charge $25–$50.

BOAT & FERRY TRAVEL

For leisurely travel between Vienna and Linz or eastward across the border into Slovakia or Hungary, consider taking a Danube boat. More than 300 km (187 mi) of Austria's most beautiful scenery awaits you as you glide past castles and ruins, medieval monasteries and abbeys, and lush vineyards. One of the lovelier sections, particularly in spring, is the *Wachau* (Danube Valley) west of Vienna. **Blue Danube Schifffahrt** offers a diverse selection of pleasant cruises, including trips to Melk Abbey and Dürnstein in the Wachau, a grand tour of Vienna's architectural sights from the river, and a dinner cruise, featuring Johann Strauss waltzes as background music. **Brandner Schifffart** offers the same kind of cruises between Krems and Melk, in the heart of the Danube Valley.

Most of the immaculate white-painted craft carry about 1,000 passengers each on their three decks. As soon as you get on board, give the steward a good tip for a deck chair and ask him to place it where you will get the best views. Be sure to book cabins in advance. Day trips are also possible on the Danube. You can use boats to move from one riverside community to the next, and along some sections, notably the Wachau, the only way to cross the river is to use the little shuttles (in the Wachau, these are special motorless boats that use the current to cross).

For the cruises up and down the Danube, the Blue Danube Steamship Company/ DDSG departs and arrives at Praterlände near Vienna's Mexikoplatz. The Praterlände stop is a two-block taxi ride or hike from the Vorgartenstrasse subway station on the U1 route of Vienna's U-Bahn. There is no pier number, but you board at Handelskai 265. Boat trips from Vienna to the Wachau are on Sundays only from May to September. The price is €19 one

way and €25 round-trip. There are other daily cruises within the Wachau, such as from Melk to Krems. Other cruises, to Budapest for instance, operate from April to early November. The Web site has dozens of options and timetables in English. For more information, see the "And the Danube Waltzes On" Close-Up box in Chapter 4.

Boat & Ferry Information Contact your travel agent or, in Austria, the **Blue Danube Schifffahrt:** ✉ Friedrichstrasse 7, A-1043 Vienna ☎ 01/588-800 🖨 01/588-8044-0 ⊕ www.ddsg-blue-danube.at For cruises from Krems to Melk, contact **Brandner Schifffahrt** ✉ Ufer 50, A-3313 Wallsee ☎ 07433/ 2590-21 ⊕ www.brandner.at.

BUS TRAVEL IN AUSTRIA

BUS LINES

Austria features extensive national networks of buses run by post offices and railroads. Where Austrian trains don't go, buses do, and you'll find the railroad and post-office buses (bright yellow for easy recognition) in even remote regions carrying passengers as well as mail. You can get tickets on the bus, and in the off-season there is no problem getting a seat, but on routes to favored ski areas during holiday periods reservations are essential. Bookings can be handled at the ticket office (there's one in most towns with bus service) or by travel agents. In most communities, bus routes begin and end at or near the railroad station, making transfers easy. Increasingly, coordination of bus service with railroads means that many of the discounts and special tickets available for trains apply to buses as well. There are private bus companies in Austria as well. Buses in Austria run like clockwork, typically departing and arriving on time. Smoking is generally allowed.

Private Bus Lines Columbus ☎ 01/53411-0. **Blaguss Reisen** ☎ 01/50180-150. **Post und Bahn** ☎ 01/71101. **Dr. Richard** ☎ 01/33100-0.

BUSINESS HOURS

BANKS & OFFICES

In most cities, banks are open weekdays 8–3, Thursday until 5:30 PM. Lunch hour is from 12:30 to 1:30. All banks are closed on Saturday, but you can change money at various locations (such as American Express offices on Saturday morning and major railroad stations around the clock), and changing machines are also found here and there in the larger cities.

GAS STATIONS

Gas stations on the major autobahns are open 24 hours a day, but in smaller towns and villages you can expect them to close early in the evening and on Sundays. You can usually count on at least one station to stay open on Sundays and holidays in most medium-size towns, and buying gas in larger cities is never a problem.

MUSEUMS & SIGHTS

Museum hours vary from city to city and museum to museum; if museums are closed one day, it is usually Monday. Few Austrian museums are open at night. In summer, the Salzburg Zoo at Hellbrunn has nighttime hours for viewing the nocturnal animals.

PHARMACIES

Pharmacies (called *Apotheken* in German) are usually open from 9 to 6, with a midday break between 12 and 2. In each area of the city one pharmacy stays open 24 hours; if a pharmacy is closed, a sign on the door will tell you the address of the nearest one that is open. Call 01/1550 for names and addresses (in German) of the pharmacies open that night. You may find over-the-counter remedies for headaches and colds much less effective than those sold in the U.S. Austrians are firm believers in natural remedies, such as herbal teas.

SHOPS

In general, you'll find shops open weekdays from 8:30 or 9 until 6, with a lunchtime closing from noon to 1 or 1:30. In smaller villages, the midday break may run until 3. Many food stores, bakeries, and small grocery shops open at 7 or 7:30 and, aside from the noontime break, stay open until 7 or 7:30 PM. Shops in large city centers forego the noon break. On Saturday, most shops stay open until 5 or 6 PM, though a few follow the old rules and close by 1 PM. Food stores stay open until 5 on Saturdays. Barbers and hairdressers traditionally take Monday off, but there

are exceptions. It is fashionable these days for hairdressers to work evenings and nights on certain "good-for-haircutting" moon days! Also in the country, many shops close on Wednesday afternoon, and in parts of Burgenland they may also close on Thursday afternoon.

CAMERAS & PHOTOGRAPHY

◪ Photo Help **Kodak Information Center** ☎ 800/242-2424. *Kodak Guide to Shooting Great Travel Pictures* ☎ 800/533-6478 ✉ $18 plus $5.50 shipping available in bookstores or from Fodor's Travel Publications.

EQUIPMENT PRECAUTIONS

Always **keep your film and tape out of the sun.** Carry an extra supply of batteries, and **be prepared to turn on your camera or camcorder** to prove to security personnel that the device is real. Always **ask for hand inspection of film,** which becomes clouded after repeated exposure to airport X-ray machines, and **keep videotapes away from metal detectors.**

FILM & DEVELOPING

All kinds of film are available for purchase in Austria, with the best prices at grocery and drug stores. Developing is very expensive, especially for one-hour service.

VIDEOS

Austrian video tapes use the PAL system, which is not compatible with NTSC players in the U.S. The same goes for DVDs.

CAR RENTAL

Rates in Vienna begin at €44 a day and €132 a weekend for an economy car with manual transmission and unlimited mileage. This includes a 21% tax on car rentals. Rates are more expensive in winter months, when a surcharge for winter tires is added. Renting a car may be cheaper in Germany, but make sure the rental agency knows that you are driving into Austria and that the car is equipped with an autobahn sticker (*see* Car Travel, *below*) for Austria. When renting an RV be sure to compare prices and reserve early. It's cheaper to arrange your rental car from the U.S., but **be sure to get a confirmation of your quoted rate in writing.**

Before you pick up a car in one city and leave it in another, **ask about drop-off charges or one-way service fees,** which can be substantial. Note, too, that some rental agencies charge extra if you return the car before the time specified in your contract.

🚗 Major Agencies **Alamo** ☎ 800/522-9696 ⊕ www.alamo.com. **Avis** ☎ 800/331-1084, 800/879-2847 in Canada, 0870/606-0100 in the U.K., 02/9353-9000 in Australia, 09/526-2847 in New Zealand ⊕ www.avis.com. **Budget** ☎ 800/527-0700, 0870/156-5656 in the U.K. ⊕ www.budget.com. **Dollar** ☎ 800/800-6000, 0124/622-0111 in the U.K., where it's affiliated with Sixt, 02/9223-1444 in Australia ⊕ www.dollar.com. **Hertz** ☎ 800/654-3001, 800/263-0600 in Canada, 020/8897-2072 in the U.K., 02/9669-2444 in Australia, 09/256-8690 in New Zealand ⊕ www.hertz.com. **National Car Rental** ☎ 800/227-7368, 020/8680-4800 in the U.K. ⊕ www.nationalcar.com.

🚗 Local Agencies **Denzel Drive** ✉ Erdberg Center/U-Bahn (U3), A-1110 Vienna ☎ 01/740-50. **Autoverleih Buchbinder** ✉ Schlachthausgasse 38, A-1030 Vienna ☎ 01/717-50-0 🖨 01/717-5022 with offices throughout Austria.

CUTTING COSTS
To get the best deal, **book through a travel agent who will shop around.** Also **ask your travel agent about a company's customer-service record.** How has the company responded to delayed plane arrivals and vehicle mishaps? Are there often lines at the rental counter? If you're traveling during a holiday period, does a confirmed reservation guarantee you a car? Make sure to fill up the tank before returning the car, and **get a confirmation in writing that it is full before leaving the dealership** to avoid being mistakenly billed for gas.

Do **look into wholesalers,** companies that do not own fleets but rent in bulk from those that do at often better rates than traditional car-rental operations. Prices are best during off-peak periods. Payment must be made before you leave home.

🚗 Wholesalers **Auto Europe** ☎ 207/842-2000 or 800/223-5555 🖨 800/235-6321 ⊕ www.autoeurope.com. **Europe by Car** ☎ 212/581-3040 or 800/223-1516 🖨 212/246-1458 ⊕ www.europebycar.com. **DER Travel Services** ✉ 9501 W. Devon Ave., Rosemont, IL 60018 ☎ 800/782-2424 🖨 800/282-

7474 for information, 800/860-9944 for brochures ⊕ www.dertravel.com. **Kemwel Holiday Autos** ☎ 800/678-0678 🖨 914/825-3160 ⊕ www.kemwel.com.

INSURANCE
When driving a rented car you are generally responsible for any damage to or loss of the vehicle. Before you rent, see what coverage your personal auto-insurance policy and credit cards already provide. Collision policies that car-rental companies sell for European rentals usually do not include stolen-vehicle coverage. Before you buy it, check your existing policies—you may already be covered.

REQUIREMENTS & RESTRICTIONS
In Austria your own driver's license is acceptable. An International Driver's Permit is a good idea; it's available from the American or Canadian automobile association, and, in the United Kingdom, from the Automobile Association or Royal Automobile Club. These international permits are universally recognized, and having one in your wallet may save you a problem with the local authorities. There is no age limit to renting a car at most agencies in Austria. However, you must have had a valid driver's license for one year. For some of the more expensive car models, drivers must be at least 25 years of age. There is no extra charge to drive over the border into Italy, Switzerland, or Germany, but there are some restrictions and possible additional charges for taking a rental car into Slovakia, Slovenia, Hungary, the Czech Republic, or Poland.

CAR TRAVEL IN AUSTRIA
Vienna is 300 km (187 mi) east of Salzburg, 200 km (125 mi) north of Graz. Main routes leading into the city are the A1 Westautobahn from Germany, Salzburg, and Linz and the A2 Südautobahn from Graz and points south.

AUTO CLUBS
Austria has two automobile clubs, ÖAMTC and ARBÖ, both of which operate motorist service patrols. You'll find emergency (orange-colored) phones along all the highways. If you break down along the autobahn, a small arrow on the

guardrail will direct you to the nearest phone. Otherwise, if you have problems, call **ARBÖ** (☎ 123) or **ÖAMTC** (☎ 120) from anywhere in the country. No area or other code is needed for either number. Both clubs charge nonmembers for emergency service. Remember to get proper coverage from your home club.

🚘 In Austria **Austrian Automobile Club/ÖAMTC** ⊠ Schubertring 1-3, A-1010 Vienna ☎ 01/71199 ⊕ www.oemtc.at.

🚘 In Australia **Australian Automobile Association** ☎ 06/247-7311.

🚘 In Canada **Canadian Automobile Association** CAA ☎ 613/247-0117.

🚘 In New Zealand **New Zealand Automobile Association** ☎ 09/377-4660.

🚘 In the U.K. **Automobile Association** AA ☎ 0990/500-600. **Royal Automobile Club** RAC ☎ 0990/722-722 for membership, 0345/121-345 for insurance.

🚘 In the U.S. **American Automobile Association** ☎ 800/564-6222.

FROM THE U.K.

The best way to reach Austria by car from England is to take North Sea/Cross Channel ferries to Oostende or Zeebrugge in Belgium or Dunkirk in northern France. An alternative is the Channel Tunnel; motoring clubs can give you the best routing to tie into the Continental motorway network. Then take the toll-free Belgian motorway (E5) to Aachen, and head via Stuttgart to Innsbruck and the Tirol (A61, A67, A5, E11, A7), or east by way of Nürnberg and Munich, crossing into Austria at Walserberg and then on to Salzburg and Vienna. Total distance to Innsbruck from London is about 1,100 km (650 mi); to Vienna, about 1,600 km (1,000 mi). The most direct way to Vienna is virtually all on the autobahn via Nürnberg, Regensburg, and Passau, entering Austria at Schärding. In summer, border delays are much shorter at Schärding than at Salzburg. The trip to Innsbruck via this route will take 2–3 days.

If this seems like too much driving, in summer you can **put the car on a train** in s'Hertogenbosch in central southern Netherlands on Thursday, or in Schaerbeek (Brussels) on Friday, for an overnight trip,

arriving in Salzburg early the following morning and in Villach three hours later.

🚘 Agencies **DER Travel Service** ⊠ 18 Conduit St., London W1R 9TD ☎ 020/7290-0111 🖷 020/ 7629-7442 has details on fares and schedules.

EMERGENCY SERVICES
See Auto Clubs, *above.*

GASOLINE
Gasoline and diesel are readily available, but on Sunday stations in the more out-of-the-way areas may be closed. Stations carry only unleaded (*bleifrei*) gas, both regular and premium (super), and diesel. If you're in the mountains in winter with a diesel, and there is a cold snap (with temperatures threatening to drop below -4°F [-20°C]), add a few liters of gasoline to your diesel, about 1:4 parts, to prevent it from freezing. Gasoline prices are the same throughout the country, slightly lower at discount and self-service stations. Expect to pay about €0.98 per liter for regular, €1 for premium, and €0.87 for diesel. If you are driving to Italy, fill up before crossing the border because gas in Italy is even more expensive. Oil in Austria is expensive, retailing at €9 upward per liter. If need be, purchase oil, windshield-wipers, and other paraphernalia at big hardware stores.

ROAD CONDITIONS
Roads in Austria are excellent and well-maintained—perhaps a bit too well-maintained judging by the frequently encountered construction zones on the autobahns.

ROAD MAPS
A set of eight excellent, detailed road maps is available from the Austrian Automobile Club/ÖAMTC (*see above*), at most service stations, and at many bookstores. The maps supplied without charge by the Austrian National Tourist Office are adequate for most needs, but if you will be covering much territory, the better ÖAMTC maps are a worthwhile investment.

RULES OF THE ROAD
Tourists from EU countries may bring their cars to Austria with no documentation other than the normal registration

papers and their regular driver's license. A Green Card, the international certificate of insurance, is recommended for EU drivers and compulsory for others. All cars must carry a first-aid kit (including rubber gloves) and a red warning triangle to use in case of accident or breakdown. These are available at gas stations along the road, or at any automotive supply store or large hardware store.

The minimum driving age in Austria is 18, and children under 12 years of age must ride in the back seat; smaller children require a restraining seat. Note that all passengers must use seat belts.

Drive on the right side of the street in Austria. Vehicles coming from the right have the right of way, except that at unregulated intersections streetcars coming from either direction have the right of way. No turns are allowed on red. In residential areas, the right of way can be switched around; the rule is, be careful at any intersection.

Drinking and driving: the maximum blood-alcohol content allowed is 0.5 parts per thousand, which in real terms means very little to drink. Remember when driving in Europe that the police can stop you anywhere at any time for no particular reason.

Unless otherwise marked, the speed limit on autobahns is 130 kph (80 mph), although this is not always strictly enforced. But if you're pulled over for speeding, fines are payable on the spot, and can be heavy. On other highways and roads, the limit is 100 kph (62 mph), 80 kph (49 mph) for RVs or cars pulling a trailer weighing more than 750 kilos (about 1,650 lbs). In built-up areas, a 50 kph (31 mph) limit applies and is likely to be taken seriously. In some towns, special 30 kph (20 mph) limits apply. More and more towns have radar cameras to catch speeders. Remember that insurance does not necessarily pay if it can be proved you were going above the limit when involved in an accident.

Sometimes the signs at exits and entrances on the autobahns are not clear—a reason why Austria has a special problem, called

the "*Geisterfahrer*," which means a driver going the wrong way in traffic. Efforts are being made to correct this problem with clearer signage.

If you're going to travel Austria's highways, make absolutely sure your car is equipped with the *Autobahnvignette,* as it is called, a little trapezoidal sticker with a highway icon and the Austrian eagle, or with a calendar marked with an M or a W. This sticker allows use of the autobahn. It costs €72.60 for a year and is available at gas stations, tobacconists, and automobile-club outlets in neighboring countries or near the border. You can also purchase a two-month Vignette for €21.80, or a 10-day one for €7.60. Prices are for vehicles up to 3.5 tons and RVs. For motorcycles it is €29 for one year, €10.90 for two months, and €4.30 for 10 days. Not having a Vignette (which is generally called the *Pickerl*) can lead to extremely high fines if you're caught. Get your Pickerl before driving to Austria!

Besides the Pickerl, if you are planning to drive around a lot, budget in a great deal of toll money: for example, the tunnels on the A10 autobahn cost €9.50, the Grossglockner Pass road will cost €26 per car, or €13 after 6 PM, while passing through the Arlberg Tunnel costs €8.50. Driving up some especially beautiful valleys, such as the Kaunertal in Tirol, or up to the Tauplitzalm in Styria, also costs money— €5.50 per person and €19 per car for the Kaunertal, and €2.55 per person and €9.45 per car for the Tauplitzalm.

The Austrian highway network is excellent, and roads are well maintained and well marked. Secondary roads may be narrow and winding. Remember that in winter you will need snow tires and often chains, even on well-traveled roads. It's wise to check with the automobile clubs for weather conditions, since mountain roads are often blocked, and ice and fog are hazards.

CHILDREN IN AUSTRIA

Be sure to plan ahead and **involve your youngsters** as you outline your trip. When packing, include things to keep them busy en route. On sightseeing days try to schedule activities of special interest to your children. If you are renting a car, don't forget to **arrange for a car seat** when you reserve. Austria is filled with wonders and delights for children, ranging from the performing Lipizzaner horses at the Spanish Riding School in Vienna to the Salzburg Marionettentheater and the rural delights of farm vacations.

☎ Baby-Sitting In Vienna, the central baby-sitting services are **Dienstleistungzentrum** ✉ Neubaugasse 66, A-1070 ☎ 01/523-4601 and **Wiener Hilfwerk** ✉ Schottenfeldgasse 29, A-1070 ☎ 01/512-3661-29. It's best to have your hotel call to make the arrangements, unless you speak German.

DINING

The best restaurants in Vienna do not welcome small children; fine dining is considered an adult pastime. With kids, **you're best off taking them to more casual restaurants and cafés.** *Heurige* are perfect for family dining, and they usually open by 4 PM. To accommodate flexible meal times, look for signs that say DURCHGEHEND WARME KÜCHE, which means warm meals are available all afternoon. Cafés offer light meals all day, and you can always get a sausage from a *Würstelstand*. Several chain restaurants have high chairs (*Hochstühle*), and a few serve children's portions (*Für den kleinen Hunger*), usually *Wienerschnitzel*, a thin slice of veal, breaded and fried.

LODGING

Most hotels in Austria allow children under a certain age to stay in their parents' room at no extra charge, but others charge for them as extra adults; be sure to **find out the cutoff age for children's discounts.**

SIGHTS & ATTRACTIONS

Places that are especially appealing to children are indicated by a rubber duckie icon—☺—in the margin.

SUPPLIES & EQUIPMENT

Supermarkets and drug stores (look for *DM Drogerie* and *Bipa*) carry *Windeln* (diapers), universally referred to as Pampers. Remember that weight is given in kilos (2.2 pounds equals 1 kilo). Baby formula is available in grocery stores, drug stores, or pharmacies. There are two

brands of formula: Milupa and Nestlé, for infants and children up to three years old. Austrian formulas come in powder form and can be mixed with tap water.

COMPUTERS ON THE ROAD

If you use a major Internet provider, getting online in Vienna and Salzburg shouldn't be difficult. Call your Internet provider to get the local access number in Austria. Many hotels have business services with Internet access and even in-room modem lines. You may, however, need an adapter for your computer for the European-style plugs. As always, if you're traveling with a laptop, carry a spare battery and adapter. Never plug your computer into any socket before asking about surge protection. IBM sells a pen-size modem tester that plugs into a telephone jack to check whether the line is safe to use.

☎ Access Numbers in Austria AOL ☎ 01/585-8483. For **Compuserve** ☎ 0049/1805-7040-70 or 0190/7500-75, you must call Germany.

CONSUMER PROTECTION

Whenever shopping or buying travel services in Austria, **pay with a major credit card** so you can cancel payment or get reimbursed if there's a problem. If you're doing business with a particular company for the first time, **contact your local Better Business Bureau and the attorney general's offices** in your own state and the company's home state, as well. Have any complaints been filed? Finally, if you're buying a package or tour, always **consider travel insurance** that includes default coverage.

CUSTOMS & DUTIES

When shopping, **keep receipts** for all purchases. Upon reentering the country, **be ready to show customs officials what you've bought.** If you feel a duty is incorrect or object to the way your clearance was handled, note the inspector's badge number and ask to see a supervisor. If the problem isn't resolved, write to the appropriate authorities, beginning with the port director at your point of entry.

IN AUSTRIA

Travelers over 17 who are residents of European countries—regardless of citizenship—may bring in, duty free,

200 cigarettes or 50 cigars or 250 grams of tobacco, 2 liters of wine and 2 liters of 22% spirits or 1 liter of over 22% spirits, and 50 milliliters of perfume. These limits may be liberalized or eliminated under terms of the European Union agreement. Travelers from all other countries (such as those coming directly from the United States or Canada) may bring in twice these amounts. All visitors may bring gifts or other purchases valued at up to €175 (about $210), although in practice you'll seldom be asked.

IN AUSTRALIA

Australian residents who are 18 or older may bring home $A400 worth of souvenirs and gifts (including jewelry), 250 cigarettes or 250 grams of tobacco, and 1,125 ml of alcohol (including wine, beer, and spirits). Residents under 18 may bring back $A200 worth of goods. Prohibited items include meat products. Seeds, plants, and fruits need to be declared upon arrival.

🔳 **Australian Customs Service** ⌂ Regional Director, Box 8, Sydney, NSW 2001 ☎ 02/9213-2000 or 1300/363263, 1800/020504 quarantine-inquiry line 🖷 02/9213-4043 ⊕ www.customs.gov.au.

IN CANADA

Canadian residents who have been out of Canada for at least 7 days may bring home C$500 worth of goods duty free. If you've been away less than 7 days but more than 48 hours, the duty-free allowance drops to C$200; if your trip lasts 24–48 hours, the allowance is C$50. You may not pool allowances with family members. Goods claimed under the C$500 exemption may follow you by mail; those claimed under the lesser exemptions must accompany you. Alcohol and tobacco products may be included in the 7-day and 48-hour exemptions but not in the 24-hour exemption. If you meet the age requirements of the province or territory through which you reenter Canada, you may bring in, duty free, 1.14 liters (40 imperial ounces) of wine or liquor *or* 24 12-ounce cans or bottles of beer or ale. If you are 16 or older you may bring in, duty free, 200 cigarettes and 50 cigars. Check ahead of time with Revenue Canada or the

Department of Agriculture for policies regarding meat products, seeds, plants, and fruits.

You may send an unlimited number of gifts worth up to C$60 each duty-free to Canada. Label the package UNSOLICITED GIFT—VALUE UNDER $60. Alcohol and tobacco are excluded.

🔳 **Revenue Canada** ⌂ 2265 St. Laurent Blvd. S, Ottawa, Ontario K1G 4K3 ☎ 613/993-0534, 800/461-9999 in Canada ⊕ www.ccra-adrc.gc.ca.

IN NEW ZEALAND

Homeward-bound residents 17 or older may bring back $700 worth of souvenirs and gifts. Your duty-free allowance also includes 4.5 liters of wine or beer; one 1,125-ml bottle of spirits; and either 200 cigarettes, 250 grams of tobacco, 50 cigars, or a combination of the three up to 250 grams. Prohibited items include meat products, seeds, plants, and fruits.

🔳 **New Zealand Customs** Head office ⌂ The Customhouse, 17–21 Whitmore St., Box 2218, Wellington ☎ 09/300-5399 or 0800/428-786 ⊕ www.customs. govt.nz.

IN THE U.K.

If you are a U.K. resident and your journey was wholly within the European Union (EU), you won't have to pass through customs when you return to the United Kingdom. If you plan to bring back large quantities of alcohol or tobacco, check EU limits beforehand. In most cases, if you bring back more than 200 cigars, 800 cigarettes, 10 liters of spirits, and/or 90 liters of wine, you have to declare the goods upon return.

🔳 **HM Customs and Excise** ⌂ Portcullis House, 21 Cowbridge Rd. E, Cardiff CF11 9SS ☎ 029/2038-6423 or 0845/010-9000 ⊕ www.hmce.gov.uk.

IN THE U.S.

U.S. residents who have been out of the country for at least 48 hours may bring home, for personal use, $400 worth of foreign goods duty-free, as long as they haven't used the $400 allowance or any part of it in the past 30 days. This exemption may include 1 liter of alcohol (for travelers 21 and older), 200 cigarettes, and 100 non-Cuban cigars. Family members from the same household who are traveling together may pool their $400 personal exemptions. For fewer than 48 hours, the duty-free allowance drops to $200, which may include 50 cigarettes, 10 non-Cuban cigars, and 150 milliliters of alcohol (or perfume containing alcohol). The $200 allowance cannot be combined with other individuals' exemptions, and if you exceed it, the full value of all the goods will be taxed. Antiques, which the U.S. Customs Service defines as objects more than 100 years old, enter duty-free, as do original works of art done entirely by hand, including paintings, drawings, and sculptures.

You may also send packages home duty free: up to $200 worth of goods for personal use, with a limit of one parcel per addressee per day (except alcohol or tobacco products or perfume worth more than $5); label the package PERSONAL USE and attach a list of its contents and their retail value. Do not label the package UNSOLICITED GIFT or your duty-free exemption will drop to $100. Mailed items do not affect your duty-free allowance on your return.

🛂 **U.S. Customs Service** ✉ 1300 Pennsylvania Ave. NW, Washington, DC 20229 ☎ 202/354–1000 inquiries ⊕ www.customs.gov ✉ Complaints c/o ✉ Office of Regulations and Rulings ✉ Registration of equipment c/o ✉ Resource Management ☎ 202/927–0540.

DINING

Austria has the largest number of organic farms in Europe, as well as the most stringent food quality standards. (Finland comes in second, followed by Italy and Sweden, though they all fall far behind Austria; France, Spain, and the U.K. are at the bottom of the list.) An increasing number of restaurants use food and produce from local farmers, ensuring the freshest ingredients for their guests.

When dining out, you'll get the best value at simpler restaurants. Most post menus with prices outside. If you begin with the *Würstelstand* (sausage vendor) on the street, the next category would be the *Imbiss-Stube,* for simple, quick snacks. Many meat stores serve soups and a daily special at noon; a blackboard menu will be posted

outside. A number of cafés also offer lunch, but watch the prices; some can turn out to be more expensive than restaurants. *Gasthäuser* are simple restaurants or country inns. Austrian hotels have some of the best restaurants in the country, often with outstanding chefs. In the past few years the restaurants along the autobahns have developed into very good places to eat (besides being, in many cases, architecturally interesting). Some Austrian chain restaurants offer excellent value for the money, such as Wienerwald, which specializes in chicken dishes, and Nordsee, which has a wide selection of fish.

In all restaurants, be aware that the basket of bread put on your table isn't free. Most of the older-style Viennese restaurants charge €0.70–€1.25 for each roll that is eaten, but more and more establishments are beginning to charge a per person cover charge—anywhere from €1.5 to €4— which includes all the bread you want, plus usually an herb spread and butter. Tap water (*Leitungswasser*) in Austria comes straight from the Alps and is among the purest in the world. Be aware, however, that a few restaurants in touristy areas are beginning to charge for tap water.

For a discussion of the delights of Austrian cuisine, *see* "Schnitzels, Strudels, and Sachertortes" *in* Pleasures and Pastimes in the Destination chapter, in the front of this book.

MEALTIMES

Besides the normal three meals—*Frühstück* (Breakfast), *Mittagessen* (Lunch), and *Abendessen* (Dinner)—Austrians sometimes throw in a few snacks in between, or forego one meal for a snack. The day begins with a very early Continental breakfast of rolls and coffee. *Gabelfrühstück* is a slightly more substantial breakfast with eggs or cold meat. A main meal is usually served between noon and 2, and an afternoon *Jause* (coffee with cake) is taken at teatime. Unless dining out, a light supper ends the day, usually between 6 and 9, but tending toward the later hour. Many restaurant kitchens close in the afternoon, but some post a notice saying DURCHGEHEND WARME KÜCHE, meaning that hot food is available even between regular mealtimes. In Vienna, some restaurants go on serving until 1 and 2 AM, a tiny number also through the night. The rest of Austria is more conservative.

Unless otherwise noted, the restaurants listed in this guide are open daily for lunch and dinner.

RESERVATIONS & DRESS

Reservations are always a good idea: we mention them only when they're essential or not accepted. Book as far ahead as you can, and reconfirm as soon as you arrive. We mention dress only when men are required to wear a jacket or a jacket and tie.

WINE, BEER & SPIRITS

Austrian wines range from unpretentious *Heurige* whites to world-class varietals. Look for the light, fruity white *Grüner Veltliner,* intensely fragrant golden *Traminer,* full-bodied red *Blaufränkisch* and the lighter red *Zweigelt.* Sparkling wine is called *Sekt,* with some of the best coming from the Kamptal region northwest of Vienna. Some of the best sweet dessert wines in the world (*Spätlesen*) come from Burgenland. Austrian beer rivals that of Germany for quality. Each area has its own brewery and local beer that people are loyal to. A specialty unique to Austria is the dark, sweet *Dunkles* beer. Look for *Kaiser Doppelmalz* in Vienna. Schnapps is an after-dinner tradition in Austria, with many restaurants offering several varieties to choose from.

DISABILITIES & ACCESSIBILITY

The Austrian National Tourist Office in New York has a guide to Vienna for people with disabilities (including hotels with special facilities) and a special map of the city's accessible sights. As a general guideline, the Hilton, InterContinental, and Marriott chain hotels, plus a number of smaller ones, are usually accessible. Once in Austria, check with the Österreichischer Zivilinvalidenverband; the Vienna Tourist Office also has a booklet on Vienna hotels and a city guide for travelers with disabilities.

⌧ Local Resources The **Austrian National Tourist Office** (*see* Visitor Information, *below*). **Österre-ichischer Zivilinvalidenverband** ✉ Wickenburggasse 15, A-1080 Vienna ☎ 01/406–4412 or 01/533–0948. For phone inquiries, call the **Vienna Tourist Office** ✉ Obere Augartenstrasse 40, A-1025 ☎ 01/211–140. For walk-in information, go to the **Vienna Tourist Office** ✉ Albertinaplatz, A-1010 near the Opera.

RESERVATIONS

When discussing accessibility with an operator or reservations agent, **ask hard questions.** Are there any stairs, inside *or* out? Are there grab bars next to the toilet *and* in the shower/tub? How wide is the doorway to the room? To the bathroom? For the most extensive facilities meeting the latest legal specifications, **opt for newer accommodations** which are more likely to have been designed with access in mind. Older buildings or ships may have more limited facilities. Be sure to **discuss your needs before booking.**

TRANSPORTATION

The railroads are both understanding and helpful. If prior arrangements have been made, taxis and private vehicles are allowed to drive right to the train platform; railway personnel will help with boarding and leaving trains; and with three days' notice, a special wheelchair can be provided for getting around train corridors. If you're traveling by plane, ask in advance for assistance or a wheelchair at your destination. A number of stations in the Vienna subway system have only stairs or escalators, but elevators are being added at major stations.

TRAVEL AGENCIES & TOUR OPERATORS

As a whole, the travel industry has become more aware of the needs of travelers with disabilities. In the United States, the Americans with Disabilities Act requires that travel firms serve the needs of all travelers. Some agencies specialize in working with people with disabilities.

⌧ Travelers with Mobility Problems Access Adventures ✉ 206 Chestnut Ridge Rd., Rochester, NY 14624 ☎ 716/889–9096 ✍ dltravel@prodigy.net, run by a former physical-rehabilitation counselor. **CareVacations** ✉ 5-5110 50th Ave., Leduc, Alberta T9E 6V4 ☎ 780/986–6404 or 877/478–7827 ⎙ 780/

986-8332 ⊕ www.carevacations.com, for group tours and cruise vacations. **Flying Wheels Travel** ✉ 143 W. Bridge St., Box 382, Owatonna, MN 55060 ☎ 507/451-5005 or 800/535-6790 ⎙ 507/451-1685 ✒ thq@ll.net ⊕ www.flyingwheels.com. **Hinsdale Travel Service** ✉ 201 E. Ogden Ave., Suite 100, Hinsdale, IL 60521 ☎ 630/325-1335 ⎙ 630/325-1342 ✒ hinstrvl@interaccess.com.

ELECTRICITY

To use your U.S.-purchased electric-powered equipment, **bring a converter and adapter.** The electrical current in Austria is 220 volts, 50 cycles alternating current (AC); wall outlets take Continental-type plugs, with two round prongs. If your appliances are dual-voltage, you'll need only an adapter. Don't use 110-volt outlets marked FOR SHAVERS ONLY for high-wattage appliances such as blow-dryers. Most laptops operate equally well on 110 and 220 volts and so require only an adapter.

EMBASSIES

🔲 Australia **Embassy of Australia** ✉ Mattiellis-trasse 2-3, 4th District, Vienna ☎ 01/50674.
🔲 Canada **Embassy of Canada** ✉ Laurenzerberg 2, on the 3rd floor of Hauptpost building complex, 1st District, Vienna ☎ 01/53138-3000.
🔲 New Zealand **Mission of New Zealand** ✉ Mattiellistrasse 2-4, 4th District, Vienna ☎ 505-3021.
🔲 United Kingdom **Embassy of United Kingdom** ✉ Jauresgasse 12, 3rd District, Vienna ☎ 01/71613-0.
🔲 United States **Embassy of the United States** ✉ Boltzmanngasse 16, A-1090, 9th District, Vienna ☎ 31339-0. **Consulate of the U.S./Passport Division** ✉ Gartenbaupromenade 2-4, A-1010, 1st District, Vienna ☎ 31339-0.

EMERGENCIES

On the street, some German phrases that may be needed in an emergency are: *Zur Hilfe!* (Help!), *Notfall* (emergency), *Rettungswagen* (ambulance), *Feuerwehr* (fire department), *Polizei* (police), *Arzt* (doctor), and *Krankenhaus* (hospital).
🔲 **Ambulance** ☎ 144. **Fire** ☎ 122. **Police** ☎ 133.

ENGLISH-LANGUAGE & LOCAL MEDIA

The *International Herald Tribune, The Wall Street Journal,* and *USA Today* are readily available in most larger cities in Austria. For local Austria-specific information in English, the choice is more limited. For a vast selection of American magazines, go to the bookstore **Morawa** (✉ Wollzeile 11, Vienna). There is no longer an exclusive English-language radio station in Austria. You can hear short English news broadcasts at 103.8 Mhz from early morning until 6 PM.

BOOKS

In Vienna and Salzburg it's fairly easy to find English-language bookstores. Bookstores in smaller towns sometimes have an English section or rack.
🔲 Local Resources **British Bookstore** ✉ Weih-burggasse 24-26, 1st District, Vienna ☎ 01/512-1945-0 ✉ Mariahilferstrasse 4, 7th District, Vienna ☎ 01/522-6730. **Shakespeare & Co.** ✉ Sterngasse 2, 1st District, Vienna ☎ 01/535-5053.

AUSTRIAN NEWSPAPERS & MAGAZINES

The most balanced coverage of any German newspaper, with the most sophisticated cultural coverage, is *Der Falter* (www.falter.at), which comes out on Wednesdays. Even though the listings are in German, it's easy to understand. The most widely read Austrian German-language newspaper is the *Kronen Zeitung,* with a culture section on Fridays. Like many of the other German newspapers, this is conservative in slant and offers what many will consider a reactionary political menu (along with a bevy of tabloid and sensationalistic photos). There is a daily newspaper in English for the international community, *Austria Today* (www.austria-today.at). Popular magazines are readily available at Tabak shops and newspaper stands and include the international weekly editions of *Time* and *Newsweek,* European editions of the fashion magazines *Marie-Claire,* and *Elle* (in German), and *Cosmopolitan,* also in German. Also look for a good magazine about dining in Austria called *A La Carte,* but it's only in German.

RADIO & TELEVISION

For news and weather broadcasts in English on the hour from early morning until 6 PM, go to the eclectic rock music station *U4* at 103.8 Mhz. For classical music interrupted with a lot of German poetry readings, tune into *Radio Stephansdom* at 107.4 Mhz. *RTL* and *Radio Wien* offer American and British soft rock music at 92.9 Mhz and 89.9 Mhz, respectively. British and American pop can be found at *Energy,* 104.2 Mhz, and *Neue Antenne,* 102.5 Mhz. There are two non-cable television stations in Austria, the state-owned ORF 1 and ORF 2. Service is entirely in German, and American and English movies are dubbed in German. ORF 1 leans more towards sports events and children's shows, while ORF 2 schedules documentaries and Austrian and American TV series and films. A private television station, ATV (Austrian TV) was granted a license in 2002 but has yet to start broadcasting.

ETIQUETTE & BEHAVIOR

The most common form of greeting in Austria is *Grüss Gott,* which literally means "God greets you." When it comes to table manners, there are some surprising differences from American usage: Austrians eat hamburgers, french fries, and pizza with a knife and fork—and even sometimes ribs. Toothpicks are sometimes found on restaurant tables, and it is normal to see people clean their teeth after a meal, discreetly covering their mouth with their free hand. Austria is a dog-loving society and you will often find dogs accompanying their masters to restaurants—some even sharing the banquette with them. Dogs are almost always beautifully behaved and accustomed to going out. Cigarette smoking is going strong in Austria, especially among the younger population. Though Ireland passed a non-smoking law in restaurants and pubs, and Italy bans smoking in many restaurants and bars, it is doubtful this will happen in Austria any time soon. The tobacco industry is subsidized by the government and very little advertising is done to discourage smoking. If you're invited to an Austrian's home for dinner, do not arrive with only your appetite. It's proper to bring flowers to your hostess, but never red roses (which are reserved for lovers).

Note that if you bring wine, it's considered a gift and is not served. Other little hostess gifts are considered appropriate, such as honey or chocolates. Austrians are comfortable with nudity, and public and hotel saunas are used by both sexes; in such facilities, people are seldom clothed (though this is an option).

GAY & LESBIAN TRAVEL

Austria is a gay-tolerant country in general. In Vienna, the twice-monthly free magazine **Xtra!** runs a calendar of daily events and addresses. Also look for the **Vienna Gay Guide,** a map showing locations of gay-friendly bars, restaurants, hotels, and saunas. Tours of historical gay Vienna are offered by the tourist office. Check ⊕ www.info-wien.at. For additional information, check the Web site ⊕ www.gayguide.at.

🔗 Gay- & Lesbian-Friendly Travel Agencies **Different Roads Travel** ✉ 8383 Wilshire Blvd., Suite 902, Beverly Hills, CA 90211 ☎ 323/651-5557 or 800/429-8747 🖷 323/651-3678 ✍ leigh@west.tzell.com. **Kennedy Travel** ✉ 314 Jericho Turnpike, Floral Park, NY 11001 ☎ 516/352-4888 or 800/237-7433 🖷 516/354-8849 ✍ main@kennedytravel.com ⊕ www.kennedytravel.com. **Now, Voyager** ✉ 4406 18th St., San Francisco, CA 94114 ☎ 415/626-1169 or 800/255-6951 🖷 415/626-8626. **Skylink Travel and Tour** ✉ 1006 Mendocino Ave., Santa Rosa, CA 95401 ☎ 707/546-9888 or 800/225-5759 🖷 707/546-9891 ✍ skylinktvl@aol.com, serving lesbian travelers.

🔗 Local Resources **Homosexuelle Initiative (HOSI)** ✉ Novaragasse 40, A-1020 Vienna ☎ 01/216-6604 ⊕ www.hosi.at ✉ Müllner Haupstrasse 11, A-5020 Salzburg ☎ 0662/435927 🖷 0662/435927-27. **Referat für gleichgeschlechtliche Lebensweisen** ✉ Rechbauerstrasse 12, A-8010 Graz ☎ 0316/873-5111.

The **Rosa Lila Villa** ✉ Linke Wienzeile 102, A-1060 Vienna ☎ 01/586-8150 women, 01/585-4343 men 🖷 01/585-4159 in Vienna is a boarding house with a restaurant catering to gay men and lesbians, with separate floors for men and women.

HEALTH

MEDICAL PLANS

No one plans to get sick while traveling, but it happens, so **consider signing up with a medical-assistance company.** Members get doctor referrals, emergency evacuation or repatriation, 24-hour telephone hot lines for medical consultation, cash for emergencies, and other personal and legal assistance. Coverage varies by plan, so **review the benefits of each carefully.** English-speaking doctors are readily available, and health care in Austria is usually excellent.

OVER-THE-COUNTER REMEDIES

You must buy over-the-counter remedies in an *Apotheke,* and most personnel speak enough English to understand what you need. Pain relievers are much milder than those available in the U.S.

SHOTS & MEDICATIONS

No special shots are required before visiting Austria, but if you will be cycling or hiking through the eastern or southeastern parts of the country, get inoculated against encephalitis; it can be carried by ticks.

HOLIDAYS

All banks and shops are closed on national holidays: New Year's Day; Jan. 6, Epiphany; Easter Sunday and Monday; May 1, May Day; Ascension Day; Pentecost Sunday and Monday; Corpus Christi; Aug. 15, Assumption; Oct. 26, National Holiday; Nov. 1, All Saints' Day; Dec. 8, Immaculate Conception; Dec. 25–26, Christmas. Museums are open on most holidays but closed on Good Friday, on Dec. 24 and 25, and New Year's Day. Banks and offices are closed on Dec. 8, but most shops are open.

LANGUAGE

German is the official national language in Austria. In larger cities and in most resort areas you will usually have no problem finding people who speak English; hotel staffs in particular speak it reasonably well, and many young Austrians speak it at least passably. However, travelers do report that they often find themselves in stores, restaurants, and railway and bus stations where it's hard to find someone who speaks English—so it's best to have some native phrases up your sleeve (*see* Chapter 11). Note that all public announcements on trams, subways, and buses are in German. Train announce-

ments are usually given in English as well, but if you have any questions, try to get answers before boarding.

LANGUAGES FOR TRAVELERS

A phrase book and language-tape set can help get you started.

🔲 Phrase Book and Language-Tape Set **Fodor's German for Travelers** ☎ 800/733-3000 in the U.S., 800/668-4247 in Canada ✉ $7 for phrasebook, $16.95 for audio set.

LODGING

You can live like a king in a real castle in Austria or get by on a modest budget. Starting at the lower end, you can find a room in a private house or on a farm, or dormitory space in a youth hostel. Next up the line come the simpler pensions, many of them identified as a *Frühstückspension* (bed-and-breakfast). Then come the *Gasthäuser,* the simpler country inns. The fancier pensions in the cities can often cost as much as hotels; the difference lies in the services they offer. Most pensions, for example, do not staff the front desk around the clock. Among the hotels, you can find accommodations ranging from the most modest, with a shower and toilet down the hall, to the most elegant, with every possible amenity.

The lodgings we list are the cream of the crop in each price category. We always list the facilities that are available—but we don't specify whether they cost extra: when pricing accommodations, always ask what's included and what costs extra (two items that occasionally fall into the latter category are parking and breakfast). Properties marked ✕▦ are lodging establishments whose restaurants warrant a special trip.

Assume that hotels operate on the European Plan (EP, with no meal provided) unless we note that they use the Breakfast Plan (BP), Modified American Plan (MAP, with breakfast and dinner daily, known as demi-pension [*halb pension*]), or Full American Plan (FAP, or *voll pension,* with three meals a day). Higher prices (inquire when booking) prevail for any meal plans. Increasingly, more and more hotels in the lower to middle price range are including breakfast with the basic room charge, but check when booking. Room rates for hotels in the rural countryside can often include breakfast and one other meal (in rare cases, all three meals are included). Happily, many of these lodgings will also offer a breakfast buffet–only rate if requested.

Faxing is the easiest way to contact the hotel (the staff is probably more likely to read English than to understand it over the phone long-distance), though calling also works, but using e-mail messages is increasingly popular. In your fax (or over the phone), specify the exact dates you want to stay at the hotel (when you will arrive and when you will check out); the size of the room you want and how many people will be sleeping there; what kind of bed you want (single or double, twin beds or double, etc.); and whether you want a bathroom with a shower or bathtub (or both). You might also ask if a deposit (or your credit card number) is required and, if so, what happens if you cancel. Request that the hotel fax you back so that you have a written confirmation of your reservation in hand when you arrive at the hotel.

Here is a list of German words that can come in handy when booking a room: air-conditioning (*Klimaanlage*); private bath (*privat Bad*); bathtub (*Badewanne*); shower (*Dusche*); double bed (*Doppelbett*); twin beds (*Einzelbetten*).

RESERVING A ROOM IN VIENNA

If you need a room upon arrival and have not made previous reservations, go to Information-Zimmernachweis, operated by the Verkehrsbüro in the Westbahnhof and in the Südbahnhof. At the airport, the information and room-reservation office in the arrivals hall is open daily 8:30 AM–9 PM. If you're driving into Vienna, get information or book rooms through the Vienna Tourist Board's hotel assistance hot line. It's open daily from 9–7.

🚩 **Information-Zimmernachweis** ☎ 01/892-3392 in Westbahnhof, 930-0031-05-0 in Südbahnhof. **Vienna Tourist Board's hotel assistance hot line** ☎ 01/24555 🖷 01/24-555-666 ⊕ www.info.wien.at.

APARTMENT & CHALET RENTALS

If you want a home base that's roomy enough for a family and comes with cooking facilities, **consider a furnished rental.** These can save you money, especially if you're traveling with a large group of people. Home-exchange directories list rentals (often second homes owned by prospective house swappers), and some services search for a house or apartment for you (even a castle, if that's your fancy) and handle the paperwork. Some send an illustrated catalog; others send photographs only of specific properties, sometimes at a charge. Up-front registration fees may apply.

🚩 International Agents **Drawbridge to Europe** ⊠ 5456 Adams Rd., Talent, OR 97540 ☎ 541/512-8927 or 888/268-1148 🖷 541/512-0978 ✉ requests@drawbridgetoeurope.com ⊕ www.drawbridgetoeurope.com. **Hometours International** 🏠 Box 11503, Knoxville, TN 37939 ☎ 865/690-8484 or 800/367-4668 ✉ hometours@aol.com ⊕ http:thor.he.net/~hometour. **Interhome** ⊠ 1990 N.E. 163rd St., Suite 110, North Miami Beach, FL 33162 ☎ 305/940-2299 or 800/882-6864 🖷 305/940-2911 ⊕ www.interhome.com. **Villas International** ⊠ 4340 Redwood Hwy., Suite D309, San Rafael, CA 94903 ☎ 415/499-9490 or 800/221-2260 🖷 415/499-9491 ⊕ www.villasintl.com.

CASTLES

🚩 **Schlosshotels und Herrenhäuser in Österreich** ⊠ Moosstrasse 60, A-5020 Salzburg ☎ 0662/8306-8141 🖷 0662/8306-8161 ⊕ www.schlosshotels.co.at.

HOME EXCHANGES

If you would like to exchange your home for someone else's, **join a home-exchange organization,** which will send you its updated listings of available exchanges for a year and will include your own listing in at least one of them. It's up to you to make specific arrangements.

🚩 Exchange Clubs **HomeLink International** 🏠 Box 650, Key West, FL 33041 ☎ 305/294-7766 or 800/638-3841 🖷 305/294-1448 ✉ usa@homelink.org ⊕ www.homelink.org 📧 $98 per year. **Intervac U.S.** 🏠 Box 590504, San Francisco, CA 94159 ☎ 800/756-4663 🖷 415/435-7440 ⊕ www.intervac.com 📧 $89 per year includes two catalogues.

HOSTELS

No matter what your age, you can **save on lodging costs by staying at hostels.** In some 5,000 locations in more than 70 countries around the world, Hostelling International (HI), the umbrella group for a number of national youth-hostel associations, offers single-sex, dorm-style beds and, at many hostels, rooms for couples and family accommodations. Membership in any HI national hostel association, open to travelers of all ages, allows you to stay in HI-affiliated hostels at member rates; one-year membership is about $25 for adults (C$35 for a two-year minimum membership in Canada, £13 in the U.K., A$52 in Australia, and NZ$40 in New Zealand); hostels run about $10–$30 per night. Members have priority if the hostel is full; they're also eligible for discounts around the world, even on rail and bus travel in some countries.

Austria has more than a hundred government-sponsored youth hostels, for which you need an International Youth Hostel Federation membership card. Inexpensively priced, these hostels are run by the Österreichischer Jugendherbergsverband and are popular with the back-pack crowd, so be sure to reserve in advance.

🔏 In Austria **Österreichischer Jugendher-bergsverband** ⊠ Schottenring 28, A-1010 Vienna ☎ 01/533-53-53 🖨 01/535-0861.

🔏 Organizations **Hostelling International–American Youth Hostels** ⊠ 733 15th St. NW, Suite 840, Washington, DC 20005 ☎ 202/783-6161 🖨 202/783-6171. **Hostelling International–Canada** ⊠ 400-205 Catherine St., Ottawa, Ontario K2P 1C3 ☎ 613/237-7884 or 800/663-5777 🖨 613/237-7868. **Youth Hostel Association of England and Wales** ⊠ Trevelyan House, Dimple Rd., Matlock, Derbyshire DE4 3YH, U.K. ☎ 0870/870-8808 🖨 0169/592-702 ⊕ www.yha.org.uk.

MAIL & SHIPPING

Post offices are scattered throughout every district in Vienna and are recognizable by a square yellow sign that says "Post." They are usually open weekdays 9–12 and 2–6, Saturday 8–10 AM. The **main post office** (⊠ Fleischmarkt 19, A-1010 Vienna), near Schwedenplatz, is open 24 hours daily. For overnight services, Federal Express, DHL, and UPS service Vienna and Austria; check with your hotel concierge for the nearest address and telephone number.

POSTAL RATES

All mail goes by air, so there's no supplement on letters or postcards. Within Europe, a letter or postcard of up to 20 grams (about ¾ ounce) costs €0.55. To the United States or Canada, a letter of up to 20 grams takes €1.25 for airmail. If in doubt, mail your letters from a post office and have the weight checked. The Austrian post office also adheres strictly to a size standard; if your letter or card is outside the norm, you'll have to pay a surcharge. Postcards via airmail to the United States or Canada need €1.25. Always place an airmail sticker on your letters or cards. Shipping packages from Austria to destinations outside the country is extremely expensive.

RECEIVING MAIL

When you don't know where you'll be staying, **American Express** (⊠ Kärntnerstrasse 21–23, A-1015 Vienna ☎ 01/515-4077-0 ⊠ Mozartplatz 5, A-5020 Salzburg ☎ 0662/8080-0 ⊠ Bürgerstrasse 14, A-4021 Linz ☎ 0732/669013) mail service is a great convenience, with no charge to anyone either holding an American Express credit card or carrying American Express traveler's checks. Pick up your mail at the local offices. You can also have mail held at any **Austrian post office** (⊠ Fleischmarkt 19, A-1010 Vienna ☎ 01/515-09-0); letters should be marked *Poste Restante* or *Postlagernd*. You will be asked for identification when you collect mail. In Vienna, if not addressed to a specific district post office, this service is handled through the main post office.

MONEY MATTERS

Prices throughout this guide are given for adults. Substantially reduced fees are almost always available for children, students, and senior citizens. For information on taxes, *see* Taxes, *below.*

ATMS

Called *Bankomats* and fairly common throughout Austria, **ATMs are one of the easiest ways to get euros.** Although ATM transaction fees may be higher abroad than at home, banks usually offer excellent, wholesale exchange rates through ATMs. Cirrus and Plus locations are easily found throughout large city centers, and even in small towns. If you have any trouble finding one, ask your hotel concierge. Note, too, that you may have better luck with ATMs if you're using a credit card or debit card that is also a Visa or MasterCard rather than just your bank card. To get cash at ATMs in Austria, **your personal identification number (PIN) must be four digits long.** Note, too, that you may be charged by your bank for using ATMs overseas; inquire at your bank about charges.

ATM Locations Cirrus ☎ 800/424-7787. Plus ☎ 800/843-7587.

COSTS

A cup of coffee in a café will cost about €3–€4; a half-liter of draft beer, €3–€4; a glass of wine, €4–€8; a Coca-Cola, €3; an open-face sandwich, €3.50; a midrange theater ticket €20; a concert ticket €30–€50; an opera ticket €40 upwards; a 1-mi taxi ride, €4. Outside the hotels, laundering a shirt costs about €4; dry cleaning a suit costs around €12–€18; a dress, €9–€12. A shampoo and set for a woman will cost around €25–€35, a manicure about €12–€15; a man's haircut about €25–€35.

CREDIT & DEBIT CARDS

In the last couple of years credit cards have been gaining broad acceptance, but always have some cash handy (easily gotten from Austrian ATM machines) and you may still wish to fall back on occasion on traveler's checks. Most grocery stores do not accept credit cards. Some establishments have a minimum sum for use of credit cards; others may accept cards grudgingly. Should you use a credit card or a debit card when traveling? Both have benefits. A credit card allows you to delay payment and gives you certain rights as a consumer. A debit card, also known as a check card, deducts funds directly from your checking account and helps you stay within your budget. When you want to rent a car, though, you may still need an old-fashioned credit card. Although you can always *pay* for your car with a debit card, some agencies will not allow you to *reserve* a car with a debit card. Otherwise, the two types of plastic are virtually the same. Both will get you cash advances at ATMs worldwide if your card is properly programmed with your personal identification number (PIN). Both offer excellent, wholesale exchange rates. And both protect you against unauthorized use if the card is lost or stolen. Your liability is limited to $50 as long as you report the card missing. Be aware that several U.S. credit card companies are now adding a 2%–3% conversion surcharge on all charges made in Europe. This can really add up on big purchases and hotel charges. Check with your credit card company, so you'll know in advance.

Throughout this guide, the following abbreviations are used: **AE**, American Express; **DC**, Diners Club; **MC**, MasterCard; and **V**, Visa.

Reporting Lost Cards American Express ☎ 336/939-1111 or 336/668-5309 call collect. Diners Club ☎ 303/799-1504 call collect. MasterCard ☎ 0800/90-1387. Visa ☎ 0800/90-1179, 410/581-9994 collect.

CURRENCY

As it is a member of the European Union (EU), Austria's unit of currency is the euro. Under the euro system there are eight coins: 1 and 2 euros, plus 1, 2, 5, 10, 20, and 50 euro cent, or cents of the euro. All coins have one side that has the value of the euro on it and the other side with each country's own unique national symbol. There are seven banknotes: 5, 10, 20, 50, 100, 200, and 500 euros. Banknotes are the same for all EU countries.

Please note that at press time (fall 2004), the euro was stronger than the dollar, but fluctuating considerably. At press time, the exchange rate was about €1.20 to the U.S. dollar, €0.67 to the British pound, €1.65

to the Canadian dollar, €1.70 to the Australian dollar, €1.94 to the New Zealand dollar. These rates can and will vary.

CURRENCY EXCHANGE

Generally, exchange rates are far less favorable outside of Austria, and there is no need to exchange money prior to your arrival. ATMs are conveniently located in city centers. Although fees charged for ATM transactions may be higher abroad than at home, Cirrus and Plus exchange rates are excellent, because they are based on wholesale rates offered only by major banks. Otherwise, the most favorable rates are through a bank. You won't do as well at exchange booths in airports or rail and bus stations, in hotels, in restaurants, or in stores, although you may find their hours more convenient than at a bank. Now that the euro has become accepted as a standard of exchange, many currency conversions have been radically simplified.

🖪 Exchange Services **Chase** *Currency To Go* ☎ 800/935–9935, 935–9935 in NY, NJ, and CT. **International Currency Express** ☎ 888/278–6628 for orders.

TRAVELER'S CHECKS

Do you need traveler's checks? It depends on where you're headed. If you're going to rural areas and small towns, go with cash; traveler's checks are best used in cities (although you can always rely on the corner ATM machine to supply ready euros). Lost or stolen checks can usually be replaced within 24 hours. To ensure a speedy refund, buy your own traveler's checks—don't let someone else pay for them; irregularities like this can cause delays. The person who bought the checks should make the call to request a refund.

PACKING

CHECKING LUGGAGE

How many carry-on bags you can bring with you is up to the airline. Most allow only one, so make sure that everything you carry aboard will fit under your seat or in the overhead bin, and get to the gate early. Note that if you have a seat at the back of the plane, you'll probably board first, while the overhead bins are still empty.

If you are flying internationally, note that baggage allowances may be determined not by piece but by weight—two checked bags weighing no more than 70 pounds each (32 kilograms). For checked bags the allowance is the same in first class, business class and economy.

Airline liability for baggage is limited to $1,250 per person on flights within the United States. On international flights it amounts to $9.07 per pound or $20 per kilogram for checked baggage (roughly $640 per 70-pound bag) and $400 per passenger for unchecked baggage. You can buy additional coverage at check-in for about $10 per $1,000 of coverage, but it excludes a rather extensive list of items, shown on your airline ticket.

Before departure, **itemize your bags' contents** and their worth, and label the bags with your name, address, and phone number. (If you use your home address, cover it so potential thieves can't see it readily.) Inside each bag, **pack a copy of your itinerary**. At check-in, **make sure that each bag is correctly tagged** with the destination airport's three-letter code. If your bags arrive damaged or fail to arrive at all, file a written report with the airline before leaving the airport.

PACKING LIST

Dressing in Austria ranges from conservative to casual, and is somewhat dependent on age. Middle-aged and older people tend to dress conventionally. Jeans and tennis shoes on women are as rare as loud sport shirts are on men. Young people tend to be very trendy, and the trend is basically U.S., with kids in baseball caps, baggy trousers, loud shirts with all kinds of things written on them in (sometimes poor) English. In the country or more rural areas of, say, Styria or Burgenland, things are a little less loud. Jeans are ubiquitous in Austria as elsewhere, but are considered inappropriate at concerts (other than pop) or formal restaurants. For concerts and opera, women may want a skirt or dress, and men a jacket; even in summer, gala performances at small festivals tend to be dressy. And since an evening outside at a Heuriger (wine garden) may be on your agenda, be sure to take a sweater or light wrap. Unless you're staying in an expensive hotel or will be in one place for more than a day or two, take hand-washables; laundry service gets complicated. Austria is a walking country, in cities and mountains alike. If intending to hike in the mountains, bring boots that rise above the ankle and have sturdy soles. For lots of city walking a good pair of sports shoes is needed.

Mountainous areas are bright, so bring sunscreen lotion, even in winter. Consider packing a small folding umbrella for the odd deluge, or a waterproof windbreaker of sorts. Sunglasses are a must as well, and if you intend to go high up in the mountains, make sure your sunglasses are good and prevent lateral rays. Mosquitoes can become quite a bother in summer around the lakes and along the rivers, especially the Danube and the swampy regions created by its old arms. Bring some good insect repellent.

In your carry-on luggage, **pack an extra pair of eyeglasses or contact lenses** and **enough of any medication you take** to last a few days longer than the entire trip. You may also ask your doctor to write a spare prescription using the drug's generic name, since brand names may vary from country to country. In luggage to be checked, **never pack prescription drugs or valuables.** To avoid customs delays, carry medications in their original packaging. And don't forget to carry with you the addresses of offices that handle refunds of lost traveler's checks.

PASSPORTS & VISAS

When traveling internationally, **carry your passport even if you don't need one** (it's always the best form of ID) and **make two photocopies of the data page** (one for someone at home and another for you, carried separately from your passport). If you lose your passport, promptly call the nearest embassy or consulate and the local police.

ENTERING AUSTRIA

U.S., Australian, Canadian, New Zealand, and U.K. citizens need only a valid passport to enter Austria for stays of up to three months.

PASSPORT OFFICES

The best time to apply for a passport or to renew is in fall and winter. Before any trip, check your passport's expiration date, and, if necessary, renew it as soon as possible. (Some countries won't allow you to enter on a passport that's due to expire in six months or less.)

▶ Australian Citizens **Australian Passport Office** ☎ 131-232 ⊕ www.passports.gov.au.

▶ Canadian Citizens **Passport Office** to mail in applications ✉ Department of Foreign Affairs and International Trade, Ottawa, Ontario K1A 0G3 ☎ 800/567-6868 toll-free in Canada or 819/994-3500 ⊕ www.dfait-maeci.gc.ca/passport.

▶ New Zealand Citizens **New Zealand Passport Office** ☎ 0800/22-5050 or 04/474-8100 ⊕ www.passports.govt.nz.

▶ U.K. Citizens **London Passport Office** ☎ 0990/210-410 ⊕ www.passport.gov.uk for fees and documentation requirements and to request an emergency passport.

▶ U.S. Citizens **National Passport Information Center** ☎ 900/225-5674 ▭ 35¢ per minute for automated service or $1.05 per minute for operator service ⊕ www.travel.state.gov.

SENIOR-CITIZEN TRAVEL

To qualify for age-related discounts, **mention your senior-citizen status up front** when booking hotel reservations (not when checking out) and before you're seated in restaurants (not when paying the bill). When renting a car, ask about promotional car-rental discounts, which can be cheaper than senior-citizen rates. Austria has so many senior citizens that facilities almost everywhere cater to the needs of older travelers, with discounts for rail travel and museum entry. Check with the Austrian National Tourist Office to find what form of identification is required, but generally if you're 65 or over (women 60), once you're in Austria the railroads will issue you a *Seniorenpass* (you'll need a passport photo and passport or other proof of age) entitling you to the senior-citizen discounts regardless of nationality.

▶ Educational Programs **Elderhostel** ✉ 75 Federal St., 3rd floor, Boston, MA 02110 ☎ 877/426-8056 ▭ 877/426-2166 ⊕ www.elderhostel.

org. **Interhostel** ✉ University of New Hampshire, 6 Garrison Ave., Durham, NH 03824 ☎ 603/862–1147 or 800/733–9753 🖷 603/862–1113 ⊕ www.learn.unh.edu.

SPORTS & OUTDOOR ACTIVITIES

BICYCLING

Cyclists couldn't ask for much more than the cycle track that runs the length of the Danube or the many cycling routes that crisscross the country, major cities included. Just about every lake is surrounded by bike paths, and there are other rivers, too, such as the Drau, that have trails. You can no longer rent a bike at train stations in Austria. The cost of renting a bike (21-gear) from a local agency is around €27 a day.

Tourist offices have details (in German), including maps and hints for trip planning and mealtime and overnight stops that cater especially to cyclists. Ask for the booklet "Radtouren in Österreich." There's also a brochure in English: "Biking Austria—On the Trail of Mozart" that provides details in English on the cycle route through the High Tauern mountains in Salzburg Province.

🚩 **Austria Radreisen** ✉ Joseph-Haydn-Strasse 8, A-4780 Schärding ☎ 07712/5511–0 🖷 07712/4811 ⊕ www.austria-radreisen.at. **Pedal Power** ✉ Ausstellungsstrasse 3, A-1020 Vienna ☎ 01/729–7234 🖷 01/729–7235 ⊕ www.pedalpower.at.

CAMPING

If your idea of a good holiday is the "great outdoors" and if your purse is a slender one, a camping holiday may be just the thing for you. Austrians love the idea and there are practically as many tourists under canvas as in hotels and Gasthäuser. You'll find more than 450 campsites throughout the country, usually run by regional organizations, a few private. Most have full facilities, often including swimming pools and snack bars or grocery shops. Charges average about €20 per day for a family of three, depending on the location and the range and quality of services offered. Many campsites have a fixed basic fee for three adults and one child, parking included. Camping is not re-

stricted to the summer season; some sites are open year-round, with about 155 specifically set up for winter camping. For details, check with the tourist offices of the individual Austrian provinces.

🚩 **Österreichischer Camping Club** ✉ Schubertring 1–3, A-1010 Vienna ☎ 01/713–6151 ⊕ www.oeamtc.at.

HIKING & CLIMBING

With more than 50,000 km (about 35,000 mi) of well-maintained mountain paths through Europe's largest reserve of unspoiled landscape, the country is a hiker's paradise. Three long-distance routes traverse Austria, including the E–6 from the Baltic, cutting across mid-Austria via the Wachau valley region of the Danube and on to the Adriatic. Wherever you are in Austria, you will find shorter hiking trails requiring varying degrees of ability. Routes are well marked, and maps are readily available from bookstores, the Österreichische Alpenverein/ÖAV, and the automobile clubs.

If you're a newcomer to mountain climbing or want to improve your skill, schools in Salzburg province will take you on. Ask the ÖAV for addresses. All organize courses and guided tours for beginners as well as for more advanced climbers.

Tourist offices have details on hiking holidays; serious climbers can write directly to **Österreichischer Alpenverein/ÖAV** (Austrian Alpine Club) for more information. Membership in the club (€333.50, about $40) will give you a 30%–50% reduction from the regular fees for overnights in the 275 mountain refuges it operates. Senior memberships have a reduced price.

🚩 **Österreichischer Alpenverein** ✉ Wilhelm-Greil-Strasse 15, A-6020 Innsbruck ☎ 0512/59547 🖷 0512/575528 ⊕ www.alpenverein.at ✉ In the U.K. ✉ 13 Longcroft House, Fretherne Rd., Welwyn Garden City, Hertfordshire AL8 6PQ ☎ 01707/324835.

WATER SPORTS & SWIMMING

Waterskiing and sail skiing are popular on the Traunsee, Attersee, and Wolfgangsee in Salzkammergut. Waterskiing is not permitted on many of the smaller Austrian lakes, so check first. There are hundreds of places to swim throughout Austria, and with very few exceptions the water is un-polluted. All the lakes in the Salzkam-mergut have excellent swimming, but are crowded in the peak season. In the Vienna area, the Alte Donau and Donauinsel arms of the Danube are accessible by public transportation and are suitable for fami-lies. It's best to go early to avoid the crowds on hot summer weekends. The Alte Donau beaches have changing rooms and checkrooms.

STUDENTS IN AUSTRIA

To save money, **look into deals available through student-oriented travel agencies.** To qualify you'll need a bona fide student ID card. Members of international student groups are also eligible. Information on student tickets, fares, and lodgings is avail-able from Jugend Info Wien (Youth Infor-mation Center) in Vienna.

🔳 Local Resources **Jugend Info Wien** ⊠ Baben-bergerstrasse 1, Vienna ☎ 01/1799 🖶 01/585-2499 🕒 Mon.-Sat., noon-7 PM.

🔳 IDs & Services **STA Travel** ⊠ CIEE, 205 E. 42nd St., 14th floor, New York, NY 10017 ☎ 212/822-2700 or 888/268-6245 🖶 212/822-2699 ✍ info@coun-cilexchanges.org ⊕ www.councilexchanges.org for mail orders only, in the U.S. **Travel Cuts** ⊠ 187 Col-lege St., Toronto, Ontario M5T 1P7, Canada ☎ 416/979-2406 or 888/838-2887 🖶 416/979-8167 ⊕ www.travelcuts.com.

🔳 Student Tours **AESU Travel** ⊠ 2 Hamill Rd., Suite 248, Baltimore, MD 21210-1807 ☎ 410/323-4416 or 800/638-7640 🖶 410/323-4498. **Contiki Holidays** ⊠ 300 Plaza Alicante, Suite 900, Garden Grove, CA 92840 ☎ 714/740-0808 or 800/266-8454 🖶 714/740-2034.

TAXES

VALUE-ADDED TAX

The Value Added Tax (VAT) in Austria is 20% generally but only 10% on food and clothing. If you are planning to take your purchases with you when you leave Aus-tria (export them), you can get a refund. The shop will give you a form or a receipt, which must be presented at the border, where the wares are inspected. The Aus-trian government will send you your re-fund, minus a processing fee.

Wine and spirits are heavily taxed—nearly half of the sale price goes to taxes. For

every contract signed in Austria (for exam-ple, car-rental agreements), you pay an extra 1% tax to the government, so tax on a rental car is 21%.

Global Refund is a V.A.T. refund service that makes getting your money back has-sle-free. The service is available Europe-wide at 130,000 affiliated stores. In participating stores, **ask for the Global Re-fund form** (called a Shopping Cheque). Have it stamped like any customs form by customs officials when you leave the Euro-pean Union. Then take the form to one of the more than 700 Global Refund coun-ters—conveniently located at every major airport and border crossing—and your money will be refunded on the spot in the form of cash, check, or a refund to your credit-card account (minus a small per-centage for processing).

🔳 **Global Refund** ⊠ 707 Summer St., Stamford, CT 06901 ☎ 800/566-9828 🖶 203/674-8709 ✍ taxfree@us.globalrefund.com ⊕ www.globalrefund.com

TELEPHONES

AREA & COUNTRY CODES

The country code for Austria is 43. When dialing an Austrian number from abroad, drop the initial 0 from the local Austrian area code. For instance, the full number to dial for the Hotel Palais Schwarzenberg in Vienna from America is 011 (international dial code)–43 (Austria's country code)–1 (Vienna's full city code is 01, but drop the "0")—798–4515 (the hotel number). All numbers given in this guide include the city or town area code; if you are calling within that city or town, dial the local number only.

DIRECTORY & OPERATOR INFORMATION

For information in EU and neighboring countries, dial 118877; for information outside Europe, dial 0900/118877. Most operators speak English; if yours doesn't, you'll be passed along to one who does.

INTERNATIONAL CALLS

You can dial direct to almost any point on the globe from Austria. However, it costs more to telephone from Austria than it does to telephone to Austria. Calls from post offices are always the least expensive and you can get helpful assistance in placing a long-distance call; in large cities, these centers at main post offices are open around the clock. To use a post office phone, you first go to the counter to be directed to a certain telephone cabin; after your call, you return to the counter and pay your bill.

To make a collect call—you can't do this from pay phones—dial the operator and ask for an *R-Gespräch* (pronounced air-ga-*shprayk*). Most operators speak English; if yours doesn't, you'll be passed to one who does.

The international access code for the United States and Canada is 001, followed by the area code and number. For Great Britain, first dial 0044, then the city code without the usual "0" (171 or 181 for London), and the number. Other country and many city codes are given in the front of telephone books (in Vienna, in the A–H book).

LOCAL CALLS

When making a local call in Vienna, **dial the number without the city prefix.** A local call costs €0.20 for the first minute, and €0.20 for every three minutes thereafter.

LONG-DISTANCE CALLS

When placing a long-distance call to a destination within Austria, you'll need to know the local area codes, which can be found by consulting the telephone numbers that are listed in this guide's regional chapters (for instance, 0662 for Salzburg and 02711 for Dürnstein in the Danube Valley). When dialing from outside Austria, the 0 should be left out. Note that calls within Austria are one-third cheaper between 6 PM and 8 AM on weekdays and from 1 PM on Saturday to 8 AM on Monday.

LONG-DISTANCE SERVICES

AT&T and MCI access codes make calling long distance relatively convenient, but you may find the local access number blocked in many hotel rooms. First ask the hotel operator to connect you. If the hotel operator balks, ask for an international operator, or dial the international operator yourself. One way to improve your odds of getting connected to your long-distance carrier is to travel with more than one company's calling card (a hotel may block Sprint, for example, but not MCI). If all else fails, call from a pay phone.

🔢 Access Codes **AT&T Direct** ☎ 01/0800-200-288, 800/435-0812 for other areas. **MCI WorldPhone** ☎ 0800-200-235, 800/444-4141 for other areas.

PHONE CARDS

If you plan to make calls from pay phones, a *Telephon Wertkarte* is a convenience. You can buy this electronic phone card at any post office for €6.90 or €3.60, which allows you to use the card at any SOS, or credit-card phone booth. You simply insert the card and dial; the cost of the call is automatically deducted from the card, and a digital window on the phone tells you how many units you have left (these are not minutes). A few public phones in the cities also take American Express, Diners Club, MasterCard, and Visa credit cards.

PUBLIC & CELL PHONES

Cell phones (called "Handys") are extremely popular in Austria for everyone over the age of 5. As a result, coin-operated pay telephones are dwindling in number, and if you're lucky enough to find one, it may be out-of-order or available only for emergency calls. But if you find one that works, a local call costs €0.20 for the first scant minute. Quickly add another €0.10 before you are cut off. If there is no response, your coin will be returned into the bin to the lower left. Most pay phones have instructions in English. When dialing an Austrian "Handy" phone from abroad (generally 0676, 0699, or 0664), dial 00–43, then the number without the 0. Faxes can be sent from post offices and received as well, but neither service is very cheap.

TIME

The time difference between New York and Austria is 6 hours (so when it's 1 PM in New York, it's 7 PM in Vienna). The time difference between London and

Vienna is 1 hour; between Sydney and Vienna, 14 hours; and between Auckland and Vienna, 13 hours.

TIPPING

Although virtually all hotels and restaurants include service charges in their rates, tipping is still customary, but at a level lower than in the United States. Tip the hotel doorman €1 per bag, and the porter who brings your bags to the room another €1 per bag. In very small country inns such tips are not expected but are appreciated. In family-run establishments, tips are generally not given to immediate family members, only to employees. Tip the hotel concierge only for special services or in response to special requests. Room service gets €1 for snacks or ice, €2 for full meals. Maids normally get no tip unless your stay is a week or more or service has been special.

In restaurants, tip about 5%–7%. You can tip a little more if you've received exceptional service. Big tips are not usual in Austrian restaurants, since 10% has already been included in the prices. Checkroom attendants get €1–€2, depending on the locale. Washroom attendants get about €0.50. Wandering musicians and the piano player get €2, €5 if they've filled a number of requests.

Round up taxi fares to the next €0.50; a minimum €0.50 tip is customary. If the driver offers (or you ask for) special assistance, such as carrying your bags beyond the curb, an added tip of €0.50–€1 is in order.

TOURS & PACKAGES

VISITING AUSTRIA

Buying a prepackaged tour or independent vacation can make your trip to Austria less expensive and more hassle-free. Because everything is prearranged, you'll spend less time planning. Operators that handle several hundred thousand travelers per year can use their purchasing power to give you a good price. Their high volume may also indicate financial stability. But some small companies provide more personalized service; because they tend to specialize, they may also be more knowledgeable about a given area.

BOOKING WITH AN AGENT

Travel agents are excellent resources. But it's a good idea to collect brochures from several agencies as some agents' suggestions may be influenced by relationships with tour and package firms that reward them for volume sales. If you have a special interest, **find an agent with expertise in that area**; ASTA (*see* Travel Agencies, *below*) has a database of specialists worldwide.

Make sure your travel agent knows the accommodations and other services of the place they're recommending. Ask about the hotel's location, room size, beds, and whether it has a pool, room service, or programs for children, if you care about these. Has your agent been there in person or sent others whom you can contact?

Do some homework on your own, too: local tourism boards can provide information about lesser-known and small-niche operators, some of which may sell only direct.

BUYER BEWARE

Every year consumers are stranded or lose their money when tour operators—even large ones with excellent reputations—go out of business. So **check out the operator**. Ask several travel agents about its reputation, and try to **book with a company that has a consumer-protection program**. (Look for information in the company's brochure.)

In the United States, members of the National Tour Association and the United States Tour Operators Association are required to set aside funds to cover your payments and travel arrangements in the event that the company defaults. It's also a good idea to choose a company that participates in the American Society of Travel Agents' Tour Operator Program (TOP); ASTA will act as mediator in any disputes between you and your tour operator.

🖪 Tour-Operator Recommendations **American Society of Travel Agents** (*see* Travel Agencies, *below*). **National Tour Association (NTA)** ⌖ 546

E. Main St., Lexington, KY 40508 ☎ 606/226–4444 or 800/682–8886 ⊕ www.ntaonline.com. **United States Tour Operators Association (USTOA)** ✉ 342 Madison Ave., Suite 1522, New York, NY 10173 ☎ 212/599–6599 or 800/468–7862 🖷 212/599–6744 ✉ ustoa@aol.com ⊕ www.ustoa.com.

COSTS

The more your package or tour includes, the better you can predict the ultimate cost of your vacation. Make sure you know exactly what is covered, and **beware of hidden costs.** Are taxes, tips, and service charges included? Transfers and baggage handling? Entertainment and excursions? These can add up. Prices for packages and tours are usually quoted per person, based on two sharing a room. If traveling solo, you may be required to pay the full double-occupancy rate. Some operators eliminate this surcharge if you agree to be matched with a roommate of the same sex, even if one is not found by departure time.

GROUP TOURS

Among companies that sell tours to Austria, the following are nationally known, have a proven reputation, and offer plenty of options. The classifications used below represent different price categories, and you'll probably encounter these terms when talking to a travel agent or tour operator. The key difference is usually in accommodations, which run from budget to better, and better-yet to best. Note that each company doesn't schedule tours to Austria every year; check by calling.

▶ Super-Deluxe **Abercrombie & Kent** ✉ 1520 Kensington Rd., Oak Brook, IL 60521–2141 ☎ 630/954–2944 or 800/323–7308 🖷 630/954–3324. **Travcoa** ✉ Box 2630, 2350 S.E. Bristol St., Newport Beach, CA 92660 ☎ 714/476–2800 or 800/992–2003 🖷 714/476–2538.

▶ Deluxe **Globus** ✉ 5301 S. Federal Circle, Littleton, CO 80123–2980 ☎ 303/797–2800 or 800/221–0090 🖷 303/347–2080. **Maupintour** ✉ 1515 St. Andrews Dr., Lawrence, KS 66047 ☎ 785/843–1211 or 800/255–4266 🖷 785/843–8351. **Tauck Tours** ✉ Box 5027, 276 Post Rd. W, Westport, CT 06881–5027 ☎ 203/226–6911 or 800/468–2825 🖷 203/221–6866.

▶ First-Class **Brendan Tours** ✉ 15137 Califa St., Van Nuys, CA 91411 ☎ 818/785–9696 or 800/421–8446 🖷 818/902–9876. **Caravan Tours** ✉ 401 N.

Michigan Ave., Chicago, IL 60611 ☎ 312/321–9800 or 800/227–2826 🖷 312/321–9845. **Collette Tours** ✉ 162 Middle St., Pawtucket, RI 02860 ☎ 401/728–3805 or 800/340–5158 🖷 401/728–4745. **DER Travel Services** ✉ 9501 W. Devon Ave., Rosemont, IL 60018 ☎ 800/937–1235 🖷 847/692–4141, 800/282–7474, 800/860–9944 for brochures. **Gadabout Tours** ✉ 700 E. Tahquitz Canyon Way, Palm Springs, CA 92262–6767 ☎ 619/325–5556 or 800/952–5068. **Trafalgar Tours** ✉ 11 E. 26th St., New York, NY 10010 ☎ 212/689–8977 or 800/854–0103 🖷 800/457–6644.

▶ Budget **Cosmos** (see Globus, *above*). **Trafalgar Tours** (*see above*).

THEME TRIPS

▶ Barge/River Cruises **Abercrombie & Kent** (see Group Tours, *above*). **KD River Cruises of Europe** ✉ 2500 Westchester Ave., Purchase, NY 10577 ☎ 914/696–3600 or 800/346–6525 🖷 914/696–0833 ⊕ www.abercrombiekent.com. **Annemarie Victory Organization** ✉ 136 E. 64th St., New York, NY 10021 ☎ 212/486–0353 🖷 212/751–3149 ⊕ www.annemarievictory.com offers luxury cruises on the River Cloud liner up and down the Danube. **Smolka Tours** ✉ 82 Riveredge Rd., Tinton Falls, NJ 07724 ☎ 732/576–8813 or 800/722–0057 ⊕ www.smolkatours.com/ offers a Beautiful Blue Danube Cruise.

▶ Bicycling **Backroads** ✉ 801 Cedar St., Berkeley, CA 94710–1800 ☎ 510/527–1555 or 800/462–2848 🖷 510/527–1444. **Butterfield & Robinson** ✉ 70 Bond St., Toronto, Ontario, Canada M5B 1X3 ☎ 416/864–1354 or 800/678–1147 🖷 416/864–0541 ⊕ www.butterfield.com. **Euro-Bike Tours** ✉ Box 990, De Kalb, IL 60115 ☎ 800/321–6060 🖷 815/758–8851. **VBT (Vermont Biking Tours)** ✉ 614 Monkton Rd., Bristol, VT 05443 ☎ 800/245–3868 ⊕ www.vbt.com offers a spectacular Salzburg Sojourn tour.

▶ Christmas/New Year's **Annemarie Victory Organization** ✉ 136 E. 64th St., New York, NY 10021 ☎ 212/486–0353 🖷 212/751–3149 ⊕ www.annemarievictory.com is known for its spectacular "New Year's Eve Ball in Vienna" excursion. This highly respected organization has been selling out this tour—which includes deluxe rooms at the Bristol, the Imperial Palace Ball, and a Konzerthaus New Year's Day concert—for 10 years running. A decade ago, Annemarie Victory premiered a "Christmas in Salzburg" trip, with rooms at the Goldener Hirsch and a side trip to the Silent Night Chapel in Oberndorf. **Smolka Tours** (*see Barge/River Cruises, above*) has also conducted festive holiday-season tours that included concerts, gala balls, and the famous Christmas Markets of Vienna and Salzburg.

🏃 Hiking/Walking **Alpine Adventure Trails Tours**
✉ 322 Pio Nono Ave., Macon, GA 31204 📠 912/
478-4007. **Mountain Travel-Sobek** ✉ 6420 Fairmount Ave., El Cerrito, CA 94530 📠 510/527-8100 or 800/227-2384 📠 510/525-7710.

🏃 Mountain Climbing **Mountain Travel-Sobek**
(*see* Hiking/Walking, *above*).

🏃 Music **Dailey-Thorp Travel** ✉ 330 W. 58th St.,
#610, New York, NY 10019-1817 📠 212/307-1555 or 800/998-4677 📠 212/974-1420 ⊕ www.daileythorp. com. **Smolka Tours** (*see* Barge/River Cruises, *above*).

TRAIN TRAVEL
TRAINS IN AUSTRIA

Austrian train service is excellent: it's fast and, for Western Europe, relatively inexpensive, particularly if you take advantage of the discount fares. Trains on the mountainous routes are slow, but no slower than driving, and the scenery is gorgeous! Many of the remote rail routes will give you a look at traditional Austria, complete with Alpine cabins tacked onto mountainsides and a backdrop of snowcapped peaks.

Austrian Federal Railways trains are identifiable by the letters that precede the train number on the timetables and posters. The IC (InterCity) or EC (EuroCity) trains are fastest, and a supplement of about €5 is included in the price of the ticket. EN trains have sleeping facilities. **Allow yourself plenty of time to purchase your ticket before boarding the train. If you purchase your ticket on board the train, you must pay a surcharge, which is around €7** or more, depending on how far you're going. All tickets are valid without supplement on D (express), E (*Eilzug;* semi-fast), and local trains. You can reserve a seat for €3.40 up until a few hours before departure. Be sure to do this on the main-line trains (Vienna–Innsbruck, Salzburg–Klagenfurt, Vienna–Graz, for example) at peak holiday times. The EC trains usually have a dining car with fairly good food. The trains originating in Budapest have good Hungarian cooking. Otherwise there is usually a fellow with a cart serving snacks and hot and cold drinks. Most trains are equipped with a card telephone in or near the restaurant car.

Make certain that you inquire about possible supplements payable onboard trains traveling to destinations outside Austria **when you are purchasing your ticket.** Austrians are not generally forthcoming with information, and you might be required to pay a supplement in cash to the conductor while you are on the train. For information, call 05/1717 from anywhere in Austria. Unless you speak German fairly well, it's a good idea to have your hotel call for you.

CLASSES

The difference between first and second class on Austrian trains is mainly a matter of space. First- and second-class sleepers, and couchettes (six to a compartment), are available on international runs, as well as on long trips within Austria. If you're driving and would rather watch the scenery than the traffic, you can put your car on a train in Vienna and accompany it to Salzburg, Innsbruck, Feldkirch, or Villach. You relax in a compartment or sleeper for the trip, and the car is unloaded when you arrive.

DISCOUNT PASSES

To save money, **look into rail passes.** But be aware that if you don't plan to cover many miles you may come out ahead by buying individual tickets.

Austria is one of 17 countries in which you can **use Eurailpasses,** which provide unlimited first-class rail travel, in all of the participating countries, for the duration of the pass. If you plan to rack up the miles, get a standard pass. These are available for 15 days ($588), 21 days ($762), one month ($946), two months ($1,338), and three months ($1,654).

In addition to standard Eurailpasses, **ask about special rail-pass plans.** Among these are the Eurail Youthpass (for those under age 26), the Eurail Saverpass (which gives a discount for two or more people traveling together), a Eurail Flexipass (which allows a certain number of travel days within a set period), the Euraildrive Pass, and the Europass Drive (which combines travel by train and rental car). Whichever pass you choose, remember that you must **purchase your pass before you leave** for Europe.

Many travelers assume that rail passes guarantee them seats on the trains they wish to ride. Not so. You need to **book seats ahead even if you are using a rail pass**; seat reservations are required on some European trains, particularly high-speed trains, and are a good idea on trains that may be crowded—particularly in summer on popular routes. You will also need a reservation if you purchase sleeping accommodations.

Another option that gives you discount travel through various countries is the European East Pass, offered by Rail Europe, good for travel within Austria, the Czech Republic, Hungary, Poland, and Slovakia: cost is $226 (first class) or $160 (second class) for any 5 days unlimited travel within a one-month period.

The ÖBB, the Austrian Austrian Federal Train Service has a Web site, but it is not particularly user-friendly. As it is often impossible to get through to them on the phone, it is best to get to the train station early for questions. The ÖBB offers a large number of discounts for various travel constellations. If you are traveling with a group of people, even small, there are percentages taken off for each member. Families can also get discounts. School children and students also get good deals. The Vorteilscard is valid for a year and costs about €100, allowing 45% fare reduction on all rail travel. If you are planning lots of travel in Austria, it could be a good deal. Ask for other special deals, and check travel agencies. Children between 6 and 15 travel at half price, under 6 years of age for free.

You can buy an Austrian Rail Pass in the United States for travel within Austria for 15 days ($158 first class, $107 second class). It's available for purchase in Austria also, but only at travel agencies, such as SNS Tours.

For €26.90 and a passport photo, women over 60 and men over 65 can obtain a Seniorenpass, which carries a 45% discount

on rail tickets. The pass also has a host of other benefits, including reduced-price entry into museums. Most rail stations can give you information.

Travelers under 26 should inquire about discount fares under the Billet International Jeune (BIJ). The special one-trip tickets are sold by Eurotrain International, travel agents, and youth-travel specialists, and at rail stations.

🚆 Information & Passes **CIT Tours Corp** ✉ 15 W. 44th St., 10th floor, New York, NY 10036 ☎ 212/730-2400, 800/248-7245 in the U.S., 800/387-0711, 800/361-7799 in Canada ⊕ www.cit-tours.com. **DER Travel Services** ✉ 9501 W. Devon Ave., Rosemont, IL 60018 ☎ 800/782-2424 🖷 800/282-7474 for information ⊕ www.dertravel.com. **ÖBB (Österreichische Bundesbahnen)** ⊕ www.oebb.at. **Rail Europe** ✉ 500 Mamaroneck Ave., Harrison, NY 10528 ☎ 914/682-5172 or 800/438-7245 🖷 800/432-1329 ⊕ www.raileurope.com ✉ 2087 Dundas E, Suite 106, Mississauga, Ontario L4X 1M2 ☎ 800/361-7245 🖷 905/602-4198. **SNS Tours** ⊕ snstours.com/ausrail.htm.

FARES & SCHEDULES

For train schedules from the Austrian rail service, the ÖBB, ask at your hotel, stop in at the train station and look for large posters labeled ABFAHRT (departures) and ANKUNFT (arrivals), or log on to their Web site. In the Abfahrt listing you'll find the departure time in the main left-hand block of the listing and, under the train name, details of where it stops en route and the time of each arrival. There is also information about connecting trains and buses, with departure details. Workdays are symbolized by two crossed hammers, which means that the same schedule might not apply on weekends or holidays. A little rocking horse means that a special playpen has been set up for children in the train. Women traveling alone may book special compartments on night trains or long-distance rides (ask for a *Damenabteilung*).

🚆 **ÖBB (Österreichische Bundesbahnen)** ⊕ www.oebb.at.

FROM THE U.K.

There's a choice of rail routes to Austria, but check services first; long-distance passenger service across the Continent is undergoing considerable reduction. There is daily service from London to Vienna via the *Austria Nachtexpress.* Check other services such as the *Orient Express.* If you don't mind changing trains, you can travel via Paris, where you change stations to board the overnight *Arlberg Express* via Innsbruck and Salzburg to Vienna. First- and second-class sleepers and second-class couchettes are available as far as Innsbruck.

When you have the time, a strikingly scenic route to Austria is via Cologne and Munich; after an overnight stop in Cologne you take the *EuroCity Express Johann Strauss* to Vienna.

🚉 Information & Reservations Contact **Eurotrain** ✉ 52 Grosvenor Gardens, London SW1W OAG ☎ 020/7730-3402, which offers excellent deals for those under 26, or **British Rail Travel Centers** ☎ 020/7834-2345. For additional information, call **DER Travel Service** ☎ 020/7408-0111 or the Austrian **National Tourist Office** (*see* Visitor Information, *below*).

TRAVEL AGENCIES

American Express, Kuoni Cosmos, Carlson/Wagons-Lit and Österreichisches Verkehrsbüro serve as general travel agencies. American Express, Kuoni Cosmos, and Vienna Ticket Service/Cityrama are agencies that offer tickets to various sights and events in Vienna.

🚉 Local Agent Referrals **American Express** ✉ Kärntnerstrasse 21–23, 1st District ☎ 01/515-4077-0 🖨 01/515-40-777. **Carlson/Wagons-Lit** ✉ Millennium Tower 94/Handelskai, 20th District ☎ 01/240600 🖨 01/24060-65. **Kuoni Cosmos** ✉ Kärntner Ring 15, 1st District ☎ 01/515-33-0 🖨 01/513-4147.**Österreichisches Verkehrsbüro** ✉ Opernring 3–5, 1st District ☎ 01/588-628 🖨 01/588-000-130. **Vienna Ticket Service/Cityrama** ✉ Börsegasse 1, 1st District ☎ 01/534130 🖨 01/534-1328.

A good travel agent puts your needs first. Look for an agency that has been in business at least five years, emphasizes customer service, and has someone on staff who specializes in your destination. In addition, **make sure the agency belongs to a professional trade organization.** The American Society of Travel Agents (ASTA), with more than 24,000 members in some 140 countries, is the largest and most influential in the field. Operating under the motto "Integrity in Travel," it maintains and enforces a strict code of ethics and will step in to help mediate any agent-client disputes if necessary. ASTA also maintains a Web site that includes a directory of agencies. (If a travel agency is also acting as your tour operator, *see* Buyer Beware *in* Tours & Packages, *above.*)

🚉 Local Agent Referrals **American Society of Travel Agents (ASTA)** ☎ 800/965-2782 24-hr hot line 🖨 703/739-3268 🌐 www.astanet.com. **Association of British Travel Agents** ✉ 68–71 Newman St., London W1P 4AH ☎ 020/7637-2444 🖨 020/7637-0713 ✉ information@abta.co.uk 🌐 www.abtanet.com. **Association of Canadian Travel Agents** ✉ 1729 Bank St., Suite 201, Ottawa, Ontario K1V 7Z5 ☎ 613/521-0474 🖨 613/521-0805 ✉ acta.ntl@sympatico.ca 🌐 www.acta.ca. **Australian Federation of Travel Agents** ✉ Level 3, 309 Pitt St., Sydney 2000 ☎ 02/9264-3299 🖨 02/9264-1085 🌐 www.afta.com.au. **Travel Agents' Association of New Zealand** 🖄 Box 1888, Wellington 6001 ☎ 04/499-0104 🖨 04/499-0827 ✉ taanz@tiasnet.co.nz.

VISITOR INFORMATION

🚉 Austrian National Tourist Office **In the U.S.** ✉ 500 5th Ave., 20th floor, New York, NY 10110 ☎ 212/944-6880 🖨 212/730-4568 🖄 Box 1142, New York, NY 10108. **In Canada** ✉ 2 Bloor St. E, Suite 3330, Toronto, Ontario M4W 1A8 ☎ 416/967-3381 🖨 416/967-4101 🖄 1010 Sherbrooke St. W, Suite 1410, Montréal, Québec H3A 2R7 ☎ 514/849-3709 🖨 514/849-9577 🖄 200 Granville St., Suite 1380, Granville Sq., Vancouver, BC V6C 1S4 ☎ 604/683-5808 or 604/683-8695 🖨 604/662-8528. **In the U.K.** ✉ 30 St. George St., London W1R OAL ☎ 020/7629-0461. **Web site** 🌐 www.anto.com.

🚉 U.S. Government Advisories **U.S. Department of State** ✉ Overseas Citizens Services Office, Room 4811 N.S., 2201 C St. NW, Washington, DC 20520 ☎ 202/647-5225 interactive hot line or 888/407-4747 🌐 www.travel.state.gov; enclose a business-size SASE.

WEB SITES

Do check out the World Wide Web when you're planning. You'll find everything from up-to-date weather forecasts to virtual tours of famous cities. Fodor's Web site, 🌐 www.fodors.com, is a great place to start your online travels—just search for the Vienna miniguide, then search for "Links." For basic information:

Austrian National Tourist Office (⊕ www.
austria-tourism.at); **Vienna** (⊕ info.
wien.at); **Burgenland** (⊕ www.
burgenland-tourism.co.at); **Carinthia**
(⊕ www.tiscover.com/carinthia);
Upper Austria (⊕ www.tiscover.com/
upperaustria); **Salzburg** (⊕ www.
salzburginfo.or.at); **Tirol** (⊕ www.
www.tiscover.com/tirol); **Vorarlberg**
(⊕ www.voralberg-tourism.at); and
Styria (⊕ www.steiermark.com). For **train
information** (⊕ www.oebb.at). Also see
the web sites for many of the tourist organizations for the big regional provinces
in Austria, listed under Visitor Information in the A to Z section at the end of
each regional chapter.

For Vienna, here are some top Web sites:
Wien Online (⊕ www.magwien.gv.at), the
city's official Web site; **Vienna Scene**
(⊕ www.austria-tourism.com), the Vienna
Tourist Board Web site; **Wienerzeitung**
(⊕ www.wienerzeitung.at), the city's leading newspaper Web site; **Die Falter**
(⊕ www.falter.at), the city's most sophisticated newspaper and best cultural listings;
Time Out Vienna (⊕ www.timeout.com/
vienna/index.html); **Vienna tickets**
(⊕ www.viennaticket.at/english); **MuseumsQuartier** (⊕ www.mqw.at) for the scoop
on the big new museum district; and the
Austrian Travel Network (⊕ www.tiscover.
com). For the main Mozart Year 2006
Web site: ⊕ www.mozart2006.net.

VIENNA

1

SWOON ALONGSIDE KLIMT'S *KISS*
at the Belvedere Palace Museum ⇨*p.57*

HUM A MOZART MOVEMENT
in his own music study at Figarohaus ⇨*p.53*

TRUMPET YOUR ENTRY INTO VIENNA
from a seat on a Ringstrasse tramcar ⇨*p.126*

OPT FOR OPULENCE
at the Habsburgs' Hofburg ⇨*p.33*

MAKE MERRY WITH THE WIDOWS
at a Volksoper operetta ⇨*p.110*

LOOK SHARP WHILE ADMIRING
the best glass and crystal at Lobmeyr's ⇨*p.119*

WHISPER *BOO!* AT HARRY LIME
from his dark *Third Man* portal ⇨*p.27*

DINE LIKE A STAATSOPER DIVA
in the baronial salons of Korso ⇨*p.72*

SOAK UP AMBIENCE-*MIT-SCHLAG*
at the kaffeehaus of Café Central ⇨*p.87*

Updated by
Bonnie Dodson
and Diane
Naar-Elphee

PROPER CITIZENS OF VIENNA, it has been said, waltz only from the waist down, holding their upper bodies ramrod straight while whirling around the crowded dance floor. The movement resulting from this correct posture is breathtaking in its sweep and splendor, and its elegant coupling of free-wheeling exuberance and rigid formality—of license and constraint—is quintessentially Viennese. The town palaces all over the inner city—built mostly during the 18th century—present in stone and stucco a similar artful synthesis. They make Vienna a Baroque city that is, at its best, an architectural waltz.

Those who tour Vienna today might feel they're keeping step in three-quarter time. As they explore churches filled with statues of gilded saints and cheeky cherubs, wander through treasure-packed museums, or take in the delights of a mecca of mocha (the ubiquitous cafés), they may feel destined to enjoy repeated helpings of the beloved *Schlagobers,* the rich, delicious whipped cream that garnishes the most famous Viennese pastry of all, the Sachertorte. The ambience of the city is predominantly ornate: White horses dance to elegant music; snow frosts the opulent draperies of Empress Maria Theresa's monument, set in the formal patterns of "her" lovely square; a gilded Johann Strauss perpetually plays midst a grove of trees; town houses present a dignified face to the outside world while enclosing lavishly decorated interior courtyards; dark Greek legends are declawed by the voluptuous music of Richard Strauss; Klimt's paintings glitter with geometric impasto; a mechanical clock intones the hour with a stately pavane. All these will create in the visitor the sensation of a metropolis that likes to be visited and admired—and which indeed is well worth visiting and admiring.

For centuries, this has been the case. One of the great capitals of Europe, Vienna was for centuries the main stamping grounds to the Habsburg rulers of the Austro-Hungarian Empire. The empire is long gone, but many reminders of the city's imperial heyday remain, carefully preserved by the tradition-loving Viennese. When it comes to the arts, the glories of the past are particularly evergreen, thanks to the cultural legacy created by the many artistic geniuses nourished here.

From the late 18th century on, Vienna's culture—particularly its musical forte—was famous throughout Europe. Haydn, Mozart, Beethoven, Schubert, Brahms, Strauss, Mahler, and Bruckner all lived in the city, composing glorious music still played in concert halls all over the world. And at the tail end of the 19th century the city's artists and architects—Gustav Klimt, Egon Schiele, Oskar Kokoschka, Josef Hoffmann, Otto Wagner, and Adolf Loos among them—brought about an unprecedented artistic revolution, a revolution that swept away the past and set the stage for the radically experimental art of the 20th century. "Form follows function," the artists of the late-19th-century Jugendstil proclaimed. Their echo is still heard in the city's contemporary arts and crafts galleries—even in the glinting, Space Needle–like object that hovers over the north end of Vienna—actually the city's waste incinerator, designed by the late, great artist Friedensreich Hundertwasser.

Magnificent, magnetic, and magical, Vienna beguiles one and all with its Old World charm and courtly grace. It is a place where headwaiters still bow as though addressing a Habsburg prince, and Lipizzaner stallions dance their intricate minuets to the strains of Mozart. Here is a city that waltzes and works in measured three-quarter time. Like a well-bred grande dame, Vienna doesn't rush about, and neither should you. Saunter through its stately streets—and rub elbows with the spirits of Beethoven and Strauss, Metternich and Freud—and marvel at its Baroque palaces. Then dream an afternoon away at a cozy *Kaffeehaus*.

1

If you have
1 day

Touring Vienna in a single day is a proposition as strenuous as it is unlikely, but those with more ambition than time should first get a quick view of the lay of the city by taking a streetcar ride around the Ringstrasse, the wide boulevard that encloses the city's heart. Then spend the time until early afternoon exploring the city center, starting at Vienna's cathedral, the **Stephansdom ①**, followed by a stroll along the Graben and Kärntnerstrasse, the two main pedestrian shopping streets in the center. About 1 PM, head for **Schönbrunn Palace ⑳** to spend the afternoon touring the magnificent royal residence, or visit the **Kunsthistoriches Museum ⑤**, one of the great art museums of the world. After the museum closes at 6 PM, relax over coffee at a café; then spend a musical evening at a concert, opera, or operetta or a convivial evening at a Heuriger, one of the wine restaurants for which Vienna is also famous.

If you have
3 days

Given three days, Day 1 can be a little less hectic, and in any case you'll want more time for the city center. Rather than going on the do-it-yourself streetcar ride around the Ringstrasse, take an organized sightseeing tour, which will describe the highlights. Plan to spend a full afternoon at **Schönbrunn Palace ⑳**. Reserve the second day for art, tackling the exciting **Kunsthistoriches Museum ⑤** before lunch, and after you're refreshed, the dazzling **MuseumsQuartier ㊾**, which comprises several major modern art collections—the Leopold Museum; the Museum moderner Kunst Stiftung Ludwig (MUMOK); the temporary shows at the Kunsthalle; plus the children's ZOOM Kinder Museum; the Architekturzentrum (Architecture Center); and the Tabak Museum, which is devoted to the subject of tobacco. If your tastes tend to the grand and royal, visit instead the magnificent collection of Old Master drawings at the **Albertina Museum ㊻** and the impressive **Belvedere Palace ㉟**. For a contrasting step into modern art in the afternoon—don't miss Klimt's legendary *The Kiss* at the Belvedere. Do as the Viennese do, and fill in any gaps with stops at cafés, reserving evenings for relaxing over music or wine. On the third day, head for the world-famous **Spanische Reitschule ㉞** and watch the Lipizzaners prance through morning training. While you're in the neighborhood, view the sparkling court jewels in the Imperial Treasury, the **Schatzkammer ㊸**, and the glitzy **Silberkammer ㊵**, the museum of court silver and tableware, and take in one of Vienna's most spectacular Baroque settings, the glorious Grand Hall of the **Hofbibliothek ㊲**. For a total contrast, head out to the Prater amusement park in late afternoon for a ride on the giant Ferris wheel and end the day in a wine restaurant on the outskirts, perhaps in Sievering or Nussdorf.

Spend your first three days as outlined in the itinerary above. Then begin your fourth day getting better acquainted with the 1st District—the heart of the city. Treasures here range from Roman ruins to the residences of Mozart and Beethoven, the **Figarohaus** 🄣 and the **Pasqualatihaus** 🄡; then, slightly afield, the **Freud Haus** 🄢 (in the 9th District) or the oddball **Hundertwasserhaus** (in the 3rd). Put it all in contemporary perspective with a backstage tour of the magnificent **Staatsoper** 🄸, the State Opera. For a country break on the fifth day, take a tour of the **Vienna Woods** (*see* Chapter 3) or the Danube Valley, particularly the glorious **Wachau district** (*see* Chapter 5), where vineyards sweep down to the river's edge. On the sixth day, fill in some of the blanks with a stroll around the **Naschmarkt** 🄧 food-market district, taking in the nearby **Secession Building** 🄤 with Gustav Klimt's famous Beethoven Frieze. Don't overlook the superb Jugendstil buildings on the north side of the market. If you're still game for museums, head for any one of the less usual offerings, such as the Jewish Museum, the Haus der Musik, or the Ephesus Museum, in the **Hofburg,** or visit the city's historical museum, **Wien Museum Karlsplatz** 🄥; by now, you'll have acquired a good concept of the city and its background, so the exhibits will make more sense. Cap the day by visiting the **Kaisergruft** 🄺 in the Kapuzinerkirche to view the tombs of the Habsburgs responsible for so much of Vienna.

At the close of World War I the Austro-Hungarian Empire was dismembered, and Vienna lost its cherished status as the seat of imperial power. Its influence was much reduced, and its population began to decline (unlike what happened in Europe's other great cities), falling from around 2 million to the current 1.8 million. Today, however, the city's future looks brighter, for with the collapse of the Iron Curtain, Vienna regained its traditional status as one of the main hubs of Central Europe.

For many first-time visitors, the city's one major disappointment concerns the Danube River. The inner city, it turns out, lies not on the river's main course but on one of its narrow offshoots, known as the Danube Canal. As a result, the sweeping river views expected by most newcomers fail to materialize.

For this the Romans are to blame, for when Vienna was founded as a Roman military encampment around AD 100, the walled garrison was built not on the Danube's main stream but rather on the largest of the river's eastern branches, where it could be bordered by water on three sides. The wide, present-day Danube did not take shape until the late 19th century, when, to prevent flooding, its various branches were rerouted and merged.

The Romans maintained their camp for some 300 years (the emperor Marcus Aurelius is thought to have died in Vindobona, as it was called, in 180) not abandoning the site until around 400. The settlement survived the Roman withdrawal, however, and by the 13th century development was sufficient to require new city walls to the south. According to legend, the walls were financed by the English: in 1192 the local duke kidnapped King Richard I (the Lion-Hearted), en route home from the Third Crusade, and held him prisoner in Dürnstein, up-river, for several months, then turning him over to the Austrian king after two years, until he was expensively ransomed by his mother, Eleanor of Aquitaine.

Vienna's third set of walls dates from 1544, when the existing walls were improved and extended. The new fortifications were built by the Habsburg dynasty, which ruled the Austro-Hungarian Empire for an astonishing 640 years, beginning with Rudolf I in 1273 and ending with Karl I in 1918. These walls stood until 1857, when Emperor Franz Josef decreed that they finally be demolished and replaced by the series of boulevards that make up the famous tree-lined Ringstrasse.

During medieval times the city's growth was relatively slow, and its heyday as a European capital did not begin until 1683, after a huge force of invading Turks laid siege to the city for a two-month period before being routed by an army of Habsburg allies. Among the supplies that the fleeing Turks left behind were sacks filled with coffee beans, and it was these beans, so the story goes, that gave a local entrepreneur the idea of opening the first public coffeehouse; they remain a Viennese institution to this day.

The passing of the Turkish threat encouraged a Viennese building boom, with the Baroque style becoming the architectural choice of the day. Flamboyant, triumphant, joyous, and extravagantly ostentatious, the new art form—imported from Italy—transformed the city into a vast theater over the course of the 17th and 18th centuries. Life became a dream—the gorgeous dream of the Baroque, with its gilt madonnas and cherubs; its soaring, twisted columns; its painted heavens on the ceilings; its graceful domes. In the early 19th century a reaction began to set in—with middle-class industriousness and sober family values leading the way to a new epoch, characterized by the Biedermeier style. Then followed the Strauss era—that lighthearted period that conjures up imperial balls, "Wine, Women, and Song," heel clicking, and hand kissing. Today's visitors will find that each of these eras has left its mark on Vienna, making it a city possessed of a special grace. It is this grace that gives Vienna the cohesive architectural character that sets the city so memorably apart from its great rivals—London, Paris, and Rome.

EXPLORING VIENNA

By George Sullivan

Updated by Bonnie Dodson

Most of Vienna lies roughly within an arc of a circle with the straight line of the Danube Canal as its chord. Its heart, the **Innere Stadt** ("Inner City"), or 1st District is bounded by the Ringstrasse (Ring) which forms almost a circle, with a narrow arc cut off by the Danube Canal, diverted from the mother river just outside the city limits and flowing through the northern sector of the city to rejoin the parent stream beyond the city line. To the Viennese, the most prestigious address of Vienna's 23 *Bezirke*, or districts, is this fabled 1st District, whose Innere Stadt contains the vast majority of sightseeing attractions. Of course, what is now the 1st District used to encompass the entire city of Vienna. In 1857 Emperor Franz Josef decided to demolish the original ancient wall surrounding the city to create the more cosmopolitan Ringstrasse, the multi-laned avenue that still encircles the expansive heart of Vienna. At that time, several small villages bordering the inner city were given district numbers and incorporated into Vienna. Today the former villages go by their official district number, but they are still known by their old village or neighborhood name, too. In conversation, the Viennese most often say the number of the district they are referring to, though sometimes they use the neighborhood name instead.

The circular 1st District is bordered on its northeastern section by the Danube Canal and 2nd District, and clockwise from there along the Ringstrasse by the 3rd, 4th, 6th, 7th, 8th, and 9th districts. Across the Danube Canal from the 1st District, the 2nd District—Leopoldstadt—is home to the venerable Prater amusement park, with its famous *Riesenrad* (Ferris wheel), as well as a huge park used for horseback riding and jogging. Along the southeastern edge of the 1st District is the 3rd District—Landstrasse—containing a number of embassies and the famed Belvedere Palace. The southern tip, the 4th District—Wieden—is fast becoming Vienna's new hip area, with trendy restaurants, art galleries, and shops opening up every week, plus Vienna's biggest outdoor market, the Naschmarkt, which is lined with dazzling Jugendstil buildings.

The southwestern 6th District—Mariahilf—includes the biggest shopping street, Mariahilferstrasse, with small, old-fashioned shops competing with smart restaurants, movie theaters, bookstores, and department stores. Directly west of the 1st District is the 7th District—Neubau. Besides the celebrated Kunsthistorisches Museum and headline-making MuseumsQuartier, the 7th District also houses the charming Spittelberg quarter, its cobblestone streets lined with beautifully preserved 18th-century houses. Moving up the western side you come to the 8th District—Josefstadt—which is known for its theaters, good restaurants, and antiques shops. And completing the circle surrounding the Innere Stadt on its northwest side is the 9th District—Alsergrund—once Sigmund Freud's neighborhood and today a nice residential area with lots of outdoor restaurants, curio shops, and lovely early-20th-century apartment buildings.

The other districts—the 5th, and the 10th through the 23rd—form a concentric second circle around the 2nd through 9th districts. These are mainly residential suburbs and only a few hold sights of interest for tourists. The 11th District—Simmering—contains one of Vienna's new architectural wonders, Gasometer, a former gas works that has been remodeled into a housing and shopping complex. The 13th District—Hietzing—whose centerpiece is the fabulous Schönbrunn Palace, is also a coveted residential area, including the neighborhood Hütteldorf. The 19th District—Döbling—is Vienna's poshest residential neighborhood and also bears the nickname the "Noble District" because of all the embassy residences on its chestnut-tree-lined streets. The 19th District also incorporates several other neighborhoods within its borders, in particular, the wine villages of Grinzing, Sievering, Nussdorf, and Neustift am Walde. The 22nd District—Donaustadt—now headlines Donau City, a modern business and shopping complex that has grown around the United

Café Society

It used to be said that there were more cafés and coffeehouses in Vienna than there were banks in Switzerland. Whether or not this can still be claimed, the true flavor of Vienna can't be savored without visiting some of its great café landmarks. Every afternoon at 4, the coffee-and-pastry ritual of *Kaffeejause* takes place from one end of the city to the other. Regulars take their *Stammtisch* (usual table), where they sit until they go home for dinner. And why not? They come to gossip, read the papers, negotiate business, play cards, meet a spouse (or someone else's), or—who knows?—perhaps just have a cup of coffee. Whatever the reason, the Viennese use cafés and coffeehouses as club, pub, bistro, and even a home away from home. (Old-timers recall the old joke: "Pardon me, would you mind watching my seat for a while so I can go out for a cup of coffee?")

In fact, to savor the atmosphere of the coffeehouse, you must allow time. There is no need to worry about outstaying one's welcome, even over a single small cup of coffee—so set aside a morning or afternoon, and take along this book. For historical overtones, head for the Café Central—Lev Bronstein, otherwise known as Leon Trotsky, at one time enjoyed playing chess here. For Old World charm, check out the opulent Café Landtmann, which was Freud's favorite meeting place, or the elegant Café Sacher (famous for its Sachertorte); for the smoky art scene, go to the Café Hawelka. Wherever you end up, never ask for a plain cup of coffee; at the very least, order a Melange *mit Schlag* (with whipped cream) from the *Herr Ober,* or any of many other delightful variations.

The Heurige

It makes for a memorable experience to sit at the edge of a vineyard on the Kahlenberg with a tankard of young white wine and listen to the *Schrammel* quartet playing sentimental Viennese songs. The wine taverns, called *Heurige* (the singular is *Heuriger*) for the new wine that they serve, are very much a part and typical of the city (although not unique to Vienna). Heurige sprang up in 1784 when Joseph II decreed that owners of vineyards could establish their own private wine taverns; soon the Viennese discovered it was cheaper to go out to the wine than to bring it inside the city walls, where taxes were levied. The Heuriger owner is supposed to be licensed to serve only the produce of his own vineyard, a rule more honored in the breach than the observance (it would take a sensitive palate indeed to differentiate between the various vineyards).

These taverns in the wine-growing districts on the outskirts of the city (in such villages as Neustift am Walde, Sievering, Nussdorf, and Grinzing) vary from the simple front room of a vintner's house to ornate settings. The true Heuriger is open for only a few weeks a year to allow the vintner to sell a certain quantity of his production, tax-free, when consumed on his own premises. The commercial establishments keep to a somewhat more regular season but still sell only wine from their own vines.

The choice is usually between a "new" and an "old" white (or red) wine, but you can also ask for a milder or sharper wine according to your taste. Most Heurige are happy to let you sample the wines before you order. You can also order a *Gespritzter,* half wine and half soda water. The waitress brings the wine, usually in a ¼-liter mug or liter carafe, but you serve yourself from the food buffet. The wine tastes as mild as lemonade, but it packs a punch. If it isn't of good quality, you will know by a raging headache the next day.

Jugendstil Jewels
From 1897 to 1907, the Vienna Secession movement gave rise to one of the most spectacular manifestations of the pan-European style known as Art Nouveau. Viennese took to calling the look *Jugendstil,* or the "young style." In such dazzling edifices as Otto Wagner's Wienzeile majolica-adorned mansion and Adolf Loos's Looshaus, Jugendstil architects rebelled against the prevailing 19th-century historicism that had created so many imitation Renaissance town houses and faux Grecian temples. Josef Maria Olbrich, Josef Hoffman, and Otto Schönthal took William Morris's Arts and Crafts movement, added dashes of Charles Rennie Mackintosh and flat-surface Germanic geometry, and came up with a luxurious style that shocked turn-of-the-century Viennese traditionalists (and infuriated Emperor Franz Josef). Many artists united to form the Vienna Secession—whose most famous member was painter Gustav Klimt—and the Wiener Werkstätte, which transformed the objects of daily life with a sleek modern look. Today, Jugendstil buildings are among the most fascinating structures in Vienna. The shrine of the movement is the world-famous Secession Building—the work of Josef Maria Olbrich—the cynosure of all eyes on the Friedrichstrasse.

Museums & Marvels
You could spend months perusing the contents of Vienna's 90 museums. Subjects range, alphabetically, from art to wine, and in between are found marvels such as carriages and clocks, memorial dedicatees such as Mozart and martyrs, and oddities such as bricks and burials. If your time is short, the one museum not to be overlooked is the Kunsthistorisches Museum, Vienna's most famous art museum and one of the great museums of the world, with masterworks by Titian, Rembrandt, Vermeer, and Velásquez, and an outstanding collection of Brueghels.

Given a little more time, the Schatzkammer, or Imperial Treasury, is well worth a visit, for its opulent bounty of crown jewels, regal attire, and other trappings of court life. The sparkling new Silberkammer, a museum of court silver and tableware, is fascinating for its "behind-the-scenes" views of state banquets and other elegant representational affairs. The best-known museums tend to crowd up in late-morning and mid-afternoon hours; you can beat the mobs by going earlier or around the noon hour, at least to the larger museums that are open without a noontime break.

The Sound—and Sights—of Music
What closer association to Vienna is there than music? Boasting one of the world's greatest concert venues (Musikverein), two of the world's greatest symphony orchestras (Vienna Philharmonic and Vienna Symphony), and one of the top opera houses (Staatsoper), it's no wonder that music and the related politics are subjects of daily conversation. During July and August—just in time for tourists—the city hosts the Vienna Summer of Music, with numerous special events and concerts.

For the music-loving tourist who is excited by the prospect of treading in the footprints of the mighty, seeing where masterpieces were committed to paper or standing where a long-loved work was either praised or damned at its first performance, Vienna is tops: the city is saturated with musical history. There is the apartment where Mozart wrote his last three symphonies, the house where Schubert was born, and, just a tram ride away, the path that inspired Beethoven's *Pastoral* Symphony. Just below, you'll find a handy list of these musical landmarks.

Of course, there is also music to delight as well as inspire. The statue of Johann Strauss II in the Stadtpark tells all. To see him, violin tucked under his chin, is to imagine those infectious waltzes, "Wine, Women, and Song," "Voices of Spring," and best of all, the "Emperor." But quite possibly you will not need to imagine them. Chances are, somewhere in the environs, an orchestra will be playing them. Head for the Theater an der Wien to hear great operetta (*Die Fledermaus* and *The Merry Widow* both premiered here) or to the Volksoper. While the traditional classics are the main fare for the conservative, traditional Viennese, acceptance of modern music is growing, as are the audiences for pop and jazz.

Musicians' residences abound, and many are open as museums. The most famous are Mozart's Figarohaus and Beethoven's Pasqualatihaus, which are discussed in the Exploring sections below. Vienna has many other music landmarks scattered over the city—here's a sample: Schubert—a native of the city, unlike most of Vienna's other famous composers—was born at **Nussdorferstrasse 54** (☎ 01/317–3601 Ⓤ U2/Schottenring; Streetcar 37 or 38 to Canisiusgasse), in the 9th District, and died in the **4th District** (☎ 01/581–6730 Ⓤ U4/Kettenbrückengasse) at Kettenbrückengasse 6. **Joseph Haydn's house** (☎ 01/596–1307 Ⓤ U4/Pilgramgasse or U3/Zieglergasse), which includes a Brahms memorial room, is at Haydngasse 19 in the 6th District. **Beethoven's Heiligenstadt residence** (☎ 01/370–5408 Ⓤ U4/Heiligenstadt; Bus 38A to Wählamt), where at age 32 he wrote the "Heiligenstadt Testament," an anguished cry of pain and protest against his ever-increasing deafness, is at Probusgasse 6 in the 19th District. All the above houses contain commemorative museums. Admission is €1.80; a block of 10 €1.80 tickets for city museums costs €11.60. All are open Tuesday–Sunday 9–12:15 and 1–4:30. The home of the most popular composer of all, waltz king Johann Strauss the Younger, can be visited at **Praterstrasse 54** (☎ 01/214–0121 Ⓤ U4/Nestroyplatz), in the 2nd District; he lived here when he composed "The Blue Danube Waltz" in 1867.

Stepping Out in Three-Quarter Time Ever since the 19th-century Congress of Vienna—when pundits laughed "*Elle danse, mais elle ne marche pas*" (the city "dances, but it never gets anything done")—Viennese extravagance and gaiety have been world famous. Fasching, the season of Prince Carnival, was given over to court balls, opera balls, masked balls, chambermaids' and bakers' balls, and a hundred other gatherings, many held within the glittering interiors of Baroque theaters and palaces. Presiding over the dazzling evening gowns and gilt-encrusted uniforms, towering headdresses, flirtatious fans, *chambres séparées*, "Wine, Women, and Song," *Die Fledermaus*, "Blue Danube," hand kissing, and gay abandon was the baton of the waltz emperor, Johann Strauss. White-gloved women and men in white tie would glide over marble floors to his heavenly melodies. They still do. Now, as in the days of Franz Josef, Vienna's old three-quarter-time rhythm strikes up anew each year during Carnival, from New Year's Eve until Mardi Gras.

During January and February, as many as 40 balls may be held in a single evening. Many events are organized by a professional group, including the Kaffeesiederball (Coffee Brewers' Ball), the Zuckerbaeckerball (Confectioners' Ball), or the Opernball (Opera's Ball). The latter is the most famous—some say too famous. This event transforms the Vienna Opera House into the world's most beautiful ballroom (and transfixes all of Austria when shown live on national television). The invitation reads *"Frack mit Dekorationen,"* which means that ball-gowns and tails are usually required for most events (you can always get your tux from a rental agency) and women mustn't wear white (reserved for debutantes). But there's something for everyone these days, including the "Ball of Bad Taste" or "Wallflower Ball." Other noted venues are the imperial Hofburg palace and the famous Musikverein concert hall. Prices usually run from about €75 to €450 and up per person. For a calendar of the main balls see www.top.wien.at/ballkalender, or ask your discerning hotel concierge for tips and pointers. If you go, remember that you must dance the *Linkswalzer*—the counterclockwise, left-turning waltz that is the only correct way to dance in Vienna. After your gala evening, finish off the morning with a *Kater Frühstuck*— a hangover breakfast—of goulash soup.

Nations center. The 22nd also has several grassy spots for bathing and sailboat watching along the Alte Donau (old Danube).

It may be helpful to know the neighborhood names of other residential districts. These are: the 5th/Margareten; 10th/Favoriten; 12th/Meidling; 14th/Penzing; 15th/Fünfhaus; 16th/Ottakring; 17th/Hernals; 18th/Währing; 20th/Brigittenau; 21st/Floridsdorf; and 23rd/Liesing. For neighborhood site listings below, information will be given for both the district and neighborhood name, *except* the 1st District, which will not include a neighborhood name.

For hard-core sightseers who wish to supplement the key attractions that follow, the tourist office has a booklet, "Vienna from A–Z" (€3.60), that gives short descriptions of some 250 sights around the city, all numbered and keyed to a fold-out map at the back, as well as to numbered wall plaques on the buildings themselves. Note that the nearest U-Bahn (subway) stop to most city attractions described below is included at the end of the service information (also listed in this chapter's Subway system map). The more important churches have coin-operated (€1–€2) tape machines that give an excellent commentary in English on the structure's history and architecture.

Vienna is a city to explore and discover on foot. The description of the city on the following pages is divided into eight areas: seven that explore the architectural riches of central Vienna and an eighth that describes Schönbrunn Palace and its gardens. Above all, *look up* as you tour Vienna: some of the most fascinating architectural and ornamental bits are on upper stories or atop the city's buildings.

Numbers in the text correspond to numbers in the margin and on the Exploring Vienna, Hofburg, and Schönbrunn Palace maps.

THE INNER CITY: HISTORIC HEART OF VIENNA

A good way to break the ice on your introduction to Vienna is to get a general picture of its layout as presented to the cruising bird or airplane pilot. There are several beautiful vantage points from which you can look down and over the city—including the terrace of the Upper Belvedere Palace or atop the Prater's famous Riesenrad Ferris wheel—but the city's preeminent lookout point, offering fine views in all directions, is from Vienna's mother cathedral, the Stephansdom, reached by toiling up the 345 steps of "der Alte Steffl" (Old Stephen, its south tower) to the observation platform. The young and agile will make it up in 8 to 10 minutes; the slower-paced will make it in closer to 20. An elevator, and no exertion, will present you with much the same view from the terrace. From atop, you can see that St. Stephan's is the veritable hub of the city's wheel.

Most of Vienna lies roughly within an arc of a circle, with the straight line of the Danube Canal as its chord. Its heart, the Innere Stadt (Inner City) or 1st District—in medieval times the entire city of Vienna—is bounded by the Ringstrasse (Ring), which forms almost a circle, with a narrow arc cut off by the Danube Canal, diverted from the main river just above Vienna and flowing through the city to rejoin the parent stream just below it. The city spreads out from the Stephansdom, accented by the series of magnificent buildings erected—beginning in the 1870s, when Vienna reached the zenith of its imperial prosperity—around the Ringstrasse: the State Opera, the Art History Museum and the Museum of Natural History, the "New Wing" of the Hofburg, the House of Parliament, the Rathaus, the University, and the Votivkirche. For more than eight centuries, the enormous bulk of the cathedral has remained the nucleus around which the city has grown. The bird's-eye view can be left until the last day of your visit, when the city's landmarks will be more familiar. First day or last, the vistas are memorable, especially if you catch them as the cathedral's famous *Pummerin* (Boomer) bell is tolling.

A Good Walk

Stephansplatz, in the heart of the city, is the logical starting point from which to track down Vienna's past and present, as well as any acquaintance (natives believe that if you wait long enough at this intersection of eight streets you'll run into anyone you're searching for). Although it's now in what is mainly a pedestrian zone, **Stephansdom** ❶, the mighty cathedral, marks the point from which distances to and from Vienna are measured. Visit the cathedral (it's quite impossible to view all its treasures, so just soak up its reflective Gothic spirit) and consider climbing its 345-step tower, der Alte Steffl, or descending into its Habsburg crypt. Vienna of the Middle Ages is encapsulated in the streets in back of St. Stephan's Cathedral. You could easily spend half a day or more just prowling the narrow streets and passageways—Wollzeile, Bäckerstrasse, Blutgasse—typical remnants of an early era.

Wander up the Wollzeile, cutting through the narrow Essiggasse and right into the Bäckerstrasse, to the **Universitätskirche** ❷ or Jesuitenkirche, a lovely Jesuit church. Note the contrasting Academy of Science diagonally opposite (Beethoven premiered his *Battle* Symphony—today more commonly known as "Wellington's Victory"—in its Ceremonial Hall). Follow the Sonnenfelsgasse, ducking through one of the tiny alleys on the right to reach the Bäckerstrasse; turn right at Gutenbergplatz into the Köllnerhofgasse, right again into tiny Grashofgasse, and go through the gate into the surprising **Heiligenkreuzerhof** ❸, a peaceful oasis (unless a handicrafts market is taking place). Through the square, enter the **Schönlaterngasse** (Beautiful Lantern Street) to admire the house fronts—film companies at times block this street to take shots of the picturesque atmosphere—on your way to the **Dominikanerkirche** ❹, the Dominican church with its marvelous Baroque interior. Head east two blocks to that repository of Jugendstil treasures, the **Museum für Angewandte Kunst** ❺, then head north along the Stubenring to enjoy the architectural contrast of the **Postsparkasse** ❻ and former War Ministry, facing each other. Retrace your steps, following Postgasse into the Fleischmarkt to savor the time-stained beauty of the famous inn, **Griechenbeisl** ❼. Nearby Hoher Markt, reached by taking Rotenturmstrasse west to Lichtensteg or Bauernmarkt, was part of the early Roman encampment, witness the Roman ruins under **Hoher Markt** ❽. The extension of Fleischmarkt ends in a set of stairs leading up past the eccentric Kornhäusal Tower. Up the stairs to the right on Ruprechtsplatz is the **Ruprechtskirche** ❾, St. Rupert's Church, allegedly the city's oldest. Take Sterngasse down the steps, turn left into Marc-Aurel-Strasse and right into Salvatorgasse to discover the lacework **Maria am Gestade** ❿, which once sat above a small river, now underground.

TIMING   If you're pressed for time and happy with facades rather than what's behind them, this route could take half a day, but if you love to look inside and stop to ponder and explore the myriad narrow alleys, figure at least a day for this walk. During services, wandering around the churches will be limited, but otherwise, you can tackle this walk any time, at your convenience.

Sights to See

❹ **Dominikanerkirche** (Dominican Church). The Postgasse, to the east of Schönlaterngasse, introduces an unexpected visitor from Rome: the Dominikanerkirche. Built in the 1630s, some 50 years before the Viennese Baroque building boom, its facade is modeled after any number of Roman churches of the 16th century. The interior illustrates why the Baroque style came to be considered the height of bad taste during the 19th century and still has many detractors today. "Sculpt 'til you drop" seems to have been the motto here, and the viewer's eye is given no respite. This sort of Roman architectural orgy never really gained a foothold in Vienna, and when the great Viennese architects did pull out all the decorative stops—Hildebrandt's interior at the Belvedere Palace, for instance—they did it in a very different style and with far greater success. ✉ *Postgasse 4, 1st District* ☎ *01/512–7460–0* Ⓤ *U3/Stubentor/Dr.-Karl-Lueger-Platz.*

7 Griechenbeisl. (The "Greeks' Tavern"). If you want to find a Vienna nook-
FodorsChoice erie where time seems to be holding its breath, head to the intersection
★ of the Fleischmarkt (Meat Market) street and the picturesque, hilly, cobblestoned, and tiny Griechengasse. Part of the city's oldest core, this street
has a medieval feel that is quite genuine, thanks to Vienna's only surviving 14th-century watchtower, houses bearing statues of the Virgin
Mary, and the enchanting scene that presents you at the intersecting streets:
an ivy-covered tavern, the Griechenbeisl, which has been in business for
some 500 years, "*zeit* 1447." Half a millennium ago, this quarter was
settled by Greek and Levante traders (there are still many Near Eastern
rug dealers here) and many of them made this tavern their "local." The
wooden carving on the facade of the current restaurant commemorates
Max Augustin—best known today from the song "Ach du lieber Augustin"—an itinerant musician who sang here during the plague of
1679. A favored Viennese figure, he managed to fall into a pit filled with
plague victims but survived intact, presumably because he was so pick-
led in alcohol. In fact, this tavern introduced one of the great Pilsner
brews of the 19th century and everyone—from Schubert to Mark Twain,
Wagner to Johann Strauss—came here to partake. Be sure to dine here
to savor its low vaulted rooms, adorned with engravings, mounted
antlers, and bric-a-brac; the Mark Twain Zimmer has the ceiling covered with autographs of the rich and famous dating back two centuries.
Adjacent to the tavern is a Greek Orthodox Church partly designed by
the most fashionable Neoclassical designer in Vienna, Theophil Hansen.
The immediate neighborhood, dotted with cobbled lanes, is one of Vienna's most time-stained areas and a delight to explore. ⊠ *Fleischmarkt
11, 1st District* ⊕ *www.griechenbeisl.at/* Ⓤ *U1 or U4/Schwedenplatz.*

3 Heiligenkreuzerhof. Tiny side streets and alleys run off Sonnenfelsgasse,
parallel to Bäckerstrasse. Amid the narrow streets is Heiligenkreuzerhof (Holy Cross Court), one of the city's most peaceful backwaters. This
complex of buildings dates from the 17th century but got an 18th-cen-
tury face-lift. Appropriately, the restraint of the architecture—with only
here and there a small outburst of Baroque spirit—gives the courtyard
the distinct feeling of a retreat. The square is a favorite site for seasonal
markets at Easter and Christmas, and for occasional outdoor art shows.
⊠ *1st District* Ⓤ *U1 or U3/Stephansplatz.*

8 Hoher Markt. This square was badly damaged during World War II, but
the famous Anker Clock at the east end survived the artillery fire. The
huge mechanical timepiece took six years (1911–17) to build and still
attracts crowds at noon when the full panoply of mechanical figures representing Austrian historical personages parades by. The figures are
identified on a plaque to the bottom left of the clock. The graceless buildings erected around the square since 1945 are not aging well and do little to show off the square's lovely Baroque centerpiece, the St. Joseph
Fountain (portraying the marriage of Joseph and Mary), designed in 1729
by Joseph Emanuel Fischer von Erlach, son of the great Johann Bernhard Fischer von Erlach. The Hoher Markt does harbor one wholly unexpected attraction, however: underground Roman ruins. ⊠ *1st District*
Ⓤ *U1 or U4/Schwedenplatz.*

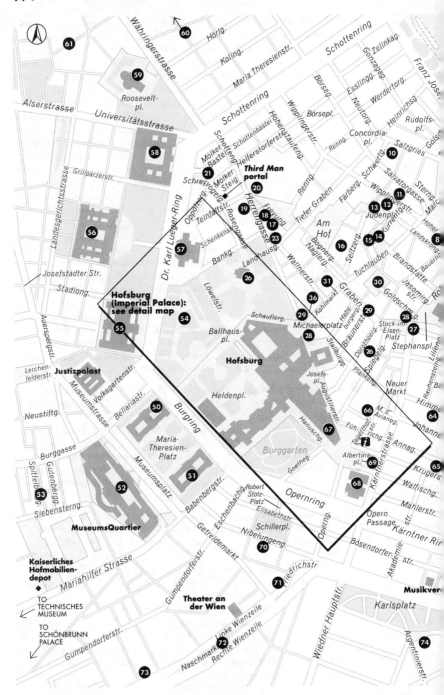

Exploring Vienna: The Historic Heart

Akademie der bildenen Künste 70
Albertina Museum 67
Altes Rathaus 11
Belvedere Palace 76
Blutgasse District 62
Bohemian Court Chancery 12
Burgtheater 57
Café Central 23
Café Sacher 69
Demel 32
Dominikanerkirche 4
Figarohaus (Mozarthaus Vienna) 63
Finanzministerium 64
Freud Haus 60
The Graben 29
Griechenbeisl 7
Haus der Musik 65
Heiligenkreuzerhof 3
Hoher Markt 8
Jewish Museum 26
Judenplatz Museum 13
Kaisergruft 66
Karlskirche 74
Kirche Am Hof 16
Kohlmarkt 31
Kunsthistorisches Museum 51
Liechtenstein Museum . . 61
Looshaus 25
Maria am Gestade 10
Michaelerplatz 24
Minoritenkirche 22
Museum für Angewandte Kunst 5
MuseumsQuartier 52
Naschmarkt 72
Naturhistorisches Museum 50
Neues Haas-Haus 28
Otto Wagner Houses 73
Palais Daum-Kinsky. 19
Palais Ferstel 17
Palais Harrach 18
Parlament 55
Pasqualatihaus 21
Pestsäule 29
Peterskirche 30
Postsparkasse 6
Puppen und Spielzeug Museum 15
Rathaus 56
Ruprechtskirche 9
Schottenkirche 20
Secession Building 71
Spittelberg Quarter 53
Staatsoper 68
Stephansdom 1
Stock-im-Eisen 27
Uhrenmuseum 14
Universität 58
Universitätskirche 2
Volksgarten 54
Votivkirche 59
Wien Museum Karlsplatz 75

KEY
🛈 Tourist Information

off the beaten path

HUNDERTWASSERHAUS – To see one of Vienna's most amazing buildings, travel eastward from Schwedenplatz or Julius-Raab-Platz along Radetzkystrasse to the junction of Kegelgasse and Löwengasse. Here you'll find the Hundertwasserhaus, a 50-apartment public-housing complex designed by the late Austrian avant-garde artist Friedensreich Hundertwasser. The structure looks as though it was decorated by a crew of mischievous circus clowns wielding giant crayons. The building caused a sensation when it was erected in 1985 and still draws crowds of sightseers. ⊠ *Löwengasse and Kegelgasse, 3rd District/Landstrasse* Ⓤ *U1 or U4/Schwedenplatz, then Tram N to Hetzgasse.*

KRIMINAL MUSEUM (CRIMINAL MUSEUM) – This might be the strangest museum in the city, and it is certainly the most macabre. The vast collection is entirely devoted to murder in Vienna of the most gruesome kind, with the most grisly displays situated, appropriately, in the cellar. Murderers and their victims are depicted in photos and newspaper clippings, and many of the actual instruments used in the killings are displayed, with axes seeming to be the most popular. The Criminal Museum is across the Danube Canal from Schwedenplatz, about a 15-minute walk from the Ruprechtskirche, the Hoher Markt, or the Heiligenkreuzerhof. ⊠ *Grosse Sperlgasse 24, 2nd District/ Leopoldstadt* ☎ *01/214–4678* ⊡ *€4.50* ⊙ *Open Thurs.–Sun. 10–5* Ⓤ *Tram: From Schwedenplatz take Tram N along Taborstrasse to Obere Augartenstrasse.*

KUNSTHAUS WIEN – Near the Hundertwasserhaus you'll find another Hundertwasser project, an art museum, which mounts outstanding international exhibits in addition to showings of the colorful Hundertwasser works. Like the apartment complex nearby, the building itself is pure Hundertwasser, with irregular floors, windows with trees growing out of them, and sudden architectural surprises, a wholly appropriate setting for modern art. ⊠ *Untere Weissgerberstrasse 13, 3rd District/Landstrasse* ☎ *01/712–0491–0* ⊕ *www.kunsthauswien.com* ⊡ *€8* ⊙ *Daily 10–7* Ⓤ *U1 or U4/ Schwedenplatz, then Tram N or O to Radetzkyplatz.*

❿ Maria am Gestade (St. Mary on the Banks). The middle-Gothic, seven-sided tower of Maria am Gestade, crowned by a delicate cupola, is a sheer joy to the eye and dispels the idea that Gothic must necessarily be austere. Built around 1400 (but much restored in the 17th and 19th centuries), the church incorporated part of the Roman city walls into its foundation; the north wall, as a result, takes a slight but noticeable dog-leg to the right halfway down the nave. Like St. Stephan's, Maria am Gestade is rough-hewn Gothic, with a simple but forceful facade. The church is especially beloved, however, because of its unusual details— the pinnacled and saint-bedecked gable that tops the front facade, the stone canopy that hovers protectively over the front door, and (most appealing of all) the intricate openwork lantern atop the south-side bell tower. Appropriately enough in a city famous for its pastry, the lantern lends its tower an engaging suggestion of a sugar caster, while some see an allusion to hands intertwined in prayer. ☒ *Passauer Platz/Salvatorgasse, 1st District* Ⓤ *U1 or U3/Stephansplatz.*

❺ **Museum für Angewandte Kunst (MAK)** (Museum of Applied Arts). This fascinating museum contains a large collection of Austrian furniture, porcelain, art objects, and priceless Oriental carpets; the Jugendstil display devoted to Josef Hoffman and his Secessionist followers at the Wiener Werkstätte is particularly fine. The museum also showcases a number of changing exhibitions of contemporary works and houses an excellent restaurant, MAK Café (closed Monday), and the museum shop sells contemporary furniture and other objects (including great bar accessories) designed by young local artists. ☒ *Stubenring 5, 1st District* ☎ *01/711–36-0* ⊕ *www.mak.at* ☜ *€7.90* ⊗ *Tues. 10 AM–midnight; Wed.–Sun. 10–6* Ⓤ *U3/Stubentor.*

❻ **Postsparkasse** (Post Office Savings Bank). The Post Office Savings Bank is one of modern architecture's greatest curiosities. It was designed in 1904 by Otto Wagner, whom many consider the father of 20th-century architecture. In his famous manifesto *Modern Architecture,* Wagner condemned 19th-century revivalist architecture and pleaded for a modern style that honestly expressed modern building methods. Accordingly, the exterior walls of the Post Office Savings Bank are mostly flat and undecorated; visual interest is supplied merely by varying the pattern of the bolts used to hold the marble slabs in place on the wall surface during construction. Later architects were to embrace Wagner's beliefs wholeheartedly, although they used different, truly modern building materials: glass and concrete rather than marble. The Post Office Savings Bank was indeed a bold leap into the future, but unfortunately the future took a different path and today the whole appears a bit dated. Go inside for a look at the restored and functioning Kassa-Saal, or central cashier's hall, to see how Wagner carried his concepts over to interior design. ☒ *Georg-Coch-Platz 2, 1st District* ☎ *01/51400* ⊗ *Lobby weekdays 8–3* Ⓤ *U1 or U4/Schwedenplatz, then Tram 1 or 2/Julius-Raab-Platz.*

off the beaten path

PRATER – You have to headout northeast from the historic city center, across the Danube Canal along Praterstrasse, to find the Prater, the city's foremost amusement park. In 1766, to the dismay of the aristocracy, Emperor Joseph II decreed that the vast expanse of imperial parklands known as the Prater would henceforth be open to the public. East of the inner city between the Danube Canal and the Danube proper, the Prater is a public park to this day, notable for its long promenade (the Hauptallee, more than 4½ km, or 3 mi, in length); its sports facilities (a golf course, a stadium, a racetrack, and a swimming pool, for starters); the landmark giant Ferris wheel (Riesenrad); the traditional, modern amusement-park rides; a number of less-innocent indoor, sex-oriented attractions; a planetarium; and a small but interesting museum devoted to the Prater's long history. If you look carefully, you can discover a handful of children's rides dating from the 1920s and '30s that survived the fire that consumed most of the Volksprater in 1945. The best-known attraction is the 200-foot Ferris wheel that figured so prominently in the 1949 film *The Third Man*. One of three built in Europe at the end of the last century (the others were in England and France but have long since been dismantled), the wheel was badly damaged during World War II and restored shortly thereafter. Its progress is slow and stately (a revolution takes 10 minutes), the views from its cars magnificent, particularly toward dusk. Try to eat at the famous **Schweizerhaus** (✉ Strasse des 1. Mai 116 ☎ 01/728–0152 ◷ Closed Nov.–Feb.), which has been serving frosty mugs of beer, roast chicken, and *Stelze* (a huge hunk of crispy roast pork on the bone) for more than 100 years. Its informal setting with wood-plank tables indoors or in the garden in summer adds to the fun. Credit cards are not accepted. ✉ *2nd District/Leopoldstadt* 🎫 *Park free, Riesenrad €7.50* ◷ *Mar.–Apr., daily 10 AM–10 PM; May–Sept., daily 9 AM–midnight; Oct., daily 10–10; Nov.–Feb., daily 10–8 PM* Ⓤ *U1/Praterstern.*

❾ **Ruprechtskirche** (St. Ruprecht's Church). Ruprechtsplatz, another of Vienna's time-warp backwaters, lies to the north of the Kornhäusel Tower. The church in the middle, Ruprechtskirche, is the city's oldest. According to legend it was founded in 740; the oldest part of the present structure (the lower half of the tower) dates from the 11th century. Set on the ancient ramparts overlooking the Danube Canal, it is serene and unpretentious. It is usually closed, but sometimes opens for local art shows and summer evening classical concerts. ✉ *Ruprechtsplatz, 1st District,* Ⓤ *U1 or U4/Schwedenplatz.*

★ **Schönlaterngasse** (Street of the Beautiful Lantern). Once part of Vienna's medieval Latin Quarter, Schönlaterngasse is the main artery of a historic neighborhood that has reblossomed in recent years. Thanks in part to government Kultur schillings—or renovation loans—the quarter has been revamped. Streets are lined with beautiful Baroque town houses (often with colorfully painted facades), now distinctive showcases for art galleries, chic shops, and coffeehouses. At No. 5, you'll find a covered passage that leads to the historic **Heiligenkreuzerhof** courtyard. The most famous house of the quarter is the **Basiliskenhaus** (House of the Basilik; ✉ Schönlaterngasse 7, 1st District). According to legend, it was first built for a baker; on June 26, 1212, a foul-smelling basilisk (half-rooster, half-toad, with a glance that could kill) took up residence in the courtyard well, poisoning the water. An enterprising apprentice dealt with the problem by climbing down the well armed with a mirror; when the basilisk saw its own reflection, it turned to stone. The petrified creature can still be seen in a niche on the building's facade. Today, modern science accounts for the contamination with a more prosaic explanation: natural-gas seepage. Be sure to take a look in the house's miniature courtyard for a trip back to medieval Vienna (the house itself is private). The picturesque street is named for the ornate wrought-iron wall lantern at Schönlaterngasse 6. Just a few steps from the Basilikenhaus, note the Baroque courtyard at Schönlaterngasse 8—one of the city's prettiest. A blacksmith's workshop, **Alte Schmiede** (Old Smithy; ✉ Schönlaterngasse 9 Ⓤ U1 or U3/Stephansplatz), is now a museum.

MOZART, MOZART, MOZART!

FOR THE MUSICAL TOURIST who is excited at the prospect of treading in the footprints of Wolfgang Amadeus Mozart (1756–91), seeing where his masterpieces were committed to paper, or standing where a long-loved work was either praised or damned at its first appearance, Vienna is saturated with Mozartiana. The great composer crammed a prodigious number of compositions into his Vienna years (the last ten of his life—he moved to Vienna in March 1781), along with the arrival of his six children and his constantly changing Viennese addresses. Certainly, it's easy to find the places he lived in or visited, all carefully marked by memorial plaques. For it was in Vienna that many of his personal peaks were achieved, both personal and artistic. He wed his beloved Constanze Weber at St. Stephen's Cathedral in August, 1782, and led the premieres of several of his greatest operas, including The Abduction from the Seraglio (July 16, 1782, at the city's Burgtheater), Così Fan Tutte (January 16, 1790, at the same theater), and The Magic Flute (September 30, 1791, at the Freihaus Theater). But a knowledge of his troubled relations with his home city of Salzburg makes his Vienna soujourn a even more poignant one.

From the beginning of Wolfgang's precocious career, his father, frustrated in his own musical ambitions at the archbishopric in Salzburg, looked beyond the boundaries of the Austro-Hungarian empire to promote the boy's fame. At the age of six, his son was presented to the royal courts of Europe and caused a sensation with his skills as an instrumentalist and impromptu composer. As he grew up, however, his virtuosity lost its power to amaze and he was forced to make his way as an "ordinary" musician, which then meant finding a position at court. In this he was not much more successful than his father had been. In Salzburg he was never able to rise beyond the level of organist (allowing him, as he noted with sarcastic pride, to sit above the cooks at table), and, in disgust, he relocated to Vienna, where despite the popularity of his operas he was able to obtain only an unpaid appointment as assistant Kapellmeister at St. Stephan's mere months before his death. By then, patronage subscriptions had been taken up in Hungary and the Netherlands that would have paid him handsomely. But it was too late. Whatever the truth about the theories still swirling around his untimely death, the fact remains that not only was he not given the state funeral he deserved, but he was buried in an unmarked grave (although most Viennese at that time were) after a hasty, sparsely attended funeral.

Only a hard-boiled cynic can fail to be moved. Only the flint-hearted can stand in Vienna's Währingerstrasse and look at the windows behind which Mozart wrote those last three symphonies in the incredible short time of six weeks in the summer of 1788 and not be touched. For this was the time when the Mozart fortunes had slumped to their lowest. "If you, my best of friends, forsake me, I am unhappily and innocently lost with my poor sick wife and my child," he wrote. And if one is inclined to accuse Mozart's fellow countrymen of neglect, they would seem to have made up for it with a vengeance. The visitor to Vienna and Salzburg can hardly ignore the barrage of Mozart candies, wine, beer, coffee mugs, T-shirts, baseball caps— not to mention the gilt statues that make do for a nonexistent monumental tomb or the 24/7 festivities scheduled for 2006, the 250th anniversary of his birth. Mozart, always one to appreciate a joke, would surely see the irony in the belated veneration.

— Gary Dodson

★ ❶ **Stephansdom** (St. Stephan's Cathedral). Vienna's soaring centerpiece, this beloved cathedral enshrines the heart of the city—although it is curious to note that when first built in 1144–47 it actually stood outside the city walls. Vienna can thank a period of hard times for the Mother Church for the cathedral's distinctive silhouette. Originally the structure was to have had matching 445-foot-high spires, a standard design of the era, but funds ran out, and the north tower to this day remains a happy reminder of what gloriously is not. The lack of symmetry creates an imbalance that makes the cathedral instantly identifiable from its profile alone. The cathedral, like the Staatsoper and some other major buildings, was very heavily damaged in World War II. Since then, it has risen from the fires of destruction like a phoenix, and like the phoenix, it is a symbol of regeneration.

It is difficult now, sitting quietly in the shadowed peace, to tell what was original and what parts of the walls and vaults were reconstructed. No matter: its history-rich atmosphere is dear to all Viennese. That noted, St. Stephan's has a fierce presence that is blatantly un-Viennese. It is a stylistic jumble ranging from 13th-century Romanesque to 15th-century Gothic. Like the exterior, St. Stephan's interior lacks the soaring unity of Europe's greatest Gothic cathedrals, with much of its decoration dating from the later Baroque era.

The wealth of decorative sculpture in St. Stephan's can be intimidating to the nonspecialist, so if you wish to explore the cathedral in detail, you may want to buy the admirably complete English-language description sold in the small room marked Dom Shop. One particularly masterly work, however, should be seen by everyone: the stone pulpit attached to the second freestanding pier on the left of the central nave, carved by Anton Pilgram around 1510. The delicacy of its decoration would in itself set the pulpit apart, but even more intriguing are its five sculpted figures. Carved around the outside of the pulpit proper are the four Latin Fathers of the Church (from left to right: St. Augustine, St. Gregory, St. Jerome, and St. Ambrose), and each is given an individual personality so sharply etched as to suggest satire, perhaps of living models. There is no satire suggested by the fifth figure, however; below the pulpit's stairs Pilgram sculpted a fine self-portrait, showing himself peering out a half-open window. Note the toads, lizards, and other creatures climbing the spiral rail alongside the steps up to the pulpit. As you walk among the statues and aisles, remember that many notable events occurred here, including Mozart's marriage in 1782 and his funeral in December 1791. The funeral service was conducted to the left of the main entrance in a small chapel beneath the Heidenturm, to the left of the cathedral's main doorway. The funeral bier on which his casket was placed is located in the Crucifix Chapel, which marks the entrance to the crypt and can be reached from outside the church. His body rested on a spot not far from the famous open air pulpit—near the apse, at the other end of the cathedral—named after the monk Capistranus who, in 1450, preached from it to rouse the people to fight the invading Turks. Continuing around the cathedral exterior at the apse you'll find a centuries-old sculpted torso of the Man of Sorrows, known irreverently as

Our Lord of the Toothache, because of its agonized expression. Inside, nearly every corner has something to savor: the Marienchor (Virgin's Choir) has the Tomb of Rudolph IV, the Wiener Neustadt altar is a wood-carved masterpiece; the gilded pulpit carved by Anton Pilgram between 1510 and 1550 with the heads of the Fathers of the Church; and the Catacombs, where the internal organs of the Habsburgs rest.

The bird's-eye views from the cathedral's beloved **Alter Steffl** tower will be a highlight for some. The tower is 450 feet high and was built between 1359 and 1433. The climb or elevator ride up is rewarded with vistas that extend to the rising slopes of the Wienerwald. ⊠ *Stephansplatz, 1st District* ☎ *01/515–5237–67* 🕾 *Guided tour, €4; catacombs, €4; elevator to Pummerin bell, €4* ◷ *Daily 6 AM–10 PM. Guided tours in English daily from Apr.–Oct. at 3:45; catacombs tour (minimum 5 people) Mon.–Sat. every half hr from 10–11:30 and 1:30–4:30, Sun. every half hr from 1:30–4:30; North Tower elevator to Pummerin bell, Apr.–Oct., daily 8:30–5:30; July–Aug., daily 8:30–6; Nov.–Mar., daily 8:30–5* Ⓤ *U1 or U3/Stephansplatz.*

> **need a break?**
>
> If you're in the mood for ice cream, head for **Zanoni & Zanoni** (⊠ Am Lugeck 7, 1st District ☎ 01/512–7979) near St. Stephan's, between Rotenturmstrasse and Bäckerstrasse, and open 365 days a year. Here you'll have trouble choosing from among 25 or more flavors of smooth, Italian-style gelato, including mango, caramel, and chocolate chip. There are also tables for those who want to rest their feet and enjoy a sundae.

❷ **Universitätskirche** (Jesuit Church). The east end of Bäckerstrasse is punctuated by Dr.-Ignaz-Seipel-Platz, named for the theology professor who was chancellor of Austria during the 1920s. On the north side is the Universitätskirche, or Jesuitenkirche, built around 1630. Its flamboyant Baroque interior contains a fine trompe-l'oeil ceiling fresco by that master of visual trickery Andrea Pozzo, who was imported from Rome in 1702 for the job. You may hear a Mozart or Haydn mass sung here in Latin on many Sundays. ⊠ *Dr.-Ignaz-Seipl-Platz, 1st District* ☎ *01/512–5232–0* Ⓤ *U3 Stubentor/Dr.-Karl-Lueger-Platz.*

BITTERSWEET VIENNA: BAROQUE GEMS & COZY CAFÉS

As the city developed and expanded, the core quickly outgrew its early confines. New urban centers sprang up, to be ornamented by government buildings and elegant town residences. Since Vienna was the beating heart of a vast empire, nothing was spared to make the edifices as exuberant as possible, with utility often a secondary consideration. The best architects of the day were commissioned to create impressions as well as buildings, and they did their job well. That so much has survived is a testimony to the solidity both of the designs and of the structures on which the ornamentation has been overlaid.

Those not fortunate enough to afford town palaces were relegated to housing that was often less than elegant and confining. Rather than suffer the discomfitures of a disruptive household environment, the city's literati and its philosophers and artists took refuge in cafés, which in effect became their combined salons and offices. To this day, cafés remain an important element of Viennese life. Many residents still have their *Stammtisch,* or regular table, at which they appear daily. Talk still prevails—but, increasingly, so do handy cell phones and even laptops.

A Good Walk

Start in the Wipplingerstrasse at the upper (west) end of Hoher Markt to find touches of both the imperial and the municipal Vienna. On the east side is the **Altes Rathaus** ⑪, which served as the city hall until 1885; on the west is the **Bohemian Court Chancery** ⑫, once diplomatic headquarters for Bohemia's representation to the Habsburg court. Turn south into the short Fütterergasse to reach Judenplatz, in the Middle Ages the center of Judaism in Vienna, and today site of the new **Judenplatz Museum** ⑬, landmarked by a memorial created by Rachel Whitehead, one of contemporary art's most important sculptors. A clock-watcher's delight is down at the end of Kurrentgasse in the form of the **Uhrenmuseum** (Clock Museum) ⑭; around the corner through the Parisgasse to Schulhof, a children's delight is the **Puppen und Spielzeug Museum** (Doll and Toy Museum) ⑮. Follow Schulhof into the huge **Am Hof** square, boasting the **Kirche am Hof** ⑯ and what must be the world's most elegant fire station. The square hosts an antiques and collectibles market on Thursday and Friday most of the year, plus other ad hoc events. Take the minuscule Irisgasse from Am Hof into the Naglergasse, noting the mosaic Jugendstil facade on the pharmacy in the Bognergasse, to your left. Around a bend in the narrow Naglergasse is the **Freyung,** an irregular square bounded on the south side by two wonderfully stylish palaces, including **Palais Ferstel** ⑰, now a shopping arcade, and the elegantly restored **Palais Harrach** ⑱ next door, now an outpost of the Kunsthistoriches Museum. The famous **Palais Daum-Kinsky** ⑲ at the beginning of Herrengasse is still partly a private residence. The north side of the Freyung is watched over by the **Schottenkirche** ⑳, a Scottish church that was, in fact, established by Irish monks; the complex also houses a small but worthwhile museum of the order's treasures. Follow Teinfaltstrasse from opposite the Schottenkirche, turning right into Schreyvogelgasse; at No. 8 is the famed **"Third Man"** Portal. Follow Teinfaltstrasse from opposite the Schottenkirche, turning right into Schreyvogelgasse. Climb the ramp on your right past the so-called Dreimäderlhaus at Schreyvogelgasse 10—note the ornate facade of this pre-Biedermeier patrician house—to reach Molker Bastei, where Beethoven lived in the **Pasqualatihaus** ㉑, now housing a museum commemorating the composer. Follow the ring south to Löwelstrasse, turning left into Bankgasse; then turn right into Abraham-a-Sancta-Clara-Gasse (the tiny street that runs off the Bankgasse) to Minoritenplatz and the **Minoritenkirche** ㉒, the Minorite Church, with its strangely hatless tower. Inside is a kitschy mosaic of the *Last Supper.* Landhausgasse will bring you to Herrengasse, and diagonally across the street, in the back corner of the Palais Ferstel, is the **Café Central** ㉓, one of Vienna's hangouts for the famous. As you go south up Herrengasse, on the left is the odd Hochhaus, a 20th-century building once renowned as Vienna's skyscraper. Opposite are elegant Baroque former town palaces, now used as museum and administration buildings by the province of Lower Austria.

TIMING   The actual distances in this walk are relatively short, and you could cover the route in 1½ hours or so. But if you take time to linger in the museums and sample a coffee with whipped cream in the Café Central, you'll develop a much better understanding of the contrasts between old and newer in the city. You could easily spend a day following this walk, if you were to take in all of the museums; note that these, like many of Vienna's museums, are closed on Mondays.

Sights to See

❶ Altes Rathaus (Old City Hall). Opposite the Bohemian Chancery stands the Altes Rathaus, dating from the 14th century but displaying 18th-century Baroque motifs on its facade. The interior passageways and courtyards, which are open during the day, house a Gothic chapel (open at odd hours); a much-loved Baroque wall-fountain (Georg Raphael Donner's **Andromeda Fountain** of 1741); and display cases exhibiting maps and photos illustrating the city's history. ⊠ *Wipplingerstrasse/Salvatorgasse 7, 1st District* Ⓤ *U1 or U4/Schwedenplatz.*

Am Hof. Am Hof is one of the city's oldest squares. In the Middle Ages the ruling Babenberg family built their castle on the site of No. 2; hence the name of the square, which means simply "at court." The grand residence hosted such luminaries as Barbarossa and Walter von der Vogelweide, the famous Minnesinger who stars in Wagner's *Tannhäuser.* The Baroque **Column of Our Lady** in the center dates from 1667, marking the Catholic victory over the Swedish Protestants in the Thirty Years' War (1618–48). The onetime **Civic Armory** at the northwest corner has been used as a fire station since 1685 (the high-spirited facade, with its Habsburg eagle, was "Baroqued" in 1731) and today houses the headquarters of Vienna's fire department. The complex includes a firefighting museum (open only on Sunday mornings). Presiding over the east side of the square is the noted Kirche Am Hof. In Bognergasse to the right of the Kirche Am Hof, around the corner from the imposing Bank Austria headquarters building, at No. 9, is the **Engel Apotheke** (pharmacy) with a Jugendstil mosaic depicting winged women collecting the elixir of life in outstretched chalices. At the turn of the 20th century the inner city was dotted with storefronts decorated in a similar manner; today this is the sole survivor. Around the bend from the Naglergasse is the picturesque Freyung square. At No. 13 is the fairly stolid 17th century **Palais Collalto**, famous as the setting for Mozart's first public engagement at the ripe age of six. This was but the first showing of the child prodigy in Vienna, for his father had him perform for three Viennese princes, four dukes, and five counts in the space of a few weeks. Having newly arrived from Salzburg, the child set Vienna on its ear and he was showered with money and gifts, including some opulent children's clothes from the Empress Maria Theresa. Next door is the Jesuit church where Leopold Mozart directed his son's *Father Dominicus Mass,* K. 66, in August 1773. Some years later, Mozart's first child, Raimund Leopold, was baptized here. Sadly, the child died two months later. ⊠ *1st District* Ⓤ *U3/Herrengasse.*

⑫ Bohemian Court Chancery. One of the architectural jewels of the Inner City can be found at Wipplingerstrasse 7, the former Bohemian Court Chancery, built between 1708 and 1714 by Johann Bernhard Fischer von Erlach. Fischer von Erlach and his contemporary Johann Lukas von Hildebrandt were the reigning architectural geniuses of Baroque-era Vienna; they designed their churches and palaces during the building boom that followed the defeat of the Turks in 1683. Both had studied architecture in Rome, and both were deeply impressed by the work of the great Italian architect Francesco Borromini, who brought to his designs a wealth and freedom of invention that were looked upon with horror by most contemporary Romans. But for Fischer von Erlach and Hildebrandt, Borromini's ideas were a source of triumphant architectural inspiration, and when they returned to Vienna they produced between them many of the city's most beautiful buildings. Alas, narrow Wipplingerstrasse allows little more than a oblique view of this florid facade. The back side of the building, on Judenplatz, is less elaborate but gives a better idea of the design concept. The building first served as diplomatic and representational offices of Bohemia (now a part of the Czech Republic) to the Vienna-based monarchy and, today, still houses government offices. ⊠ *Wipplingerstrasse 7, 1st District* Ⓤ *U1 or U4/ Schwedenplatz.*

㉓ Café Central. Part of the **Palais Ferstel** complex, the Café Central is one of Vienna's more famous cafés, its full authenticity blemished only by complete restoration in recent years. In its prime (before World War I), the café was "home" to some of the most famous literary figures of the day, who dined, socialized, worked, and even received mail here. The denizens of the Central favored political argument; indeed, their heated discussions became so well known that in October 1917, when Austria's foreign secretary was informed of the outbreak of the Russian Revolution, he dismissed the report with a facetious reference to a well-known local Marxist, the chess-loving (and presumably harmless) "Herr Bronstein from the Café Central." The remark was to become famous all over Austria, for Herr Bronstein had disappeared and was about to resurface in Russia bearing a new name: Leon Trotsky. Today, things are a good deal more yuppified and shiny (thanks to a big renovation some years ago): The coffee now comes with a little chocolate biscuit and is overpriced and the man tickling the piano keys is more likely to play Sinatra than Strauss. But no matter how crowded the café may become, you can linger as long as you like over a single cup of coffee and a newspaper from the huge international selection provided. Across the street at Herrengasse 17 is the **Café Central Konditorei,** an excellent pastry and confectionery shop associated with the café. ⊠ *Herrengasse 14, 1st District* ☎ *01/533–3763–26* ⊕ *www.palaisevents.at* ⊟ *AE, DC, MC, V* Ⓤ *U3/Herrengasse.*

FodorsChoice
★

The Freyung. Naglergasse, at its curved end, flows into Heidenschuss, which in turn leads down a slight incline from Am Hof to one of Vienna's most prominent squares, the Freyung, meaning "freeing." The square was so named because for many centuries the monks at the adjacent Schottenhof had the privilege of offering sanctuary for three days. In the center of the square stands the allegorical **Austria Fountain** (1845), notable because its Bavarian designer, one Ludwig Schwanthaler, had the statues cast in Munich and then supposedly filled them with cigars to be smuggled into Vienna for black-market sale. Around the sides of the square are some of Vienna's greatest patrician residences, including the Ferstel, Harrach, and Kinsky palaces. ⊠ *At the intersection of Am Hof and Herrengasse, 1st District* Ⓤ *U3/Herrengasse.*

⑬ Judenplatz Museum. In what was once the old Jewish ghetto, construction workers discovered the remains of a 13th-century synagogue while digging for a new parking garage. Simon Wiesenthal (a Vienna resident) helped to turn it into a museum dedicated to the Austrian Jews who died in World War II. Marking the outside is a rectangular concrete cube resembling library shelves, signifying Jewish love of learning, designed by Rachel Whitehead. Downstairs are three exhibition rooms on medieval Jewish life and the synagogue excavations. Also in Judenplatz is a statue of the 18th-century playwright Gotthold Ephraim Lessing, erected after World War II. ⊠ *Judenplatz 8, 1st District* ☏ *01/535–0431* ⊕ *www. jmw.at* ⌸ *€3; combination ticket with Jewish Museum €7* ☉ *Sun.–Fri. 10–6, Thurs. 10–8 PM.*

⑯ Kirche Am Hof. On the east side of the Am Hof square, the Kirche Am Hof, or the Church of the Nine Choirs of Angels, is identified by its sprawling Baroque facade, designed by Carlo Carlone in 1662. The somber interior lacks appeal, but the checkerboard marble floor may remind you of Dutch churches. ⊠ *Am Hof 1, 1st District* Ⓤ *U3/Herrengasse.*

㉒ Minoritenkirche (Church of the Minorite Order). The Minoritenplatz is named after its centerpiece, the Minoritenkirche, a Gothic affair with a strange stump of a tower, built mostly in the 14th century. The front is brutally ugly, but the back is a wonderful, if predominantly 19th-century, surprise. The interior contains the city's most imposing piece of kitsch: a large mosaic reproduction of Leonardo da Vinci's *Last Supper,* commissioned by Napoléon in 1806 and later purchased by Emperor Francis I. ⊠ *Minoritenplatz 2A, 1st District* ☏ *01/533–4162* Ⓤ *U3/Herrengasse.*

⑲ Palais Daum-Kinsky. Just one of the architectural treasures that comprise the urban set piece of the Freyung, the Palais Kinsky is the square's best-known palace, and is one of the most sophisticated pieces of Baroque architecture in the whole city. It was built between 1713 and 1716 by Hildebrandt, and its only real competition comes a few yards farther on: the Greek-temple facade of the Schottenhof, which is at right angles to the Schottenkirche, up the street from the Kinsky Palace. The palace now houses Wiener Kunst Auktionen, a public auction business offering artworks and antiques. If there is an auction viewing, try to see the palace's spectacular 18th-century staircase, all marble goddesses and crowned with a trompe-l'oeil ceiling painted by Marcantonio Chiarini. ⊠ *Freyung 4, 1st District* ☏ *01/532–4200* 🖷 *01/532–42009* ☉ *Mon.–Fri. 10–6* Ⓤ *U3/Herrengasse.*

⑰ Palais Ferstel. At Freyung 2 stands the Palais Ferstel, which is not a palace at all but a commercial shop-and-office complex designed in 1856 and named for its architect, Heinrich Ferstel. The facade is Italianate in style, harking back, in its 19th-century way, to the Florentine palazzi of the early Renaissance. The interior is unashamedly eclectic: vaguely Romanesque in feel and Gothic in decoration, with here and there a bit of Renaissance or Baroque sculpted detail thrown in for good measure. Such eclecticism is sometimes dismissed as mindlessly derivative, but here the architectural details are so respectfully and inventively combined that the interior becomes a pleasure to explore. The 19th-century stock-exchange rooms upstairs are now gloriously restored and used for conferences and concerts. ⊠ *Freyung 2, 1st District* Ⓤ *U3/Herrengasse.*

⑱ Palais Harrach. Next door to the Palais Ferstel is the newly renovated Palais Harrach, part of which now houses a small but worthwhile gallery of paintings and art objects from the main Kunsthistorisches Museum (which has far more treasures than space in which to display them) as well as special exhibits. Mozart and his sister, Nannerl, performed here when children for Count Ferdinand during their first visit to Vienna in 1762. The palace looks much different from Mozart's day, however, since it was altered after 1845 and severely damaged by World War II. Many of the state rooms have lost their historical lustre but the Marble Room, set with gold boiseries, and the Red Galley, topped with a spectacular ceiling painting, still offer grand settings for receptions, readings, and exhibitions. ⊠ *Freyung 3, 1st District* ☎ *01/523–1753* ⊕ *www.khm.at* ⊡ *€7* ◷ *During special exhibits, daily 10–6* Ⓤ *U3/Herrengasse.*

㉑ Pasqualatihaus. Beethoven lived in the Pasqualatihaus while he was composing his only opera, *Fidelio,* as well as his Seventh Symphony and Fourth Piano Concerto. Today his apartment houses a small commemorative museum (in distressingly modern style). After navigating the narrow and twisting stairway, you might well ask how he maintained the jubilant spirit of the works he wrote there. Some exhibits are fascinating: note particularly the prints that show what the window view out over the Mölker bastion was like when Beethoven lived here and the piano that dates from his era—one that was beefed-up to take the banging Beethoven made fashionable. This house is around the corner from the *Third Man* Portal. ⊠ *8 Mölker Bastei, 1st District* ☎ *01/535–8905* ⊕ *www.wienmuseum.at* ⊡ *€2* ◷ *Tues.–Sun. 9–12:15 and 1–4:30* Ⓤ *U2/Schottentor.*

Ⓒ ⑮ Puppen und Spielzeug Museum (Doll and Toy Museum). As appealing as the clockworks of the Uhrenmuseum located just next door is this doll and toy museum, with its collections of dolls, dollhouses, teddy bears, and trains. ⊠ *Schulhof 4, 1st District* ☎ *01/535–6860* ⊡ *€4.70* ◷ *Tues.–Sun. 10–6* Ⓤ *U1 or U3/Stephansplatz.*

Schottenhof. Found on the Freyung square and designed by Joseph Kornhäusel in a very different style from his Fleischmarkt tower, the Schottenhof is a shaded courtyard. The facade typifies the change that came over Viennese architecture during the Biedermeier era (1815–48). The Viennese, according to the traditional view, were at the time so relieved to be rid of the upheavals of the Napoleonic Wars that they accepted without protest the iron-handed repression of Prince Metternich, chancellor of Austria, and retreated into a cozy and complacent domesticity. Restraint also ruled in architecture, with Baroque license rejected in favor of a new and historically "correct" style that was far more controlled and reserved. Kornhäusel led the way in establishing this trend in Vienna; his Schottenhof facade is all sober organization and frank repetition. But in its marriage of strong and delicate forces it still pulls off the great Viennese-waltz trick of successfully merging seemingly antithetical characteristics. ⊠ *1st District* Ⓤ *U2/Schottentor.*

need a break?

In summer, **Wienerwald** restaurant, in the delightful tree-shaded courtyard of the Schottenhof at Freyung 6, is ideal for relaxing over lunch or dinner with a glass of wine or frosty beer. The specialty here is chicken, and you can get it just about every possible way. Especially good is the spit-roasted *Knoblauch* (garlic) chicken. It's open daily.

㉟ Schottenkirche. From 1758 to 1761, the noted Italian *vedutiste* (scene-painter), Bernardo Bellotto, did paintings of the Freyung square looking north toward the Schottenkirche; the pictures hang in the Kunsthistorisches Museum, and the similarity to the view you see about 240 years later is arresting. In fact, a church has stood on the site of the Schottenkirche since 1177; the present edifice dates from the mid-1600s, when it replaced its predecessor, which had collapsed after the architects of the time had built on weakened foundations. The interior, with its ornate ceiling and a decided surplus of cherubs and angels' faces, is in stark contrast to the plain exterior. The adjacent small **Museum im Schottenstift** includes the best of the monastery's artworks, including the celebrated late-Gothic high altar, dating from about 1470. The winged altar is fascinating for its portrayal of the Holy Family in flight into Egypt—with the city of Vienna clearly identifiable in the background. ⊠ *Freyung 6, 1st District* ☎ *01/534-98-600* ⊕ *www.schottenstift.at* 🎟 *Church free, museum €4* ⊘ *Museum Mon.–Sat. 10–5* Ⓤ *U2/Schottentor.*

Third Man Portal. The doorway at Schreyvogelgasse 8 (up the incline) was made famous in 1949 by the classic film *The Third Man* (see the Close-up box, *below*); it was here that Orson Welles, as the malevolently knowing Harry Lime, stood hiding in the dark, only to have his smiling face illuminated by a sudden light from the upper-story windows of the house across the alley. The film enjoys a renaissance each summer in the Burg Kino and is fascinating for its portrayal of a postwar Vienna still in ruins. To get here from the nearby and noted Schottenkirche, follow Teinfaltstrasse one block west to Schreyvogelgasse on the right. ⊠ *1st District* Ⓤ *U2/Schottentor.*

★ ⑭ Uhrenmuseum (Clock Museum). Kurrentgasse leads south from the east end of Judenplatz; the beautifully restored 18th-century houses on its east side make this one of the most unpretentiously appealing streets in the city. And at the far end of the street is one of Vienna's most appealing museums: the Uhrenmuseum, or Clock Museum (enter to the right on

TRACKING DOWN THE THIRD MAN

NOTHING HAS DONE MORE TO CREATE THE MYTH OF POSTWAR VIENNA than Carol Reed's classic 1949 film The Third Man. The bombed-out ruins of this proud, imperial city created an indelible image of devastation and corruption in the war's aftermath.

Vienna was then divided into four sectors, each commanded by one of the victorious American, Russian, French, and British armies. But their attempts at rigid control could not prevent a thriving black market.

Reed's film version of the great Graham Greene thriller features Vienna as a leading player, from the top of its Ferris wheel in the Prater to the depth of its lowest sewers—"which run right into the Blue Danube"—thrillingly used for the famous chase scene. It is only fitting to note that this was the first British film to be shot entirely on location.

In the film, Joseph Cotten plays Holly Martins, a pulp-fiction writer who comes to Vienna in search of his friend Harry Lime (Orson Welles). He makes the mistake of delving too deeply into Lime's affairs, even falling in love with his girlfriend, Anna Schmidt (Alida Valli), with fatal consequences.

Many of the sites where the film was shot still remain and are easily visited. Harry Lime appears for the first time nearly one hour into the film in the doorway of Anna's apartment building at No. 8 Schreyvogelgasse, around the corner from the Mölker-Bastei (a remnant of the old city wall). He then runs to Am Hof, a lovely square lined with Baroque town houses and churches, which appears much closer to Anna's neighborhood than it actually is.

The famous scene between Lime and Martins on the Ferris wheel was filmed on the Riesenrad at the Prater, the huge amusement park across the Danube canal. While the two friends talk in the enclosed compartment, the wheel slowly makes a revolution, with all Vienna spread out below them.

In the memorable chase at the end of the movie, Lime is seen running through the damp, sinister sewers of Vienna, hotly pursued by the authorities. In reality, he would not have been able to use the sewer system as an escape route because the tunnels were too low and didn't connect between the different centers of the city.

But a movie creates its own reality. In fact, a more feasible, if less cinematic, possibility of escape was offered by the labyrinth of cellars that still connected many buildings in the city.

Lime's funeral is held at the Zentralfriedhof (Central Cemetery), reachable by the 71 streetcar. This is the final scene of the movie, where Anna Schmidt walks down the stark, wide avenue (dividing sections 69 and 70), refusing to acknowledge the wistful presence of Holly Martins.

After touring sewers and cemeteries, a pick-me-up might be in order. You couldn't do better than to treat yourself to a stop at the Hotel Sacher, used for a scene in the beginning of the movie when Holly Martins is using the telephone in the lobby.

The bar in the Sacher was a favorite hangout of director Carol Reed, and when filming finally wrapped, he left a signed note to the bartender, saying: "To the creator of the best Bloody Marys in the whole world."

— Bonnie Dodson

the Schulhof side of the building). The museum's three floors display a splendid parade of clocks and watches—more than 3,000 timepieces—dating from the 15th century to the present. The ruckus of bells and chimes pealing forth on any hour is impressive, but for the full cacophony try to be here at noon. Right next door is the Puppen und Spielzeug Museum. ⊠ *Schulhof 2, 1st District* ☎ *01/533–2265* 🎫 *€4, Sun. free* 🕐 *Tues.–Sun. 9–4:30* Ⓤ *U1 or U3/Stephansplatz.*

VIENNA'S SHOP WINDOW: FROM MICHAELERPLATZ TO THE GRABEN

The compact area bounded roughly by the back side of the Hofburg palace complex, the Kohlmarkt, the Graben, and Kärntnerstrasse belongs to the oldest core of the city. Remains of the Roman city are just below the present-day surface. This was and still is the commercial heart of the city, dense with shops and markets for various commodities; today, the Kohlmarkt and Graben in particular offer the choicest luxury shops, overflowing into the Graben end of Kärntnerstrasse. The area is marvelous for its visual treats, ranging from the squares and varied architecture to shop windows. The evening view down Kohlmarkt from the Graben is an inspiring classic, with the night-lit gilded dome of Michael's Gate to the palace complex as the glittering backdrop. Sights in this area range from the sacred—the Baroque church of Peterskirche—to the more profane pleasures of Demel, Vienna's beloved pastry shop, and the modernist masterwork of the Looshaus.

A Good Walk

Start your walk through this fascinating quarter at **Michaelerplatz** ㉔, one of Vienna's most evocative squares, where the feel of the imperial city remains very strong; the buildings around the perimeter present a synopsis of the city's entire architectural history: medieval church spire, Renaissance church facade, Baroque palace facade, 19th-century apartment house, and 20th-century bank. Look in the Michaelerkirche (St. Michael's Church). Opposite the church is the once-controversial **Looshaus** ㉕, considered a breakthrough in modern architecture (visitors are welcome to view the restored lobby). From Michaelerplatz, take the small passageway to the right of the church; in it on your right is a relief dating from 1480 of Christ on the Mount of Olives. Follow the Stallburggasse through to Dorotheergasse, and turn right to discover the **Dorotheum**, the government-run auction house and Viennese equivalent of Christie's or Sotheby's. On your right in the Dorotheergasse (toward the Graben) is the enlarged **Jewish Museum** ㉖, which includes a bookstore and café. On the left is the famous Café Hawelka, haunt to the contemporary art and literature crowd. Turn right in the Graben to come to **Stock-im-Eisen** ㉗; the famous nail-studded tree trunk is encased in the corner of the building with the Bank Austria offices. Opposite and impossible to overlook is the aggressive **Neues Haas-Haus** ㉘, an upmarket restaurant and shopping complex. Wander back through the **Graben** ㉙ for the full effect of this harmonious street and look up to see the ornamentation on the buildings. Pass the Pestsäule, or Plague Column, which shoots up from the middle of the Graben like a geyser of whipped cream. Just off to the north side is the **Peterskirche** ㉚, St. Peter's Church, a Baroque gem almost hidden by its surroundings. At the end of the Graben, turn left into the **Kohlmarkt** ③ for the classic view of the domed arch leading to the Hofburg, the imperial palace complex. Even if your feet aren't calling a sit-down strike, finish up at **Demel** ㉜, at Kohlmarkt 14, for some of the best *Gebäck* (pastries) in the world.

TIMING   Inveterate shoppers, window or otherwise, will want to take time to pause before or in many of the elegant shops during this walk, which then could easily take most of a day or even longer. If you're content with facades and general impressions, the exercise could be done in a bit over an hour, but it would be a shame to bypass the narrow side streets. In any case, look into St. Michael's and consider the fascinating Dorotheum, itself easily worth an hour or more.

Sights to See

㉜ **Demel.** Vienna's best-known pastry shop, Demel offers a dizzying selection,
Fodor'sChoice so if you have a sweet tooth, a visit will be worth every euro. And in a
★ city famous for its tortes, their Senegaltorte takes the cake. Chocolate lovers will want to participate in the famous Viennese Sachertorte debate by sampling Demel's version and then comparing it with its rival at the **Café Sacher,** which is in the Hotel Sacher. Don't forget to press your nose against Demel's shop windows, whose displays are among the most mouthwatering and inventive in Austria. And during the hours of noon and 4 PM, Thursday–Saturday, you can visit the Demel museum in the basement. ⊠ *Kohlmarkt 14, 1st District* ☎ *01/535–1717–0* Ⓤ *U1 or U3/Stephansplatz.*

Dorotheum. The narrow passageway just to the right of St. Michael's, with its large 15th-century relief depicting Christ on the Mount of Olives, leads into the Stallburggasse. The area is dotted with antiques stores, attracted by the presence of the Dorotheum, the famous Viennese auction house that began as a state-controlled pawnshop in 1707 (affectionately known as "Aunt Dorothy" to its patrons). Merchandise coming up for auction is on display at Dorotheergasse 17. The showrooms—packed with everything from carpets and pianos to cameras and jewelry and postage stamps—are well worth a visit. Some wares are not for auction but for immediate sale. ⊠ *Dorotheergasse 17, 1st District* ☎ *01/515–60–200* ⊕ *www.dorotheum.com* ☉ *Weekdays 10–6, Sat. 9–5* Ⓤ *U1 or U3/Stephansplatz.*

㉙ **The Graben.** One of Vienna's major crossroads, the Graben, leading west from Stock-im-Eisen-Platz, is a street whose unusual width gives it the presence and weight of a city square. Its shape is due to the Romans, who dug the city's southwestern moat here (Graben literally means "moat" or "ditch") adjacent to the original city walls. The Graben's centerpiece is the effulgently Baroque **Pestsäule,** or Plague Column. Erected by Emperor Leopold I between 1687 and 1693 as thanks to God for delivering the city from a particularly virulent plague, today the representation looks more like a host of cherubs doing their best to cope with the icing of a wedding cake wilting under a hot sun. Staunch Protestants may be shocked to learn that the foul figure of the Pest stands also for the heretic plunging away from the "True Faith" into the depth of hell. But they will have to get used to the fact that the Catholic Church has triumphed over Protestantism in Austria and frequently recalls the fact in stone and on canvas. ⊠ *At the intersections of Kärntnerstrasse and Kohlmarkt, 1st District* Ⓤ *U1 or U3/Stephansplatz.*

㉖ Jewish Museum. The former Eskeles Palace, once an elegant private residence, now houses the city's Jüdisches Museum der Stadt Wien. Permanent exhibitions tell of the momentous role that Vienna-born Jews played in realms from music to medicine, art to philosophy, both in Vienna—until abruptly halted in 1938—and in the world at large. Changing exhibits add contemporary touches. The museum complex includes a café and bookstore. ⊠ *Dorotheergasse 11, 1st District* ☎ *01/535–0431* 🎫 *€5* ◔ *Sun.–Fri. 10–6, Thurs. 10–8* Ⓤ *U1 or U3/Stephansplatz.*

㉛ Kohlmarkt. The Kohlmarkt, aside from its classic view of the domed entryway to the imperial palace complex of the Hofburg, is best known as Vienna's most elegant shopping street—here you can buy Demel's chocolate goodies and purchase Thonet's ever-stylish bentwood chairs. The shops, not the buildings, are remarkable, although there is an entertaining odd-couple pairing: No. 11 (early 18th century) and No. 9 (early 20th century). The mixture of architectural styles is similar to that of the Graben, but the general atmosphere is low-key, as if the street were consciously deferring to the showstopper dome at the west end. The composers Haydn and Chopin lived in houses on the street, and indeed, the Kohlmarkt lingers in the memory when flashier streets have faded. ⊠ *At the intersections of Hofburg Palace and Kohlmarkt, 1st District* Ⓤ *U3/Herrengasse.*

★ ㉕ Looshaus. In 1911, Adolf Loos, one of the founding fathers of 20th-century modern architecture, built the Looshaus on august Michaelerplatz, facing the Imperial Palace entrance. It was considered nothing less than an architectural declaration of war. After two hundred years of Baroque and neo-Baroque exuberance, the first generation of 20th-century architects had had enough. Loos led the revolt against architectural tradition; *Ornament and Crime* was the title of his famous manifesto, in which he inveighed against the conventional architectural wisdom of the 19th century. Instead, he advocated buildings that were plain, honest, and functional. When he built the Looshaus for Goldman and Salatsch (men's clothiers) in 1911, the city was scandalized. Archduke Franz Ferdinand, heir to the throne, was so offended that he vowed never again to use the Michaelerplatz entrance to the Imperial Palace. Today the Looshaus has lost its power to shock, and the facade seems quite innocuous; argument now focuses on the postmodern Neues Haas-Haus opposite St. Stephan's Cathedral. The recently restored interior of the Looshaus remains a breathtaking surprise; the building now houses a bank, and you can go inside to see the stylish chambers and staircase. To really get up close and personal with Loos, head to the splendor of his Loos American Bar, five blocks or so to the east at No. 10 Kärntnerdurchgang. ⊠ *Michaelerplatz 3, 1st District* Ⓤ *U3/Herrengasse.*

㉔ Michaelerplatz. One of Vienna's most historic squares, this small plaza is now the site of an excavation revealing Roman plus 18th- and 19th-century layers of the past. The excavations are a latter-day distraction from the Michaelerplatz's most noted claim to fame—the eloquent entryway to the palace complex of the Hofburg.

In 1945 American soldiers forced open the doors of the crypt in the **Michaelerkirche** for the first time in 150 years and made a singular discovery. Found lying undisturbed, obviously for centuries, were the mummified remains of former wealthy parishioners of the church—even the finery and buckled shoes worn at their burial had been preserved by the perfect temperatures contained within the crypt.

Fascinatingly ghoulish tours are offered from Easter to the end of November (at 11, 1, and 3, Monday to Friday; on Saturdays and other times of the year, check the posted announcement at the church, or phone 0699/104–74–828). The cost is €4. The tour is given first in German and then in English. Visitors are led down into the shadowy gloom and through a labyrinth of passageways, pausing at several tombs (many of which are open in order to view the remains), with a brief explanation of the cause of death given at each site. ⊠ *At the intersections of Hofburg Palace and Kohlmarkt, 1st District* Ⓤ *U3/Herrengasse.*

㉘ Neues Haas-Haus. Stock-im-Eisen-Platz is home to central Vienna's most controversial (for the moment, at least) piece of architecture: the Neues Haas-Haus designed by Hans Hollein, one of Austria's best-known living architects. Detractors consider its aggressively contemporary style out of place opposite St. Stephan's, seeing the cathedral's style parodied by being stood on its head; advocates consider the contrast enlivening. Whatever the ultimate verdict, the restaurant and shopping complex has not proved to be the anticipated commercial success; its restaurants may be thriving, but its boutiques are not. ⊠ *Stephansplatz 12, 1st District* ⊙ *Shops weekdays 9–6, Sat. 9–noon* Ⓤ *U1 or U3/Stephansplatz.*

★ ㉚ Peterskirche (St. Peter's Church). Considered the best example of church Baroque in Vienna—certainly the most theatrical—the Peterskirche was constructed between 1702 and 1708 by Lucas von Hildebrandt. According to legend, the original church on this site was founded in 792 by Charlemagne, a tale immortalized by the relief plaque on the right side of the church. The facade has angled towers, graceful turrets (said to have been inspired by the tents of the Turks during the siege of 1683), and an unusually fine entrance portal. Inside the church, the Baroque decoration is elaborate, with some fine touches (particularly the glass-crowned galleries high on the walls to either side of the altar and the amazing tableau of the martyrdom of St. John Nepomuk), but the lack of light and the years of accumulated dirt create a prevailing gloom, and the much-praised ceiling frescoes by J. M. Rottmayr are impossible to make out. Just before Christmastime each year, the basement crypt is filled with a display of nativity scenes. The church is shoehorned into tiny Petersplatz, just off the Graben. ⊠ *Petersplatz, 1st District* Ⓤ *U1 or U3/Stephansplatz.*

㉗ Stock-im-Eisen. In the southwest corner of Stock-im-Eisen-Platz, set into the building on the west side of Kärntnerstrasse, is one of the city's odder relics: the Stock-im-Eisen, or the "nail-studded stump." Chronicles first mention the Stock-im-Eisen in 1533, but it is probably far older, and for hundreds of years any apprentice metalsmith who came to Vienna to learn his trade hammered a nail into the tree trunk for good luck. During World War II, when there was talk of moving the relic to a museum in Munich, it mysteriously disappeared; it reappeared, perfectly preserved, after the threat of removal had passed. ⊠ *At the intersections of the Graben and Singerstrasse, 1st District* Ⓤ *U1 or U3/ Stephansplatz.*

AN IMPERIAL CITY: THE HOFBURG

A walk through the Imperial Palace, known as the Hofburg, brings you back to the days when Vienna was the capital of a mighty empire. You can still find in Vienna shops vintage postcards and prints that show the revered and bewhiskered Emperor Franz Josef leaving his Hofburg palace for a drive in his carriage. Today, at the palace—which faces Kohlmarkt on the opposite side of Michaelerplatz—you can walk in his very footsteps, gaze at the old tin bath the emperor kept under his simple iron bedstead, marvel at his bejeweled christening robe, and, along the way, feast your eyes on great works of art, impressive armor, and some of the finest Baroque interiors in Europe.

Until 1918 the Hofburg was the home of the Habsburgs, rulers of the Austro-Hungarian Empire. As a current tourist lure, it has become a vast smorgasbord of sightseeing attractions: the Imperial Apartments, two Imperial treasuries, six museums, the National Library, and the famous Winter Riding School all vie for attention. The newest Hofburg attraction is a museum (opened April 2004) devoted to "Sisi," the beloved Empress Elisabeth, wife of Franz Josef, whose beauty was the talk of Europe and whose tragic death was mourned by all. The entire complex takes a minimum of a full day to explore in detail; if your time is limited (or if you want to save most of the interior sightseeing for a rainy day), you should omit the Imperial Apartments and all the museums mentioned below except the new museum of court silver and tableware, the Silberkammer, and probably the Schatzkammer. An excellent multilingual, full-color booklet describing the palace in detail is for sale at most ticket counters within the complex; it gives a complete list of attractions and maps out the palace's complicated ground plan and building history wing by wing.

Vienna took its imperial role seriously, as evidenced by the sprawling Hofburg complex, which is still today, as then, the seat of government. But this is generally understated power; while the buildings cover a considerable area, the treasures lie within, not to be flamboyantly flaunted. Certainly under Franz Josef II the reign was beneficent—witness the broad Ringstrasse he ordained and the panoply of museums and public buildings it hosts. With few exceptions (Vienna City Hall and the Votive Church), rooflines are kept to an even level, creating an ensemble effect that helps integrate the palace complex and its parks into the urban landscape without making a domineering statement. Diplomats still bustle in and out of high-level international meetings along the elegant halls. Horse-drawn carriages still traverse the Ring and the roadway that cuts through the complex. Ignore the cars and tour buses and you can easily imagine yourself in a Vienna of a hundred or more years ago.

Architecturally, the Hofburg—like St. Stephan's—is far from refined. It grew up over a period of 700 years (its earliest mention in court documents is from 1279, at the very beginning of Habsburg rule), and its spasmodic, haphazard growth kept it from attaining any sort of unified identity. But many of the bits and pieces are fine, and one interior (the National Library) is a tour de force.

A Good Walk

When you begin to explore the Hofburg you realize that the palace complex is like a nest of boxes, courtyards opening off courtyards and wings (*Trakte*) spreading far and wide. First tackle **Josefsplatz** ㉝, the remarkable square that interrupts Augustinerstrasse, ornamented by the equestrian statue of Josef II—many consider this Vienna's loveliest square. Indeed, the beautifully restored imperial decor adorning the roof of the buildings forming Josefsplatz is one of the few visual demonstrations of Austria's onetime widespread power and influence. On your right to the north is the **Spanische Reitschule** ㉞, the Spanish Riding School—one emblem of Vienna known throughout the world—where the famous white horses reign. Across Reitschulgasse under the arches are the **Lipizzaner Museum** ㉟ and the Imperial Stables. To the south stands the **Augustinerkirche** ㊱, St. Augustine's Church, where the Habsburg rulers' hearts are preserved in urns. The grand main hall (Prunksaal) of the **Hofbibliothek** ㊲, the National Library, is one of the great Baroque treasures of Europe, a site not to be missed (enter from the southwest corner of Josefsplatz).

Under the Michaelerplatz dome is the entrance to the **Kaiserappartements** ㊳, hardly the elegance you would normally associate with royalty, but Franz Josef II, the residing emperor from 1848 to 1916, was anything but ostentatious in his personal life. For the representational side, however, go through into the **In der Burg** ㊴ courtyard and look in at the elegant **Silberkammer** ㊵ museum of court silver and tableware. Go through the **Schweizertor** ㊶, the Swiss gate, to the south off In der Burg, to reach the small Schweizer Hof courtyard with stairs leading to the **Hofburgkapelle** ㊷, the Imperial Chapel where the Vienna Boys Choir makes its regular Sunday appearances. In a back corner of the courtyard is the entrance to the **Schatzkammer** ㊸, the Imperial Treasury, overflowing with jewels, robes, and royal trappings. From In der Burg, the roadway leads under the Leopold Wing of the complex into the vast park known as **Heldenplatz** ㊹, or Hero's Square. The immediately obvious heroes are the equestrian statues of Archduke Karl and Prince Eugene of Savoy. The Hofburg wing to the south with its concave facade is the **Neue Burg** ㊺, the "new" section of the complex, now housing four specialized museums. Depending on your interests, consider the **Ephesus Museum** ㊻, with Roman antiquities; the **Musical Instrument Collection** ㊼, where you also hear what you see; and the impressive **Weapons Collection** ㊽, with tons of steel armor. Ahead, the Burgtor gate separates the Hofburg complex from the Ringstrasse. The quiet oasis in back of the Neue Burg is the **Burggarten** ㊾, home to the magical **Schmetterlinghaus** (Butterfly

House). Catch your breath and marvel that you've seen only a small part of the Hofburg—a large part of it still houses the offices of the Austrian government and is not open to the public.

TIMING   You could spend a day in the Hofburg complex. For most of the smaller museums, figure on anything from an hour upward.

Sights to See

36 Augustinerkirche (Augustinian Church). Across Josefsplatz from the Riding School is the entrance to the Augustinerkirche, built during the 14th century and presenting the most unified Gothic interior in the city. But the church is something of a fraud; the interior, it turns out, dates from the late 18th century, not the early 14th. A historical fraud the church may be, but a spiritual fraud it is not. The view from the entrance doorway is stunning: a soaring harmony of vertical piers, ribbed vaults, and hanging chandeliers that makes Vienna's other Gothic interiors look earthbound by comparison. Note the magnificent **Tomb of the Archduchess Maria-Christina,** sculpted by the great Antonio Canova in 1805, with mournful figures of her and her family (her husband founded the Albertina) trooping into a temple. The imposing Baroque organ sounds as heavenly as it looks, and the Sunday-morning high mass sung here—frequently by Mozart or Haydn—can be the highlight of a trip. To the right of the main altar in the small Loreto Chapel stand silver urns containing the hearts of Habsburg rulers. This rather morbid sight is viewable after early mass on Sunday, Monday, or by appointment. ⊠ *Josefsplatz, 1st District* ☎ *01/533–7099–0* Ⓤ *U3/Herrengasse.*

★ **49 Burggarten.** The intimate Burggarten in back of the Neue Burg is a quiet oasis that includes a statue of a contemplative Kaiser Franz Josef and an elegant statue of Mozart, moved here from the Albertinaplatz after the war, when the city's charred ruins were being rebuilt. Today, the park is one of the most favored time-out spots for the Viennese; the alluring backdrop is formed by the striking former greenhouses that are now the gorgeous Palmenhaus restaurant and the **Schmetterlinghaus.** Total enchantment awaits you here at Vienna's unique Butterfly House. Inside are towering tropical trees, waterfalls, a butterfly nursery, and more than 150 species on display (usually 400 winged jewels are in residence). ⊠ *Access from Opernring and Hanuschgasse/Goethegasse, 1st District* ☎ *€4.70* ⊙ *Apr.–Oct., Mon.–Fri. 10–4:45, Sat.–Sun. 10–6:15; Nov.–Mar., daily 10–3:45* ⊕ *www.schmetterlinghaus.at* Ⓤ *U2/MuseumsQuartier; Tram: 1, 2, and D/Burgring.*

46 Ephesus Museum. One of the museums in the Neue Burg, the Ephesus Museum contains exceptional Roman antiquities unearthed by Austrian archaeologists in Turkey at the turn of the century. ⊠ *Hofburg, 1st District* ☎ *Combined ticket with Musical Instrument Collection and Weapons Collection €8* ⊙ *Wed.–Mon. 10–6* Ⓤ *Tram: 1, 2, and D/ Burgring.*

44 Heldenplatz. The long wing with the concave bay on the south side of the square is the youngest section of the palace, called the Neue Burg. Although the Neue Burg building plans were not completed and the Heldenplatz was left without a discernible shape, the space is nevertheless

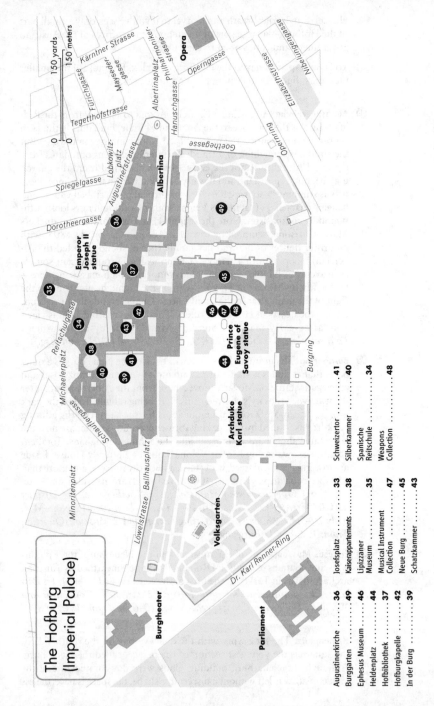

The Hofburg (Imperial Palace)

150 yards
150 meters

Opera

Burgtheater

Parliament

Volksgarten

Emperor
Joseph II
statue

Albertina

Prince
Eugene of
Savoy statue

Archduke
Karl statue

Augustinerkirche **36**
Burggarten **49**
Ephesus Museum......**46**
Heldenplatz **44**
Hofbibliothek **37**
Hofburgkapelle **42**
In der Burg **39**

Josefsplatz **33**
Kaiserappartements......**38**
Lipizzaner
Musical Instrument
Collection **47**
Neue Burg **45**
Schatzkammer **43**

Museum **35**

Schweizertor **41**
Silberkammer **40**
Spanische
Reitschule **34**
Weapons
Collection **48**

punctuated by two superb equestrian statues depicting Archduke Karl and Prince Eugene of Savoy. The older section on the north includes the offices of the federal president. ⊠ *Hofburg, 1st District* Ⓤ *Tram: 1, 2, and D/Burgring.*

③⑦ **Hofbibliothek** (formerly Court, now National Library). This is one of the

Fodor'sChoice grandest Baroque libraries in the world, in every sense a cathedral of

★ books. Its centerpiece is the spectacular Prunksaal—the Grand Hall of the National Library—which probably contains more book treasures than any comparable collection outside the Vatican. The main entrance to the ornate reading room is in the left corner of Josefsplatz. Designed by Fischer von Erlach the Elder just before his death in 1723 and completed by his son, the Grand Hall is full-blown High Baroque, with trompe-l'oeil ceiling frescoes by Daniel Gran. This floridly Baroque library may not be to everyone's taste, but in the end it is the books themselves that come to the rescue. They are as lovingly displayed as the gilding and the frescoes, and they give the hall a warmth that the rest of the palace decidedly lacks. On the third floor is an intriguing museum of cartographic globes that should not be overlooked. Beginning in 1782, Mozart performed regularly at the Sunday matinees of Baron Gottfried van Swieten, who lived in a suite of rooms in the grand, palace-like library. Four years later, the baron founded the Society of Associated Cavaliers, which set up oratorio performances with Mozart acting as conductor. Across the street at Palais Palffy, Mozart reportedly first performed *The Marriage of Figaro* before a select, private audience to see if it would pass the court censor. ⊠ *Josefsplatz 1, 1st District* ☎ *01/534-100* ⊕ *www.hofburg-wien.at* ⊠ *€5* ⊙ *May–Oct., daily 10–4, Thurs. 10–7; Nov.–Apr., Mon.–Sat. 10–2* Ⓤ *U3/Herrengasse.*

④② **Hofburgkapelle** (Chapel of the Imperial Palace). Fittingly, this is the main venue for the beloved Vienna Boys' Choir (Wiener Sängerknaben), since they actually have their earliest roots in the Hofmusikkapelle choir founded by Emperor Maximilian I four centuries ago (Haydn and Schubert as young boys were both participants). Today, the troop sings mass here at 9:15 on Sundays from mid-September to June (and, yes, even though this is a mass tickets are sold to hear the choir, ranging from €5 to €30). Alas, the arrangement is such that you *hear* the choirboys but don't see them; their soprano and alto voices peal forth from a gallery behind the seating area. But the choir can be seen in all their apple-cheeked splendor at other places around town, notably the Musikverein and Schönbrunn Palace; see their Web site for their concert schedule. For ticket information, *see* Nightlife and the Arts, *below.* ⊠ *Hofburg, Schweizer Hof, 1st District* ☎ *01/533-9927* ⊕ *www.wsk.at; www.bmbwk.gv.at/kultur/musik.xml* ⊟ *01/533-9927-75* Ⓤ *U3/Herrengasse.*

③⑨ **In der Burg.** This prominent courtyard of the Hofburg complex is centered around a statue of Francis II and the noted **Schweizertor** gateway. Note the **clock** on the far upper wall at the north end of the courtyard: It tells time by the sundial, also gives the time mechanically, and even, above the clock face, indicates the phase of the moon. ⊠ *Hofburg, 1st District* Ⓤ *U3/Herrengasse.*

③③ Josefsplatz. Josefsplatz is the most imposing of the Hofburg courtyards, with an equestrian **statue of Emperor Joseph II** (1807) in the center. ✉ *Herrengasse, 1st District* Ⓤ *U3/Herrengasse.*

③⑧ Kaiserappartements (Imperial Apartments). Entering the spectacular portal gate of the Michaelertor—you can't miss the four gigantic statues of Hercules and his Labors—you enter and climb the marble Kaiserstiege (Emperor's Staircase) to begin a tour of a long, repetitive suite of 18 conventionally luxurious state rooms. The red-and-gold decoration (19th-century imitation of 18th-century Rococo) tries to look regal, but much like the empire itself in its latter days it is only going through the motions and ends up looking merely official. Still, these are the rooms where the ruling family of the Habsburg empire ate, slept, and dealt with family tragedy—in the emperor's study on January 30, 1889, Franz Josef was told about the tragic death of his only son, Crown Prince Rudolf, who had shot himself and his soulmate, 17-year-old Baroness Vetsera, at the hunting lodge at Mayerling. Among the few signs of genuine life are Emperor Franz Josef's spartan, iron field bed, on which he slept every night, and his Empress Elisabeth's wooden gymnastics equipment (obsessed with her looks, "Sisi" suffered from anorexia and was fanatically devoted to exercise). To commemorate the 150th wedding anniversary of this mismatched pair in 2004, a Sisi Museum was inaugurated, which is actually part of the regular tour. Five rooms are given over to the myths and realities of this Princess Diana of the 19th century; exhibits are displayed in high-style fashion, with colored spotlights, painted murals, and many of her treasured items, including her jewels, the gown she wore the night before her marriage, her dressing gown, and the reconstructed, opulent Court Salon railroad car she used. There is also a death mask made after her assassination in Geneva in 1898 by an anarchist. ✉ *Hofburg, Schweizer Hof, 1st District* ⊕ *www.hofburg-wien.at* ☎ *01/533–7570* 💶 *€7.50, with guided tour €9.40* ◔ *Daily 9–5; July–Aug., daily 9–5:30* Ⓤ *U3/Herrengasse.*

③⑤ Lipizzaner Museum. If you're interested in learning more about the Lipizzaners, visit this museum, located in what used to be the old imperial pharmacy. Exhibitions document the history of the Lipizzans, including paintings, photographs, and videos giving an overview from the 16th century to the present. A highlight is a visit to the stables, where you can see the horses up close, through a glass window. ✉ *Reitschulgasse 2, 1st District* ☎ *01/533–7811* ⊕ *www.lipizzaner.at* 💶 *€5; combined ticket with morning training session €14.50* ◔ *Daily 9–6* Ⓤ *U3/Herrengasse.*

④⑦ Musical Instrument Collection. This Neue Burg museum houses pianos that belonged to Brahms, Schumann, and Mahler. An acoustic guided tour allows you actually to hear the various instruments on headphones as you move from room to room. ✉ *Hofburg, 1st District* 💶 *Combined ticket with Ephesus Museum and Weapons Collection €8, more for special exhibits)* ◔ *Wed.–Mon. 10–6* Ⓤ *U2/MuseumsQuartier.*

④⑤ Neue Burg. The Neue Burg stands today as a symbol of architectural overconfidence. Designed for Emperor Franz Josef in 1869, this "new château" was part of a much larger scheme that was meant to make the

Hofburg rival the Louvre, if not Versailles. The German architect Gottfried Semper planned a twin of the present Neue Burg on the opposite side of the Heldenplatz, with arches connecting the Neue Burg and its twin with the other pair of twins on the Ringstrasse, the Kunsthistorisches Museum (Museum of Art History), and the Naturhistorisches Museum (Museum of Natural History). But World War I intervened, and with the empire's collapse the Neue Burg became merely the last in a long series of failed attempts to bring architectural order to the Hofburg. (From its main balcony, in April 1938, Adolf Hitler, telling a huge cheering crowd below of his plan for the new German empire, declared that Vienna "is a pearl! I am going to put it into a setting of which it is worthy!") Today crowds flock to the Neue Burg because it houses no fewer than four specialty museums: the **Ephesus Museum, Musical Instruments Collection, Ethnological Museum,** and **Weapons Collection.** For details on these museums, see separate listings. ✉ *Heldenplatz, 1st District* ☎ *01/525240* Ⓤ *U2/MuseumsQuartier.*

🔳 **Schatzkammer** (Imperial Treasury). The entrance to the Schatzkammer, with its 1,000 years of treasures, is tucked away at ground level behind the staircase to the Hofburgkapelle. The elegant display is a welcome antidote to the monotony of the Imperial Apartments, for the entire Treasury was completely renovated in 1983–87, and the crowns and relics and vestments fairly glow in their surroundings. Here you'll find such marvels as the Holy Lance—reputedly the lance that pierced Jesus' side—the Imperial Crown (a sacred symbol of sovereignty once stolen on Hitler's orders), and the Saber of Charlemagne. Don't miss the Burgundian Treasure, connected with that most romantic of medieval orders of chivalry, the Order of the Golden Fleece. ✉ *Schweizer Hof, 1st District* ☎ *01/525240* 💶 *€8* 🕐 *Wed.–Mon. 10–6* Ⓤ *U3/Herrengasse.*

🔳 **Schweizertor** (Swiss Gate). Dating from 1552 and decorated with some of the earliest classical motifs in the city, the Schweizertor leads from In der Burg through to the oldest section of the palace, a small courtyard known as the Schweizer Hof. The gateway is painted maroon, black, and gold; it gives a fine Renaissance flourish to its building facade. ✉ *Hofburg, Schweizertor, 1st District* Ⓤ *U3/Herrengasse.*

🔳 **Silberkammer** (Museum of Court Silver and Tableware). The large courtyard on the far side of the Michaelertor rotunda is known as In der Burg; here on the west side is the entrance to the sparkling new Silberkammer. There's far more than forks and finger bowls here; stunning decorative pieces vie with glittering silver and gold for attention. Highlights include Franz Josef's vermeil banqueting service, the jardinière given to Empress Elisabeth by Queen Victoria, and gifts from Marie-Antoinette to her brother Josef II. The presentation of full table settings gives an idea of court life both as lived daily and on festive occasions. ✉ *Hofburg, Michaelertrakt, 1st District* ☎ *01/533–7570* 💶 *€7.50, including Kaiserappartements* 🕐 *Daily 9–5; July–Aug., daily 9–5:30* Ⓤ *U3/Herrengasse.*

★ 🔳 **Spanische Reitschule** (Spanish Riding School). Between Augustinerstrasse and the Josefsplatz is the world-famous Spanish Riding School, a favorite for centuries, and no wonder: who can resist the sight of the stark-white Lipizzan horses going through their masterful paces? For the last 300 years they have been perfecting their *haute école* riding demonstrations to the sound of Baroque music in a ballroom that seems to be a crystal-chandeliered stable. The breed was started in 1580, and the horses proved themselves in battle as well as in the complicated "dances" for which they are famous. The interior of the riding school, the 1735 work of Fischer von Erlach the Younger, is itself an attraction—surely Europe's most elegant sports arena—and if the prancing horses begin to pall, move up to the top balcony and examine the ceiling. The school's popularity is hardly surprising, and tickets to some performances must be ordered in writing many weeks in advance, or through their Web site. Information offices have a brochure with the detailed schedule (performances are usually March–December, with the school on vacation in July and August). Generally the full, 80-minute show takes place Sundays at 11 AM plus selected Fridays at 6 PM. There are two yearly classical dressage final rehearsals with music, at the end of August and the end of December. Check the Web site for details.

Morning training sessions with music are held Tuesday–Saturday 10–12. Tickets are available at the visitor center, Michaelerplatz 1, Tuesday to Saturday (except holidays) 9–5, and at Josefsplatz, Gate 2 on the day of the morning exercise 9–12:30. It's best to get there early to get a place in line. Note that if you purchase your tickets through a ticket agency for an actual performance, they can legally add a commission of 22%–25% to the face price of the ticket. For performance ticket orders, write to **Spanische Reitschule** (⊠ Hofburg, A-1010 Vienna). Pick up reserved tickets at the office under the Michaelerplatz rotunda dome. ⊠ *Michaelerplatz 1, Hofburg, A-1010, 1st District* ☎ *01/533–9031-0* 🖷 *01/535–0186* ⊕ *www.srs.at* ✉ *€33–€145; standing room €22–€25, morning training sessions €11.60; Sat. classical dressage final rehearsal, €20* ⊙ *Mar.–June and late Aug.–mid-Dec. Closed tour wks.* Ⓤ *U3/Herrengasse.*

❽ Weapons Collection. Rivaling the armory in Graz as one of the most extensive arms and armor collections in the world is this Neue Burg museum. Enter at the triumphal arch set into the middle of the curved portion of the facade. ⊠ *Heldenplatz, 1st District* ✉ *Combined ticket with Ephesus Museum and Musical Instrument Collection €8, more for special exhibits* ⊙ *Wed.–Mon. 10–6* Ⓤ *U2/MuseumsQuartier.*

THE RINGSTRASSE: GEMS OF THE "RING"

Along with the Hofburg, the Ringstrasse comprises Vienna's major urban set piece. This grand series of thoroughfares circles the heart of Vienna, the Innere Stadt (Inner City), or 1st District. It follows the lines of what were, until an imperial decree ordered them leveled in 1857, the city's defenses. By the 1870s Vienna had reached the zenith of her imperial prosperity, and this found ultimate expression in the series of magnificent buildings erected around the Ringstrasse—the Opera House, the Kunsthistoriches Museum, the Naturhistorisches Museum, and the Rathaus, the University, and the Votivkirche. In and around the Ring ribbon, you'll find an array of other unmissable gems: the quaint-now-trendy Spittelberg Quarter, Freud's apartment, and Vienna's new/old daz-zler, the Liechtenstein "garden palace," now home to princely Old Masters, including a fabled collection of paintings by Peter Paul Rubens.

A Good Walk

Is there a best way to explore the Ring? You can walk it from one end to the other—from where it begins at the Danube Canal to where it returns to the canal after its curving flight. Or, you can explore it whenever you happen to cross it on other missions. While it is a pleasant sequence of boulevards, seeing its succession of rather pompous buildings all in one walk can be overpowering. Or, you can obtain the best of both options by following this suggested itinerary, which leavens the bombast of the Ring with some of Vienna's most fascinating sights. If you just want to do the highlights, plan on spending the morning at the Kunsthistorisches Museum, then take in the MuseumsQuartier (and lunch in the complex), followed by a leisurely afternoon spent at the Freud-Haus and the spectacular Liechtenstein Museum.

Your walk begins at the twin buildings, both museums. across the Ringstrasse from the Hofburg. To the west is the **Naturhistorisches Museum** 🟡; to the east, the **Kunsthistorisches Museum** 🟡, the art museum packed with world-famous treasures. Allow ample time for exploration here. Not far away is the new, headline-making **MuseumsQuartier** 🟡, a museum complex that includes several highly important modern art collections, including the Leopold Collection of Austrian Art and the Museum Moderner Kunst. Farther west of the museum square is the compact and hip **Spittelberg Quarter** 🟡 of tiny streets between Burggasse and Sibensterngasse, often the site of handicraft and seasonal fairs. For more, and superspectacular, evidence of handicraft of an earlier era, detour south to Mariahilferstrasse and the **Kaiserliches Hofmobiliendepot**, the repository of much of the sumptuous furnishings of the old Habsburg palaces.

Heading back to the Ring, the **Volksgarten** 🟡 on the inside of the Ringstrasse to the north of the museum square includes a café and rose garden among its attractions; look also for the small memorial to Franz Josef's wife, Empress Elisabeth, in the rear corner. Tackle the Ringstrasse buildings by the **Parlament** 🟡, the **Rathaus** 🟡 (City Hall), the **Burgtheater** 🟡 opposite on the inside of the Ring, then the **Universität** 🟡 (the main building of Vienna's university) beyond, again on the outside of the Ring. Next to the university stands the neo-Gothic **Votivkirche** 🟡. If you still have time and energy, walk farther along the Ring to discover the Börse at the corner of the Ring and Wipplingerstrasse. The outside end of Hohenstaufengasse leads into Liechtensteinstrasse, which will bring you to Berggasse. Turn right to reach No. 19, the **Freud Haus** 🟡, now a museum and research facility. Not far from Freud's apartment and just off the Liechtensteinstrasse on Fürstengasse, is the **Liechtenstein Museum** 🟡, home of the Prince of Liechtenstein's fabulous private art collection, housed in the family's summer palace.

TIMING   If you can, plan to visit Vienna's Louvre—the Kunsthistorisches Museum—early in the day before the crowds arrive, although the size of crowds depends greatly on whatever special shows the museum may be exhibiting. As for the main sights off the Ringstrasse, you could easily lump together visits to the Freud Apartment and the MuseumsQuartier, figuring on about a half day for the two combined.

Sights to See

㊐ Burgtheater (National Theater). One of the most important theaters in the German-speaking world, the Burgtheater was built between 1874 and 1888 in the Italian Renaissance style, replacing the old court theater at Michaelerplatz. Emperor Franz Josef's mistress, Katherina Schratt, was once a star performer here, and famous Austrian and German actors still stride across this stage. The opulent interior, with its 60-foot relief *Worshippers of Bacchus* by Rudolf Wyer and foyer ceiling frescoes by Ernst and Gustav Klimt, makes it well worth a visit. For information about performances here, *see* Theater *in* Nightlife and the Arts, *below.* ⊠ *Dr.-Karl-Lueger-Ring 2, 1st District* ☏ *01/514-4441-40* 🖾 *€4.50* ⊙ *Guided tours Mon.–Sat. at 3, Sun. at 11 and 3* Ⓤ *Tram: 1, 2, and D/Burgtheater, Rathaus.*

㊐ Freud Haus. Not far from the historic Hofburg district, beyond the Votivkirche at the Schottenring along the Ringstrasse, you can skip over several centuries and visit that outstanding symbol of 20th-century Vienna: Sigmund Freud's apartment at Berggasse 19 (Apartment 6, one flight up; ring the bell and push the door simultaneously); this was his residence from 1891 to 1938. The five-room collection of memorabilia is mostly a photographic record of Freud's life, with some documents, publications, and a portion of his collection of antiquities also on display. The waiting-room furniture is authentic, but the consulting room and study furniture (including the famous couch) can be seen only in photographs. ⊠ *Berggasse 19, 9th District/Alsergrund* ☏ *01/319-1596* ⊕ *www.freud-museum.at* 🖾 *€5* ⊙ *Jan.–June and Oct.–Dec., daily 9–5; July–Sept., daily 9–6* Ⓤ *U2/Schottentor.*

㊐ Kunsthistorisches Museum (Museum of Fine Art). However short your stay

FodorsChoice ★ in Vienna, you will surely want to pay a visit to one of the greatest art collections in the world, that of the Kunsthistorisches Museum. For this is no dry-as-dust museum illustrating the history of art, as its name implies. Rather its collections of Old Master paintings reveal the royal taste and style of many members of the mighty House of Habsburg, who during the 16th and 17th centuries ruled over the greater part of the Western world. Today you can enjoy what this great ruling house assiduously (and in most cases, selectively) brought together through the centuries. The collection stands in the same class with those of the Louvre, the Prado, and the Vatican. It is most famous for the largest collection of paintings under one roof by the Netherlandish 16th-century master Pieter Brueghel the Elder—just seeing his sublime *Hunters in the Snow* is worth a trip to Vienna, many art historians will tell you. Brueghel's depictions of peasant scenes, often set in magnificent landscapes, distill the poetry and magic of the 16th century as few other paintings do. Room RX is the Brueghel shrine—on its walls, in addition to *Hunters in the Snow,* hang *Children's Games,* the *Tower of Babel,* the *Peasant Wedding,* the *Nest-Robber,* and eight other priceless canvases. But there are also hundreds of other celebrated Old Master paintings here, most assembled by the Habsburgs over many centuries. Even a cursory description would run on for pages, but a brief selection of the museum's most important works will give you an idea of the riches to be enjoyed. The large-scale works concentrated in the main galleries shouldn't distract you from the equal share of masterworks in the more intimate side wings.

The Flemish wing also includes Rogier van der Weyden's *Triptych Crucifixion,* Holbein's *Portrait of Jane Seymour, Queen of England,* a fine series of Rembrandt portraits, and Vermeer's peerless *Allegory of the Art of Painting.* The grand style of the 17th century is represented by Rubens' towering altarpieces and his *Nude of Hélène Fourment.* In the Italian wing are works by Titian, including his *Portrait of Isabella d'Este,* whose fiercely intelligent eyes make you realize why she was the first lady of the Renaissance, and Giorgione's *The Three Philosophers,* an enigmatic composition in uniquely radiant Venetian coloring. A short list of other highlights include Raphael's *Madonna in the Meadow,* Correggio's *Jupiter Embracing Io,* Parmigianino's *Cupid Cutting a Bow,* Guercino's *Return of the Prodigal Son,* and Caravaggio's *Madonna of the Rosary.* One level down is the remarkable, less-visited *Kunstkammer,* displaying priceless objects created for the Habsburg emperors. These include curiosities made of gold, silver, and crystal (including Cellini's famous salt cellar), and more exotic materials, such as ivory, horn, and gemstones. In addition, there are rooms devoted to Egyptian antiquities, Greek and Roman art, sculpture (ranging from masterworks by Tilmann Riemenschneider to Italian Mannerist bronzes, which the Habsburgs collected by the roomful) and the decorative arts, and numerous other collections. Sadly, Benevenuto Cellini's legendary salt cellar, valued at €50 million, was stolen in 2003. When your feet are ready to call a sit-down strike, repair to the wonderful café on the museum's second floor. Set under a grand dome, adorned with paintings, sculpture, and framed by gilt-tipped black marble columns, this spot is run by Gerstner, the famed pastry-shop. The fruit tortes and comfy armchairs here add up to a refined time-out. ✉ *Maria-Theresien-Platz, 7th District/ Neubau* ☎ *01/525240* 🌐 *www.khm.at* 🎫 *€10* ⏲ *Tues.–Sun. 10–6; extended hours for picture galleries, Thurs. until 9* PM Ⓤ *U2/MuseumsQuartier, U2, or U3/Volkstheater.*

61 Fodor'sChoice ★ **Liechtenstein Museum.** For the first time since 1938, Palais Liechtenstein is again home to the Prince of Liechtenstein's fabulous private art collection, an accumulation so vast only a tenth of it is on display. Prince Karl I of Liechtenstein began collecting art back in the 17th century, with each of his descendents adding to the family treasure trove. The palace itself is a splendid example of Baroque architecture. While this was built up on the then-outskirts of the city, a mere "summer palace" was not grand enough for Prince Johann Adam Andreas I, who had already erected five other Liechtenstein palaces, including his family's gigantic Vienna "winter palace" on the Bankgasse. He instead commissioned a full-blown town palace from plans drawn up by Domenicio Martinelli. A Marble Hall, grand staircases, impressive stucco work by Santino Bussi (who was paid with forty buckets of wine in addition to a tidy sum), and sump-

tuous ceiling frescoes by Marcantonio Franceschini and Andrea Pozzo made this a residence fitting for one of the J. Paul Gettys of his day. Surrounding the palace was a great swampland soon dubbed "Lichtenthal" when it was transformed into a magnificent baroque-style garden; today, it has been restored along the lines of an English landscape park with baroque statues and topiaries.

The pride of the museum is the Peter Paul Rubens Room, showcasing the tremendous Decius Mus cycle, which illustrates episodes from the life of the heroic ancient Roman consul who waged a war against the Latins. The grandest picture of the eight-painting cycle illustrates the death of the consul and it is high drama, indeed: Decius Mus gazes up to heaven as he falls off his massive grey steed as a lance pierces his throat in the middle of a pitched battle. All these paintings were made as models for a tapestry series, which is why Rubens' panels are so enormous. There are other Rubens gems here, including one of his best children's portraits, that of his daughter, *Clara Serena Rubens*. It's easy to spend the greater part of a day here. Behind the palace is the exquisite landscaped park—after wandering through the museum, stroll through the prince's shaded gardens. Even better, try to book a table at Ruben's Palais, the important new restaurant masterminded by top chef Ruben Brunhart. ⊠ *Fürstengasse 1, 9th District/Alsergrund* ☎ *01/319–6757–0* ⊕ *www.liechtensteinmuseum.at* 🎫 *€10* ⊙ *Wed.–Mon. 9–8* Ⓤ *Bus: 40A/Bauernfeldplatz, Tram: D/Bauernfeldplatz.*

Ⓒ 🔢 **MuseumsQuartier.** (Museum Quarter). New and old, past and present,
FodorśChoice Baroque and Modernism dazzlingly collide in this headline-making,
★ vast culture center, newly opened in 2001. Claiming to be the largest of its kind in the world, the MuseumsQuartier—or **MQ** as many now call it—is housed in what was once the Imperial Court Stables, the 250-year-old Baroque complex designed by Fischer von Erlach and ideally situated in the heart of the city, near the Hofburg and set, appropriately, between the great Old Master treasures of the Kunsthistorisches Museum and the Spittelberg neighborhood, today one of Vienna's hippest enclaves. Where once 900 Lipizzaner horses were housed, now thousands of artistic masterworks of the 20th century and beyond are exhibited, all in a complex that is architecturally an expert and subtle blending of historic and cutting-edge—the original structure (fetchingly adorned with pastry-white stuccoed ceilings and rococo flourishes) was retained, while ultra-modern wings were added to house five museums, most of which showcase modern art at its best. Once ensconced in the Palais Liechtenstein, the **Leopold Museum** comprises the holdings amassed by Rudolf and Elizabeth Leopold and famously contains one of the greatest collections of Egon Schiele in the world, as well as impressive works by Gustav Klimt and Oskar Kokoschka. Other artists worth noting are Josef Dobrowsky, Anton Faistauer, and Richard Gerstl. Emil Jakob Schindler's landscapes are well-represented, as are those by Biedermeier artist Ferdinand Georg Waldmüller. Center stage is held by Schiele (1890–1918), who died young, along with his wife and young baby, in one of Vienna's worst Spanish flu epidemics. His colorful, appealing landscapes are here, but all eyes are invariably drawn to the artist's

THE "NEUE" CITY

ONE MORNING IN 1911 *the revered and bewhiskered Emperor Franz Josef, starting out on a morning drive in his carriage from the Hofburg, opened his eyes in amazement as he beheld the defiantly plain Looshaus, constructed just opposite the Michaelerplatz entrance to the imperial palace. Never again, it was said, did the royal carriage ever use the route, so offensive was this modernist building to His Imperial Highness. One can, then, only imagine the Josefian reaction to the Neues Haas-Haus, built in 1985 on Vienna's Stephansplatz. Here, across from the Gothic cathedral of St. Stephen's, famed architect Hans Hollein has designed a shopping and restaurant complex whose elegant curved surfaces and reflecting glass interact beautifully—critics now unanimously agree—with its environment. It proves an intelligent alternative to the demands of historicism on one hand and aggressive modernism on the other.*

This balancing act has always been a particular challenge in Vienna. For a few critics, the Gaudiesque eccentricities of the late Friedensreich Hundertwasser (besides the Kunsthaus museum by the Danube canal he is also responsible for the multicolored, golden globe-topped central heating tower that has become almost as much a part of the skyline as St. Stephen's spire) did the trick. But for all their charm, they have now been overshadowed by the Viennese modernism of today. Indeed, the current architectural scene is the most creative since the heyday of the Jugendstil master Otto Wagner. A generation of Austrian architects who tried out their ideas in small private and commercial commissions in the 1960s and '70s have now made their mark in a very public way, in part spurred on by the city's

expansion following the fall of the Iron Curtain in 1989.

If a single building can stand as the manifesto of the present revival, it would have to be the Neues Haas-Haus. But if it is the most prominent example of Vienna's new architecture, the vast MuseumsQuartier is by necessity the most discreet. Hidden behind the Baroque facade of the former imperial stables, the design by Laurids and Manfred Ortner uses its enclosed space to set up a counterpoint between Fischer von Erlach's riding school and the imposing new structures built to house the Leopold Museum and the Modern Art Museum. From the first, old and new collide: to enter the complex's Halle E + G, you pass below the Emperor's Loge, whose double-headed Imperial eagles now form a striking contrast to a silver-hued steel double staircase. Again, the modern buildings manage to complement the historical surroundings dynamically, breathing new life into a construction whose original purpose had long ago become obsolete. Other important projects—notably the new underground museum devoted to Jewish history on the Judenplatz (landmarked by a stark cube memorial by award-winning English sculptor Rachel Whitehead); the Gasometer complex, an entire planned community recycled from the immense brick drums of the 19th-century gasworks to the east of the city; and ecologically responsible Donau City—are among the architectural landmarks on tours now organized by the Architecture Center (AZW) of the MuseumsQuartier; their maps and brochures can be used for self-guided tours.

— Gary Dodson

tortured and racked depictions of nude mistresses, orgiastic self-portraits, and provocatively sexual couples, all elbows and organs.

Adjacent, in a broodingly modernistic, dark stone edifice, is the **Museum moderner Kunst Stiftung Ludwig (MUMOK)**, or Modern of Modern Art, which houses the national collection of 20th-century art on eight floors, mainly a bequest of Herr Ludwig, a billionaire industrialist who collected the cream of the cream of 20th-century art. Top works here are of the American Pop Art school, but all the trends of the last century—Nouveau Réalisme, Radical Realism, and Hyperrealism of the '60s and '70s, Fluxus, Viennese Actionism, Conceptual Art and Minimal Art, Land Art and Arte Povera, as well as installation art vie for your attention. Names run from René Magritte and Max Ernst to Andy Warhol, Jackson Pollock, Cy Twombly, Nam June Paik, and the very latest superstars of contemporary art, such as Chris Burden (whose installation was of $1 million worth of gold ingots) and Kara Walker's daringly revisionist silhouettes. Kids will make a beeline for Claes Oldenburg's walk-in sculpture in the shape of Mickey Mouse.

Nearby, the **Kunsthalle** is used for temporary exhibitions—gigantic halls used for the installation of avant-avant-garde art. The emphasis is on the ethos of "temporariness," so these halls are used to show off myriad works of contemporary art in an ever-changing schedule of installations and happenings—one recent exposition was called "Scandal and Myth," so you can take it from there. A definite change of pace is offered by the **ZOOM Kinder Museum,** which caters to children. In the ZOOM lab, kids age 7 and up can experience the fine line between the real and virtual world, making their imagined screenplays come to life by becoming directors, sound technicians, authors, and actors. For the little ones there's the ZOOM Ozean (ocean), where with their parents they can enter a play area inhabited by magical creatures from the underwater world, featuring a ship with a captain's quarters and lighthouse. It's probably a good idea to reserve tickets in advance for this museum. The **Architekturzentrum** (Architecture Center) displays new architecture models, with computers showing the latest techniques used in restoring old buildings. And the often overlooked **Tabak Museum** (Tobacco Museum) has a fascinating collection of elaborate snuff boxes and pipes.

The **Quartier21** showcase up-and-coming artists and musicians in the huge Fischer von Erlach wing facing the Museumsplatz. Artists will have their own studios, open to the public for free, and at the end of two years their output will be judged by a panel of visiting museum curators who will decide—*Survivor*-fashion?—if they should be invited to remain another two years. In addition to all this, the annual Wiener Festwochen (theater-arts festival) and the International Tanzwochen (dance festival) are held every year in the former Winter Riding Hall, and a theater for the annual Viennale Film Festival is planned. All in all, modern-art lovers will find it very easy to spend the entire day at MuseumsQuartier (even that may not be enough), and with several cafés, restaurants, gift shops, and bookstores, they won't need to venture outside. ⊠ *Museumsplatz 1–5, 7th District/Neubau* ☎ *01/523–5881, 01/*

524–7908 ZOOM Kinder Museum ⊕ *www.mqw.at; www.kindermuseum.at* ✉ *Leopold Museum €9; Kunst Stiftung Ludwig €8; Kunsthalle €6.50; Architekturzentrum €5; ZOOM Kindermuseum €5; ZOOM Ozean €4, including one companion for this only; combination ticket to all museums €25* ⊙ *Open daily 10–7* Ⓤ *U2 MuseumsQuartier/U2 or U3/Volkstheater.*

🄐 **Naturhistorisches Museum** (Natural History Museum). The palatial, archetypally "Ringstrasse" 19th-century museum complex just outside the Ring has two elements—to the east is the celebrated Kunsthistorisches Museum, to the west is the Naturhistorisches Museum, or Natural History Museum. This is the home of, among other artifacts, the famous Venus of Willendorf, a tiny statuette (actually, replica—the original is in a vault) thought to be some 20,000 years old; this symbol of the Stone Age was originally unearthed in the Wachau Valley, not far from Melk. The reconstructed dinosaur skeletons understandably draw the greatest attention. ✉ *Maria-Theresien-Platz, 7th District/Neubau* 🕿 *01/521-77-0* ✉ *€3.60* ⊙ *Wed. 9–9, Thurs.–Mon. 9–6:30* Ⓤ *U2 or U3/Volkstheater.*

🄑 **Parlament.** This sprawling building reminiscent of an ancient Greek temple is the seat of Austria's elected representative assembly. An embracing, heroic ramp on either side of the main structure is lined with carved marble figures of ancient Greek and Roman historians. Its centerpiece is the **Pallas-Athene-Brunnen** (fountain), designed by Theophil Hansen, which is crowned by the goddess of wisdom and surrounded by water nymphs symbolizing the executive and legislative powers governing the country. ✉ *Dr. Karl-Renner-Ring 1, 1st District* 🕿 *01/401-110-2570* ⊕ *www.parlament.gv.at* ✉ *€3* ⊙ *Tours mid-Sept.–June, Mon., Wed. 10 and 11, Tues., Thurs. 2 and 3, Fri. 11, 1, 2, and 3 (except on days when Parliament is in session); July–mid-Sept., Mon.–Fri. 9, 10, 11, 1, 2, and 3* Ⓤ *Tram: 1, 2, or D/Stadiongasse, Parlament.*

🄒 **Rathaus** (City Hall). Designed by Friedrich Schmidt and resembling a Gothic fantasy castle with its many spires and turrets, the Rathaus was actually built between 1872 and 1883. The facade holds a lavish display of standard-bearers brandishing the coats of arms of the city of Vienna and the monarchy. Guided tours include the banqueting hall and various committee rooms. A regally landscaped park graces the front of the building and it is usually brimming with activity. In winter it is the scene of the *Christkindlmarkt*, the most famous Christmas market in Vienna; in summer, concerts are performed here. ✉ *Rathausplatz 1, 1st District* 🕿 *01/5255-0* ✉ *Free* ⊙ *Guided tours Mon., Wed., Fri., at 1. Five person minimum* Ⓤ *Tram: 1, 2, or D/Rathaus.*

Ringstrasse. Late in 1857, Emperor Franz Josef issued a decree announcing the most ambitious piece of urban redevelopment Vienna had ever seen. The inner city's centuries-old walls were to be torn down, and the *glacis*—the wide expanse of open field that acted as a protective buffer between inner city and outer suburbs—was to be filled in. In their place was to rise a wide, tree-lined boulevard, upon which would stand an imposing collection of new buildings that would reflect Vienna's special status as the political, economic, and cultural heart of the Austro-Hungarian Empire. During the 50 years of building that followed, many factors combined to produce the Ringstrasse as it now stands, but the most important was the gradual rise of liberalism after the failed Revolution of 1848. By the latter half of the Ringstrasse era, support for constitutional government, democracy, and equality—all the concepts that liberalism traditionally equates with progress—was steadily increasing. As the Ringstrasse went up, it became the definitive symbol of this liberal progress; as Carl E. Schorske put it in his *Fin-de-Siècle Vienna*, it celebrated "the triumph of constitutional *Recht* (right) over imperial *Macht* (might), of secular culture over religious faith. Not palaces, garrisons, and churches, but centers of constitutional government and higher culture dominated the Ring."

The highest concentration of public building is found in the area around the Volksgarten, where are clustered (moving from south to north, from Burgring to Schottenring) the **Kunsthistorisches Museum,** the **Naturhistorisches Museum,** the **Justizpalast** (Central Law Courts), the **Parliament,** the **Rathaus** (City Hall), the **Burgtheater** (National Theater), the **Universität** (University of Vienna), the **Votivkirche** (Votive Church), and slightly farther along, the **Börse** (Stock Exchange) on Schottenring (for most of these sights, see either *above* or *below*). As an ensemble, the collection is astonishing in its architectural presumption: it is nothing less than an attempt to assimilate and summarize the entire architectural history of Europe. As critics were quick to notice, however, the complex suffers from a serious organizational flaw: most of the buildings lack effective context. Rather than being the focal points of an organized overall plan, they are plunked haphazardly down on an avenue that is itself too wide to present a unified, visually comprehensible character.

To some the monumentality of the Ringstrasse is overbearing; others find the architectural panorama exhilarating, and growth of the trees over 100 years has served to put the buildings into a different perspective. There is no question but that the tree-lined boulevard with its broad sidewalks gives the city a unique ribbon of green and certainly the distinction that the emperor sought. ⊠ *1st, 7th Districts* Ⓤ *U2 or U3/Volkstheater, U2/MuseumsQuartier, U3/Volkstheater, U2/Schottentor; Tram: 1, 2, and D/Burgtheater, Rathaus.*

㉓ **Spittelberg Quarter.** People like to come to the Spittelberg because it's a
FodorśChoice slice of Old Vienna, a perfectly preserved little enclave that allows you
★ to experience the 18th century by strolling along cobblestone pedestrian streets lined with pretty Baroque town houses. As such, the quarter—situated one block northwest of Maria-Theresien-Platz off the Burggasse—offers a fair visual idea of the Vienna that existed outside of the city walls a century ago. Most buildings have been replaced, but the engaging 18th-century survivors at Burggasse 11 and 13 are adorned with religious and secular decorative sculpture, the latter with a niche statue of St. Joseph, the former with cherubic work-and-play bas-reliefs. For several blocks around—walk down Gutenberggasse and back up Spittelberggasse—the 18th-century houses have been beautifully restored. The sequence from

A HOP THROUGH HIP VIENNA

PARIS HAS THE LATIN QUARTER AND LONDON HAS NOTTING HILL, *but until recently, Vienna didn't have the Bohemian district it always longed for. Now, the* **Freihaus** *sector makes its claim as Vienna's trendiest neighborhood. In the 17th-century, this enclave, within what is now the 4th District (Wieden), provided free housing to the city's poor, hence its name "Freihaus" or Free House. Destroyed in the Turkish siege of 1683, the complex was rebuilt on a much larger scale, becoming arguably the largest housing project in Europe at that time. It was a city within a city, including shops and even the old Theater auf der Wieden, in which Mozart's "The Magic Flute" premiered. A slow decline followed, spanning Franz Josef's reign from the mid-19th century to the early 20th century, with some of it being razed to the ground before WWI. During WWII, bombing raids practically finished it off. But then in the late 1990s a group of savvy local merchants decided to bring Freihaus back to life. With some government assistance, but mostly through their own panache, they revitalized the area, opening funky art galleries, antiques shops, espresso bars, trendy restaurants, fashion boutiques, and the city's coolest video and DVD store, Alphaville. Freihaus is quite small, stretching from Karlsplatz to Kettenbrückengasse, which encompasses part of the Naschmarkt, the city's largest open air market. To best experience Freihaus and all it has to offer, take time to stroll along two of its most fascinating streets, Operngasse and Schleifmühlgasse. For an advance preview, check out ⊕ www.freihausviertel.at.*

What do you do with four immense gasometers over 100 years old? Turn them into a cool, urban complex combining living and shopping, that's what. Looming large on the Vienna horizon, the gigantic complex known as the **Gasometer** *(⊕ www.gasometer.org) has generated a lot of publicity. Just to give an idea of their size, Vienna's giant Ferris wheel (the Riesenrad) at the Prater Amusement Park, would fit easily inside each one. Top architects were hired to accomplish the sleek and modern interior renovations, and today the former gasworks contain over 600 modern apartments and a huge shopping mall with movie theaters and restaurants. It's located in Simmering, Vienna's 11th District, and is just 8 minutes from the heart of the city on the U3 subway.*

A visit to Vienna during the summer months would not be complete without a few hours spent on the Donauinsel (Danube Island), more popularly known as the **Copa Kagrana.** *("Kagrana" is taken from the name of the nearby local area known as "Kagran.") It was originally built as a safeguard against flooding, but now this 13-square-mi island is where the Viennese head for bicycling, skateboarding, jogging, swimming, or just a leisurely stroll and dinner by the water. There are dozens of stalls and restaurants to choose from, offering grilled steaks, fried chicken, or freshly caught fish to go along with a mug of ice cold draft beer or Austrian wine. Every year for three days in June, an admission-free summer festival, the Donaufest (⊕ www.donauinselfest.at) is held. Billed as Europe's largest outdoor party, two million visitors converge on the island to listen to bands ranging from pop, rock, and hip hop to country and western— or if you'd prefer, you can make your own musical debut on a karaoke stage. Entertainment is also offered for kids, including an old-fashioned merry-go-round and sports activities. The Copa Kagrana can be reached by subway: either the U1 to Donauinsel or the U6 to Handelskai.*

Spittelberggasse 5 to 19 is an especially fine array of Viennese plain and fancy. Around holiday times, particularly Easter and Christmas, the Spittelberg quarter, known for arts and handicrafts, hosts seasonal markets offering unusual and interesting wares. Promenaders will be able to also enjoy some art galleries and loads of restaurants. ✉ *Off Burggasse, 7th District/Spittelberg* Ⓤ *U2 or U3/Volkstheater.*

> **off the beaten path**

KAISERLICHES HOFMOBILIENDEPOT (IMPERIAL FURNITURE MUSEUM) – In the days of the Habsburg empire, palaces remained practically empty if the ruling family was not in residence. Cavalcades laden with enough furniture to fill a palace would set out in anticipation of a change of scene, while another caravan accompanied the royal party, carrying everything from traveling thrones to velvet-lined portable toilets. Much of this furniture is now on display here, allowing you a fascinating glimpse into everyday court life. The upper floors contain recreated rooms from the Biedermeier to the Jugendstil periods, and document the tradition of furniture-making in Vienna. Explanations are in German and English. ✉ *Mariahilferstrasse 88/ entrance on Andreasgasse, 7th District/Neubau* ☎ *01/524–3357–0* 💶 *€6.90* ⊙ *Tues.–Sun. 9–5* Ⓤ *U3 Zieglergasse/follow signs to Otto-Bauer-Gasse/exit Andreasgasse.*

⑤⑧ Universität (University of Vienna). After the one in Prague, Vienna's is the oldest university in the German-speaking world. The main section of the university is a massive block in Italian Renaissance style designed by Heinrich Ferstel and built between 1873 and 1884. Thirty-eight statues representing important men of letters decorate the front of the building, while the rear, which encompasses the library (with nearly 2 million volumes), is adorned with *sgraffito*. ✉ *Dr.-Karl-Lueger-Ring/ Universitätstrasse, 1st District* Ⓤ *U2/Schottentor.*

⑤④ Volksgarten. Just opposite the Hofburg is a green oasis with a beautifully planted rose garden, a 19th-century Greek temple, and a rather wistful white marble monument to Empress Elisabeth—Franz Josef's Bavarian wife, who died of a dagger wound inflicted by an Italian anarchist in Geneva in 1898. If not overrun with latter-day hippies, these can offer appropriate spots to sit for a few minutes while contemplating Vienna's most ambitious piece of 19th-century city planning: the famous Ringstrasse. ✉ *Volksgarten, 1st District* Ⓤ *Tram: 1, 2, or D/ Rathausplatz, Burgtheater.*

⑤⑨ Votivkirche (Votive Church). When Emperor Franz Josef was a young man, he was strolling along the Mölker Bastei, now one of the few remaining portions of the old wall that once surrounded the city, when he was taken unawares and stabbed in the neck by an Italian tailor. The assassination attempt was unsuccessful, and in gratitude for his survival Franz Josef ordered that a church be built exactly at the spot he was gazing at when he was struck down. The neo-Gothic church was built of gray limestone with two openwork turrets between 1856 and 1879. ✉ *Rooseveltplatz, 9th District/Alsergrund* ☎ *01/406–1192* ⊙ *Tours by prior arrangement* Ⓤ *U2/Schottentor.*

MONARCHS & MOZART: FROM ST. STEPHAN'S TO THE OPERA HOUSE

The cramped, ancient quarter behind St. Stephan's Cathedral offers a fascinating contrast to the luxurious expanses of the Ringstrasse and more recent parts of Vienna. This was—and still is—concentrated residential territory in the heart of the city. Mozart lived here; later, Prince Eugene and others built elegant town palaces as the smaller buildings were replaced. Streets—now mostly reserved for pedestrians—are narrow, and tiny alleyways abound. Facades open into courtyards that once housed carriages and horses. The magnificent State Opera shares with St. Stephan's the honor of being one of the city's most familiar and beloved landmarks.

A Good Walk

To pass through these streets is to take a short journey through history and art. In the process—as you visit former haunts of Mozart, kings, and emperors—you can be easily impressed with a clear sense of how Vienna's glittering Habsburg centuries unfolded. Start from St. Stephan's Cathedral by walking down Singerstrasse to Blutgasse and turn left into the **Blutgasse District** ⑫—a neighborhood redolent of the 18th century. At the north end, in Domgasse, is the so-called **Figarohaus** ⑬, now a memorial museum, the house in which Wolfgang Amadeus Mozart lived when he wrote the opera *The Marriage of Figaro*. Follow Domgasse east to Grünangergasse, which will bring you to Franziskanerplatz and the Gothic-Renaissance Franziskanerkirche (Franciscan Church). Follow the ancient Ballgasse to Rauhensteingasse, turning left onto **Himmelpfortgasse**—Gates of Heaven Street. Prince Eugene of Savoy had his town palace here at No. 8, now the **Finanzministerium** ⑭, living here when he wasn't enjoying his other residence, the Belvedere Palace. Continue down Himmelpfortgasse to Seilerstätte to visit a museum devoted to the wonders of music, the **Haus der Musik** ⑮. Then turn into Annagasse with its beautiful houses, which brings you back to the main shopping street, **Kärnterstrasse,** where you can find everything from Austrian jade to the latest Jill Sander fashion turnouts. Turn left, walking north two blocks, and take the short Donnergasse to reach **Neuer Markt** square and the Providence Fountain. At the southwest corner of the square is the **Kaisergruft** ⑯ in the Kapuzinerkirche (Capuchin Church), the burial vault for rows of Habsburgs. Tegetthofstrasse south will bring you to Albertinaplatz, the square noted for the obvious war memorial and even more for the **Albertina Museum** ⑰, one of the world's great collections of Old Master drawings and prints. The southeast side of the square is bounded by the famous **Staatsoper** ⑱, the State Opera House; check for tour possibilities or, better, book tickets for a great *Rosenkavalier*. Celebrate with a regal time-out at the famed **Café Sacher** ⑲.

TIMING A simple walk of this route could take you a full half day, assuming you stop occasionally to survey the scene and take it all in. The restyled Figarohaus is worth a visit, and the Kaisergruft in the Kapuzinerkirche is impressive for its shadows of past glories, but there are crowds, and you may have to wait to get in; the best times are early morning and around lunchtime. Tours of the State Opera House take place in the afternoons;

check the schedule posted outside one of the doors on the arcaded Kärntnerstrasse side. Figure about an hour each for the various visits and tours.

Sights to See

★ ⑦ **Albertina Museum.** Home to some of the greatest Old Master drawings in Vienna—including Dürer's iconic *Praying Hands* and beloved *Alpine Hare*—this unassuming building contains the world's largest collection of drawings, sketches, engravings, and etchings. Partly built into Augustinerbastei—part of the original old city walls—and occupying the 17th-century Sylva-Tarouca palace, which is famed for its gilded Neoclassical rooms, the museum reopened in 2003 after a major renovation and new extension. In a seamless marvel of Baroque and modern styles, the Albertina now has an attached four-floor contemporary building designed by Austrian architects Steinmayer and Mascher. The core collection of nearly 65,000 drawings and almost a million prints was begun by the 18th-century Duke Albert of Saxon Teschen. All the legendary names are here, from Leonardo da Vinci, Michelangelo, Raphael, and Rembrandt on down. The mansion's glorious early-19th-century salons—all gilt-boiserie and mirrors—provide a jewelbox setting. An excellent in-house restaurant with an immense patio long enough for an empress's promenade offers splendid vistas of the historical center and the Burggarten—the perfect place to take a break for a meal. ⊠ *Augustinerstrasse 1, 1st District* ☎ *01/534–830* ☉ *Closed for renovation, scheduled to reopen Mar. 2003; check with tourist office for opening hours* Ⓤ *U3/Herrengasse.*

⑥ **Blutgasse District.** The small block bounded by Singerstrasse, Grünangergasse, and Blutgasse is known as the Blutgasse District. Nobody knows for certain how the gruesome name—*Blut* is German for "blood"—originated, although one legend has it that Knights Templar were slaughtered here when their order was abolished in 1312, although in later years the narrow street was known in those unpaved days as Mud Lane. Today the block is a splendid example of city renovation and restoration, with cafés, small shops, and galleries tucked into the corners. You can look inside the courtyards to see the open galleries that connect various apartments on the upper floors, the finest example being at Blutgasse 3. At the corner of Singerstrasse sits the 18th-century **Neupauer-Breuner Palace,** with its monumental entranceway and inventively delicate windows. Opposite at Singerstrasse 17 is the **Rottal Palace,** attributed to Hildebrandt, with its wealth of classical wall motifs. For contrast, turn up the narrow Blutgasse, with its simple 18th-century facades. ⊠ *1st District* Ⓤ *U1 or U3/Stephansplatz.*

⑥ **Café Sacher.** Popular with prominent Viennese and tourists alike since the Sacher Hotel opened in 1876, the Sacher Café is steeped in tradition, and though it's elegant and dignified, you don't need to wear a suit and tie to be admitted. Choose a table in either the formal café with its sparkling chandeliers and plush wine-red banquettes, the more modern Wintergarten, or the small outdoor café with its glimpse of the Opera and try to decide among an abundance of tempting pastries—though here, and only here, can you sample the original Sachertorte. After decades of court battles with their rival, Demel, the Sacher was finally granted the distinction of possessing the secret, original recipe for the densely rich chocolate cake. Order it with a generous dollop of *Schlag* (barely sweetened whipped cream) on the side, and a *Melange*, for a truly Viennese experience. There is live piano music every day from 4:30 to 7 PM. ⊠ *Philharmonikerstrasse 4, 1st District* ☎ *514–5666–1* ▤ *AE, DC, MC* ⊘ *Open daily, 8 AM–11:30 PM* Ⓤ *U1, U2, or U4/Karlsplatz.*

㊛ Figarohaus (Mozarthaus Vienna). One of Mozart's 11 rented Viennese residences, the Figarohaus has its entrance at Domgasse 5, on the tiny alley behind St. Stephan's (although the facade on Schulerstrasse is far more imposing). During the nearly three years Mozart lived in this house, he wrote dozens of piano concertos, as well as *The Marriage of Figaro,* and the six quartets dedicated to Joseph Haydn (who once called on Mozart here, saying to Leopold, Mozart's father, "your son is the greatest composer that I know in person or by name"). For two weeks in April 1787 Mozart taught a pupil who would become famous in his own right, the 16-year-old Beethoven. The apartment he occupied now contains a small commemorative museum—"created" by an architect more interested in graphic blandishment than a sense of history; you'll have to use your imagination to picture how Mozart lived here. ⊠ *Domgasse 5, 1st District* ☎ *01/513–6294* ▧ *€4* ⊘ *Tues.–Sun. 9–6* Ⓤ *U1 or U3/Stephansplatz.*

㊚ Finanzministerium (Ministry of Finance). The architectural jewel of Himmelpfortgasse, this imposing abode—designed by Fischer von Erlach in 1697 and later expanded by Hildebrandt—was originally the town palace of Prince Eugene of Savoy. As you study the Finanzministerium, you'll realize its Baroque details are among the most inventively conceived and beautifully executed in the city; all the decorative motifs are so softly carved that they appear to have been freshly squeezed from a pastry tube. The Viennese are lovers of the Baroque in both their architecture and their pastry, and here the two passions seem visibly merged. Such Baroque elegance may seem inappropriate for a finance ministry, but the contrast between place and purpose could hardly be more Viennese. ⊠ *Himmelpfortgasse 8, 1st District* Ⓤ *U1 or U3/ Stephansplatz.*

★ ☾ ㊛ Haus der Musik (House of Music). It would be easy to spend an entire day at this ultra-high-tech museum housed on several floors of an early-19th-century palace near Schwarzenbergplatz. Pride of place goes to the special rooms dedicated to each of the great Viennese composers—Haydn, Mozart, Beethoven, Strauss, and Mahler—complete with music samples and manuscripts. Other exhibits trace the evolution of sound (from primitive noises to the music of the masters) and illustrate the mechanics of the human ear (measure your own frequency threshold). There are also dozens of interactive computer games. You can even take a turn as conductor of the Vienna Philharmonic—the conductor's baton is hooked to a computer, which allows you to have full control of the computer-simulated orchestra. ⊠ *Seilerstätte 30, 1st District* ☎ *01/ 51648–51* ▧ *€8.50* ⊘ *Daily 10–10* ☾ *Restaurant, café* Ⓤ *U1, U2, or U4/Karlsplatz, then Tram D/Schwarzenbergplatz.*

need a
break?

Take a break at a landmark café in one of the most charming squares in Vienna, between Himmelpfortgasse and Singerstrasse. The **Kleines Cafe** (⊠ Franziskanerplatz 3, 1st District), open daily, is more for coffee, cocktails, and light snacks than for pastries, and few places are more delightful to sit in and relax on a warm afternoon or evening. In summer, tables are set outside on the intimate cobblestone square where the only sounds are the tinkling fountain and the occasional chiming of bells from the ancient Franciscan monastery next door. Before heading on, be sure to take a short stroll up Ballgasse, the tiny 18th-century street opposite the café.

Himmelpfortgasse. The maze of tiny streets including Ballgasse, Rauhensteingasse, and Himmelpfortgasse (literally, "Gates of Heaven Street") masterfully conjures up the Vienna of the 19th century. The most impressive house on the street is the Ministry of Finance. The back side of the Steffl department store on Rauhensteingasse now marks the site of the house in which Mozart died in 1791. There's a commemorative plaque that once identified the streetside site together with a small memorial corner devoted to Mozart memorabilia that can be found on the fifth floor of the store. ⊠ *1st District* Ⓤ *U1 or U3/Stephansplatz.*

66 **Kaisergruft** (Imperial Burial Vault). In the basement of the Kapuzinerkirche, or Capuchin Church (on the southwest corner of the Neuer Markt), is one of the more intriguing sights in Vienna: the Kaisergruft, or Imperial Burial Vault. The crypts contain the partial remains of some 140 Habsburgs (the hearts are in the Augustinerkirche and the entrails in St. Stephan's) plus one non-Habsburg governess ("She was always with us in life," said Maria Theresa, "why not in death?"). Perhaps starting with their tombs is the wrong way to approach the Habsburgs in Vienna, but it does give you a chance to get their names in sequence as they lie in rows, their coffins ranging from the simplest explosions of funerary conceit—with decorations of skulls and other morbid symbols—to the lovely and distinguished tomb of Maria Theresa and her husband. Designed while the couple still lived, their monument shows the empress in bed with her husband—awaking to the Last Judgment as if it were just another weekday morning, while the remains of her son (the ascetic Josef II) lie in a simple casket at the foot of the bed as if he were the family dog. ⊠ *Neuer Markt/Tegetthofstrasse 2, 1st District* ☎ *01/512–6853–12* 🎫 *€3.60* ⊙ *Daily 9:30–4* Ⓤ *U1, U3/Stephansplatz or U1, U4/Karlsplatz.*

Kärntnerstrasse. The Kärntnerstrasse remains Vienna's leading central shopping street. These days Kärntnerstrasse is much maligned. Too commercial, too crowded, too many tasteless signs, too much gaudy neon—the complaints go on and on. Nevertheless, when the daytime tourist crowds dissolve, the Viennese arrive regularly for their evening promenade, and it is easy to see why. Vulgar the street may be, but it is also alive and vital, with an energy that the more tasteful Graben and the impeccable Kohlmarkt lack. For the sightseer beginning to suffer from an excess of art history, classic buildings, and museums, a Kärntnerstrasse window-shopping respite will be welcome. ⊠ *1st District* Ⓤ *U1, U4/ Karlsplatz, or U1, U3/Stephansplatz.*

★ ⑥⑧ **Staatsoper** (State Opera House). The famous Vienna Staatsoper on the Ring vies with the cathedral for the honor of marking the emotional heart of the city—it is a focus for Viennese life and one of the chief symbols of resurgence after the cataclysm of World War II. Its directorship is one of the top jobs in Austria, almost as important as that of president, and one that comes in for even more public attention. Everyone thinks he or she could do it just as well, and since the huge salary comes out of taxes, they feel they have every right to criticize, often and loudly. The first of the Ringstrasse projects to be completed (in 1869), the opera house suffered disastrous bomb damage in the last days of World War II (only the outer walls, the front facade, and the main staircase area behind it survived). The auditorium is plain when compared to the red and gold eruptions of London's Covent Garden or some of the Italian opera houses, but it has an elegant individuality that shows to best advantage when the stage and auditorium are turned into a ballroom for the great Opera Ball.

The construction of the Opera House is the stuff of legend. When the foundation was laid, the plans for the Opernring were not yet complete, and in the end the avenue turned out to be several feet higher than originally planned. As a result, the Opera House lacked the commanding prospect that its architects, Eduard van der Nüll and August Sicard von Sicardsburg, had intended, and even Emperor Franz Josef pronounced the building a bit low to the ground. For the sensitive van der Nüll (and here the story becomes a bit suspect), failing his beloved emperor was the last straw. In disgrace and despair, he committed suicide. Sicardsburg died of grief shortly thereafter. And the emperor, horrified at the deaths his innocuous remark had caused, limited all his future artistic pronouncements to a single immutable formula: *"Es war sehr schön, es hat mich sehr gefreut"* ("It was very nice, it pleased me very much").

Renovation could not avoid a postwar look, for the cost of fully restoring the 19th-century interior was prohibitive. The original basic design was followed in the 1945–55 reconstruction, meaning that sight lines from some of the front boxes are poor at best. These disappointments hardly detract from the fact that this is one of the world's half-dozen greatest opera houses, and experiencing a performance here can be the highlight of a trip to Vienna. Tours of the Opera House are given regularly, but starting times vary according to opera rehearsals; the current schedule is posted at the east-side entrance under the arcade on the Kärntnerstrasse marked GUIDED TOURS, where the tours begin. Alongside under the arcade is an information office that also sells tickets to the main opera and the Volksoper. ✉ *Opernring 2, 1st District* ☎ *01/ 514–44–2613* 🎫 *€4* ☉ *Tours year-round when there are no rehearsals, but call for times* Ⓤ *U1, U2, or U4 Karlsplatz.*

POMP & CIRCUMSTANCE: SOUTH OF THE RING TO THE BELVEDERE

City planning in the late 1800s and early 1900s clearly was essential to manage the growth of the burgeoning imperial capital. The elegant Ringstrasse alone was not a sufficient showcase, and anyway, it focused on public rather than private buildings. The city fathers as well as private individuals commissioned the architect Otto Wagner to plan and undertake a series of projects. The area around Karlsplatz and the fascinating open food market remains a classic example of unified design. Not all of Wagner's concept for Karlsplatz was realized, but enough remains to be convincing and to convey the impression of what might have been. The unity concept predates Wagner's time in the former garden of Belvedere Palace, one of Europe's greatest architectural triumphs.

A Good Walk

The often overlooked **Akademie der bildenen Künste** ㊆, or Academy of Fine Arts, is an appropriate starting point for this walk, as it puts into perspective the artistic arguments taking place around the turn of the century. While the Academy represented the conservative viewpoint, a group of modernist revolutionaries broke away and founded the Secessionist movement, with its culmination in the gold-crowned **Secession Building** ㊐. Now housing changing exhibits and Gustav Klimt's provocative *Beethoven Frieze,* the museum stands appropriately close to the Academy; from the Academy, take Makartgasse south one block. The famous **Naschmarkt** ㊒ open food market starts diagonally south from the Secession; follow the rows of stalls southwest. Pay attention to the northwest side of the Linke Wienzeile, to the Theater an der Wien at the intersection with Millöckergasse (Mozart and Beethoven personally premiered some of their finest works at this opera house–theater) and to the **Otto Wagner Houses** ㊓. Head back north through the Naschmarkt; at the top end, cross Wiedner Hauptstrasse to your right into the park complex that forms Karlsplatz, creating a frame for the classic **Karlskirche** ㊔. Around **Karlsplatz,** note the Technical University on the south side, and the Otto Wagner subway station buildings on the north. Across Lothringer Strasse on the north side are the Künstlerhaus art exhibit hall and the Musikverein. The out-of-place and rather undistinguished modern building to the left of Karlskirche houses the worthwhile **Wien Museum Karlsplatz** ㊕. Cut through Symphonikerstrasse (a passageway through the modern complex) and take Brucknerstrasse to **Schwarzenbergplatz.** The Jugendstil edifice on your left is the French Embassy; ahead is the Russian War Memorial. On a rise behind the memorial sits Palais Schwarzenberg, a jewel of a onetime summer palace and now a luxury hotel. Follow Prinz-Eugen-Strasse up to the entrance of the **Belvedere Palace** ㊖ complex on your left. Besides the palace itself are other structures and, off to the east side, a remarkable botanical garden. After viewing the palace and the grounds, you can exit the complex from the lower building, Untere Belvedere, into Rennweg, which will steer you back to Schwarzenbergplatz.

TIMING The first part of this walk, taking in the Academy of Fine Arts and the Secession, plus the Naschmarkt and Karlsplatz, can be accomplished in an easy half day. The Museum of the City of Vienna is good for a couple of hours, more if you understand some German. Give the Belvedere Palace and grounds as much time as you can. Organized tours breeze in and out—without so much as a glance at the outstanding modern art museum—in a half hour or so, not even scratching the surface of this fascinating complex. If you can, budget up to a half day here, but plan to arrive fairly early in the morning or afternoon before the busloads descend. Bus tourists aren't taken to the Lower Belvedere, so you'll have that and the formal gardens to yourself.

Sights to See

70 **Akademie der bildenen Künste** (Academy of Fine Arts). If the teachers here had admitted Adolf Hitler as an art student in 1907 and 1908, instead of rejecting him, history may have proved very different. The Academy was founded in 1692, but the present Renaissance Revival building dates from the late 19th century. The idea was conservatism and traditional values, even in the face of a growing movement that scorned formal rules. The Academy includes a museum focusing on Old Masters. The collection is mainly of interest to specialists, but Hieronymus Bosch's famous *Last Judgment* triptych hangs here—an imaginative, if gruesome, speculation on the hereafter. ⊠ *Schillerplatz 3, 1st District* ☎ *01/588–16–225* 🖼 *€3.63* ⊙ *Tues.–Sun. 10–4* Ⓤ *U1, U2, or U4 Karlsplatz.*

off the
beaten
path

AM STEINHOF CHURCH – Otto Wagner's most exalted piece of Jugendstil architecture is not in the inner city but in the suburbs to the west: the Am Steinhof Church, designed in 1904 during his Secessionist phase. You can reach the church by taking the U4 subway line, which is adjacent to the Otto Wagner Houses. On the grounds of the Vienna City Psychiatric Hospital, Wagner's design unites mundane functional details (rounded edges on the pews to prevent injury to the patients and a slightly sloped tile floor to facilitate cleaning) with a soaring, airy dome and glittering Jugendstil decoration (stained glass by Koloman Moser). The church is open Saturdays at 3 for a guided tour (in German) for €4. English tours can be arranged in advance at €4 per person *if* it's a group of ten people. If there are only two of you, then you still must pay the total price for ten. You may come during the week to walk around the church on your own, but you must call first for an appointment. In 2003 the exterior of the church will be renovated, but it won't affect the guided tours of the interior. Renovations are planned for the interior in 2004, so check first to see if it's open before going. ⊠ *Baumgartner Höhe 1, 13th District/ Hütteldorf* ☎ *01/91060–11–204* 🖼 *Free* ⊙ *Sat. 3–4* Ⓤ *U4/Unter- St.-Veit, then Bus 47A to Psychiatrisches Krankenhaus; or U2/ Volkstheater, then Bus 48A.*

76 **Belvedere Palace (including the Österreichische Galerie).** One of the most

Fodor'sChoice splendid piece of Baroque architecture anywhere, the Belvedere Palace—

★ actually two imposing palaces separated by a 17th-century French-style garden parterre—is one of the masterpieces of architect Lucas von Hildebrandt. The palace is wedged between Rennweg (entry at No. 6A) and Prinz Eugen-Strasse (entry at No. 27). In fact the Belvedere is two palaces with extensive gardens between. Built outside the city fortifications between 1714 and 1722, the complex originally served as the summer palace of Prince Eugene of Savoy; much later it became the home of Archduke Franz Ferdinand, whose assassination in 1914 precipitated World War I. Though the lower palace is impressive in its own right, it is the much larger upper palace, used for state receptions, banquets, and balls, that is acknowledged as Hildebrandt's masterpiece. The usual tourist entrance for the Upper Belvedere is the gate on Prinz-Eugen-Strasse; for the Lower Belvedere, use the Rennweg gate—but for the most impressive view of the upper palace, approach it from the south garden closest to the South Rail Station. The upper palace displays a remarkable wealth of architectural invention in its facade, avoiding the main design problem common to all palaces because of their excessive size: monotony on the one hand and pomposity on the other. Hildebrandt's decorative manner here approaches the Rococo, that final style of the Baroque era when traditional classical motifs all but disappeared in a whirlwind of seductive asymmetric fancy. The main interiors of the palace go even further: columns are transformed into muscle-bound giants, pilasters grow torsos, capitals sprout great piles of symbolic imperial paraphernalia, and the ceilings are set aswirl with ornately molded stucco. The result is the finest Rococo interior in the city. On the garden level, you are greeted by the celebrated **Sala Terrena** whose massive Atlas figures shoulder the marble vaults of the ceiling and, it seems, the entire palace above. The next floor is centered around a gigantic Marble Hall, covered with trompe l'oeil frescoes, while down in the Lower Belvedere palace, there are more 17th-century salons, including the Grotesque Room painted by Jonas Drentwett and another Marble Hall (which really lives up to its name).

Today both the upper and lower palaces of the Belvedere are noted museums devoted to Austrian painting. The **Österreichisches Barockmuseum** (Austrian Museum of Baroque Art) in the lower palace at Rennweg 6a displays Austrian art of the 18th century (including the original figures from Georg Raphael Donner's Providence Fountain in the Neuer Markt)—and what better building to house it? Next to the Baroque Museum (outside the west end) is the converted Orangerie, devoted to works of the medieval period.

The main attraction in the upper palace's **Galerie des 19. und 20. Jahrhunders** (Gallery of the 19th and 20th Centuries) is the legendary collection of 19th- and 20th-century Austrian paintings, centering on the work of Vienna's three preeminent early-20th-century artists: Gustav Klimt, Egon Schiele, and Oskar Kokoschka. Klimt was the oldest, and by the time he helped found the Secession movement he had forged a highly idiosyncratic painting style that combined realistic and decorative elements in a way that was completely revolutionary. *The Kiss*—his greatest painting and one of the icons of modern art—is here on display. Schiele and Kokoschka went even further, rejecting the decorative appeal of Klimt's glittering abstract designs and producing works that completely ignored conventional ideas of beauty. Today they are considered the fathers of modern art in Vienna. Modern music, too, has roots in the Belvedere complex: the composer Anton Bruckner lived and died here in 1896 in a small garden house now marked by a commemorative plaque. ✉ *Prinz-Eugen-Strasse 27, 3rd District/Landstrasse* ☎ *01/795-57-134* 💶 *€7.50* 🕐 *Apr.–Oct., daily 10–6, Nov.–Mar., Tues.–Sun. 10–5* Ⓤ *U1, U2, or U4 Karlsplatz, then Tram D/Belvederegasse.*

★ ⑦ **Karlskirche.** Dominating the Karlsplatz is one of Vienna's greatest buildings, the Karlskirche, dedicated to St. Charles Borromeo. At first glance, the church seems like a fantastic vision—one blink and you half expect the building to vanish. For before you is a giant Baroque church framed by enormous freestanding columns, mates to Rome's famous Trajan's Column. These columns may be out of keeping with the building as a whole, but were conceived with at least two functions in mind: one was to portray scenes from the life of the patron saint, carved in imitation of Trajan's triumphs, and thus help to emphasize the imperial nature of the building; and the other was to symbolize the Pillars of Hercules, suggesting the right of the Habsburgs to their Spanish dominions, which the emperor had been forced to renounce. Whatever the reason, the end result is an architectural tour de force.

The Karlskirche was built in the early 18th century on what was then the bank of the River Wien and is now the southeast corner of the park complex. The church had its beginnings in a disaster. In 1713 Vienna was hit by a brutal plague outbreak, and Emperor Charles VI made a vow: if the plague abated, he would build a church dedicated to his namesake, St. Charles Borromeo, the 16th-century Italian bishop who was famous for his ministrations to Milanese plague victims. In 1715 construction began, using an ambitious design by Johann Bernhard Fischer von Erlach that combined architectural elements from ancient Greece (the columned entrance porch), ancient Rome (the Trajanesque columns), contemporary Rome (the Baroque dome), and contemporary Vienna (the Baroque towers at either end). When it was finished, the church received a decidedly mixed press. History, incidentally, delivered a negative verdict: in its day the Karlskirche spawned no imitations, and it went on to become one of European architecture's most famous curiosities. Notwithstanding, seen lit at night, the building is magical in its setting.

The main interior of the church utilizes only the area under the dome and is surprisingly conventional given the unorthodox facade. The space and architectural detailing are typical High Baroque; the fine vault frescoes, by J. M. Rottmayr, depict St. Charles Borromeo imploring the Holy Trinity to end the plague. ⊠ *Karlsplatz, 4th District/Wieden* ☎ *01/504–61–87* ⊙ *Daily 8–6* Ⓤ *U1, U2, or U4 Karlsplatz.*

Karlsplatz. Like the space now occupied by the Naschmarkt, Karlsplatz was formed when the River Wien was covered over at the turn of the century. At the time, Wagner expressed his frustration with the result—too large a space for a formal square and too small a space for an informal park—and the awkwardness is felt to this day. The buildings surrounding the Karlsplatz, however, are quite sure of themselves: the area is dominated by the classic **Karlskirche,** made less dramatic by the unfortunate reflecting pool with its Henry Moore sculpture, wholly out of place, in front. On the south side of the Resselpark, that part of Karlsplatz named for the inventor of the screw propeller for ships, stands the **Technical University** (1816–18). In a house that occupied the space closest to the church, Italian composer Antonio Vivaldi died in 1741; a plaque marks the spot. On the north side, across the heavily traveled roadway, are the **Künstlerhaus** (the exhibition hall in which the Secessionists refused to exhibit, built in 1881 and still in use) and the famed **Musikverein.** The latter, finished in 1869, is now home to the Vienna Philharmonic. The downstairs lobby and the two halls upstairs have been gloriously restored and glow with fresh gilding. The main hall has what may be the world's finest acoustics; this is the site of the annual, globally televised New Year's Day concert.

Some of Otto Wagner's finest Secessionist work can be seen two blocks east on the northern edge of Karlsplatz. In 1893 Wagner was appointed architectural supervisor of the new Vienna City Railway, and the matched pair of small pavilions he designed, the **Otto Wagner Stadtbahn Pavilions,** at No. 1 Karlsplatz, in 1898 are among the city's most ingratiating buildings. Their structural framework is frankly exposed (in keeping with Wagner's belief in architectural honesty), but they are also lovingly decorated (in keeping with the Viennese fondness for architectural finery). The result is Jugendstil at its very best, melding plain and fancy with grace and insouciance. The pavilion to the southwest is utilized as a small, specialized museum. In the course of redesigning Karlsplatz, it was Wagner, incidentally, who proposed moving the fruit and vegetable market to what is now the Naschmarkt. ⊠ *4th District/Wieden* Ⓤ *U1, U2, or U4/Karlsplatz.*

㊆ Naschmarkt. The area between Linke and Rechte Wienzeile has for 80 years been address to the Naschmarkt, Vienna's main outdoor produce market, certainly one of Europe's—if not the world's—great open-air markets, where packed rows of polished and stacked fruits and vegetables compete for visual appeal with braces of fresh pheasant in season; the nostrils, meanwhile, are accosted by spice fragrances redolent of Asia or the Middle East. It's open Monday to Saturday 6:30–6:30 (many stalls close two hours earlier in winter months). When making a purchase, be sure you get the correct change. ⊠ *Between the Linke and Rechte Wienzeile, 4th District/Wieden* Ⓤ *U1, U2, or U4 Karlsplatz (follow signs to Secession).*

> ## need a break?
> Who can explore the Naschmarkt, located just two blocks southeast of the Karlsplatz square, without picking up a snack? A host of Turkish stands offer tantalizing *Döner* sandwiches—thinly sliced lamb with onions and a yogurt sauce in a freshly baked roll. If you're in the mood for Italian *tramezzini*—crustless sandwiches filled with tuna and olives or buffalo mozzarella and tomato, there are a couple of huts to choose from on the Linke Wienzeile side about midway through the market. You can also have sushi and other fish snacks at the glass-enclosed seafood huts at the Karlsplatz end.

㊆ Otto Wagner Houses. The Ringstrasse-style apartment houses that line the Wienzeile are an attractive, if generally somewhat standard, lot, but two stand out: **Linke Wienzeile 38 and 40**—the latter better known as the "Majolica House"—designed (1898–99) by the grand old man of Viennese fin-de-siècle architecture, Otto Wagner, during his Secessionist phase. A good example of what Wagner was rebelling against can be seen next door, at **Linke Wienzeile 42,** where decorative enthusiasm has blossomed into Baroque Revival hysteria. Wagner had come to believe that this sort of display was nothing but empty pretense and sham; modern apartment houses, he wrote in his pioneering text *Modern Architecture,* are entirely different from 18th-century town palaces, and architects should not pretend otherwise. Accordingly, he banished classical decoration and introduced a new architectural simplicity, with flat exterior walls and plain, regular window treatments meant to reflect the orderly layout of the apartments behind them. There the simplicity ended. For exterior decoration, he turned to his younger Secessionist cohorts Joseph Olbrich and Koloman Moser, who designed the ornate Jugendstil patterns of red majolica-tile roses (No. 40) and gold stucco medallions (No. 38) that gloriously brighten the facades of the adjacent houses—so much so that their Baroque-period neighbor is ignored. The houses are privately owned. ⊠ *4th District/ Wieden* Ⓤ *U1, U2, or U4/Karlsplatz.*

Schwarzenbergplatz. A remarkable urban ensemble, the Schwarzenbergplatz comprises some notable sights. The center of the lower square off the Ring is marked by an oversize equestrian sculpture of Prince Schwarzenberg—he was a 19th-century field marshal for the imperial forces. Admire the overall effect of the square and see if you can guess which building is the newest; it's the one on the northeast corner (No. 3) at Lothringer Strasse, an exacting reproduction of a building destroyed by war damage in 1945 and dating only from the 1980s. The military monument occupying the south end of the square behind the fountain is the **Russian War Memorial,** set up at the end of World War II by the Soviets; the Viennese, remembering the Soviet occupation, call its unknown soldier the "unknown plunderer." South of the memorial is the stately **Schwarzenberg Palace,** designed as a summer residence by Johann Lukas von Hildebrandt in 1697, completed by Fischer von Erlach father and son, and now (in part) a luxury hotel. The delightful formal gardens wedged between Prinz Eugen-Strasse and the Belvedere gardens can be enjoyed from the hotel restaurant's veranda. ⊠ *Schwarzenbergplatz, 3rd District/Landstrasse* Ⓤ *Tram: Schwarzenbergplatz.*

★ ❼ **Secession Building.** If the Academy of Fine Arts represents the conservative attitude toward the arts in the late 1800s, then its antithesis can be found in the building immediately behind it to the southeast: the Secession Pavilion. Restored in the mid-1980s after years of neglect, the Secession building is one of Vienna's preeminent symbols of artistic rebellion. Rather than looking to the architecture of the past, like the revivalist Ringstrasse, it looked to a new antihistoricist future. It was, in its day, a riveting trumpet-blast of a building and is today considered by many to be Europe's first example of full-blown 20th-century architecture.

The Secession began in 1897, when 20 dissatisfied Viennese artists, headed by Gustav Klimt, "seceded" from the Künstlerhausgenossenschaft, the conservative artists' society associated with the Academy of Fine Arts. The movement promoted the radically new kind of art known as Jugendstil, which found its inspiration in both the organic, fluid designs of Art Nouveau and the related but more geometric designs of the English Arts and Crafts movement. (The Secessionists founded an Arts and Crafts workshop of their own, the famous Wiener Werkstätte, in an effort to embrace the applied arts.) The Secession building, designed by the architect Joseph Olbrich and completed in 1898, was the movement's exhibition hall. The lower story, crowned by the entrance motto *Der Zeit Ihre Kunst, Der Kunst Ihre Freiheit* ("To Every Age Its Art, To Art Its Freedom"), is classic Jugendstil: the restrained but assured decoration (by Koloman Moser) beautifully complements the facade's pristine flat expanses of cream-color wall. Above the entrance motto sits the building's most famous feature, the gilded openwork dome that the Viennese were quick to christen "the golden cabbage" (Olbrich wanted it to be seen as a dome of laurel, a subtle classical reference meant to celebrate the triumph of art). The plain white interior—"shining and chaste," in Olbrich's words—was also revolutionary; its most unusual feature was movable walls, allowing the galleries to be reshaped and redesigned for every show. One early show, in 1902, was an exhibition devoted to art celebrating the genius of Beethoven; Gustav Klimt's *Beethoven Frieze,* painted for the occasion, has now been restored and is permanently installed in the building's basement. ☒ *Friedrichstrasse 12, 4th District/Wieden* ☎ *01/587–5307–0* ⊕ *www.secession.at* ☒ *€4 exhibition, €5.50 exhibition with Beethoven Frieze, €1.50 guided tour* ⊙ *Tues.–Sun. 10–6, Thurs. 10–8, guided tours Sat. at 3 and Sun. at 11.*

❼❺ **Wien Museum Karlsplatz** (Museum of Viennese History). Housed in an incongruously modern building at the east end of the regal Karlsplatz, this museum possesses a dazzlement of Viennese historical artifacts and treasures: everything from 16th-century armor to great paintings by Schiele and Klimt and the preserved facade of Otto Wagner's *Die Zeit* offices. ☒*Karlsplatz, 4th District/Wieden* ☎*01/505–8747–0* ⊕*www.wienmuseum. at/94.htm* ☒ *€4* ⊙ *Tues.–Sun. 9–6* Ⓤ *U1, U2, or U4 Karlsplatz.*

off the
beaten
path

ZENTRALFRIEDHOF – Taking a streetcar out of Schwarzenbergplatz, music lovers will want to make a pilgrimage to the **Zentralfriedhof** (Central Cemetery), which contains the graves of most of Vienna's great composers: Ludwig van Beethoven, Franz Schubert, Johannes Brahms, the Johann Strausses (father and son), and Arnold Schönberg, among others. The monument to Wolfgang Amadeus Mozart is a memorial only; the approximate location of his unmarked grave can be seen at the now deconsecrated St. Marx-Friedhof at Leberstrasse 6–8. ☒ *Simmeringer Hauptstrasse, 11th District/Simmering* Ⓤ *Tram: 71 to St. Marxer Friedhof, or on to Zentralfriedhof Haupttor/2.*

SPLENDORS OF THE HABSBURGS: A VISIT TO SCHÖNBRUNN PALACE

The glories of imperial Austria are nowhere brought together more convincingly than in the Schönbrunn Palace (Schloss Schönbrunn) complex. Brilliant "Maria Theresa yellow"—she, in fact, caused Schöbrunn to be built—is everywhere in evidence. An impression of imperial elegance, interrupted only by tourist traffic, flows unbroken throughout the grounds. This is one of Austria's primary tourist sites, although sadly, few stay long enough to discover the real Schönbrunn (including the little maiden with the water jar, after whom the complex is named). While the assorted outbuildings might seem eclectic, they served as centers of entertainment when the court moved to Schönbrunn in the summer, accounting for the zoo, the priceless theater, the fake Roman ruins, the greenhouses, and the walkways. In Schönbrunn you step back three hundred years into the heart of a powerful and growing empire and follow it through to defeat and demise in 1917.

A Good Walk

The usual start for exploring the Schönbrunn complex is the main palace. There's nothing wrong with that approach, but as a variation, consider first climbing to the **Gloriette** ⑦ on the hill overlooking the site, for a bird's-eye view to put the rest in perspective (take the stairs to the Gloriette roof for the ultimate experience). While at the Gloriette, take a few steps west to discover the **Tiroler House** ⑱ and follow the zigzag path downhill to the palace; note the picture-book views of the main building through the woods. Try to take the full tour of **Schönbrunn Palace** ⑲ rather than the shorter, truncated version. Check whether the ground-floor back rooms (*Berglzimmer*) are open to viewing. After the palace guided tour, take your own walk around the grounds. The Schöner Brunnen, the namesake fountain, is hidden in the woods to the southeast; continue along to discover the convincing (but fake) Roman Ruins. At the other side of the complex to the west are the excellent **Tiergarten** ⑳ (zoo), and the **Palmenhaus** ㉛ (tropical greenhouse). Closer to the main entrance, both the **Wagenburg** ㉜ (carriage museum) and Schlosstheater (palace theater) are frequently overlooked treasures. Before heading back to the city center, visit the **Hofpavillon** ㉝, the private subway station built for Emperor Franz Josef, located to the west across Schönbrunner Schlossstrasse.

TIMING If you're really pressed for time, the shorter guided tour will give you a fleeting impression of the palace itself, but try to allot at least half a day to take the full tour and include the extra rooms and grounds as well. The 20-minute hike up to the Gloriette is a bit strenuous but worthwhile, and there's now a café as reward at the top. The zoo is worth as much time as you can spare, and figure on at least a half hour to an hour each for the other museums. Tour buses begin to unload for the main building about mid-morning; start early or utilize the noon lull to avoid the worst crowds. The other museums and buildings in the complex are far less crowded.

Sights to See

⑦ **Gloriette.** At the crest of the hill, topping off the Schönbrunn Schlosspark, sits a Baroque masterstroke: Johann Ferdinand von Hohenberg's incomparable Gloriette, now restored to its original splendor. Perfectly scaled, the Gloriette—a palatial pavilion that once offered royal guests a place to rest and relax on their tours of the palace grounds and that now houses an equally welcome café—holds the whole vast garden composition together and at the same time crowns the ensemble with

Gloriette **77**
Hofpavillon . . . **83**
Palmenhaus . . **81**
Schönbrunn
Palace **79**
Tiergarten **80**
Tiroler House . **78**
Wagenburg . . .**82**

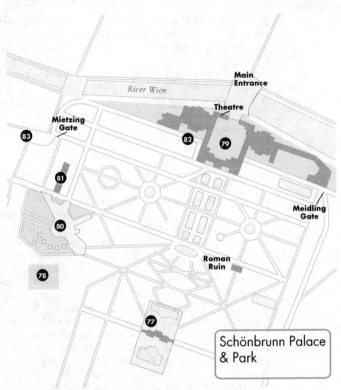

Schönbrunn Palace & Park

a brilliant architectural tiara. This was a favorite spot of Maria Theresa's, though in later years she grew so obese it took six men to carry her in her palanquin to the summit. ⊠ *13th District* Ⓤ *U4/Schönbrunn.*

83 Hofpavillon. The most unusual interior of the Schöbrunn Palace complex, the restored imperial subway station known as the Hofpavillon is just outside the palace grounds (at the northwest corner, a few yards east of the Hietzing subway station). Designed by Otto Wagner in conjunction with Joseph Olbrich and Leopold Bauer, the Hofpavillon was built in 1899 for the exclusive use of Emperor Franz Josef and his entourage. Exclusive it was: the emperor used the station only once. The exterior, with its proud architectural crown, is Wagner at his best, and the lustrous interior is one of the finest examples of Jugendstil decoration in the city. ⊠ *Schönbrunner Schloss-Strasse, next to Hietzing subway station, 13th District/Hietzing* ☎ *01/877–1571* ✉ *€2* ☉ *Sun. 11–12:30* Ⓤ *U4/Hietzing.*

81 Palmenhaus. On the grounds to the west of Schönbrunn Palace is a huge greenhouse filled with exotic trees and plants. ⊠ *Nearest entrance Hietzing, 13th District/Hietzing* ☎ *01/877–5087* ✉ *€3.50* ☉ *May–Sept., daily 9:30–6; Oct.–Apr., daily 9:30–5.*

79 **Schönbrunn Palace.** Designed by Johann Bernhard Fischer von Erlach in
Fodor'sChoice   1696, Schönbrunn Palace, the huge Habsburg summer residence, lies
★   well within the city limits, just a few subway stops west of Karlsplatz
on line U4. The vast and elegantly planted gardens are open daily from
dawn until dusk, and multilingual guided tours of the palace interior
are offered daily. A visit inside the palace is not included in most general city sightseeing tours, which offer either a mercilessly tempting drive
past or else an impossibly short half hour or so to explore. The four-
hour commercial sightseeing-bus tours of Schönbrunn offered by tour
operators cost several times what you'd pay if you tackled the easy excursion yourself; their advantage is that they get you there and back with
less effort. Go on your own if you want time to wander through the
magnificent grounds.

The most impressive approach to the palace and its gardens is through
the front gate, set on Schönbrunner Schloss-Strasse halfway between the
Schönbrunn and Hietzing subway stations. The vast main courtyard is
ruled by a formal design of impeccable order and rigorous symmetry:
wing nods at wing, facade mirrors facade, and every part stylistically
complements every other. The courtyard, however, turns out to be a mere
appetizer; the feast lies beyond. The breathtaking view that unfolds on
the other side of the palace is one of the finest set pieces in all Europe
and one of the supreme achievements of Baroque planning. Formal *al-
lées* (garden promenades) shoot off diagonally, the one on the right toward
the zoo, the one on the left toward a rock-mounted obelisk and a fine
false Roman ruin. But these, and the woods beyond, are merely a frame
for the astonishing composition in the center: the sculpted fountain; the
carefully planted screen of trees behind; the sudden, almost vertical rise
of the grass-covered hill beyond, with the **Gloriette** a fitting crown.

Within the palace, the magisterial state salons are quite up to the splendor of the gardens, but note the contrast between these chambers and
the far more modest rooms in which the rulers—particularly Franz
Josef—lived and spent most of their time. Of the 1,400 rooms, 40 are
open to the public on the regular tour, of which two are of special note:
the Hall of Mirrors, where the six-year-old Mozart performed for Empress Maria Theresa in 1762 (and where he met six-year-old Marie Antoinette for the first time, developing a little crush on her), and the Grand
Gallery, where the Congress of Vienna (1815) danced at night after carving up Napoléon's collapsed empire during the day. Ask about viewing
the ground-floor living quarters (*Berglzimmer*), where the walls are fascinatingly painted with palm trees, exotic animals, and tropical views.
As you go through the palace, glance occasionally out the windows; you'll
be rewarded by a better impression of the beautiful patterns of the formal gardens, punctuated by hedgerows and fountains. These window
vistas were enjoyed by rulers from Maria Theresa and Napoléon to Franz
Josef. ☒ *Schönbrunner-Schloss-Strasse, 13th District/Hietzing* ☎ *01/
81113–239* ⊕ *www.schoenbrunn.at* ✉ *Guided grand tour of palace interior (40 rooms) €13, self-guided tour €10.50* ☉ *Apr.–June and
Sept.–Oct., daily 8:30–5; July–Aug., daily 8:30–6; Nov.–Mar., daily
8:30–4:30* Ⓤ *U4/Schönbrunn.*

Schönbrunn Schlosspark (Palace Park). The palace grounds entice with a bevy of splendid divertissements, including a grand zoo (the Tiergarten) and a carriage museum (the Wagenburg). Climb to the Gloriette for a panoramic view out over the city as well as of the palace complex. If you're exploring on your own, seek out the intriguing Roman ruin, now used as a backdrop for outdoor summer opera. The marble *schöner Brunnen* ("beautiful fountain"), with the young girl pouring water from an urn, is nearby. The fountain gave its name to the palace complex. ⊠ *Schönbrunner Schlosspark, 13th District/Hietzing* ⊕ *www. schoenbrunn.at* ⊘ *Apr.–Oct., daily 6 AM–dusk; Nov.–Mar., daily 6:30 AM–dusk* Ⓤ *U4/Schönbrunn.*

Ⓒ ⑧⓪ **Tiergarten.** Claimed to be the world's oldest, the Tiergarten zoo has retained its original Baroque decor and today has acquired world-class recognition under director Helmut Pechlaner. New settings have been created for both animals and public; in one case, the public looks out into a new, natural display area from one of the Baroque former animal houses. The zoo is constantly adding new attractions and undergoing renovations, so there's plenty to see. ⊠ *Schönbrunner Schlosspark, 13th District/Hietzing* ☎ *01/877–9294–0* ⊕ *www.zoovienna.at* 🖾 *€12; combination ticket with Palmenhaus €16* ⊘ *Nov.–Jan., daily 9–4:30; Feb., daily 9–5; Mar. and Oct., daily 9–5:30; Apr.–Sept., daily 9–6:30* Ⓤ *U4/Schönbrunn.*

⑦⑧ **Tiroler House.** This charming "Tyrolean-style" building to the west of the Gloriette was a favorite retreat of Empress Elisabeth; it now includes a small restaurant (open according to season and weather). ⊠ *Schönbrunner Schlosspark, 13th District/Hietzing* Ⓤ *U4/Schönbrunn.*

Ⓒ ⑧② **Wagenburg** (Carriage Museum). Most of the carriages are still roadworthy and, indeed, Schönbrunn dusted off the gilt-and-black royal funeral carriage that you see here for the burial ceremony of Empress Zita in 1989. ⊠ *Schönbrunner Schlosspark, 13th District/Hietzing* ☎ *01/877–3244* ⊕ *www.schoenbrunn.at* 🖾 *€4.50* ⊘ *Apr.–Oct., daily 9–6; Nov.–Mar., daily 10–4* Ⓤ *U4/Schönbrunn.*

---

off the beaten path

Ⓒ

TECHNISCHES MUSEUM – About a 10-minute walk from Schönbrunn Palace is Vienna's version of the Smithsonian, the **Technical Museum**, which provides a fascinating learning experience by tracing the evolution of industrial development over the past two centuries. On four floors you'll find actual locomotives from the 19th century, a Tin Lizzie, airplanes from the early days of flying, as well as examples of factory life, how electric lighting took the place of gas lamps, and how mountain highway tunnels are constructed. And, appropriate for such a music-loving city, a whole section is devoted to the work involved in creating different musical instruments. You can only marvel at man's ingenuity in designing the everyday things that we take for granted. ⊠ *Mariahilferstrasse 212, 14th District/Penzing* ☎ *01/899–9860–00* ⊕ *www.tmw.ac.at* 🖾 *€7* ⊘ *Mon.–Sat. 9–6, Thurs. 9–8, Sun. 10–6* Ⓤ *U3 or U6/Westbahnhof, then Tram 52 or 58/Penzingerstrasse.*

WHERE TO EAT

By Diane
Naar-Elphee

To appreciate how far the restaurant scene in Vienna has come in recent years, it helps to recall the way things used to be. Up until five years ago, Austria was still dining in the 19th century. Most dinners were a *mittel-europisch* sloshfest of *Schweinsbraten, Knoedel,* and *Kraut* (pork, cabbage, and dumplings). Bouillon soups were lacking in everything but the soup-cube taste. Starchy sauces seem to come straight from *Hunger*-y. And strudel desserts proved as heavy as a main course. Clearly, Austrian cuisine dated back to the *wurst* traditions of the imperial past. No one denies that such courtly delights as *Tafelspitz*—the blush-pink boiled beef famed as Emperor Franz Josef's favorite dish— is delicious, but most traditional carb-loaded, nap-inducing meals left you stuck to your seat like a suction pad. If you consumed a plate-filling Schnitzel and were able to eat anything after it, you were looked upon as a phenomenon—or an Austrian. A lighter, more nouvelle take on cuisine had difficulty making incursions because many meals were centered around *Rehrücken* (venison), served up in wine-cellar recipes of considerable—nay, medieval—antiquity.

Today, Austrian cuisine is far from Middle-Aged. It is now hip-hopping to a brand new beat. The marvel is that Vienna's dining scene is as lively, experimental, and as good as it is, thanks in part to changing epicurean tastes and a rising generation of chefs dedicated to taking the culinary heritage of the nation to a new phase of *Neu Wiener Küche* (New Vienna Cuisine). No longer tucked away in anonymous kitchens, cooks now create signature dishes that rocket them to fame; they earn fan clubs and host television shows. The Austrian chef has become a star, a phenomenon that has also been seen in the U.S., as witness New York's David Bouley and Hollywood's Wolfgang Puck. Back in Vienna, chefs want to delight an audience hungry for change. Schmaltzy schnitzels have been replaced by Styrian beef, while soggy *Nockerl* (small dumplings) are traded in for seasonal delights like Carinthian asparagus, Styrian wild garlic, or the common alpine-garden stinging nettle. The old Gulasch and Bratwurst have given way to true gustatory excitement. Thanks to their nouvelle touch, the new chefs have taken the starch—in both senses— out of Vienna's dining scene. But you can always find the time-honored standards of Wiener Küche at the famous *Beisln,* Vienna's answer to Paris's bistros and London's gastro-pubs. Be aware that the basket of bread put on your table is not free. Most of the older-style Viennese restaurants charge €0.80–€1.50 for each roll that is eaten, but more and more establishments are beginning to charge a per person cover charge—anywhere from €1.50 to €4—which includes all the bread you want, plus usually an herb spread and butter.

WHAT IT COSTS In euros				
$$$$	$$$	$$	$	¢
over €28	€23–€28	€17–€22	€10–€16	under €10

Prices are per person for a main course at dinner.

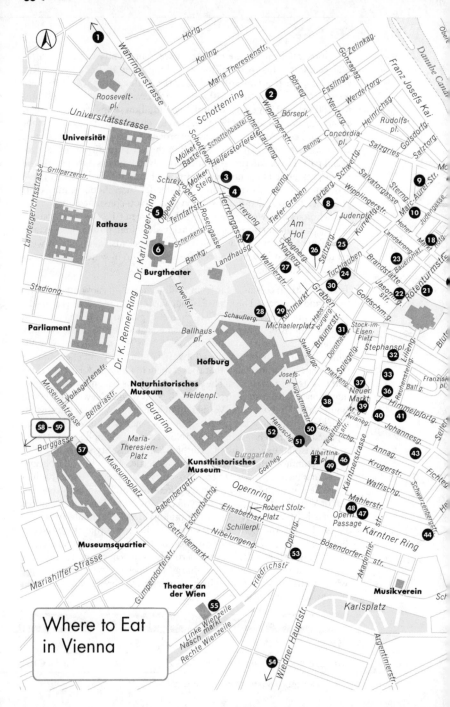

Where to Eat in Vienna

Restaurants ▼

Alt Wien	**16**
Anna Sacher	**49**
Beim Czaak	**15**
Bohème	**58**
Brezl Gwölb	**8**
Cantino	**43**
Coburg	**35**
Culinarium Österreich	**39**
DO & CO Albertina	**51**
DO & CO Stephansplatz	**22**
Fabios	**24**
Figlmüller	**19**
Gasthaus Puerstner	**34**
Gmoa Keller	**45**
Gösser Bierklinik	**25**
Griechenbeisl	**11**
Hansen	**2**
Julius Meinl am Graben	**30**
Korso	**48**
Lusthaus	**12**
Morwald im Ambassador	**40**
Palmenhaus	**53**
Reinthaler	**38**
Ruben's Palais	**1**
Salzgries	**9**
Spatzennest	**59**
Steirereck	**46**
Strandcafé	**13**
Tancredi	**55**
Theatercafe Wien	**56**
Una	**57**
Urania	**14**
Vestibül	**6**
Wrenkh	**23**
Zu den Drei Husaren	**32**
Zum Finsteren Stern	**10**
Zum Kuckuck	**41**
Zum Schwarzen Kameel	**26**

Munch-on-the-Run ▼

Bizi Pizza	**21**
Karlsplatz Mall	**47**
Meinl am Graben	**30**
Radatz	**3**
Würstelstand	**18**

Wine Taverns ▼

Augustinerkeller	**52**
Esterházykeller	**27**
Melker Stiftskeller	**4**
Zwölf-Apostelkeller	**17**

Cafés ▼

Café Central	**7**
Café Frauenhuber	**42**
Café Griensteidl	**28**
Café Hawelka	**31**
Café Landtmann	**5**
Café Mozart	**46**
Café Museum	**53**
Café Sacher	**49**
Café Schwarzenberg	**44**

Pastry Shops ▼

Demel	**29**
Gerstner	**33**
Heiner	**20, 36**
Oberlaa	**37**

Restaurants

$$$$ ✕ **Anna Sacher.** Sacher is a name that almost has as many reverberations as Strauss's: The legendary Sachertorte cake, the family saga that began with Franz Sacher, Prince von Metternich's pastry chef, and the famed 19th-century hotel that was opened by Franz's son and his wife, the redoubtable Anna, Vienna's "hostess with the mostess." Near this entrance to the hotel's main dining room, the Restaurant Anna Sacher, pay your respects to her oil portrait nearby—it reveals her formidable character and her weakness for cigars and bull dogs (shades of Churchill). Up until 2005, that is all you can pay, as this landmark restaurant is undergoing a refurbishment. When it reopens during that year, this showcase for "internationale und typische Wiener Küche" will hopefully still exude the monarchical magic of former glory: wainscotted oak walls, beige silk fabrics, gilt-framed oil paintings, and sparking chandeliers create a suitably aristo ambience. Adjacent is the Rote Bar, which may fulfill your fantasy of a Viennese red ambience of baroque-ed velvet and crystal luxury—a truly fitting spot for a pre- or post-theater dinner (the state opera house is a skip and jump away). Sacher offers one of the city's best Tafelspitz (boiled beef), garnished with creme spinach and hash brown potatoes, with chive creme sauce and apple horse-radish adding extra flavor to this favorite dish of Emperor Franz Josef. If you're not into that stiff discipline of regimental restaurant rules, then choose the more informal Sacher Café for your slice of the world's most famous chocolate sponge cake, the Sachertorte (even if you're calorie counting, you'll still want that dollop of *Schlag Obers* to enhance the chocolate and apricot jam). ⊠ *Philharmonikerstrasse 4, 1st District* ☎ *01/5145–6840* ⊕ *www.sacher.com* ⌲ *Reservations essential* 🏛 *Jacket and tie* ⊟ *AE, DC, MC, V* ⊘ *No lunch in Restaurant Anna Sacher* Ⓤ *U1, U2, or U4/Karlsplatz/Opera.*

$$$$ ✕ **Cantino.** After a visit to the Haus der Musik—Vienna's inspiring museum devoted to music—just take its glass elevator to the roof, climb the few stairs to the attic, and discover a wonderful new restaurant with a view overlooking the towers, roofs, and steeples of the city. Chef Richard Rainer's lemon risotto is unbeatable, while his *Bonito del Norte* (White Spanish Tuna) on rocket salad with lemon-olive oil dressing is a delight. Another winner is the pasta shells stuffed with essence of chanterelle—pure poetry. Wines are mainly home-grown Austrian, but there is also a fine array of Italian vintages. When you've tired of the view out of the enormous windows, study the historic prints and photos decorating the slanting ceiling to see if you can recognize any of the celebrated conductors and composers. ⊠ *Seilerstätte 30, 1st District* ☎ *01/512–54–46* ⊟ *AE, DC, MC, V* ⊘ *Closed Sun. evening* Ⓤ *U1 or U3/Stephansplatz.*

★ **$$$$** ✕ **Julius Meinl am Graben.** You might think you're in the wrong place when you arrive at Meinl, one of Vienna's best restaurants. Who goes to a *delikatessen* when dining out? This is no ordinary eatery, of course: Just a few doors down from the Hofburg Palace, Meinl opened as a caterer to the Habsburgs in 1862, and has remained Vienna's poshest grocery store ever since. But if you go straight down the aisle through the fruit and pastry sections, head upstairs past the cheese bar, and then turn the corner, you'll find a cozy salon, all deep orange banquettes and dark wood. The window tables have stunning views over the pedestrian crossroads of Graben/Kohlmarkt. The maestro in command is Joachim Gradwohl—opt for his lobster terrine and its side of lobster bisque (adorably served in an espresso cup), then go on to sizzling duck, carved tableside and served with roasted chestnuts and apple-studded *Rotkraut* (red cabbage). ⊠ *Graben 19 (entrance after 7 PM from outdoor elevator on Naglergasse), 1st District* ☎ *01/532–3334–99* ⌕ *Reservations essential* 🖃 *AE, DC, MC, V* ⊗ *Closed Sun.* Ⓤ *U3/Herrengasse.*

★ **$$$$** ✕ **Mörwald im Ambassador.** The sleek renovation of the century-old Ambassador Hotel brought with it this restaurant, now acclaimed as one of the very best places for eating out. Overlooking the famous Neuer Markt, one half of the restaurant is set in an elegant glassed-in "Wintergarten" with a lovely view of the square's Donnerbrunnen, the Baroque-era fountain. On the other side of the restaurant is the Schau Kueche (open kitchen), with dark wood floors, blue-green curtains, and inquisitive diners who can watch the cooks at work behind glass. You can't blame them because chef Christian Domschitz is now one of the best "new Austrian" chefs. His classic cuisine "with a twist" carries the day with his signature dishes, such as his famous Szegediner lobster and cabbage dish or his breast of pigeon with beans and olives. ⊠ *Kärntnerstrasse 22, 1st District* ☎ *01/96161161* ⌕ *Reservations essential* 🍽 *Jacket and tie* 🖃 *AE, DC, MC, V* Ⓤ *U1, U2, or U4/Karlsplatz/Opera.*

$$$$ ✕ **Steirereck.** Possibly the most raved-about restaurant in Austria, Steirereck completed its 2004 move to a location worthy of its status as a culinary temple: the former Milkhauspavilion, a grand Jugendstil-vintage "drinking hall" overlooking the Wienfluss promenade in the centrally located Stadtpark, the main city park on the Ringstrasse. You are first greeted by a huge, 20-foot-long rococo banqueting table, above which a video screen allows a preview peek into the famed kitchen. The dining room itself is *eine Fantasie,* with uniquely structured floors and ceilings styled to form the leaves from indigenous Styrian trees; if you want the real thing, opt for a table on the two terraces so you can enjoy the lushest of the Stadtpark's green landscapes. The main rooms are suitably impressive stages for longtime chef Helmut Österreicher, who has been voted Austria's chef of the year twice. Warm artichoke cocktail will be accompanied by caviar and artichoke cream, while crayfish is garnéed with basil bread and sweet organic cherry tomatoes. Styrian venison soars with sauteed *Eierschwammerl* (chanterelle) mushrooms. Other winners include delicate smoked catfish, turbot in an avocado crust, or char with mashed potatoes on a bed of white garlic sauce. Extra touches include a bread trolley overflowing with freshly baked breads and, at the end of the meal, an outstanding selection of cheeses from Steirereck's own cheese cellar. If you don't want the gala Steirereck experience, opt for a bite in the first-floor restaurant—a "milk hall" now given a 21st-century spin. This eaterie showcases the delights of dairy—from cheeses to curds and beyond—in a striking decor: The floor, hand-painted, resembles a huge slab of Roquefort, the arty furniture is in shades of milky

FodorsChoice ★

white, while the milk bar shimmers with a milky-glass wall. For a restaurant that is fully booked every night, the wait staff handles itself with a Benedictine calm. ⊠ *Im Stadtpark, 3rd District/Landstrasse* ☎ *01/713–3168* ⊕ *www.steirereck.at* ⚑ *Reservations essential* ▤ *AE, DC, MC, V* Ⓤ *U4/Stadtpark.*

★ **$$$–$$$$** ✕ **Coburg.** Just off the Ringstrasse, the massive Neoclassical Palais Coburg stands proud—or, rather, prouder than ever. Recently renovated to become the sleek and airy Hotel Coburg, this masterpiece of 19th-century architecture has also become home to top *chef de cuisine* Christian Petz, who offers delights in the dinner-only Restaurant Coburg, the Gartenpavilion (Garden Pavilion), for lunch, or the Basteibar (Bastion Bar), adjacent to 16th-century fortifications. Petz was Austria's Chef of the Year 2002, trained at Meinl am Graben, and has earned three Gault-Millau crowns. At dinner, you can savor his obsession with pure flavor and carefully chosen ingredients. Roasted breast of duck with artichoke puree, salmon trout tartare on savoy cabbage with almonds, goose liver on quince cabbage, or pheasant with roast apple, goose liver, and poppyseed polenta are just some of the extravaganzas that await. ⊠ *Coburgbastei 4, 1st District* ☎ *1/5181–8800* ⚑ *Reservations essential* ▤ *AE, DC, MC, V* Ⓤ *U3/Stubentor.*

$$$–$$$$ ✕ **Fabios.** The easiest way for Viennese to visit sleek, suave, power-dining New York—short of paying $800 for a round-trip ticket—is to book a table at this cool hot spot. If they can, that is. Exceedingly popular and wait-listed weeks in advance, this modernist extravaganza has brought a touch of big-city glamour to Alt Wien, and foodies to fashionistas love it. With soaring mirrored walls, towering black-leather banquettes, a levitating pine ceiling, and acres of wood floor so polished women can check their make-up in it, Fabios has a decor that is high dramas. Chef Christoph Brunnhuber has a truly sophisticated touch, as you'll see with his octopus carpaccio with paprika, crispy pork with orange pesto on fennel, or duckling breast on kumquat-Cassis-sauce with potato-olive puree. ⊠ *Tuchlauben 6, 1st District* ☎ *01/532–2222* ⊕ *www.fabios.at* ⚑ *Reservations essential* ▤ *AE, DC, MC, V* ☉ *Closed Sun.*

★ **$$$–$$$$** ✕ **Korso.** In the Bristol Hotel, just across from the Staatsoper (don't be surprised if you see Domingo at the next table), the Korso bei Der Oper has always been one of the great favorites of Vienna's posherie. Chef Reinhard Gerer is known throughout Austria for his creative touch, and the salons for such gastronomic excellence are appropriately delicious, with gleaming wood-paneled walls, beveled glass, tables set with fine linen, sparkling Riedel crystal, fresh flowers, and a massively baronial fireplace, complete with period columns. Fish is Gerer's specialty, and he prepares it in ways like no other chef in Vienna. Delicately fried *Rotbarsch* (rosefish) is paired with tiny, crispy fried parsley and the smoothest of pureed polenta, Salzkammergut lake trout is grilled and drizzled with a sensational shallot sauce, and *Saibling* (char) caviar is enhanced by organic olive oil. Service can be a little stiff and formal, but it goes with the surroundings. ⊠ *Mahlerstrasse 2, 1st District* ☎ *01/515–16–546* 🖷 *01/515–16–550* ⚑ *Reservations essential* 🎩 *Jacket and tie* ▤ *AE, DC, MC, V* ☉ *Closed 3 wks in Aug. No lunch Sat.* Ⓤ *U4/Karlsplatz.*

$$$–$$$$ ✕ **Ruben's Palais.** Once your aesthetic liver is crying for mercy after view-
Fodor'sChoice ing the incomparable Old Master paintings on view at the newly reopened
★ Palais Liechtenstein, wouldn't it be wonderful to enjoy a feast for the
tastebuds along with this feast for the eyes? Well, the Princes of Liecht-
enstein aim to please and have now opened this restaurant in their im-
maculately restored family palace. Having just seen the Decius Mus cycle
upstairs, you might think that the place's name refers to the great Peter
Paul Rubens canvases on view, but the honor goes to *chef de cuisine*
Ruben A. Brunhart, who himself looks like he stepped out of a 17th-
century portrait, with his amazingly long red beard (twisted into two
long thin threads). Brunhart's inspiration comes from the creations of
the great cook Escoffier, but he takes "classic" and "exclusive" into new
realms, as you can see with one taste of his dandelion omelette. For starters,
the grilled duck liver with rhubarb-coconut ragout is a sensation, as is
the terrine of green asparagus, mozzarella cheese, and smoked ham. The
restaurant setting is exquisite—nut-wood floors, dark walls, and beau-
tifully upholstered furniture. For a slightly cheaper take on Brunhart's
creations, repair to the museum's Ruben's Brasserie, which is set around
a chic bar. Both restaurants also feature wonderful alfresco dining on
the palace's Baroque Ehrenhof terrace. ⊠ *Fürstengasse 1, at the Palais
Liechtenstein, 9th District/Alsergrund* ☎ *01/3123–9613* ⊕ *www.rubens.
at* ⌨ *Reservations essential* ▤ *AE, DC, MC, V* ☉ *Closed Mon.–Tues.*
Ⓜ *U4/Friedensbruecke.*

$$$–$$$$ ✕ **Zu den Drei Husaren.** *Ou est les néiges d'antan?* Here, in the snowy
linen, table-topped time-warp of Vienna's oldest luxury restaurant. The
interior has the elegance of a mansion, the warmth of refined hospital-
ity, and the cuisine blends the many nostalgic flavors of the Habsburg
Empire. The clientele is also something of an old-fashioned imperial mix,
too. The "Three Hussars" was created by Lord Paul Pálffy and two other
soldierly noblemen who served together in World War I, decided to open
a restaurant together in 1933, and then made it the place for Viennese
society. The mâitre d' stands at attention at the end of a long, decorous
corridor made for showy entrances, ready to lead you to your table
through a series of sedate rooms accented in Biedermeier yellows and
dark greens. Having been renovated one too many times, the salons are
too shiny for some, but some of the old time-burnished charm remains
in the Library room, adorned with sculpted busts and leather-bound vol-
umes. If iconic presentations of Wiener Schnitzel and *Tafelspitz* (boiled
beef) don't tempt you, opt for such exotica as the pork-stew Serbian style,
"Baron Fodermayer." ⊠ *Weihburggasse 4, 1st District* ☎ *01/512–
1092–0* ☐ *01/512–1092–18* ⊕ *www.drei-husaren.at* ⌨ *Reservations
essential* ⌂ *Jacket and tie* ▤ *AE, DC, MC, V.*

$$$–$$$$ ✕ **Zum Schwarzen Kameel.** The Ladies Who Lunch love to shop and dine
at "the Black Camel," a foodie landmark 200 years ago, back when
Beethoven used to send his man-servant here to buy wine and ham. In
timeless Viennese fashion, this provisioner split into both a *delikatessen*
and a restaurant. You can use the former if you're in a hurry—the fab-
ulously fresh sandwiches are served at the counter. But if you want to
dine in elegance and intimacy then choose the glossy and gleaming
glass-and-brass Art Nouveau dining area just to the right of the entrance.

Let the head waiter do his number—he's the one with the Emperor Franz Josef beard—who, in almost perfect English, will rattle off the specials of the day. ⊠ *Bognergasse 5, 1st District* ☎ *01/533–8125* ⚲ *Reservations essential* 🖃 *AE, DC, MC, V* ☉ *Closed Sun.* Ⓤ *U3/Herrengasse.*

★ **$$–$$$** ✕ **DO & CO Stephansplatz.** For front-row seats for the medieval splendor of St. Stephan's Cathedral, the best perch in town is a window seat at this restaurant, set across the square atop the semi-circular glass-fronted Haas House. You have to head up to the seventh floor in this Hans Hollein–designed landmark but the reward is a gorgeously relaxing setting—all dark blue furniture, deep blue carpets, and those large windows featuring That View. Some couldn't care less about dining on Gothic and take a table instead bordering the open kitchen. Don't laugh—the food is very spiffy here. Cooks hurry about preparing everything from stir-fry wok dishes to carpaccio parmigiana to Tafelspitz. The locals know a good thing and continue to cram this place and overtip the pretty waitresses in their short black miniskirts. ⊠ *Stephansplatz 12, 1st District* ☎ *01/535–3969* ⊕ *www.doco.com* ⚲ *Reservations essential* 🖃 *V* Ⓜ *U1 or U3/Stephansplatz.*

$$–$$$ ✕ **Griechenbeisl.** Beethoven, Mozart, Schubert, and Gina Lollabrigida
Fodor'sChoice all dined here—so how can you resist? Neatly tucked away in a quiet
★ and quaint area of the old city, this ancient inn goes back half a millennium. You can hear its age in the creaking floor boards when you walk through some of the small dark-wood panelled rooms (don't forget to look into the cellar to see the mannequined figure of Augustine, the drunkard bagpipe player, who, according to legend, fell in a pit full of plague corpses, passed the night comfy and warm, and returned home the next day fit as a fiddle). An inn has been on this site since 1457, next to the glittering gold Greek Orthodox church, and its name refers to the many Levantine merchants who used to hang out here back when. Yes, it's historic and touristy yet the food, including all the classic hearty dishes like the goulash soup, Wiener Schnitzel, and *Apfelstrudel,* is as good as in many other Beisln. Savor, also, the Styrian wrought-iron chandeliers, the zither music (showcased in the Zitherstüberl room), and the time-stained ambience, most impressively on show in the high vaulted Karlsbader room, adorned with relics from the Bohemia spa of Carlsbad. The Mark Twain room has the famous walls and ceiling covered with signatures of the famed who have chowed down here—get the waiter to point out the most famous. ⊠ *Fleischmarkt 11, 1st District* ☎ *01/533–1941* ⊕ *www.griechenbeisl.at* 🖃 *AE, DC, MC, V* Ⓤ *U1 or U4/Schwedenplatz.*

$$–$$$ ✕ **Lusthaus.** When the sun is shining and the romance of Old Vienna beckons, why not splurge on a Fiaker carriage and take a trip back to the 19th century? Head to the Prater park, where, along the grand and imperial Hauptallee, you'll find a pleasure pavilion designed for Emperor Josef II by Isidore Canevale, now one of Vienna's most romantic restaurants. As you alight in princely fashion from your horse-drawn cab you'll climb the steps and enter a Baroque world of yesteryear. Octagonal in shape, with a fanciful roof, and elegant garden windows, the Lusthaus sparkles with crystal chandeliers, white stuccoed ceilings, fine white damask, silver cutlery, and candles. Recalling the 19th century (when the Habsburgs ruled Italy), the menu has one foot in Austria, the other in the Mediterranean. You can also head here in the afternoon for a high tea, replete with whipped-cream cakes. Champagne, anyone? ⊠ *Freudenau 254 on the Prater Hauptallee, 2nd District/Leopoldstadt* ☎ *01/728– 9565* ⊕ *www.lusthaus-wien.at* ⌕ *Reservations essential* ⊟ *DC, MC, V* ⊘ *Closed Wed.* Ⓤ *U3, 77/Lusthaus.*

★ $$–$$$ ✕ **Theatercafe Wien.** Up until recently, it was practically a scandal there were so few options for fine dining in the Mariahilf District. After all, it is home to not only Vienna's legendary Theater an der Wien but Olbrich's iconic Secession Pavilion, Otto Wagner's Majolikahaus, and Beethoven's residence. Historic ground, indeed. Now, not only is Beethoven's room being reconstructed, but eight new restaurants have opened up in the immediate area, including this spot, just next door to Vienna's finest theater. Although Ludwig might have have wondered at the style of this place—a cool/hot creation of Hermann Czech, it is polished and puristic, with light pine furniture, metal trim, and white walls—he would have adored the food. Saddle of lamb on zucchini mousse, the finely cut carpaccio with Venetian mustard sauce, and the curd dumplings with rhubarb and strawberry sauce are all creations of Martin Stein, whose style is Austrian with a soupçon of Asia, a pinch of Mediterranean spice, and a celebrity or two thrown in—Michel Piccoli, Luc Bondy, and Pierre Boulez have all dined here. ⊠ *Linke Wienzeile 6, 6th District/Mariahilf* ☎ *01/585–6262* ⊕ *www.theatercafe-wien. at/* ⌕ *Reservations essential* ⊟ *AE, DC, MC, V* ⊘ *Closed Sun.* Ⓤ *U4/ Karlsplatz.*

$$–$$$ ✕ **Urania.** The year 1910 saw the inauguration of the Urania under the auspices of Franz Josef. Nearly a hundred years later this Jugendstil building has been beautifully restored. Today, Wolfgang Reichl is the charming cosmopolitan chap who is responsible for making this one of Vienna's trendiest locations. The interior design, conceived entirely by him, matches his persona—cool, modern, and urban. His chef, young Norbert Fiedler, is ditto and doesn't like the use of the word fusion to describe his cooking. Best bets include the creamy cauliflower soup with Thai asparagus, the fillet of trout on chanterelle risotto, and tender duck served with ginger ravioli. You can sit inside to take in the crowd and some of the handsomest waiters in town (rumor has it they are mostly models). Or sit outside on the upper or lower terrace overlooking the Danube Canal. Friendly opening times run from 9 AM until 2 AM, but the big hour on Sundays is Brunch. ⊠ *Uraniastrasse 1, 1st District* ☎ *01/7133066* ⌕ *Reservations essential* ⊟ *AE, DC, MC, V* Ⓤ *U1 or U4/Schwedenplatz.*

$$–$$$ ✕ **Vestibül.** Even if you're not attending a play at the extravagantly sumptuous Burgtheater, it's fun to dine in this thoroughly theatrical setting, located in what was once the carriage vestibule of the emperor's court theater. In the Marmorsaal room, Corinthian marble columns, coffered arcades, and lots of candlelight add romance to the scene. Don't expect high drama: as an example of Ringstrasse architecture, the Burgtheater offers up splendor at its most staid. In fact, you might opt instead for a lighter meal in the adjoining bar salon, which has gigantic glassed-in doors overlooking the grand boulevard, sculpted 19th-century putti, modernist

lighting, and a sense of fun. The menu changes frequently and may include such Viennese classics as veal goulash and Wiener Schnitzel as well as some classical *Beuschel* (a hash made of heart and lung, Viennese-style), plus a full array of nouvelle novelties. It's open late to accommodate theatergoers. In warm weather, you can also choose a table on the Ringstrasse garden terrace. ⊠ *Burgtheater/Dr.-Karl-Lueger-Ring 2* ☎ *01/532–4999* 🖷 *01/532–4999–10* ⊕ *www.vestibul.at* ▤ *AE, DC, MC, V* ⊘ *Closed Sun. No lunch Sat.* Ⓤ *Tram: 1 or 2.*

$$–$$$ ✕ **Zum Kuckuck.** If you want to leave the modern world behind and escape to Old Vienna, head for this cocoon-cum-sanctorum. The warm wooden interior gets high marks for *Gemütlickeit* (coziness), thanks to its vaulted ceilings, tiled ceramic stoves, and walls covered with old prints from Emperor Franz Josef's time. Small and old-fashioned, yes, but foodwise the kitchen is quite innovative. Take a seat at a table set with pink linen, pewter candlestick, and fresh flowers to sip a glass of *Sekt* (sparkling wine) with blood-orange juice and peruse the surprisingly extensive menu. Freshwater catfish oven-cooked with dried tomatoes and artichoke? Wild boar sausages served up on elderberry cabbage? Roast Barbarie-duckbreast with honey-pepper sauce and almond fritters? If you still have room for dessert, dive into the sweet cottage-cheese dumplings with stewed plums. ⊠ *Himmelpfortgasse 15, 1st District* ☎ *01/ 512–8470* 🖷 *01/774–1855* ▤ *AE, DC, MC, V* ⊘ *Closed Sun.*

$–$$$ ✕ **Palmenhaus.** Vienna has rarely looked better than from a table at Pal-
Fodor'sChoice   menhaus. A soaring glass-and-marble conservatory—created in 1904 by
★   Friedrich Ohlmann, whose Jugendstil designs pleased even the fussy Habsburgs—it once harbored the orchids grown for Emperor Franz Josef's dinner table. Renovated in 1998, it is now one of the city's most popular scene-arenas, where Viennese love to preen and parade. It's hard to beat the view from the terrace that looks across the idyllic Burggarten to the grandiose facade of the Hofburg palace, and in good weather, you'll want to wait for a table outside. Fortunately, there is plenty of space inside and the garden atmosphere is just as impressive: Twenty-foot-high palm trees soar up to the glass-paned vault while one side of the hall abuts the historic Schmetterlinghaus, allowing you to study butterflies as you munch on pumpkin gnocchi. As the evening wears on, the bar crowd—artists, writers, and clubsters—takes center stage and things tend to become a bit boisterous (and smoky). But for lunch or dinner—or even just a quick coffee and bitter-chocolate mousse—don't miss this extraordinary setting. ⊠ *Burggarten (entrance through Goethegasse gate after 8 PM), 1st District* ☎ *01/533–1033* ⚇ *Reservations essential* ▤ *DC, MC, V* ⊘ *Closed Mon.–Tues. during Nov.–Mar.* Ⓤ *U1, U2, or U4/Karlsplatz/Opera.*

$$ ✕ **Culinarium Öesterreich.** Vienna's version of Fauchon, this is a sort of pan-Austrian foodie emporium and that's just what this place delivers (and delivers—the take-out business is big here). Bringing together dishes, wines, and produce from every corner of the country—be it the Styrian rosé Schilcher or the Bregenzer Bergkaese, the friendly pumpkin-seed oil ("Styrian Viagra") or the hand-stirred apricot jams from the Wachau—chances are you'll find it here. Offering a menu with a definite Austrian stamp to it, the upstairs dining room is no-frills bright and airy, while downstairs an outside garden tempts many. In the vaulted brick cellar, the Winery has over 400 different Austrian wines which can be sampled with delicious whole-meal breads and an astonishingly delectable array of cheeses. ⊠ *Neuer Markt 10, 1st District* ☎ *01/ 5138281* ⊕ *www.culinarium.at* ☰ *AE, DC, MC, V* Ⓜ *U1, U2, or U4/ Karlsplatz/Opera.*

\$\$ ✕ **DO & CO Albertina.** When you're ready to drop from taking in all the art treasures at the fabulous Albertina, then just drop into the museum's new Do & Co café. Not only will the five huge painted copies of some of Egon Schiele's most famous works prolong the art experience, you'll be dining on one of the liveliest menus in town and be allured by a Vienna Moderne room, all glass, red marble, high-backed, camel-colored leather seating, and windowsills with large vases filled with flowers. Go for the Albertina BLT-Burger, a grand-sized fist of the finest Styrian beef, complete with crispy bacon, tomatoes, and classic potato goulash. For exotic, the Thai vegetable wok dish with steamed rice, oysters, and sweet chili sauce can be served plain or, for that extra energy boost, with prawns or beef. If you fancy just a snack, sit at the bar and enjoy the Baguette Albertina, stuffed with juicy smoked salmon, cream cheese, arugula, and sundried tomatoes. Last but not least, this place is open all day, every day, 10 AM to midnight (and is handy to the opera house). On summery days, you can also sit outside on the terrace overlooking the Burggarten. ⊠ *Albertinaplatz 1, 1st District* ☎ *01/ 532–9669* ⊕ *www.doco.com* ⌒ *Reservations essential for dinner only* ☰ *V* Ⓤ *U1, U2, or U4/Karlsplatz/Opera.*

\$\$ ✕ **Hansen.** One foot past the entrance of the beautiful Lederleitner garden store and you're enjoying a walk through paradise in spring (or fall, winter, and summer, for that matter). This fashionable establishment, housed in the basement of the 19th-century Vienna Stock Exchange, is home to countless flowers and plants, and, as it turns out, an elegant restaurant. As you walk to your table passing all those scented shrubs, it is hard to say what's better: the sweet perfume of the tuberoses or the tantalizing whiff of the truffle. The restaurant is at one end of the flower shop, so diners can see shoppers browsing for everything from a single rose to a \$2,000 lemon tree. Although this eatery is named after Theophil Hansen—the ornament-crazy architect of the Börse—its decor is sleek and modern. Tables set a bit too close together are compensated by the fantastic Austrian-Mediterranean menu. Lunch is the main event here, though you can also come for breakfast or a pre-theater dinner. ⊠ *Wipplingerstrasse 34, 1st District* ☎ *01/532–0542* ⌒ *Reservations essential* ☰ *AE, DC, MC, V* ◷ *Closed Sun. and after 9 PM weekdays. No dinner Sat.* Ⓤ *U2/Schottenring.*

★ **\$\$** ✕ **Tancredi.** Ever since this upscale Beisl with a Sicilian name opened, it's been the talk of the town because of the kitchen's fresh approach to Austrian cooking. *Beisln* (a cross between a pub and a café) are traditionally known for their solid, old-fashioned renditions of Austrian standards like Wiener Schnitzel and *Tafelspitz,* but Tancredi has set out to revamp the Beisl image. No plain, dark wood tables, lace curtains, and smoke-stained walls here—instead the decor is elegantly light and modern, dominated by a huge bar along one wall and clean-lined tables fronting the window opposite. The menu changes seasonally and may include crispy fried chicken and chunky potato salad (using home-made mayonnaise), tender, succulent steak topped with matchstick fried onions and light, grilled dumplings, or *Wels G'röstl* (hunks of catfish, vegetables, potatoes, and *Spätzle* cooked in a blackened skillet). ☒ *Grosse Neugasse 5, 4th District/Wieden* ☎ *01/941–0048* 🍴 *Reservations essential* 🖃 *No credit cards* ⊗ *Closed Sun. No lunch Sat.* Ⓤ *U1, U2, or U4/Karlsplatz, then Tram 62 or 65/Mayerhofgasse.*

$–$$ ✕ **Bohème.** If Rodolfo, Mimi, and all the other bohemians of Puccini's
FodorsChoice   *La Boheme* lived in Vienna instead of Paris, there is a good chance this
★   would have been their neighborhood hangout. As charming and casual as Café Momus must have been, Bohème occupies a former 18th-century bakery and is located on a boutique-lined passageway in the heart of Vienna's luxe-bohemian quarter of Spittelberg. A low-vaulted ceiling, cherry-wood walls, a menu divided into "overtures," "preludes," and "first and second acts," and Bellini on the soundtrack make for a setting frequently favored by stars appearing across town at the Staatsoper (as you'll see from the autographed pictures of some of the opera-loving owner's more famous patrons on the walls). Bravi to chef Robert Rauch. The cream of pumpkin soup is a fine start, perhaps accompanied by a tasty salad of field greens and fried zucchini in a yogurt dressing; two favorite entrées are the pork medallions with potato cakes in a mushroom cream sauce and the more traditional roast duck with dumplings and *Rotkraut* (red cabbage). ☒ *Spittelberggasse 19, 7th District/Neubau* ☎ *01/523–3173* 🖃 *AE, DC, MC, V* ⊗ *Closed Sun. No lunch* Ⓤ *U2 or U3/Volkstheater.*

$–$$ ✕ **Figlmüller.** The Wiener Schnitzel institution, known for its gargantuan breaded veal and pork cutlets, which are so large they overflow the plate, Figlmüller is always packed. The cutlet is so large because it has been hammered into a two-fisted portion (you can hear the kitchen's pounding mallets from a block away). They wind up wafer-thin but delicious because the quality, as well as the size, is unrivaled (a quarter kilo of quality meat for each schnitzel). At first sight, it seems there is no room for anything else on the plate, but if you just dive into the middle of the cut your side order of salad, potato, or vegetable (everything is à la carte) will fit nicely. As the Viennese are fond of saying, "A Schnitzel should swim," so don't forget the lemon juice. ☒ *Wollzeile 5, 1st District* ☎ *01/512–6177* 🖃 *AE, DC, MC, V* ⊗ *Closed first 2 wks Aug.* Ⓤ *U1 or U3/Stephansplatz.*

$–$$ ✕ **Strandcafé.** When the going gets hot in the center of town, the over-heated get going (via the U1 subway) to the lake area known as the Alte Donau (or Old Danube). Since the construction of the Danube Canal, this lake has become a highly popular recreation area for city dwellers. Sitting on the Strandcafé's wooden pier directly over the water and watching swans glide beneath the weeping willows and paddle-boats paddle by is a great way to spend a relaxing afternoon. That, in itself, would be reason enough to come but there is an even stronger appeal. The spare ribs. These beautifully barbecued pork ribs come in huge meaty portions and are served with scrumptious roast potatoes. Have a glass of house wine or a cold beer to wash them down and enjoy this Edenic setting just a stone's skip from the bustling city. ✉ *Florian-Berndl-Gasse 20, 22nd District/Donaustadt* ☎ *01/203–6747* ⚄ *Reservations essential* ▭ *No credit cards* Ⓤ *U1/Alte Donau.*

$–$$ ✕ **Wrenkh.** Once Vienna's vegetarian pioneer extraordinaire, Christian Wrenkh now prefers a mixed cuisine in his house (over in the 15th District his ex-wife keeps up with the healthy kitchen). Happily, those delightful dishes like the wild-rice risotto with mushrooms, or the Greek fried rice with vegetables, sheep's cheese, and olives, or the tofu and tomato and basil-pesto tarts still carry his signature. Now, however, you can also be tempted by steak, fish, and fowl. The minimalist-style café section offers inexpensive lunch specials, while the more elegant adjacent dining room is perfect for a nice, relaxed lunch or dinner. Fortunately Christian hasn't changed the no-smoking policy in his restaurant. ✉ *Bauernmarkt 10, 1st District* ☎ *01/533–1526* ⊕ *www.wrenkh.at* ▭ *AE, DC, MC, V* Ⓤ *U1 or U3/Stephansplatz.*

$–$$ ✕ **Zum Finsteren Stern.** Paging all Mozart maniacs: This is the old Gothic
Fodor'sChoice cellar of the one and only Palais Collalto, the site where six-year-old
★ Amadeus made his first public appearance ever. Being the playful chappy he was, he was probably scampering along these ancient walls and right out into the street (where the cobblestones are the same) when he "played the palace" with his father. Not much has changed in the *Keller* since 1762—the vaulted ceiling, cool white walls, and dark wooden-planked floor are just as they have always been. It takes courage in Vienna to only offer a choice of two three-course menus but the success of Ella de Silva's establishment proves her right. If available, go for the rabbit with sweet and sour lentils or the lamb steak with polenta tomato, zucchini cakes. and red-wine shallot sauce. Opening hours are 5 PM until 1 AM and on a warm summer's evening there is a lovely seating area outside in the quietest of corners underneath an old bluebell tree. ✉ *Schulhof 8 at Parisergasse, 1st District* ☎ *01/535–2100* ▭ *MC, V* ☉ *Closed Sun.* Ⓤ *U3/Herrengasse.*

$ ✕ **Gasthaus Puerstner.** Ever fancied sitting in an enormous wine barrel for dinner? Turned on its side and cut almost in half, this one seats four and, after a while, the bouquet of its former contents reaches the olfactory organ and mingles oh-so-pleasantly with the aromas of Austrian cooking. That's what dining at Puerstner's is all about. This is one of those places proud to offer classic Austrian fare—no surprises or creativity, please (you'd be surprised how many people prefer it that way). Although a large establishment, separate seating areas lend a pleasant, intimate air. Even better, there's lots of dark wood and rustic Tyrolean carpentry work; the alpine atmosphere is enhanced by the folklore vests the waiters wear. You can't go wrong with the carpaccio of Styrian beef with Parmesan cheese or the veal goulash with potato gnocci. The place does fill up for dinner—but the waiters will always try to find room for you. ✉ *Riemergasse 10, 1st District* ☎ *01/512–6357* ⊕ *www.puerstner. com/* ▭ *MC, V* Ⓜ *U3/Schottenring.*

¢–$ ✕ **Alt Wien.** Gulasch and a glass of beer, that's all you need for lunch,
Fodor'sChoice no? Ageing Vienna Pop–idols Danzer and Ambros sang that refrain in
★ 1975 and for many Viennese, nearly 30 years later, that line is truer than ever. One of the best, most succulent goulashes is served up in defini-

tive Viennese style here at Old Vienna (the small portion is €4.75, the large, €6.90). The gravy is, of course, the most important part of the dish—for dunking (don't worry about table manners) use the crispy semmel or, even better, a couple of the slices of dark bread. Oh, and don't forget the glass of beer—ask for a Seidl herbes Gösser, which harmonizes just perfectly with the dish. The cultured and chic clientele (writers, journalists, artists, poets) and the interior—replete with huge vaulted ceilings and walls covered with artsy posters—give the place a quintessentially Vienna feel. ⊠ *Bäckerstrasse 9, 1st District* ☎ *01/512–5222* ▭ *No credit cards* Ⓤ *U3/Stephansplatz.*

¢–$ ✕ **Beim Czaak.** Pronounced "bime chalk," this homey spot with friendly service is a favorite with locals. It's long and narrow, with forest-green wainscoting, framed caricatures of a few well-known Viennese on the walls, and a small outside seating area. Choose a glass of excellent Austrian wine to go along with Waldviertler pork stuffed with bacon, onions, and mushrooms, spinach dumplings drizzled with Parmesan and browned butter, or a big Wiener Schnitzel. ⊠ *Postgasse 15, corner of Fleischmarkt, 1st District* ☎ *01/513–7215* ▭ *No credit cards* ◷ *Closed Sun.* Ⓤ *U1, U2, or U4/Karlsplatz/Opera.*

¢–$ ✕ **Brezl Gwölb.** A real medieval cellar which looks like a stage set from *Phantom of the Opera*, tiny wooden nooks and crannies, and no fancy frills, make this a great choice for chilling out after all those extravagant luxury eateries. Indeed, this snuggery fills up fast at night. Tucked away just off Am Hof down a cobbled alley, this tavern is housed in a former 15th-century pretzel factory. The comfort level is great, the wine selection impressive, and the food scrumptious: *Tyroler G'röstl* (home-fried potatoes, ham, onions, and cheese served in a blackened skillet) or the *Kasnockerl* (spätzle in a pungent cheese sauce) are two best bets. Try to get a table downstairs in the most historic part and then try not to remember the story about Haydn's head being found in a jar in this very same cellar. ⊠ *Ledererhof 9 (near Am Hof), 1st District* ☎ *01/533–8811* ▭ *AE, DC, MC, V* Ⓤ *U3/Herrengasse.*

★ ¢–$ ✕ **Gmoa Keller.** One of the friendliest places in Vienna, this wonderful old vaulted spot—just across the street from the Konzert Haus concert hall offers some of the most *gutbürgerlich* (hearty) home cooking in town. Come here to enjoy dishes that hail from Carinthia, one of the best being the *Kasnudeln* (potatoes and spinach pasta filled with cheese and onion), served best with green leaf salad. Needless to say, a real favorite here is the *Tafelspitzsulz mit Kernoel und Zwiebeln* (cold cut of beef in aspic served with onions and lashings of dark green pumpkin seed oil)—like everyone else, you'll wind up using the *Semmel* (the white bread roll) to sop up that last drop of wonderful oil. Choose from various seating areas, all similar with dark wood panelled walls, wooden chairs, and alcoves, with one room showcasing an enormous modern mural painting. ⊠ *Am Heumarkt 25, 3rd District/Landstrasse* ☎ *01/712–5310* ▭ *AE, DC, MC, V* ◷ *Closed Sun.* Ⓤ *U4/Stadtpark.*

¢–$ ✕ **Gösser Bierklinik.** In the very heart of Vienna, where the cobblestone streets remain a hazard to high-heel wearers, one comes across this engaging Old World house, which dates back four centuries. Ambience freaks will love its dark wood trim and Gothic stained-glass windows. One of the top addresses for beer connoisseurs in Austria, this serves up brews, both draft and bottled, *dunkeles* (dark) and *helles* (light) from the Gösser brewery in Styria. Of the four dining areas (including a no-smoking room), many diners opt for the covered courtyard, where your beer will taste better no matter the weather. Besides the obligatory (but first-class) Wiener Schnitzel there are substantial, dark whole-wheat sandwiches stuffed with ham, cheese, and different vegetables, along with *Kas'nocken* (little pasta dumplings topped with melted Tyrolean mountain cheese and crispy fried onions) and the bountiful *Bauernsalat* (farmer's salad) with sheep's cheese. ⊠ *Steindlgasse 4, 1st District* ☎ *01/533–7598* ▭ *DC, MC, V* ☉ *Closed Sun.* Ⓤ *U3/Herrengasse.*

★ ¢–$ ✕ **Reinthaler.** Not many "tourists" meander down this lane with the idea of finding one of the best home-cooked Viennese lunches, but just between you and us, tucked away in this hidden corner is the vintage-1950s Reinthaler Gasthaus. Because this place is so popular with the locals it's packed at lunchtime so don't hesitate to sit down at one of the big communal tables. If you see there are a few diners eating alone at a table that would easily seat at least another four, ask if you could join them with a *"Ist hier frei bitte?"* (easy to pronounce as "is here fry bitta?"). First, see what the others are tucking into, or consult the daily specials for pot-luck. Or, if you prefer to be on the safe side, choose the classic *Griess Knockerl* (bouillon with small fluffy semolina dumplings) followed by *Krautrouladen* (juicy meat-filled cabbage rolls) or *Kraut Fleisch*, a tasty cabbage-meat dish. ⊠ *Gluckgasse 5, 1st District* ☎ *01/512–3366* ▭ *No credit cards* ☉ *Closed weekends* ☉ *Closed weekends* Ⓤ *U1, U2, or U4/Karlsplatz/Opera.*

¢–$ ✕ **Spatzennest.** This is simple, hearty Viennese cooking at its best, located on a quaint, cobblestone pedestrian street straight out of a 1930s Hollywood movie set in Old Vienna. Tasty dishes include Wiener Schnitzel, roast chicken, and pillowy fried spätzle with slivers of ham and melted cheese. It's especially delightful in summer, when tables are set outside. It can be smoky indoors. ⊠ *Ulrichsplatz 1, 7th District/Neubau* ☎ *01/526–1659* ▭ *MC, V* ☉ *Closed Fri.–Sat.* Ⓤ *U2, U3/Volkstheater.*

¢–$ ✕ **Una.** Set in one of the former imperial stables that were renovated to become part of Vienna's mammoth MuseumsQuartier, this spot has drawn crowds attracted by its unpretentious air, knowing menu, and spectacular decor. Or, to, be precise, its vaulted tiled ceiling that has now become an extravaganza with a vaguely Turkish/Indian look. Under this white-and-turquoise fantasia of arabesques, camels, and Bosporus blues, an arty crowd ponders a menu that is varied, reasonably priced, and comes with plenty of vegetarian dishes. Try the couscous and herb salad with a sprinkling of mint or the tangy prawn and watercress sandwich. Adjacent to the unpretentious main room is a comfortable lounge-like seating area with coffee tables set with magazines and newspapers. If you want a different degree of reading matter, go through to the directly adjoining AC (Architecture Center) to check up on what's new on Vienna's architectural front. ⊠ *Museumsplatz 1, MuseumsQuartier, 7th District/Neubau* ☎ *1/523–6566* ▭ *No credit cards* Ⓤ *U2/MuseumsQuartier.*

¢ ✕ Salzgries. A typical old Viennese *Beisl,* which is somewhere between a café and a pub, the Salzgries has an unpretentious, rather worn atmosphere. It's known for having good schnitzels, and you can get either pork, milk-fed veal, or chicken breast (*Gebackenes Hühnerfilet*), all fried to a golden crispness, with potato salad on the side. The *Vanillerostbraten* (garlicky rump steak) is also worth trying, and the *Moor im Hemd* (warm chocolate cake with whipped cream) is scrumptious. ✉ *Marc-Aurel-Strasse 6, 1st District* ☎ *01/968–9645* ▭ *No credit cards* Ⓤ *U1 or U4/Schwedenplatz.*

Munch on the Run

If you don't have time for a leisurely lunch, or you'd rather save your money for a splurge at dinner, here's a sampling of the best places in the city center to grab a quick, inexpensive, and tasty bite to eat. In the lower level of the Ringstrasse Galerie shopping mall, the gourmet supermarket **Billa Corso** (✉ Kärntner Ring 9–13, 1st District ☎ 01/512–6625 ☉ Closed Sun.) has a good salad bar, and will prepare the sandwich of your choice at the deli counter. (The Ringstrasse Galerie is in two similar buildings, so make sure you're in the one on the Kärntner Ring.) The best pizza by-the-slice can be found near St. Stephan's at **Bizi Pizza** (✉ Rotenturmstrasse 4, 1st District ☎ 01/513–3705). Next to the produce section on the ground floor of Vienna's premier gourmet grocery store, **Meinl am Graben** (✉ Graben 19, 1st District ☎ 01/532–3334 ☉ Closed Sun.) is a smart, stand-up café where you can choose from a selection of soups, sandwiches, or antipasti (don't confuse it with the full-service restaurant upstairs). Near the Freyung, the epicurean deli **Radatz** (✉ Schottengasse 3a, 1st District ☎ 01/533–8163 ☉ Closed Sun.) offers made-to-order sandwiches from a vast selection of mouthwatering meats and cheeses. Around the corner from Am Hof, **Zum Schwarzen Kameel** (✉ Bognergasse 5, 1st District ☎ 01/533–8967 ☉ Closed Sun.) serves elegant little open-faced sandwiches and baby quiches in their stand-up section. Directly beneath the Vienna State Opera House, discover the **"Karlsplatz" underground mall** (✉ Opern Passage, 1st District), where you'll find a huge choice of quick-food alternatives within the space of a hundred yards. Take the escalator at the corner of the Opera across from Hotel Bristol and descend to the subway station "Karlsplatz" mall.

A sure way to spike a lively discussion among the Viennese is to ask which *Würstelstand* serves the most delicious grilled sausages. Here are three that are generally acknowledged to be the best: **Ehrenreich's** (✉ Naschmarkt, on the Linke Wienzeile side across from Piccini, under the clock, 1st District ☉ Closed Sun.) serves scrumptious *Käsekrainer* (beef sausages oozing with melted cheese), alongside a *Semmel* (soft roll) and mild, sweet mustard. Behind the Opera House, **Oper** (✉ Corner of Philharmonikerstrasse/Hanuschgasse, 1st District) entices passersby with its plump, sizzling *Bratwurst.* **Würstelstand am Hoher Markt** (✉ Hoher Markt, corner of Marc-Aurel-Strasse, 1st District) serves American-style hot dogs and is open daily from 7 AM to 5 AM.

Wine Taverns

In the city center, wine taverns are known as *Weinkeller.* Hundreds of years ago, Vienna's vintners started taking advantage of the cavernous spaces found below ancient monasteries and old houses and converted them into underground wine cellars. The fact that these subterranean "Kellers" were some of the coolest spots in summertime Vienna have always proved a big drawing card.

★ **$–$$** ✕ **Augustinerkeller.** Built into the old brick vaults of the 16th-century historic fortifications surrounding the old city, this is one of the last monastic wine-cellars in central Vienna. The atmosphere is very gemütlichkeit—vaulted brick ceiling, wooden "cow-stall" booths, street lanterns, Austrian bric-a-brac, and a lovely troupe of roaming musicians (dig that accordian!) in the evenings. The spit-roasted chicken is excellent, as is the filling *Stelze* (roast knuckle of pork). ✉ *Augustinerstrasse 1, Albertinaplatz, 1st District* ☎ *01/533–1026* ⊕ *http://members.aon. at/augustinerkeller/eframe.htm* ▭ *DC, MC, V* Ⓤ *U3/Herrengasse.*

$–$$ ✕ **Esterházykeller.** The roots here go way back to 1683 when this opened as one of the official "Stadtheuriger" (city wine taverns). Below the Esterházy palace, the atmosphere is like a cozy subterranean cave, with low hanging vaults and alpine wooden booths. The maze of rooms offers some of the best Keller wines in town plus a typical Vienna menu noontime and evenings, as well as a hot and cold buffet. ✉ *Haarhof 1, 1st District* ☎ *01/533–3482* ⊕ *www.esterhazykeller.at/* ▭ *No credit cards* ✆ *No lunch weekends. Closed weekends in summer* Ⓤ *U1 or U4/ Stephansplatz.*

★ **$** ✕ **Melker Stiftskeller.** Down and down you go, into one of the friendliest Keller in town, where Stelze is a popular feature, along withoutstanding wines by the glass or, rather, mug. Part of the fabled Melkerhof complex—dating from 1438 but rebuilt in the 18th century—this originally was the storage house for wines from the great Melk Abbey in the Danube Valley. This is a complex of six cavernous rooms, with the most atmospheric having low-hanging vaults right out of a castle dungeon. ✉ *Schottengasse 3, 1st District* ☎ *01/533–5530* ⊕ *http://members. aon.at/melkerstiftskeller/* ▭ *AE, DC, MC, V* ✆ *Closed Sun., Mon. No lunch* Ⓤ *U2/Schottentor.*

¢–$ ✕ **Zwölf-Apostelkeller.** You pass a huge wood statue of St. Peter on the way downstairs to the two underground floors in this deep-down cellar in the oldest part of Vienna. The atmosphere is rather crammed; the Apostelstüberl has some rather cheesy folk reliefs of the twelve apostles. The young crowd comes for the good wines and the atmosphere, and there's buffet food as well. ✉ *Sonnenfelsgasse 3, 1st District* ☎ *01/ 512–6777* ⊕ *www.zwoelf-apostelkeller.at/* ▭ *AE, DC, MC, V* ✆ *No lunch* Ⓤ *U1, U2/Stephansplatz.*

Heurige

The city's light and slightly fizzy "new wine"—the *Heurige,* harvested every September and October in hills around the city—has been served up for centuries in suburban taverns known as "Heuriger." These are charmingly set in the picturesque wine villages that dot Vienna's out-skirts: Stammersdorf, Grinzing, Sievering, Nussdorf, and Neustift (tram lines to take from the city center are listed under the reviews below). Grinzing is a particularly enchanting destination: Although colonized by faux-heurige and tour buses, it has enough winding streets, antique lanterns, stained-glass windows, and oh-so-cozy taverns that you may feel you're wandering through a stage set for an "Old Austria" operetta (don't forget to look for the town organ-grinder). The best times to visit the Heurige are in the summer and fall, when many of these places fa-mously hang a pine branch over their doorway to show they are open, though often the more elegant and expensive establishments, called *Noble-Heurige,* stay open year-round. Begin by ordering the classic *Ein Viertel*—a quarter liter of wine—then check out the buffet. In the old days, the *Salamutschi* (sausage seller) would trot his wares from one tav-ern to another. Today, increasingly, full dinners are available. If you go to a Heurige in the fall, be sure to order a glass of Sturm, a cloudy drink halfway between grape-juice and wine, with a delicious yeasty fizz.

$$–$$$ ✕**Kronprinz Rudolfshof.** Named after the crown prince who died a tragic death at Mayerling, this heuriger has always been one of Grinzing's most famous. Sigmund Freud, C. G. Jung, and Albert Einstein sipped glasses of Viennese wine here. Although it might be hard to channel their spir-its—a new Hundertwasser modern pavilion has been added here—you might enjoy the kitschy blast of the "1st Grinzinger Heurigen Show," which features a troupe of costumed singers and musicians warbling the heart out of "Wiener Blut." The price is €40 a ticket. If not, if you're lucky, you might catch a *Natursänger* roaming the village streets. ⊠ *Cobenzl-gasse 8, 19th District/Grinzing* ☎ *01/524–7478* ⊕ *www.heuriger.com/* ⊟ *AE, DC, MC, V* Ⓤ *U2/Schottentor; Tram: 38/Grinzing.*

★ **$$–$$$**   ✕**Mayer am Pfarrplatz.** Heiligenstadt is home to this legendary Heuriger in one of Beethoven's former abodes. Ludwig van Beethoven lived in this house on Pfarrplatz in the summer of 1817. At that time there was a spa in Heiligenstadt, which Beethoven visited, hoping to find a cure to his deafness. In this town he composed his 6th Symphony (Pastoral), and while staying in this house, had also created parts of his famous 9th Symphony ("Ode to Joy"). The atmosphere in the collection of rooms is genuine, with vaulted rooms filled with Tyrolean iron chandeliers, an-tique engravings, and mounted antlers. The à la carte offerings and buf-fet are more than abundant and the house wines among the most excellent of all heurigen nectars. You'll find lots of Viennese among the tourists here. ⊠*Heiligenstädter Pfarrplatz 2, 19th District/Nussdorf* ☎*01/ 370–1287* ⊕ *www.mayer.pfarrplatz.at/* ⊟ *DC, MC, V* ✆ *No lunch weekdays or Sat.* Ⓤ *Tram: D/Nussdorf from the Ring.*

$$–$$$ ✕**Weingut Reinprecht.** The grandest heurigen in Grinzing (the town has
FodorśChoice   more than 30 of them), Reinprecht is *gemütlichkeit*-heaven: Tyrolean
★   wood beams, 19th-century oil paintings, Austrian-eagle banners, por-traits of army generals, globe lanterns, marble busts, trellised tables, and the greatest collection of corkscrews in Austria. The building—a former monastery—is impressive, as is the garden, which can hold up to 700 people (to give you an idea of how popular this place is). If you ignore the crowds, get a cozy corner table, and focus on the archety-

WINE-WIEN-WEIN-VIENNA

T MAKES FOR A MEMORABLE EXPERIENCE to sit at the edge of a vineyard on the Kahlenberg with a tankard of young white wine and listen to the Schrammel quartet playing sentimental Viennese songs. The wine taverns, called Heurige (the singular is Heuriger) for the new wine that they serve, sprang up in 1784 when Joseph II decreed that owners of vineyards could establish their own private wine taverns; soon the Viennese discovered it was cheaper to go out to the wine than to bring it inside the city walls, where taxes were levied. The Heuriger owner is supposed to be licensed to serve only the produce of his own vineyard, a rule more honored in the breach than the observance. These taverns in the wine-growing districts on the outskirts of the city vary from the simple front room of a vintner's house to ornate settings. The true Heuriger is open for only a few weeks a year to allow the vintner to sell a certain quantity of his production, tax-free, when consumed on his own premises. The choice is usually between a "new" and an "old" white (or red) wine, but you can also ask for a milder or sharper wine according to your taste. Most Heurige are happy to let you sample the wines before you order. You can also order a Gespritzter, half wine and half soda water. The waitress brings the wine, usually in a ¼-liter mug or liter carafe, but you serve yourself from the food buffet. The wine tastes as mild as lemonade, but it packs a punch. If it isn't of good quality, you will know by a raging headache the next day.

pal *atmosphäre,* you might have a great time. ⊠ *Cobenzlgasse 20, 19th District/Grinzing* ☎ *01/320–1389* ⊕ *http://heuriger-reinprecht.at/* 🖃 *AE, DC, MC, V* ☺ *Closed Dec.–Feb.* Ⓤ *U2/Schottentor; Tram: 38/ Grinzing.*

★ $ ✕ **Schreiberhaus.** In Neustift am Walde, the Schreiberhaus heuriger has one of the prettiest terraced gardens in the city, with picnic tables stretching straight up into the vineyards. The buffet offers delicious treats such as spit-roasted chicken, salmon pasta, and a huge selection of tempting grilled vegetables and salads. The golden Traminer wine is excellent. ⊠ *Rathstrasse 54, 19th District/Neustift am Walde* ☎ *01/440– 3844* 🖃 *AE, DC, MC, V* Ⓤ *U4, U6/Spittelau; Bus 35A/Neustift am Walde.*

¢–$ ✕ **Passauerhof.** If you want live folk music (offered nightly) to accompany your meal, this is the place to go. But you may have to share the experience with the tour groups that descend on Grinzing. The food from the heurigen menu, such as roast chicken and Wiener Schnitzel, is tasty, while the buffet offers a limited selection. It's a pleasant five-minute walk up the hill from the town center. ⊠ *Cobenzlgasse 9, 19th District/ Grinzing* ☎ *01/320–6345* 🖃 *AE, DC, MC, V* ☺ *No lunch. Closed Jan.–Feb.* Ⓤ *U2/Schottentor; Tram: 38/Grinzing.*

★ ¢–$ ✕ **Wieninger.** Heurigen wine and food are both top-notch here, and the charming, tree-shaded inner courtyard and series of typical vintner's rooms are perfect for whiling away an evening. Wieninger's bottled wines are ranked among the country's best. It's located across the Danube in Stammersdorf, one of Vienna's oldest Heurige areas. ⊠ *Stammersdorferstrasse 78, 21st District/Floridsdorf* ☎ *01/292–4106* ⊟ *V* ☻ *Closed late Dec.–Feb. No lunch except Sun.* Ⓤ *U2, U4/Schottenring; Tram: 31/ Stammersdorf.*

¢–$ ✕ **Zimmermann.** East of the Grinzing village center, the Zimmermann heuriger has excellent wines, an enchanting tree-shaded garden, and an endless series of small paneled rooms and vaulted cellars. You can order from the menu or choose from the tempting buffet. This well-known Heuriger attracts the occasional celebrity, including fashion model Claudia Schiffer when she's in town. ⊠ *Armbrustergasse 5/Grinzingerstrasse, 19th District/Grinzing* ☎ *01/370–2211* ⊟ *AE, DC, MC, V* ☻ *No lunch* Ⓤ *U2/Schottentor; Tram: 38/Grinzing.*

Cafés & Coffeehouses

Is it the coffee they come for, or the coffeehouse? This question is one of the hot topics in town as Vienna's café scene has become increasingly overpopulated with Starbucks branches and Italian outlets. The ruckus over whether the quality of the coffee or the *atmosphäre* is more important is not new, but is becoming fiercer as competition from all sides increases. The result is that the legendary landmark Wiener Kaffeehäuser—the famous cafés known for a century as the "Viennese Parlors," where everyone from Mozart and Beethoven to Lenin and Andy Warhol were likely to hang out—are smarting from the new guys on the block. On the plus side, their ageless charms remain mostly intact: the sumptuous red-velvety padded booths, the marble-topped tables, the rickety yet indestructible Thonet bentwood chairs, the waiter—still the *Herr Ober* dressed in a Sunday-best outfit—pastries, cakes, strudels, and rich tortes, newspapers, magazines, and journals, and, last but not least, a sense that here, time stands still. To savor the traditional coffeehouse experience, set aside a morning or an afternoon, or at least a couple of hours, and settle down in the one you've chosen. Read a while or catch up on your letter writing or plan tomorrow's itinerary: there is no need to worry about overstaying one's welcome, even over a single small cup of coffee, though don't expect refills. (Of course, in some of the more opulent coffeehouses, your one cup of coffee may cost as much as a meal somewhere else.)

And remember that in Austria coffee is never merely coffee. It comes in countless forms and under many names. Ask for *ein Kaffee* from a waiter and you'll get a vacant stare. If you want a black coffee, you must ask for a *kleiner* or *grosser Schwarzer* (small or large black coffee, with small being the size of a demitasse cup). If you want it strong, add the word *gekürst* (shortened); if you want it weaker, *verlängert* (stretched). If you want your coffee with cream, ask for a *Brauner* (again *gross* or *klein*); say *Kaffee Creme* if you wish to add the cream yourself. Others opt for a *Melange,* a mild roast with steamed milk (which you can even get *mit Haut,* with skin, or *Verkehrter,* with more milk than coffee). The usual after-dinner drink is espresso. Most delightful are the coffee-and-whipped-cream concoctions, universally cherished as *Kaffee mit Schlag,* a taste that is easily acquired and a menace to all but the very thin. A customer who wants more whipped cream than coffee asks for a *Doppelschlag.* Hot black coffee in a glass with one knob of whipped cream is an *Einspänner* (literally, "one-horse coach"—as coachmen needed one hand free to hold the reins). Then you can go to town on a *Mazagran,* black coffee with ice and a tot of rum, or *Eiskaffee,* cold coffee with ice cream, whipped cream, and cookies. Or you can simply order a *Portion Kaffee* and have an honest pot of coffee and jug of hot milk. And watch out: if you naively request a Menu, you'll wind up with a Schwarzer with a double shot of pear liqueur. As for the actual *Speisekarte* (menu), most places offer hot food, starting with breakfast, from early morning until around 11 AM, lunch menus in some, and many offer a great variety of meals until about an hour before closing time.

Fodor'sChoice ✕ **Café Central.** The coffeehouse *supreme.* Made famous by its illustri-
★ ous guests, the Café Central is probably the world's most famous coffeehouse—outside of Florian's in Venice. Although recently somewhat over-restored (by its Donald Trump–like new owner), its old vibes remain attached to it as though by suction-pad. Don't expect a cozy-hole-in-the-wall kaffeehaus: With soaring ceiling and gigantic columns giving it the look of an apse strayed from St. Stephan's cathedral, it provided a rather sumptuous home-away-from-home for Leon Trotsky, who mapped out the Russian Revolution here under the portraits of the imperial family. It's just across from the Spanish Riding School. Piano music fills the marble pillared hall in the afternoons and although it will never again be all that it used to be, Central should be on the "must see" list. ✉ *Herrengasse 14, corner Strauchgasse 1st District* ☎ *01/5333–76424* ⊕ *www.palaisevents.at/* Ⓤ *U3/Herrengasse.*

✕ **Café Frauenhuber.** Repair here to find some peace and quiet away from the Himmelpfortgasse's busy shoppers. A visual treat is the original turn-of-the-20th-century interior with the obligatory red-velvet seating and somewhat tired upholstery (if you don't suffer from back problems you'll be fine). The breakfasts served here are legendary, having never lost that original "egg-in-a-glass" touch. You'll find fewer tourists here than in other typical Viennese cafés, so head here for real patina, which it has earned as this establishment first opened its doors in 1824. ✉ *Himmelpfortgasse 6, 1st District* ☎ *01/512–4323* Ⓤ *U1 or U3/Stephansplatz.*

✕ **Café Griensteidl.** Once the site of one of Vienna's oldest coffeehouses and named after the pharmacist Heinrich Griensteidl—the original dated back to 1847 but was demolished in 1897—this café was resurrected in 1990. Here, Karl Kraus, the sardonic critic, spent many hours writing his feared articles, and here, Hugo von Hofmannsthal took time-outs from writing libretti for Richard Strauss. Although this establishment is still looking for the patina needed to give it back its real flair, locals are pleased by the attempt to re-create the former atmosphere that exuded history. The daily, reasonably priced midday menu is a winner. Numerous newspapers and magazines hang on the rack (with a goodly number in English). ✉ *Michaelerplatz 2 1st District* ☎ *01/533–2692* Ⓤ *U3/Herrengasse.*

Fodor'sChoice ✗ **Café Hawelka.** Practically a shrine, nearly a museum, the beloved
★ Hawelka has been presided over for more than 70 years by Josefine and
Leopold Hawelka, in person, day in, day out. Josefine, sometimes working 14 hours a day, rules the empire (except on Tuesdays) with circumspect, incredible energy and an iron glove—she is the one who decides
which of her "beloved guests" sits where. Will this institution live on
forever? This troubles many of the regulars. Well, if the Hawelka becomes a museum, it will be ready. This was the hang-out of most of Vienna's modern artists and the café has acquired quite an admirable art
collection over the years. As you enter the rather dark interior, wait to
be seated—unusual in Vienna—and then speak up and ask to have a
look at the guest book, in itself a work of art, with entries including
some very illustrious names (Elias Canetti, Andy Warhol, Tony Blair, et
al.). Back in the 1960s, the young John Irving enjoyed the atmosphere
here, too, as you can see when reading *The Hotel New Hampshire.* If
you want to try what the Hawelka is most famous for, then ask for
Buchteln, a baked bun with a sweet filling that goes down well with a
Melange. ✉ *Dorotheergasse 6, 1st District* ☎ *01/512–8230* Ⓤ *U1 or
U3/Stephansplatz.*

✗ **Café Landtmann.** A recent $500,000 government-sponsored renovation has brought new lustre to the chandeliers of Landtmann, a century-old favorite of politicians, theater stars (the Burg is next door), and
celeb-watchers. Sigmund Freud, Burt Lancaster, Hillary Rodham Clinton, and Sir Paul McCartney are just of few of the famous folk who have
patronized this vaguely Secession-ish looking café, whose glass and
brass doors have been open since 1873. If you want a great meal, at almost any time of the day, there are few places that can beat this one. If
you just want coffee and cake, then choose the right-hand-side seating
area (just beyond the door). But if it is bustle and star-sightings, head
for the elongated salon that runs parallel with the Ring avenue, just opposite the main University building. At night lots of theatergoers turn
up after the Burg has turned out. ✉ *Dr.-Karl-Lueger-Ring 4, 1st District* ☎ *01/532–0621* Ⓤ *U2/Schottenring.*

★ ✗ **Café Mozart.** Graham Greene, staying in the Hotel Sacher next door,
loved having his coffee here while working on the script for *The Third
Man* (in fact, Greene had the café featured in the film and Anton Karas,
the zither player who did the famous Harry Lime theme, wrote a waltz
for the place). The café was named after the monument to Mozart (now
in the Burggarten) that once stood outside the building; reputedly,
Wolfie came here to enjoy his coffee, but the decor is entirely changed
from his era. Although overrun with sightseers, the waiters are charming as all get out and manage to remain calm even when customers run
them ragged. Crystal chandeliers, a brass-and-oak interior, comfortable
seating, and delicious food—the excellent Tafelspitz here has to be mentioned—add to its popularity. With the state opera house just behind
the café, this is a fine place for an after-performance snack. Be on the
lookout for opera divas doing just the same. ✉ *Albertinaplatz 2 1st*

District ☎ *01/2410–0210* ⊕ *www.cafe-wien.at/* Ⓤ *U1, U2, or U4/Karl-splatz/Opera.*

$$ ✕ **Café Museum.** The controversial architect Adolf Loos (famed for his pronouncement: "Ornament is a sin") laid the foundation stone for this "puristically" styled coffeehouse in 1899. Throughout the past century, this was a top rendezvous spot for Wien Secession artists, along with actors, students, and professors due to the proximity of the Secession Pavilion, the Academy of Fine Arts, the Theater an der Wien, and Vienna's Technical University. Gustav Klimt, Egon Schiele, and Josef Hoffmann all enjoyed sipping their Melange here. Today, after years of intensive and painstaking restoration (following Loos's detailed documents discovered in the Albertina), it once again lives up to its former glory. ⊠ *Friedrichstrasse 6, 1st District* ☎ *01/586–5202* Ⓤ *U1, U2, or U4/Karlsplatz/Opera.*

✕ **Café Sacher.** You'll see people wandering out of this legendary café in a whipped-cream stupor. Yes, you can famously enjoy life at its sweetest here. This legend began life as a *delikatessen* opened by Sacher, court confectioner to Prince von Metternich, the most powerful prime minister in early-19th-century Europe and fervent chocoholic (*see also* "Monarchs & Mozart: From St. Stephan's to the Opera House" *in* Exploring Vienna, *above*). Back then, cookbooks of the day devoted more space to desserts than to main courses and Sacher's creations were practically ranked on the order of painting and sculpture. When the populace at large was allowed to enjoy the prime minister's favorite chocolate cake—a sublime mixture of flour, eggs, butter, chocolate, and apricot preserves—the fashion for Sachertorte was created. War-weary Metternich must have been amused to see a battle break out between Sacher and Demel—a competing confectioner—as to who served the real Sachertorte, but the jury has now awarded the prize to Sacher, after a much-publicized trial, which came to a decision worthy of Solomon, that the original article should be spelled as one word, those others using the similar recipe must use two words. The difference between the Demel version? Sacher puts its apricot jam in the cake middle, while Demel puts it just below the icing. Which do you prefer (gossip has it that a true Viennese likes Demel's version best). Red flocks the drapes, walls, and floors here, mirrors and chandeliers add glitter, and there is live piano music every day from 4:30 until 7 PM. ⊠ *Philharmonikerstrasse 4, 1st District* ☎ *01/514560* Ⓤ *U1, U2, or U4/Karlsplatz/Opera.*

✕ **Café Schwarzenberg.** A bright yellow facade and a large terrace welcomes all to this café. Wall-to-wall mirrors reflect the elegant clientele perched on green leather seats. Across from the Hotel Imperial, this location is perfect if you want a snack after a concert at the Musikverein or the Konzerthaus, both just a couple of minutes away. Open until midnight, this has a good choice of food and pastries and, even though the waiters can be a little condescending, the overall atmosphere is still nice enough to encourage longer stays. Piano music can be heard until late on Wednesdays and Fridays, and from 5 until 7 PM on Saturdays and Sundays. ⊠ *Kärntner Ring 17, 1st District* ☎ *01/512–8998* Ⓤ *U2/Schottentor.*

CloseUp

VIENNA'S SWEETEST VICE

MANY THINK THAT THE CHIEF contribution of the people who created the Viennese waltz and the operetta naturally comes with the dessert course, in the appropriate form of rich and luscious pastries, and in the beloved and universal Schlagobers (whipped cream). Most people would agree that the finest pastry shops and confectioners are found in Vienna. There is even one place where you can stand and watch the confectioner at work. Watch the cakes being iced, marzipan figures shaped to form flower petals, strudels being rolled, or chocolate being poured over the dark sponge. Mmmmmmmmm . . . Spend an afternoon at one of these places and you'll understand why the Viennese consider whipped cream to be one of the four main food groups.

First stop for sweet lovers, pastry fans, and marzipan maniacs has to be **Demel** (✉ Kohlmarkt 14, 1st District ☎ 01/535-1717-0), a 200-year-old confectioner famous for its sweetmeats that make every heart beat faster (and eventually slower). The display cases are filled to the brim; all you have to do is point at what you want and then go and sit where you want. But don't forget to watch the pastry chef at work in the glassed-over, glassed-in courtyard. If you belong to those who like to see freak shows, then peep into the cellar and see the Marzipan Museum with a strange display of famous heads—among others Bill Clinton, Barbara Cartland, and Kofi Annan—in colored marzipan.

Beyond the shop proper are stairs that lead to dining salons where the decor is almost as sweet as the chocolates, marzipan, and sugar-coated almonds on sale. **Gerstner** (✉ Kärntnerstrasse 13–15 ☎ 01/5124963) is in the heart of the bustling Kärntnerstrasse and is one of the best places for the dark, moist, mouthwatering

poppy-seed cake (Mohntorte), carrot cake, and chocolate-dipped strawberries. Its decor is modern but the place has been here since the mid-18th century. **Heiner** (✉ Kärntnerstrasse 21–23 ☎ 01/512-6863 ✉ Wollzeile 9 ☎ 01/512-2343) is dazzling for its crystal chandeliers as well as for its pastries. The great favorite here has to be the almond-orange torte. **Oberlaa** (✉ Neuer Markt 16 ☎ 01/513-2936 ✉ Babenbergerstrasse 7, opposite Kunsthistoriches Museum ☎ 01/5867-2820 ✉ Landstrasser Hauptstrasse 1 ☎ 01/7152-7400) has irresistible confections such as the "Oberlaa Kurbad Cake," Truffle Cake, and Chocolate Mousse Cake. Highly popular with the locals and great value for money, there are now six Oberlaa branches to choose from. **Sperl** (✉ Gumpendorferstrasse 11, 6th District/Mariahilf ☎ 01/586–4158), founded in 1880, has an all-around Old Viennese ambience.

It doesn't really matter which of the many branches of **Aida** (✉ Neuer Markt 16 ☎ 01/513-2936 ✉ Opernring 7 ☎ 01/533-1933 ✉ Bognergasse 3 ☎ 01/533-9442 ✉ Stock-im-Eisen-Platz 2 ☎ 01/512-2977 ✉ Wollzeile 28 ☎ 01/512-3724 ✉ Praterstrasse 78 ☎ 01/216-2137 ✉ Rotenturmstrasse 24 ☎ 01/58-2585) you go to as they are all quite similar. Aida is most famous for the cheapest cup of (excellent) coffee in town, but the incredibly inexpensive pastries are just fantastic. Since 1971 200 million "Topfengolatschen" (cream-cheese pastries) have been counted and consumed.

WHERE TO STAY

By Bonnie
Dodson

If you're lucky enough to stay at one of Vienna's better hotels, chances are you'll be deposited at one of those grand Ringstrasse palais that once housed assorted Imperial Highnesses. Their red velvet–gilt mirror–and–crystal chandelier opulence still stands supreme even in today's world of lavish hospitality, and these establishments pride themselves on staff that appear to anticipate, like fairy-guardians, your every desire. Of course, for those with more modest requirements, and purses, ample rooms are available in less costly but still alluring hotels. Even when the high-flown elegance may be sparse and the layers of charm a bit thin, most of our lower-priced options offer the best in location, value, and, in many instances, a quaint echo of Alt Wien (Old Vienna) atmosphere.

When you have only a short time to spend in Vienna, you will probably choose to stay in the inner city (the 1st District, or 1010 postal code), to be within walking distance of the most important sights, restaurants, and shops. But outside of the 1st, there are any number of other delightful neighborhoods to rest your head. The "Biedermeier" quarter of Spittelberg, in the 7th District of Neubau, has cobblestone streets, lots of 19th-century houses, and a wonderful array of art galleries and restaurants and, increasingly, hotel options. Just to its east is the fabulous MuseumsQuartier, an area that has some nice hotel finds. Schwedenplatz is the area fronted by the Danube Canal—a neighborhood that is one of the most happening in the city, although just a stroll from the centuries-old lanes around Fleischmarkt. Other sweet hotel options are set in the 8th District of Josefstadt, an area noted for antiques shops, good local restaurants, bars, and theater.

Because of the famous Christmas markets, the weeks leading up to the holidays are also a popular time, as well as the week around New Year's (*Silvester*), with all the orchestral concerts. Expect to pay accordingly, and, at the very top hotels, a lot (around €300–€550 a night). Surprisingly, summer months are not as busy, perhaps because the opera is not in season. You'll find good bargains at this time of year, especially in August. Vienna summers are usually full of warm, sunny days, and it hardly ever gets uncomfortably hot. Air-conditioning is customary in the top categories only, but since Vienna has very few extremely hot days, with temperatures cooling off at night, it's usually not necessary.

The Vienna tourist office can assist in getting hotel rooms, even at the last minute. Note that neighborhoods are *only* listed for those hotels and pensions that are outside the 1st District. Assume that all guest rooms have air-conditioning, room phones, and room TVs unless noted otherwise.

WHAT IT COSTS In euros				
	$$$$	**$$$**	**$$**	**$**	**¢**
FOR 2 PEOPLE	over €270	€170–€270	€120–€170	€80–€120	under €80

Prices are for two people in a standard double room. Assume that hotels operate on the European Plan (EP, with no meal provided) unless we note that they use the Breakfast Plan (BP).

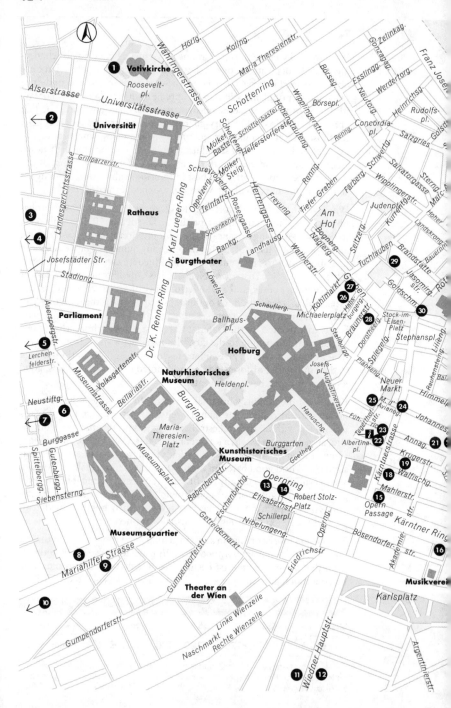

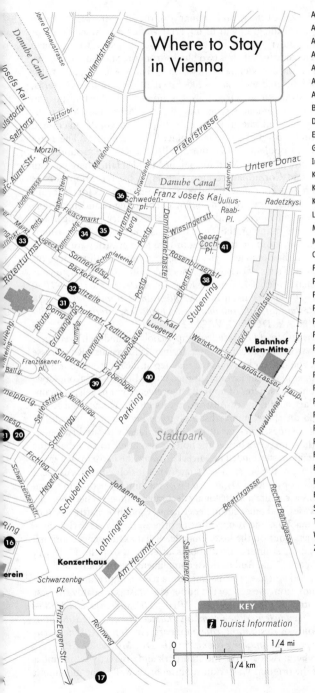

Where to Stay in Vienna

Academia 2
Altstadt .7
Ambassador 24
Am Stephanplatz 30
Arenberg 38
Astoria 23
Austria 35
Bristol 15
Das Triest 12
Erzherzog Rainer 11
Graben 28
Imperial 16
Kärntnerhof 34
König von Ungarn 32
Kummer 8
Le Méridien 13
Mailberger Hof 21
Museum 6
Opernring 14
Palais Coburg 39
Palais Schwarzenberg 17
Pension Aviano 25
Pension Christina 36
Pension City 33
Pension Dr. Geissler, ...41
Pension Domizil 31
Pension Nossek 27
Pension Pertschy 26
Pension Reimer 10
Pension Riedl 37
Pension Suzanne 18
Pension Wild 5
Pension Zipser 3
Radisson 40
Rathaus Wine & Design 4
Regina .1
Römischer Kaiser 20
Sacher 22
Tyrol 9
Wandl 29
Zur Wiener Staatsoper 19

KEY

𝑖 Tourist Information

0 — 1/4 mi

0 — 1/4 km

$$$$ ⊞ **Imperial.** One of the great landmarks of the Ringstrasse, this hotel
FodorśChoice has exemplified the grandeur of imperial Vienna ever since Emperor
★ Franz Josef formerly opened its doors in 1873. Adjacent to the famed
Musikverein concert hall and two blocks from the Staatsoper, the emphasis here is on Old Vienna elegance and privacy, which accounts for
a guest book littered with names like Elizabeth Taylor, José Carreras,
and Bruce Springsteen. Originally the home of Duke Philipp von
Württenberg, this remains a symphony of potted-palm luxe. Don't overlook, as if you could, the grand marble staircase, a wonder in colored
marbles modeled on the one in Munich's court library. The main
lobby looks as opulent as a Hofburg ballroom. On the ground floor
is the true showpiece: the Marmorsaal, or Marble Hall, where you can
now dine amid Corinthian columns. Upstairs, the reception floor is
filled with rooms done in whipped cream neo-rococo. As for the beautiful guest rooms, they are furnished with sparkling chandeliers, gorgeously swagged fabrics, and original 19th-century paintings. The
larger suites are found on the lower floor; as you ascend, guest rooms
get smaller, but those on the top floor (the former attic) are done in
an enchanting Biedermeier style, and several have small terraces offering amazing views of the city. *Ja,* indeeed, suites do come with your
own personal butler. ⊠ *Kärntner Ring 16, A-1010* ☎ *01/501–10–0*
🖷 *01/501–10–410* ⊕ *www.luxurycollection.com/imperial* ⇥ *138
rooms* ⚹ *Restaurant, café, minibars, gym, piano bar, Internet, no-smoking rooms* ▤ *AE, DC, MC, V* ⦾ *EP.*

★ **$$$$** ⊞ **Le Méridien.** One of Le Méridien's super-cool "art and tech" ventures,
their Vienna outpost occupies three former 19th-century Ringstrasse
palaces but you'd never know it after one step inside the front door. Sleek
as a *Wallpaper* magazine layout, adorned with Mies van der Rohe–style
sofas and ottomans, acres of nouvelle fluorescent light panels, and contemporary art renditions of Austrian actors Oskar Werner and Romy
Schneider in the spare, minimalist lobby, you know you're in a different kind of Viennese five-star at first glance. Ideally located two minutes from the state opera house, the hotel is also home to Shambala, the
luxe restaurant masterminded by Michel Rostang, the Parisian chef-guru,
so you can enjoy the latest in Austrian/Asian fusion cuisine. Adjacent
is a bar that hops with a DJ and some of the hippest people in town.
Guest rooms are white and strikingly decorated with glass headboards,
contempo vases, and other cutting-edge items. Cloudlike mattresses, flat-
screen plasma TVs, and roomy "tower of power" showers with three
massaging jets pour on the luxe. Outside, visual excitements continue,
as the tranquil, soundproofed rooms offer views of the Hofburg,
Burggarten, and Ring. Add to this a complimentary minibar and Internet service, and you have the makings for a truly pampered stay, which
you can enjoy from the get-go: the buffet breakfast is arguably the best
in the country. ⊠ *Opernring 13, A-1010* ☎ *01/588–900* 🖷 *01/588–
9090–90* ⊕ *www.lemeridien.com/austria/vienna/hotel_at1806.shtml*
⇥ *294 rooms* ⚹ *Restaurant, café, minibars, bar, Internet, fitness center, indoor pool, no-smoking rooms* ▤ *AE, DC, MC, V* ⦾ *EP.*

★ **$$$$** ⊞ **Palais Coburg.** Across from the Stadtpark and discreetly set behind a
fraction of the original Wasserkunst *bastei* brick wall is the mammoth

19th-century white palace once known throughout the city as "Fort Aspargus," due to the slender marble columns that adorn the garden facade. Built as the home for the princes of Saxe-Coburg-Kohary, the palace has received a complete modernist make-over, starting with the lobby all ablaze with white stone and plate glass. The old princes, however, would find comfort in the fact that up the grand staircase his Blue Salon and Chinese Salon remain the same, as does the hyperopulent pink and yellow marble ballroom where Johann Strauss conducted his orchestra as dancers waltzed across the parquet floor. There are no double rooms here, only deluxe modern or imperial-style suites, all named after Coburg titles. Many of them are spectacular two-storied showpieces, the best done in a gilded-yellow 19th-century Biedermeier or Empire style. All offer fresh flowers, fully equipped kitchenettes with a complimentary stock of champagne, wine, beer, and soft drinks, espresso makers, laptops with free Internet, and two bathrooms, some with gigantic whirlpool baths and saunas. Some of the suites have a large terrace with lordly views of the Stadtpark or St. Stephan's spire (others look out on unprepossessing modern hotels). Popular in its own right is the house restaurant, manned by one of the most famous chefs in the country, Christian Petz. ⊠ *Coburgbastei 4, A-1010* ☎ *01/51818-0* 🖷 *01/51818-1* ⊕ *www.palaiscoburg.at* ➧ *33 suites* ⌂ *Restaurant, bar, minibars, Internet, indoor pool, fitness room* ▤ *AE, DC, MC, V* ❙❂❙ *EP.*

$$$$ 🖾 **Palais Schwarzenberg.** It's not every day you get to call a palace de-
FodorśChoice signed by Lukas von Hildebrandt (architect of the nearby Belvedere Palace)
★ and Fischer von Erlach (whose Karlskirche crowns the nearby skyline) your home-away-from-home. But this enchanting residence allows you to feel like a prince—Prince Adam Franz zu Schwarzenberg, to be exact, who completed the mansion in 1716—or his princess. Complete with five historic salons, including the Marmorsaal, one of Vienna's most glittering ballrooms, this hotel has everything, including a 16-acre private park. Though it's just a few minutes' walk from the heart of the city, the hotel feels like a country estate—the loudest sounds you'll often hear are the thwack of croquet balls on the lawn. Guest rooms are individually and luxuriously appointed, with the family's original artwork adorning the walls; only those with ultramodern tastes will want to book the suites by Italian designer Paolo Piva, in a separate wing in the park. All bathrooms are sleekly done, with heated towel racks and long, deep bathtubs. Happily, you don't have to be a guest here to come for a drink, coffee, or light lunch, served outside on the terrace in summer overlooking the formal gardens studded with marble statues. ⊠ *Schwarzenbergplatz 9, 3rd District/Landstrasse* ☎ *01/798-4515* 🖷 *01/798-4714* ⊕ *www. palais-schwarzenberg.com* ➧ *44 rooms* ⌂ *Restaurant, minibars, tennis court, bar, Internet, free parking* ▤ *AE, DC, MC, V* ❙❂❙ *EP.*

★ $$$$ 🖾 **Sacher.** One of Europe's legends, originally founded by Eduard Sacher, chef to Prince Metternich, the Sacher dates from 1876. It has retained its sense of history over the years while providing luxurious, modern-day comfort. In fact, the entire hotel got a 2004 refurbishment, which is now complete except for the third floor and the Restaurant Anna Sacher, both of which will reopen sometime in 2005. In our experience, the staff has proved unfailingly helpful and gracious, in great contrast to decades gone by when most guests got the chilly monocle treatment. Sacher's widow, Anna, turned the hotel into the phenomenon that it still is. In an age when every moment had to be lived in public, her *separé* dining rooms offered privacy and comfort to archdukes and their mistresses, to dancers and their hussars. It was an empire that she watched over, supreme and always with a cigar in her mouth. Today, the corridors serve as a veritable art gallery, and the exquisitely furnished bedrooms also contain original artwork. The location directly behind the Opera House could hardly be more central, and the ratio of staff to guests is more than two to one. Meals in the Red Room or Anna Sacher Room are first-rate, with both a Continental and Viennese menu. The Café Sacher, of course, is legendary. British director Carol Reed filmed some of his classic 1949 film *The Third Man* in the reception area. ⊠ *Philharmonikerstrasse 4, A-1010* ☎ *01/514–56–0* 🖷 *01/514–56–810* ⊕ *www.sacher.com* 🖉 *113 rooms* ♨ *2 restaurants, café, minibars, bar, Internet, no-smoking rooms* 🖃 *AE, DC, MC, V* ⦿ *EP.*

$$$–$$$$ 🏨 **Ambassador.** Franz Lehár, Marlene Dietrich, the Infanta Isabel of Spain, and Mick Jagger are just a few of the celebrities who have stayed at this old dowager (from 1866), given a face-lift overhaul in 2001. The lobby is small but grand, and the high-ceilinged guest rooms, differing only in size, are uniformly decorated with pale yellow-striped wallpaper, deep blue carpets, and faux Empire furniture. Unless you want the excitement of a direct view onto the lively pedestrian Kärntnerstrasse, ask for one of the quieter rooms on the Neuer Markt side. The Ambassador also houses the top-flight restaurant Mörwald, which offers stunning views of the square. ⊠ *Kärntnerstrasse 22/Neuer Markt 5, A-1010* ☎ *01/961610* 🖷 *01/5132–999* ⊕ *www.ambassador.at* 🖉 *86 rooms* ♨ *Restaurant, minibars, bar, Internet* 🖃 *AE, DC, MC, V* ⦿ *EP.*

$$$–$$$$ 🏨 **Bristol.** A Bösendorfer grand of a hotel, this venerable landmark, dating from 1892, has one of the finest locations in the city, on the Ring next to the state opera house. The accent here is on tradition—a note struck by the lobby, which is fairly and disappointingly standard-issue when it comes to luxe: the usual oval salons, domed ceilings, traditional overstuffed chairs, modern wood paneling, and potted palms. There are enough chandeliers, surely, but too bad there are so many ugly recessed ceiling lights. For real grandeur, you have to book one of the top penthouses and suites, gloriously furnished in Biedermeier style with decorative fireplaces, thick carpets, wing-back chairs, crystal chandeliers, and lace curtains. Penthouse rooms have terraces with staggering views of the Opera. Other rooms miss out on this Ringstrasse splendor but are most comfortable and stylish nevertheless. The Bristol also houses the acclaimed Korso restaurant and a music salon complete with a pianist playing tunes on a time-burnished—yes—Bösendorfer. ⊠ *Kärntner Ring 1, A-1010* ☎ *01/515–16–0* 🖷 *01/515–16–550* ⊕ *www.westin.com/ bristol* 🖉 *141 rooms* ♨ *2 restaurants, minibars, health club, bar, Internet, business services* 🖃 *AE, DC, MC, V* ⦿ *EP.*

$$$ 🏨 **Astoria.** Built in 1912 and still retaining the outward charm of that era, the Astoria is one of the grand old Viennese hotels and in a superb location on the Kärnterstrasse between the Opera and St. Stephan's. You are greeted by a wood-paneled lobby that is an essay in Wiener Werkstätte style. Two of the floors have been renovated and have a lovely, soft contemporary style with pretty fabrics in beige tones, polished dark wood, and Oriental rugs. The other floors retain their old-fashioned appeal, though some are a little worn around the edges. ☒ *Kärntnerstrasse 32–34, A-1010* ☎ *01/51577* 🖷 *01/515–7782* ⊕ *www. austria-trend.at/asw* ⤴ *118 rooms* ⚭ *Bar, minibars, Internet; no a/c* ▤ *AE, DC, MC, V* ⊧⊙⊧ *BP.*

★ **$$$** 🏨 **Das Triest.** A single yellow tulip perched—toothbrush-fashion—against a white closet. Beige-on-beige fabrics offset by glowing pine headboards the size of walls. A staircase suave as a Bauhaus image. Yes, this is Sir Terrence Conran country: the Vienna outpost of the man who has, since the 1970s, colonized every hip neighborhood in the world with his signature flair. Totally redone with the Conran look, this hotel gives one the feeling of being on board an ultrasleek ocean liner—a bit surprising, considering this was once the stable of the old Vienna-Trieste mail-route posthouse. All of this has attracted the requisite celebrities, including Johnny Depp (who set off the fire alarm twice in one evening because of cigarette smoke in his room). They would certainly appreciate the extra (and plentiful) little touches in the rooms; even the doorknobs feel nice to the touch. Decor is delightful—linen-fresh, with accents of blue carpeting and honey-hued woods, and high-style as only a Conran hotel can be. The hotel also allures with an excellent Austro-Italian restaurant, Collio. Das Triest may be a little off the beaten track but is still within easy walking distance of the city center. ☒ *Wiedner Hauptstrasse 12, A-1040, 4th District/Wieden* ☎ *01/589–180* 🖷 *01/589–1818* ⊕ *www.dastriest.at.* ⤴ *73 rooms* ⚭ *Restaurant, café, minibars, health club, bar, Internet; no a/c in some rooms* ▤ *AE, DC, MC, V* ⊧⊙⊧ *BP.*

$$$ 🏨 **König von Ungarn.** In a dormered, 16th-century house in the shadow of St. Stephan's Cathedral, this hotel began catering to court nobility in 1815—many Hungarian aristos rented rooms here back when. Famously, the complex is joined to the Figarohaus—an adjacent house where, as it turns out, Mozart lived when he wrote *The Marriage of Figaro.* Wolfie would undoubtedly cotton to this hostelry, now outfitted with the glowing Mozartstuberl restaurant, which is beautifully aglow in "Schönbrunn yellow"; a courtyard-atrium (so gigantic a tree sprouts in the middle of it); and guest rooms that radiate charm: some with Styrian wood-paneled walls are furnished with country antiques and have walk-in closets and double sinks in the sparkling bathrooms. The eight suites are two-storied, and two have balconies with rooftop views of Old Vienna. ☒ *Schulerstrasse 10, A-1010* ☎ *01/515–840* 🖷 *01/515–848* ⊕ *www.kvu.at* ⤴ *33 rooms* ⚭ *Restaurant, minibars, bar, Internet* ▤ *DC, MC, V* ⊧⊙⊧ *BP.*

FodorśChoice
★

$$$ 🏨 **Opernring.** With an ideal location on the Ringstrasse and catercorner from the state opera house, the Opernring has rooms that are nicer than you would imagine considering the rather unprepossessing entrance and lobby. Guest rooms are spacious with good carpets, cheerful and soigne furniture done up in Swedish woods, and sitting areas, and about half have small terraces. ☒ *Opernring 11, A-1010* ☎ *01/587–5518* 🖷 *01/*

587–5518–29 ⊕ *www.opernring.at* ✒ *35 rooms* ⚬ *Minibars, Internet; no a/c* ☰ *AE, DC, MC, V* ⊜ *BP.*

★ **$$$** ▦ **Radisson.** One of the handsomest of all Ringstrassen palaces comprises the core of Radisson's Vienna outpost. Along with the fin-de-siècle Palais Leitenberger, the Palais Henckel von Donnersmarck, built in 1872, was occupied by an exceedingly patrician family, and their taste shows in the superbly designed facade, articulated with window pediments and caryatids. Inside, a grand staircase leads you up to a gallery of ancestral portraits, spotlighted in a sober marble hall. The location is also princely—directly across from the Stadtpark, Vienna's main city park. Inside, the rooms are done in an understated, traditional, and soigné manner. Quiet and comfortable, some have pretty floral drapes and matching bedspreads, others allure with a more masculine Biedermeier look. Le Siecle restaurant offers food as stylish as its decor. ✉ *Parkring 16, A-1010* ☎ *01/515170* 🖷 *01/512–2216* ⊕ *www.radissonsas.com* ✒ *246 rooms* ⚬ *2 restaurants, café, minibars, gym, bar, Internet* ☰ *AE, DC, MC, V* ⊜ *EP.*

★ **$$–$$$** ▦ **Kummer.** With a lobby that is as old-world Viennese as they come, this 19th-century landmark has a distinguished history dating back to 1872 (the Strauss family once resided in a hotel on the site; Friedrich Schlögl, one of the founding fathers of the Viennese literature tradition, began a literary and art salon in this hotel's reception rooms). You enter and are caught up in a waltz of beveled glass, gilded globe-lanterns, colored marble trim, and painted boiserie, all surrounding a grand staircase atrium. Upstairs, each comfortably furnished room is different, and the ones facing the busy Mariahilferstrasse have soundproof windows. Some rooms have an alcove sitting area; single rooms are very much on the bijou side. Yes, you are in the very heart of the shopping district, which means crowds and neon-signs, but the hotel is close to the Westbahnhof, major museums, and you may feel you've wandered onto a set for *Die Fledermaus* when you see that lobby. ✉ *Mariahilferstrasse 71/a, 6th District/Mariahilf* ☎ *01/58895* 🖷 *01/587–8133* ⊕ *www. hotelkummer.at* ✒ *100 rooms* ⚬ *Restaurant, minibars, bar, Internet, parking (fee); no a/c* ☰ *AE, DC, MC, V* ⊜ *BP.*

★ **$$–$$$** ▦ **Mailberger Hof.** The Knights of Malta—those famous "Hospitallers"— knew something about hospitality and their former Vienna palace continues to offer travelers a comforting welcome mat. You arrive at this Baroque mansion to find an atmospheric carriage entrance and a cobblestoned and captivating courtyard, set in a wonderful location just off the Kärntnerstrasse. A recent renovation has given some of its formerly rather dour rooms some charm, with lovely golden and crimson bedspreads, reproduction furniture, and soft carpets, but most remain traditional in the extreme. The rooms on the first floor are the most attractive; try to get one facing the pretty Baroque street. In summer, the inner courtyard is set with tables for dining; at other times, you'll dine on Vienna specialities and "Naturküche" under rather regal vaulted arches. ✉ *Annagasse 7, A-1010* ☎ *01/512–0641* 🖷 *01/512–0641–10* ⊕ *www.mailbergerhof.at* ✒ *40 rooms, 5 apartments with kitchenettes (available by the month)* ⚬ *Restaurant, minibars, Internet; no a/c in some rooms* ☰ *AE, DC, MC, V* ⊜ *BP.*

$$–$$$ 🏨 **Römischer Kaiser.** A pastel pink confection of a hotel (with whipped-
FodorsChoice cream white stone trim), housed in a late-17th-century former town palace
★ between the Opera and St. Stephan's, the Roman Emperor has been host
to an impressive musical clientele over the years—Mozart, Liszt, Wagner, Bruckner, and Grieg, to name a few. Happily, a sense of history still
pervades throughout, and the elegant guest rooms have real charm, with
lots of burnished wood trim and armoires, crystal chandeliers, pale
pink or yellow wallpaper, expensive fabrics, and in some of the larger
doubles, dramatic tie-back curtains separating the sleeping area. The style
of most is staidly, wonderfully "Viennese." A few of the baths—called
Versace-style (trumped up with the historicizing motifs of the famous
fashion house)—are fit for an empress, with pink, white, and gold accents. Breakfast is served in an adorable Louis XVI nook. Pretty, *non*?
✉ *Annagasse 16, A-1010* 🕾 *01/512–7751–0* 🖶 *01/512–7751–13*
🌐 *www.bestwestern-ce.com/roemischerkaiser* 🛏 *24 rooms* ♨ *Minibars, Internet* 🖃 *AE, DC, MC, V* ❙⊙❙ *BP.*

★ **$$–$$$** 🏨 **Tyrol.** On a busy corner of Mariahilferstrasse, this small, luxurious
hotel is a good choice for those who want to be close to the MuseumsQuartier and some fun shopping, too. Rooms are exceptionally pleasing, with fabrics and tony furniture from posh Viennese stores like
Backhausen, Thonet, and Wittmann. There are many nice touches,
from the exquisite bedcovers, stylish high-backed chairs and fashionable, elongated lamps to the elegant, subtle drapes that dress the long
windows. It's in a neighborhood that has everything, including a host
of good restaurants to choose from. ✉ *Mariahilferstrasse 15, A-1060*
🕾 *01/587–5415* 🖶 *01/587–5415–9* 🌐 *www.das-tyrol.at* 🛏 *30 rooms*
♨ *Bar, minibars, Internet* 🖃 *AE, DC, MC, V* ❙⊙❙ *BP.*

$$–$$$ 🏨 **Wandl.** The restored facade identifies a 300-year-old house that has
been in family hands as a hotel since 1854. You couldn't find a better
location, tucked behind St. Peter's Church, just off the Graben. The hallways are punctuated by cheerful, bright openings along the glassed-in
inner court. The rooms are modern, but some are a bit plain and charm-
less, despite parquet flooring and red accents. If you can, ask for one of
the rooms done in period furniture, with decorated ceilings and gilt mirrors; they're rather palatial, with plush Victorian chairs, carved wood
trim, and velvet throws. ✉ *Petersplatz 9, A-1010* 🕾 *01/534–55–0*
🖶 *01/534–55–77* 🌐 *www.hotel-wandl.com* 🛏 *138 rooms* ♨ *Bar, Internet; no a/c* 🖃 *AE, DC, MC, V* ❙⊙❙ *BP.*

$$ 🏨 **Altstadt.** A cognoscenti favorite, this small hotel was once a patrician
FodorsChoice home and is in one of Vienna's most pampered neighborhoods—and
★ we mean neighborhood: a plus here is being able to really interact with
real Viennese, their stores (hey, supermarkets!), and residential streets.
In fact, you are lucky enough to be in the chic and quaint Spittelberg
quarter. The Altstadt is blessed with a personable and helpful manage-
ment. Palm trees, a Secession-style, wrought-iron staircase, modernist
fabrics, and halogen lighting make for a very design-y interior. Guest
rooms are large with all the modern comforts, though they retain an
antique feel. The English-style lounge has a fireplace and plump floral
sofas. Upper rooms have lovely views out over the city roofline. Last
but not least, you are one streetcar stop or a pleasant walk from the main

museums. ⊠ *Kirchengasse 41, 7th District/Neubau* ☎ *01/526–3399–0* 🖷 *01/523–4901* ⊕ *www.altstadt.at* ⤴ *25 rooms* ⌂ *Minibars, bar; no a/c* ⊟ *AE, DC, MC, V* ⦿| *BP.*

$$ ⌸ **Am Stephansplatz.** You can't get a better location than this, directly across from the magnificent front entrance of St. Stephan's Cathedral. Despite this modern hotel's gray, lackluster facade, it offers surprisingly nice, spacious rooms furnished with Turkish carpets, lovely prints and paintings, and elegant furniture. Some rooms are a bit over the top with red wallpaper, but others have more subtle shades of pale yellow and beige. If the bells from the cathedral pose a problem, ask for a room facing the inner courtyard. ⊠ *Stephansplatz 9, A-1010* ☎ *01/53405–0* 🖷 *01/53405–710* ⊕ *www.nethotels.com/am_stephansplatz* ⤴ *57 rooms* ⌂ *Café, minibars, Internet; no a/c* ⊟ *AE, DC, MC, V* ⦿| *BP.*

$$ ⌸ **Arenberg.** Near Schwedenplatz and the Danube Canal, the Arenberg is an old-fashioned pension with lots of character. Despite its corner location on the Ringstrasse, serenity reigns, because the pension is on the upper floors of the building. Rooms have a charming, old-fashioned appearance, with plump beds, overstuffed chairs, and patterned carpets. The No. 1 streetcar is virtually outside the front door, allowing easy access to the city center, or you can walk about 10 minutes up the Ring. ⊠ *Stubenring 2, A-1010* ☎ *01/512–5291* 🖷 *01/513–9356* ⊕ *www.arenberg.at* ⤴ *22 rooms* ⌂ *Internet; no a/c* ⊟ *AE, DC, MC, V* ⦿| *BP.*

$$ ⌸ **Erzherzog Rainer.** On a fountained square in a good location near the Naschmarkt and within walking distance of Karlsplatz and the city center, the lovely pale green Archduke Rainer opened in 1913 as a grand hotel, with its restaurant a meeting place for prominent Viennese society. Guest rooms are extremely pleasant, with a mixture of modern and antique reproduction furniture providing a regal touch, and baths are well designed. Breakfast is ample. ⊠ *Wiedner Hauptstrasse 27–29, 4th District/Wieden* ☎ *01/501110* 🖷 *01/50111–350* ⊕ *www.schick-hotels.com* ⤴ *84 rooms* ⌂ *Restaurant, minibars, Internet; no a/c* ⊟ *AE, DC, MC, V* ⦿| *BP.*

$$ ⌸ **Pension Domizil.** Around the corner from the house where Mozart wrote *The Marriage of Figaro*, the Domizil offers quiet, well-equipped rooms furnished with rather bland contemporary furniture. Breakfast is a notch above the average, with both hot and cold selections. Another nice thing about staying here is free access to the Internet in the lobby. The staff is pleasant, and you're right in the middle of a series of charming Old World cobblestone streets near St. Stephan's. ⊠ *Schulerstrasse 14* ☎ *01/513–3199–0* 🖷 *01/512–3484* ⊕ *www.hoteldomizil.at* ⤴ *40 rooms* ⌂ *Internet; no a/c* ⊟ *AE, DC, MC, V* ⦿| *BP.*

★ $$ ⌸ **Pension Pertschy.** Housed in the former Palais Cavriani just off the Graben, this pension is as central as you can get—just behind the Hofburg and down the street from the Spanish Riding School. One of those typical Viennese mansion-turned-apartment-houses, the structure is still graced with a massive arched portal and yellow-stone courtyard, around which the 18th-century edifice was built. A few guest rooms contain lovely old ceramic stoves (just for show). Most rooms are spacious, and each one is comfortable. Some rooms are sweet, with bed canopies and chandeliers, although others are decorated with "repro"–antique furniture which verges on the kitsch. As for noise, the street outside gets a lot of fiaker carriages (and street sweepers at night), so opt for a courtyard room if you need complete peace and quiet. Use the elevator, but don't miss the palatial grand staircase. ⊠ *Habsburgergasse 5, A-1010* ☎ *01/534–49–0* 🖷 *01/534–49–49* ⊕ *www.pertschy.com* ⋈ *43 rooms* ⚭ *Minibars; no a/c* ⊟ *AE, DC, MC, V* ⭕ *BP.*

$$ 🏨 **Rathaus Wine & Design.** As if Josef Hoffman, Otto Wagner, and other
Fodor'sChoice great designers of the Wiener Werkstatte and Secession movements de-
★ signed a hotel for the 21st century, this new option on the Vienna lodging scene conjures up that soigné past with moderne color schemes, striking Werkstatte light fixtures, and the kind of Bauhaus-y chairs that Marlene Dietrich would have liked to perch on. But that is just the half of it. The brainchild of entrepreneurs Petra und Klaus Fleischhaker of Salzburg, this exclusive boutique hotel also pays homage to the winemakers of Austria. The spacious, high-ceilinged, ultra-modern guest rooms have polished wooden floors and accent wood walls, with warm orange, yellow, ocher, and cream accents. On each door is the name of a different winemaker, with a bottle of the vintner's wine inside (sorry, it's not included in the room price) and some of the greatest Austrian winemakers are represented, such as Bründelmayer, Gesellmann, Sattlerhof, and Markowitsch. Guests can take a grape escape in the chic, minimalist lounge, where vintages and snacks are served. ⊠ *Langegasse 13, A-1080* ☎ *01/400–1122* 🖷 *01/400–1122–88* ⊕ *www.hotel-rathaus-wien.at* ⋈ *33 rooms* ⚭ *Wine bar, minibars, Internet* ⊟ *AE, DC, MC, V* ⭕ *EP.*

$$ 🏨 **Regina.** Sitting regally on the edge of the Altstadt, this is a quintessen-
Fodor'sChoice tially Viennese hotel: The building is "grand" in the Ringstrasse style,
★ with French mansard roof, Italianate pilasters, the works; Inside, the decor is dignified grande dame—nothing showy, slightly matronly, but with solid good taste and refinement, with thick velvet drapes, vaulted hallways, baroque-style chandeliers, and an air that everything function *exactly* as it should, in a very proper Austrian manner. Little wonder that Freud, who lived nearby, used to eat breakfast in the hotel café every morning—this hotel's "correctness" must have given him much needed balance and ballast. Beyond the grand reception rooms, the high-ceilinged guest rooms are quiet, spacious, and decorated in a subdued, staid, nearly Germanic manner; many come with charming sitting areas. ⊠ *Rooseveltplatz 15, 9th District/Alsergrund* ☎ *01/404–460* 🖷 *01/408–8392* ⊕ *www.hotelregina.at* ⋈ *125 rooms* ⚭ *Restaurant, minibars, Internet; no a/c* ⊟ *AE, DC, MC, V* ⭕ *BP.*

$–$$ 🏨 **Kärntnerhof.** Behind the "Maria Theresa yellow" facade of this 100-year-old building, on a quiet corner, lies one of the friendliest small hotels in the center of the city. Take the restored Biedermeier elevator to the guest rooms upstairs, which are standard-issue, with antique-"styled" repros and modern baths. ⊠ *Grashofgasse 4, A-1010* ☎ *01/512–1923–0* 🖷 *01/513–1923–39* ⊕ *www.karntnerhof.com* ⋈ *43 rooms* ⚭ *Internet, some pets allowed; no a/c* ⊟ *AE, DC, MC, V* ⭕ *BP.*

★ **$–$$** 🏨 **Pension Nossek.** A family-run establishment on the upper floors of a 19th-century office and apartment building, the Nossek lies at the heart of the pedestrian and shopping area. The rooms have high ceilings and are eclectically but comfortably furnished; those on the front have a magnificent view of the Graben. Mozart worked on *The Abduction from the Seraglio* while he lived here in the early 1780s. Do as the many regular guests do: book early. ⊠ *Graben 17, A-1010* ☎ *01/533–7041–0* 🖷 *01/535–3646* ⊕ *www.pension-nossek.at* ⇱ *27 rooms, 25 with bath* ⚭ *Internet; no a/c* ☰ *No credit cards* ⊤◯⊦ *BP.*

$–$$ ▦ **Zur Wiener Staatsoper.** A great deal of loving care has gone into this family-owned hotel near the State Opera, reputed to be one of the Viennese settings in John Irving's *The Hotel New Hampshire*. The florid facade, with oversize torsos supporting its upper bays, is pure 19th-century Ringstrasse style. Rooms are small but have high ceilings and are charmingly decorated with pretty fabrics and wallpaper. ⊠ *Krugerstrasse 11, A-1010* ☎ *01/513–1274–0* 🖷 *01/513–1274–15* ⊕ *www.zurwienerstaatsoper.at* ⇱ *22 rooms* ⚭ *No a/c* ☰ *AE, MC, V* ⊤◯⊦ *BP.*

$ ▦ **Graben.** A small, family-run hotel in the heart of the city, the Graben has been in business since the late 18th century. Its tavern was a once popular literati hangout, and Franz Grillprazer, Franz Kafka, and Peter Altenberg made it into a mini-Bohemia—today, they would simply head to the famous and beloved Café Hawelka, located across the street. Guest rooms offer an assortment of high ceilings, chandeliers, and antique paintings mixed with durable carpets and modern, unexciting furniture, but several of them have a graceful "Biedermeier" stylistic echo. The best part of staying here is that you can walk virtually everywhere. Insist on a written confirmation of your booking. ⊠ *Dorotheergasse 3, A-1010* ☎ *01/512–1531–0* 🖷 *01/512–1531–20* ⊕ *www.kremslehner.at* ⇱ *41 rooms* ⚭ *Restaurant, bar, minibars, Internet; no a/c* ☰ *AE, DC, MC, V* ⊤◯⊦ *BP.*

★ $ ▦ **Museum.** In a beautiful Belle Epoque mansion just a five-minute walk from the Kunsthistorisches Museum, Naturhistorisches Museum, and the MuseumsQuartier, this elegant pension offers good-size rooms mixed in with few that are a bit squeezy. Considering this is an old-style pension, the need for renovation can be excused, especially since the price is reasonable for such a great location. There is also a pretty, sunny sitting room with deep, overstuffed sofas and wingback chairs, perfect for curling up with a good book. ⊠ *Museumstrasse 3, 7th District/Neubau* ☎ *01/523–44–260* 🖷 *01/523–44–2630* ⇱ *15 rooms* ⚭ *No a/c* ☰ *AE, DC, MC, V* ⊤◯⊦ *BP.*

$ ▦ **Pension Aviano.** Tucked away in a corner of the Neuer Markt, this small pension is part of the group that owns the well-known Pension Pertschy. Like its sister, this one is set in a vast 19th-century apartment house, now mostly given over to private apartments, offices, and stores. On the third and fourth floors you'll find the Aviano, whose guest rooms are cheerful and quiet. Some are rather regal, with flocked wallpapers, tiny chandeliers, bed canopies, and other Biedermeier grace notes. The two junior suites have a charming turret where you can sit and gaze out over the rooftops of Vienna. Music lovers favor this option since it is close to the Opera House. ⊠ *Marco d'Avianogasse 1, A-1010* ☎ *01/512–8330* 🖷 *01/512–8330–6* ⊕ *www.pertschy.com* ⇱ *17 rooms* ⚭ *Minibars, Internet; no a/c* ☰ *DC, MC, V* ⊤◯⊦ *BP.*

$ ▦ **Pension Christina.** Just steps from Schwedenplatz and the Danube Canal, this quiet pension offers mainly smallish modern rooms, warmly decorated with attractive dark-wood furniture set off against beige walls. The location is extremely convenient, near the U-Bahn and tram lines, or just a short, pleasant walk through ancient streets to the heart of the Altstadt. For night owls, the Bermuda Triangle, a late-night hot spot of bars and cafés clustered around the Rupertskirche, is close by. ⊠ *Hafnersteig 7, A-1010* ☎ *01/533–2961–0* 🖷 *01/533–2961–11* ⊕ *www.pertschy. com* 🗪 *33 rooms* ♨ *Minibars; no a/c* ▤ *MC, V* ⑩ *BP.*

$ 🏨 **Pension City.** You'll be on historic ground here: in 1791 the noted Austrian playwright and critic Franz Grillparzer was born in the house that then stood here; a bust and plaques in the entryway commemorate him. On the second floor of the present 100-year-old house, about three minutes away from St. Stephan's Cathedral, the rooms are outfitted in a successful mix of modern and 19th-century antique furniture against white walls. ⊠ *Bauernmarkt 10, A-1010* ☎ *01/533–9521* 🖷 *01/535–5216* ⊕ *www.inthotels.com* 🗪 *19 rooms* ♨ *Minibars; no a/c* ▤ *AE, DC, MC, V* ⑩ *BP.*

$ 🏨 **Pension Riedl.** Not far from Schwedenplatz, and across the square from the Postsparkasse, the 19th-century postal savings bank designed by Otto Wagner, this small establishment set back from the Ring offers modern, pleasant rooms with cable TV. One pretty room has a small balcony filled with flower pots. As an added touch, breakfast is delivered to your room. Cheerful owner Maria Felser is happy to arrange concert tickets and tours. The Stubentor tram and U-Bahn stop is just steps away. ⊠ *Georg-Coch-Platz 3/4/10, A-1010* ☎ *01/512–7919* 🖷 *01/512–79198* ⊕ *www. pensionriedl.at* 🗪 *8 rooms* ♨ *No a/c* ▤ *DC, MC, V* ⊙ *Closed first 2 wks of Feb.* ⑩ *BP.*

$ 🏨 **Pension Suzanne.** The Opera House is a stone's throw from this 1950s building on a small side street off the Ring. Don't be deceived by the nondescript exterior; once you step inside the doors of the pension you'll be enveloped in Viennese warmth and coziness. Most rooms are not spacious, but all are charmingly and comfortably furnished in 19th-century Biedermeier style. ⊠ *Walfischgasse 4, A-1010* ☎ *01/513–2507–0* 🖷 *01/513–2500* ⊕ *www.pension-suzanne.at* 🗪 *26 rooms* ♨ *Internet; no a/c* ▤ *AE, MC, V* ⑩ *BP.*

¢–$ 🏨 **Austria.** This older house, tucked away on a tiny cul-de-sac, offers the ultimate in quiet and is only five minutes' walk from the heart of the city. The high-ceiling rooms are pleasing in their combination of dark wood and lighter walls; the decor is mixed, with Oriental carpets on many floors. Rooms without full bath are a bit cheaper. There is a nice courtyard terrace that is perfect for sipping coffee after a day of sightseeing. You'll feel at home here, and the staff will help you find your way around town. ⊠ *Wolfengasse 3 (Fleischmarkt), A-1010* ☎ *01/ 515–23–0* 🖷 *01/515–23–506* ⊕ *www.hotelaustria-wien.at* 🗪 *46 rooms, 42 with bath* ♨ *Minibars, Internet; no a/c* ▤ *AE, DC, MC, V* ⑩ *BP.*

¢–$ 🏨 **Pension Zipser.** With an ornate facade and gilt-trimmed coat of arms, this 1904 house is one the city's better values. It's in the picturesque Josefstadt neighborhood of small cafés, shops, bars, and good restaurants, yet within steps of the J streetcar line to the city center. The rooms are in browns and beiges, with modern furniture and well-equipped baths. The balconies of some of the back rooms overlook tree-filled neighborhood courtyards. The accommodating staff will help get theater and concert tickets. ☒ *Langegasse 49, A-1080, 8th District/Josefstadt* ☎ *01/404–540* ⊟ *01/404–5413* ⊕ *www.zipser.at* ⟿ *47 rooms* ⚐ *Bar, Internet; no a/c* ⊟ *AE, DC, MC, V* ⦿⎸ *BP.*

¢ ⊞ **Academia.** Vienna has some exceptional student residences, which operate as hotels July to September and which can provide excellent bargains. Most rooms are single or double, and all come with bath, TV, and phones in the rooms. Among seasonal hotels, this is a fairly luxurious choice. ☒ *Pfeilgasse 3a, 8th District/Josefstadt* ☎ *01/40176* ⊟ *01/40176–20* ⟿ *300 rooms* ⚐ *Restaurant, bar* ⊟ *AE, MC, V.*

¢ ⊞ **Pension Dr. Geissler.** If this friendly pension only dates from the 1960s, no matter. You're just a few blocks from ground central of "old Vienna"— the Fleischmarket square and its enchanting cobblestoned alleyway. ☒ *Postgasse 14, A-1010* ☎ *01/533–2803* ⊟ *01/533–2635* ⊕ *www.hotelpension. at/dr-geissler/english/index.htm* ⟿ *23 rooms* ⊟ *No credit cards.*

¢ ⊞ **Pension Reimer.** Friendly and comfortable, this hotel is in a prime location just off Mariahilferstrasse. The modern rooms have high ceilings and large windows, and the atmosphere throughout is cheerful, though plain. Note, however, this place is located on the fourth floor and access is via an elevator which can only be operated with a key, leaving you and your arriving luggage at a bit of a loss. But not to worry—if you're willing to leap up the stairs first, the elevator key is happily handed over. ☒ *Kirchengasse 18, A-1070, 7th District/Neubau* ☎ *01/523–6162* ⊟ *01/524–3782* ⟿ *14 rooms* ⚐ *No a/c, no room phones, no room TVs* ⊟ *MC, V* ⦿⎸ *BP.*

★ ¢ ⊞ **Pension Wild.** This friendly, family-run pension on several floors of an older apartment house draws a relaxed, younger crowd to one of the best values in town. Rooms are simple, modern, and welcoming, with light-wood furniture. An ample breakfast is included in the room rate. The close proximity to the major museums makes this a top choice. This is a gay-friendly pension. ☒ *Langegasse 1, A-1080, 8th District/Josefstadt* ☎ *01/406–5174* ⊟ *01/402–2168* ⊕ *www.pension-wild.com* ⟿ *19 rooms* ⚐ *Kitchenette, minibars; no a/c* ⊟ *AE, DC, MC, V* ⦿⎸ *BP.*

NIGHTLIFE & THE ARTS

Updated by Diane Naar-Elphee

Vienna's nightlife and arts scenes confront you with a tantalizing myriad of choices, so only by combining Admiral Byrd-ish foresight with a movie editor's ruthless selectivity can you hope to ride herd on it all. What shall it be? Do you want to time-warp back to the 18th century at Mozart concerts featuring bewigged musicians in the opulent surrounds of the court theater at Schönbrunn Palace? Or at the tiny jewelbox Sala Terrena (which has seats for no more than 50 and shimmers with Venetian-style frescoes)? Or do you want to catch a Broadway-musical extravaganza devoted to the life of the tragic empress Elisabeth at the Theater an der Wien (where Beethoven's *Fidelio* premiered in 1805)? Or bravo! the divas at the grandest of grand opera at the Staatoper? Or dive into the Franz-Josef splendor of an evening concert of Strauss waltzes? Or catch a recital of the greatest *Altemusik* (Old Music) ensemble, Nikolaus Harnoncourt's Concentus Musicus? Or enjoy a trombone troupe at a "jazzkeller"? Or take in an operetta at the beloved Volksoper? Or, or, or . . . ?

The Arts

Tickets

With a city as music mad and opera crazy as Vienna, it is not surprising to learn that the bulk of major performances are sold out in advance. But with thousands of seats to be filled every night, you may luck out with a bit of planning and the State Theatre Booking Office, or **Österreichischer Bundestheaterkassen** (⊠ Theaterkassen, back of Opera, Hanuschgasse 3, in courtyard ☎ 01/513–1513 ⊕ www.bundestheater. at). They sell tickets for the Akademietheater, Schauspielhaus, Staatsoper, Volksoper, and Burgtheater. Call the (frequently busy) phone line Monday to Friday, 8 AM to 5 PM. To purchase tickets at the box office, the above address also operates as a central clearing house, open Monday to Friday, 8 AM to 6 PM, weekends from 9 AM to noon. Tickets for the Staatsoper and Volksoper go on sale one month before the date of performance; credit-card reservations are taken up to six days before the performance. You can also purchase tickets using the Web site; tickets to opera performances can be purchased online (⊕ www.culturall.at). As for other ticket agencies, the most trusted is **Liener Brünn** (☎ 01/533–0961 ⊕ www.ims.at/lienerbruenn)—charging a minimum 22% markup and generally dealing in the more expensive seats. Tickets to musicals and some events including the Vienna Festival are available at the **"Salettl" gazebo** kiosk alongside the Opera House on Kärntnerstrasse, open daily 10 AM to 7 PM. Tickets to that night's musicals are reduced by half after 2 PM.

Dance

A small revolution has been brewing on the modern dance front, thanks to **Tanzquartier Wien** (⊠ Museumsplatz 1, 7th District/Neubau ☎ 01/581–35–91 ⊕ www.tqw.at). DanceQuarter Vienna is now Austria's foremost center for contemporary dance and performances. The Tanzquartier season lasts from October through April. In May and June, it is followed by the so-called "Factory Season," when the center concentrates solely on the projects presented in its dance studios. The **ballet evenings** (☎ 01/514–44–0 ⊕ www.wiener-staatsoper.at ⊕ www. volksoper.at) on the Staatsoper and Volksoper seasonal schedule measure up to international standards and are seeing far more contemporary pieces performed. **Dietheater Wien** (⊠ Karlsplatz 5, 1st District ☎ 01/587–0504–0 ⊠ 01/587–8774–31) is a popular venue for cutting-edge dance arts.

Film

The film schedule in the daily newspapers *Der Standard* and *Die Presse* lists foreign-language films (*Fremdsprachige Filme*) separately. In film listings, *OmU* means original language with German subtitles. Vienna has a thriving film culture, with viewers seeking original rather than German-dubbed versions. There are several theaters offering English-language films.

Just around the corner from Tuchlauben street, the **Artis** (⊠ Corner of Shultergasse/Jordangasse, 1st District ☎ 01/535–6570) has six screens altogether, showing the latest block-busters three to four times a day.

The **Burg Kino** (⊠ Opernring 19, 1st District ☎ 01/587–8406) features Carol Reed's Vienna-based classic *The Third Man*, with Orson Welles and Joseph Cotton, every Friday and Sunday. Otherwise all the new releases are usually shown in the original English version. The **Haydn** (⊠ Mariahilferstrasse 57, 6th District/Mariahilf ☎ 01/587–2262) is a multiplex theater. Most English films are shown with German subtitles. Set in the famous Albertina museum, the **Filmmuseum** (⊠ Augustinerstrasse 1, 1st District ☎ 01/533–7054 ⊕ www.filmmuseum.at) has one of the most ambitious and sophisticated schedules around, with original-version classics and a heavy focus on English-language films. The theater is closed July, August, and September. The arty **Votiv-Kino** (⊠ Währingerstrasse 12, 9th District/Alsergrund ☎ 01/317–3571) usually features less mainstream, more alternative fare, with most films being shown in their original version with German subtitles. In winter the Votiv Kino offers a leisurely Sunday-brunch/feature-film package.

Galleries

With new and hip contemporary art museums springing up across Austria (notably the Kunsthaus in Graz and the Museum der Moderne Kunst in Salzburg), art in Vienna needs to remain cutting-edge, and that it has succeeded in doing thanks to notable galleries that have opened up in two quarters of the city. The first is behind the MQ (MuseumsQuartier) complex, while the second is located in the 4th District—the Freihaus-Quartier, where some of the most exciting contemporary galleries in town have set up shop, appropriately within range of the famed Secession Pavilion. Today, Freihaus has become one of the hottest areas in Vienna for everything that's trendy, fashionable, and fun. The more traditional art galleries are still grouped around the now privatized Dorotheum auction house (see our chapter on shopping) in the city center.

The leading address for contemporary galleries in the Freihaus-Quartier is Schleifmuehlgasse. Here is where you'll find, in a former printing shop, ★ **Gallery Georg Kargl** (⊠ Schleifmuehlgasse 5, 4th District/Wieden ☎ 01/585–4199), which shows art that sidesteps categorization and is a must for serious art collectors. Another of the "Schleifmuehlgasse" galleries is **Gallery Christine Koenig** (⊠ Schleifmuehlgasse 1a, 4th District/Wieden ☎ 01/585–7474). A presence at cutting-edge art fairs around the world, **Krinzinger Gallery** (⊠ Schottenfeldgasse 45, 7th District ☎ 01/513–30 06) has been going strong since the 1970s, when it pushed Vienna Actionism. Its Krinzinger Projects are among the most important blips on the contemporary Austrian art radar screen, and it is close to the MQ (MuseumsQuartier), a very appropriate backdrop. **Gallery Julius Hummel** (⊠ Bäckerstrasse 14, 1st District ☎ 01/512–1296) concentrates mainly on themes concerning the human body in art. It is situated in an old Gothic building in one of the most charming spots in Vienna, nestled between the likes of such venerable institutions as Café Alt-Wien and Oswald & Kalb. Franz West is one of the artists shown here.

Music

Vienna is one of the main music centers of the world. Contemporary music gets its due, but it's the hometown standards—the works of Beethoven, Brahms, Haydn, Mozart, and Schubert—that draw the Viennese public and make tickets to the Wiener Philharmoniker the hottest of commodities. A monthly printed program, the *Wien-Programm,* put out by the city tourist board and available at any travel agency or hotel, gives a general overview of what's going on in the worlds of opera, concerts, jazz, theater, and galleries, and similar information is posted on billboards and fat advertising columns around the city. Vienna is home to four full symphony orchestras: the great Wiener Philharmoniker (Vienna Philharmonic), the outstanding Wiener Symphoniker (Vienna Symphony), the broadcasting service's ORF Symphony Orchestra, and the Niederösterreichische Tonkünstler. There are also hundreds of smaller groups, from world-renowned trios to chamber orchestras.

The most important concert halls are in the buildings of the Gesellschaft Fodor'sChoice der Musikfreunde, called the **Musikverein** (✉ Dumbastrasse 3; ticket office at Karlsplatz 6 ☎ 01/505–8190 🖷 01/505–8190–94 ⊕ www.
★ musikverein.at). There are actually six auditoria in this magnificent theater but the one that everyone knows is the venue for the annually televised New Year's Day Concert—the "Goldene Saal," the Golden Room, officially called the Grosser Musikvereinssaal. Possibly the most beautiful in the world, this Parthenon of a music hall was designed by Theophil Hansen, the Danish 19th-century architect, a passionate admirer of ancient Greece. For his 1869 design of the hall, he arrayed an army of gilded caryatids in the main concert hall, planted Ionic columns in the 660-seat Brahmssaal, and placed the figure of Orpheus in the building pediment. But the surprise is that his smaller Brahmssal is even more sumptuous—a veritable Greek temple with more caryatids and lots of gilding and green malachite marble. What Hansen would have made of the four newly constructed (2004) subsidiary halls, set below the main theater, must remain a mystery, but the avant-garde Glass, Metal, Wooden, and Stone Halls (Gläserne, Hölzerne, Metallene, Steinerne Saal) make fitting showcases for contemporary music concerts. The Musikverein, in addition to being the main venue for such troupes as the Wiener Philharmoniker and the Wiener Symphoniker, also hosts many of the world's finest orchestras. A three-minute walk from the ★ Musikverein, crossing Schwarzenbergplatz, is the **Konzerthaus** (✉ Lothringerstrasse 20, 1st District ☎ 01/242002 🖷 01/242–0011–0 ⊕ www.konzerthaus.at), home to the Grosser Konzerthaussaal, Mozartsaal, and Schubertsaal halls. The first is a room of magnificent size, with red velvet and gold accents. The calendar of Grosser Konzerthaussaal is packed with goodies, including the fabulous early-music group, Concentus Musicus Wien, headed by Nicolaus Harnoncourt, and concerts of the Wiener Philharmoniker and the Wiener Symphoniker.

If the white-gloved, whirling waltzes of Strauss are your thing, head to the "Johann Strauss Konzerte im Wiener Kursalon" concerts at the ★ **Wiener Kursalon** (✉ Johannesgasse 33, 1st District ☎ 01/513–2477 🖷 01/512–5791 ⊕ www.strauss-konzerte.at/), a majestic palace-like structure set in Vienna's sylvan Stadtpartk, which was built in the Italian Renaissance Revival style in 1865. Here, in (somewhat distressingly overrenovated) gold and white salons, the Salonorchester "Alt Wien" performs concerts, accompanied at times by dancers, of the works of

"Waltz King" Johann Strauss and his contemporaries, with waltzes, polkas, parade themes, operetta melodies, traditional "Schrammeln," and *Salonmusik* at the fore. In addition, the Wiener Johann Strauss Capelle, dressed in period costume, also presents concerts of the Strauss era in "Original Viennese Waltz Show" evenings, replete with singers, dancers, and your very own glass of champagne (no dancing by the audience allowed).

★ Happily, there is a plethora of period-era, chocolate-box, jeweled concert salons in Vienna. Perhaps the most opulent is the **Schlosstheater Schönbrunn** (✉ Schönbrunner Schloss-strasse, 13th District/Hietzing ☎ 01/71155–158 ⊕ www.mdw.ac.at), built for Empress Maria Theresa in the Valerie Wing of the palace, with glittering chandeliers and a gigantic mural painted on the ceiling. For an grand evening of Strauss and Mozart in imperial surroundings, head to the Wiener Hofburgorchester concerts given in the Hofburg palace auditoria of the Redoutensaal and the mammoth 19th-century **Festsaal** (✉ Heldenplatz, 1st District ☎ 01/587–2552 🖷 01/587–4397 ⊕ www.hofburgorchester.at/). The concerts are offered Tuesdays, Thursdays, and Saturdays, May through October. The most enchanting place to hear Mozart in Vienna (or anywhere, for that matter?) is the exquisite 18th-century Sala Terrena of the

Fodor'sChoice **Deutschordenskloster** (✉ Singerstrasse 7, 1st District ⊕ www.
★ mozarthaus.at). Here, in a tiny room—seating for no more than 50 people—a bewigged chamber group offers Mozart concerts in a jewel box overrun with Rococo frescoes in the Venetian style. The concerts are scheduled by the nearby Mozarthaus. Said to be the oldest concert "hall" in Vienna, the Sala Terrena is part of the German Monastery, where, in 1781, Mozart worked for his despised employer, Archbishop Colloredo of Salzburg.

Although the well-known summer-season Vienna Festival, the **Wiener Festwochen** (☎ 01/589–22–11 ⊕ www.festwochen.at), held mid-May to mid-June, wraps up the primary season, the rest of the summer musical scene, from mid-July to mid-August, nowadays brims with activities. One top event is the **Festival KlangBogen** (✉ Stadiongasse 9, 1st District ☎ 01/42717 ⊕ www.klangbogen.at), which features rare and contemporary operas starring some famous singers and performers.

Fodor'sChoice The beloved Vienna Boys' Choir, the **Wiener Sängerknaben** (✉ Hof-
★ burg, Schweizer Hof, 1st District ☎ 01/533–9927 🖷 01/533–9927–75 ⊕ www.wsk.at) are far from just being living "dolls" out of a Walt Disney film (remember the 1962 movie, *Almost Angels*?). Their pedigree is royal, and their professionalism such that they regularly appear with the best orchestras around the world. The troupe originated as a choir founded by Emperor Maximilian I in 1498, but with the demise of the Habsburg empire in 1918, they were on their own and became a private outfit, subsidizing themselves by giving public performances starting in the 1920s. When the troupe lost its imperial patronage, they traded in their court costume for these charming costumes, then the height of fashion (a look even sported by Donald Duck, who was also born in that era).

JUST LIKE TAKING CANDY FROM MOZART

A FITTING TITLE FOR A SPECIAL FESTIVAL offered by the Vienna Kammeroper to honor the 250th birthday year of Mozart. Just the maraschino cherry atop of a multi-layered cake of events scheduled for 2006—hundreds of concerts, operas, and recitals years in the planning—it is only appropriate that this chamber-opera troupe (⊕ www.wienerkammeropera.at) present the baby composer's earliest works in their Fleischmarkt theater. Considering the wunderkind started composing at age 8, he would probably delight in the Marionettentheater Schloss Schönbrunn's production of The Magic Flute (⊕ www.marionettentheater.at) or its "Greatest Hits" Mozart show, mounted at Empress Maria Theresa's palace. But these are only two of the sweetest birthday offerings. The grandest? Perhaps the concert-spectacular on Rathausplatz on May 12 to kick off the annual Vienna Festival (⊕ www.festwochen.at); another open-air concert will be held on Josefsplatz on July 9. One of the most moving events will be the Easter Night concert on April 16 at St. Stephan's Cathedral, scene of Mozart's marriage and burial service. The Mozart Year will reach its crescendo on December 5th—the day of the composer's death—when the Wiener Philharmoniker will perform his last work, the Requiem, under Christian Thielemann at the Staatsoper, while Nikolaus Harnoncourt's Concentus Musicus will mount Mozart's Mass in C Minor at the Musikverein (⊕ www.musikverein.at).

This legendary concert hall has a 2006 calendar packed with Mozart. Under the auspices of the Osterklang Wien festival (⊕ www.osterklang.at), the Wiener Philharmoniker will perform the last three symphonies on April 7 and 8; during May and June, Rudolf Buchbinder will play the piano concertos; in October, German star violinist Anne Sophie Mutter will grace Mozart's violin sonatas, while "Mozart and More" will showcase the Vienna Boys' Choir (⊕ www.mondial.at). Over at one of the world's premier opera houses, the Vienna Staatsoper (⊕ www.wiener-staatsoper.at), Mozart will be bravi-ed with January 2006 performances of The Magic Flute, Don Giovanni, The Marriage of Figaro and Così fan tutte, with May bringing The Abduction from the Seraglio. More opera will be on tap over at the Vienna Volksoper (⊕ www.volksoper.at): The Magic Flute (date of premiere, 12/17/05); The Marriage of Figaro (2/26/06); La Clemenza di Tito (4/28/06); Don Giovanni (9/16/06) and Così fan Tutte (9/29/06). Perhaps the best house in the world to hear a Mozart opera, the Theater an der Wien (opened 1801), has some special treats (⊕ www.klangbogen.at): Neil Shicoff in Idomeneo (late January, early Feb., late June); the rare Lucio Silla (March); Patrice Chereau's provocative Così fan tutte (early June, late Nov.); and Sir Simon Rattle conducting the Wiener Philharmoniker in the last three symphonies (early Dec). Other events include free open-air showing of Mozart films, like Amadeus and Ingmar Bergman's Magic Flute on Rathausplatz, every dusk July 1 to September 3 (⊕ www.wien-event.at); a series of Mozart Galas at the Palais Auersperg (⊕ www.wro.at); and the "New Crowned Hope" fall festival (⊕ www.festwochen.at) directed by the noted Peter Sellars. Museum shows? Mozart's most notable Viennese residence, the Figarohaus—now rechristened the Mozart Haus Vienna (⊕ www.mozarthausvienna.at)—has a new exhibition gallery. Over at the Haus der Musik (⊕ www.hdm.at), you'll be able to "conduct" some Mozart ditties, make your own custom-tailored Magic Flute, and marvel at the autograph Requiem. Finally, the regal Albertina museum (⊕ www.albertina.at) will host an extensive exhibition of Mozartiana mid-March through August. For the complete rundown of concerts and special events, log on to http://b2b.wien.info/data/mozart-sales-wien-e.pdf

From mid-September to late-June, the apple-cheeked lads sing mass at 9:15 AM Sundays in the Hofburgkapelle. Written requests for seats should be made at least eight weeks in advance (✆ Verwaltung der Hofmusikkapelle, Hofburg, A-1010 Vienna). You will be sent a reservation card, which you exchange at the box office (in the Hofburg courtyard) for your tickets. Tickets are also sold at ticket agencies and at the box office (open Friday, 11 AM–1 PM and 3–5 PM; any remaining seats may be available Sunday morning, 8:15 to 8:45). General seating costs €5, prime seats in the front of the church nave €29. It's important to note that only the ten side balcony seats allow a view of the actual choir; those who purchase floor seats, standing room, or center balcony will not have a view of the boys. On Sunday at 8:45 AM any unclaimed, pre-ordered tickets are sold. You can also opt for standing room, which is free. If you miss hearing choir at a Sunday mass, you may be able to catch them in a more popular program in the Musikverein or Konzerthaus or, in August, at the Schönbrunn Palace.

Opera & Operetta

★ The **Staatsoper** (State Opera House ⊠ Opernring 2, 1st District ☎ 01/514–440 ⊕ www.wiener-staatsoper.at), one of the world's great opera houses, has been the scene of countless musical triumphs and a center of unending controversies over how it should be run and by whom. (When Lorin Maazel was unceremoniously dumped as head of the Opera not many years ago, he pointed out that the house had done the same thing to Gustav Mahler half a century earlier.) A performance takes place virtually every night September–June, drawing on the vast repertoire of the house, with emphasis on Mozart and Verdi works. Guided tours of the Opera House are held year-round.

★ Opera and operetta are also performed at the **Volksoper** (⊠ Währingerstrasse 78 ☎ 01/514–440 ⊕ www.volksoper.at), outside the city center at Währingerstrasse and Währinger Gürtel (third stop on Streetcar 41, 42, or 43, which run from "downstairs" at Schottentor, U2, on the Ring). Prices here are significantly lower than in the Staatsoper, and performances can be every bit as rewarding. This theater has a fully packed calendar, with offerings ranging from the grandest opera, such as Mozart's *Don Giovanni,* to an array of famous Viennese operettas, such as Johann Strauss's *Wiener Blut* and *Die Fledermaus,* to modern Broadway musicals (during 2004, Rodgers & Hammerstein's *The Sound of Music* finally received its first Austrian staging here ever). Most operas are sung here in German.

You'll also find musicals and operetta at several theaters. The **Raimundtheater** (⊠ Wallgasse 18 ☎ 01/599–77–0 ⊕ www.musicalvienna.at) mostly offers musicals by local composers. For cabaret and traveling music groups, try the **Ronacher** (⊠ Seilerstätte/Himmelpfortgasse ☎ 01/514–110 ⊕ www.musicalvienna.at). **Theater an der Wien** (⊠ Linke Wienzeile 6 ☎ 01/588–30–0 ⊕ www.musicalvienna.at ⊕ www.elisabeth-musical.de/) has glitzy musicals, such as *Mozart!* and *Elisabeth,* the extravaganza about the Empress "Sisi." Opera and operetta are performed on an irregular schedule at the **Kammeroper** (⊠ Fleischmarkt 24 ☎ 01/512–01–000 ⊕ www.wienerkammeroper.at). In summer, light opera or operetta performances by the Kammeroper ensemble are given in the exquisite **Schlosstheater** at Schönbrunn. Send a fax to 01/51201–00–30 for details.

Theater

Vienna's **Burgtheater** (✉ Dr.-Karl-Lueger-Ring 2, 1st District, Vienna) is one of the leading German-language theaters of the world. The repertoire has recently begun mixing German classics with more modern and controversial pieces. The Burg's smaller house, the **Akademietheater** (✉ Lisztstrasse 1), draws on much the same group of actors for classical and modern plays. Both houses are closed during July and August. The **Kammerspiele** (✉ Rotenturmstrasse 20 ☎ 01/42700–304) does modern plays. The **Theater in der Josefstadt** (✉ Josefstädterstrasse 26,, 8th District/Josefstadt ☎ 01/42700–306) stages classical and modern works year-round in the house once run by the great producer and teacher Max Reinhardt. The **Volkstheater** (✉ Neustiftgasse 1, 7th District/Neubau ☎ 01/523–3501–0) presents dramas, comedies, and folk plays.

For theater in English (mainly standard plays), head for **Vienna's English Theater** (✉ Josefsgasse 12, 8th District/Josefstadt ☎ 01/402–1260). Another option is the equally good **International Theater** (✉ Porzellangasse 8, 9th District/Alsergrund ☎ 01/319–6272).

Nightlife

Balls

The gala Vienna evening you've always dreamed about can become a reality: among the many **balls** given during the Carnival season, several welcome the public—at a wide range of prices, from about €65 to €350 and up per person. Dates change every year, but most balls are held in January and February. Some of the more popular balls are the Blumen Ball (Florists' Ball), Kaffeesieder Ball (Coffee Brewers' Ball), Bonbon Ball (Confection Ball), and the most famous and expensive of them all, the Opernball (Opera Ball). You can book tickets through **hotel concierges** (for more information call ☎ 01/211140 🖷 01/216–8492).

Bars, Lounges & Nightclubs

Where once night-owls had to head to Vienna's *Bermuda Dreieck* ("Bermuda Triangle," around St. Ruprecht's church on the Ruprechtsplatz, two blocks south of the Danube Canal), today's nightclub scene has blossomed with a profusion of delightful and sophisticated bars, clubs, and lounges. Many of the trendoisie like to head to the clubs around the Naschmarkt area, then move on to nearby Mariahilferstrasse to shake their groove thing. A sort of spaceship has landed smack between the Hofburg palace and the Kunsthistorisches Museum—just look for the glowing orange kiosk at the intersection of the Ring and Mariahilferstrasse and head downstairs to find **Babenberger Passage** (✉ Passagecorner of Ringstrasse at Babenbergerstrasse, 1st District ☎ 01/961–8800 ⊕ www.sunshine.at/ Ⓤ U2/MuseumsQuartier), one of the hippest places in Vienna these days. State-of-the-art lighting systems, futuristic decor, and adaptable design elements come together in a blush-hued bar and a sizzling-blue dance room. One of the most dazzling settings for a Viennese club is in one of the city's cavernous subway stations and **Café**

Carina (✉ Josefstädterstrasse 84/Stadtbahnbogen, 8th District/Josefstadt ☏ 01/406–4322 Ⓤ U6/Josefstädterstrasse) has one of the best—an actual Otto Wagner original. Vienna's new "subway-station clubs" are proof positive that nightlife is no longer centered in and around the old city center. Carina is very off-beat, artistic, and action-packed—anything can happen here, from an airguitar competition to an evening with 1980s hits. Near the Naschmarkt, **Kaleidoskop** (✉ Schleifmühlgasse 13, 4th District/Wieden ☏ 01/920–3343 Ⓤ U4/Kettenbrückengasse) sits shoulder to shoulder with a number of top art galleries, so the hip and happening art crowd tends to come here. Chic, chic, and once again chic, the designer café-bar **Shultz** (✉ Siebensterngasse 31, 7th District/Neubau ☏ 01/522–9120 ⊕ www.schultz.at Ⓤ U4/Kettenbrückengasse) seduces fashionable folk with its long drinks, retro cocktails, and its Vienna Moderne setting. Back in 1870, Viennese used to come to the **Volksgarten** (✉ Burgring 2, 1st District ☏ 01/532–0907 ⊕ www.volksgarten.at Ⓤ U2/3 MuseumsQuartier) to waltz, share champagne, and enjoy the night in candlelit garden. Today, they come to the same site to *diskothek* the night away under pink strobes, enjoy some boogie-woogie or tango dancing in the Tanzcafe (Dance Café), and sip a beer against the greenery. A best bet when you don't know where else to head, this one-in-all club complex is set within a lush garden and has a pretty, vaguely Jugendstil dining salon, with a vast curved wall of windows overlooking a terrace set with tables. Beyond lies the Pavilion, a 1950s jewel that looks airlifted from California, which serves brews and nibbles.

Disco

Occupying one of the former stables of the Habsburgs in the MuseumsQuartier, **Café Leopold** (✉ Museumsplatz 1 (MuseumsQuartier), 1st District ☏ 01/523–6732 ⊕ www.cafe-leopold.at/ Ⓤ U2 or 3/MuseumsQuartier) is located in the big modern white cube that is the Leopold Museum. After frugging to the house and electro music, you can escape ★ to a table outdoors in the plaza. "U" stands for underground and **Club U im Otto-Wagner-Café** (✉ Karlsplatz/Kuenstlerhauspassage, 4th District/Wieden ☏ 01/505–9904 ⊕ www.club-u.at Ⓤ U1, U2, or U4/Karlsplatz) is located just underneath one of the two celebrated Jugendstil pavilions that Otto Wagner built on the Karlsplatz square when designing Vienna's subway, the Stadtbahn. Which means this disco is easy to find. One of the best dance halls for alternative music, it is open on Sunday, has outdoor seating, live music, a great atmosphere, and excellent DJs who turn this place into a real Soul City most nights. In the middle of one of Vienna's latest hipster districts, the Freihaus-Quarter, **Club Schikaneder** (✉ Margaretenstrasse 22–24, 4th District/Wieden ☏ 01/585–2867 ⊕ www.schikaneder.at Ⓤ U1, U2, or U4/Karlsplatz) is a former cinema has become a multimedia art and dance center. There are three to five films screened every day, exhibitions, and first-class DJ–lines to groove to. The Freihaus-Quarter sizzles with cafés and shops. For all the poop, ★ log on to ⊕ www.freihausviertel.at. **Flex** (✉ Donaukanal/Augartenbrücke, 1st District ☏ 01/533–7525 ⊕ www.flex.at Ⓤ U1, U2, or U4/Karlsplatz) has the grooviest grunge—quite literally, as this is set in a dark, dungeon-like cave—with an internationally famed sound system. Practically an institution, the disco **Queen Anne** (✉ Johannesgasse 12, 1st District ☎ 01/512–0203 Ⓤ U4/Stadtpark) offers a retro trip, complete with a marble dance floor (paging John Travolta) and a bar where the tunes date from the '50s.

Jazz Clubs

The jazz scene in Vienna is one of the hottest in Europe. The biggest splash has recently been made by **Birdland** (✉ Am Stadtpark 3 [enter Landstrasser Hauptstrasse 2], 3rd District ☎ 01/2196–39315 ⊕ www.birdland.at), opened in the newly renovated Hilton Hotel in 2004. This club has been a dream come true for the great jazz legend Joe Zawinul who named it after one of his most renowned compositions and New York City's legendary temple of jazz. Set in a cellar under St. Ruprecht's church and the granddaddy of Vienna's jazz clubs, **Jazzland** (✉ Franz-Josefs-Kai 29, 1st District ☎ 01/533–2575 ⊕ www.jazzland.at) opened more than 30 years ago when there was just a small local jazz scene. But thanks to the pioneering work of the club's founder, Axel Melhardt, Austrian jazz musicians have vibed with the best American stars. The club also serves excellent and authentic Viennese cuisine. In the course of a few years, **Porgy & Bess** (✉ Riemergasse 11, 1st District ☎ 01/512–8811 ⊕ www.porgy.at) has become a fixed point in the native and international jazz scene.

SPORTS & OUTDOOR ACTIVITIES

Participant Sports

Bicycling

Look for the special pathways either in red brick or marked with a stylized cyclist image in yellow. Note and observe the special traffic signals at some intersections. You can take a bike on the subway (except during rush hours) for an additional half fare, but only in cars with a blue shield on the door, and only on stairs or elevators with the "bike" shield, not on escalators. The city tourist office has a brochure in German with useful cycling maps, plus a leaflet, "See Vienna by Bike," with tips in English. At most bookstores you can purchase a cycling map of Vienna put out by a local cycling organization known as ARGUS.

It's possible to rent a bike in the Prater. **Radverleih Hochschaubahn** (☎ 12/729–5888) is open mid-March–October and is located in the Prater amusement park by the Hochschaubahn, slightly right after the Ferris wheel. **Radverleih Praterstern** is open April–October and can be found at street level under the Praterstern North rail station.

Pedal Power (✉ Ausstellungsstrasse 3, 2nd District/Leopoldstadt ☎ 01/729–7234 🖷 01/729–7235) offers guided bike tours of Vienna and the surrounding vicinity in English from April to October, including the main sights of the city, or tours to the outlying vineyards for a glass of wine. It's also possible to rent a bike and do your own exploring. Rentals cost €5 per hour; a three-hour guided tour costs €23 (€19 for students); a four-hour bike rental on your own is €17; for a full day, €27. Pedal Power will also deliver a bike to your hotel for an additional fee.

Ice-Skating

The **Wiener Eislaufverein** (⊠ Lothringerstrasse 22, behind InterContinental Hotel, 3rd District ☎ 01/713–6353–0) has outdoor skating with skate rentals, October–mid-March. Weekends are crowded. For indoor skating, check the **Wiener Stadthalle** (⊠ Vogelweidplatz 14, 15th District ☎ 01/981–00–0).

Swimming

Head for the swimming areas of the Alte Donau or the Donauinsel, an area built up along the stream of the Danube Canal. The pools and the Alte Donau (paid admission) will be filled on hot summer weekends, so the Donauinsel can be a surer bet. But don't be tempted to jump into the Danube Canal itself; the water is definitely not for swimming, nor is the Danube itself, because of heavy undertows and a powerful current.

Donauinsel Nord is a huge, free recreation area with a children's section and nude bathing. **Donauinsel Süd** is free and offers good swimming and boating and a nude bathing area. It's harder to get to and less crowded than other areas, and food facilities are limited. **Gänsehäufel** is a bathing island in the Alte Donau with paid admission, lockers, changing rooms, children's wading pools, topless and nude areas, and restaurants; on sunny weekends it's likely to be full by 11 AM or earlier. **Krapfenwaldbad** is an outdoor park-pool tucked among the trees on the edge of the Vienna Woods, full of Vienna's beautiful people and singles. Get there early on a sunny Sunday or you won't get in. **Stadionbad** is an enormous sports complex popular with the younger crowd; go early. For the fun of it, ride the miniature railway (*Liliputbahn*) from behind the Ferris wheel in the Prater amusement park to the Stadion station and walk the rest of the way.

SHOPPING

Shopping Districts

Updated by
Diane Naar-
Elphee

The Kärntnerstrasse, Graben, and Kohlmarkt pedestrian areas in the 1st District, **Inner City,** claim to have the best shops in Vienna, and for some items, such as jewelry, some of the best anywhere, although you must expect high prices. The side streets within this area have developed their own character, with shops offering antiques, art, clocks, jewelry, and period furniture. **Ringstrasse Galerie,** the indoor shopping plaza at Kärntner Ring 5–7, brings a number of shops together in a modern complex, although many of these stores have other, larger outlets elsewhere in the city. Outside the center, concentrations of stores are on **Mariahilferstrasse,** straddling the 6th and 7th districts; **Landstrasser Hauptstrasse** in the 3rd District; and, still farther out, **Favoritenstrasse** in the 10th District.

A collection of attractive small boutiques can be found in the **Palais Ferstel** passage at Freyung 2 in the 1st District. A modest group of smaller shops has sprung up in the **Sonnhof** passage between Landstrasser Hauptstrasse 28 and Ungargasse 13 in the 3rd District. The **Spittelberg** market, on the Spittelberggasse between Burggasse and Siebensterngasse in the 7th District, has drawn small galleries and handicrafts shops and is particularly popular in the weeks before Christmas and Easter. Christmas is the time also for the tinselly **Christkindlmarkt** on Rathausplatz in front of City Hall; in protest over its commercialization, smaller markets specializing in handicrafts have sprung up on such traditional spots as Am Hof and the Freyung (1st District), also the venue for other seasonal markets.

Vienna's **Naschmarkt** (between Linke and Rechte Wienzeile, starting at Getreidemarkt) is one of Europe's great and most colorful food and produce markets. Stalls open at 5 or 6 AM, and the pace is lively until 5 or 6 PM. Saturday is the big day, when farmers come into the city to sell at the back end of the market, but shops close around 3 PM. Also Saturdays there's a huge flea market at Kettenbrückengasse end. It is closed Sunday.

Flea Markets

Every Saturday (except holidays), rain or shine, from about 7:30 AM to 4 or 5, the **Flohmarkt** in back of the Naschmarkt, stretching along the Linke Wienzeile from the Kettenbrückengasse U4 subway station, offers a staggering collection of stuff ranging from serious antiques to plain junk. Haggle over prices. On Thursdays and Fridays from late spring to mid-fall, an outdoor combination arts-and-crafts, collectibles, and flea market takes place on **Am Hof.** On Saturday and Sunday in summer from about 10 to 6, an outdoor **art and antiques market** springs up along the Danube Canal, stretching from the Schwedenbrücke to beyond the Salztorbrücke. Lots of books are sold, some in English, plus generally better goods and collectibles than at the Saturday flea market. Bargain over prices.

Department Stores

Steffl (✉ Kärntnerstrasse 19, 1st District) is moderately upscale without being overly expensive. The larger department stores are concentrated in Mariahilferstrasse. By far the best is **Peek & Cloppenburg** (✉ Mariahilferstrasse 26–30, 6th District). Farther up the street you will find slightly cheaper goods at **Gerngross** (✉ Mariahilferstrasse and Kirchengasse, 6th District).

Specialty Stores

ANTIQUES You will find the best antiques shops located in the 1st District, many clustered close to the Dorotheum auction house, in the Dorotheergasse, Stallburggasse, Plankengasse, and Spiegelgasse. You'll also find interesting shops in the Josefstadt (8th) District, where prices are considerably lower than those in the center of town. Wander up Florianigasse and back down Josefstädterstrasse, being sure not to overlook the narrow side streets.

Just around the corner from the Opera House, **Gallery Dr. Sternat** (✉ Lobkowitzplatz 1 ☎ 01/512–2063) is one of the most traditional art galleries, with a focus on fine Austrian paintings, Viennese bronzes, ★ Thonet furniture, and beautiful Biedermeier pieces. **Bel Etage** (✉ Mahlerstrasse 15 ☎ 01/512–2379) has wonderful works by Josef Hoffmann, Dagobert Peche, and other Wiener Werkstätte masters, all of which entice onlookers to spend more than just time here. **D & S Antiquitäten** (✉ Dorotheergasse 13 ☎ 01/512–5885) has a striking entrance designed by Oskar Hoefinger; inside are rare Austrian clocks, 18th-cen-

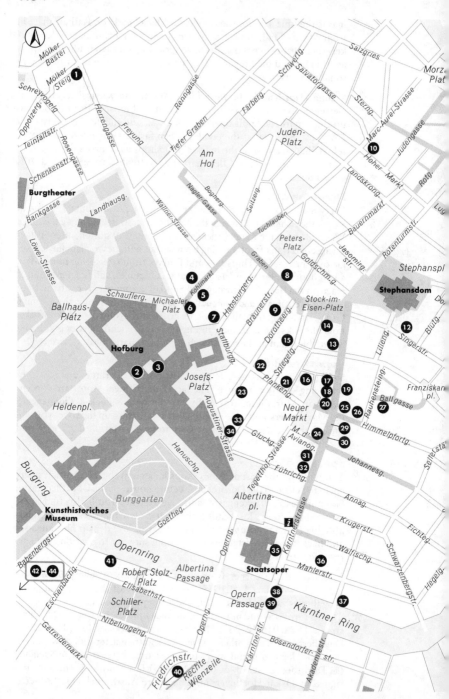

Vienna Shopping

Map labels:

Morzin-Platz

Marienb...

Danube

Art & Antiques Flea Market

Franz Josefs Kai

Schweden br.

Canal

Schwedenpl.

Raben Steig

Dominikanerbastei

Fleischmarkt

Laurenzerberg.

Postg.

Rosenbursenstr

Lugeck

Köllnerhofg.

Sonnenfelsg.

Bäckerstr.

nspl.

11

Wollzeile

Biberstr.

Dom-Gasse

Schulerstr.

Postg.

lutg

Grünangerg.

Kumpfg.

Riemerg.

Dr. Karl Lueger-Platz

Zedlitzg.

Stubenbastei

skaner-pl.

Liebenbgg.

Weihburg.

Stadtpark

28

Schelling.

Parkring

eiterstätte

Schubertring

Johannesg.

Hegelg.

Lothringerstr

Konzerthaus

| 0 | 110 yards |
| 0 | 100 meters |

KEY

i *Tourist Information*

A. E. Köchert 16
Albin Denk 9
Alt-Österreich 26
Arcadia 35
Augarten 14
Bel Etage 36
Berger 24
British Bookshop 28
Burgenland 38
Collins Hüte 39
D & S Antiquitäten 22
Doppeladler 41
Dorotheum 23
EMI 32
Flohmarkt 40
Freytag & Berndt 7
Galerie Dr. Sternat 33
Geiger Boutique 29
Gerngross 42
Giesswein 37
Golden Genius 5
Haban 17
Helmut Lang 21
House of Gentlemen 4
Kober 8
Lobmeyr 31
Loden-Plankl 6
Morawa 11
Österreichische Werkstätten 20
Palais Kinsky 10
Pawlata 17
Peek & Cloppenburg 44
Petit Point Kovacec . . .18
Resi Hammerer 30
Schella Kahn 12
Sir Anthony 25
Souvenir in der Hofburg 3
Spielzeugschachtel 27
Steffl 19
Stransky 2
Swarovski 13
Tostmann 1
Virgin Megastore 43
Wiener Blut 15
Wolfrum 34

tury paintings, and beautiful 19th-century furniture. Set in a beautiful history palais, the **Dorotheum** (⊠ Dorotheergasse 17 ☎ 01/515–60–0 ⊕ www.dorotheum.at) is a state institution dating from 1707, when Emperor Josef I determined that he didn't want his people being exploited by pawnbrokers. The place is intriguing, with goods ranging from furs to antique jewelry to paintings and furniture auctioned almost daily. Information on how to bid is available in English. Some items are for immediate cash sale. Also check out **Palais Kinsky** (⊠ Freyung 4 ☎ 01/532–42009) for paintings and antiques.

AUSTRIAN CLOTHING & TRACHTEN
★

For military memorabilia, including uniforms, medals, and weapons from the Austrian monarchy through World War I, go to **Doppeladler** ⊠ Opernring 9 ☎ 01/581–6232. If you want to dress like Captain von Trapp and Maria, perhaps the best place for that extra special piece of folklore wear, **Loden-Plankl** (⊠ Michaelerplatz 6 ☎ 01/533–8032) stocks some really gorgeous hand-embroidered jackets, not to mention the "Leder Hosen" leather breeches for kids (famed for being just about indestructible). The building, opposite the Hofburg, is a centuries-old treasure. **Giesswein** (⊠ Kärntnerstrasse 5–7 ☎ 01/512–4597) is one of the most noted places to shop for a selection of dirndls and women's *Trachten,* the typical Austrian costume with white blouse, print skirt, and apron. **Resi Hammerer** (⊠ Kärntnerstrasse 29–31 ☎ 01/512–6952) offers Folklore fashion with a touch of the trendy. The color and fabric mix has that certain casual, sportive touch but still is conservative enough to suit most fraus. Fancy having your very own tailor-made Austrian dirndl dress because you can't find the one that you really want? **Tostmann** (⊠ Schottengasse 3a ☎ 01/533–5331) is the place to exquisitely fulfill your wishes.

BOOKS
★

The biggest Harry Potter launch in Austria took place at the **British Bookshop** (⊠ Weihburggasse 24 ☎ 01/512–1945 ⊕ www.britishbookshop.at) always well stocked with all the latest editions and best sellers. The staff encourages browsing. If you are planning a hiking holiday in Austria then stock up on the necessary maps at **Freytag & Berndt** (⊠ Kohlmarkt 9 ☎ 01/533–8685 ⊕ www.freytagberndt.at), the best place for maps and travel books in Vienna. The biggest book store in Vienna, **Morawa** (⊠ Wollzeile 11 ☎ 01/513–7513 ⊕ www.morawa.at), has titles on everything under the sun. Thankfully, help is always at hand if you can't find that one book. The magazine and newspaper section is vast and don't pass over some of the cute printed gifts, such as a calendar made out of paper shopping bags (put the bags to good use when the year has
★ passed). If you're an art book lover, **Wolfrum** (⊠ Augustinerstrasse 10 ☎ 01/512–5398) will be your home-away-from-home. If you have money to burn, you can also spring for a Schiele print or special art edition to take home.

CERAMICS, GLASS & PORCELAIN

The best porcelain in town can be found at **Augarten** (⊠ Graben/Stock-im-Eisen-Platz 3 ☎ 01/512–1494–0 ⊕ www.augarten.at). The Lippizaner stallion balancing on two hind hoofs is an expensive piece but an eye-catcher. The manufactory in the 2nd District in Vienna offers tours

A GLITTERING TROVE

F YOU ARE LOOKING FOR *that something truly special—an 18th-century oil portrait or a fake fur, a Rococo mirror or a fine silk fan, modern or retro jewelry, a china figurine or solid silver spoon, an old map of the Austrian Empire or even a stuffed parrot—the one place that may have the answer is the* **Dorotheum** *(⊠ Dorotheergasse 17 ☎ 01/515–60–0 ⊕ www.dorotheum.at), Vienna's fabled auction house. Have you ever wanted to see how the Austrian aristocracy once lived, how their sumptuous homes were furnished? Well, don't bother with a museum—you can inspect their antique furnishings, displayed as if in use, for free, and without the eagle eyes of sales personnel following your every move, in peace and quiet in the gilded salons here. This was the first imperial auction house (oops, pawn-shop), established in 1707 by Emperor Joseph I. Occupying the former site of the Dorothy Convent (hence the name), the Dorotheum has built up a grand reputation since it was privatized in the early 1990s. The neo-Baroque building was completed in 1901 and deserves a walk-through (you can enter from Spiegelgasse and exit Dorotheergasse) just to have a look, even if it is only to admire the gorgeous stuccoed walls and palatial interiors, or to take a peek into the glass-roofed patio stocked with early-20th-century glass, furniture, and art. With more than 600 auctions a year, this has become one of the busiest auction houses in Europe. There are auctions held daily except Sunday. And if you don't fancy bidding for something, there are large cash-sale areas in the ground and second floors where loads of stuff (that didn't sell at auction) can simply be bought off the floor.*

of the palais Augarten is housed in, and you can study the steps involved in making these precious pieces. Is it a "Maria-Theresia," ornately cut diamanté chandelier with a 30%–34% lead content, you're looking for?

★ If it is, head and hunt here at **Lobmeyr** (⊠ Kärntnerstrasse 26 ☎ 01/512–0508–0 ⊕ www.lobmeyr.at), one of the world's finest addresses for the best in glass and crystal. Even if you're not buying, go upstairs and have a look at the museum on the second floor. Pottery from **Berger** (⊠ Weihburggasse 17 ☎ 01/512–1434) may be just the great gift you're looking for—how about a decorative wall plate blooming with a hand-painted flowering gentian? If you want to enter an old-fashioned interior that makes time stand still and is little changed from the time when Empress Elisabeth shopped here, **Albin Denk** (⊠ Graben 13 ☎ 01/512–4439 ⊕ www.albindenk.at) is the place to head. The shop entrance itself is a vitrine, as it is lined with glass cases and filled with a wonderful-if-kitschy army of welcoming porcelain figurines. Gmunden ceramics have been the Hausfrau's favorite for centuries. The typical green-and-white design with the tiny painted buttercups or the irregular bands of color are present in nearly every Austrian country home. But these quaint pieces can add that rustic touch to any dinner table, so stock up at **Pawlata** (⊠ Kärntnerstrasse 14 ☎ 01/512–1764). Ireland has its Waterford,

★ France its Baccarat, and Austria has **Swarovski** (✉Kärntnerstrasse 8 ☎01/ 5129032 ⊕ www.swarovski.com), purveyors of some of the finest cut crystal in the world and, thanks to the newer generation of Swarovskis, trinkets increasingly fashionable in style and outlook. There are your typical collector items and gifts here, but also high-style fashion accessories (Paris couturiers now festoon their gowns with Swarovski crystals the way they used to with ostrich feathers), crystal figurines, jewelry, and home accessories. This flagship store opened recently is one heck of a cave of coruscating crystals that gleam and glitter.

GIFTS THAT SAY "VIENNA"
★ Are you looking for an old postcard, a hand-carved walking stick, an old record or ball gift, or even an old photograph of the Opera House from before the war? Head to **Alt-Österreich** (✉Himmelpfortgasse 7 ☎01/ 5121296)—its name translates as "Old Austria" and this treasure trove has just about everything dealing with that time-burnished subject. Trachten for the toddlers, dirndl for the dames, and cute hand-embroidered cardigans for the kids are all found at **Giesswein** (✉ Kärntnerstrasse 5–7 ☎01/512–4597), famed for some of the best traditional clothing in town. Austria's one and only cooperative for art and crafts, **Österreichische Werkstätten** (✉Kärntnerstrasse 6 ☎01/512–2418), stocks Austrian handicrafts of the finest quality. The range covers home accessories, from brass or pewter candlesticks to linen tablecloths, to quality souvenirs, ranging from enamel jewelry to embroidered brooches. For that Alt Wien flourish, choose a needlepointed handbag, pill boxes, or brooch from **Petit Point Kovalcec** (✉Kärntnerstrasse 16 ☎01/512–4886). Fancy a composers portrait–bust collection? Schubert, Mozart, Beethoven, Haydn,
★ and the rest of the gang can be had at **Souvenir in der Hofburg** (✉ Hofburgpassage 1 and 7 ☎ 01/533–5053). While you're at it, you might want to go for a ceramic figure of a Lippizaner stallion, too (it may not be an Augarten porcelain original, but it is certainly more affordable). Postcards, vintage booklets on Vienna, imperial memorabilia, small busts of former Habsburg rulers, and petite gifts for the folks back home will tempt one and all connoisseurs at **Stransky** (✉ Hofburgpassage 2 ☎ 01/533–6098).

CHRISTKINDLMÄRTE
Vienna keeps the Christmas olympic flame burning perhaps more brightly than any other metropolis in the world. Here, during the holiday season, no less than five major *Christkindmärte* (Christmas Markets) proffer their wares, with stands selling enough woodcarved Austrian toys, crêche figures, and Tannenbaum ornaments to tickle anybody's mistletoes. Many of the markets offers food vendors selling dee-scrumptious *Glühwein* mead and *Kartoffelpuffer* potato patties. Here are the best of the markets. **Altwiener Christkindlmarkt** (✉ The Freynung ☎ 01/ 5121296) is held on one of Vienna's biggest squares. **Karlsplatz** (✉ Karlsplatz) has some of the more refined stands in town.The biggest holiday market is the famous **Rathausplatz** (✉ Rathausplatz) held in front of the magnificently Gothic fantasy that is Vienna's Rathaus city hall. All the glitter and gilt of the season frames the market held at the Habsburgs' splendid **Schönbrunn** (✉ Schönbrunn Palace) The cognoscenti love the arty market held in the enchanting Biedermeier quarter of **Spittelberg** (✉ Burggasse and Siebensterngasse)

JEWELRY   The finest selection of watches in Vienna can be found at **Haban** (✉ Kärntnerstrasse 2 ☎ 01/512–6730–0 ✉ Kärntnerstrasse 17 ☎ 01/512–6750), and the gold and diamond jewelry selection is top-notch, too. In the city of Freud, father of psychoanalysis, what else can you expect but the sort of jewelry at the **Golden Genius** (✉ Kohlmarkt 3 ☎ 01/470–94–82), where dream symbols are individually cast in different shades of gold as a surround for colorful precious stones. One of Vienna's fabled K & K (*Kaiserlich und Königlich*—Imperial and Royal) suppliers,

★ **A. E. Köchert** (✉ Neuer Markt 15 ☎ 01/512–5828–0), has been Vienna's jeweler of choice for nearly two centuries. Almost 150 years ago Empress Elisabeth ordered some diamond studded stars here to adorn her legendary auburn hair (so long she could sit on it). Guess what? Those diamonded stars are more fashionable than ever since Köchert has started reissuing them. And if you're ever in need of a crown, Köchert will even craft your very own. Discover interesting pieces of Austrian jade at **Burgenland** (✉ Opernpassage ☎ 01/587–6266).

MEN'S CLOTHING Although his shops now span the globe, Vienna-born **Helmut Lang** (✉ Seilergasse 6 ☎ 01/5132588 ⊕ www.helmutlang.com) rightly has an outlet in his old home town. His choice colors are black and white, with just a touch of beige, and his minimalist designs represent the peak of understatement in fashion. **Peek & Cloppenburg** (✉ Mariahilferstrasse 26–30, ☎ 01/525610 ⊕ www.peekundcloppenburg.at) is the right place for those who hate having to go to various shops to find what they are looking for. It's all here with brand names, designer labels, and excellent value for money. Austrians love their hats and **Collins Hüte** (✉ Opernpassage ☎ 01/587–1305) is one of the best sources in town—not only for hats but also for accessories, such as scarves, gloves, and the stray sombrero (for that glaring summer sun on the slopes at Lech). For that high classic look, **Sir Anthony** (✉ Kärntnerstrasse 21-23, 1st District ☎ 01/512–6835) is the place.

MUSIC You just might bump into Placido, Jose, or even Dame Joan Sutherland—and if you do, you know where to buy that picture postcard and then run

★ and have it autographed—at Vienna's noted **Arcardia** (✉ Staatsoper Opera House, Opernring 2 ☎ 01/513–9568–0), which is stocked with not only a grand selection of latest CD releases from the operatic world, but quite a few classic rareties, too. Helpful sales assistants are at the ready if you're looking for any special titles at **EMI** (✉ Kärntnerstrasse 30 ☎ 01/512–3675)—one of the big mainstays for classical music (find it upstairs) plus the whole gamut from ethno to pop. **Virgin Megastore** (✉ Mariahilferstrasse 37–39, 6th District ☎ 01/588370) is the well-known music store found all over the world.

Toys

Emperor Franz Josef in his horse-drawn carriage, the K & K Infantry cheering him on, and the Prussian emperor to meet him at the battle-

★ field—here at **Kober** (✉ Graben 14–15 ☎ 01/533–6018) you can find all of the historic tin soldiers you'll ever need to relive those eventful last years of the empire. If you prefer something a little less military-like, go for the full Johann Strauss Orchestra, it's a scream. Mozart, that "eternal child." would have loved **Spielzeugschachtel** ✉ Rauenstein-gasse 5 ☎ 01/512–3994—he lived just across the street.

Fashion designer Doris is very often in her own shop so she can help you with decision making. Vienna-born **Helmut Lang** (✉ Seilergasse 6 ☎ 01/5132588 ⊕ www.helmutlang.com) has become one of the fashion Masters of the Universe, so those who want the chicest in modern, minimalist clothes head here to pay homage. **Wiener Blut** (✉ Spiegelgasse 19 ☎ 01/5132015) has lots of temptations. Monika Bacher's zippy knitwear, striking pieces by Berlin designers, zany shoes from Canada, and the finest crafted handbags from Italy. Fashionistas make a bee line for the studio of Austrian designer **Schella Kann** (✉ Singerstrasse 14/2 ☎ 01/513–2287)—extravagant and trendy, these are clothes one never wants to take off. For conservative, high-quality clothing, go to the **Geiger Boutique** (✉ Kärntnerstrasse 19 ☎ 01/513–1398) in the Steffl Department Store.

VIENNA A TO Z

To research prices, get advice from other travelers, and book travel arrangements, visit www.fodors.com.

ADDRESSES
Vienna is divided into 23 numbered districts; for a complete rundown on the various districts, or *Bezirke,* see the introductory text to the Exploring Vienna section near the top of this chapter. Taxi drivers may need to know which district you seek, as well as the street address. The district number is coded into the postal code with the second and third digits; thus A-1010 (the "01") is the 1st District, A-1030 is the 3rd, A-1110 is the 11th, and so on. Some sources and maps still give the district numbers, either in Roman or Arabic numerals, as Vienna X or Vienna 10.

AIR TRAVEL
Austrian Airlines flies into Schwechat from North America.
🚩 Airlines & Contacts **Austrian Airlines** ☎ 05/1789.

AIRPORTS & TRANSFERS
Vienna's airport is at Schwechat, about 19 km (12 mi) southeast of the city.
🚩 Airport Information **Schwechat Airport (Vienna)** ☎ 01/7007–0 for flight information.

The fastest way into Vienna from Schwechat Airport is the sleek, double-decker **City Train.** The journey from the airport to Wien–Mitte (the center of the city) takes only 16 minutes and operates daily every 30 minutes between 5:30 AM and midnight. The cost is €8 one-way and €15 round-trip.

The cheapest way to get to Vienna from the airport is the **S7 train,** called the *Schnellbahn,* which shuttles twice an hour between the airport basement and the Landstrasse/Wien–Mitte (city center) and Wien–Nord (north Vienna) stations; the fare is €3 and it takes about 35 minutes (19 minutes longer than the City Train). Your ticket is also good for an immediate transfer to your destination within the city on the streetcar, bus, or U-Bahn. Another cheap option is the **bus,** which has two separate lines. One line goes to the City Air Terminal at the Hilton Hotel (near the city's 1st District) every 20 minutes between 6:30 AM and 11 PM, and every 30 minutes after that; traveling time is 20 minutes. The other line goes to the South and West train stations (Südbahnhof and Westbahnhof) in 20 and 35 minutes, respectively. Departure times are every 30 minutes from 8:10 AM to 7:10 PM, hourly thereafter, and not at all 12:10–3:30 AM. Fare is €5.80 one-way, €10.90 for a round-trip. Prices may be higher in 2005 and beyond. Another possibility is via taxi with C+K Airport Service (☎ 01/44444 🖷 01/689–6969), charging a set price of €25 (don't forget to tip). C+K will also meet your plane at no extra charge if you let them know your flight information in advance.

🔢 Taxis & Shuttles **C+K Airport Service** ☎ 01/44444 🖷 01/689–6969. **City Air Terminal** ✉ Am Stadtpark ☎ 01/5800–33369 or 01/2300.

BOAT & FERRY TRAVEL

If you arrive in Vienna via the Danube, the Blue Danube Steamship Company/DDSG will leave you at Praterlände near Mexikoplatz. The Praterlände stop is a two-block taxi ride or hike from the Vorgartenstrasse U1/subway station, or you can take a taxi directly into town.

🔢 Boat & Ferry Information **Blue Danube Schifffahrt (Steamship Company)/DDSG** ✉ Friedrichstrasse 7, A-1043 Vienna ☎ 01/588-800 🖷 01/588-8044-0 ⊕ www.ddsg-blue-danube.at.

BUS TRAVEL TO & FROM VIENNA

International long-distance bus service (Bratislava, Brno) and most postal and railroad buses arrive at the Wien–Mitte central bus station, across from the Hilton Hotel on the Stadtpark.

🔢 Bus Information **Wien-Mitte** ✉ Landstrasser Hauptstrasse 1b ☎ 01/711-01.

CAR RENTAL

Rental cars can be arranged at the airport or in town. Major firms include the following. Buchbinder is a local firm with particularly favorable rates and clean cars.

🔢 Major Agencies **Avis** ✉ Airport ☎ 01/7007-32700 ✉ Opernring 5 ☎ 01/587-6241. **Buchbinder** ✉ Schlachthausgasse 38 ☎ 01/71750-0. **Budget** ✉ Airport ☎ 01/7007-32711 ✉ Hilton Hotel, Am Stadtpark ☎ 01/714-6565. **Europcar** ✉ Airport ☎ 01/7007-33316 ✉ Erdberg Park & Ride ☎ 01/799-6176. **Hertz** ✉ Kärntner Ring 17 ☎ 01/512-8677.

CAR TRAVEL

Vienna is 300 km (187 mi) east of Salzburg, 200 km (125 mi) north of Graz. Main routes leading into the city are the A1 Westautobahn from Germany, Salzburg, and Linz and the A2 Südautobahn from Graz and points south.

PARKING   The entire 1st and 6th through 9th districts of Vienna are limited-parking zones and require that a *Parkschein,* a paid-parking chit available at most newsstands and tobacconists, be displayed on the dash during the day. Parkscheine cost €0.40 for 30 minutes, €0.80 for 1 hour, and €1.20 for 90 minutes. You can park 10 minutes free of charge, but you must get a violet "gratis" sticker to put in your windshield. You can also park free in the 1st District on Saturday and Sunday, but not overnight. Overnight street parking in the 1st and 6th through 9th districts is restricted to residents with special permits; all other cars are subject to expensive ticketing or even towing, so in these districts be sure you have off-street garage parking.

EMBASSIES & CONSULATES

🏴 Canada ⊠ Laurenzerberg 2, on the 3rd floor of Hauptpost building complex, 1st District ☎ 01/53138-3000.

🏴 United Kingdom ⊠ Jauresgasse 12 Landstrasse, 3rd District/Landstrasse ☎ 01/71613-5151.

🏴 United States **Embassy of the United States** ⊠ Boltzmanngasse 16, A-1090, 9th District, Vienna ☎ 31339-0. **Consulate of the U.S./Passport Division** ⊠ Gartenbaupromenade 2-4, A-1010, 1st District, Vienna ☎ 31339-0.

EMERGENCIES

If you need a doctor and speak no German, ask your hotel, or in an emergency, phone your consulate. In each area of the city one pharmacy stays open 24 hours; if a pharmacy is closed, a sign on the door will tell you the address of the nearest one that is open. Call the number listed below for names and addresses (in German) of the pharmacies open that night.

🏴 Emergency Services **Ambulance** ☎ 144. **Fire** ☎ 122. **Police** ☎ 133.

🏴 Late-night Pharmacies **Pharmacy information** ☎ 01/1550.

LODGING

RESERVING A ROOM If you need a room upon arrival and have not made previous reservations, go to Information-Zimmernachweis, operated by the Verkehrsbüro in the Westbahnhof and in the Südbahnhof. At the airport, the information and room-reservation office in the arrivals hall is open daily 8:30 AM–9 PM. If you're driving into Vienna, get information or book rooms through the Vienna Tourist Board's hotel assistance hot line. It's open daily from 9–7.

🏴 **Information-Zimmernachweis** ☎ 01/892-3392 in Westbahnhof, 01/505-3132 in Südbahnhof. **Vienna Tourist Board's hotel assistance hot line** ☎ 01/24555 🖶 01/24-555-666 ⊕ www.info.wien.at.

TOURS

BUS TOURS When you're pressed for time, a good way to see the highlights of Vienna is via a sightseeing bus tour, which gives you a once-over-lightly of the heart of the city and allows a closer look at Schönbrunn and Belvedere palaces. You can cover almost the same territory on your own by taking either Streetcar 1 or 2 around the Ring and then walking through the heart of the city. For tours, there are a couple of reputable firms: Vienna Sightseeing Tours and Cityrama Sightseeing. Both run daily "get acquainted" tours lasting about three hours (€34), including visits to the Schönbrunn and Belvedere palace grounds. The entrance fee and guided tour of Schönbrunn is included in the price, but not a guided tour of Belvedere, just the grounds. Both firms offer a number of other tours as well (your hotel will have detailed programs) and provide hotel pickup for most tours. These tour operators offer short trips outside the city. Check their offerings and compare packages and prices to be sure you get what you want. Your hotel will have brochures.

🛈 Fees & Schedules **Cityrama Sightseeing** ⊠ Börsegasse 1 ☎ 01/534-130 🖷 01/534-13-28 ⊕ www.cityrama.at. **Vienna Sightseeing Tours** ⊠ Graf Starhemberggasse 25 ☎ 01/712-4683-0 🖷 01/714-1141 ⊕ www.viennasightseeingtours.com.

STREETCAR TOURS From early May to early October, a 1929 vintage streetcar leaves each Saturday at 11:30 AM and 1:30 PM and Sundays and holidays at 9:30, 11:30 AM, and 1:30 PM from the Otto Wagner Pavilion at Karlsplatz for a guided tour. For €15 (€13.50 if you have the Vienna-Card), you'll go around the Ring, out past the big Ferris wheel in the Prater and past Schönbrunn and Belvedere palaces in the course of the two-hour trip. Prices may go up in 2005, and departure times may change; be sure to check ahead. The old-timer trips are popular, so make your reservation at the transport-information office underground at Karlsplatz, weekdays 7 AM–6 PM, weekends and holidays 8:30–4. You must buy your ticket on the streetcar.

🛈 Fees & Schedules **Transport-information office** ☎ 01/7909-43426.

WALKING TOURS Guided walking tours (in English) are a great way to see the city highlights. The city tourist office offers around 40 tour topics, ranging from "Unknown Underground Vienna" to "Hollywood in Vienna," "For Lovers of Music and Opera," "Old World Vienna–Off the Beaten Track," "Jewish Families and Their Past in Vienna," and many more. Vienna Walks and Talks offers informative walks through the old Jewish Quarter and a *Third Man* tour from the classic film starring Orson Welles, among other subjects. Tours take about 1½ hours, are held in any weather provided at least three people turn up, and cost €11, plus any entry fees. No reservations are needed for the city sponsored tours. Get a full list of the guided-tour possibilities at the city information office. Ask for the monthly brochure "Walks in Vienna," which details the tours, days, times, and starting points. You can also arrange to have your own privately guided tour for €120 for a half day.

If you can, try to get a copy of "Vienna Downtown Walking Tours" by Henriette Mandl from a bookshop. The six tours take you through the highlights of central Vienna with excellent commentary and some entertaining anecdotes that most of your Viennese acquaintances won't know. The booklet "Vienna from A–Z" (in English, €3.60; available at bookshops and city information offices) explains the numbered plaques attached to all major buildings.

🛈 **City information office** ⊠ Am Albertinaplatz 1. **Vienna Guide Service** ⊠ Werdertorgasse 9/2 ☎ 01/774-8901 ⊕ www.wienguide.at. **Vienna Walks and Talks** ⊠ Werdertorgasse 9/2, 1st District ☎ 01/774-8901 🖷 01/774-8933 ⊕ www.viennawalks.tix.at.

TRAIN TRAVEL

Trains from Germany, Switzerland, and western Austria arrive at the Westbahnhof (West Station), on Europaplatz, where Mariahilferstrasse crosses the Gürtel. If you're coming from Italy or Hungary, you'll generally arrive at the Südbahnhof (South Station). There are two current stations for trains to and from Prague and Warsaw: Wien Nord (North Station) and Franz-Josef Bahnhof. Central train information will have details about schedule information for train departures all over Austria. However, it's hard to find somebody who can speak English, so it's best to ask your hotel for help in calling.

🚩 Train Information **Central train information** ☎ 05/1717. **Westbahnhof** ✉ Westbahnhof, 15th District/Fünfhaus. **Franz-Josef Bahnhof** ✉ Julius-Tandler-Platz, 9th District/Alsergrund. **Südbahnhof** ✉ Wiedner Gürtel 1, 4th District/Wieden. **Wien Nord** ✉ Praterstern, 2nd District/Leopoldstadt.

TRANSPORTATION WITHIN VIENNA: BUS, TRAM & U-BAHN
When it comes to seeing the main historic sights, Vienna is a city to tackle on foot. With the exception of the Schönbrunn and Belvedere palaces and the Prater amusement park, most sights are concentrated in the center, the 1st District (A-1010), much of which is a pedestrian zone anyway. Happily, Vienna's subway system, called the U-Bahn, does service the core of the inner city. The main city center subway stops in the 1st District are Stephansplatz, Karlsplatz, Herrengasse, Schottenring, and Schwedenplatz. Stephansplatz is the the very heart of the city, at St. Stephan's cathedral, with exits to the Graben and Kärntnerstrasse. You can reach the famous amusement park of the Prater from Stephansplatz by taking the U1 to Praterstern. Near the southern edge of the Ringstrasse, the major Karlsplatz stop is right next to the Staatsoper, the pedestrian Kärntnerstrasse, and the Ringstrasse, with an easy connection to Belvedere Palace via the D Tram. You can also take the U4 from Karlsplatz to Schönbrunn Palace (Schönbrunn stop). Herrengasse is also directly in the city center, close to the Hofburg and Graben. Schottenring is on the Ringstrasse, offering quick tram connections or a short walk on foot to the Graben. Schwedenplatz is ideally situated for a 10-minute walk to St. Stephan's through some of Vienna's oldest streets, or you can hop on a tram and be on the Ringstrasse in five minutes. You can also take the U1 from Schwedenplatz to the Prater, getting off at Praterstern. Karlsplatz is serviced by the train lines U4, U2, U1, while U3 goes to Herrengasse and U2 to Schottentor. In addition, there are also handy U-Bahn stops along the rim of the city core, such as MuseumsQuartier, Stadtpark, Volkstheater, and Rathaus. You can also hop around the 1st District by using bus lines 1A, 2A, and 3A, and there are also useful crosstown buses if you don't want to walk 10 minutes from one U-Bahn stop to another.

Each sight write-up in our Exploring Vienna chapter lists its nearest public transportation stop. Vienna's public transportation system, run by the VOR, or Vorverkaufsstellen der Wiener Linen, is fast, clean, safe, and easy to use. Get public transport maps at a tourist office or at the transport-information offices (*Wiener Verkehrsbetriebe*), underground at Karlsplatz, Stephansplatz, and Praterstern. You can transfer on the same ticket between subway, streetcar, bus, and long stretches of the fast suburban railway, *Schnellbahn* (*S-Bahn*).

Five subway (*U-Bahn*) lines, whose stations are prominently marked with blue U signs, crisscross the city. Karlsplatz and Stephansplatz are the main transfer points between lines. The last subway (U4) runs at about 12:30 AM. Track the main lines of the U-Bahn system by their color-codes on

Vienna
Subways

Floridsdorf
Leopoldau
Heiligenstadt
Großfeldsiedlung
Neue Donau
Aderklaaer Straße
Rennbahnweg
Handelskai
Dresdner Str.
Kagraner Platz
Spittelau
Jägerstr.
Nussdorfer
Str.
Friedens-
brücke
Kargran
Währinger Str.
Alte Donau
Volksoper
Kaisermühlen - VIC
Michelbeuern
Rossauer
Donauinsel
Allg. Krankenhaus
Lände
Vorgartenstraße
Alser Str.
Praterstern–Wien Nord
Ottakring
Josefstädter Str.
Schottenring
Messe
Aspernstraße
Schottentor
Trabrennstraße
Thaliastr.
Rathaus
Schwedenplatz
Lerchenfelder
Johnstr.
Burgg.-
Str.
Stadthalle
Schweglerstr.
Ziegierg.
Volkstheater
Herreng.
Stephanspl.
Stadion

Donaustadt.
Seestern
Stadiau
Hardegg-gasse
Donauspital
Landstr.–Wien Mitte
Rochusgasse
Hütteldorf
Ober St. Veit
Längenfeldg.
Margareten-
gürtel
Museums-
quartier
Stubentor
Kardinal-Nagl-Platz
Schlacthausg.
Unter St. Veit
Braunschweigg.
Hietzing
Schönbrunn
Pilgramg.
Kettenbrückeng.
Stadtpark
Erdberg
Gasometer
Zippererstr.
Niederhofstr.
Taubstummeng.
Enkplatz
Meidling
Simmering
Philadelphiabrücke
Südtiroler
Platz
Keplerplatz
Tschertteg.
Am Schöpfwerk.
Alterlaa
Reumannplatz
Erlaaer Str.
Perfektastr.
Siebenhirten

the subway maps: U1 is red; U2, purple; U3, orange; U4, green; and U6, brown. Note that you have to open the subway door when the train stops, either by pushing a lighted button or pulling the door handle aside. The first streetcars (*Strassenbahnen*) run from about 5:15 AM. From then on, service (barring gridlock on the streets) is regular and reliable, and most lines operate until about midnight. The most famous tram lines are No. 1, which travels the great Ringstrasse avenue clockwise, and No. 2, which travels its counter-clockwise; each offers a cheap way to sightsee the glories of Vienna's 19th-century Ringstrasse monuments. Where streetcars don't run, buses—the word in German is *Autobus*—do; route maps and schedules are posted at each bus or subway stop.

Within the heart of the city, bus lines 1A, 2A, and 3A are useful crosstown routes. Should you miss the last streetcar tram or bus, special night buses with an N designation operate at half-hour intervals over several key routes; the starting (and transfer) points are the Opera House and Schwedenplatz. The night-owl buses now accept all normal tickets. There is no additional fare.

Tickets for public transportation are valid for all public transportation—buses, trams, and the subway. It's best to buy your ticket at a U-Bahn stop before boarding a bus or tram. Though there are ticket machines on trams, and bus drivers sell tickets, you'll pay €0.50 more. Passengers can enter and exit buses and trams through any door. You'll need to punch your ticket before entering the boarding area at U-Bahn stops, but for buses and trams, you'll punch it on board. Though Vienna public transportation operates on the honor system; if you're caught without a ticket you'll pay a hefty fine.

Buy single tickets for €2 from dispensers on the streetcar tram or from your bus driver; you'll need exact change for the former. Note that it's €0.50 cheaper to buy your ticket in advance from a ticket machine located at subway stations, and also good for buses and trams. The ticket machines at subway stations (*VOR-Fahrkarten*) give change and dispense 24-hour, 72-hour, and eight-day tickets, as well as single tickets separately and in blocks of two and five. Tickets are sold singly or as strip tickets, *Streifenkarten*. At Tabak-Trafik (cigarette shops/newsstands) or the underground Wiener Verkehrsbetriebe offices you can get a block of five tickets for €7.50, each ticket good for one uninterrupted trip in more or less the same general direction with unlimited transfers. Or you can get a three-day ticket for €12, good on all lines for 72 hours from the time you validate the ticket; there's also a 24-hour ticket for €5. If you're staying longer, get an eight-day ticket (€24), which can be used on eight separate days or by any number of persons (up to eight) at any one time. Prices may go up in 2005. Children under six travel free on Vienna's public transport system; children under 15 travel free on Sundays, public holidays, and during Vienna school holidays. If you don't speak German, opt to purchase your transport tickets from a person at a Tabak or main U-Bahn station.

As with most transport systems within European cities, it is essential to "validate," or punch, your ticket when you start your trip. You'll find the validations machines on all buses, trams, and at the entrance of each U-Bahn station—look for the blue box and slide your ticket into the machine until you hear a "punch." Tabak-Trafik Almassy is open every day from 8 AM to 7 PM and has tickets as well as film and other items.

A *Fiaker,* or horse cab, will trot you around to whatever destination you specify, but this is an expensive way to see the city. A short tour of the inner city takes about 20 minutes and costs €40; a longer one including the Old Town and part of the Ringstrasse lasts about 40 minutes and costs €65, and an hour-long tour of the inner city and the whole Ringstrasse costs €95. The carriages accommodate four (five if someone sits next to the coachman). Starting points are Heldenplatz in front of the Hofburg, Stephansplatz beside the cathedral, and across from the Albertina, all in the 1st District. For longer trips, or any variation of the regular route, agree on the price first.

🚃 **Tabak-Trafik Almassy** ✉ Stephansplatz 4, to the right behind cathedral ☎ 01/512-5909. **VOR, or Vorverkaufsstellen der Wiener Linien** ☎ 7909/105 ⊕ www.wienerlinien.at.

TRAVEL AGENCIES
American Express, Kuoni Cosmos, Carlson/Wagons-Lit, and Österreichisches Verkehrsbüro serve as general travel agencies. American Ex-

press, Kuoni Cosmos, and Vienna Ticket Service/Cityrama are agencies that offer tickets to various sights and events in Vienna.

Local Agent Referrals American Express ✉ Kärntnerstrasse 21–23, 1st District ☎ 01/515-40-0 📠 01/515-40-777. **Carlson/Wagons-Lit** ✉ Millennium Tower 94/Handelskai, 20th District ☎ 01/240600 📠 01/24060-65. **Kuoni Cosmos** ✉ Kärntner Ring 15, 1st District ☎ 01/515-33-0 📠 01/513-4147. **Österreichisches Verkehrsbüro** ✉ Friedrichstrasse 7, 4th District, opposite the Secession Building ☎ 01/588-00-0 📠 01/588-000-280. **Vienna Ticket Service/Cityrama** ✉ Börsegasse 1, 1st District ☎ 01/534130 📠 01/534-1328.

VIENNA TAXIS

Taxis in Vienna are relatively reasonable. The initial charge is €3 for as many as four people daytime, and about 5% more from 11 PM until 6 AM. Radio cabs ordered by phone have an initial charge of €6. They also may charge for each piece of luggage that must go into the trunk, and a charge is added for waiting beyond a reasonable limit. It's customary to round up the fare to cover the tip. Service is usually prompt, but when you hit rush hour, the weather is bad, or you need to keep to an exact schedule, call ahead and order a taxi for a specific time. If your destination is the airport, ask for a reduced-rate taxi. There are several companies that offer chauffeured limousines, which are listed below.

Taxi Companies Göth ☎ 01/713-7196. **Mazur** ☎ 01/604-2530. **Peter Urban** ☎ 01/713-5255.

VISITOR INFORMATION

The main center for information (walk-ins only) is the Vienna City Tourist Office, open daily 9–9 PM and centrally located between the Hofburg and Kärntnerstrasse.

Ask at tourist offices or your hotel about a Vienna-Card; costing €15.25, the card combines 72 hours' use of public transportation and discounts at certain museums and shops.

If you've lost something valuable, check with the police at the Fundangelegenheiten (Lost and Found). If your loss occurred on a train in Austria, call the central number and ask for Reisegepäck. Losses on the subway system or streetcars can be checked by calling the Fundstelle U-Bahn.

Tourist Information Fundstelle U-Bahn ☎ 01/7909-43500. **Reisegepäck (Central Train Information)** ☎ 05/1717. **Vienna City Tourist Office** ✉ Am Albertinaplatz 1, 1st District ☎ 01/24555 📠 01/216-84-92 or 01/24555-666.

SIDE TRIPS FROM VIENNA

FROM THE VIENNA WOODS TO THE WEINVIERTEL

2

EAT HEARTY AND DRINK UP
in the wine village of Gumpoldskirchen ⇨ *p.138*

ENJOY A LITTLE SCHUBERT WITH YOUR SPA
treatments at fashionable Baden ⇨ *p.138*

RELIVE THE HAUNTING ROMANCE
of the legend of Mayerling ⇨ *p.140*

TOUR THE MAGNIFICENT COMPLEX
of the abbey of Helligenkreuz ⇨ *p.140*

DO A TASTING TOUR OF THE BEST WINE
Kellergassen of Poysdorf ⇨ *p.144*

MEET AN ANIMAL OR TWO
in the castle zoo at Schlosshof ⇨ *p.145*

WALK THE ANCIENT PATHS
of the Roman fortress at Carnuntum ⇨ *p.146*

Updated by
Bonnie Dodson

THE VIENNESE ARE UNDENIABLY LUCKY. Few populaces enjoy such glorious—and easily accessible—options for day-tripping. Droves of stressed-out city residents strap their bicycles to the roof racks of their Mercedeses on Saturdays and Sundays; vacationers stopping in Vienna can share in the natives' obvious pleasure in the city's outer environs any day of the week. For many the first destination is, of course, the Wienerwald, the deservedly fabled Vienna Woods—a rolling range of densely wooded hills extending from Vienna's doorstep to the outposts of the Alps in the south (and not a natural park or forest, as you might think from listening to Strauss or the tourist blurbs). This region is crisscrossed by country roads and hiking paths, dotted with forest lodges and inns, and solidifies every now and then into quaint little villages and market towns.

In addition to such natural pleasures, the regions outside of Vienna offer satisfactions for every interest. Keen on history and mystery? Turning south to Mayerling leads you to the site where in 1889 the successor to the Austrian throne presumably took his own life after shooting his secret love—a mystery still unresolved. Prefer scenic beauty? Head northeast, into the area's wonderfully encompassing woods and sweetly rolling hills sprinkled with elegant summer palaces. To the north, you can sip and taste your way down the Weinstrasse (Wine Road), along which vast expanses of vineyards produce excellent, mainly white, wines. Here, you'll find Gumpoldskirchen, one of Austria's most famous wine-producing villages and the source of one of Europe's most pleasant white wines. Vintners' houses line its main street, their gates leading into vine-covered courtyard-gardens where the Heuriger (wine of the most recent vintage) is served at wooden tables, sometimes to the tune of merry or plaintive melodies played on an accordion. Another choice is to follow the trail of the defensive castles that protected the land from invaders arriving from the north; or you can even trace the early days of Masonic lore in Austria—both Haydn and Mozart were members of what was then a secret and forbidden brotherhood. For dramatic contrast, head to the elegant spa town of Baden, where Beethoven passed 15 summers and composed large sections of the Ninth Symphony.

These sub-regions of Lower Austria (which derives its name from the fact that for centuries it was the "lower"—defined by the Danube's course—part of the archduchy of Austria) are simple, mainly agricultural, country areas. People live in close harmony with the earth, and on any sunny weekend from March through October you may see whole families out working the fields. This isn't to suggest that pleasure is neglected; just as often, you'll stumble across a dressy parade with the local brass band decked out in lederhosen and feathered hats. Sundays here are still generally days of rest, with many families venturing to morning mass, then retiring to the local Gasthaus to discuss weather and politics over lunch. Whatever destination you choose in this area, however, the lakes are waiting, the biking paths are open, and the lovely countryside cafés beckon.

Exploring Vienna's Environs

The region surrounding Vienna divides itself logically into two main areas. The Vienna Woods, that huge, unspoiled belt of forest green stretching westward south of the Danube, was celebrated by composers Beethoven, Schubert, and Strauss and remains beloved by the Viennese today. The towns to its south—Mödling, Baden, and Bad Vöslau—mark the east end of these rolling, wooded hills. There the fertile Vienna Basin begins, sweeping east to the low, wooded Leitha Mountains, which shelter the Puszta plain extending on into Hungary.

North of the Danube, and east of the Kamp River, are the undulating hills of the agricultural Weinviertel (or Wine District), bordering on the Czech Republic and on Slovakia, where the March River flows into the Danube.

About the Restaurants & Hotels

Dining in the countryside outside Vienna is a casual affair. It's not un-usual to see locals arrive in traditional lederhosen and dirndl, and you'll be sure to see a well-behaved dog or two accompanying their owners right to the table. Meal times are usually from noon to 2 PM for lunch and from 6 to 10 PM for dinner. It's rare to find a restaurant that serves all afternoon, so plan ahead. It's a good idea to reserve a table, espe-cially for Sunday lunch, which is a popular time for families to get to-gether. Tipping 5%–7% is customary.

Accommodations in the countryside around Vienna are pretty basic. This is underdeveloped tourist territory, prime turf for the more adventure-some, with rooms frequently to be found as an adjunct to the local *Gasthaus*. Nearly all such establishments are family-run; the younger members will speak at least some school-level English. You'll probably have to carry your own bags, and elevators are scarce. Booking ahead is a good idea, as most places have relatively few rooms, particularly ones with full bath. Window screens are almost unknown in Austria, as bugs are few, but in farming areas both flies and occasionally mosquitoes can be a nuisance in the warmer seasons. Since you may want windows open at night, take along a can of bug spray to sleep more soundly. The standard country bed covering is a down-filled feather bed, so if you're allergic to feathers or want more warmth, ask for blankets.

Some hotels offer half-board, with dinner in addition to buffet break-fast. The half-board room rate is usually an extra €15–€30 per per-son. Occasionally, quoted room rates for hotels already include half-board accommodations, though a "discounted" rate is usually offered if you prefer not to take the evening meal. Inquire when booking. Room rates include taxes and service, and usually breakfast—although you should always ask about the latter.

Is it the sun, or the soil? Or the dreamy, castle-crowned peaks? Whatever the lure, the idyllic regions that lie beyond Vienna's environs have always offered irresistible pastoral escapes for the Viennese. Besides being rich in scenic splendor, this countryside is also saturated with musical history: here Beethoven was inspired to write his *Pastoral* Symphony, Johann Strauss transformed the tales of the Vienna Woods into exhilarating music, and a glass of intoxicating Retzer Wein moved Richard Strauss to compose the "Rosenkavalier Waltz." From the elegant spa of Baden to mysterious Mayerling, the region offers a multitude of delights to the day-tripper.

The districts surrounding Vienna are compact, and each can be explored in a day or two. To pursue the lives of the famous composers Schubert and Beethoven, take the route to the south, to Mödling and Baden; for Haydn's birthplace, go to the east to Rohrau, then possibly on to Eisenstadt (*see* Chapter 3). To enjoy rolling hills and vast expanses of vineyards and to sample their output, seek out the Weinviertel to the north.

Numbers in the text correspond to numbers in the margin and on the Baden and Environs and the Weinviertel maps.

If you have 1 day

South of the Danube To get a taste of the fringes of the Vienna Woods to the capital's south and west, head for **Mödling** ❷ and **Baden** ❼. Both are smaller communities with unspoiled 17th-century town centers on a scale easy to assimilate. The route to Baden runs through the band of rolling wooded hills that mark the eastern edge of the Vienna Woods. These hills are skirted by vineyards forming a "wine belt," which also follows the valleys south of Vienna.

If you have 6 days

With more time, you might spend two days in the Vienna Woods area, starting off with two particularly picturesque towns, **Perchtoldsdorf** ❶ and **Mödling** ❷—with perhaps a look at the grand garden of **Schloss Laxenburg** ❸—then following the scenic Weinstrasse (Wine Road) through lush vineyard country to the noted wine-producing village of **Gumpoldskirchen** ❻. Overnight in ⬚ **Baden** ❼; then spend your second day taking in the sights of this fashionable spa town, including its grand Kurpark and Casino. Set out in the afternoon for mysterious ⬚ **Mayerling** ❽. After an evocative dawn and morning there, head for the great abbey at **Heiligenkreuz** ❾, continuing on to Vienna, and up north through the farmlands to the heart of the capital of the Weinviertel, ⬚ **Poysdorf** ⬚. After touring this famous wine center on the morning of your fifth day, track the castles around **Marchegg** ⬚, including Schloss Niederweiden and Johann Lukas von Hildebrandt's Schlosshof. Overnight in ⬚ **Strasshof** ⬚. On your sixth day, pay a call on the ancient Roman site of **Carnuntum** ⬚, then head down to the tiny village of Rohrau, to see the cottage where Haydn was born. For a grand finale, visit the Schloss Rohrau, home to one of the grandest ancestral Old Master painting collections in Europe.

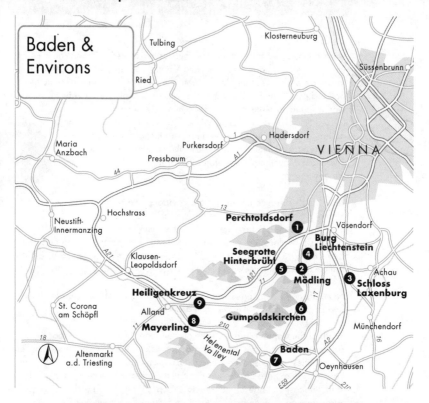

WHAT IT COSTS In euros					
	$$$$	**$$$**	**$$**	**$**	**¢**
RESTAURANTS	over €22	€18–€22	€13–€17	€7–€12	under €7
HOTELS	over €175	€135–€175	€100–€135	€70–€100	under €70

Restaurant prices are per person for a main course at dinner. Hotel prices are for a standard double room in high season, including taxes and service. Assume that hotels operate on the European Plan (EP, with no meal provided) unless we note that they use the Breakfast Plan (BP), Modified American Plan (MAP, with breakfast and dinner daily, known as "halb pension"), or Full American Plan (FAP, or "voll pension," with three meals a day). Higher prices (inquire when booking) prevail for any meal plans.

Timing

Most of the regions around Vienna are best seen in the temperate months between mid-March and mid-November. The Waldviertel, however, with its vast stands of great forest, offers picture-book scenery throughout the year. The combination of oaks and evergreens offers a color spectrum ranging from intense, early-spring green, through the deep green of summer, and into traces of autumn foliage, particularly in the Kamp River valley; in winter, occasional spectacular displays of hoar-

2

Bicycling

The Carnuntum region and the southeast corner of the Weinviertel, a region known as the Marchfeld, offer outstanding cycling, with a number of marked routes. Cycle paths follow the southern bank of the Danube past Carnuntum (Petronell) through Bad Deutsch–Altenburg to Hainburg, and other parts of the region are flat enough to offer fine cycling without overexertion. One of the marked routes close to the March River includes the Baroque castles at Marchegg and Schlosshof.

Castles

Taking advantage of the natural line of defense formed by the course of the Danube, barons and bailiffs decided centuries ago to erect fortifications on the bluffs along the river. Castles were the best answer, and a wonderful string of these dot the Weinviertel, including Schloss Niederweiden and Schlosshof. A more polished estate awaits at Schloss Rohrau. The 17th- and 18th-century structures vary from turreted hilltop fortresses to more elegant moated bastions, but all were part of a chain designed to repel invaders. Several are basically intact while others have been restored, but all are impressive relics worth visiting. Castle concerts have become popular during summer months, when the buildings are open for tours as well.

Dining

With very few exceptions, food in this region, while influenced by Viennese cuisine, is on the simple side. The basics are available in abundance: roast meats, customary schnitzel variations, game in season, fresh vegetables, and standard desserts such as *Palatschinken* (crepes filled with jam or nuts, topped with chocolate sauce). Imaginative cooking is rare; this is not tourist territory, and the local population demands little beyond reasonable quality and quantity.

Wines are equally taken for granted, although four of the areas included here are designated as separate wine regions—the Weinviertel, or wine quarter to the north of Vienna; the Kamptal, which divides the Weinviertel from the Waldviertel to the west; the Carnuntum–Petronell region, just below the Danube to the southeast of Vienna; and the Thermen region, south and southwest of the capital. The specialties are mainly white wines, with the standard types, Grüner Veltliner and Rieslings and increasingly Weissburgunder, predominating. Reds are coming more into favor, with lighter reds such as Zweigelt and even rosés to be found in the northern areas. The heavier reds such as Blaufränkisch and St. Laurent and the spicier Gewürztraminer and Müller–Thurgau whites are found in the south. Most vintners work small holdings, so output is limited. The wine market in Poysdorf, center of one of Austria's largest wine regions, offers an opportunity to sample a wide choice of area vintages.

Hiking & Walking

The celebrated Vienna Woods to the west and southwest of Vienna are crisscrossed by hundreds of easy hiking paths, numbered, color-coded, and marked for destinations. Excellent hiking maps available from most bookstores will give ideas and routes. Paths will take you through woods, past meadows and vineyards, alongside streams and rivers, occasionally revealing a tavern hidden away deep in the woods where you can stop for refreshment or a cold snack. Deer, wild boar, and a host of small animals inhabit these preserves. The area is protected, and development is highly restricted, making it ideal for pleasurable hiking.

frost and snowswept vistas turn the region into a glittering three-dimensional Christmas card.

ON THE ROAD TO BADEN & MAYERLING

This brief though history-rich tour takes you to Baden through the part of the legendary Vienna Woods that borders Vienna on the west. The hills are skirted by vineyards forming a "wine belt," which also follows the valleys south of Vienna. You can tour this area easily in a day, either by car or by public transportation, or you can spend the night in Baden, Mödling, or Alland to allow for a more leisurely exploration of Mayerling, Heiligenkreuz, and a few other sights in the area.

Perchtoldsdorf

❶ *12 km (7½ mi) southwest of Vienna center.*

Just over the Vienna city line to the southwest lies Perchtoldsdorf, a charming market town with many wine taverns, a 13th-century Gothic Pfarrkirche (parish church), and the overarching symbol of the town—an imposing stone tower completed in 1511, once forming a piece of the town's defense wall. Familiarly known as Pedersdorf, the town is a favorite excursion spot for the Viennese, who come mainly for the good local wines. Wander around the compact town square to admire the Renaissance houses, some with arcaded courtyards. The Pestsäule (Plague Column) in the center of the square, which gives thanks for rescue from the dread 16th-century plague, was created by the famous Baroque architect Fischer von Erlach and is similar to the Plague Column that adorns the Graben in Vienna (⇨ Vienna's Shop Window: From Michaelerplatz to the Graben *in* Chapter 1). The 1993 version of *The Three Musketeers*, starring Chris O'Donnell and Charlie Sheen, was partly filmed here within the old defense walls. Without a car, you can reach Perchtoldsdorf from Vienna by taking the S-Bahn, or train, from the Westbahnhof, to Liesing, and then a short cab ride to the town.

Where to Eat

$–$$ ✕ **Sonnberghaus.** A former 19th-century carriage house, the Sonnberghaus offers country casual dining with a friendly welcome. You can order from the menu or choose from the plentiful hot and cold buffet. Tasty standards include *Käsespätzle* (little pasta dumplings baked with cheese) and a salad, or Wiener Schnitzel. The wine list is good and reasonably priced. Dining at a picnic table in the inviting courtyard is a delightful way to spend a summer evening. ⊠ *Sonnbergstrasse 22* ☎ *01/869–8181* ▤ *AE, DC, MC, V* ◷ *Closed Mon. and Tues. No lunch.*

Mödling

❷ *20 km (12½ mi) southwest of Vienna.*

Founded in the 10th century, Mödling has a delightful town center, now a pedestrian zone. Here you can admire centuries-old buildings, most of them one- or two-story, which give the town an intimate scale. Composers Beethoven and Schubert appreciated this in the early 1800s;

Mödling was one of Beethoven's favored residences outside of Vienna. Note the domineering **St. Othmar Gothic Pfarrkirche** on a hill overlooking the town proper, a Romanesque 12th-century charnel house (where the bones of the dead were kept), and the town hall, which has a Renaissance loggia. Later eras added Art Nouveau, which mixes happily with the several 16th- and 17th-century buildings.

❸ A couple of miles east of Mödling is **Schloss Laxenburg,** a complex consisting of a large Baroque Neues Schloss (New Castle), a small 14th-century Altes Schloss (Old Castle), and an early-19th-century neo-Gothic castle set into the sizable lake. The large park is full of birds and small game, such as roe deer and hare, and is ornamented with statues, cascades, imitation temples, and other follies. The park and grounds are a favorite with the Viennese for Sunday outings. The Altes Schloss was built in 1381 by Duke Albrecht III as his summer residence, and several Habsburg emperors spent summers in the Neues Schloss, which now houses the International Institute of Applied Systems Analysis. Opposite is the large Baroque convent of the order of the Charitable Sisters. The castle is currently occupied by a research institute and is generally not open to the public, but the gardens are open daily. ⊠ *Schlossplatz 1* ☎ *02236/712–26–0* ⊕ *www.schloss-laxenburg.at* ☒ *Garden €1.30, boat to castle €0.40, tour €4.20* ⊙ *Tours daily at 11, 2, and 3.*

❹ A couple of miles east of Mödling is **Burg Liechtenstein,** an imposing medieval castle perched formidably on a crag overlooking the Vienna Woods. The pale stone walls and turrets have withstood marauding armies and the elements for more than 800 years, but the interior has been largely restored and includes a squires' hall, kitchen, bedchambers, a chapel, and even a medieval toilet. Not to be missed is the Tower Room, with its 13th-century red Italian marble fireplace and carved wooden spiral staircase. The Tower Room was the last refuge in case of an attack, and you can see where boiling water and refuse were poured onto the attackers. In summer, concerts are held in the courtyard. ⊠ *Maria Enzersdorf* ☎ *02236/ 44294 or 0664/301–6066* ☒ *€4.50* ⊙ *Apr.–Oct., daily 9:30–5.*

❺ West of Mödling on Route 11 is the **Seegrotte Hinterbrühl,** a fascinating but now somewhat commercialized underground sea, created years ago when a mine filled up with water. You can take a 45-minute motorboat trip and look at the reflections through the arched caverns of the mine. Some of the film *The Three Musketeers,* starring Charlie Sheen and Chris O'Donnell, was filmed here. ⊠ *Grutschgasse 2, Hinterbrühl* ☎ *02236/ 26364* ☒ *€6* ⊙ *Apr.–Oct., daily 9–noon and 1–5; Nov.–Mar., weekdays 9–noon and 1–3, weekends 9–3:30.*

Where to Eat

$–$$ ✕ **Hotel-Restaurant Höldrichsmühle.** A former mill with parts dating from the 12th century, the Höldrichsmühle has been a famed country inn for more than 200 years. Legend holds that the linden tree and the well found here inspired composer Franz Schubert to compose one of his better-known pieces. Stop at this traditional restaurant for fish, game, or wild mushroom dishes in season. ⊠ *Gaadnerstrasse 34* ☎ *02236/26274–0* 🖷 *02236/ 48729* ⊕ *www.hoeldrichsmuehle.at* ▭ *AE, DC, MC, V* ⦿ *BP.*

Gumpoldskirchen

❻ *4 km (2½ mi) west of Mödling.*

From Mödling, follow the scenic Weinstrasse (an unnumbered road to the west of the rail line) through the lush vineyard country to the famous wine-producing village of Gumpoldskirchen. This tiny village on the eastern slopes of the last Alpine rocks has lived for wine for two thousand years, and its white wines enjoy a fame that is widespread. At one stage, there was more Gumpoldskirchner on the world markets than the village could ever have produced—a situation reminiscent of the medieval glut of fragments of the True Cross. **Vintners' houses** line the main street, many of them with the typical large wooden gates that lead to vine-covered courtyards where the Heuriger (wine of the latest vintage) is served by the owner and his family at simple wooden tables with benches. Gumpoldskirchen also has an arcaded Renaissance town hall, a market fountain made from a Roman sarcophagus, and the (private) castle of the Teutonic Knights, whose descendants still own some of the best vineyard sites in the area.

Where to Eat

$ ✕ **Altes Zechhaus.** Perched at the top of the Altstadt (Old Town), this centuries-old drinking tavern is still going strong. Choose from the tempting panoply of salads downstairs and then order a hearty schnitzel, spit-roasted chicken, or duck, which will be brought to your table piping hot. Try to get a table upstairs in the wood-beamed Gothic Room, where plank tables are set against ancient stone walls and mullioned windows. Be sure to check out the house wine with its bawdy label, on display in the foyer. ⊠ *Kirchenplatz 1* ☎ *02252/62247* 📠 *02252/62247-4* ▭ *V* ☺ *No lunch.*

Baden

★ **❼** *7 km (4½ mi) south of Gumpoldskirchen, 32 km (20 mi) southwest of Vienna.*

The Weinstrasse brings you to the serenely elegant spa town of Baden. Since antiquity, Baden's sulfuric thermal baths have attracted the ailing and the fashionable from all over the world. When the Romans came across the springs, they dubbed the town Aquae; the Babenbergs revived it in the 10th century; and with the visit of the Russian czar Peter the Great in 1698, Baden's golden age began. Austria's emperor Franz II spent 31 successive summers here. Every year for 12 years before his death in 1835, the royal entourage moved here from Vienna for the season. Later in the century, Emperor Franz Josef II was a regular visitor, his presence inspiring much of the regal trappings the city still displays. In Baden, Mozart composed his "Ave Verum"; Beethoven spent 15 summers here and wrote large sections of his Ninth Symphony and *Missa Solemnis* when he lived at Frauengasse 10; Franz Grillparzer wrote his historical dramas here; and Josef Lanner, both Johann Strausses (father and son), Carl Michael Ziehrer, and Karl Millöcker composed and directed many of their waltzes, marches, and operettas here.

For many people the primary reason for a visit to Baden is the lovely, sloping **Kurpark** in the center of town, where occasional outdoor public concerts still take place. Operetta is performed under the skies in the Summer Arena (its roof closes if it rains); in winter, performances are moved to the Stadttheater. People sit quietly under the old trees or walk through the upper sections of the Kurpark for a view of the town from above. The old Kurhaus now incorporates a convention hall. ⊠ *Kaiser Franz-Ring.*

The ornate **Casino**—with a bar, restaurant, and gambling rooms—still includes traces of its original 19th-century touches but has been enlarged and, in the process, overlaid with glitz rivaling that of Las Vegas. Casual dress is acceptable. ⊠ *Kaiser Franz-Ring 1–3, Kurpark* ☎ *02252/ 44496–0* ⊡ *Free* ☉ *Casino daily from 1* PM, *gambling daily from 3* PM.

Music lovers will want to visit the **Beethoven Haus,** just one of several addresses Beethoven called his own hereabouts—the great man was always on the run from his creditors and moved frequently. ⊠ *Rathausgasse 10* ☎ *02252/86800–231* ⊡ *€3* ☉ *Tues.–Fri. 4–6, weekends 9–11 and 4–6.*

Children of all ages will enjoy the enchanting **Badener Puppen und Spielzeugmuseum** (Doll and Toy Museum). ⊠ *Erzherzog Rainer-Ring 23* ☎ *02252/41020* ⊡ *€3* ☉ *Tues.–Fri. 4–6, weekends 9–11 and 4–6.*

One of the pleasures associated with Baden is getting there. You can reach the city directly from Vienna by bus or, far more fun, by interurban streetcar, in about 50 minutes—the bus departs from the Ring directly opposite the Opera; the blue streetcar departs from the Ring across from the Bristol Hotel. Both drop you off in the center of Baden. By car from Vienna, travel south on Route A2, turning west at the junction of Route 305. It is possible, with advance planning, to go on to Mayerling and Heiligenstadt on post office buses (☎ 01/79444).

Where to Stay & Eat

★ **$$$$** ✕⌂ **Grand Hotel Sauerhof.** "Maria Theresa yellow" marks this appealing country house, which has elegant rooms in the Old Vienna style. The hotel caters heavily to seminars and group activities, but individual guests are not ignored, and accommodations are very comfortable. It is also possible to go for a day's outing to their Beauty Farm and pamper yourself with the full body treatment. The hotel's Rauhenstein restaurant is famous in Baden (try the veal with a red-wine mushroom sauce and, for dessert, the house crepes). ⊠ *Weilburgstrasse 11–13, A-2500* ☎ *02252/41251–0* ⊟ *02252/48047* ⊕ *www.sauerhof.at* ↪ *88 rooms* ⌂ *Restaurant, minibars, tennis court, indoor pool, gym, sauna, bar, Internet, meeting rooms; no a/c* ⊟ *AE, DC, MC, V* ⦿⧧ *BP.*

★ **$$$$** ✕⌂ **Schloss Weikersdorf.** A restored Renaissance castle whose earliest foundations go back to 1233, the Weikersdorf is just minutes away from the center of Baden. Set on the edge of a vast public park, the hotel estate offers bonuses of a rose garden featuring 600 varieties and boating on the lake. Rooms and baths are luxuriously outfitted. The restaurant is excellent—make a beeline for the angler in a saffron sauce with morel risotto, or pork ribs in a tomato-olive crust. In fine weather, tables are set outside on the Renaissance loggia overlooking the rose garden. The hotel sometimes offers special last-minute rates. ⊠ *Schlossgasse 9–11, A-2500* ☏ *02252/48301* 📠 *02252/48301–150* ⊕ *www. hotelschlossweikersdorf.at* 🛏 *107 rooms ⅗ Restaurant, minibars, tennis courts, indoor pool, sauna, bowling, bar, Internet, meeting rooms; no a/c* ▤ *AE, DC, MC, V* ⧑ *BP.*

$$–$$$ ✕⊞ **Krainerhütte.** About 5 km (3 mi) from Baden, this friendly house, in typical Alpine style with balconies and lots of natural wood, has been family-run since 1876. The site on the outskirts of town is ideal for relaxing or exploring the surrounding woods. Facilities are up-to-date, and the restaurant offers a choice of cozy rooms or an outdoor terrace along with international and Austrian cuisine, with fish and game from the hotel's own reserves. ⊠ *Helenental, A-2500* ☏ *02252/44511–0* 📠 *02252/ 44514* ⊕ *www.krainerhuette.at* 🛏 *60 rooms ⅗ Restaurant, tennis court, indoor pool, sauna; no a/c* ▤ *AE, DC, MC, V* ⧑ *BP.*

Mayerling

❽ *11 km (7 mi) northwest of Baden, 29 km (18 mi) west of Vienna.*

Scenic Route 210 takes you through the quiet Helenental valley west of Baden to Mayerling, scene of a tragedy that is still passionately discussed and disputed by the Austrian public, press, and historians at the slightest provocation, and still provides a torrid subject for moviemakers and novelists in many other parts of the world. On the snowy evening of January 29, 1889, the 30-year-old Habsburg heir, Crown Prince Rudolf, Emperor Franz Josef's only son, and his 17-year-old mistress, Baroness Marie Vetsera, met a violent and untimely end at the emperor's hunting lodge at Mayerling. Most historians believe it was a suicide pact between two desperate lovers (the Pope had refused an annulment to Rudolf's unhappy marriage to Princess Stephanie of Belgium). There are those, however, who feel Rudolf's pro-Hungarian political leanings might be a key to the tragedy. Given information gleaned from private letters that have more recently come to light, it is also possible Rudolf was hopelessly in love with a married woman and killed himself in despair, taking Marie Vetsera with him. In an attempt to suppress the scandal—the full details are not known to this day—the baroness's body, propped up between two uncles, was smuggled back into the city by carriage (she was buried hastily in nearby Heiligenkreuz). The bereaved emperor had the hunting lodge where the suicide took place torn down and replaced with a rather nondescript Carmelite convent. Mayerling remains beautiful, haunting—and remote: the village is infrequently signposted.

Heiligenkreuz

❾ *4 km (2½ mi) west of Mayerling, 14 km (8¾ mi) west of Mödling.*

Heiligenkreuz, in the heart of the southern section of the Vienna Woods, is a magnificent Cistercian abbey with a famous Romanesque and Gothic church, founded in 1135 by Leopold III. The church itself is lofty and serene, with beautifully carved choir stalls (the Cistercians are a singing order) surmounted by busts of Cistercian saints. The great treasure here is the relic of the cross that Leopold V is said to have brought back from his crusade in 1188. The cloisters are interesting for the Chapel of the Dead, where the brothers lie in state guarded by four gesticulating skeletons holding a candelabra. The chapter house contains the tombs of Babenberg rulers. In a corner of the abbey grounds, you can follow the Baroque stations of the cross along paths lined with chestnut and linden trees. ✉ *Heiligenkreuz 1* ☎ *02258/8703* 🌐 *www.heiligenkreuz.at* 🎟 *Abbey free, tour €6* 🕓 *Tours Mon.–Sat. at 10, 11, 2, 3, and 4, Sun. at 11, 2, 3, and 4.*

From Vienna, reach Heiligenkreuz by taking Route A21 southwest or via bus from Südtirolerplatz.

Where to Stay & Eat

$ ✕🏨 **Landgasthof Zur Linde.** In the heart of the Vienna Woods, some 24 km (15 mi) northwest of Mayerling, lies the small town of Laaben bei Neulengbach—equidistant from Mayerling and Heiligenkreuz, in the shadow of the 2,900-foot Schöpfl Mountain. This family-run country inn offers an excellent base from which to explore the countryside. Rooms are modest but complete and comfortable, with rustic trimmings. The rambling restaurant, with its several wood-beamed rooms, serves standard tasty Austrian fare, with seasonal specialties such as lamb, asparagus, and game. ✉ *Hauptplatz 28, A-3053 Laaben bei Neulengbach* ☎ *02774/8378–0* 📠 *02774/8378–20* 🛏 *10 rooms* 👍 *Restaurant; no a/c* 💳 *MC, V* 🕓 *Hotel closed Tues. and Wed. and 1 wk in Mar.* 🍽 *BP.*

THE WEINVIERTEL

Luckily, Austria's Weinviertel (Wine District) has been largely neglected by the "experts," and its deliciously fresh wines reward those who enjoy drinking wine but dislike the all-too-frequent nonsense that goes with it. This region takes its name from the rustic and delightful rolling countryside north of Vienna. The Weinviertel is bounded by the Danube on the south, the Thaya River and the reopened Czech border on the north, and the March River and Slovakia to the east. No well-defined line separates the Weinviertel from the Waldviertel to the west; the Kamp River valley, officially part of the Waldviertel, is an important wine region. Whether wine, crops, or dairies, this is farming country, its broad expanses of vineyards and farmlands broken by patches of forest and neat villages. A tour by car, just for the scenery, can be made in a day; you may want two or three days to savor the region and its wines—these are generally on the medium-dry side. Don't expect to find here the elegant facilities found elsewhere in Austria; prices are low by any standard, and village restaurants and accommodations are mainly *Gasthäuser* that meet local needs. This means that you'll be rubbing shoulders with the country folk over your glass of wine or beer.

Göllersdorf

❿ *10 km (6 mi) north of Stockerau West interchange on Rte. 303/E59.*

The verdant hills and agricultural lands of the southwest Weinviertel around Hollabrunn offer little excitement other than panoramas and

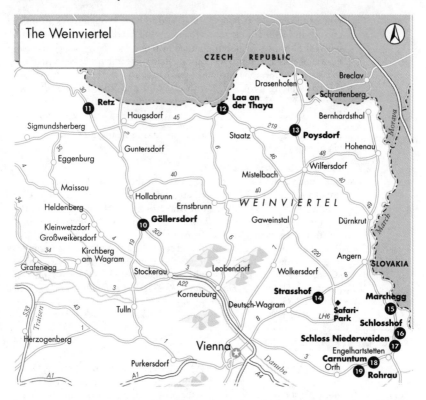

The Weinviertel

CZECH REPUBLIC

Breclav
Drasenhofen
Schrattenberg
Laa an
11 **Retz**
der Thaya
Haugsdorf 45
12
Bernhardsthal
Sigmundsherberg
Staatz 219
13 **Poysdorf**
Guntersdorf
Hohenau
Eggenburg
46 48
Wilfersdorf
40
Mistelbach
Maissau
40
Hollabrunn
Heldenberg
Ernstbrunn **W E I N V I E R T E L**
Kleinwetzdorf
10 **Göllersdorf** Gaweinstal
Dürnkrut
Großweikersdorf 303
34
Kirchberg 6
am Wagram
Angern
Grafenegg Stockerau Leobendorf Wolkersdorf **SLOVAKIA**
A22 8
3
Korneuburg **Strasshof**
Tulln Deutsch-Wagram **14** **Marchegg**
LH6 8 **15**
Safari-
Park **Schlosshof**
Herzogenberg **Schloss Niederweiden** **16**
Engelhartstetten **17**
Vienna **Carnuntum** **18**
Purkersdorf Orth
Danube **19** **Rohrau**
A1 A1 A4

scenic pleasures, but one exception is **Schloss Schönborn,** about 2 km (1 mi) south of Göllersdorf on Route 303. The castle was laid out in 1712 by that master of Baroque architecture Johann Lukas von Hildebrandt. Today the castle is in private hands, but the harmony of design can be appreciated from the outside. The Pfarrkirche in Göllersdorf is also a Baroque Hildebrandt design from 1740 imposed on a Gothic structure dating from the mid-1400s.

Retz

★ **11** *43 km (27 mi) north of Göllersdorf, 70 km (44 mi) north of Vienna.*

Retz, at the northwest corner of the Weinviertel, is a charming town with an impressive rectangular central square formed by buildings dating mainly from the 15th century. Take time to explore Retz's tiny streets leading from the town square; the oldest buildings and the wall and gate-tower defenses survived destruction by Swedish armies in 1645, during the Thirty Years' War. The Dominican church (1295) at the southwest corner of the square also survived, and it is interesting for its long, narrow design. The pastel Biedermeier facades along with the *sgraffiti* (painted facades) add appeal to the square, which is further marked by the impressive city hall with its massive Gothic tower in the center. The landmark of the town is the pretty **Windmühle,** a Dutch windmill set incongruously in the middle of vineyards on the edge of town. Follow the markers leading up to the summit, where you can sit and rest on benches offering a stunning view of the surrounding countryside.

Retz is best known for its red wines. Here you can tour the **Retzer Erlebniskeller,** Austria's largest wine cellar, tunneled 65 feet under the town, and at the same time taste wines of the area. Some of the tunnels go back to the 13th century, and at the end of the 15th century each citizen was permitted to deal in wines and was entitled to storage space in the town cellars. Efforts to use the cellars for armaments production during World War II failed because of the 88% humidity. The temperature remains constant at 8°C–10°C (47°F–50°F). Entrance to the cellars is at the Rathauskeller, in the center of town. ⊠ *Hauptplatz* ☎ *02942/2700* ☒ *Tour €6.50* ⊙ *Tours May–Oct., daily at 10:30, 2, and 4; Mar., Apr., Nov., and Dec., daily at 2; Jan. and Feb., weekends at 2.*

Where to Stay & Eat

$–$$$ ✕▥ **Althof.** The big, yellow "Old Courtyard"—a former medieval estate just off the town square—has a sloping terra-cotta roof, a narrow second-story loggia, and a tranquil grassy courtyard perfect for relaxing. Rooms, done in beige and white with red accents, are modern and don't have the charm of the building's exterior, but they're comfortable and up-to-date. In summer you can dine in the cool courtyard. The excellent wines naturally come mainly from the area. ⊠ *Althofgasse 14, A-2070* ☎ *02942/3711–0* ☒ *02942/3711–55* ⊕ *www.althof.at* ⤴ *95 rooms* ⚭ *3 restaurants, Internet; no a/c* ⊟ *AE, DC, MC, V* � � *BP.*

Laa an der Thaya

⑫ *39 km (24 mi) east of Retz, 65 km (41 mi) north of Vienna.*

From 1948 until about 1990, Laa an der Thaya was a town isolated by the Cold War, directly bordering what was then Czechoslovakia. Laa is considerably livelier now that the border is open. (As long as you have your passport with you, you can cross into the Czech Republic and return without complication.) The town's huge central square is adorned with a massive neo-Gothic city hall, in stark contrast to the low, colorful buildings that form the square. A good time to visit is mid-September, during the Onion Festival, when all varieties of onions are prepared in every imaginable way in food stalls set up throughout the village. If you're traveling from Retz to Laa an der Thaya, retrace your way south on Route 30 to Route 45.

Laa is noted for its **Bier Museum,** located in the town fortress, that traces the history of beer (the nearby Hubertus brewery has been in business since 1454) and displays an imposing collection of beer bottles. ☎ *02522/ 2501–29* ☒ *€2* ⊙ *May–Sept., call for opening times.*

Where to Eat

★ **$** ✕ **Restaurant Weiler.** Light woods and country accessories set the tone in this family-run restaurant; in summer, dinner is served in the outdoor garden. Try the delicate cream of garlic soup or the house specialty, game in season. For dessert, the delicious cakes of the house are temptingly displayed in a showcase. ⊠ *Staatsbahnstrasse 60* ☎ *02522/2379* ☰ *No credit cards* ⊘ *Closed Mon., 2 wks in Feb., and variable weeks in July.*

Poysdorf

⑬   *22 km (13 mi) southeast of Laa an der Thaya, 61 km (38 mi) north of Vienna.*

Poysdorf is considered by many the capital of the Weinviertel. Wine making here goes back to the 14th century. Poysdorf vintages, mainly whites, rank with the best Austria has to offer. Narrow paths known as *Kellergassen* (cellar streets) on the northern outskirts are lined with wine cellars set into and under the hills. A festival in early September marks the annual harvest. At the **wine market** (⊠ Weinmarktplatz 1) in the center of town, you can taste as well as buy; the market is open June to October on weekdays 8–noon and 12:30–8 PM, and on weekends 10–noon and 1–8 PM. From November to May it's open Monday through Thursday 8–5, Fridays 8–6, and weekends 10–noon and 1–6.

The town **Museum** includes a section on viticulture and wine making. ⊠ *Brünnerstrasse 9* ☎ *02552/3209* ≊ *€4* ⊘ *Easter–Oct., Wed.–Mon. 9–noon and 1–5; call to confirm.*

Where to Stay & Eat

$ ✕ **Gasthaus Schreiber.** Choose the shaded garden under huge trees or the country-rustic indoors. The typical Austrian fare—roast pork, stuffed breast of veal, boiled beef, fillet steak with garlic—is commendable, as is the house-made ice cream. The wine card lists more than 60 area labels. ⊠ *Bahnstrasse 2* ☎ *02552/2348* ☰ *AE, DC, MC, V* ⊘ *Closed Sun. and Tues. and late Jan.–Feb. No dinner Mon.*

★ $-$$ ✕▦ **Zur Linde.** This friendly family-run restaurant with rustic decor 16 km (10 mi) south of Poysdorf is setting higher standards for such traditional fare as roast pork, stuffed breast of veal, flank steak, and fresh game in season. Desserts are excellent; try the extraordinary *Apfelstrudel*. A major attraction here is the remarkable parade of wines from the neighborhood at altogether reasonable prices. The Zur Linde also has several well-equipped, modern rooms for overnighters. ⊠ *Bahnhofstrasse 49, Mistelbach* ☎ *02572/2409* ⊕ *www.zur-linde.at* ⤴ *19 rooms* ⚏ *Restaurant, minibars, Internet; no a/c* ☰ *AE, DC, MC, V* ⊘ *Closed Mon. No dinner Sun.* ⫶⬤⫶ *BP.*

Strasshof

⑭   *25 km (16 mi) northeast of Vienna.*

☾ The **Eisenbahnmuseum Das Heizhaus,** north of Strasshof, is a fascinating private collection of dozens of steam locomotives and railroad cars stored in a vast engine house. Enthusiasts have painstakingly rebuilt and restored many of the engines; steam locomotives are up and running on the first Sunday of each month. The complex includes a transfer table, water towers, and a coaling station, and few can resist climbing around among many of the locomotives awaiting restoration. ✉ *Sillerstrasse 123* ☎ *01/603–5301* ✍ *€5.50, steam days €7, including tour* ☉ *Apr.–Oct. 26, Mon. and Wed.–Sat. 9–6, Tues. 9–8, Sun. 10–6.*

Where to Eat

$$–$$$ ✕ **Marchfelderhof.** In nearby Deutsch Wagram, this sprawling complex, with its eclectic series of rooms bounteously decorated with everything from antiques to hunting trophies, has a reputation for excess in the food department as well. The menu's standards—Wiener Schnitzel, roast pork, lamb—are more successful than the more expensive efforts at innovation. Deutsch Wagram is 9 km (5½ mi) southwest of Strasshof on Route 8, 17 km (11 mi) northeast of Vienna on Route 8. ✉ *Bockfliesserstrasse 31, Deutsch Wagram* ☎ *02247/2243–0* 🖨 *02247/2236–13* ▭ *DC, MC, V.*

> **off the beaten path**
>
> **ZUR ALTE SCHULE** – Less than 40 minutes (by car) northeast of Vienna, this former 19th-century cheery yellow schoolhouse has had its classrooms turned into charming dining rooms. Chef and owner Manfred Buchinger went back to his Weinviertler roots to open a reasonably priced restaurant close to his heart. The menu changes seasonally, but look for veal with creamy mustard sauce and the Austrian standard, fried chicken with potato salad. Zur Alte Schule is in the tiny village of Riedenthal, five minutes from Wolkersdorf on the B7. ✉ *Wolkersdorferstrasse 6, Riedenthal ob Wolkersdorf* ☎ *02245/82500* ⊕ *www.buchingers.at* ☉ *Closed Mon.–Wed.*

Marchegg

⓯ *43 km (27 mi) east of Vienna.*

The tiny corner of the lower Weinviertel is known as the Marchfeld, for the fields stretching east to the March River, forming the border with Slovakia. In this region—known as the granary of Austria—a pair of elegant Baroque castles are worth a visit; while totally renovated, these country estates have lost none of their gracious charm over the centuries. They have since been given over to changing annual exhibits, concerts, and other public activities.

🖐 ⓰ The castle at **Schlosshof** is a true Baroque gem, a product of that master designer and architect Johann Lukas von Hildebrandt, who in 1732 reconstructed the four-sided castle into an elegant U-shape building, opening up the eastern side to a marvelous Baroque formal garden that gives way toward the river. The famed landscape painter, Bernardo Bellotto, noted for his Canaletto-like vistas of scenic landmarks, captured the view before the reconstruction (now that the gardens are being restored to their Baroque state, Bellotto's three paintings of the hof are proving the most important sources for this work). The castle was once owned by Empress Maria Theresa (the mother of Marie Antoinette), and beginning in May 2005 you can visit the suite the empress used during her royal visits, faithfully recreated down to the tiniest details, as well as the two-story chapel in which she prayed. For kids there's a menagerie and petting zoo featuring exotic wild animals and old breeds of gentle pets. You can walk through the garden and grounds without paying admission, but the castle itself is open for guided tours only. The castle is about 8 km (5 mi) south of Marchegg. ⊠ *Schlosshof* ☎ *02285/6580* ⊕ *www.schlosshof.at* ✉ *€5* ⊙ *Tours Apr.–Oct., daily at 11, 2, and 3:30.*

⑰ About 4 km (2½ mi) southwest of Schlosshof and north of Engelhartstetten, **Schloss Niederweiden** was designed as a hunting lodge and built in 1694 by that other master of the Baroque, Fischer von Erlach. This jewel was subsequently owned in turn by Prince Eugene and Empress Maria Theresa, who added a second floor and the mansard roof. Annual exhibits take place here, and in a vinothek you can sample the wines of the surrounding area. Schloss Niederweiden is closed indefinitely for renovations; call for information. ☎ *02285/20000.*

Carnuntum

⑱ *32 km (20 mi) east of Vienna.*

The remains of the important Roman legionary fortress Carnuntum, which once numbered 55,000 inhabitants, is in the tiny village of Petronell, reachable by the S7, a local train that departs from Wien–Mitte/Landstrasse or Wien–Nord. Though by no means as impressive as Roman ruins in Italy and Spain, Carnuntum still merits a visit, with three amphitheaters (the first one seating 8,000) and the foundations of former residences, baths, and trading centers, some with mosaic floors. The ruins are quite spread out, with the impressive remains of a Roman arch, the **Heidentor** (Pagans' Gate), a good 15 minutes' walk from the main excavations. A pleasant path along the north end of the ruins leads past a dilapidated 17th-century palace once belonging to the counts of Traun, to the remains of a Roman bath. In summer Greek plays are sometimes performed in English at the **main amphitheater** (☎ *02163/3400*). ⊠ *Petronell* ☎ *02163/33770* ⊕ *www.carnuntum.co.at* ✉ *€7, includes admission to Carnuntium Museum* ⊙ *Late Mar.–mid-Nov., daily 9–5.*

Many of the finds from excavations at Carnuntum are housed 4 km (2½ mi) northeast of Petronell in the village of Bad Deutsch-Altenburg, in the Museum **Carnuntium.** The pride of the collection is a carving of Mithras killing a bull. ⊠ *Badgasse 40–46, Petronell* ☎ *02163/33770* ⊕ *www.carnuntum.co.at* ✉ *€7, includes admission to amphitheater* ⊙ *Late Mar.–mid-Nov., Mon. noon–5, Tues.–Sun. 10–5; mid-Nov.–mid-Dec., weekends 11–5.*

⑲ Just 5 km (3 mi) south of Petronell, in the tiny village of **Rohrau,** is the birthplace of Joseph Haydn. The quaint reed-thatched cottage where the composer, son of the local blacksmith, was born in 1732, is now a small museum, with a pianoforte he is supposed to have played, as well as letters and other memorabilia. After Haydn had gained worldwide renown, he is said to have returned to his native Rohrau and knelt to kiss the steps of his humble home. ⊠ *Hauptstrasse 60, Rohrau* ☎ *02164/2268* ✉ *€2* ⊙ *Tues.–Sun. 10–4.*

Also in Rohrau is the cream-and-beige palace, **Schloss Rohrau,** where Haydn's mother worked as a cook for Count Harrach. The palace has one of the best private art collections in Austria, with emphasis on

17th- and 18th-century Spanish and Italian painting. ☎ *02164/225318* ⊕ *harrach.nwy.at* ✉ €7 ⊘ *Apr.–Oct., Tues.–Sun. 10–5.*

off the beaten path

ARTNER WEINBAU – Some of the best wines and freshly made *Ziegenkäse* (goat cheese) in the region can be found in the tiny village of Höflein, 12 km (7½ mi) southwest of Petronell. Artner has been a family business since 1650, and owner Hannes Artner is proud to offer tastings of his wines, including Chardonnay Barrique, cabernet sauvignon, and Blauer Zweigelt Kirchtal. Check for the opening times of the outdoor *Heuriger* during selected weeks from May to August, when full meals of tasty Austrian standards can be had along with the new wine. ⊠ *Heuriger, Dorfstrasse 43; winery, Dorfstrasse 93, Höflein* ☎ *02162/63142* ⊕ *www.artner.co.at.*

SIDE TRIPS FROM VIENNA A TO Z

To research prices, get advice from other travelers, and book travel arrangements, visit www.fodors.com.

BUS TRAVEL

Buses are a good possibility for getting around, although if you're not driving, a combination of bus and train is probably a better plan in many cases. Frequent scheduled bus service runs between Vienna and Baden, departing from across from the Opera House in Vienna to the center of Baden. Connections are available to other towns in the area. Bus service runs between Vienna and Carnuntum–Petronell, and on to Hainburg. In the Weinviertel, bus service is fairly good between Vienna and Laa an der Thaya and Poysdorf.

CAR RENTAL

Cars can be rented from all leading companies at the Vienna airport (⇨ Vienna A to Z *in* Chapter 1). In Baden, try Autoverleih Buchbinder.
🚘 Local Agencies **Autoverleih Buchbinder** ☎ 02252/48693.

CAR TRAVEL

The autobahn A1 traverses the Vienna Woods in the west; the A2 autobahn runs through the edge of the Vienna Woods to the south. The A4 autobahn is a quick way to reach the Carnuntum region. The Weinviertel is accessed by major highways but not by autobahns.

Driving through these regions is by far the best way to see them, since you can wander the byways and stop whenever and wherever you like. To get to the Weinviertel, follow signs to Prague, taking Route E461 toward Mistelbach and Poysdorf if you want to go northeast. Or take the A22 toward Stockerau, changing to Route 303 or the E49 in the northwesterly direction of Horn and Retz. If you're going east to Carnuntum, follow signs to the A23 and the airport (Schwechat). And if you're going to Baden and the surrounding villages, take the A2 south in the direction of Graz, getting off in Baden and taking Route 210 west.

EMERGENCIES

For any medical emergency, dial 144.

🔢 Emergency services **Ambulance** ☎ 144. **Fire** ☎ 122. **Police** ☎ 133.

TOURS

The Vienna Woods is one of the standard routes offered by the sightseeing-bus tour operators in Vienna, and it usually includes a boat ride through the "underground sea" grotto near Mödling. These short tours give only a quick taste of the region; if you have more time, investigate further. For details, check with your hotel or with Cityrama Sightseeing. Another good option is Vienna Sightseeing Tours.

🔢 Fees & Schedules **Cityrama Sightseeing** ☎ 01/534-130. **Vienna Sightseeing Tours** ☎ 01/712-4683-0.

TRAIN TRAVEL

The main east–west train line cuts through the Vienna Woods; the main north–south line out of Vienna traverses the eastern edge of the Vienna Woods. Train service in the Weinviertel is regular to Mistelbach, irregular after that. The rail line east out of Vienna to the border town of Wolfstal cuts through the Carnuntum region. The line to the north of the Danube to Bratislava runs through the middle of the Marchfeld. You can get to the Weinviertel from Vienna's Franz Josef Bahnhof, with buses running between the small villages.

The Schnellbahn No. 7 (suburban train) running from Wien–Mitte (Landstrasser Hauptstrasse) stops at Petronell, with service about once an hour. Carnuntum is about a 10-minute walk from the Petronell station. Trains go on to Hainburg, stopping at Bad Deutsch-Altenburg.

🔢 Train Information **ÖBB–Österreichisches Bundesbahn** ☎ 05/1717.

VISITOR INFORMATION

For information on Lower Austria, call the Niederösterreich Tourismus in Vienna. Local tourist offices in the Vienna Woods, which include ones in Baden, Gumpoldskirchen, Mödling, and Perchtoldsdorf, are generally open weekdays. The Waldviertel district has numerous tourist offices, including Gars am Kamp, Gmünd, Waidhofen an der Thaya, and Zwettl. The Weinviertel region also has several tourist centers: Laa an der Thaya, Poysdorf, and Retz.

🔢 Tourist Information **Baden** ✉ Brusattiplatz 3 ☎ 02252/22600-600 🖨 02252/80733 ⊕ www.baden.at. **Gars am Kamp** ✉ Hauptplatz 83 ☎ 02985/2680 🖨 02985/2680. **Laa an der Thaya** ✉ Stadtplatz 17/Altes Rathaus ☎ 02522/250129 🖨 02522/250129. **Mödling** ✉ Elisabethstrasse 2 ☎ 02236/26727 🖨 02236/26727-10 ⊕ www.moedling.at. **Niederösterreich Tourismus** ☎ 01/53610-6200 🖨 01/53610-6060. **Perchtoldsdorf** ✉ Marktplatz 11 ☎ 01/86683-34. **Poysdorf** ✉ Weinmarktplatz 1 ☎ 02552/20371 🖨 02552/20877 ⊕ www.poysdorf.at. **Retz** ✉ Hauptplatz 30 ☎ 02942/2700 ⊕ www.retz.at. **Weinviertel** ✉ Kolpingstrasse 7, A-2170 Poysdorf ☎ 02552/3515 🖨 02552/3515-4 ⊕ www.weinviertel.at. **Wienerwald** ✉ Hauptplatz 11, A-3002 Purkersdorf ☎ 02231/62176 🖨 02231/65510. **Zwettl** ✉ Hauptplatz 4 ☎ 02822/54109-0 🖨 02822/54109-36.

EASTERN AUSTRIA

3

HEAR AN OPERETTA PERFORMED
on Mörbisch's open-air floating stage ⇨*p.161*

SHADOW-JOUST WITH A LANCE
at the vast armorial museum in Graz ⇨*p.175*

WATCH STORKS ATOP CHIMNEY NESTS
in Mother Goose country ⇨*p.159*

ATTEND A HEAVENLY HAYDN CONCERT
the magnificent at Schloss Esterházy ⇨*p.162*

SEE THE WHITE STALLIONS DANCE
at the Lipizzaner Stud Farm in Piber ⇨*p.182*

LET THE SCENT OF GINGERBREAD
guide you through Mariazell ⇨*p.186*

PEEK AT SCHNEEBERG'S PEAK
from the Puchberg cogwheel train ⇨*p.189*

Updated by
Bonnie Dodson

NO PART OF THE NATION offers a greater panoply of scenery than the area loosely defined as Eastern Austria, yet despite its proximity to Vienna it is often overlooked by foreign tourists. Not that the region lacks for visitors—long a favorite of the Austrians themselves, it is now becoming increasingly popular with Hungarians and other Eastern Europeans. Most of these travelers, being cost-conscious, demand strict value for their money, which ensures that prices will remain lower here than in other parts of the country for some time.

There are no singularly great sights in the region—no Schönbrunn Palace, no Salzburg, no major five-star attractions; nevertheless, its aggregate of worthwhile sights is most impressive. You'll find a largely unspoiled land of lakes, farms, castles, villages, and vineyards. The area has a rich history and a distinguished musical past, as well as—yes—one genuine city, Graz, whose sophistication and beauty may surprise you. It also happens to be a sports-lover's paradise. In short, this is an ideal destination for experienced travelers who have already explored Vienna, Salzburg, the Tirol, and other better-known parts of Austria.

Eastern Austria, as it is defined here, consists of Burgenland, most of Styria (Steiermark), and a small section of Lower Austria (Niederösterreich)—three wholly distinct provinces that have little in common with one another. The geography varies from haunting steppes and the mysterious Lake Neusiedl (Neusiedler See) in the east to the low, forested mountains of the south; the industrial valleys of the center and west; and the more rugged mountains of the north, where Austrian skiing began. Culturally, Eastern Austria is strongly influenced by neighboring Hungary and Slovenia, most especially in its earthy and flavorful cuisines. Along with hearty food, the region produces notable wines, many of which never travel beyond the borders.

This chapter begins with Burgenland, intriguing both for its flatness and for shallow Lake Neusiedl, whose reed-lined shore forms a natural nature preserve. Storks come in the thousands to feed in the lake, and stork families, in turn, obligingly nest atop nearby chimneys—allegedly bringing luck to the household below (and assuring travelers of some great photos). Off to the east, the lake gives way to the vast Hungarian plain, interrupted by occasional thatch-roof farmhouses and picturesque pole-and-pail wells. Music lovers will want to make the pilgrimage to Eisenstadt, where the great composer Joseph Haydn (1732–1809) was in the employ of Prince Esterházy. The impressive Esterházy Castle stands just as it did in Haydn's time, with its spacious theater-auditorium in which Haydn conducted his own operas and orchestral works almost nightly for the prince's entertainment.

The route from Burgenland southwest to Graz achieves an end-around run, circling the eastern tail of the Alps through a territory marked by monumental defensive castles, built to ward off invaders from the east. Graz, Austria's second-largest city, headlines one of Europe's best-preserved Renaissance town centers, dating to an era when Graz, not Vi-

In contrast to the excitements that abound in vibrant Vienna, the charms of Eastern Austria are mostly those of rustic pleasures and simple treasures: a stork alighting on the chimney atop a Mother Goose house; the haunting sounds of Gypsy music; heady vistas of lush vineyards; magical castles; and the city of Graz, whose preserved Old City is a time-warp marvel. In Burgenland, discover Lake Neusiedl—so shallow you can wade across its vast expanse—and Eisenstadt, alive with the sound of Joseph Haydn's celebrated music. Travelers who tackle Eastern Austria usually design their trip around three different destinations—Burgenland, the city of Graz, and the mountain route to Vienna—and the following suggested itineraries highlight these destinations.

3

Numbers in the text correspond to numbers in the margin and on the Burgenland, Eastern Styria and Lower Austria, and Graz maps.

If you have 1 day

Travelers with only a day at their disposal could head for Haydn's former haunting grounds, the elegant town of **Eisenstadt** ⑧ and along the west shore of **Lake Neusiedl** to picturesque **Rust** ⑥—famed for its stork nests—then return to Vienna via **Wiener Neustadt** ㊱, a modern city with some medieval must-sees. Other good (but full) one-day excursions are to **Mariazell** ㉜, for its famous basilica and narrow-gauge mountain railway, or to **Puchberg am Schneeberg** ㉟, both reachable from Vienna by car or train.

If you have 6 days

A leisurely pursuit of Eastern Austria is highly rewarding. Get better acquainted with the curiously flat puszta on the eastern side of **Lake Neusiedl**; then head back over to the western side and spend your first overnight in ⌂ **Rust** ⑥. The next day head to the historic town of ⌂ **Eisenstadt** ⑧ and follow in the footsteps of famed Baroque-era composer Joseph Haydn and the Esterházy princes. Follow the Burgenland wine route south, and for contrast, spend two nights and a day discovering the delightful Altstadt and bustling metropolis that is ⌂ **Graz** ⑭–㉖, one studded with riveting sights, from grandly Baroque palaces to the latest in cutting-edge modern-art museums. From Graz, head northward via **Bruck an der Mur** ㉛, to see its fine historic center, then on to magnificent ⌂ **Mariazell** ㉜. After an overnight, continue north to ⌂ **Semmering** ㉞—already famous in the 19th century as a ski and spa destination—and **Wiener Neustadt** ㊱ to Vienna.

enna, was the capital. The compact pedestrian zone that forms the city core sets imaginations on fire, with eye-catching sights waiting to be discovered around every corner. History notwithstanding, the city today is a pulsating metropolis, surprising even many Austrians, and it is now home to two of Austria's most dazzling creations of contemporary architecture, the Kunsthaus and the Murinsel island-complex. Styria offers the chance to visit one of Europe's oldest and still-revered religious pilgrimage sites, at Mariazell. The dramatic onward route northward can be accomplished by rail or road; the latter climbs to above 3,000 feet at Annaberg via a series of more than a dozen challenging hairpin turns. The easier route to Vienna via the Semmering Pass achieves the same elevation and also offers some magnificent panoramas, including views of the snowcapped Schneeberg.

Exploring Eastern Austria

The Eastern Austrian countryside has been fought over many times, which in part explains the host of defensive hilltop castles overlooking the level outlands to the east. Both conqueror and conquered have left their marks. The topography here, which ranges from the flat puszta of the north to the wheat-fleeced hills of the south, demonstrates that there's more to Austria than the Alps. Graz is the only real city here; most other centers are little more than villages in comparison.

About the Restaurants & Hotels

When choosing a restaurant, keep in mind that each province has its own cooking style. In Burgenland, the local Pannonian cooking, strongly influenced by neighboring Hungary, showcases such spicy dishes as *gulyas* (goulash) flavored with paprika. You'll also find fish from Lake Neusiedl, goose, game, and an abundance of fresh, local vegetables. Styria, bordering on Slovenia (formerly northern Yugoslavia), has a hearty cuisine with Slavic overtones; a typical dish is *Steirisches Brathuhn* (roast chicken turned on a spit). The intensely nutty *Kürbiskernöl* (pumpkin-seed oil) is used in many soup and pasta dishes, as well as in salad dressings. Such Balkan specialties as *cevapcici* (spicy panfried sausages) are also often found on Styrian menus. You are most likely to encounter the more urbane Viennese cooking in Lower Austria, where you can get the traditional Wiener Schnitzel nearly everywhere.

Many of the restaurants listed in the chapter are actually country inns that provide overnight accommodations as well as meals, as noted in the reviews.

Accommodations in Eastern Austria range from luxury city hotels to mountain and lakeside resorts to castles and romantic country inns, and all are substantially lower in price than those in Vienna or Salzburg. Every town and village also has the simpler *Gasthäuser,* which give good value as long as you don't expect a private bath. Accommodations in private homes are cheaper still. These bargains are usually identified by signs reading ZIMMER FREI (room available) or FRÜHSTÜCKSPENSION (bed-and-breakfast).

In larger centers, many hotels offer half-board, with dinner in addition to buffet breakfast (although most $$$$ hotels will charge extra for breakfast). On the chart below, hotel prices are listed for room rates that include no meals (EP, European Plan) or, if indicated, CP (with Continental breakfast) or BP (Breakfast Plan, with full breakfast). Higher prices pre-

Wines & Weinstrasse

Eastern Austria vies with Lower Austria as a source of the country's best wines. In both Burgenland and Styria you can travel between villages along "wine routes," stopping to sample the local vintages. Outstanding white wines predominate, although, increasingly, there are excellent reds and rosés as well. Burgenland's vineyards, mostly around Lake Neusiedl, produce wines that tend to be slightly less dry, with perhaps the best examples coming from the villages of Rust and the areas around Donnerskirchen, Jois, Gols, and Deutschkreuz. Some of the sweet dessert wines (*Spätlese,* late harvest, and *Eiswein,* pressed from frozen grapes) are extraordinary, and all Burgenland wines are gaining a reputation for high quality. Many vintners happily share samples of their wares and will provide bread and cheese as accompaniment. In Styria, the increasingly popular region south of Graz along the Slovenian border (known among Austrians as "South of Styria") offers award-winning wines, with most of them coming from the area around tiny, picturesque Gamlitz, which also prides itself on being the flower capital of Europe. With its lush, softly rolling hills, the area is reminiscent of Tuscany, and the well-marked *Weinstrasse* will take you from winery to winery, where it is possible to do some tasting. Southern Styria is also known for the tart, pale orange Schilcher wine. The *Schilcherstrasse* offers an ideal route to stop and taste at small family-run wineries.

3

The Great Outdoors

Eastern Austria is prime hiking country, and most tourist regions have marked trails. You'll need a local hiking map (*Wanderkarte*), usually for sale at a town's tourist office—whose staff can also suggest short rambles in the vicinity. Some particularly good places for walks are around Lake Neusiedl and Güssing in Burgenland; in the Mur Valley of Styria, especially the Bärenschützklamm at Mixnitz; around Mariazell; and atop the Schneeberg, Rax, and Semmering in Lower Austria. For the truly ambitious, several long-distance trails cut through this region, among them the Nordalpen-Weitwanderweg past the Raxalpe to Rust, and the Oststeiermärkischer-Hauptwanderweg from western Austria to Riegersburg. There's no need to carry either food or a tent, because you stay overnight in staffed huts. Camping is strongly discouraged for both safety and environmental reasons. The *puszta* (steppe) to the east of Lake Neusiedl is known as the Seewinkel, a perfect place for horseback riding; horses (*Pferde*) can be hired in several villages. Ask at the local tourist office. Weekends are particularly popular, so book your steed well in advance.

---

vail for board plans such as MAP (Modified American Plan, with breakfast and dinner; the half-board room rate is usually an extra €15–€30 per person). Occasionally, quoted room rates for hotels already include half-board accommodations, though a "discounted" rate is usually offered if you prefer not to take the evening meal. Inquire when booking. Pets are welcome unless otherwise noted.

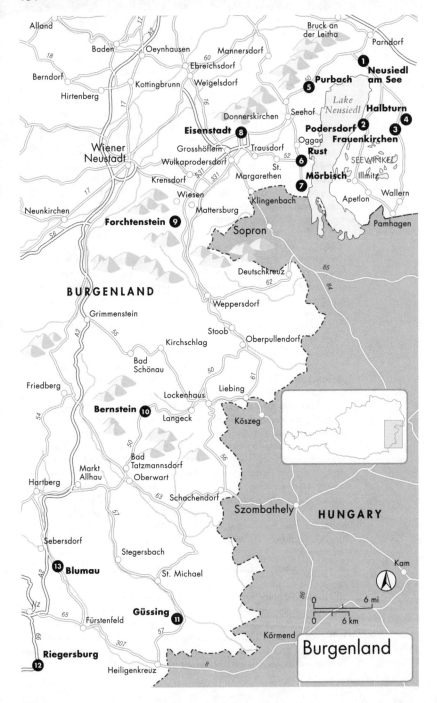

Burgenland

WHAT IT COSTS In euros				
$$$$	**$$$**	**$$**	**$**	**¢**
RESTAURANTS over €22	€18–€22	€13–€17	€7–€12	under €7
HOTELS over €175	€135–€175	€100–€135	€70–€100	under €70

Restaurant prices are per person for a main course at dinner. Hotel prices are for a standard double room in high season, including taxes and service. Assume that hotels operate on the European Plan (EP, with no meal provided) unless we note that they use the Breakfast Plan (BP), Modified American Plan (MAP, with breakfast and dinner daily, known as "halb pension"), or Full American Plan (FAP, or "voll pension," with three meals a day). Higher prices (inquire when booking) prevail for any meal plans.

Exploring Eastern Austria

The Eastern Austrian countryside has been fought over many times, which in part explains the host of defensive hilltop castles overlooking the level outlands to the east. Both conqueror and conquered have left their marks. The topography here, which ranges from the flat puszta of the north to the wheat-fleeced hills of the south, demonstrates that there's more to Austria than the Alps. Graz is the only real city here; most other centers are little more than villages in comparison.

Timing

Spring, summer, and fall are the seasons for Eastern Austria, unless you're a winter-sports enthusiast, when downhill skiers head for Lower Austria and the less crowded slopes of Styria. Other than coming across festival-goers and, in summer, visitors to the shores of Lake Neusiedl, you'll find relatively few tourists in this region. Graz functions year-round, but its treasures are modestly touted and crowds are unknown; Christmas in Graz is a visual spectacle, with whole sections of the city turned into a Christmas market. Winter in the area is an enigma: the Semmering mountains mark the eastern tail end of the Alps—north of the divide can be overcast and dreary while the area to the south basks in sunshine.

LAND OF CASTLES

This tour demonstrates that there's more to Austria than the Alps; it travels the length of Burgenland from the flat puszta of the north to the rolling castle-capped hills of the south before turning west to Styria, ending at Austria's second city, Graz. Although it is possible to cover the entire route of about 300 km (185 mi) in a single day, a leisurely pace is, of course, preferable.

Burgenland, a region of castles, grain fields, and vineyards, is a narrow, fertile belt of agricultural land stretching some 170 km (106 mi) from the Slovak (formerly Czechoslovak) border, along the Hungarian frontier, and south to Slovenia (formerly northern Yugoslavia). Only 65 km (40 mi) across at its widest point, the region at its narrowest is a mere 4 km (2½ mi).

The name Burgenland, meaning land of castles, dates only from 1921; prior to World War I this area was a part of Hungary. Throughout its long history it has been a battleground between east and west. It was part of the ancient Roman province of Pannonia, occupied by Celts, Roman settlers, Ostrogoths, and Slavs. After them came the Bavarians, Hungarians, and Austrians, followed by invading Turks. This legacy of conflict continued into the late 20th century, with the tensions of the Iron Curtain a stark fact of life until 1989. The opening of the Hungarian border has again brought change and increased Burgenland's appeal to tourists.

Lake Neusiedl

In the north part of Burgenland, and one of the region's chief attractions, Lake Neusiedl occupies a strange world. One of the largest lakes in Europe, it is the Continent's only true steppe lake—a bizarre body of warm brackish water. Its sole tributary is far too small to replenish the water lost through evaporation, and there is no outflow at all. Underground springs feed it, but when they fail it dries up, which last happened in the 1860s. At present the water is not more than about 7 feet deep at any spot; its many shallower sections make it possible (but still hazardous) to wade across the lake. Its depth has varied dramatically, however, at times nearly engulfing the villages on its banks. Most of its 318-square-km (124-square-mi) surface area is in Austria, but the southern reaches extend into Hungary.

What really sets Lake Neusiedl apart is the thick belt of tall reeds—in some places more than a mile deep—that almost completely encircles it. This is the habitat of large and varied flocks of birds (more than 250 species) that nest near the water's edge. The lake is also a magnet for anglers, boaters, and windsurfers; other activities include swimming and, along its banks, bicycling.

The flat plains around Lake Neusiedl, with their tiny hamlets and unspoiled scenery, are perfect for leisurely bicycling. Practically every village has a bike-rental shop (*Fahrradverleih* or *Radverleih*), but demand is so great that it's a good idea to reserve in advance. A bike route encircles the lake, passing through Hungary on the southern end (you can shorten the route by taking the ferry between Illmitz beach and Mörbisch). This and many other routes are described in a German-language map-brochure called "Radeln in Burgenland," available for the asking at tourist offices.

Neusiedl am See

❶ *51 km (32 mi) southeast of Vienna.*

Neusiedl am See, at the north end of the lake for which it is named, is a pleasant resort town with good facilities. Direct hourly commuter trains from Vienna have made it very popular, so you won't be alone here. To reach the lake itself, follow the main street for three blocks east of the Hauptplatz and turn right on Seestrasse, a mile-long causeway that leads through the reeds to the lake, where you can rent small boats, swim, or just laze on the beach.

In Neusiedel am See itself, visit the ruins of the 13th-century hill fortress Ruine Tabor, a 15th-century parish church near the town hall.

Where to Stay & Eat

★ **$$$–$$$$** ✕ **Zur Blauen Gans.** The lakeside Blue Goose is manned by Alsatian dynamo Alain Weissberger, who is fast becoming one of the most well-known chefs in the country. You can dine inside the charming, thatch-roof cottage or on the patio at the edge of a green park, with sweeping views of sailboats in Neusiedl harbor. Besides the dreamlike scenery, the unusual table settings catch your eye: beautiful serving dishes, bracelets of apricot pits for napkin rings, and remarkable potted plants. The kitchen casts its own spell, with delights like *Zander* (pike perch) fillet with *Eierschwammerl* (chanterelle) mushrooms and baby asparagus, or the classic, tender *Tafelspitz* beef in a chive sauce. Desserts are bursting with flavor, such as the zingy lemon-thyme sorbet. Signposts to the Blue Goose are aplenty in the minuscule town of Weiden, 4 km (2½ mi) south of Neusiedl. ⊠ *Seepark, Weiden, A-7121* ☏ *02167/7840* ⌖ *Reservations essential* ▭ *No credit cards* ⊘ *Closed Tues.–Wed.; in summer closed Tues. only.*

$–$$ ✕ **Nyikospark.** Located on the main street of Neusiedl, this upscale yet casual eatery is ill-marked, but worth the trouble to search for (it's on the left side about halfway down as you're driving through town from north to south). The unique, modern glass-and-wood structure looks like a feature in an architectural magazine, with one side opening onto an inviting terrace shaded by canvas sheets attached to chestnut trees. Begin with an *amuse guele* of refreshing cucumber soup with a dollop of spicy fried ground beef, continue with big, tender chunks of veal goulash with homemade spinach *Nockerln* (similar to *Spätzle*), opt for the *Perlhuhnbrust* (guinea fowl) with crispy fried polenta balls and *Eierschwammerl* (chanterelle) ragout. ⊠ *Untere Hauptstrasse 59* ☏ *02167/40222* ⌖ *Reservations essential* ▭ *AE, DC, MC, V* ⊘ *Closed Mon.–Tues.*

$$$ ✕▦ **Hotel Wende.** This sprawling three-story hotel complex is close to the lake and has many standard amenities, but don't expect the charm of a country inn. The comfortable rooms with balconies are of adequate size, the restaurant is quite well regarded, and half-pension is included in the room price. ⊠ *Seestrasse 40, A-7100* ☏ *02167/8111* ⎙ *02167/8111–649* ⊕ *www.hotel-wende.at* ⇆ *106 rooms* ⌖ *Restaurant, minibars, indoor pool, gym, sauna, bicycles; no a/c* ▭ *MC, V* ⊘ *Closed Christmas wk and 1st 2 wks of Feb.* ⍾ *BP, MAP.*

Podersdorf

❷ *14 km (8½ mi) south of Neusiedl am See.*

The region east of Lake Neusiedl is the beginning of the unusual Hungarian puszta, the great flat steppe marked with occasional windmills and wells with the long, characteristic wooden poles for drawing up water—a circular tour of about 70 km (44 mi) by car (or bicycle) would cover nearly everything of interest before returning you to Neusiedl am See. Some of the picturesque houses in Podersdorf have typical thatched roofs, and in summer their chimneys are often occupied by storks nesting after wintering in Egypt. Podersdorf has excellent swimming.

Where to Stay & Eat

$$$-$$$$ ✕ **Presshaus.** At first glance, this seems like a traditional country restaurant, with pickled pine walls, cheerful blue curtains at the windows, tables covered in crisp white linen, and lit by old-fashioned hanging lamps. But the Presshaus offers some of the most innovative Austrian cuisine in the area—seasonal *Bärlauch* (wild wood garlic) cream soup, asparagus risotto, or the house specialty, spicy ricotta strudel drizzled with browned butter deliciously push that Austrian envelope. Main courses include plenty of fish choices, naturally, and flavorful grilled steak from local Apetloner cattle, served with a golden potato gratin. There's a big selection of wines from the region, including their own label, which you can sample by the glass. It's located in Illmitz, 11 km (7 mi) south of Podersdorf. ⊠ *Apetlonerstrasse 6* ☎ *02175/2730* ⚓ *Reservations essential* ▤ *AE, DC, MC, V* ☉ *Closed Mon.–Tues.*

★ **$$** ✕ **Gasthof zur Dankbarkeit.** The kitchen offers fine local fare as well as creative dishes with occasional Hungarian touches, served in a comfortable *Stuben,* or outdoors, at picnic tables under centuries-old shady trees. Look for grilled Zanderfilet (pike perch) in a pumpkin orange sauce with pumpkin risotto, roast lamb with garlicky spinach, or skirt steak in a sensational creamy chive sauce with crispy roast potatoes. Schnitzels, homemade sausages, and venison are always found on the menu, while the excellent wines come from neighboring vineyards. ⊠ *Hauptstrassse 39* ☎ *02177/2223* ▤ *DC, MC, V* ☉ *Closed Wed.–Thurs.; from Dec.–Easter closed Mon.–Thurs.*

$$ ✕▦ **Haus Attila.** In this small, simple, family-run lakefront hotel the balconied rooms overlooking the lake are especially appealing. The Karner family also runs the nearby smaller (and slightly cheaper) **Seewirt** (⊠ Strandplasse 1 ☎ 02177/2415). ⊠ *Strandplatz 8, A-7141* ☎ *02177/ 2415* 🖨 *02177/2465–30* ⊕ *www.tiscover.at/gasthof.seewirt* ⇗ *34 rooms* ⚘ *Restaurant, sauna; no a/c* ▤ *No credit cards* ☉ *Closed Dec.–Feb.* ⊘ *BP, MAP.*

Frauenkirchen

❸ *7½ km (4½ mi) east of Podersdorf, 16½ km (10¼ mi) southeast of Neusiedl am See.*

Frauenkirchen is known mainly for its **pilgrimage church,** rebuilt in 1702 after its 14th-century predecessor was destroyed by invading Turks, and again restored following World War II. The Baroque interior has a much-venerated wooden statue of the Virgin from the 13th century. Note the miniature Mount Calvary depiction alongside the church.

Halbturn

❹ *5 km (3 mi) northwest of Frauenkirchen, 14 km (8½ mi) southeast of Neusiedl am See.*

★ Halbturn contains the exquisite Baroque **Schloss Halbturn,** an imperial hunting lodge built in 1710 by Lukas von Hildebrandt, the great architect of the period. This restored jewel was once used by Empress Maria Theresa as a summer residence and is noted for its ceiling frescoes. Devastated by Russian troops in the occupation following World War II, then re-built in the 1970s, the castle now houses special annual exhibitions. A stroll through the large, wooded surrounding park is pleasant anytime, but in late spring when the red and pink chestnut trees are in bloom, the spectacle easily rivals a Monet painting. In the courtyard, a shop sells excellent wines from the Halbturn vineyards, and a small art museum displays a copy of Gustav Klimt's impressive *Beethoven Frieze*, with the decided advantage over the Vienna original that here you can see the details up close. ⊠ *Schloss Halbturn* ☎ *02172/8577* ⊕ *www.schlosshalbturn.at* 🖂 *€7* ⊘ *Mid-Apr.–late Oct., Tues.–Sun. 10–6.*

Purbach

❺ *13 km (8½ mi) southwest of Neusiedl am See.*

Purbach, like the nearby wine villages of Breitenbrunn and Donner-skirchen, retains traces of its medieval fortifications. Look for the bust of a Turk atop a chimney in the town center; legend has it that when the invaders withdrew in 1532, one badly hungover, sleepy Turk missed the retreat and, fearing retribution, climbed down a chimney for safety. He was discovered, became an honored citizen, and lived in Purbach happily ever after. The wines of this area, the reds in particular, are outstanding and merit stopping for samples. In late fall and early winter you'll still see bunches of shriveled grapes on the leafless vines; these will be turned into rare Spätlese and still-rarer Eiswein dessert wines.

Where to Stay & Eat

$$$–$$$$ ✕🏨 **Am Spitz.** This country inn, at the end of an attractive row of wine cellars, is known for its local Burgenland and Pannonian cooking. The restaurant is in a former cloister, and the outside garden is a veritable bower of flowers, looking down over the lake. The menu changes daily but always spotlights fresh fish, possibly including a spicy Hungarian fish soup, a cassoulet of lake fish in basil cream, and roast veal steak. The somewhat plain and modern associated Gasthof is pleasant but less gemütlich in feeling. ⊠ *Waldsiedlgasse 2, A-7083* ☎ *02683/5519* ⊕ *www.klosteramspitz.at* 🖨 *02683/5519–20* 🛏 *14 rooms* ⚲ *Restaurant; no a/c* ⊟ *MC, V* ⊘ *Restaurant closed Jan.–mid-Mar.; Mon.–Wed. from mid-Mar.–mid-Dec.; Mon.–Tues. July–Aug.* 🍴 *BP.*

Rust

★ ❻ *14 km (9 mi) south of Purbach, 28 km (17½ mi) southwest of Neusiedl am See.*

Picturesque Rust is easily the most popular village on the lake for the colorful pastel facades of its houses and for lake sports. Tourists flock here in summer to see for themselves the famed sight of storks nesting atop the Renaissance and Baroque houses in the town's well-preserved historic center. Be sure to look for *Steckerl,* a delicious local fish caught from the Neusiedlersee and grilled barbecue-style with spices. It's available in most restaurants, but only in the hot months of summer. If you're heading from Purbach, leave Route 50 at Seehof and follow the local road past Oggau to arrive in Rust.

Visit the restored Gothic **Fischerkirche** (Fishermen's Church) off the west end of the Rathausplatz. Built between the 12th and 16th centuries, it is surrounded by a defensive wall and is noted for its 15th-century frescoes and an organ from 1705. ✉ *Conradplatz 1* ☎ *02685/295 or 0676/970–3316* 🎫 *€1, €2 with tour* ⏲ *Apr. and Oct., Mon.–Sat. 11–12 and 2–3, Sun. 11–12 and 2–4; May–Sept., Mon.–Sat. 10–12 and 2:30–5, Sun. 11–12 and 2–5.*

A causeway leads through nearly a mile of reeds to the **Seebad** beach and boat landing, where you can take a sightseeing boat either round-trip or to another point on the lake, rent boats, swim, or enjoy a waterside drink or snack at an outdoor table of the Seerestaurant Rust.

Rust is also renowned for its outstanding wines. There are wine-tasting opportunities at the **Weinakademie** (✉ Hauptstrasse 31 ☎ 02685/6853). There are a couple of family-owned wineries offering tastings that are a cut above the rest **Weingut Feiler-Artinger** (✉ Hauptstrasse 3 ☎ 02685/237) and **Ernst Triebaumer** (✉ Raiffeisenstrasse 9 ☎ 02685/528).

You can sample the excellent local vintages, along with a light lunch, in a number of friendly cafés, cellars, and the typical *Heurige,* where young wines are served by their makers. A favorite spot is the **Rathauskeller** (✉ Rathausplatz 1), open daily except Wednesday from 11:30 AM. The Ruster Blaufränkisch red wine is particularly good, its taste similar to a well-rounded Burgundy.

Where to Stay & Eat

$ ✕ **Schandl.** For good, simple food to go along with the excellent wine from the family's winery, join the locals at this popular *Buschenschank* (inn). The buffet offers a selection of sausages, salads, cheeses, and pickles, as well as a few hot dishes that change daily. There is a pleasant courtyard for outdoor dining in summer. ✉ *Hauptstrasse 20* ☎ *02685/265* 💳 *No credit cards* ⏲ *No lunch weekdays. Closed Nov.–Mar.*

$$$–$$$$ ✕🏨 **Rusterhof.** A lovingly renovated burgher's house—the town's oldest—at the top of the main square houses an excellent and imaginative restaurant. Light natural woods and vaulted ceilings set the tone in a series of smaller rooms; in summer there's an outside garden. The menu depends on what's fresh and might include grilled fish or saddle of hare in *Eiswein* sauce. Finish with a rhubarb compote. The complex also includes four comfortable, though plain, apartments. ✉ *Rathausplatz 18, A-7071* ☎ *02685/6416* 📠 *02685/6416–11* 🌐 *www.rusterhof.at* 4 *apartments* *Restaurant; no a/c* 💳 *AE, MC, V* ⏲ *Restaurant closed Mon.* 🍽 *BP, MAP.*

$ ✕🏨 **Sporthotel Rust.** An imposing, modern structure modeled after castles of yore, complete with miniature towers topped by red turrets, the Sporthotel is just a five-minute walk from the beach. The emphasis here is on the sporting life, as can be deduced from the hotel's name. Nordic walking with a *Leihstöcken* (walking stick), water sports, Tibetan exercise, and deep body massages are popular here. Rooms have a clean, simple design, some with soothing, golden walls. This is also a good base for those who simply want to lie on the beach, eat well, and sample the village wines. ✉ *Mörbischerstrasse 1, A-7071* ☎ *02685/6418* 📠 *02685/*

6418–58 ⊕ *www.drescher.at* ⟷ *45 rooms* ☼ *Restaurant, bar, indoor pool, Internet; no a/c* ⊟ *AE, DC, MC, V* ⦿❘ *BP, MAP.*

Nightlife & the Arts

Between Rust and Eisenstadt, outside the tiny village of St. Margarethen, is **Römersteinbruch** (☎ 02680/2188 ⊠ 02680/218822 ⊕ www. roemersteinbruch.at), a delightful rock quarry used for outdoor opera performances for six or seven weeks in July and August. It's one of the three largest outdoor opera venues in Europe, seating 7,000 nightly. Performances are a spectacular extravaganza—a recent run of Verdi's *Aida* included horse-drawn chariots, a dozen galloping horses, and even two well-trained elephants. Performances also include a dazzling fireworks display. Ticket prices range from €26 to €85. It's a good idea to bring a seat cushion, if possible, because seating is on metal chairs.

Mörbisch

★ ➐ *5½ km (3½ mi) south of Rust.*

Mörbisch is the last lakeside village before the Hungarian border. Considered by many to be the most attractive settlement on the lake, the town is famous for its low, whitewashed, Magyar-style houses, whose open galleries are colorfully decorated with flowers and bunches of grain. The local vineyards produce some superb white wines, especially the fresh-tasting Welschriesling and the full-bodied Muscat-Ottonel. Here, too, a causeway leads to a beach on the lake, where an international operetta festival is held each summer. A leisurely activity is to tour the countryside in a typical, open **horse-drawn wagon.** Operators in several lakeside villages will arrange this, including **Johann Mad** (⊠ Ruster Strasse 14 ☎ 02685/8250) and **Evi Wenzl** (⊠ Weinberggasse 1 ☎ 02685/8401).

Where to Stay & Eat

$ ✕⚇ **Hotel Drescher.** Though in the center of the village, the family-run Drescher is also close to the vineyards and Lake Neusiedl. The somewhat plain modern exterior conceals rustic-style accommodations with all the conveniences. ⊠ *Hauerstrasse 1, A-7072* ☎ *02685/8444* ⊠ *02685/844–643* ⊕ *www.drescher.at* ⟷ *70 rooms* ☼ *Restaurant, indoor pool, sauna, bicycles; no a/c* ⊟ *AE, DC, MC, V* ☉ *Closed Nov.–Mar.* ⦿❘ *BP, MAP.*

Nightlife & the Arts

At the **Mörbisch Lake Festival,** held on Fridays, Saturdays, and Sundays mid-July–August on Burgenland's Lake Neusiedl, operettas are performed outdoors on a floating stage. For information, contact the Mörbisch tourist office or the **festival office** (Seefestspiele Mörbisch ☎ 02682/66210–0 ⊠ 02682/662–1014 ⊕ www.seefestspiele-moerbisch.at) in Schloss Esterházy in Eisenstadt or, from June through August, in **Mörbisch** (☎ 02685/8181 ⊠ 02685/8334).

Eisenstadt

★ ➑ *22 km (14 mi) northwest of Mörbisch, 48 km (30 mi) south of Vienna, 26 km (16¼ mi) west of Wiener Neustadt.*

Burgenland's provincial capital, Eisenstadt, scarcely more than a village, nevertheless has an illustrious history and enough sights to keep you busy for a half, if not quite a full, day. It is connected to Vienna and Neusiedl am See by train and to places throughout Burgenland by bus. From Rust, take Route 52 west past St. Margarethen and Trausdorf to the capital.

Although the town has existed since at least the 12th century, it only became at all significant in the 17th, when it became the seat of the Esterházys, a princely Hungarian family that traces its roots to Attila the Hun. The original Esterházy made his fortune by marrying a succession of wealthy landowning widows. Esterházy support was largely responsible for the Habsburg reign in Hungary under the Dual Monarchy. At one time the family controlled a far-flung agro-industrial empire, and it still owns vast forest resources. The composer Joseph Haydn lived in Eisenstadt for some 30 years while in the service of the Esterházys. When Burgenland was ceded to Austria after World War I, its major city, Sopron, elected to remain a part of Hungary, so in 1925 tiny Eisenstadt was made the capital of the new Austrian province.

In addition to the list below, Eisenstadt has a few other attractions that its tourist office can tell you about, including the Museum of Austrian Culture, the Diocesan Museum, the Fire Fighters Museum, Haydn's little garden house, and an assortment of churches.

🏛 **Schloss Esterházy,** the yellow-facaded former palace of the ruling princes, reigns over the town. Built in the Baroque style between 1663 and 1672 on the foundations of a medieval castle and later modified, it is still owned by the Esterházy family, who lease it to the provincial government for use mostly as offices. The Esterházy family rooms are worth viewing, and the lavishly decorated **Haydn Room,** an impressive concert hall where the composer conducted his own works from 1761 until 1790, is still used for presentations of Haydn's works, with musicians often dressed in period garb. The hall can be seen on guided tours (in English on request if there is a minimum of 10 people) lasting about 30 minutes. The **park** behind the Schloss is pleasant for a stroll or a picnic; in late August it is the site of the Burgenland wine week. ⊠ *Esterházy Platz* ☎ *02682/719–3000* ⊕ *www.schloss-esterhazy.at* ⊠ *€5* ☼ *Early Apr.–mid-Nov., daily 9–5, guided tour hourly; mid-Nov.–Mar., Mon.–Fri., guided tour at 10 and 2.*

At the crest of Esterházystrasse perches the **Bergkirche,** an ornate Baroque church that includes the strange *Kalvarienberg,* an indoor Calvary Hill representing the Way of the Cross with life-size figures placed in cave-like rooms along an elaborate path. At its highest point, the trail reaches the platform of the belfry, offering a view over the town and this section of Burgenland. The magnificent wooden figures were carved and painted by Franciscan monks more than 250 years ago. The main part of the church contains the tomb of Joseph Haydn, who died in 1809 in Vienna. When the body was returned to Eisenstadt for burial 11 years later at the request of Prince Esterházy, it was unaccountably headless. A search for the head ensued, but it was not discovered until 1932. It had been under glass in the possession of the Gesellschaft der Musikfreunde, the main Viennese musical society. Finally, in 1954 Haydn's head was returned to Eisenstadt, where it was buried with his body in a crypt inside the church. ⊠ *Josef Haydn Platz 1* ☎ *02682/62638*

⊕ *www.haydnkirche.at* ☒ *€2.50* ⊗ *Late Mar.–Oct., daily 9–noon and 2–5; other months by appointment.*

Wertheimergasse and Unterbergstrasse were boundaries of the Jewish ghetto from 1671 until 1938. During that time, Eisenstadt had a considerable Jewish population; today the **Österreichisches Jüdisches Museum** (Austrian Jewish Museum) recalls the experience of Austrian Jews throughout history. A fascinating private synagogue in the complex survived the 1938 terror and is incorporated into the museum. ☒ *Unterbergstrasse 6* ☎ *02682/65145* ⊕ *www.ojm.at* ☒ *€3.70* ⊗ *May 2–late Oct., Mon.–Thurs. 9–4, Fri. 9–1, by appointment Nov.–Apr.*

The **Landesmuseum** (Burgenland Provincial Museum) brings the history of the region to life with displays on such diverse subjects as Roman culture and the area's wildlife. There's a memorial room to the composer Franz Liszt, along with more relics of the town's former Jewish community. ☒ *Museumgasse 1–5* ☎ *02682/62652–0* ⊕ *www.burgenland. at* ☒ *€3* ⊗ *Tues.–Sun. 9–noon and 1–5.*

Joseph Haydn lived in the simple house on Joseph Haydn-Gasse from 1766 until 1778. Now the **Haydn Museum,** it contains several of the composer's original manuscripts and other memorabilia. The house itself, and especially its flower-filled courtyard with the small back rooms, is unpretentious but quite delightful. ☒ *Joseph-Haydn-Gasse 19–21* ☎ *02682/ 719–3900* ⊕ *www.burgenland.at* ☒ *€3* ⊗ *Apr.–Oct., daily 9–5.*

Where to Stay & Eat

$$$ ✕ **Zum Eder.** This sunny atrium restaurant in the center of town offers friendly service and numerous specialties. The emphasis here is on light, healthy dishes, featuring salads with strips of grilled chicken breast or pork, and Asian favorites, particularly sushi and wok dishes. There are also several vegetarian items to choose from as well, such as tasty carrot and celery lasagne. ☒ *Hauptstrasse 25* ☎ *02682/62645* ▭ *AE, DC, MC, V.*

$$$–$$$$ ✕▥ **Taubenkobel.** Consistently ranked as one of the Top 10 restaurants
Fodor's Choice in Austria (reservations essential), the "Dovecote" is a rambling, elegantly
★ restored 19th-century farmhouse 5 km (3 mi) from Eisenstadt in the village of Schützen. Owner and award-winning chef Walter Eselböck and his wife, Evelyne, have created a series of strikingly beautiful dining rooms, some with stone-vaulted ceilings, others with rough-hewn wooden beams and glass walls facing the garden. The seasonally changing menu may offer potato and goat-cheese soup, *Zander* (pike perch) from the Neusiedlersee with Rösti and fried basil, or saddle of lamb with mangold blossoms and asparagus in a saffron sauce. Desserts are innovative, such as the liquid chocolate cake and white-pepper ice cream. They sell some of the best wines in the country under their own label. The former stables and outbuildings have been converted to luxurious, unique bedrooms with unusual mirrors, wooden beams, fabrics, cathedral ceilings, along with objets d'art the Eselböcks have collected on their frequent visits to India and France. ☒ *Hauptstrasse 33, A-7081 Schützen* ☎ *02684/ 2297* ☒ *02684/2297–18* ⊕ *www.taubenkobel.at* ⇆ *5 rooms* ♻ *Shop, Internet; no a/c* ▭ *AE, DC, MC, V accepted in restaurant only* ❝❞ *BP.*

$$ ✕⊞ **Hotel Burgenland.** Considered one of the province's best, this big, early-1980s hotel in the town center has everything you'd expect in a first-class establishment. The staff is especially friendly, voluntarily going out of its way to assist guests. The well-maintained, spacious rooms are classic modern, with lots of shuttered windows offering views of the town and countryside. Baths are roomy and have a separate tub and shower. And every floor has something both kids and adults love: an ice machine. The restaurant is superb, showcasing Austrian dishes with a Pannonian slant, due to the city's close proximity to Hungary. Be sure to order the special aperitif, Burgenland's own Hahnenkamp Traminer Auslese, which tastes like a fine, dry sherry. You'll need to book a year in advance for the music festivals. ✉ *Schubertplatz 1, A-7000* ☎ *02682/696* 📠 *02682/65531* ⊕ *www.austria-hotels.co.at* ⤶ *88 rooms* ♲ *Restaurant, bar, minibars, indoor pool, sauna, Internet; no a/c* ⊟ *AE, DC, MC, V* ⍥| *BP, MAP.*

$–$$ ✕⊞ **Gasthof Ohr.** This personal, family-run hotel and restaurant is within an easy 10-minute walk of the town center. The immaculate rooms are comfortably attractive, done in natural woods and white with pastel accents; those in the back are quieter. The rustic wood-paneled restaurant offers specialty weeks—goose, game, fresh asparagus—in addition to Austrian and regional standards such as schnitzel and Hungarian fish soup. A favorite is the saffron risotto with lobster and chicken. In summer, the canopied outdoor dining terrace is a green oasis. Wine comes from the family vineyards. ✉ *Rusterstrasse 51, A-7000* ☎ *02682/62460* 📠 *02682/624609* ⊕ *www.hotelohr.at* ⤶ *30 rooms* ♲ *Restaurant; no a/c* ⊟ *MC, V* ⊘ *Closed 3 wks in Feb.* ⍥| *BP (MAP available for stays of 3 days).*

Nightlife & the Arts

Eisenstadt devotes much cultural energy to one of its favorite sons. In the first half of September, it plays host to the annual **Haydn Festival** in the Esterházy Palace. Many of the concerts are by renowned performers, and admission prices vary with the event. Other concerts featuring the works of Joseph Haydn run from mid-May to early October. Contact the **Haydnfestspiele office** (☎ 02682/61866–0 📠 02682/61805 ⊕ www.haydnfestival.at) in Schloss Esterházy or the local tourist office. Eisenstadt's **Schloss Trio Eisenstadt, Haydn Quartet,** and **Haydn Brass,** in 18th-century costumes, play short matinee concerts of the master's works at 11 AM Wednesday, Thursday, and Friday in July and August at the **Esterházy Palace** (☎ 02682/719–3000 📠 02682/719–3223 ⊕ www.schloss-esterhazy.at). Tickets are €8.

en route Heading southwest from Eisenstadt brings you to the waist of Burgenland, the narrow region squeezed between Lower Austria and Hungary. The leading attraction here is Forchtenstein; take Route S31 for 20 km (12½ mi) to Mattersburg, then a local road 3 km (2 mi) west.

Forchtenstein

⊙ *23 km (14½ mi) southwest of Eisenstadt.*

In the summer people throng to the small village of Forchtenstein for its strawberries, but its enduring dominant landmark is the medieval hilltop castle **Burg Forchtenstein.** This formidable fortress was built in the early 14th century, then enlarged by the Esterházys around 1635, and twice it successfully defended Austria against invading Turks. Captured enemy soldiers were put to work digging the castle's 466-foot-deep well, famous for its echo. As befits a military stronghold, there is a fine collection of weapons in the armory and booty taken from the Turks; there's also an exhibition of stately carriages. ☒ *Burgplatz 1* ☎ *02626/63125* ⊕ *www.forchtenstein.at* ☒ *€5* ⊙ *Apr.–Oct., daily 9–6.*

Where to Stay & Eat

$$–$$$ ✕ **Reisner.** The delicately prepared traditional food served at this popular restaurant attracts people from all over the region. You can eat in the somewhat formal dining room or in the rustic tavern favored by the locals. Some typical dishes are grilled salmon trout with asparagus tips or chicken breast filled with mushroom risotto, and, for dessert, a nougat charlotte. ☒ *Hauptstrasse 141* ☎ *02626/63139* ▭ *No credit cards* ⊙ *Closed Mon.–Tues.*

¢ ✕▦ **Gasthof Sauerzapf.** This simple country inn on the main road just five minutes west of the castle has comfortably furnished modern rooms. ☒ *Rosalienstrasse 39, A-7212* ☎ *02626/81217* ⇝ *8 rooms* ◊ *Restaurant; no a/c, no room phones, no room TVs* ▭ *No credit cards* ⊙ *Closed Wed.* ▐◉▌ *BP.*

en route You can get to Bernstein from Forchtenstein by returning to the highway from Burg Forchtenstein and taking S31 and Route 50 south past Weppersdorf and Stoob, the latter famous for its pottery. The road then goes through Oberpullendorf and close to Lockenhaus, where a renowned music festival is held each summer in the 13th-century castle (*see* Nightlife & the Arts *in* Bernstein, *below*).

Bernstein

⑩ *73 km (45 mi) south of Forchtenstein.*

The small village of Bernstein is one of the very few sources of *Edelserpentin,* a dark green serpentine stone also known as Bernstein jade. Jewelry and objets d'art made locally from the town's stone are on display in the **Felsenmuseum** (Stone Museum), housed partly within a former mine. ☒ *Potsch, Hauptplatz 5* ☎ *03354/6620-0* ⊕ *www.felsenmuseum.at* ☒ *€4.50* ⊙ *Mar.–May and Aug.–Oct., daily 9–noon and 1:30–6; June–July, daily 9–6; Dec.–Feb., Sat. 1:30–5.*

off the beaten path **SOUTH BURGENLAND OPEN-AIR MUSEUM** – South of Bernstein in Bad Tatzmannsdorf is the Freilichtmuseum (South Burgenland Open-Air Museum), which displays wonderfully restored old barns, farmhouses, and stables from the region, giving a feeling of life as experienced a century or more ago. You can arrange in advance for a personal guided tour. ☒ *Josef-Hölzel-Allee 2* ☎ *033537015* ☒ *€1* ⊙ *Apr.–Oct., daily 9–5, Nov.–Mar., daily 9–4.*

THE CASTLE ROAD

IF YOU ARE HEADING SOUTH FROM VIENNA TO GRAZ *on the A2 autobahn, the flat plains give way suddenly to steeply wooded hills and rocky gorges, with tantalizing glimpses of proud and seemingly inaccessible castles perched atop craggy promontories. More than a dozen castles along the Schlösserstrasse (Castle Road) have withstood the invading armies of the Huns and Turks to repose today in all their splendor as museums or hotels.*

You can begin the tour by dipping into the eastern edge of Styria, leaving the autobahn at the Hartberg exit to visit **Schloss Hartberg,** *a castle dating from the 13th century and now a museum and the venue for occasional summer concerts.*

From Hartberg take Highway 54 south to Kaibing, where there will be signs for St. Johann bei Herberstein and **Schloss Herberstein,** *famous for its Florentine-style courtyard and animal and nature park. You can also inspect the castle's weaponry collection and stroll in the Baroque garden.* **Schloss Stubenberg,** *north along the lakeside drive Stubenbergsee, is a fortresslike structure with an impressive ceramics display and summer concerts.*

The Allhau exit off the A2 autobahn a short distance north of Hartberg takes you to Highway 50 and Bernstein. This is the home of **Burg Bernstein,** *now a hotel but once the castle owned by Count Almásy, the character played by Ralph Fiennes in The English Patient.*

East of Bernstein on Highway 50 is **Lockenhaus** *(☎ 02616/2394 ☏ 02616/ 2766), the castle with the most grisly history in Austria. In the 16th century, Countess Elisabeth Bathory was infamous for luring peasant girls to her employ with promises of a dowry after two years' servitude; most girls never made it out alive.*

Obsessed with retaining her beauty, the depraved countess tortured and killed more than 500 girls, believing that their virginal blood would keep her young. As a member of the nobility, the countess was never tried for her crimes. The castle is now a very nice hotel, with a medieval restaurant serving simple food like roast chicken and sausages.

Highway 50 south of Bernstein takes you to Stadtschlaining, the home of **Burg Schlaining,** *famous for its weaponry collection, chapel, and palatial rooms (closed Monday).*

Highway 57 south of Highway 50 leads to **Burg Güssing,** *not far from the Slovenian and Hungarian borders. After this the Castle Road continues on into Styria, southeast of Graz, with several more noteworthy castles to visit or stay in.*

A drive along the Castle Road can take anywhere from four or five hours to a couple of days, depending on how many of the castles you stop to visit—either to tour or to spend the night in. Even if you're in a hurry, it's relatively easy to get off and on the A2 autobahn to visit a castle.

The best time to visit this area is between April and October, because most of the castles are closed during the winter months. For more information about the Castle Road, contact the **Büro Die Schlösserstrasse** *(✉ Schloss Stubenberg, A-8223 Stubenberg am See ☎ 03176/ 20050 ☏ 03176/20060 ⊕ www. schloesserstrasse.com).*

— Bonnie Dodson

Where to Stay

★ **$$$–$$$$** ⌨ **Burg Bernstein.** This massive medieval castle, built in the 12th century, became a hotel in 1953, with indoor plumbing being the only concession to modern life. It has gained a certain fame of late because it once belonged to Count Almásy, the character portrayed by Ralph Fiennes in *The English Patient.* It's now owned by an offshoot of the family, and you can still find Count Almásy's books on the shelves in the corridors, and his room is preserved the way he left it. The hilltop location gives it a bird's-eye view of the peaceful Tauchen Valley, just west of the village of Bernstein. The rooms, which tend to be large, look much as they must have in the mid-1800s; the reception salons are decorated with historic 19th-century writing tables and armoires, several of which are for sale. Meals, prepared by Countess Berger-Almásy herself, are served with regional wines in the Rittersaal, a baronial hall in the 18th-century style. ☒ *Schlossweg 1, A-7434* ☎ *03354/6382* 🖷 *03354/6520* ⊕ *www.burgbernstein.at* 🛏 *10 rooms* ⚒ *Restaurant, pool, sauna, fishing; no a/c, no room phones, no room TVs* ⊟ *AE, DC, MC, V* ⊘ *Closed mid-Oct.–Apr.* ⦿ *BP, MAP.*

Nightlife & the Arts

The **International Chamber Music Festival** (Kammermusikfest; ☎ 02616/2225 🖷 02616/22225–16 ⊕ www.lockenhaus.at) of Lockenhaus, 15 km (9½ mi) east of Bernstein, takes place during the first half of July in a 13th-century castle. World-famous musicians are invited to this intimate festival, and the audience may attend morning rehearsals. Call for information, reservations, and accommodations.

Güssing

⓫ *54 km (34 mi) south of Bernstein, 13 km (8½ mi) north of Heiligenkreuz, Hungary.*

Güssing is yet another of Burgenland's castle-dominated villages. From Bernstein many travelers arrive via Route 50 past Bad Tatzmannsdorf, then follow Route 57. The classic 12th-century fortress **Burg Güssing,** perched high on a solitary volcanic outcrop, has wonderful views of the surrounding countryside. It also has a fine collection of Old Master paintings (including portraits by Lucas Cranach), weapons and armor, and a Gothic chapel with a rare 17th-century cabinet organ. The castle has special exhibits. ☎ *03322/43400* 🖷 *€5.50* ⊘ *Apr.–Oct., Tues.–Sun. 10–5.*

If you stop in Güssing to explore its castle, consider also visiting the nearby ☾ game park, **Naturpark Raab-Örsg-Goricko,** where wild animals indigenous to Eastern Austria reside in more than a square mile of open space. Observation posts are scattered throughout, and you should exercise patience—the animals need time to come to you. The park is in Jennersdorf, 1 km (½ mi) northeast of Güssing. ☒ *Eisenstädterstrasse 11, A-8380* ☎ *03329/48453* 🖷 *03329/48453–21* ⊕ *www.naturpark-raab.at* 🖷 *Free* ⊘ *Daily dawn–dusk.*

Where to Stay & Eat

¢–$ ✗⌨ **Gasthof Gibiser.** Its proximity to Hungary has inspired the creative dishes served at this classic, white, villa-style country inn. The Pannonian cuisine combines the best of Austrian and Hungarian culinary traditions to produce such specialties as cabbage soup, and steak stuffed with goose liver. For overnighters, there are several quiet rooms plus a few rustic thatch-roof cottages surrounded by gardens. ⊠ *Heiligenkreuz 81, A-7561* ☎ *03325/4216–0* ⊟ *03325/4246–44* ⊕ *www.g-gibiser.at* ⇝ *12 rooms, 4 cottages* ⊟ *MC, V* ⊙ *Restaurant closed Mon.* ⏐◯⏐ *BP, MAP.*

Riegersburg

⑫ *57 km (35 mi) southwest of Güssing, 56 km (34¾ mi) east of Graz.*

To arrive at Riegersburg from Güssing, stay on Route 57 to the frontier village of Heiligenkreuz-im-Laftnitztal; then take Route 65 west to Fürstenfeld, leaving Burgenland and crossing into Styria. Continue on to Ilz, and then turn south on Route 66 to Riegersburg. Riegersburg is a quiet agricultural community overshadowed by the massive fortress that perches atop an extraordinary volcanic outcropping. The rock has steadily increased in interest over the centuries; archaeological finds have established that there were settlements here more than 6,000 years ago.

Rising some 600 feet above the valley is the mighty and well-restored **Schloss Riegersburg,** one of Austria's great defensive bastions. Originally built in the 11th century on the site of Celtic and Roman strongholds, it has never been humbled in battle, not even in 1945, when its German occupants held out against the Russians. The present structure dates from the 17th century and is entered by way of a heavily defended, winding path, so be prepared to climb for 20 to 30 minutes. The castle has weapons displays and rooms with period furnishings. Needless to say, the views are magnificent. ☎ *03153/82131* ⊕ *www.riegersburg.com* ▣ *€9.50* ⊙ *Apr.–Oct., daily 9–6 (last admission at 5).*

Adjacent to the Riegersburg Castle you can observe free-flying birds of prey at **Greifvogelwarte Riegersburg** (Birds-of-Prey Keep). At various hours, falcons and eagles are set loose from a stand within the aviary preserve (always returning to the keepers' care—and tempting meals, of course). ☎ *03153/7390* ▣ *€6* ⊙ *Apr.–Oct., Mon.–Sat. at 11 and 3, Sun. at 11, 2, and 4, weather permitting.*

Where to Stay & Eat

¢ ✕⏐☰⏐ **Gasthof Fink Zur Riegersburg.** This venerable, family-run country inn near the foot of the castle is prettily adorned with flowerboxes and shutters. Its large, paneled dining room—complete with ceiling beams—is bright and airy, and there's also garden dining in season. The Austrian cuisine is hearty, with such dishes as bratwurst with sauerkraut and dumplings, and roast beef with fried polenta. A fine selection of Styrian wines is offered. ⊠ *Riegersburg 29, A-8333* ☎ *03153/8216* ⊟ *03153/7357* ⊕ *www.finkwirt.at* ⇝ *30 rooms* ☆ *Restaurant; no a/c* ⊟ *AE, DC, MC, V* ⊙ *Restaurant and hotel closed Thurs., hotel closed 3 wks sometime in winter* ⏐◯⏐ *BP, MAP.*

Blumau

⑬ *60 km (37 mi) northeast of Graz.*

Midway between Vienna and Graz, this tiny hamlet was known until recently as one of the poorest farming communities in the country. Then in the late 1970s an oil exploration company drilling for gas unexpectedly found a thermal spring instead. Not realizing its value, they blocked it up, but the people in the area didn't forget about it. It wasn't until the mid-1990s that permission was granted to drill again, and when the volcanic springs were released, the area became fashionable for spa treatments and cures.

Where to Stay & Eat

$$$$ ✕▦ **Schloss Obermayerhofen.** The queen of all the castle hotels along the
Fodor'sChoice   Castle Drive from Vienna to Graz (*see* the Close-up box, *above*) is just
★   a little over 3 km (2 mi) northwest of Blumau. No expense was spared in providing luxurious modern-day comfort while retaining the ancient feel of the castle. No two rooms are alike, some being furnished in French Empire style, others with gleaming Biedermeier antiques, canopied beds, and museum-worthy tapestries. The serious restaurant serves such tempting items as salmon tartare on a bed of crispy potato strips or pan-fried pike perch with white-truffle mashed potatoes. The menu changes frequently. ✉ *A-8272 Sebersdorf/Bad Waltersdorf* ☎ *03333/2503* 🖷 *03333/2503–50* ⊕ *www.obermayerhofen.at* ⇆ *22 rooms* ⚐ *Restaurant; no a/c, no pets* ⊟ *DC, MC, V* ⊙ *Closed Jan. 6–Feb.* ⑩ *BP.*

★ **$$$–$$$$** ✕▦ **Bad Blumau.** Designed by the late visionary artist Friedensreich Hundertwasser, this phenomenal spa hotel complex resembles a fantasy by Gaudí—undulating walls covered by a brilliant checkered patchwork, with turrets, mismatched windows, as well as sloping rooftop gardens and multicolored ceramic pillars. Rooms have curved walls, soothing fabrics, and oddly angled bathrooms. Take an evening swim (even in winter) in the outdoor thermal pool, whose natural hot springs keep the water at a constant 34°C (92°F). Your days can be filled with spa treatments, from sound therapy to qi-gong to hay wraps—anything is possible here. The spa restaurants serve tasty Austrian fare, using produce and meat provided by local farmers. ✉ *A-8283 Blumau* ☎ *03383/5100–0* 🖷 *03383/5100–9100* ⊕ *www.blumau. com* ⇆ *271 rooms, 59 suites* ⚐ *2 restaurants, minibars, indoor-outdoor pool, massage, sauna, bar, shops, Internet; no a/c, no pets* ⊟ *AE, DC, MC, V* ⑩ *BP, MAP.*

GRAZ AND ITS ENVIRONS

★   *200 km (125 mi) southwest of Vienna, 285 km (178 mi) southeast of Salzburg.*

Native son Arnold Schwarzenegger hasn't managed to give Graz quite the cultural cachet that Mozart bestowed on Vienna and Salzburg, so this second-largest Austrian city (and capital of the province of Styria) has had to work harder to grab the spotlight. But its efforts paid off— Graz was chosen as the "Cultural Capital of Europe" for 2003. And though the city may have said, *Hasta la vista, Europa* to the coveted title, the Altstadt retains an exciting, vibrant atmosphere, due in part to the large university population who keep the sidewalk cafés, trendy bars, and chic restaurants humming. There's a new modern art museum, the Kunsthaus, whose startling biomorphic blue shape looms over rooftops like some alien spaceship. Over at the River Mur, New York avant-gardist Vito Acconci created a bit of a splash with his Murinsel island-complex; depending on who you speak to, Acconci's design, connected by walkways to the river banks and containing a popular café, amphitheater, and playground, looks like a giant open mussel or a kitchen colander. Along with this, the annual Styriarte summer music festival has become one of the most prestigious cultural events in the country, and the city opera theater now attracts top companies like the Bolshoi. Graz is far from the cultural backwater it once was.

With its skyline dominated by the squat 16th-century clock tower, this stylish city has a gorgeous and well-preserved medieval center whose Italian Renaissance overlay gives it, in contrast to other Austrian cities, a Mediterranean feel. There are scenic delights galore, ranging from Rococo facades to marble churches and glittering Baroque palaces. Lying in a somewhat remote corner of the country and often overlooked by tourists, Graz is easily reached from Vienna or Salzburg and provides the urban highlight of an itinerary through southeastern Austria. The name Graz derives from the Slavic *gradec,* meaning "small castle"; there was probably a fortress atop the Schlossberg hill as early as the 9th century. This strategic spot guarded the southern end of the narrow Mur Valley—an important approach to Vienna—from invasion by the Turks. By the 12th century, a town had developed at the foot of the hill, which in time became an imperial city of the ruling Habsburgs. Graz's glory faded in the 17th century when the court moved to Vienna, but the city continued to prosper as a provincial capital, especially under the enlightened 19th-century rule of Archduke Johann.

If you're staying in the city for more than a day, you might want to make a short excursion or two into the countryside. Ask at the information office for the detailed folder in English, "Excursions Around Graz," with suggestions as well as travel directions. Three favorite trips—to Stübing bei Graz, Piber, and Bärnbach—can each be done in a few hours. Sometimes called the "Tuscany of Austria," the lush, wine-terraced area 30 minutes south of Graz is home to some of the best wineries in the country. If you don't have time to take a couple of days to explore this enchanting part of Styria on your own, the Graz tourist office offers a bus excursion that takes just a few hours, allowing you to visit a few wineries and do some tasting. The tour, which is conducted in German and English, also includes a *Brettjause* (a snack of cheese, home-cured meats, and bread, served on a wooden plank). Excursions are from April to October, departing Sundays at 2 PM from the tourist office at Herrengasse 16, and returning around 7. The cost is €24 for adults and €9 for children under 15. To reserve a spot, contact the tourist office at 0316/8075–0 or e-mail them at info@graztourismus.at.

A Good Walk

On the left bank of the River Mur at the center of the Old City is the **Hauptplatz** ⑭, which was converted from a swampy pastureland to a town square by traveling merchants in 1164. It wasn't until 1550 that the sumptuously opulent Rathaus (City Hall) was built, but little remains now of the original structure. Modernized over the centuries until it began to look out of place in the Renaissance-style square, its facade was restored to the initial design in 1966. Facing the Rathaus is the impressive Erzherzog Johann Brunnen (Archduke Johann Fountain). Before leaving the Hauptplatz, go to the corner of Sporgasse for a look at the Baroque Luegg Haus, which gets its name from the German phrase *ums Eck lugen,* or "peer around the corner."

Backtrack toward the Rathaus and take the second right from the Hauptplatz onto the narrow, medieval Franziskanergasse. Walk its short length to the Franziskanerplatz and the Franziskanerkirche, a church and Franciscan monastery dating from 1240, with a 14th-century choir, a 16th-century nave, and a 17th-century tower. The area is known as the Kälbernes Viertel, or Butchers Quarter, because in the Middle Ages it was where butchers tended their stalls offering meat and sausages for sale. Return to the Hauptplatz and go past the Rathaus on the right side, which is Schmiedgasse, or Blacksmith Lane. A block ahead it is lined with old burgher houses in pretty pastel shades. If you're up for visiting a series of museums, make a detour by going right on Landhausgasse, then an almost immediate left onto Raubergasse to the entrance to the natural-history section of the **Landesmuseum Joanneum** ⑮. The entrance to the Applied Arts department, displaying works by Lucas Cranach and Pieter Brueghel the Younger, is on Neutorgasse, parallel to but west of Raubergasse.

Go back to Landhausgasse and turn right onto Herrengasse. Across the street to your left at No. 3 is the famous Gemaltes Haus, a centuries-old ducal residence with lovely frescoes. At the corner of Herrengasse and Stempfergasse, note the Bären Apotheke (Chemist at the Sign of the Bear) for its Rococo exterior. Opposite the Apotheke is the **Landhaus** ⑯, the home of the Styrian parliament. Take a moment to enter the arcaded courtyard, which was designed by Italian architect Domenico dell'Allio in glorious Renaissance Lombard style. Adjoining the Landhaus is the **Landeszeughaus** ⑰, once the most important armory of southern Austria. Today it houses more than 30,000 exhibition pieces, mainly from the 16th and 17th centuries. Across the street at Herrengasse 13 is a house where Napoléon allegedly once spent the night.

Continue south on Herrengasse to the **Stadtpfarrkirche** ⑱, a splendid church dating from the early 16th century (worth a visit), and on to Hans-Sachs-Gasse. Exit the church and turn left, then left again onto Schlossergasse (Locksmith Lane), passing Bischofsplatz and going on to **Glockenspielplatz** ⑲, famous for the wood-carved, life-size Styrian couple who dance to the sound of the Glockenspiel (chimes). Just past the square is the Mehlplatz, which is lined with historic houses and has a number of bars. This is popularly known as the Bermuda Triangle, because the university students have such a good time here that they "never come out

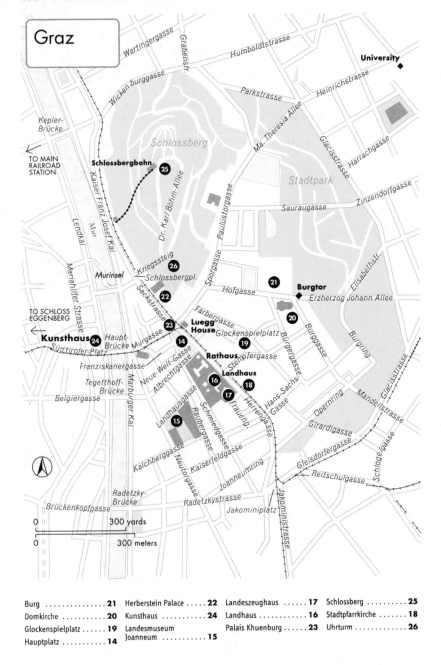

Graz

Burg **21**
Domkirche **20**
Glockenspielplatz **19**
Hauptplatz **14**

Herberstein Palace **22**
Kunsthaus **24**
Landesmuseum
Joanneum **15**

Landeszeughaus **17**
Landhaus **16**
Palais Khuenburg **23**

Schlossberg **25**
Stadtpfarrkirche **18**
Uhrturm **26**

again." In summer it's perfect for sipping a beer while watching the passing crowd. Go back through Glockenspielplatz and go left on Abraham-A-Sancta-Clara-Gasse, then left again onto Bürgergasse. Almost immediately to your right, some steps lead to the late-Gothic **Domkirche** ⑳ and the Mausoleum of Emperor Ferdinand II. From the Mausoleum go through the passageway that leads to Burggasse (not Bürgergasse). Across the street the castle gateway (Burgtor) leads to the Stadtpark, the vast city park, with its fountains, pathways, and park benches offering relaxation.

Just left of the Burgtor on Hofgasse is another grand archway, which is the entrance to the **Burg** ㉑, or old imperial palace, now used for government offices, but worth stepping inside the courtyard to see the Gothic staircase. Exiting the Burg, turn right onto Hofgasse, or Court Lane, and follow it to Sporgasse. Sporgasse (Spur Lane) was where spur makers and weaponry makers of the 14th and 15th centuries lived and worked. Go left on Sporgasse, and if you're still game after passing Luegg Haus from the beginning of the tour, go right onto Sackstrasse to **Herberstein Palace** ㉒, now housing a collection of modern Styrian art, and the **Palais Khuenburg** ㉓, which now houses the city museum. Emerging from the Stadtmuseum, go west toward the Mur river and across the Haupt-Brücke bridge to the riverside avenue known as Lendkai. Here, looming over all is the modernistic "space-ship" that is Graz's new **Kunsthaus** ㉔. If you're into cutting-edge modern art, you'll want to check out the impressive calendar of temporary exhibitions here. There's also a pedestrian walkway from the Haupt-Brücke to the **Murinsel**, a man-made river island designed by modernist Vito Acconci, set below the Kunsthaus, with a trend-setting café and amphitheater. If modern art doesn't appeal to you, you'll want to stick to the Altstadt side of the river and, from the Palais Khuenburg, go right to Schlossbergplatz.

Schlossbergplatz is the base of the **Schlossberg** ㉕, or Palace Mountain. This is where the fortress guarding Graz was located and where you'll mount an amazing flight of zig-zagging steps leading to the famous **Uhrturm** ㉖. This clock tower is the most famous landmark in Graz. Continue following the path upward to the Glockenturm, the bell tower that is part of the original fortress on the Schlossberg. This winds up the end of the walking tour, and if you're too tired to go back on foot to the center of the city, consider taking the Schlossbergbahn, the funicular that carries the weary down to Kaiser-Franz-Josef-Kai at 15-minute intervals. Outside the city center are is the hyper-grand and regal **Schloss Eggenberg,** located at the eastern edge of the city suburbs.

TIMING   Nearly all tourist attractions in Graz are conveniently located in the compact Altstadt, or Old City quarter, which can easily be explored on foot in an hour or so, not including any stops. With several stops, a walk through the Old City of Graz can take all day. If you're pressed for time, choose which part of the Old City you'd rather see: the lower section, with its churches, historical houses, and museums, or the upper town, with its winding wooded paths, famous clock tower, and the Schlossberg, the lookout point of the city. The best time to visit is between April and October, when the weather is at its most inviting, although most tourist attractions are open year-round.

Sights to See

㉑ Burg. The scanty remains of this former imperial palace now house government offices. Most of this uninspired structure is from the 19th and 20th centuries, but two noteworthy vestiges of the original 15th-century stronghold remain: the **Burgtor** (palace gate), which opens into the sprawling **Stadtpark** (municipal park); and the unusual 49-step, 26-foot carved stone double-spiral **Gothic staircase** of 1499, in the hexagonal tower at the far end of the first courtyard.

㉚ Domkirche. On the south exterior wall is a badly damaged 15th-century fresco called the *Landplagenbild*, which graphically depicts contemporary local torments—the plague, the locusts, and the Turks. Step inside to see the outstanding high altar made of colored marble, the choir stalls, Raphael Donner's 1741 tomb of Count Cobenzl, and Konrad Laib's *Crucifixion* of 1457. The 15th-century reliquaries on either side of the triumphal arch leading to the choir were originally the hope chests of Paola Gonzaga, daughter of Ludovico II of Mantua. The Baroque **Mausoleum** of Emperor Ferdinand II, who died in 1637, adjoins the cathedral. Its sumptuous interior is partly an early design by native son Fischer von Erlach and his only work to be seen in Graz. ⊠ *Burggasse 3* ☎ *0316/ 821683* ✆ *Domkirche, free; Mausoleum €4* ☉ *Domkirche open daily 11–7 approx.; Mausoleum, Nov.–Dec. and early Jan.–Apr., daily 10:30–12 and 1:30–3; May–Oct. daily, 10–12, 1–4.*

⑲ Glockenspielplatz. Every day at 11 AM and 3 and 6 PM two mullioned windows open in the mechanical clock high above the square, revealing a wooden man adorned in lederhosen, a tankard of beer in his upraised fist, accompanied by a dirndl-clad Austrian maiden. An old folk tune plays and they dance on the window ledges before returning to their hidden perch. The musical box was erected in 1903 by the owner of the house. Look into the courtyard at No. 5, which has an impressive 17th-century open staircase. The house at No. 7 has an arcaded Renaissance courtyard.

need a break?   Part deli, part café, **Frankowitsch** (⊠ Stempfergasse 2–4) is worth a stop just to look at the selection of artistic pastries (which invariably sell out by late afternoon). Choose from a series of rooms, both upstairs and down, where you can nibble on little open-faced sandwiches and sip excellent coffee or a glass of Styrian wine. Make sure you look upstairs at the selection of exquisite chocolates on display. Frankowitsch is closed in the evenings and Sunday.

★ **⑭ Hauptplatz** (Main Square). This triangular area was first laid out in 1164 and is used today as a lively open-air produce market. In its center stands the **Erzherzog Johann Brunnen** (Archduke Johann Fountain), dedicated to the popular 19th-century patron whose enlightened policies did much to develop Graz as a cultural and scientific center. The four female figures represent what were Styria's four main rivers; today only the Mur and the Enns are still within the province. The **Luegg House,** at the corner of Sporgasse, is noted for its Baroque stucco facade. On the west side of the square are Gothic and Renaissance houses. The spectacular, late-19th-century **Rathaus** (City Hall) totally dominates the south side. From the Neue-Welt-Gasse and Schmiedgasse you get a superb view of the Hauptplatz.

22 Herberstein Palace. Another instance of old and new colliding magnificently in time-burnished Graz, this 17th-century former city residence of the ruling princes now houses the **Neue Galerie** (New Gallery), which features an array of temporary modern-art exhibitions of the newest trends in Styrian art. The permanent collection dates back to the 19th century with works by such masters as Egon Schiele. ⊠ *Sackstrasse 16* ☎ *0316/ 829155* ⊕ *www.neuegalerie.at* ✆ *€6* ◷ *Tues.–Sun. 10–6, Thurs. 10–8.*

24 Kunsthaus. Across the River Mur from the Alstadt is a new modern-art museum, nicknamed the "Friendly Alien"—and indeed, it does look like an alien ship landed smack in the middle of the town's medieval orange-tiled, gabled roofs. Designed by London-based architects Peter Cook and Colin Fournier, with an aim at forging an interaction between the traditional landmarks of Graz and the avant-garde, it resembles a gigantic blue beached whale with spiky tentacles—which light up at night. Inside, the vast exhibition rooms are linked by escalators and spiraling walkways, with an open arena at the top offering spectacular views. There is no permanent collection here, only temporary exhibits of renowned modern artists. Just a short walk back to the River Mur, you'll find a pedestrian walkway (set off the Haupt-Brücke) that will take you to the **Murinsel** island-complex, designed by famed modern artist Vito Acconci. There's a café and a theater but the complex itself remains a conceptual piece of sculpture that has set the tongues of Graz wagging. ⊠ *Lend-kai 1* ☎ *0316/8017–9200* ⊕ *www.kunsthausgraz.at* ✆ *€6* ◷ *Open Tues.–Sun. 10–6, Thurs. 10–8.*

★ 15 Landesmuseum Joanneum. This is the oldest public museum in Austria, founded by Archduke Johann in 1811. Actually, this is part of a large complex of museums—with collections ranging from natural history exhibits to Old Master paintings—several of which are in other parts of town. The **Alte Galerie** (Old Gallery) is a world-famous collection of art from the Middle Ages through the Baroque period. Among its treasures are works by Pieter Brueghel the Younger and both Hans and Lucas Cranach, the noted *Admont Madonna* wood carving from 1400, and a medieval altarpiece depicting the murder of Thomas à Becket. ⊠ *Alte Galerie and Applied Arts: Neutorgasse 45; Natural History Museum: Raubergasse 10* ☎ *0316/8017–9740 Alte Galerie and Applied Arts, 0316/ 8017–9770 Natural History Museum* ⊕ *www.museum-joanneum.at* ✆ *€4.50* ◷ *Alte Galerie and Applied Arts: Tues.–Sun. 10–6, Thurs. 10–8; Natural History Museum: Tues.–Sun. 9–4.*

☾ 17 Landeszeughaus. This provincial arsenal is possibly the most noted attraction in Graz. Virtually unchanged since it was built in 1643, this four-story armory still contains the 16th- and 17th-century weapons intended for use by Styrian mercenaries in fighting off the Turks. Nearly 30,000 items are on display, including more than 3,000 suits of armor (some of which are beautifully engraved), thousands of halberds, swords, firearms, cannons, and mortars. Probably the most important collection of its type in the world, the sheer quantity of displays can be daunting, so thankfully the most unusual items are highlighted, sometimes in very striking displays. ✉ *Herrengasse 16* ☎ *0316/8017–9810* 💰 *€4.50* ⏱ *Apr.–Oct., Tues.–Sun. 10–6, Thurs. 10–8; Nov.–Mar., Tues.–Sun. 10–3.*

⑯ Landhaus. The Styrian provincial parliament house was built between 1557 and 1565 by Domenico dell'Allio in the Renaissance Lombard style. Its three-tiered arcaded courtyard is magnificently proportioned and surrounds a 16th-century fountain that is an unusually fine example of old Styrian wrought-iron work. ✉ *Herrengasse 16.*

㉓ Palais Khuenburg. This was the birthplace in 1863 of Archduke Franz Ferdinand, heir to the throne of the Austro-Hungarian Empire. His assassination at Sarajevo in 1914 led directly to the outbreak of World War I. The palace is now address to the **Stadtmuseum** (City Museum), whose exhibits trace the history of Graz and include an old-time pharmacy. ✉ *Sackstrasse 18* ☎ *0316/822580* 💰 *€7* ⏱ *Tues. 10–9, Wed.–Sat. 10–6, Sun. 10–1.*

㉕ Schlossberg (Palace Mountain). The view from the summit of Graz's midtown mountain takes in all of the city and much of central Styria. A zigzagging stone staircase beginning at Schlossbergplatz leads to the top, but since it is a 395-foot climb, you may prefer to use the **Schlossbergbahn** funicular railway (Kaiser-Franz-Josef-Kai 38) for €1.60 or an elevator, carved through the rockface, that leaves from Schlossbergplatz. The defensive fortress, whose ramparts were built to prevent the invading Turks from marching up the Mur Valley toward Vienna, remained in place until 1809, when a victorious Napoléon had them dismantled after defeating the Austrians. The town paid a large ransom to preserve two of the castle's towers, but the rest was torn down and is today a well-manicured and very popular park. Atop the Schlossberg and a few steps east of the funicular station is the **Glockenturm** (bell tower), an octagonal structure from 1588 containing Styria's largest bell, the famous 4-ton Liesl. This is also the departure point for guided walking tours of the Schlossberg, conducted daily (except in winter), every hour from 9 to 5, if there are more than five people. The cost is €2.15 for adults, and €1.05 for children. The **Open-Air Theater,** just yards to the north, is built into the old casements of the castle and has a sliding roof in case of rain. Both opera and theater performances are held here in summer.

need a
break?

★

At the top of the Schlossberg is **Aiola** (☎ 0316/818797), a toney café and bar serving drinks and light snacks. Relax under crisp white canvas umbrellas while sipping a glass of Styrian wine or coffee with all of Graz spread out below you. For €1.60 you can let the futuristic, clear elevator whisk you up through the center of the mountain, reached from Schlossbergplatz.

Schloss Eggenberg. This 17th-century palace is on the very eastern edge of the city and is surrounded by a large deer park. Built around an arcaded courtyard lined with antlers, this fine example of the high Baroque style contains the gorgeous **Prunkräume** (State Apartments) noted for their elaborate stucco decorations and frescoes, as well as three branch museums of the Joanneum. The **Jagdmuseum** (Hunting Museum), on the first floor, displays antique weapons, paintings, and realistic dioramas. The **Abteilung für Vor- und Frühgeschichte** (Archaeological Museum) has a remarkable collection of Styrian archaeological finds, including the small and rather strange Strettweg Ritual Chariot dating from the 7th century BC. The **Münzensammlung** (Numismatic Museum) is tucked away in a corner on the ground floor. The attractive outdoor café in the park surrounding the castle is the perfect place to fortify yourself before or after visiting the museums. ⊠ *Eggenberger Allee 90* ☎ *0316/583–264–0* ⊠ *Prunkräume with guided tour €6; for grounds only, €1; Abteilung für Vor- und Frühgeschichte and Münzensammlung €4.50* ☉ *Prunkräume and Jagdmuseum, Mar.–Nov., Tues.–Sun. hourly tours from 9–4; Abteilung für Vor- und Frühgeschichte and Münzensammlung, daily 9–4.*

⑱ Stadtpfarrkirche. The city parish church was built early in the 16th century and later received its Baroque facade and 18th-century spire. Tintoretto's *Assumption of the Virgin* decorates the altar. Badly damaged in World War II, the stained-glass windows were replaced in 1953 by a Salzburg artist, Albert Birkle, who included portrayals of Hitler and Mussolini as malicious spectators at the scourging of Christ (left window behind the high altar, fourth panel from the bottom on the right). Across the street begins a narrow lane named after Johann Bernhard Fischer von Erlach, the great architect of the Austrian Baroque, who was born in one of the houses here in 1666. ⊠ *Herrengasse 23* ☎ *0316/829684–20* ☉ *Daily, 7–7.*

㉖ Uhrturm (Clock Tower). This most famous landmark of Graz dates from the 16th century, though the clock mechanism is two centuries younger. The clock has four giant faces that might at first confuse you—until you realize that the *big* hands tell the hour and the *small* hands the minutes. At the time the clock was designed, this was thought to be easier to read at a distance. The 16th-century wooden parapet above the clock was once a post for firefighters, who kept a lookout on the city and sounded the alarm in case of fire.

Where to Stay & Eat

$$$–$$$$ ✕ **Iohan.** A flickering torch marks the Renaissance portal entrance to this chic restaurant, set under a low vaulted ceiling and enhanced by dramatic lighting from wall sconces and candles. Start with a selection of fish on a skewer over a bed of mango rice and shiitake mushrooms, then go on to grilled salmon and sautéed greens, or veal with a light cheese crust and crisp shoestring potatoes. The homemade mango sherbet with coconut milk is sublime. ⊠ *Landhausgasse 1* ☎ *0316/821312–0* ⚑ *Reservations essential* ▤ *AE, DC, MC, V* ☉ *Closed Sun.–Mon. No lunch.*

$$$–$$$$ ✕ **Stainzerbauer.** Known for its homestyle Styrian recipes that have been handed down for generations, this beloved Graz institution is located just a block down from the town cathedral and has charming, *gemütlich* rooms and servers wearing traditional dirndls and lederhosen. The tasty *Zwiebelrostbraten* (skirt steak) topped with loads of crispy fried onions would be better without a salty tomato-based sauce, while the grilled *Zander* (pike perch) doesn't quite click with its accompaniment of *Kraut* in paprika sauce. The *Häuptelsalat* is simply iceberg lettuce in a light vinaigrette, so try the Styrian salad with creamy pumpkin-seed oil dressing instead. In summertime, head for the cool courtyard and hone in on the meaty spare ribs, served on a wooden plank with garlic bread. ✉ *Bürgergasse 4* ☎ *0316/821106* ▤ *MC, V* ☉ *Closed Sun. and holidays.*

★ $$$ ✕ **Hofkeller.** With its vaulted ceiling and dark, gleaming wainscoting, the elegantly appointed Hofkeller offers the most innovative Italian cuisine in the city. The engaging waitstaff lets you linger over complimentary appetizers—Gaeta olives, cheese sticks, a variety of fresh-baked breads and jewel-green olive oil, as well as a plate of Parma ham, which is thinly sliced before your eyes on a big oak table in the center of the room—before bringing the huge blackboard menu to your table. Look for the generous arugula salad with loads of shaved Parmesan, pasta with salami and cherry tomatoes, and the lightly fried John Dory atop a mound of grilled vegetables. Guests are urged to sample a wine before ordering by the glass. ✉ *Hofgasse 8* ☎ *0316/832439* ⌂ *Reservations essential* ▤ *MC, V* ☉ *Closed Sun.*

$–$$$ ✕ **Sacher.** Joining the expanding enterprise of Sacher cafés in Austria's most prominent cities, the Graz Sacher's imperious location at the juncture of the Hauptplatz and Herrengasse lets you know it is *the* café in town. Everything is what you would hope for and expect from a Sacher Café—lots of gilt, crimson upholstery, and sparking chandeliers, and of course, the famous rich chocolate Sachertorte. Full meals are also served. ✉ *Herrengasse 6* ☎ *0316/8005–0* ▤ *AE, DC, MC, V* ☉ *Open daily.*

★ $–$$ ✕ **Altsteirische Schmankerlstub'n.** Arguably the best place in the city to experience authentic Styrian cooking, this old Graz institution is reminiscent of a cozy country cottage. Salads are a must here, prepared with that Styrian specialty, *Kürbiskernöl,* pumpkin-seed oil. Main courses include *Rinderschulterscherzl,* boiled beef with pumpkin puree and roasted potatoes, or chicken breast in a creamy herb sauce. A vegetarian menu is always offered. ✉ *Sackstrasse 10* ☎ *0316/833211* ▤ *No credit cards* ☉ *Open daily.*

$–$$ ✕ **Landhauskeller.** The magnificent centuries-old Landhaus complex, which houses Graz's provincial parliament and its armory, also includes a favorite traditional restaurant containing a labyrinth of charming Old World dining rooms set within the ancient arcaded Landhaus itself. Styrian beef is the main event here, but there are lots of other dishes to choose from, such as chicken breast in a sesame crust with herbed buttered noodles or *Käsespätzle,* little pasta dumplings in baked cheese with fried onions. ✉ *Schmiedgasse 9* ☎ *0316/830276* ▤ *AE, DC, MC, V* ☉ *Closed Sun. and late Dec.–mid-Jan.*

¢–$ ✕ **Mangold's Vollwertrestaurant.** Located near Südtirolerplatz, this popular vegetarian restaurant offers tasty dishes, served cafeteria-style. ✉ *Griesgasse 10* ☎ *0316/718002* ▤ *No credit cards* ☉ *No dinner Sat. Closed Sun.*

★ $$$$ ✕▨ **Grand Hotel Wiesler.** With five stars and a supreme location just across the Mur River from the Old City, the Wiesler is the grande dame of Graz hotels. Arnold Schwarzenegger checks in when he's in town, and Alfred Hitchcock was once a guest. It dates from the turn of the last century, as evidenced by its high ceilings and gracious proportions, and the decoration has Secessionist echoes. The modern guest rooms are subtly fetching with cherry-wood accents, plush carpeting, and striking fabrics. Striking, too, is the hotel's contempo-modern restaurant, Wiesler, which features one of the best and most daring menus in town. No foodie should miss chef Andreas Schabelreiter's spruce-needle melon sherbet, crépinette of lamb chop on balsamico lentils, or rabbit with asparagus-orange risotto. ⊠ *Grieskai 4–8, A-8020* ☎ *0316/7066–0* 🖷 *0316/ 7066–76* ⊕ *www.hotelwiesler.com* ⇨ *98 rooms* ᗡ *Restaurant, mini-bars, Internet, parking (fee)* ▭ *AE, DC, MC, V* �📶 *BP.*

$$$$ 🏨 **Schlossberg.** This robin's-egg-blue town house, tucked up against the foot of the Schlossberg, is owned by a former racecar driver who turned it into a hotel in 1982. The owner's wife is an avid art collector, and the tastefully furnished rooms display provincial antiques as well as 18th-century portraits, while the corridors are filled with modern art-works and an interesting display of old Styrian lamps. The outdoor pool, on a rocky terrace, offers a spectacular view of the city. ⊠ *Kaiser-Franz-Josef-Kai 30, A-8010* ☎ *0316/8070–0* 🖷 *0316/8070–160* ⊕ *www. schlossberg-hotel.at* ⇨ *55 rooms* ᗡ *Minibars, pool, gym, sauna, bar, Internet, meeting rooms, parking (fee)* ▭ *AE, DC, MC, V* 📶 *BP.*

★ $$$ 🏨 **Augarten.** A glass and chrome structure in the middle of a residen-tial neighborhood, the Augarten is Graz's newest, most chic hotel. It is also a virtual modern-art gallery (make sure to take the steps instead of the elevator to view the art at each landing), practically vying with the new Kunsthaus museum for the number of artworks displayed. The spa-cious guest rooms, all with terraces, are decorated with a cool, lean touch, yet offer the ultimate in luxury—heated wood floors, feather beds, and eye-catching, expensive fabrics. In a place like this, the clientele is equally stylish, and the young staff eager to please. Want to go for a midnight swim in the heated indoor pool? No problem—all facilities are open 24 hours. Breakfast is especially good, with little extras like can-dlelight and fresh-squeezed orange juice. The only drawback is that it's a 15-minute walk from the Altstadt. ⊠ *Schönaugasse 53, A-8010* ☎ *0316/20800* 🖷 *0316/20800–80* ⊕ *www.augarten.at* ⇨ *56 rooms* ᗡ *Restaurant, bar, minibars, indoor pool, sauna, fitness center, Inter-net, parking (fee)* ▭ *AE, DC, MC, V* 📶 *BP.*

$$$ 🏨 **Dom.** Occupying the 18th century Palais Inzaghi, the Dom has, hands down, the best location in Graz, smack in the center of the lively Alt-stadt. The high-ceilinged rooms are whimsically decorated, some with rather eye-popping color combinations, and each door has its own de-lightfully grotesque figurehead. The theme of the hotel is to indulge in the senses, and for that they provide CD players, mounted bottles of designer perfume for spritzing the air (a different fragrance for each room), and a bar of decadent handmade Styrian chocolate from the Zotter choco-late factory on your bed pillow. (Try the hot chocolate at breakfast, swiz-zling a melting chunk of Zotter chocolate in a cup of steaming milk.) Baths are on the small side, but have a lot of shelf space. The rooftop suite has a Jacuzzi on a secluded terrace. There is also a gourmet restau-rant in the courtyard called Mod (Dom backwards). ⊠ *Bürgergasse 14, A-8010* ☎ *0316/824800* 🖷 *0316/824800–8* ⊕ *www.domhotel.co.at* ⇨ *55 rooms* ᗡ *Restaurant, bar, minibars, a/c on upper floors, Inter-net, parking (fee)* ▭ *AE, DC, MC, V* 📶 *BP.*

$$$ ✕🏨 **Erzherzog Johann.** Travelers who prefer a traditionally elegant city hotel will be happy with this historic establishment in a 16th-century building. Its location, just steps from the Hauptplatz in the Old City, is perfect for tourists. Rooms are furnished charmingly, some in Biedermeier style, some with exotic themes and canopied beds in red or purple velvet. All rooms open onto a sunny atrium. ⊠ *Sackstrasse 3–5, A-8010* ☎ *0316/811616* 🖷 *0316/811515* ⊕ *www.erzherzog-johann. com* ↝ *62 rooms* ⚒ *Restaurant, café, minibars, sauna, bar, parking (fee); no a/c* ⊟ *AE, DC, MC, V* ❑ *BP, MAP.*

$$–$$$ 🏨 **Gollner.** A popular hotel since the mid-1800s and family-owned for four generations, the friendly Gollner is close to the Jakominiplatz and about a 10-minute walk from the Old City. Rooms are mostly contemporary in design, with soothing beige walls, soundproofed windows and plentiful space for toiletries in the bathrooms. More than half the Gollner's rooms are no-smoking, and there is no smoking allowed at breakfast, unusual for Austria. The staff is helpful, and sassy is the only word to describe the resident parrot. ⊠ *Schlögelgasse 14, A-8010* ☎ *0316/ 822521-0* 🖷 *0316/822521-7* ⊕ *www.hotelgollner.at* ↝ *50 rooms* ⚒ *Sauna, bar, Internet, parking (fee); no a/c* ⊟ *AE, DC, MC, V* ❑ *BP.*

$$ 🏨 **Kirchenwirt.** An inn has stood on this lofty knoll since 1695, initially providing beds to those who made the pilgrimage to Mariatrost, the magnificent, Rococo, daffodil-yellow hued basilica next door. Just 4 km (2.5 mi) northeast of Graz, the cheerful Kirchenwirt is in the middle of the quiet, lushly rolling countryside, so you may be awakened by a crowing rooster or muted church bells calling the monks faithful to prayer. A charming exterior of yellow walls and green shutters gives way to modern, pleasant rooms, with gorgeous vistas. And though you may be looking for rest and and relaxation, each room offers a high-speed Internet connection, with two hours free every day. A truly outstanding restaurant makes it worth your while to come for a meal, even if you're not staying here. In fine weather tables are spread under hundred-year-old chestnut trees overlooking the basilica, offering the perfect setting for a glass of Styrian wine from the award-winning wine cellar. ⊠ *Kaiser-Franz-Josef-Kai 30, A-8010* ☎ *0316/391112-0* 🖷 *0316/391112-49* ⊕ *www. kirchenwirtgraz.at* ↝ *55 rooms* ⚒ *Restaurant, minibars, sauna, Internet, meeting rooms, free parking; no a/c* ⊟ *AE, DC, MC, V* ❑ *BP, MAP.*

$ 🏨 **Mariahilf.** A comfortable old hotel in the center of things, the Mariahilf is just across the river from the Old City. Though the modern rooms are nothing fancy, the hotel is in a pedestrian zone, so the only noises you'll hear will be church bells and the sound of people hurrying to and fro. A tram stop is just steps away to take you to the city center, or you can cross one of the two nearby bridges and, in a short while, reach the Altstadt by foot. ⊠ *Mariahilferstrasse 9, A-8020* ☎ *0316/713163* 🖷 *0316/717652* ↝ *44 rooms* ⚒ *Parking (fee); no a/c* ⊟ *AE, DC, MC, V* ❑ *BP.*

¢ 🏨 **Strasser.** This friendly budget hotel, just two blocks south of the main train station, offers acceptable accommodations at rock-bottom prices. There is no elevator, the toilets are down the hall, and it can be a bit noisy, but, on the plus side, the rooms are large, comfortable, and clean, and the restaurant is a good value. Credit cards are not accepted for stays of only one night. ⊠ *Eggenberger Gürtel 11, A-8020* ☎ *0316/ 713977* 🖷 *0316/716856* ↝ *40 rooms, most without bath* ⚒ *Restaurant, parking (fee); no a/c, no TV in some rooms* ⊟ *MC, V* ❑ *BP.*

Nightlife & the Arts

Graz is noted for its avant-garde theater and its opera, concerts, and jazz. The Graz tourist office distributes the quarterly "Graz Guide," with information in English, and the "Graz Stadtanzeiger" ("City Informer"), a free monthly guide in German.

The **Styriarte** festival (late June to mid-July), under the direction of native son Nikolaus Harnoncourt—one of the most famous names in the early-music world—gathers outstanding musicians from around the world. Performances take place at Schloss Eggenburg and various halls in Graz. For program details contact the tourist office or **Styriarte** (✉ Palais Attems, Sackstrasse 17, A-8010 Graz ☎ 0316/812–9410 🖷 0316/825000–15 ⊕ www.styriarte.com www.steirischerbst.at).

The annual Steirische Herbst, or **Styrian Autumn Festival** (⊕ www.steirischerbst.at), a celebration of the avant-garde with the occasional shocking piece in experimental theater, music, opera, dance, jazz, film, video, and other performing arts, is held in Graz in October. Contact Styriarte or the tourist office for details.

A 19th-century opera house, the **Graz Opernhaus** (✉ Kaiser-Josef-Platz 10 ☎ 0316/8000 🖷 0316/8008–565 ⊕ www.buehnen-graz.com), with its resplendent Rococo interior, is a famed showcase for young talent and experimental productions as well as more conventional works; it stages three to five performances a week during its late September–June season. Tickets are generally available until shortly before the performances; call for information.

Graz, a major university town, has a lively theater scene known especially for its experimental productions. Its **Schauspielhaus,** built in 1825, is the leading playhouse, and there are smaller theaters scattered around town. Contact the tourist office for current offerings.

Graz's **after-hours scene** is centered on the area around Prokopigasse, Bürgergasse, and Glockenspielplatz. Here you'll find activity until the early-morning hours. The crowd is always on the move, so check with the tourist office for the current "in" spots. The **Casino Graz** (✉ Landhausgasse 10 ☎ 0316/832578), at the corner of Landhausgasse and Schmiedgasse in the Old City, is open daily from 3 PM. It offers French and American roulette, blackjack, baccarat, and punto banco. The entrance fee is €25. A passport is required, you must be at least 21, and men are expected to wear a jacket and tie, though it is not required.

Shopping

Graz is a smart, stylish city with great shopping. In the streets surrounding Sackstrasse you'll find top designer boutiques and specialty shops. Be on the lookout for traditional skirts, trousers, jackets, and coats of gray and dark green loden wool; dirndls; modern sportswear and ski equipment; handwoven garments; and objects of wrought iron. Take time to wander around the cobblestone streets of the Altstadt near the cathedral, where you'll come across several little specialty shops selling exotic coffees, wine, and cheese. The **Heimatwerk** shops at Paulustorgasse 4 and Herrengasse 10 are associated with the local folklore museum and stock a good variety of regional crafts and products. For a wide selection of wine and cheese, as well as hard-to-find Styrian cheese varieties, go to **Alles Käse**, at Paradeisgasse 1, near the Hauptplatz. **The English Bookshop** (✉ Tummelplatz 7 ☎0316/826266) is the only English-language bookstore in Graz, offering a great collection of current hardbacks as well as paperbacks and magazines. It's open Monday–Friday 9–6 and Saturday 9–noon.

Stübing bei Graz

⟳ ㉗ *15 km (9 mi) northwest of Graz.*

The attraction in Stübing bei Graz is the **Austrian Open-Air Museum** (Österreichisches Freilichtmuseum), which covers some 100 acres of hilly woodland. A fascinating collection of about 80 authentic farmhouses, barns, Alpine huts, working water mills, forges, and other rural structures dating from the 16th century through the early 20th century has been moved to this site from seemingly every province of Austria. Buildings that otherwise would have been lost in the rush to "progress" have been preserved complete with their original furnishings. Most are open to visitors, and in several of them artisans can be seen at work, sometimes in period costume. There is a restaurant and outdoor café by the entrance. You can reach Stübing bei Graz from Graz via Route 67 to Gratkorn, by train (15 minutes) to Stübing and a 2-km (1½-mi) walk from there, or by municipal bus (40 minutes) from Lendplatz. ✉ *Stübing bei Graz* ☎ *03124/ 53700* 🎟 *€7* ⊘ *Apr.–Oct., Tues.–Sun. 9–5 (last admission at 4).*

Piber

★ ⟳ ㉘ *44 km (27 mi) west of Graz.*

The hamlet of Piber on the northeast outskirts of Köflach (take Route 70 to and beyond Köflach) is devoted to raising horses, and from the **Lipizzaner Stud Farm** come the world-famous stallions that perform at the Spanish Riding School in Vienna. These snow-white horses trace their lineage back to 1580, when Archduke Karl of Styria established a stud farm at Lipica near Trieste, using stallions from Arabia and mares from Spain. After World War I, when Austria lost Lipica, the farm was transferred to the estate of Piber Castle (which can be seen when concerts are offered during the summer months). Born black, the steeds gradually turn white between the ages of two and seven. To get to Piber from Graz you can drive (take Route 70) or take a bus (75 minutes) or a train (about an hour), with departures every hour or two. Some trains split en route; be sure to board the correct car. Walk or take a taxi the 3 km (2 mi) between Köflach and Piber. There is a fine and festive restaurant, the Spanish Caballero ("The Spanish Horseman") on site in the castle. ✉ *Bundesgestüt Piber* ☎ *03144/3323* ⊕ *www.piber.com* 🎟 *Tour, €11* ⊘ *Nov.–Mar., daily 9–10:30 and 1:30–3:30, Apr.–Oct., daily 9–5:30 (last entrance at 4).*

Bärnbach

33 km (21 mi) west of Graz, 3 km (2 mi) north of Voitsburg.

Bärnbach offers the amazing vision of the **Church of St. Barbara**. Completely redone in 1988 by the late Austrian painter and architect Friedensreich Hundertwasser, its exterior is a fantasy of abstract religious symbols in brilliant colors and shapes.

At the interesting **Stölzle Glass Center** you can watch glass blowing and purchase original glass articles. ⊠ *Hochtregisterstrasse 1–3* ☎ *03142/ 62950* ⊕ *www.stoelzle.at* 🖃 *€5.50* ⊙ *Weekdays 9–5, Sat. 9–1; May–Oct. Last admission 1 hr prior to closing.*

THROUGH STYRIA TO VIENNA

The mountainous green heartland of Styria embraces a region where ancient Romans once worked the surrounding mines of what are accurately called the Iron Alps. Here in West Styria, the atmosphere can change abruptly from industrial to tourist. The prime destination, however, remains Mariazell. In the past, royalty—not only the Habsburgs but princes of foreign countries as well—went there, not for social pleasures but for religious reasons, for Mariazell has a double personality. It is a summer and winter pleasure resort as well as a renowned place of pilgrimage. The evening candlelit processions through the village to its famed basilica are beautiful and inspiring. To tour this region, you can head southwest, enjoying a scenic ride north through the Mur Valley to the historic crossroads of Bruck an der Mur. Here, where several highways and rail lines converge, you can head north to Mariazell and then continue on one of the country's most scenic mountain drives (or rail trips) back to the Danube Valley. The most direct route from Bruck an der Mur northward to Vienna, in fact, is also in some ways the most interesting. It takes you through the cradle of Austrian skiing, past several popular resorts, and over the scenic Semmering Pass, and offers an opportunity to ride a 19th-century steam cogwheel train to the top of the highest mountain in this part of the country, a peak that often remains snowcapped into summer. It also takes you to Wiener Neustadt, a small, historic city. This area's proximity to Vienna makes day trips or weekend excursions from the capital practical.

Peggau

㉙ *20 km (12 mi) north of Graz.*

Just north of the industrial town of Peggau (rail stop: Peggau-Deutschfeistritz) is the famous **Lurgrotte**, the largest stalactite and stalagmite cave in Austria. Guided tours lasting an hour follow a subterranean stream past illuminated sights, and there is a small restaurant at the entrance. To get to Peggau from Graz, head north on Route 67, driving through the heavily forested, narrow Mur Valley toward Bruck an der Mur. (A rail line parallels the road, with trains every hour or two making local stops near the points of interest.) ☎ *03127/2580* 🖃 *1-hr tour €5, 2-hr tour €8* ⊕ *www.lurgrotte.com* ⊙ *Apr.–Oct., daily 9–4.*

Mixnitz

20 km (12 mi) north of Peggau.

Mixnitz is the starting point for a rugged 4½-hour hike through the wild ㉚ **Bärenschützklamm,** a savage gorge that can be negotiated only on steps

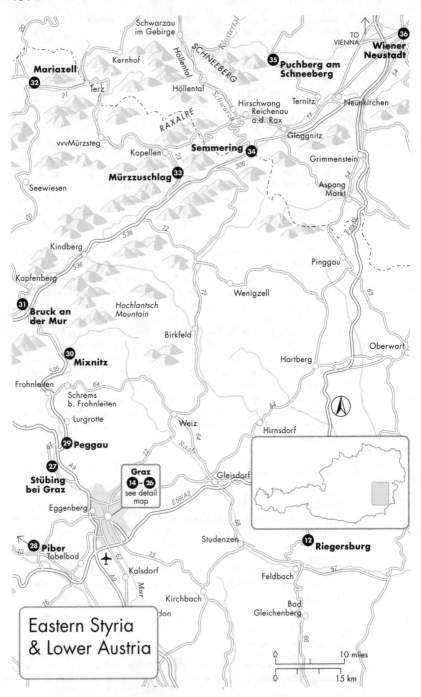

Eastern Styria
& Lower Austria

and ladders but is nevertheless worth visiting for its spectacular foaming waterfalls. Beyond it are peaceful mountain meadows and finally the 5,650-foot Hochlantsch mountain.

Bruck an der Mur

③ *55 km (34 mi) north of Graz.*

Bruck an der Mur is known primarily as Styria's major traffic junction, a point where four valleys and two rivers converge and where several highways and main rail lines come together. Although most of the busy town is devoted to industry, its compact historic center, dating partially from the 13th century, is well worth a short visit.

The architecturally distinguished main square, **Koloman-Wallisch-Platz**, is four blocks west of the train station. On the square's northeast corner stands the late-15th-century **Kornmesserhaus**, a magnificent example of secular architecture in the late-Gothic style, noted especially for its elaborate loggia and arcades. The filigreed **Eiserner Brunnen** is across the square. This ornamental wrought-iron well housing dating from 1620 is considered to be the best piece of ironwork in Styria, a province noted for fine metalwork. The **Rathaus** (Town Hall; ⊠ Hauptplatz ☎ 03862/890111) facing it is also attractive and houses a small museum of local life. On the hill behind the square is the **Pfarrkirche** (Parish Church), built between the 13th and 15th centuries, which has an interesting late-Gothic sacristy door of wrought iron.

Overlooking the town, just two blocks northeast of its center, are the remains of **Burg Landskron**, a 13th-century fortress that once defended the confluence of the Mur and Mürz rivers. Today only its clock tower remains intact, but the view is worth the short climb. The small park surrounding the Landskron ruins, on the Schlossberg hill, makes a wonderful spot for a picnic. Buy your supplies at one of the shops in the streets below.

Where to Eat

★ **$$$$** ✕ **Wirtshaus Steirereck.** The sign "Griasdi"—Styrian dialect for "Greetings"—welcomes all to this charming, green-shuttered farmhouse. It's northwest of Bruck an der Mur, but it's well worth the trek to get here, as owner and chef Heinz Reitbauer—son of the owner of the famous Steirereck in Vienna—has created possibly the most unusual restaurant in the country, one-half gourmand restaurant, one-half working farm. There are goats and other farm animals in a fenced enclosure, while indoors the many dining rooms retain the farmhouse-rustic decor of the early part of the 20th century. Especially good are the crispy farm duck for two, served with light homemade dumplings, *Backhendl* (fried chicken adorably served in a toy-sized feeding trough), Styrian beef, and fresh fish. The restaurant also offers its own microbrewed beer and a good selection of wines by the glass. To get to Wirtshaus Steirereck, take Route 116 north toward St. Lorenzen, exiting at St. Marein. From there follow signs to Pogusch. ⊠ *Pogusch 21, St. Lorenzen* ☎ *03863/2000* 🖷 *03863/515151* ⌖ *Reservations essential* ▭ *No credit cards* ☉ *Closed Mon.–Wed. and first 3 wks of Jan.*

Mariazell

★ *50 km (29 mi) north of Bruck an der Mur.*

An excursion to Mariazell—famed for its pilgrimage church and gingerbread—is an adventure, thanks to the winding road that brings you there. The town has been a place of pilgrimage since 1157, when the Benedictines established a priory here. After Louis I, King of Hungary, attributed his victory over the Turks in 1377 to the intervention of its Virgin, Mariazell's reputation for miracles began to spread. As a year-round resort, Mariazell offers a wide panoply of sports and recreation; in winter there's a good ski school for beginners and young people. The impressive **Mariazeller Basilica** stands resolutely over the town square. The present structure replaced the original church during the 14th century and was itself enlarged in the late 17th century by the Italian architect Domenico Sciassia. Its exterior is unusual, with the original Gothic spire and porch flanked by squat, bulbous Baroque towers. Step inside to see the incredibly elaborate plasterwork and paintings. In the **Gnadenkapelle** (Chapel of Miracles), the nave holds the main object of pilgrimage: the 12th-century statue of the Virgin of Mariazell. It stands under a silver baldachin (canopy) designed in 1727 by the younger Fischer von Erlach and behind a silver grille donated by Empress Maria Theresa, who took her first communion here. Following her example, thousands of youngsters neatly turned out in white are brought annually from all over Austria to Mariazell for their first communion, usually on or around Whitsun. The **high altar** of 1704, by the elder Fischer von Erlach—the leading architect of the Austrian Baroque—is in the east end of the nave. Don't miss seeing the **Schatzkammer** (treasury) for its collection of votive offerings from medieval times to the present. Walls are covered with plaques, many of them illustrated, given in thanks for assorted blessings, including rescues from a variety of hazards ranging from runaway horses to shipwrecks. ✉ *Basilica free, Schatzkammer €3* ☉ *Schatzkammer May–Oct., Tues.–Sat. 10–3, Sun. 11–4.*

Pay a visit to the **Heimatmuseum** (Regional Museum of Local Life; ✉ Wienerstrasse 35 ☎ 03382/2366). Bruno Habertheuer's **mechanical Nativity figurines** are at the **stations of the cross** (✉ Kalvarienberg 1) on Calvary Hill. The nativity scene with its 130 moving figures took 18 years to build. Admission to the museum is €3.50.

☾ The **Museumtramway,** the world's oldest steam tramway, dating from 1884, operates between Mariazell and the Erlaufsee, for a 20-minute ride of about 3½ km (2 mi) to a lovely lake. For €10 extra charge, you can accompany the engineer in the cab. ✉ *Bahnhof Mariazell* ☎ *03882/3014* ✉ *Round-trip €8* ☉ *July–Sept., weekends only, 10–5.*

The famous narrow-gauge **Mariazellerbahn** rail line ambles over an 84-km (52½ mi) route between Mariazell and St. Pölten, coursing through magnificent valleys and surmounting mountain passes in the process. This remarkable engineering achievement—the line incorporates 21 tunnels and 75 bridges and viaducts—was built in 1907 and electrified in 1911. The cars are modern but the sensation is one of ages long past. About five trains a day traverse the route in each direction. In St. Pölten, the narrow-gauge line connects with the main east–west rail route. For schedules, contact the Tourist Office (☎ 03882/2366).

Where to Stay & Eat

★ **$$** ✕ **Alpenhotel Gösing.** A breathtaking alpine road leads to this gabled early-20th-century hotel, which looks like it was the setting for Alfred Hitchcock's *The Lady Vanishes.* There is nothing up here except the hotel, a story-book train station, the woods with hiking trails, and gorgeous scenery everywhere you turn. The spacious, *gemütlich* lobby with its cozy groupings of chintz-covered chairs and sofas is the perfect place to relax with a book and a cup of tea. Rooms are really charming, with cheery floral curtains and duvets in pastel shades. Try to get one with a panoramic balcony facing Ötscher mountain. Some of the baths have stunning original 1930s tiles and fixtures, others are more modern. Half-pension is optional, but the remote location doesn't give you much choice, and, though the kitchen isn't exactly innovative, healthy dishes are emphasized. ⊠ *Gösing an der Mariazellerbahn, A-3221* ☎ *02728/ 217* 🖷 *02728/ 217–116* ⊕ *www.goesing.at* 🖘 *74 rooms* 🖑 *Restaurant, indoor pool, sauna, bar; Internet, no a/c* 🖃 *DC, MC, V* ❣ *BP, MAP.*

$ ✕ **Mariazellerhof.** This small, cheerfully modern chalet-style hotel one block west of the basilica is known for its gingerbread snacks; the spicy aroma fills the house. Its comfortable rooms have balconies. ⊠ *Graz- erstrasse 10, A-8630* ☎ *03882/2179–0* 🖷 *03882/2179–51* 🖘 *10 rooms with bath, 4 with shower* 🖑 *Café, minibars; no a/c* 🖃 *MC, V* ❣ *BP.*

Sports

The skiing on 4,150-foot **Bürgeralpe** is quickly reached by the Bürger- alpebahn cable car from a lower station just two blocks north of the basilica. Paths from the upper station fan out in several directions for country walks in summer. ⊠ *Wienerstrasse 28* ☎ *03882/2555* 🖾 *Round- trip €10* ☉ *Daily 9–5.*

Shopping

Parts of town are permeated by the spicy aroma of baking **gingerbread**, for which Mariazell is famous, and you'll see the decorated cookies every- where.

Mürzzuschlag

❸ *37 km (23 mi) northeast of Bruck an der Mur, 92 km (57 mi) north of Graz.*

The resort town of Mürzzuschlag is popular for both winter and sum- mer sports. From Bruck an der Mur, head northeast on S6, past the in- dustrial town of Kapfenberg, and take the exit marked for the resort. It is regarded as the birthplace of Austrian skiing and, in a sense, of the Winter Olympics, since the first Nordic Games were held here in 1904, but the main focus of ski activity has long since moved west to the Tirol.

Mürzzuschlag is popular with the Viennese and preserves its past glo- ries in the excellent **Winter-Sports-Museum**, which displays equipment past and present from around the world. ⊠ *Wienerstrasse 13* ☎ *03852/3504* 🖾 *€4* ☉ *Tues.–Sun. 9–noon and 2–5.*

The **Brahms Museum,** Austria's only museum dedicated to composer Johannes Brahms, a German who adopted Austria as his home, is in Mürzzuschlag, where he spent many summers. The museum also hosts a number of chamber music concerts and recitals. ⊠ *Wienerstrasse 4* ☎ *03852/3434* ⊕ *www.brahmsmuseum.at* ⊠ *€4* ⊗ *Open daily 9–noon and 2–5.*

Semmering

★ ㉞ *14 km (8½ mi) northeast of Mürzzuschlag, 90 km (56¼ mi) southwest of Vienna.*

Climbing along Route 306, high atop the Semmering Pass, at a height of 3,230 feet, lies the boundary between the provinces of Styria and Lower Austria. A bridle path has existed on this mountainous route since at least the 12th century, but the first road was not built until 1728. Today's highway is an engineering wonder, particularly on the Lower Austrian side, where the road, high on concrete stilts, leaps over deep valleys; the old road snakes up in a series of switchback curves. The Styrian side is less dramatic, but offers distant Alpine vistas. Given the technologies of the era, the railway—completed in 1854—that crosses the divide is a technical marvel, with its great viaducts and tunnels, and is still the main north–south rail route. At the top is Semmering, the first town in Lower Austria, a resort on a south-facing slope overlooking the pass. Sheltered by pine forests and built on terraces reaching as high as 4,250 feet, Semmering is considered to have a healthy atmosphere and has several spa-type hotels and pensions. In the early 20th century, Sigmund Freud, Oskar Kokoschka, Arthur Schnitzler, and Gustav Mahler were frequent visitors. Wealthy Viennese also came here for their *Sommerfrische* (summer vacation), and many built grand villas for the purpose, whose exteriors you can observe. The Semmering area plus the nearby Rax and Schneeberg regions are immensely popular with Viennese skiers in winter. This is the area in which most Viennese first learn to ski, meaning that there are slopes ranging from gentle inclines to the more challenging, although they are no match for the rugged Alpine stretches of Tirol and Salzburg province.

off the beaten path

HÖLLENTAL – A delightful side trip can be made from Semmering into the Höllental (Valley of Hell), an extremely narrow and romantic gorge cut by the Schwarza stream between two high mountains, the Raxalpe and the Schneeberg. From Hirschwang, at the beginning of the valley, you can ride the **Raxbahn cable car** to a plateau on the Raxalpe at 5,075 feet. ☎ *02666/52497* ⊠ *Round-trip €17* ⊗ *High season, Mon.–Fri. 8–5:30, Sat.–Sun. 8–6, at ½-hr intervals; other months, daily 9–4:30 at ½-hr intervals.*

Where to Stay & Eat

¢–$ ✕ **Seewirts Haus.** A rustic Tyrolean-style cottage at the base of the Hirschkogel in the center of town, the Seewirts has a large terrace for dining in summer (or for ski-watching on sunny winter days), and a cozy country-kitchen feel indoors. The menu is simple and hearty, offering such mountain staples as goulash soup, *Kasnockerl,* little pasta dumplings baked with cheese and served in a skillet, or grilled Bratwurst with french fries. ☒ *Zauberberg 2* ☎ *02664/20030* ☰ *DC, MC, V* ⊘ *Closed Mon.–Tues. in summer.*

★ **$$$–$$$$** ✕🍴 **Hotel Panhans.** Built in 1888, the Panhans is a classic and popular mountain-lodge resort near the center of town. The main lodge has retained its characteristic Art Nouveau ambience, while a luxurious modern annex is connected by an enclosed walkway to the main building. Rooms are varied and quite large, some with faux French Empire furniture and others with alcove-equipped sleeping areas and a Jugendstil slant. A few rooms offer balconies, but all have spectacular views. The elegant Wintergarten restaurant offers fine dining at reasonable prices, and the menu may include poached char in a light crayfish butter sauce with cilantro noodles, or crispy duck breast with leek ravioli. The more casual Kaiser Karl is for guests choosing half-pension. Wines are excellent, and the hotel has its own Vinotek for tastings. ☒ *Hochstrasse 32, A-2680* ☎ *02664/8181–0* 🖷 *02664/8181–513* ⊕ *www.panhans.at* ⤵ *113 rooms* ⟡ *2 restaurants, café, minibars, indoor pool, gym, sauna, bar, dance club, Internet; no a/c* ☰ *AE, DC, MC, V* 🍴 *BP, MAP.*

★ **$$$** 🍴 **Panoramahotel Wagner.** One of a handful of "bio" (ecologically friendly) hotels in Austria, this unique family-owned establishment offers rooms with beechwood floors, attractive unbleached fabrics, clean-lined furniture entirely free of nails, and balconies with panoramic views. Walls are a serene sea-green or butterscotch. Baths are state-of-the-art, with temperature-controlled showers and heated towel racks. Dedicated owner Josef Wagner is also the chef, and his delicious buffet dinners are a tribute to the organic produce of the area. Half-pension is included in the room price. The hotel is no-smoking, except for a few tables in the restaurant. ☒ *Hochstrasse 267, A-2680* ☎ *02664/2512–0* 🖷 *02664/2512–61* ⊕ *www.panoramahotel-wagner.at* ⤵ *24 rooms* ⟡ *Restaurant, sauna; no a/c, no room TVs* ☰ *No credit cards* ⊘ *Closed various weeks in Nov. and Apr.* 🍴 *BP, MAP.*

Puchberg am Schneeberg

③⑤ *33 km (21 mi) north of Semmering.*

People flock to the quiet mountain resort of Puchberg am Schneeberg mostly to ride to the top of the Schneeberg mountain, Lower Austria's highest peak. You get to Puchberg via regular trains from Vienna, Wiener Neustadt, or points south. From Vienna, the railroads have a package ticket that includes the regular rail connection, the cog railway, and a chit for lunch at one of the mountaintop restaurants. From Höllental, continue north into the valley for 18 km (11 mi), passing through the wildest section, to Schwarzau im Gebirge. Then circle the north slope of the Schneeberg via the Klostertal to the resort.

🜂 The marvelous old narrow-gauge **Puchberg cog-wheel steam train** ascends to a plateau near Schneeberg's summit. Although many use the rail line as a starting point for mountain hiking, the journey itself is an exciting outing. Allow the better part of a day for this trip, since the ride takes nearly 90 minutes each way and the trains are none too frequent, some running on a schedule and others according to demand. This excursion is very popular; make reservations well in advance—particularly for weekends and holidays—at any rail station in Europe. If you haven't already made them, be sure to make reservations at Puchberg for the return trip before you board for the trip up. Bring along a light sweater or jacket even in summer; it can be both windy and cool at the top. Ordinary walking shoes are sufficient unless you wander off the main trails, in which case you'll need hiking boots, along with some mountain experience. (You can also take the quicker, more frequent **Salamander diesel train,** which takes less than an hour.)

The steam engines, dating from the 1890s, are built at a peculiar angle to the ground to keep their fireboxes level while climbing. The wooden cars they haul are of equal vintage, with hard seats. Near the upper station hut at an altitude of 5,892 feet are the small **Elizabeth Chapel** and the **Berghaus Hochschneeberg,** a simple lodge with a restaurant and overnight guest facilities. From here, you can walk to the **Kaiserstein** for a panoramic view and to the **Klosterwappen** peak, at 6,811 feet. Real stick-to-your-ribs mountain food, draft beer, and plenty of gemütlichkeit are served up at the inexpensive **Damböck Haus,** a rustic hut operated by the Austrian Touring Club (*ÖTK*). It's only a 15-minute walk from the upper station of the Puchberg line.

Allow about two to three hours total for these walks. Maps are available at the lodge. For departure times for the Salamander diesel train and Puchberg cog-wheel train, check the Web site below. ✉ *Schneeberg Bahn, Bahnhof Puchberg* ☎ *02636/3661–20* 📠 *02636–3262* ⊕ *www. schneebergbahn.at* 🚂*Cog-wheel steam train, round-trip €28; Salamander diesel train, round-trip €27* 🕑 *Cog-wheel steam train, late June–Sept. 1; Salamander diesel train, late Apr.–early Nov.*

Don't miss a drive along the **Hohe Wand** (High Wall), a scenic nature park east of Puchberg (from Puchberg, go east past Grünbach to Oberhöflein, where you turn left at the sign for Hohe Wand). The spectacular route has many twists and turns leading to the limestone plateau, and there are several simple country inns along the way that provide good bases for hiking. The 4 km (2½ mi) road ends at the top at Kleine Kanzel in the west and Herrgottschnitzerhaus in the east, so you must retrace your route down along the Panoramastrasse, unless you're mountain biking, or hiking. Also worth a visit is the **Heimatmuseum** (open mid-April to mid-September, on Saturday 3–5 and Sunday 9:30–11:30 and 3–5), with displays of local artifacts.

Where to Stay & Eat

★ **$$–$$$** ✕🏨 **Schneeberghof.** Across the street from Puchberg am Schneeberg's tiny train station, this 100-year-old chalet-hotel with a modern annex is nestled at the foot of the towering Schneeberg. It's a popular spot for sports lovers, and King Juan Carlos of Spain is a regular guest during hunting season. Rooms are large, with contemporary furnishings and pastel fabrics, and all have balconies. The restaurant, with live folk music on weekends, has a selection of delicious fish and meat dishes, including grilled *Welsfilet* (catfish) and pork medallions in a honey herb sauce. The Schneeberghof also offers a "Teddy Bear" weekend year-round, which provides two nights with half pension at great value. ✉ *Wiener Neustädterstrasse*

24, A-2734 ☎ *02636/3500* 🖨 *02636/3233* ⊕ *www.tiscover.com/ schneeberghof* 🖪 *74 rooms* ⚭ *Restaurant, minibars, tennis courts, indoor pool, sauna, Internet; no a/c* ▤ *AE, DC, MC, V* ⅠⓄⅠ *BP, MAP.*

Wiener Neustadt

㉞ *19 km (12 mi) southeast of Puchberg am Schneeberg, 45 km (28¼ mi) south of Vienna, 38 km (23¾ mi) northeast of Semmering, 27 km (16¾ mi) west of Eisenstadt.*

Although today's Wiener Neustadt is a busy industrial center built on the ashes of its prewar self, enough of its past glories survived World War II's bombings to make a visit worthwhile. The small city was established in 1194 as a fortress to protect Vienna from the Hungarians. During the mid-15th century it was an imperial residence, and in 1752 it became, and still is, the seat of the Austrian Military Academy.

Begin your exploration of the Old City at the **Hauptplatz,** the largely traffic-free main square, which contains several rebuilt medieval houses with Gothic arcades standing opposite the 16th-century **Rathaus** (City Hall). The mighty **Stadtpfarrkirche** (town parish church), also known as the Liebfrauenkirche, rises imposingly out of the center of Domplatz, or Cathedral Square. Begun in the 13th century, the church had cathedral status from 1468 until 1784, and a number of choirs and chapels were added during that period. Note the ornate entryway on the south side, dating from about 1230. Styles are mixed between Romanesque and Gothic, but the interior is impressive for its unity of columned walls and ribbed ceiling. Look for the painted wooden figures of the Apostles dating from about 1500, a mural of the Last Judgment from about 1300, and the splendid tomb of Cardinal Khlesl with a bust carved in 1630 attributed to the school of Giovanni Bernini, the master of the Italian Baroque.

A narrow lane called the Puchheimgasse leads to the 12th-century **Reckturm,** a defensive tower said to have been built with part of the ransom money paid to free Richard the Lion-Hearted. Down Baumkirchnerring at the corner of Wienerstrasse is the 14th-century **Church of St. Peter-an-der-Sperr,** once a defense cloister, now an exhibition gallery. The greatest treasure in the **Stadtmuseum,** which is in a onetime Jesuit residence on Wienerstrasse, is the Corvinusbecher, an elegant 32-inch-high goblet from 1487 that was a gift from the Hungarian king who conquered the town. To the east of the Hauptplatz, on Neuklostergasse, is the **Neukloster Church,** part of a Cistercian convent founded in 1250. Behind the high altar in the richly Baroque interior is the tomb of Eleanor of Portugal (died 1467), wife of the emperor Frederick III. Mozart's Requiem was first performed here in 1793. The massive **Burg** on Grazerstrasse, a castle begun in the 13th century and rebuilt as an imperial residence in the 15th century, was designated the Austrian Military Academy by order of Empress Maria Theresa in 1752. The Nazis took it over in 1938, and its first German commandant was General Erwin Rommel, the Desert Fox. The complex was battered by bombing in 1943 and 1945 but subsequently rebuilt. Enter its grounds through the south gate to visit the famous 15th-century **Church of St. George** (you will need to be escorted by a guard), whose exterior gable is decorated with, among others, 14

Habsburg coats of arms. Beneath the gable is a statue of Friedrich III, curiously inscribed with "A.E.I.O.U.," which some believe stands for the Latin words meaning "Austria will last until the end of the world." Inside the church, under the steps of the high altar, the remains of Emperor Maximilian I are buried.

Where to Stay & Eat

$$$$ ✕ **Gelbes Haus.** The 1906 art deco "Yellow House," slightly north of the center, offers limited but outstandingly prepared dishes served in tasteful surroundings. Look for grilled *Steinbutt* (turbot) with *Eierschwammerl* (chanterelle) lasagne, tender medallions of venison with cranberry sauce, and, for dessert, silky mango crepes with fresh ginger and berries. The homemade sherbets are also outstanding. The wine selection is broad, by the glass as well as the bottle. ⊠ *Kaiserbrunngasse 11* ☎ *02622/26400* ⊟ *DC, MC* ⊘ *Closed Sun.–Mon.*

$$ ✕☷ **Hotel Corvinus.** A modern, unexceptional hotel next to the city park, the Corvinus is the best choice in town. Located two blocks east of the train station and only a few minutes' stroll from the main square, it caters primarily to business travelers. Rooms are spartan but clean and have all the amenities. The restaurant serves surprisingly sophisticated fare. ⊠ *Bahngasse 29–33, A-2700* ☎ *02622/24134* ⊠ *02622/24139* ⊕ *www.hotel-corvinus.at* ⊷ *68 rooms* ⟁ *Restaurant, minibars, sauna, Internet, meeting rooms; no a/c* ⊟ *AE, DC, MC, V* ☷ *BP, MAP.*

Nightlife

The **Wiesen Jazz Festival** (⊕ www.wiesen.at) attracts top-name performers from America and around the world for a couple of days in early July in Wiesen, Burgenland (12 km [7½ mi], southeast of Wiener Neustadt). For information, contact Landesverband Burgenland Tourismus or check out the Wiesen Web site.

EASTERN AUSTRIA A TO Z

To research prices, get advice from other travelers, and book travel arrangements, visit www.fodors.com.

AIR TRAVEL

The northern part of Eastern Austria is served by Vienna's international airport at Schwechat, 19 km (12 mi) southeast of the city center (*see* Vienna A to Z *in* Chapter 1).

Graz has its own international airport at Thalerhof, just south of the city, with flights to and from Vienna, Innsbruck, Linz, Munich, Frankfurt, Düsseldorf, and Zürich. Austrian Airlines and its subsidiary Tyrolean Airways, as well as Lufthansa, are the major carriers. Call the number listed below for information.

🛈 Airlines and Contacts **Graz Airport** ☎ 0316/2902–0.

BIKE TRAVEL

Bicycling is enormously popular in the flatlands around Lake Neusiedl. There are several places that rent bikes, listed below.

🛈 Bike Rentals **Fahrradverleih Waldherr** ⊠ Hauptstrasse 42, Podersdorf ☎ 02177/2297. **Hotel Wende** ⊠ Seestrasse 40, Neusiedl am See ☎ 02167/8111–0. **Mike's Rad-**

verleih ✉ Strandgasse 9, Podersdorf ☎ 02177/2411. **Mürner** ✉ Friedhofgasse 5, Illmitz ☎ 02175/2756 ⊕ www.radverleih.at. **Posch** ✉ Blumentalgasse 9, Mörbisch ☎ 02685/8242. **Schneeberger** ✉ Rathausplatz 15, Rust ☎ 02685/6442.

BUS TRAVEL

There is good bus service to Neusiedl am See, Eisenstadt, and Güssing in Burgenland; Mariazell in Styria; and Wiener Neustadt in Lower Austria. Direct express service to Graz is infrequent. Most buses leave Vienna from the Wien Mitte Bus Station on Landstrasser Hauptstrasse, opposite the air terminal and Hilton Hotel, but be sure to check first, since some services to the south may depart from the bus terminal area at Südtirolerplatz, to the west of the Südbahnhof rail station. A major bus service connecting Vienna to towns in Eastern Austria is Blaguss Reisen.

Post office and railroad buses cover the area thoroughly, although services are less frequent in the less populated areas more distant from city centers. Take trains for the main routes.

🚌 Bus Information **Blaguss Reisen** ☎ 01/501-80-0 🖷 01/501-80-299 ⊕ www.blaguss.at.

CAR RENTAL

Cars can be rented at all airports. Within Graz there are also several locations.

🚗 Major Agencies **Avis** ✉ Schlögelgasse 10, Graz ☎ 0316/812920 🖷 0316/841178. **Buchbinder** ✉ Keplerstrasse 93–95, Graz ☎ 0316/717330 🖷 0316/718843. **Budget** ✉ Airport, Graz ☎ 0316/2902–342 ✉ Europaplatz 12, Graz ☎ 0316/722074 🖷 0316/722076. **Hertz** ✉ Andreas-Hofer-Platz 1, Graz ☎ 0316/825007 🖷 0316/810288.

CAR TRAVEL

Two main autobahns traverse this region: the A3 between Vienna and Eisenstadt and the heavily traveled A2 between Vienna and past Wiener Neustadt to Graz and farther south. Northern Burgenland can be reached via the A4 autobahn east out of Vienna.

Driving is the most scenic way to explore Eastern Austria, especially if you're visiting the smaller towns and villages. Route 10 from Vienna to Lake Neusiedl in Burgenland is the preferred scenic alternative to the A4 autobahn. Graz is connected to Vienna by both A2 and a more scenic mountain road, Route S6 over the Semmering Pass to Bruck an der Mur, then south through the Mur Valley. Driving in the Graz city center is not advisable, because there are many narrow, one-way, and pedestrian streets and few places to park.

EMERGENCIES

Each Apotheke (pharmacy) posts a sign with information about the nearest pharmacy that will be open late. Also, the daily regional newspaper *Kleine Zeitung* lists those pharmacies with late-night hours in the area.

🚑 Emergency services **Ambulance** ☎ 144. **Fire** ☎ 122. **Medical Service** ✉ Graz ☎ 141. **Police** ☎ 133.

SPORTS & OUTDOOR ACTIVITIES

BOATING You can hire boats (*Bootsvermietung* or *Bootsverleih*) around Lake Neusiedl. Expect to pay about €4 per hour for a rowboat, €6 for a pedal boat, and €10–€20 for an electric boat; sailboat prices vary widely. There are several businesses in the area.

🏢 **Baumgartner** ⊠ Neusiedl am See ☎ 02167/2782. **Knoll** ⊠ Podersdorf ☎ 02177/2443. **Ruster Freizeitcenter** ⊠ Rust ☎ 02685/595.

SKIING   The best place to ski near Vienna is Semmering. Near Mariazell is the Bürgeralpe. Another good option is the Schneeberg, where you can take a train to the summit. Great cross-country skiing can be found in western Styria on the 50-km (31-mi) Murtal Loipe, the 30-km (19-mi) Tauern-Süd-Loipe, and the 12-km (7½-mi) Katschtal-Sonnen-Loipe, all near Murau. Adults and children can learn to ski at the Franz Skazel Ski School.

🏢 **Bürgeralpe** ⊠ Mariazell, A-8630 ☎ 03882/2555 🖳 03882/2555–15. **Cross-Country Ski Information (Murtal Loipe, Tauern-Süd-Loipe, and Katschtal-Sonnen-Loipe)** ⊠ Murau, A-8850 ☎🖳 03532/2720. **Franz Skazel Ski School** ⊠ Mariazellerstrasse 19, Mürzzuschlag, A-8680 ☎ 03852/2615–2. **Schneeberg** ⊠ Puchberg am Schneeberg, A-2734 ☎ 02636/2256 or 02636/3605 🖳 02636/3262. **Semmering** ⊠ A-2680 ☎ 02664/20025 🖳 02664/20029 ⊕ www.semmering.com.

TOURS

Relatively few guided tours visit Eastern Austria, and those that do are conducted in German, although English may be available on request. Inquire when booking. General orientation tours depart from Vienna and last one to four days. The one-day tours are usually to Lake Neusiedl and include a boat ride or to the Semmering mountain region with a cable-car ride. There are a couple of reputable operators, listed below.

🏢 **Fees & Schedules Cityrama Sightseeing** ⊠ Börsegasse 1, A-1010 Vienna ☎ 01/534-130 🖳 01/534-13-28. **Vienna Sightseeing Tours** ⊠ Stelzhammergasse 4/11, 1030 Vienna ☎ 01/712-4683-0 🖳 01/714-1141.

WALKING TOURS   Guided walking sightseeing tours of Graz in English and German are conducted Tues.–Wed. and Fri.–Sun. at 2:30, April–October, and on Saturdays at 2:30 November–March. The meeting point for these tours is Tourist Information at Herrengasse 16. The cost is €7.50. Guided tours of the Schlossberg are conducted daily Easter–October, departing hourly 9–5 from the Glockenturm (Bell Tower) near the upper station of the Schlossberg funicular. The cost is €2.15, with a minimum of five people. For more information, contact the city tourist office.

TAXIS

In Graz, taxis can be ordered by phone.

🏢 Taxi Companies **Taxis** ☎ 0316/1718, 0316/2204, 0316/222, or 0316/2801.

TRAIN TRAVEL

Vienna and Graz are the logical rail arrival or departing points for this part of Austria. The main international north–south route connecting Vienna and northeastern Italy runs through this region and is traversed by EuroCity trains from Munich, Salzburg, Linz, Klagenfurt, and Venice, as well as other cities in neighboring countries. Nearly all long-distance trains going through this region meet at Bruck an der Mur, where connections can be made.

If you're not driving, take trains on the main routes; services are fast and frequent. Trains depart from Vienna's Südbahnhof (South Station) hourly for the one-hour ride to Neusiedl am See. Connections can be made there for Eisenstadt and Pamhagen. There is also express service every two hours from the same station in Vienna to Graz, 2½ hours away, with intermediate stops at Wiener Neustadt, Mürzzuschlag, and Bruck an der Mur, and connections to Puchberg am Schneeberg, Semmering, and points west. Trains for Mariazell depart from Vienna's Westbahnhof (West Station), with a change at St. Pölten. Call the number listed below for information on departures throughout Austria.

🚆 Train Information **ÖBB−National Train Information Line** ☎ 05/1717.

TRANSPORTATION AROUND EASTERN AUSTRIA

In Graz, streetcars and buses (see below for information) are an excellent way of traveling within the city. Single tickets (€1.45) can be bought from the driver, and one-day and multiple-ride tickets are also available. All six streetcar routes converge at Jakominiplatz near the south end of the Old City. One fare may combine streetcars and buses as long as you take a direct route to your destination.

🚌 **Bus Information−Stadtbus Verkehr** ☎ 0316/887411.

TRAVEL AGENCIES

There are two popular travel agencies in Graz.

🧳 Local Agents **Reisebüro Kuoni** ✉ Sackstrasse 6 ☎ 0316/824571-0 🖨 0316/824571-6. **Ruefa** ✉ Opernring 9 ☎ 0316/829775-0 🖨 0316/829775-32.

VISITOR INFORMATION

The regional tourist information office for Burgenland province is the Landesverband Burgenland Tourismus. For information on Lower Austria, call the Niederösterreich Tourismus in Vienna. For Styria, the provincial tourist office is Steirische Tourismus. There are several helpful local *Fremdenverkehrsämter* (tourist offices), listed below by town.

🛈 Tourist Information **Bruck an der Mur Tourismusverband** ✉ Koloman-Wallisch-Platz 1, A-8600 ☎ 03862/890-121 🖨 03862/890-102 ⊕ www.bruckmur.at/wirtschaft/u1194.htm. **Eisenstadt Tourismus** ✉ Schloss Esterházy, A-7000 ☎ 02682/67390 🖨 02682/67391 ⊕ www.burgenland.at. **Grazer Tourismus** ✉ Herrrengasse 16, A-8010 ☎ 0316/80750 ⊕ www.graztourismus.at 🖨 0316/8075-15 ✉ Platform 1 of main train station ☎ 0316/80750. **Landesverband Burgenland Tourismus** ✉ Schloss Esterházy, A-7000 Eisenstadt ☎ 02682/63384-0 🖨 02682/63384-32 ⊕ www.burgenland-tourismus.at. **Mariazell Tourismusverband** ✉ Hauptplatz 13, A-8630 ☎ 03882/2366 🖨 03882/3945. **Neusiedl am See Tourismusbüro** ✉ Hauptplatz 1, A-7100 ☎ 02167/2229 🖨 02167/2637 ⊕ www.neusiedlamsee.at. **Niederösterreich Tourismus** ✉ Fischhof 3/3rd floor, A-1010 Vienna ☎ 01/53610-6200 🖨 01/53610-6060 ⊕ www.oesterreich.tourismus.net/noe. **Rust Gästeinformation** ✉ Conradplatz 1, A-7071 ☎ 02685/502 🖨 02685/502-10 ⊕ www.rust.at. **Steirische Tourismus** ✉ St. Peter-Hauptstrasse 243, A-8042 Graz ☎ 0316/4003-0 🖨 0316/4003-10 ⊕ www.steiermark.com. **Wiener Neustadt** Fremdenverkehrsverein ✉ Hauptplatz 3, A-2700 ☎ 02622/373310 or 02622/373311 🖨 02622/82065 ⊕ www.wiener-neustadt.at.

THE DANUBE VALLEY

4

NIBBLE A LINZER TORTE
as you stroll through Linz's Old City ⇨*p.215*

CLIMB FROM TOWER TO TURRET
of the fantastic Burg Kreuzenstein ⇨*p.204*

HUM STRAUSS'S LILTING WALTZ
while cruising the Blue Danube River ⇨*p.203*

GO FOR BAROQUE
at Melk's majestic abbey ⇨*p.231*

NAME TWO FAMED COMPOSERS
inspired by postcard-perfect Steyr ⇨*p.228*

DINE WITH *GEMÜTLICHKEIT*
at the Landhaus Bacher restaurant ⇨*p.233*

GET BECALMED AND CHARMED
in the riverside town of Dürnstein ⇨*p.209*

Updated by
Bonnie Dodson

TO THE SIGHTSEER, a trip along the Austrian Danube unfolds like a treasured picture-book. Roman ruins (some dating to Emperor Claudius), remains of medieval castles-in-air, and Baroque monasteries with "candle-snuffer" cupolas perching precariously above the river stimulate the imagination with their historic legends and myths. This is where Isa—cousin of the Lorelei—lured sailors onto the shoals; where Richard the Lion-Hearted was locked in a dungeon for a spell; and where the Nibelungs—later immortalized by Wagner—caroused operatically in battlemented forts. Here is where Roman sailors threw coins into the perilous whirlpools near Grein, in hopes of placating Danubius, the river's tutelary god. Today, thanks to the technology of modern dams, travelers have the luxury of tamely observing this part of Austria from the deck of a comfortable river steamer. In clement weather, the nine-hour trip upriver to Linz is highly rewarding. If your schedule allows, continuing onward to Passau may be less dramatic but gives more time to take in the picturesque vineyards and the castles perched on crags overlooking the river.

Even more of the region's attractions can be discovered if you travel by car or bus. You can explore plunging Gothic streets, climb Romanesque towers, then linger over a glass of wine in a Weinkeller. River and countryside form an inspired unity here, with fortress-topped outcroppings giving way to broad pastures that end only at the riverbanks. Many visitors classify this as one of Europe's great trips: you feel you can almost reach out and touch the passing towns and soak up the intimacy unique to this stretch of the valley. This chapter follows the course of the Danube upstream from Vienna as it winds through Lower Austria (Niederösterreich) and a bit of Upper Austria (Oberösterreich) to Linz, on the way passing monasteries and industrial towns, the riverside vineyards of the lower Weinviertel, and fragrant expanses of apricot and apple orchards.

Linz, Austria's third-largest city (and some say its most underrated), is a key industrial center. It is also a fine town for shopping; the stores are numerous and carry quality merchandise, often at more reasonable prices than in Vienna or the larger resorts. Concerts and operas performed at Linz's modern Brucknerhaus offer every bit as good listening as those staged in Vienna or Salzburg.

It is, however, the Danube itself, originating in Germany's Black Forest and emptying into the Black Sea, that is this chapter's focal point. The route that brought the Romans to the area and contributed to its development remains one of Europe's most important waterways, with four national capitals on its banks—Vienna, Bratislava, Budapest, and Belgrade. "Whoever controls the Danube controls all Europe" is attributed to the Romans, but the Kuenringer (robber knights who built many of the hilltop castles), followed suit, thriving by sacking the baggage caravans of the early Crusaders. With the passing of time, castles came to be financed through somewhat more commercial means—Frederick Barbarossa, leading his army downstream, had to pay a crossing toll at Mauthausen. Subsequently, settlements evolved into ports for the salt, wood, ores, and other cargo transported on the river, and today, modern railroads and highways parallel most of the blue Danube's course.

This is a wonderful trip to take in early spring or after the grape harvest in the fall, when the vineyards turn reddish-blue and a bracing chill settles over the Danube—the Empress Maria Theresa made it a point to arrive in Linz in May, just as the fruit trees were about to bloom. No matter when you come, be sure to try some of those fruits in a Linzer torte (a filling of brandy-flavored apricots, raspberries, or plums under a latticed pastry crust), a treat as rich and satisfying as the scenic wonders of the Danube Valley itself.

Exploring the Danube Valley

Although much of the river is tightly wedged between steep hills rising from a narrow valley, the north and south banks of the Danube present differing vistas. The hills to the north are terraced to allow the vineyards to catch the full sun; to the south, the orchards, occasional meadows, and shaded hills have just as much visual appeal, if a less dramatic sight. Upstream from the Wachau region the valley broadens, giving way to farmlands and, straddling the river, the industrial city of Linz.

About the Restaurants & Hotels

Wherever possible, restaurants make the most of the river view, and alfresco dining overlooking the Danube is one of the region's unsurpassed delights. Simple *Gasthäuser* are everywhere, but better dining is more often found in country inns. The cuisine usually runs along traditional lines, but the desserts are often brilliant inventions, including the celebrated Linzertorte and Linzer Augen, jam-filled cookies with three "eyes" planted in the top layer. A specialty found only in the Wachau region of the Danube Valley is *Wachauer Semmel,* freshly baked rolls which are crisped golden on the outside and wonderfully dense and chewy inside.

Wine is very much the thing in the lower part of the Weinviertel, particularly on the north bank of the Danube in the Wachau region. Here you'll find many of Austria's best white wines, slightly dry with a hint of fruitiness. In some of the smaller villages, you can sample the vintner's successes right on the spot in his cellars. Restaurants, whether sophisticated and stylish or plain and homey, are often rated by their wine offerings as much as by their chef's creations.

Accommodation options range from castle-hotels, where you'll be treated like royalty, to the often family-managed, quiet and elegant country inns, to standard city hotels in Linz. The region is compact, so you can easily lodge in one place and drive to a nearby locale to try a different restaurant. Rates understandably reflect the quality of service and amenities but usually include breakfast, which may range from a fast to a feast. Summers days are never uncomfortably hot, and nights are delightfully cool, so most hotels don't need air-conditioning. Some hotels offer half-board, with dinner included in addition to buffet breakfast (although most $$$$ hotels charge extra for breakfast). The half-board room rate is usually an extra €15–€30 per person. Occasionally, quoted room rates for hotels already include half-board, though a "discounted" rate may be available if you prefer not to take the evening meal. Inquire about any pension food plans when booking. Room rates in-

4

The Wachau section of the Danube Valley is a favorite outing for Viennese seeking a pleasant Sunday drive and a glass or two of good wine, but for foreign sojourners to treat the region this casually would cause them to miss some of Austria's greatest treasures. Once there, castles and abbeys beckon, picturesque villages beg to be explored, and the vine-covered wine gardens prove nearly irresistible, as are the pastry shops of the cheery town of Linz, which produce the best Linzertortes around.

Numbers in the text correspond to numbers in the margin and on the Lower Danube Valley, Upper Danube Valley, and Linz maps.

If you have
3 days

Start out early from Vienna, planning for a stop to explore the medieval center of **Krems** ③. The Vinotek Und's eponymous Kloster will give you a good idea of the regions's best wines. Along the northern, Krems side of the Danube, you can opt to spend a night in a former cloister, now an elegant hotel, in ⊡ **Dürnstein** ⑤, probably the most famous, if not prettiest, town of the Danube Valley. Here you'll find the ruined castle where Richard the Lion-Hearted was imprisoned—an early-morning climb up to the ruin or a jog along the Danube shoreline will reward you with great views. Take time to explore enchanting Dürnstein before heading west along the Danube crossing over to ⊡ **Melk** ㊱, rated one of the greatest abbeys in Europe. This is high Baroque at its most glorious. Follow the river road back east to ⊡ **Göttweig** ㊴ and have lunch on the terrace at the abbey. The abbey's 17th-century chapel is breathtaking. Continuing eastward, follow the river as closely as possible (signs indicate Zwentendorf and Tulln) to **Klosterneuburg** ㊷, the imposing abbey that was once the seat of the powerful Babenburger kings, and onward to Vienna.

If you have
5 days

A more leisurely schedule would follow the same basic route but permit a visit at either the fairytale castle of Burg Kreuzenstein, near **Korneuburg** ① or the more staid and mammoth castle of **Schloss Grafenegg,** near **Haitzendorf** ②, before stopping in attractive **Krems** ③ to tour its wine museum, the Weinkolleg Kloster, then overnighting in ⊡ **Dürnstein** ⑤. Spend the morning exploring Dürnstein, including the colorfully restored Baroque Stiftskirche. In the afternoon, discover the wine villages of **Weissenkirchen** ⑥ and **Spitz** ⑦. Plan on two overnights in the capital city of the region, ⊡ **Linz** ⑪–㉘, to tour the entire city. On day four, take in the spectacular abbey of **St. Florian** ㉙ (where composer Anton Bruckner spent a good deal of time) and the palatial halls of the abbey at **Kremsmünster** ㉚, both southeast of Linz and south of the Danube; then proceed east to the grandest abbey of all, ⊡ **Melk** ㊱. The fifth day will be full, but start with the Melk abbey, then continue east to the religious complex at **Göttweig** ㊴, and move onward to the abbey at **Klosterneuburg** ㊷.

If you have
7 days

Additional time allows for a far better acquaintance with this region. Located to the northwest of the Wachau, the Mühlviertel—the mill region north of Linz—turned out thousands of yards of linen from flax grown in the neighboring fields in the 19th century. You might follow the "textile trail," which takes you to museums tracing this bit of history. On your way along the northern Danube bank, visit the fascinating theater in **Grein** ⑨ and view the curious chancel in the church at **Baumgartenberg** ⑩. From ⚌ **Linz** ⑪–㉘, take a trip south to the gorgeously time-hallowed ⚌ **Steyr** ㉜—you might also consider an overnight in this charming medieval city with its vast central square framed with pastel facades. From Steyr, instead of trying to pack three abbeys into one day, spread out the pleasures, dining in **Mautern** ㊳ and overnighting in ⚌ **Tulln** ㊵ before heading on to **Klosterneuburg** ㊷ and, finally, returning to Vienna.

---

clude taxes and service, and usually breakfast—although, again, always ask. Assume all rooms have TV, telephones, and private bath, unless otherwise noted; air-conditioning, in rare instances, is noted.

WHAT IT COSTS In euros				
	$$$$	**$$$**	**$$**	**$**	**¢**
RESTAURANTS	over €22	€18–€22	€13–€17	€7–€12	under €7
HOTELS	over €175	€135–€175	€100–€135	€70–€100	under €70

Restaurant prices are per person for a main course at dinner. Hotel prices are for a standard double room in high season, including taxes and service. Assume that hotels operate on the European Plan (EP, with no meal provided) unless we note that they use the Breakfast Plan (BP), Modified American Plan (MAP, with breakfast and dinner daily, known as "halb pension"), or Full American Plan (FAP, or "voll pension," with three meals a day). Higher prices (inquire when booking) prevail for any meal plans.

Timing

The Wachau—both north and south Danube banks—is packed wall-to-wall with crowds in late April to early May, but of course there's a reason: apricot and apple trees are in glorious blossom, and bright orange poppies blanket the fields. Others prefer the chilly early- to mid-autumn days, when a blue haze curtains the vineyards. Throughout the region, winter is drab. Seasons notwithstanding, crowds jam the celebrated abbey at Melk; you're best off going first thing in the morning, before the tour buses arrive, or at midday, when the throngs have receded.

THE WACHAU: ALONG THE NORTH BANK OF THE DANUBE

Unquestionably the loveliest stretches of the Danube's Austrian course run from the outskirts of Vienna, through the narrow defiles of the Wachau to the Nibelungengau—the region where the mystical race of dwarfs, the Nibelungs, are supposed to have settled, at least for a while. If you're taking the tour by train, take Streetcar D to Vienna's Franz Josef Bahnhof, for your departure point. If you're driving, the trickiest part may be getting out of Vienna. Follow signs to Prague to get across the Danube, but once across, avoid the right-hand exit marked Prague—which leads to the autobahn—and continue ahead, following signs for Prager Strasse and turning left at the traffic light. Prager Strasse (Route 3) heads toward Langenzersdorf and Korneuburg.

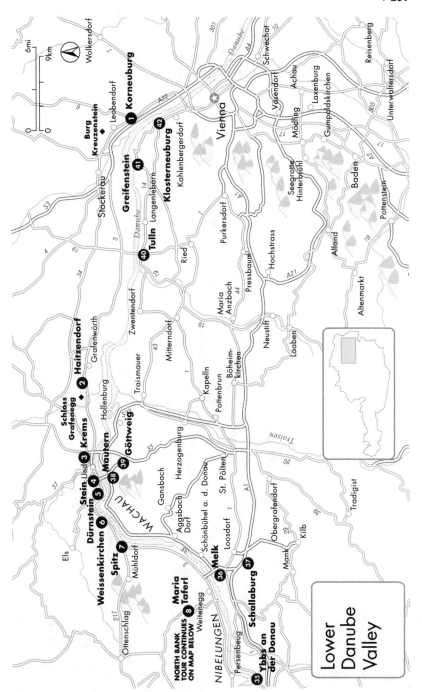

Lower
Danube
Valley

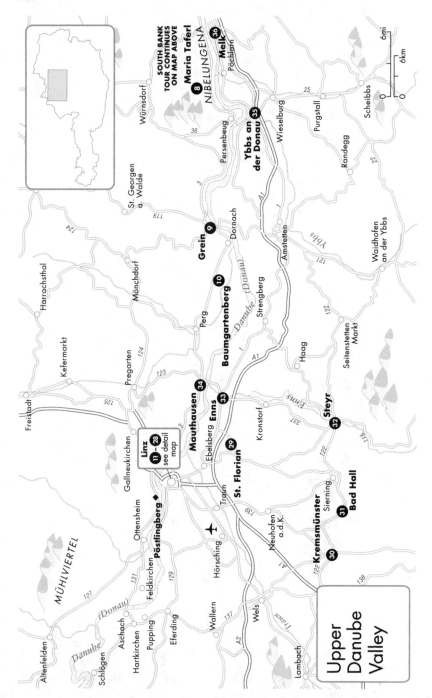

Upper Danube Valley

SOUTH BANK TOUR CONTINUES ON MAP ABOVE

8 Maria Taferl
36 Melk
NIBELUNGENA
Pöchlarn

35 Ybbs an der Donau
Persenbeug
Wieselburg
Purgstall
Randegg
Scheibbs

9 Grein
Dornach
Amstetten
Waidhofen an der Ybbs
Ybbs

10 Baumgartenberg
Strengberg
Perg
Haag
Seitenstetten Markt

Danube (Donau)

34 Mauthausen
33 Enns
Ebelsberg
Kronstorf
32 Steyr
Enns

Linz 11–28 see detail map
Pregarten
Kefermarkt
Freistadt
Gallneukirchen

29 St. Florian
31 Bad Hall
Sierning
Neuhofen a.d.K.

Pöstlingberg
Feldkirchen
Ottensheim

30 Kremsmünster

Hörsching
Traun
Wels
Wallern
Lambach

MÜHLVIERTEL
Altenfelden
Aschach
Harkirchen
Pupping
Eferding
Schlögen

Danube (Donau)

St. Georgen a. Walde
Mönchdorf
Harrachsthal
Wurmdorf

0 6km
0 6mi

And the Danube Waltzes On

The whole world sighs when it hears the opening strains of the Blue Danube waltz. Who, then, can resist a cruise upon the river immortalized by Johann Strauss II's unforgettable melody? Below, you'll find information about these popular day-trip cruises, which originate from Vienna's piers along the city's Danube Canal. As it turns out, when Strauss composed this piece, he was living on Vienna's Praterstrasse, a river's breath away from the Danube Canal, and enamored of a poem by Karl Beck whose refrain "By the Danube, beautiful blue Danube" he couldn't get out of his mind. It comes as a surprise to learn that the "waltz king" was, in fact, a terrible dancer and never took to the floor. But if you listen to the first motif of "An der schonen blauen Donau" (Strauss's title)—developing from the D major triad (D–F#–A)—it seems the composer must have been a wonderful swimmer. Sublimely, the melody suggests flowing waters—to be exact, the interplay of main current and subsidiary little whirlpools you often find on the Danube as you cruise its banks. When Strauss composed "On the Beautiful Blue Danube" for a war memorial concert given by the Men's Choral Association at Vienna's Imperial Winter Riding School in 1867, it was politely applauded, then forgotten the next week. Austria had been trounced by Prussia the year before and was licking its wounds, so hopes were high for the premiere, when the piece was accompanied by a chorus singing lyrics by poet Josef Weyl— "Vienna, be gay!" But once the chorus was banished (the words were fighting the waltzing rhythm), and once it was taken up at the great World Exposition given that year in Paris, "The Blue Danube" exploded around the world.

Now, as in Strauss's time, a cruise up the Danube to the Wachau valley is a tonic in any season. A parade of storybook-worthy sights—fairy-tale castles-in-air, medieval villages, and Baroque abbeys crowned with "candle-snuffer" cupolas—unfolds before your eyes. The main company that offers these cruises is the Blue Danube Schifffahrt/DDSG (Donau-Dampfschifffahrts-Gesellschaft's "Blue Danube") for contact information; see Boat Travel in this chapter's Danube Valley A to Z section. Their boats leave from the company's piers at Handelskai 265 every Sunday between May 11 and September 28 at 8:45 AM. Departing from the Reichsbrücke (Vienna Piers) on the city's Danube Canal, they arrive in Krems at 1:55 PM, Dürnstein at 2:30 PM, returning from Dürnstein at 4:30 PM, Krems at 4:50 PM, and get back to Vienna by 8:45 PM. One-way is €17.50—the ticket office is at the Vienna piers (take the U-Bahn line U1 to Vorgartenstrasse).

Another way to cruise the Danube is to leapfrog ahead by train from Vienna to Krems, where a short walk will lead you to the Schiffstation Krems piers, where river cruises run by Brandner Schifffahrt depart (10:15 AM; 1 PM; 3:45 PM; for contact information, *see* Boat Travel *in* this chapter's A to Z section) for a ride to glorious Melk Abbey and Dürnstein. Tickets for one-way are €16.50, but their Web site offers an enticing array of extra goodies—"ump-pah" band concerts, wine cruises, and the like—for extra prices. If you opt for either cruise, remember that it takes longer to travel north: the trip up the canal to Krems,

Dürnstein, and Melk will be shorter than the return back to Vienna, which is why many travelers opt to return to the city by train, not boat. Keep your fingers crossed: Rumor has it that the river, on the proper summer day, takes on an authentic shade of Johann Strauss blue.

Heavenly Mansions
While castles galore dot the area—ranging from crumbling mountaintop ruins to wonderfully restored edifices replete with gargoyles—the real gems in these environs are the abbeys, majestic relics of an era when bishops were as wealthy and as influential as kings. The greatest are Melk, Klosterneuburg, Kremsmünster, St. Florian, and Göttweig, all of which have breathlessly imposing scope and elegance.

Biking & Hiking
The trail alongside the Danube must be one of the great bicycle routes of the world. For much of the way (the exception being the Korneuburg–Krems stretch) you can bike along either side of the river. Some small hotels will even arrange to pick up you and your bike from the cycle path. You'll find bicycle rentals at most riverside towns and at rail stations. The terrain around Linz is relatively level, and within the city there are 89 km (55 mi) of marked cycle routes. In the areas of Eferding, St. Florian, through the Enns River valley, and around Steyr, the territory, with its gentle hills and special routes, is generally good for cycling.

You could hardly ask for better hiking country: from the level ground of the Danube Valley hills rise on both sides, giving great views when you reach the upper levels. There are *Wanderwege* (marked hiking paths) virtually everywhere; local tourist offices have maps and route details. Around Linz you might retrace the route of the Linz–Budweis horse-drawn tramway, Continental Europe's first railway, or trek from one castle to another. You can hike in the Mühlviertel from Freistadt to Grein and even arrange to get your pack transferred from hotel to hotel.

Korneuburg

❶ *18 km (11¼ mi) northwest of Vienna.*

FodorsChoice
★

Castle lovers, prepare yourself. Seemingly lifted from the pages of a Germanic fairy tale, **Burg Kreuzenstein**, bristling with storybook turrets and towers, might have made Albrecht Dürer drop his sketch pad in a second. Sitting atop a hillside 3 km (2 mi) beyond Korneuburg along Route 3, "Castle Cross-stone," in fact, is a 19th-century architectural fantasy built to conjure up "the last of the knights"—Emperor Maximilian I himself. Occupying the site of a previously destroyed fort, the enormous structure was built by Count Nepomuk Wilczek between 1879 and 1908 to house his collection of late-Gothic art objects and armor, including the "Brixner Cabinet" dating from 15th-century Salzburg. Using old elements and Gothic and Romanesque bits and pieces, the castle was carefully laid out according to the rules of yore, complete with a towering Burgtor, "Kennel" corridor (where attackers would have been cornered), Gothic arcades, and tracery parapet walls. The Burghof courtyard, with its half-timbered facade and Baltic loggia, could be a stand-in for a stage-set for Wagner's *Tannhäuser*. Inside, the medieval thrills continue with rooms full of armaments, a festival and banquet hall, a library, a stained-glass chapel, vassal kitchens, and the Narwalzahn, a room devoted to hunting trophies (if you've ever wanted to see a "unicorn horn," here's your chance). It is possible to reach Kreuzenstein from Vienna via the suburban train (S-Bahn) to Leobendorf, followed by a ¾-hour hike up to the castle. Until recently, the town of Korneuburg was the center of Austrian shipbuilding, where river passenger ships, barges, and transfer cranes were built to order for Russia, among other customers. Stop for a look at the imposing neo-Gothic city hall (1864), which dominates the central square and towers over the town. ⊠ *Leobendorf bei Korneuburg* ☎ *01/283–0308* ⊕ *www.kreuzenstein.com and www. werbeka.com/wien/kreuzend.htm* ⌑ *€8* ⊙ *Apr.–Oct., daily 10–4, guided tour on the hour.*

Haitzendorf

❷ *51 km (38½ mi) west of Korneuburg.*

The tiny farming community of Haitzendorf (to reach it from Korneuburg, take Route 3, 33 km [21 mi] past Stockerau, then turn right at Graftenwörth) is landmarked by a church dating from the 14th century. In early summer, the vast strawberry fields surrounding the town yield a delicious harvest, which you can pick yourself. A lush meadow ★ and woodland area also surrounds the best-known site, the **Schloss Grafenegg**. The moated Renaissance castle dating from 1533 was stormed by the Swedes in 1645 and rebuilt from 1840 to 1873 in the English Gothic Revival style, although its most dominant feature is a gigantic central tower in the Bohemian style, complete with four mini-turrets like those of spooky Prague Castle. Greatly damaged during the 1945–55 occupation, the vast structure was extensively restored in the 1980s and has been owned for centuries by the Metternich-Sándor family. Inside, you can be regaled by the Bibliothek (library), Rittersaal (Knights' Hall), and Wappenstube (coat of arms room). Look for such fascinating details as the gargoyle waterspouts, and don't miss the chapel. The castle has a packed calendar filled with temporary art exhibits and classical music concerts. ☎ *02735/2205–17* ⊕ *www.grafenegg.com* ⌑ *€5* ⊙ *Early Mar.–Oct., Tues.–Sun. 10–5.*

Where to Stay & Eat

★ **$$–$$$** ✕⌂ **Mörwald.** Just past the manicured lawns of Schloss Grafenegg, this elegant tavern is part of the culinary empire founded by owner Toni Mörwald. Here, the showcase is on classic Austrian dishes with a fresh slant. The menu is seasonal, and may include Waldviertler duck with asparagus and *Schupfnudeln* (Austrian-style gnocchi), or grilled *Saiblingsfilet* (char) with tomato and zucchini risotto. Mörwald has his own winery, and a glass of his golden Gelbe Muskateller or sauvignon blanc provides the perfect accompaniment. In summer dine in the sunny garden under hunter-green umbrellas and linden trees—or better yet, opt for one of the €30 picnics the restaurant will prepare for you to enjoy on the castle grounds. Mörwald also has a few stylishly attractive rooms upstairs that are in the $$ category. ⊠ *A-3485, Haitzendorf* ☎ *02735/*

2616–0 🖴 *02735/2616–60* ⊕ *www.moerwald.at* ↩ *9 rooms* ⚲ *Restaurant; no a/c* 🖃 *AE, DC, MC, V* ☯ *Closed Mon.–Tues. and Jan.* ⍥ *BP.*

Krems

★ ❸ *12 km (7 mi) west of Haitzendorf, 80 km (50 mi) northwest of Vienna, 26 km (16¼ mi) north of St. Pölten.*

Krems marks the beginning (when traveling upstream) of the Wachau section of the Danube. The town is closely tied to Austrian history; here the ruling Babenbergs set up a dukedom in 1120, and the earliest Austrian coin was struck here in 1130. In the Middle Ages, Krems looked after the iron trade while neighboring Stein traded in salt and wine, and over the years Krems became a center of culture and art. Today the area is the heart of a thriving wine production, while Krems is most famed for the cobbled streets of its Altstadt (Old Town), which is virtually unchanged since the 18th century. The lower Old Town is an attractive pedestrian zone, while up a steep hill (a car can be handy) you'll find the upper Old Town, with its Renaissance Rathaus town hall and a parish church that is one of the oldest in Lower Austria.

Opened in 2001 (with Robert Crumb, the renowned comic-strip artist, at the ribbon-cutting ceremony), the **Karikaturmuseum** (Caricature Museum) houses more than 250 works of cartoon art from the 20th century to the present, including a large collection of English-language political satire and caricature. ⊠ *Steiner Landstrasse 3a* ☎ *02732/908020* ⊕ *www.karikaturmuseum.at* 🎟 *€8* ☯ *Daily 10–6.*

A 14th-century former Dominican cloister now serves as the **Weinstadt Museum Krems,** a wine museum that holds occasional tastings. ⊠ *Körnermarkt 14* ☎ *02732/801–567* ⊕ *www.weinstadtmuseum.at* 🎟 *€3.60* ☯ *Mar.–Nov., Tues.–Sun. 10–6.*

Where to Stay & Eat

$$$ ✕ **Jell.** Located in the heart of Krems' medieval Altstadt, this storybook stone cottage run by Ulli Amon-Jell (pronounced "Yell") is a cluster of cozy rooms with lace curtains, dark wood banquettes, candlelight, and Biedermeier knickknacks on the walls, making it seem like you've stepped into an early-20th-century grandmother's house. Your meal begins with tantalizing breads and dips, fine starters like cream of asparagus soup, then delicious main courses like the pheasant breast wrapped in their own home-cured bacon. For vegetarians there's a superb dish of peppers stuffed with smoked tofu in a sweet, organic tomato sauce. And for that warm glow at the end of your repast, have a glass of homemade apricot schnapps. In summer, book ahead for a table under the grape arbor in the small, secluded outdoor dining area. ⊠ *Hoher Markt 8–9* ☎ *02732/82345* 🖴 *02732/82345–4* ⚲ *Reservations essential* 🖃 *AE, DC, MC, V* ☯ *Closed Mon., no dinner weekends.*

★ **$$$** ✕ **M. Kunst. Genuss.** Another popular, hip restaurant belonging to entrepreneur Toni Mörwald (who owns a string of hot dining spots, including Mörwald, adjacent to nearby Schloss Grafenegg), this strikingly minimalistic, cathedral-roofed, glass-sided structure is situated at the Karikaturmuseum and has a name that signifies "Mörwald, Art, and

GRAPE EXPECTATIONS

OR A "GRAPE ESCAPE," there are few pleasanter ways to spend an afternoon than to travel to the fabled wineries of the Danube Valley and sample the golden nectar coaxed from their vines. For many the epitome of Austrian viticulture is found in the Wachau, those few precious kilometers of terraced vineyards along the north bank of the river.

Here you can discover some of the finest white wines in Europe. The elegant, long-lived Rieslings are world-renowned, but the special glory of Austria is the Grüner Veltliner, an indigenous grape that can produce anything from simple Heuriger thirst-quenchers to wines of a nobility that rival the best of Burgundy.

The area has its own unique three-tiered classification system, ranging from the young, fresh Steinfeder and medium-bodied Federspiel to the rich, ripe Smaragd. Some of the already legendary vintners include F. X. Pichler, Prager, Knoll, and Hirtzberger, as well as the exemplary cooperative of the Freie Weingärtner Wachau.

It is usually possible to stop in and meet the winemaker, who will be happy to pour you a taste from the latest vintage and share some of the secrets of the trade. A late spring drive through the charming villages of Loiben, Weissenkirchen, and Dürnstein, when the apricots are in blossom, is an idyllic experience not easily forgotten.

Straddling both sides of the Danube is the Kremstal, centering on the medieval town of Krems, the hub of the area's wine trade. Here, you can get a good idea of the regional wines with a visit to the Vinotek Und's eponymous Kloster. The range of grape varieties expands here to include intensely fragrant Traminer, Grauburgunder (more familiar as pinot gris), and even some full-bodied reds from cabernet sauvignon and pinot noir. To sample some of these wines, you may be tempted to make an excursion to one of the nearby wineries like Nigl, Salomon, and Malat.

Venturing farther from the Danube takes you through lush, rolling hills to the Kamptal, the valley that follows the winding course of the gentle Kamp River. Here is another premium wine region, this one dominated by Langenlois, the country's largest wine producing town.

Newly opened is the Loisium (✉ Kornplatz A-3550, Langenlois ⊕ www.loisium.at), the sleek, ultramodern emporium that provides a comprehensive selection of wines and other delectables from the area; for a fine web site on Wachau wineries, log on to ⊕ www.vinea-wachau.at/. Top producers include Hirsch, Loimer, and Bründlmayer, who makes one of Austria's best sparkling wines as well as chardonnay and Alte Reben (old-vine) Grüner Veltliner and Riesling of exceptional character.

After you've had your fill of wine tasting, you might want to relax over a good meal at one of these distinguished wineries. Several have very nice restaurants on-site, including Jamek, near Dürnstein, and Bründlmayer in Langenlois.

— Gary Dodson

Pleasure." Look for the big salad of field greens topped with a generous skirt steak, or the perfectly cooked wild salmon fillet with basmati rice and a profusion of colorful grilled vegetables. Service is without fault. This is one of the few restaurants in the area open for lunch all day. ⊠ *Franz-Zeller-Platz 3* ☎ *02732/908–0102–1* 🖷 *02732/908011* ▤ *AE, DC, MC, V.*

$$$ ✕ **Zum Kaiser von Österreich.** At this landmark in Krems' Old City district, you'll find excellent regional cuisine along with an outstanding wine selection (some of these vintages come from the backyard). The inside rooms are bright and pleasant, and the outside tables in summer are even more inviting. Owner-chef Haidinger learned his skills at Bacher, across the Danube in Mautern, so look for fish dishes along with specialties such as potato soup and roast shoulder of lamb with scalloped potatoes. ⊠ *Körnermarkt 9* ☎ *02732/86001* 🖷 *02732/86001–4* ⌂ *Reservations essential* ▤ *AE, DC, V* ۞ *Closed Sun. from Easter–Sept. and last 2 wks in June.*

★ **$$$** ✕🖃 **Am Förthof.** An inn has existed on the riverside site of this small, multi-windowed hotel for hundreds of years. Comfortably set back from the busy main road, it gives a sense of seclusion because of the large front garden shaded by 200-year-old chestnut trees and a multitude of flowers. The charming rooms are done in pale yellow, blue, or pink, and have antique pieces and soft carpets. Those in front have views of the Danube and Göttweig Abbey across the river while the back rooms overlook a swimming pool. Rooms on the second floor have more sweeping views of the river, but are a bit smaller. At dinnertime, there's no need to leave the premises as the kitchen is nearly more touted than the hotel. Partake of the optional 5-course Degustation menu, with a different local wine to accompany each course. Breakfast is a sumptuous feast of organic products and fresh-baked *Wachauer Semmel,* as well as silver tureens of sweet strawberries, red currants, and apricots picked from the *Marillen* trees of the neighboring medieval village of Stein. For those settling in to do a bit of wine tasting in the Wachau, friendly owner Frau Figl will gladly arrange wine tours. ⊠ *Förthofer Donaulände 8, A-3500* ☎ *02732/83345* 🖷 *02732/83345–40* ⊕ *www.tiscover.com/ feinschmecker.foerthof* ⊅ *16 rooms* ⌂ *Restaurant, minibars, pool, sauna, Internet, some no-smoking rooms; no a/c, free parking* ▤ *AE, DC, MC, V* ۞ *Closed. Jan.–Feb.* ⍾◎ *BP.*

★ **$** ✕🖃 **Alte Post.** The oldest inn in Krems, for centuries the mail-route posthouse for the region, this hostelry is centered around an adorable Renaissance-style courtyard, which is topped with a flower-bedecked arcaded balcony and storybook mansard roof. If you're a guest here, you'll be able to drive into the pedestrian zone of the Old Town and pull up next to the Steinener Tor (Stone Gate) to find this inn. The rooms are in comfortable yet elegant country style (full baths are scarce), but the real draw here is dining on regional specialties or sipping a glass of the local wine in the courtyard. The staff is friendly (though English is a struggle), and cyclists are welcome. ⊠ *Obere Landstrasse 32, A-3500 Krems* ☎ *02732/82276–0* 🖷 *02732/84396* ⊕ *www.altepost-krems.at* ⊅ *23 rooms, 4 with bath* ⌂ *Restaurant; no a/c* ▤ *No credit cards* ۞ *Closed Dec.–Mar.* ◎ *BP.*

Stein

④ *5 km (3 mi) east of Krems.*

A frozen-in-time hamlet that has, over the years, become virtually a suburb of the adjacent city of Krems, Stein is dotted with lovely 16th-century houses, many on the town's main street, Steinlanderstrasse. The 14th-century **Minoritenkirche,** just off the main street in the pedestrian zone, now serves as a museum with changing exhibits. A few steps beyond the Minoritenkirche, an imposing square Gothic tower identifies the 15th-century **St. Nicholas parish church,** whose altar painting and ceiling frescoes were done by Kremser Schmidt. The upper part of the Gothic charnel house (1462), squeezed between the church and the hillside, has been converted to housing. Notice, too, the many architecturally interesting houses, among them the former tollhouse, which has rich Renaissance frescoes. Stein was the birthplace of Ludwig Köchel, the cataloger of Mozart's works, still referred to by their Köchel numbers.

Dürnstein

⑤ *4 km (2½ mi) west of Stein, 90 km (56 mi) northwest of Vienna, 34 km (21¼ mi) northeast of Melk.*

If a beauty contest were held among the towns along the Wachau Danube, chances are Dürnstein would be the winner, hands down—as you'll see when you arrive along with droves of tourists. The town is small; leave the car at one end and walk the narrow streets. The main street, Hauptstrasse, is lined with picturesque 16th-century residences. The trick is to overnight here—when the daytrippers depart, the storybook spell of the town returns. The top night to be here is the Summer Solstice, when hundreds of boats bearing torches and candles sail down the river at twilight to honor the longest day of the year—a breathtaking sight best enjoyed from the town and hotel terraces over the Danube. In October or November, the grape harvest from the surrounding hills are gathered by volunteers from villages throughout the valley—locals garnish their front doors with straw wreaths if they can offer tastes of the new wine, as members of the local wine cooperative, the Winzergenossenschaft Wachau.

Set among terraced vineyards, the town is landmarked by its gloriously Baroque **Stiftskirche,** dating from the early 1700s, which sits on a cliff overlooking the river—this cloister church's combination of luminous blue facade and stylish Baroque tower is considered the most beautiful of its kind in Austria. After taking in the Stiftskirche, head up the hill, climbing 500 feet above the town, to the famous **Richard the Lion-Hearted Castle** where Leopold V held Richard the Lion-Hearted of England, captured on his way back home from the Crusades. Leopold had been insulted, so the story goes, by Richard while they were in the Holy Land and when the English lord was shipwrecked and had to head back home through Austria, word got out—even though Richard was disguised as a peasant—and Leopold pounced. In the tower of this castle, the Lionheart was imprisoned (1192–93) until he was located by Blondel, the faithful minnesinger. It's said that Blondel was able to locate his imprisoned king when he heard his master's voice completing the verse of a song Blondel was singing aloud—a bit famously recycled in Sir Walter Scott's *Ivanhoe* (and the Robert Taylor MGM film). Leopold turned his prisoner over to the emperor, Henry VI, who held him for months longer until the ransom was paid by Richard's mother, Eleanor of Aquitaine. The rather steep 30-minute climb to the ruins will earn you a breathtaking view up and down the Danube Valley and over the hills to the south.

Where to Stay & Eat

★ $$$ ╳ **Loibnerhof.** It's hard to imagine a more idyllic frame for a memorable meal, especially if the weather is fine and tables are set out in the invitingly fragrant apple orchard. The kitchen offers inventive variations on regional themes: Wachauer fish soup, crispy roast duck, and various grilled fish or lamb specialties. The house is famous for its *Butterschnitzel,* an exquisite variation on the theme of ground meat (this one's panfried veal with a touch of pork). To reach Loibnerhof, look for the Unterloiben exit a mile east of Dürnstein. ⊠ *Unterloiben 7* ☎ *02732/82890-0* 🖷 *02732/82890-3* ⌂ *Reservations essential* ▤ *MC, V* ⊘ *Closed Mon.–Tues. and early Jan.–mid-Feb.*

$$$$ ╳▥ **Richard Löwenherz.** Built up around the former church of a vast 700-year-old convent, this noted inn occupies a fine point overlooking the Danube. If you can tear yourself away from its bowered terrace and balcony walkways, you'll enter the hotel and discover impressive, vaulted reception rooms beautifully furnished with antiques, reflecting the personal warmth and care of the family management. The inviting open fire, stone floors, grandfather clock, and bowls of fresh roses make this one of the most romantic of the Romantik Hotels group. Though all rooms are spacious and comfortable, the balconied guest rooms in the newer part of the house have more modern furnishings. Wander through the grounds among the roses, oleanders, and fig trees, all set against the dramatic backdrop of 600-year-old stone walls. The outstanding restaurant—with an impressively Danubian decor—is known for its local wines and regional specialties, such as crispy duck with dumplings and red cabbage. In summer, dine on that enchanting terrace under maple and chestnut trees, and admire the lushly wooded hills and languid Danube. ⊠ *A-3601* ☎ *02711/222* 🖷 *02711/222–18* ⊕ *www. richardloewenherz.at* ⇆ *38 rooms* ⌂ *Restaurant, minibars, pool, bar; no a/c* ▤ *AE, DC, MC, V* ⊘ *Closed Nov.–Easter or mid–Apr.* ⏺❙ *BP.*

Fodor'sChoice
★

★ $$$$ ╳▥ **Schloss Dürnstein.** Once the preserve of the princes of Starhemberg, this 17th-century early Baroque castle, on a rocky terrace with exquisite views over the Danube, is one of the most famous hotels in Austria. Its classic elegance and comfort have been enjoyed by the ilk of King Juan Carlos of Spain, Prince Hirohito of Japan, Rudolf Nureyev, and a bevy of other celebs. The best guest rooms look onto the river, but all are elegantly decorated, some in grand Baroque or French Empire style. Biedermeier armoires, ceramic stoves, and country antiques grace public rooms. The restaurant is cozily nestled under coved ceilings—half-board is standard and a good value, but not required. The kitchen matches the quality of the excellent wines from the area, and the tables set outside on the large stone balcony overlooking the river make dining here a memorable experience, with pike perch from the Danube, Waldviertler beef, or roast pheasant stuffed with apricots among the menu's delights. Even if you don't stay at the hotel, it's worth a stop for lunch or a leisurely afternoon Wachauer torte and coffee. ⊠ *A-3601* ☎ *02711/ 212* 🖥 *02711/351* ⊕ *www.schloss.at* ➶ *37 rooms* ♌ *Restaurant, minibars, 2 indoor-outdoor pools, gym, sauna, bar, Internet; no a/c* ⊟ *AE, DC, MC, V* ☉ *Closed Nov.–Mar.* ⦿❘ *BP.*

$–$$ 🏨 **Sänger Blondel.** Nearly under the shadow of the exquisitely Baroque spire of Dürnstein's parish church, this *gasthof-pension* welcomes you with a lovely, sunny-yellow, flower-bedecked facade. Owned by the same family since 1729, the inn—named after the minstrel famous for tracking Richard the Lion-Hearted—has a large garden, quite the treat to enjoy in the heart of town. The simply furnished, country-style rooms are of medium size and have attractive paneling and antique decorations. The staff is particularly helpful and can suggest excursions in the area. The hotel's restaurant serves hearty Austrian food, and offers zither music on Thursday evenings. In summer, meals are served in the pretty courtyard under a huge chestnut tree. ⊠ *No. 64, A-3601* ☎ *02711/253–0* 🖥 *02711/253–7* ⊕ *www.saengerblondel.at* ➶ *16 rooms* ♌ *Restaurant; no a/c* ⊟ *V* ☉ *Closed mid-Nov.–mid-Mar.* ⦿❘ *BP.*

Weissenkirchen

❻ *5 km (3 mi) west of Dürnstein, 22 km (14 mi) northeast of Melk.*

Tucked among vineyards, just around a bend in the Danube, is Weissenkirchen, a picturesque town that was fortified against the Turks in 1531. A fire in 1793 laid waste to much of the town, but the 15th-century parish church of **Maria Himmelfahrt**, built on earlier foundations, largely survived. The south nave dates from 1300, the middle nave from 1439, the chapel from 1460. The Madonna on the triumphal arch goes back to the Danube school of about 1520; the Baroque touches date from 1736; and to complete the picture, the rococo organ was installed in 1777. On the Marktplatz, check out the 15th-century **Wachaumuseum** (Wachau museum), which has a charming Renaissance arcaded courtyard. The building now contains many paintings by Kremser Schmidt. ⊠ *Marktplatz* ☎ *02715/2268* ⊕ *www.weissenkirchen.at/ museum.php* 💶 *€2.20* ☉ *Apr.–Oct., Tues.–Sun. 10–5.*

Where to Stay & Eat

★ $$$ ✕ **Gasthaus Erwin Schwarz.** Natives will tell you this is the best restaurant in the area, offering delicious regional cooking in a former farmhouse and butcher shop. There is virtually nothing in the village of Nöhagen, which is 7 km (4½ mi) north of Weissenkirchen, yet people come from miles around to dine here. The restaurant raises its own animals, and all produce is grown on the premises. You're in luck if the succulent crispy duck with *Rotkraut* (red cabbage) and dumplings is on the menu. For information on the pleasant drive to this countryside spot, see the En Route below. ⊠ *Nöhagen 13* ☎ *02717/8209* ♘ *Reservations essential* ⊟ *AE, MC, V* ☉ *Closed Mon.–Tues., and Mon.–Thurs. Nov.–mid-Apr.*

$$–$$$ ✕ **Jamek.** The Jamek family's country inn on the Danube is well known throughout Austria, and though Josef and Edeltraud have handed over the management to their daughter, the quality remains the same. You dine either in one of several rooms tastefully decorated with 19th-century touches, or outdoors in the shady garden. Start with the vegetable torte gratin, then go on to lightly fried Zanderfilet (pike perch) on a bed of garlicky spinach, or pork cutlet with fried dumplings. Don't miss the house specialty, the surprisingly light chocolate cake with whipped cream and chocolate sauce. Wines are from the nearby family vineyards. Jamek is located just west of Weissenkirchen in Joching. ⊠ *Joching 45* ☎ *02715/2235* 🖷 *02715/2235–22* ⌔ *Reservations essential* ▭ *DC, MC, V* ⊗ *Closed Sun. and mid-Dec.–mid-Jan., no lunch Mon.–Thurs.*

$$ 🏛 **Raffelsbergerhof.** This lovely Renaissance building (1574), once a shipmaster's house, has been tastefully converted into a hotel with every comfort. The friendly family management and peaceful surroundings make this a good lodging choice. Guest rooms, with beautiful original wooden floors, are furnished with charming country pieces, pretty fabrics, and fresh flowers, and most have sitting areas. Baths are modern and well equipped. The buffet breakfast is excellent. There's an extra charge of €5 for stays of only one night. ⊠ *A-3610* ☎ *02715/2201* 🖷 *02715/2201–27* ⊕ *www.raffelsbergerhof.at/* ⇨ *15 rooms* ⌂ *Minibars, Internet; no a/c* ▭ *DC, MC, V* ⊗ *Closed Nov.–Easter.* ⏐◯⏐ *BP.*

en route | One of the prettiest drives in the Wachau leads from Weissenkirchen to the renowned Gasthaus Erwin Schwarz in Nöhagen. From the main entrance to the town of Weissenkirchen, follow the road (Route L7094) north through the village, veering to your right and continuing upward. Soon the village gives way to a forested incline, after which you'll emerge into a verdant landscape of soft-contoured hills and vineyards and an occasional old farmhouse, passing through Weinzierl on Route L7090 on your way north to Nöhagen. From Nöhagen, take Route L7040 east toward Reichau, then to sleepy, rambling Senftenberg ("Mustard Mountain") with its romantic castle ruin perched above the town. A few kilometers east of Senftenberg, change to Route 218, going northeast to Langenlois. From here there will be signs to Vienna or back to Krems.

Spitz

❼ *5 km (3 mi) southwest of Weissenkirchen, 17 km (10½ mi) northeast of Melk.*

Picturesque Spitz is off the main road and set back from the Danube, sitting like a jewel in the surrounding vineyards and hills. One vineyard, the "Thousand Bucket Hill" is so called for the amount of wine it is said to produce in a good year. A number of interesting houses in Spitz go back to the 16th and 17th centuries. The late-Gothic 15th-century **parish church** contains Kremser Schmidt's altar painting of the martyrdom of St. Mauritius. Note the carved wood statues of Christ and the 12 apostles, dating from 1380, on the organ loft. Just beyond Spitz and above the road is the ruin of the **castle Hinterhaus,** to which you can climb.

Where to Stay

$$ 🏰 **Burg Oberranna.** About 7 km (4½ mi) beyond the village of Mühldorf, directly west of Spitz, stands this well-preserved castle-hotel, surrounded by a double wall and dry moat. The original structure dates from the early 12th century, and the St. George chapel possibly even earlier. Some of the charming antiques-filled suites include a kitchenette and sitting room. This is a great base for hiking and also perfect for those who just want to get away. ✉ *Ober-Ranna 1, A-3622 Mühldorf* ☎ *02713/8221* 🖷 *02713/8366* ⊕ *www.schlosshotels.co.at* 🛏 *5 rooms, 7 suites* △ *Café, kitchenettes; no a/c* ▭ *AE, DC, MC, V* ⊙ *Closed Nov.–Apr.* ◎I *BP.*

> **en route** The vistas are mainly of the other side of the Danube, looking across at Schönbühel and Melk, as you follow a back road via Jauerling and Maria Laach to Route 3 at Aggsbach. Shortly after Weitenegg the Wachau ends, and you come into the part of the Danube Valley known as the **Nibelungenau,** where the Nibelungs—who inspired the great saga *Das Nibelungenlied,* source of Wagner's *Ring*—are supposed to have settled for a spell. If you have always thought of the Nibelungs as a mythical race of dwarfs known only to old German legends and Wagner, dismiss that idea. The Nibelungs actually existed, though not as Wagner describes them, and this area was one of their stomping grounds.

Maria Taferl

❽ *49 km (31 mi) southwest of Spitz, 13 km (8 mi) west of Melk, 7½ km (4¾ mi) northeast of Persenbeug/Ybbs an der Donau.*

Crowning a hill on the north bank is the two-towered **Maria Taferl Basilica,** a pilgrimage church with a spectacular outlook. It's a bit touristy, but the church and the view are worth the side trip. About 5 km (3 mi) up a back road is **Schloss Artstetten,** a massive square castle crowned with no less than seven "candle-snuffer" turrets—a touch of *mittel-europa* style befitting this family seat of the Austro-Hungarian Habsburgs. To be exact, this was the former country retreat of no less than Archduke Franz Ferdinand and his wife, Sophie, whose double assassination in 1914 in Sarajevo was one of the immediate causes of World War I. The castle has rooms given over to their collected memorabilia as well as their marble vaults. ✉ *Artstetten* ☎ *07413/8302 or 07413/8006* ⊕ *www. schloss-artstetten.at* 🖾 *€6.50* ⊙ *Apr.–Oct., daily 9–5:30.*

Where to Stay

$–$$ 🏰 **Krone–Kaiserhof.** Two hotels—both rather large, barn-like, and uncomely modern structures—-share each other's luxurious facilities. The Krone looks out over the Danube Valley, while the Kaiserhof has views of the nearby Baroque pilgrimage church. Both have rooms done a bit slickly in country style, and the restaurants are popular. Cyclists staying overnight will be picked up free at Marbach or Klein Pöchlarn landing stations on the Danube. ✉ *A-3672* ☎ *07413/6355-0* 🖷 *07413/6355–83* ⊕ *www.hotel-schachner.at* 🛏 *72 rooms* △ *2 restaurants,*

café, miniature golf, indoor-outdoor pools, sauna, bar; no a/c ▭ *AE,
DC, MC, V* ☉ *Closed Jan.–Feb., Nov.–Dec.* ⦿ *BP.*

Grein

9 *32 km (20 mi) west of Maria Taferl, 20 km (12 mi) west of Persenbeug/
Ybbs an der Donau.*

Set above the Danube, Grein is a picture-book town complete with castle. The river bend below, known for years as the "place where death
resides," was one of the river's most hazardous stretches until the reefs
were blasted away in the late 1700s. Take time to see the intimate rococo **Stadttheater** in the town hall, built in 1790 and still occasionally
used for concerts or plays. ⊠ *Rathaus* ☎ *07268/7055* ⊕ *www.
museumsland.at/museen/greinst/daten.htm* 🖾 *€3* ☉ *May 2–Oct. 26,
tours Mon.–Sat. at 9, 11, 1:30, and 4, Sun. at 3.*

Baumgartenberg

10 *11 km (7 mi) west of Grein, 17½ km (11 mi) east of Mauthausen.*

The small village of Baumgartenberg is worth a visit for its ornate
Baroque **parish church.** Note the lavish stucco-work and exquisitely
carved 17th-century pews—and the unusual pulpit supported by a tree
trunk. The church is the only reminder of a once-famed Cistercian
abbey, founded in 1141 by Otto von Machland, that once stood here.
Outside the town is the picturesque **castle of Klam,** which used to belong to Swedish playwright August Strindberg; it now contains a small
museum.

LINZ:
"RICH TOWN OF THE RIVER MARKETS"

*48 km (22 mi) northwest of Baumgartenberg, 130 km (81¼ mi) east of
Salzburg, 185 km (115½ mi) west of Vienna.*

Linz, the capital of Upper Austria—set where the Traun River flows into
the Danube—has a fascinating Old City core and an active cultural life.
In 1832 it had a horse-drawn train to Czechoslovakia that functioned
as the first rail line on the Continent. Once known as the "Rich Town
of the River Markets" because of its importance as a medieval trading
post, it is today the center of Austrian steel and chemical production,
both started by the Germans in 1938. Linz is also a leader in computer
technology—every September the city hosts the internationally renowned
Ars Electronica Festival, designed to promote artists, scientists, and the
latest technical gadgets. A city where past and present collide, Linz has
Austria's largest medieval square and is now address to one of the country's most modern multipurpose halls, the Brucknerhaus, which is used
for concerts and conventions.

With the city's modern economic success, Linz's attractions for tourists
have been generally overlooked. Nevertheless, Linz can cast a spell, thanks
to the beautiful old houses on the Hauptplatz; a Baroque cathedral with

twin towers and a fine organ over which composer Anton Bruckner once presided; and its "city mountain," the Pöstlingberg, with a unique railway line to the top. As you tour the city, you may want to do so with Mozart's "Linz Symphony" on your Walkman. Mozart *en famille* often stayed here as his family relentlessly traveled up and down Europe, most notably in November 1783, when he was a guest of Count Johann Thun-Hohenstein at his Thun Palace. Staying for nearing a month allowed the composer to relax and tour Linz's sights, use its Minoritenkirche (across from the palace) for mass and, in so doing, was inspired enough to write his great symphony. Today, extensive redevelopment, ongoing restoration, and the creation of traffic-free zones continue to transform Linz. The heart of the city—the Altstadt (Old City)—has been turned into a pedestrian zone; either leave your car at your hotel or use the huge parking garage under the main square in the center of town. Distances are not great, and you can take in the highlights in the course of a two-hour walking tour.

A Good Walk

The center of the Old City is the Hauptplatz, with its pretty pastel town houses. Dominating the square is the **Pillar to the Holy Trinity** ⑪, erected in 1723 in gratitude for Linz's survival after threats of war, fire, and the dreaded plague. Head down Klostergasse to the magnificent **Minoritenkirche** ⑫, which is definitely worth a stop to inspect the church's Rococo interior before visiting the adjacent **Landhaus** ⑬, once Linz's college and the place where famed astronomer Johannes Kepler taught, which occupies a rambling Renaissance building with two inner courtyards. In the arcaded courtyard is the Fountain of the Planets, with Jupiter as the crowning glory.

At No. 20 Klostergasse is the Thun Palace, now known as the **Mozart Haus** ⑭, where Mozart stayed as a guest of the Count of Thun-Hohenstein and composed the Linz Symphony in his "spare time." Turn right at the corner onto Altstadtgasse. At No. 10 is the **Kremsmünsterhaus** ⑮, with its turrets and onion domes, where Emperor Friedrich III supposedly died in August 1493. Turn left from Altstadtgasse onto Hofgasse (one of the prettiest corners in the city), and climb the quaint narrow street that leads up to the Rudolfstor, one of the entrances to **Schlossmuseum Linz** (Linz Castle) ⑯. Since its early days as a prime fortress on the Danube, it has served as a hospital, army barracks, and even a prison, before becoming a provincial museum. The view from the castle promontory is one of the most impressive in Linz. Walk through the castle grounds to the end of the parking lot and turn left, going through the archway to the **Martinskirche**, one of the oldest churches in Austria, with its nave dating from 799.

Go back along Römerstrasse, which veers right down the hill. At the bottom it becomes the Promenade. Go straight on the Promenade, following it around to the left, then turn right onto Herrenstrasse. Where Bichofstrasse meets Herrenstrasse is the **Bischofshof** ⑰, which was built between 1721 and 1726 for the Kremsmünster monastery and is still the seat of the bishop of Linz. The west end of Bishofstrasse angles onto Baumbachstrasse, the site of the **Neuer Dom** ⑱, a massive 19th-century

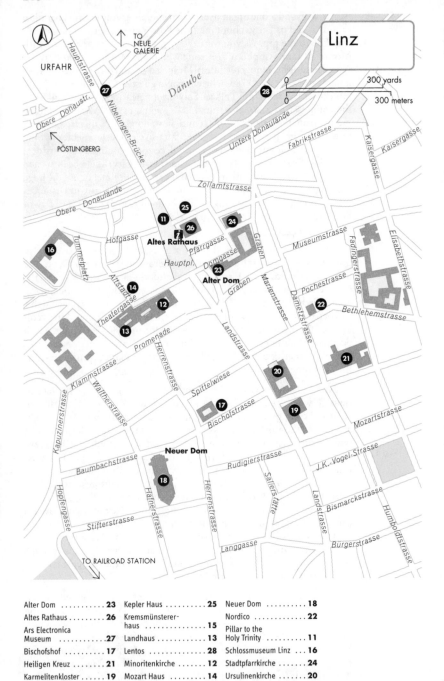

Alter Dom **23**
Altes Rathaus **26**
Ars Electronica
Museum **27**
Bischofshof **17**
Heiligen Kreuz **21**
Karmelitenkloster **19**

Kepler Haus **25**
Kremsmünsterer-
haus **15**
Landhaus **13**
Lentos **28**
Minoritenkirche **12**
Mozart Haus **14**

Neuer Dom **18**
Nordico **22**
Pillar to the
Holy Trinity **11**
Schlossmuseum Linz . . . **16**
Stadtpfarrkirche . . . **24**
Ursulinenkirche **20**

cathedral capable of holding 20,000 worshipers. Note the Linz Window, depicting the history of Linz, before heading back to Herrenstrasse.

Turn right and shortly afterward left onto Rudigierstrasse. Follow this to Landstrasse, where you'll make another left. Two Baroque churches are located here, that of the **Karmelitenkloster** ⑲, modeled after St. Joseph's in Prague, and down the street the **Ursulinenkirche** ⑳. Between these two churches is Harrachstrasse, which holds another Baroque gem, the **Heiligen Kreuz** ㉑, a seminary church, located shortly after you cross Dametzgasse. After inspecting the high altar by Hildebrandt, backtrack along Harrachstrasse to Dametzstrasse, where you'll turn right. At the corner of Dametzstrasse and Bethlehemstrasse is the **Nordico** ㉒, the city museum, which was originally an early-17th-century town house used by the Kremsmünster monastery for nearly 200 years as a Jesuit training center for young Scandinavian men. Now it houses a collection that ranges from archaeological finds to the Biedermeier era.

Keep going along Dametzstrasse until you reach the Graben, where you turn left and walk for a short while before turning right on Domgasse. Here is the **Alter Dom** ㉓, the old city cathedral where Anton Bruckner played the organ for 12 years, beginning in 1856. From here follow Domgasse around to the **Stadtpfarrkirche** ㉔, near the intersection to Kollegiumgasse. This was originally a Romanesque basilica before being rebuilt in the Baroque style in the mid-17th century. In the entrance hall and approach to the tower staircase you can see Gothic cross-ribbing on the vaulted ceiling.

Go left from the church onto Kollegiumgasse, then left into the Pfarrplatz. From the northwest edge of the square, head down Rathausgasse to No. 5, to view the **Kepler Haus** ㉕, home of astronomer Johannes Kepler. He lived here with his family for 10 years, beginning in 1612. More than a hundred years later, Linz's first printing shop was established here. Opposite the Kepler house, head across the Rathausgasse into the neo-Renaissance courtyard of Linz's **Altes Rathaus** ㉖—a neo-Renaissance Town Hall. Back at the central Hauptplatz square, you can decide to chill out at a café or blast forward to the 21st century by heading across the Nibelungen-Brücke bridge to see two hyper-modern sights, the **Ars Electronica Museum** ㉗ and the dazzling new contemporary art museum, **Lentos** ㉘, gleaming on the banks of the Danube.

TIMING Of course the best time to visit Linz is between May and September, but fortunately the main tourist attractions are open year-round. Touring the Old City takes two to three hours, depending on how many of the sights you stop to visit. If you're pressed for time, head straight for Linz Castle. You'll pass through the loveliest parts of the city, and from the heights of the castle grounds you'll be able to enjoy stupendous views of the Danube.

Numbers in the text correspond to numbers in the margin and on the Linz map.

What to See

23 **Alter Dom** (Old Cathedral). Hidden away off the Graben, a narrow side street off of the Taubenmarkt above the Hauptplatz, is this Baroque gem (1669–78), whose striking feature is the single nave together with the side altars. Anton Bruckner was organist here from 1856 to 1868. ⊙ *Daily 7–7.*

26 **Altes Rathaus** (Old City Hall). Located at the lower end of the main square, the original 1513 building was mostly destroyed by fire and replaced in 1658–59. Its octagonal corner turret and lunar clock, as well as some vaulted rooms, remain, and you can detect traces of the original Renaissance structure on the Rathausgasse facade. The present exterior dates from 1824. The approach from Rathausgasse 5, opposite the Kepler Haus, leads through a fine, arcaded courtyard. On the facade here you'll spot portraits of Emperor Friedrich III, the mayors Hoffmandl and Prunner, the astronomer Johannes Kepler, and the composer Anton Bruckner. ⊠ *Hauptplatz.*

27 **Ars Electronica Museum.** Just across the Nibelungen Bridge from the Hauptplatz, this futuristic museum allows visitors to try out all kinds of modern technology gadgets. Ever thought you could water a "telegarden" through the services of a robot? On the cyberdeck, you can be suspended aloft in a special flight suit and determine your own flight movements, and the virtual reality "cave" lets you experience, with the aid of 3-D glasses, the sensation of flying over Renaissance cathedrals, speeding through a labyrinth of underground tunnels, or entering a painting. Instructions for all exhibits are also in English. ⊠ *Hauptstrasse 2* ☎ *0732/72720* ⊕ *www.aec.at* ⊠ *€6* ⊙ *Wed.–Thurs. 9–5, Fri. 9–9, Sat.–Sun. 10–6.*

17 **Bischofshof** (Bishop's Residence). At the intersection of Herrenstrasse and Bischofstrasse is this impressive mansion, which dates from 1721. The residence of Mozart's friend, Count Herberstein, who was later appointed Bishop of Linz, this remains the city's most important Baroque secular building. Graced by a fine wrought-iron gateway, the building was designed by Jakob Prandtauer, the architectural genius responsible for the glorious Melk and St. Florian abbeys.

21 **Heiligen Kreuz.** This former seminary church from 1723 is a beautiful yellow-and-white Baroque treasure with an elliptical dome designed by Johann Lukas von Hildebrandt, who also designed its high altar. ⊠ *Harrachstrasse 7* ☎ *0732/771205* ⊙ *Daily 7–5.*

19 **Karmelitenkloster.** This magnificent Baroque church on Landstrasse was modeled on St. Joseph's in Prague. ⊠ *Landstrassse 33* ☎ *0732/770217* ⊙ *Daily 7–11:30 and 3–6:30.*

Märchengrotte (Fairy-tale Grotto) Railroad. Trains run through a colorful imaginary world at the top of the **Pöstlingberg**. It is entertaining for the rest of the family, as well as the kids. ☎ *0732/3400–7506* ⊕ *www.linzag. at* ⊠ *€4.50* ⊙ *Mar.–May, daily 10–5; June–Aug., daily 10–6; Sept.–Nov., daily 10–5.*

㉕ Kepler Haus. The astronomer Johannes Kepler lived here from 1612 to 1622; Linz's first printing shop was established in this house in 1745. The interior is closed to the public. ⊠ *Rathausgasse 5.*

⑮ Kremsmünsterhaus. Emperor Friedrich III is said to have died here in 1493. The building was done over in Renaissance style in 1578–80, and a story was added in 1616, with two turrets and onion domes. There's a memorial room to the emperor here; his heart is entombed in the Linz parish church, but the rest of him is in St. Stephen's cathedral in Vienna. The traditional rooms now house one of Linz's best restaurants, Herberstein. ⊠ *Altstadt 10.*

⑬ Landhaus. The early Renaissance monastery adjoining the **Minoritenkirche** is now the Landhaus, with its distinctive tower, seat of the provincial government. Look inside to see the arcaded courtyard with the Planet Fountain (honoring Johannes Kepler, the astronomer who taught here when it was Linz's college) and the Hall of Stone on the first floor, above the barrel-vaulted hall on the ground floor. This hall, the Steineren Saal, was probably the setting for a noted concert given by the Mozart children in October 1762 (from which Count Pálffy hurried back to Vienna to spread the word about the musical prodigies). For a more extensive look at the interior, inquire at the local tourist office about their scheduled guided tours. The beautiful Renaissance doorway (1570) is of red marble. ⊠ *Klosterstrasse 7.*

㉘ Lentos. Taking its name from the ancient Celtic settlement that was the origin of the city of Linz, this new contemporary art museum hugs the banks of the Danube on the Altstadt side of the river. Designed by Zürich architects Weber and Hofer, its long, low-slung gray glass structure picks up the reflection of the water and, at night, lit in shimmering blue or red, really stands out. The collection contains an impressive number of paintings by Austrian Secession artists Klimt, Schiele, and Kokoschka, along with works by other artists, including sculptures by Alfred Hrdlicka and one of those famous silkscreen portraits of Marilyn Monroe by Andy Warhol. All in all, the museum has about 1,500 artworks, with roughly a third of them on display. Plans for exhibit rotation are in the works, but considering the vast space, it seems more pieces could be shown at one time. The museum also houses a nice restaurant with beautiful views of the river. ⊠ *Ernst-Koref-Promenade 1* ☎ *0732/707–0360–0* 🖷 *0732/707–0360–4* ⊕ *www.lentos.at* 💲 *€6.50* ⊘ *Wed.–Mon., Thurs. 10–10.*

★ ⑫ Minoritenkirche. Situated at the end of Klosterstrasse, this church was once part of a monastery. The present building dates from 1752 to 1758 and has a delightful Rococo interior with side altar paintings by Kremser Schmidt and a main altar by Bartolomeo Altomonte. Mozart probably worshipped here when he stayed at the Thun Palace across the way. ⊠ *Klosterstrasse 7* ☎ *0732/772–01136–4* 💲 *Free* ⊘ *Nov.–Mar., daily 8–11 AM; Apr.–Oct., daily 8–4.*

⑭ Mozart Haus. This three-story Renaissance town house, actually the Thun Palace, has a later Baroque facade and portal. Mozart arrived here in 1783 with his wife to meet an especially impatient patron (Mozart was late by 14 days). As the composer forgot to bring any symphonies along with him, he set about writing one and completed the sublime Linz Symphony in the space of four days. The palace now houses private apartments, but the courtyard can be viewed (entering from Altstadt 17, around the corner). ⊠ *Klostergasse 20.*

⑱ Neuer Dom (New Cathedral). In 1862 the bishop of Linz engaged one of the architects of Cologne cathedral to develop a design for a cathedral in neo-Gothic French-cathedral style and modestly ordered that its tower not be higher than that of St. Stephen's in Vienna. The result was the massive 400-foot tower, shorter than St. Stephan's by a scant 6½ feet. The cathedral contains gorgeous stained-glass windows. ⊠ *Herrenstrasse 26* ☎ *0732/777885* ⊡ *Free* ☉ *Mon.–Sat. 7:30–7, Sun. 8–7.*

㉒ Nordico. At the corner of Dametzstrasse and Bethlehemstrasse, you'll find the city museum, dating from 1610. Its collection follows local history from pre-Roman times to the mid-1880s. ⊠ *Dametzstrasse 23* ☎ *0732/7070–1900* ⊕ *www.nordico.at* ⊡ *€4* ☉ *Weekdays 9–6, weekends 2–5.*

⑪ Pillar to the Holy Trinity. One of the symbols of Linz is the 65-foot Baroque column in the center of the Hauptplatz square. Completed in 1723 of white Salzburg marble, the memorial offers thanks by an earthly trinity—the provincial estates, city council, and local citizenry—for deliverance from the threats of war (1704), fire (1712), and plague (1713). From March through October there's a flea market here each Saturday (except holidays), from 7 AM to 2 PM.

★ ⑯ Schlossmuseum Linz (Linz Castle). The massive four-story building on Tummelplatz was rebuilt by Friedrich III around 1477, literally on top of a castle that dated from 799. Note the **Friedrichstor** (the Friedrich Gate), with the same *A.E.I.O.U.* monogram also found in Krems, and the two interior courtyards. This is widely known as one of the best provincial museums in the country. The interior of the castle is well worth a visit, with a 17th-century inlaid walnut portal from Schloss Hartheim, historical musical instruments (including Beethoven's Hammerklavier), recreations of rooms from 19th-century Austrian homes, fine 19th-century portraits and landscapes by Dutch and Austrian artists, as well as weaponry, coins, and ceramics. ⊠ *Tummelplatz 10* ☎ *0732/774–419* ⊕ *www.schlossmuseum.at* ⊡ *€4* ☉ *Tues.–Fri. 9–6, weekends 10–5.*

㉔ Stadtpfarrkirche. This city parish church dates from 1286 and was rebuilt in Baroque style in 1648. The tomb in the right wall of the chancel contains Friedrich III's heart. The ceiling frescoes are by Altomonte, and the figure of Johann Nepomuk (a local saint) in the chancel is by Georg Raphael Donner, with grand decoration supplied by the master designer Hildebrandt. ⊠ *Pfarrplatz 4* ☎ *0732/7761–200* ☉ *Daily 8–6.*

⑳ Ursulinenkirche. The towers at this Baroque church are one of the identifying symbols of Linz. Inside is a blaze of gold and crystal ornamentation. Note the Madonna figure wearing a hooded Carmelite cloak with huge pockets, used to collect alms for the poor. ⊠ *Landstrasse 31* ☎ *0732/7610–3151* ☉ *Daily 8–6.*

ON A CLEAR DAY
YOU CAN FLEE FOREVER

WHEN YOU WANT TO ESCAPE the hustle and bustle of Linz, just hop on electric railway, the *Pöstling-bergbahn*, for a scenic ride up to the famous mountain belvedere, the **Pöstling-berg**. With a glass of chilled white wine in hand, drink in the grand vista over Linz and the Danube from one of the flower-hung restaurants located at the top of Linz's "city mountain." At the summit is the **Church of Sieben Schmerzen Mariens**, an immense and splendidly opulent twin-towered Baroque pilgrimage church (1748), visible for miles as a Linz landmark. Also on the mountain is the **Märchengrotte (Fairy-tale Grotto)** Railroad. To reach the base station for the railway, take Streetcar 3 to the Bergbahnhof stop, which crosses the river to Urfahr, Linz's left bank. Note the railway's unusual switches, necessary because the car-wheel flanges ride the outside of the rails rather than the (usual) inside. When the line was built in 1898, it boasted the steepest incline of any non-cog railway in Europe. In summer, the old open-bench cars are used. On a clear day the view at the top takes in a good deal of Upper Austria south of the Danube, with a long chain of the Austrian Alps visible on the horizon. ☎ 0732/7801–7002 ⊕ www.linzag.at ✉ Round-trip €3.20, combined ticket with Tram 3 €5.60 (combination tickets only available at Tourist Information) ⊙ Daily, every 20 min (Sun. mornings beginning at 7:15 AM) 5:40 AM–8:20 PM.

Where to Stay & Eat

$$$$ ✕ **Herberstein.** In a historic town house in the heart of Linz's Altstadt you'll find this newly renovated restaurant, which was formerly the Kemsmünster Stuben of long standing. A fortune has been spent on the interior design, which is well integrated within the 15th-century walls, with a kind of clubby, 1960s-retro look, defined by cozy tables, muted lighting, and attractive stonework. The cuisine is Austrian with a slice of Asia, as evidenced by the selection of wok dishes and crispy, delicate fish tempura with Thai basil. Also good is the duck in a port wine sauce. Service, however, can be uneven. If the weather is fine, you can also opt to sit outside in the inviting, enclosed *Hof* (courtyard). A separate enoteca is also part of the restaurant, with surprisingly few open wines to taste by the glass. ✉ *Altstadt 10* ☎ *0732/786161* 🖷 *0732/786161–11* 🖋 *Reservations essential* ▤ *AE, DC, MC, V* ⊙ *No lunch Sat.–Mon.*

$$$ ✕ **Donautal.** Fish is the main event at this quaint old house perched above the Danube—even the warm, fresh rolls come in a fish shape. Green-striped banquette tables offer gorgeous views of the river, and there's a terrace for dining in fine weather. The menu offers such choices as grilled *Saibling* (char) served simply with lemon and capers, or crispy *Zanderfilet* (pike perch) with gnocchi in a paprika sauce. You can also get fried chicken (*Backhendl*), or vegetarian pasta. Desserts are delicious here, from the simple vanilla ice-cream sundae with chocolate sauce to caramel cannelloni stuffed with praline ice cream. Donautal is about five minutes from the Alstadt by taxi. It's also possible to walk, though it could be hazardous at night because of traffic. ⊠ *Obere Donaulände 105* ☎ *0732/795566* 🖷 *07327/795566–7* ⌦ *Reservations essential* ▭ *AE, DC, MC, V (credit cards not allowed on Sundays or holidays)* ⊘ *Closed Sun. eve., Mon.*

$$ ✕ **Goldenes Schiff.** Four generations of the Rauscher family have served traditional Austrian dishes in this rambling yellow house across the river (and about a 10-minute walk) from the Altstadt. The rustic, cozy rooms have stone walls and vaulted ceilings, and the old-fashioned kitchen proudly showcases a stone oven, which turns out delectable *Schweinsbraten* and roast duck. Vegetarian dishes are always offered. Be sure to finish with homemade apple strudel. It's particularly charming to eat here in nice weather, when tables are set out by the river with stunning views of the Altstadt. ⊠ *Ottensheimerstrasse 74* ☎ *0732/739879* 🖷 *0732/715420* ▭ *AE, DC, MC, V* ⊘ *Closed Mon.–Tues. and 2 wks around late Sept./early Oct.*

★ **$$** ✕ **Verdi Einkehr.** The trendy, less pricey bistro (Austrian-style) accompaniment to Verdi—a noted Linz dinner restaurant—Verdi Einkehr shares the same house and kitchen. The rooms are done in rustic chic, with stone fireplaces, chintz-covered chairs, and lots of polished wood. There is also a terrace for summer dining. Delights are many, ranging from guinea fowl with Venetian-style gnocchi to a *Saiblingschnitzel* (golden-fried char) served with lime radicchio risotto. If you don't have a car, you'll need a taxi to get here. It's set in Lichtenberg, about 3 km (2 mi) north of the center, off Leonfelderstrasse. You must specify that you want to be seated in the Einkehr. ⊠ *Pachmayrstrasse 137* ☎ *0732/733005* 🖷 *07327/733005–4* ⌦ *Reservations essential* ▭ *DC, MC, V* ⊘ *Closed Sun., no lunch.*

★ **$–$$** ✕ **Schloss Café.** A more pleasant spot for casual dining in Linz can hardly be imagined, tucked to the side of the town's landmark castle and affording lordly views of the Danube and opposite bank. Tables are set outside under shady trees and take full advantage of the scenery, but it's alluring inside as well, thanks to the smart red leather banquettes and modern artwork. The menu offers dishes for every taste, from the bubbling hot spinach and feta crepes or a big chicken salad with pumpkin seed oil dressing. Zipfer beer is fresh on tap, and wines from the Danube Valley are featured. ⊠ *Tummelplatz 10* ☎ *0732/781574* ▭ *MC, V.*

★ **$** ✕ **Traxlmayr.** Proud with the patina of age, this is one of Austria's great old-tradition coffeehouses. You can linger all day over a single cup of coffee, reading the papers (*Herald Tribune* included) in their bentwood holders, and then have a light meal. In winter it's extremely smoky from European cigarettes, but in summer you can sit outside on the terrace, enjoy the cleaner air, and watch passersby. Ask for the specialty, Linzertorte (almond cake with jam), with your coffee. ⊠ *Promenade 16* ☎ *0732/773353* ▭ *No credit cards* ⊘ *Closed Sun.*

$$$$ 🏨 **Arcotel Nike.** Next door to the Brucknerhaus concert hall, the Arcotel Nike is a good 10-minute walk from the Altstadt. Rooms in this modern high-rise on the banks of the Danube are smallish, and though lacking charm, they're comfortable and well-equipped. Ask for a river view. There's also a generous breakfast buffet. Check for special low rates at certain times of the year. ⊠ *Untere Donaulände 9, A-4020* ☎ *0732/76260* 🖷 *0732/76262* ⊕ *www.arcotel.at* 📞 *176 rooms* ♨ *2 restaurants, minibars, indoor pool, gym, 2 bars, Internet, meeting rooms, parking (fee)* ▤ *AE, DC, MC, V.*

★ **$$$** 🏨 **Drei Mohren.** Legend has it that three "moors" were stranded here in a snowstorm in 1770 and took such a liking to the place they made Linz their home. You, too, may cotton to this inn, which faces the Landhaus Park in the very heart of the city center. Occupying three 16th-century buildings (with lots of modernizations), this pretty, family-owned hotel has some guest rooms beautifully decorated in regal blue and gold with large, state-of-the art baths; others are smaller and more modestly furnished. The showpiece is the elegant drawing room, replete with card tables, wing-back chairs, and a fireplace. ⊠ *Promenade 17, A-4020* ☎ *0732/772626–0* 🖷 *0732/772626–6* ⊕ *www.drei-mohren.at* 📞 *22 rooms* ♨ *Bar, free parking; no a/c* ▤ *AE, DC, MC, V* ⊙| *BP.*

$$ 🏨 **Landgraf.** Set in an adorably turn-of-the-century 1904 redbrick building, this new, ultra-chic hotel is next door to the Ars Electronica Museum and just a 5-minute walk across the bridge from the Altstadt. Guest rooms are enormous, so much so that although they have a good-sized bed, desk, bookcases, and seating arrangements, they still seem rather bare. Accent walls are sometimes jarring, such as bright orange. Baths are small but efficient. The four cool suites are the real bargain here, at €185–€255. Rolf Benz designed the striking leather furniture and colorful works by artists Anatol Ak and Christian Sery adorn the walls. And, as the ultimate in luxury, their Philippe Starck bathrooms feature an open-style bath. If you don't book a suite, try to get a room on an upper floor or you might be kept awake by the faint sound of loud music emanating nightly from the trendy downstairs bar. ⊠ *Hauptstrasse 12, A-4020* ☎ *0732/700712* 🖷 *0732/700712–411* ⊕ *www.landgraf.at* 📞 *32 rooms* ♨ *Restaurant, bar, Interet; no a/c* ▤ *AE, DC, MC, V* ⊙| *BP.*

$$ 🏨 **Wolfinger.** A 500-year-old former nunnery, the centrally located Wolfinger has been a hostelry since the late 1700s. Some rooms have real charm, with vaulted ceilings and antique headboards; others are furnished with a mixture of kitsch and modern pieces. Those in the front are less quiet but offer a view of city activities. Baths are satisfactory. Rooms without bath are in the $ category. The breakfast room allures with flowing curtains and baroque-style chandeliers—a lovely way to greet the day. ⊠ *Hauptplatz 19, A-4020* ☎ *0732/773291–0* 🖷 *0732/773291–55* ⊕ *www.oberoesterreich.at/wolfinger* 📞 *45 rooms, 4 without bath* ♨ *Parking (fee); no a/c* ▤ *AE, DC, MC, V* ⊙| *BP.*

$–$$ 🏨 **Zum Schwarzen Bären.** The birthplace of the renowned Mozart tenor Richard Tauber (1891–1948), the "Black Bear" is a fine, traditional house on a quiet side street in the center of the Old City, a block from the pedestrian zone. Over the last couple of years the hotel has undergone a total overhaul, with an extremely pleasing result. The floors and walls are of gleaming wood, sprightly curtains decorate the windows, and the low, modern beds have fluffy white comforters. Some rooms contain imaginative bathrooms with brick-and-gray-tile bathtubs set out in the open. The hotel also has a very good Heuriger-style restaurant. ✉ *Herrenstrasse 9–11, A-4020* ☎ *0732/772477–0* 🖷 *0732/772477–47* ⊕ *www.linz-hotel.at* 🛏*35 rooms* ⚴ *Restaurant, bar, parking (fee); no a/c* ☰ *MC, V* ᵀᴼᶦ *BP.*

Nightlife & the Arts

Linz is far livelier than even most Austrians realize. The local population is friendlier than those of either Vienna or Salzburg, and much less cliquish. Nor has Linz lagged behind other Austrian cities in developing its own hot section, known as the Bermuda Triangle. Around the narrow streets of the Old City (Klosterstrasse, Altstadt, Hofgasse) are dozens of fascinating small bars and lounges; as you explore, you'll probably meet some Linzers who can direct you to the current "in" location.

THE ARTS The **Linz opera company** is talented and often willing to mount venturesome works and productions. Most performances are in the Landestheater, with some in the Brucknerhaus.

The tourist office's monthly booklet "Was ist los in Linz und Oberösterreich" ("What's On in Linz and Upper Austria") will give you details of theater and concerts. Two **ticket agencies** are **Linzer Kartenbüro** (✉ Herrenstrasse 4 ☎ 0732/778800) and **Kartenbüro Pirngruber** (✉ Landstrasse 34 ☎ 0732/772833 🖷 0732/772833–76).

A vast array of concerts and recitals are held in the noted **Brucknerhaus**, the modern hall on the bank of the Danube. From mid-September to early October, it's the center of the International Bruckner Festival. In mid-June the hall hosts the biggest multimedia event in the area, the Ars Electronica, a musical and laser-show spectacle. ✉ *Untere Donaulände 7* ☎ *0732/775230* ⊕ *www.brucknerhaus.at* ☉ *Box office weekdays 12–6:30, Sat. 10–1.*

NIGHTLIFE A good starting point, where both the young and the older will feel comfortable, is the below-stairs, fanciful Moroccan-style bar in the **Landgraf Hotel** (✉ Hauptstrasse 12), which is just across the bridge from the Altstadt and open Tuesday–Saturday from 6 PM until the wee hours.

The Linz **casino,** with roulette, blackjack, poker, and slot machines, is in the Hotel Schillerpark; the casino complex includes a bar and the Rouge et Noir restaurant. A passport is required for admission. Parking in the garage is free. ✉ *Rainerstrasse 2–4* ☎ *0732/654487–0* 🖷 *0732/654487–17222* 💳 *€21 (includes €25 worth of tokens)* ☉ *Daily (Except Christmas Eve) 3 PM–3 AM.*

For the young crowd there are several choices for popular late-night clubs. One of the most frequented is **Bluu Club** (✉ Graben 18/Kollegiumgasse ☎ 0732/785528), in the Altstadt, which has great cocktails and convivial groupings of deep leather sofas and chairs. It's open from 4 PM, Tuesday to Saturday. **Josef Stadtbräu** (✉ Landstrasse 49 ☎ 0732/773165) is another hopping establishment with its own home-brewed beer on tap, light snacks, or hearty regional dishes, open every day from 10 AM until very late.

Shopping

Linz is a good place to shop; prices are generally lower than those in resorts and the larger cities, and selections are varied. The major shops are found in the main square and the adjoining side streets, in the old quarter to the west of the main square, in the pedestrian zone of the Landstrasse and its side streets, and in the Hauptstrasse of Urfahr, over the Nibelungen Bridge across the Danube.

For local handmade goods and good-quality souvenirs, try **O. Ö. Heimatwerk** (⊠ Landstrasse 31 ☎ 0732/773–3770), where you'll find silver, pewter, ceramics, fabrics, and some clothing. Everything from clothing to china is sold at the **Flea Market,** open every Saturday from 7–2, on the Hauptplatz (main square). Check with the tourist office about other flea markets. At the state-run **Dorotheum auction house** (⊠ Fabrikstrasse 26 ☎ 0732/773132–0 ⊕ www.dorotheum.at), auctions take place on varying days—see the auction calendar on the Dorotheum Web site. The auction house is open to the public Monday to Friday 9–5.

For antiques, head for the Old City and these shops on the side streets around the main square. **Otto Buchinger** (⊠ Bethlehemstrasse 5 ☎ 0732/770117) is the place to go for modern graphic drawings and 19th-century furniture and artworks. **Richard Kirchmayr** (⊠ Bischofstrasse 3a ☎ 0732/797711) has a tempting collection of paintings and furniture. **Kunst-Haus Dr. Pastl** (⊠ Wischerstrasse 26 ☎ 0699/117221–44) is known throughout Linz for the great selection of sculpture and 18th-century paintings, ceramics, and porcelain. **Ferdinand Saminger** (⊠ Waldeggstrasse 20 and Hopfengasse 15 ☎ 0732/654081) sells antique paintings and objets d'art.

There are two superior places in the city center to shop for elegant jewelry at reasonable prices, **Lucas Drobny** (⊠ Herrenstrasse 20 ☎ 0732/779218–5) and **Wild** (⊠ Landstrasse 49 ☎ 0732/774105–0). For nice, less costly jewelry and souvenirs, go to **Egger Peter** (⊠ Graben 34 ☎ 0732/774670).

Outdoor Activities & Sports

BICYCLING Cyclists appreciate the relatively level terrain around Linz, and within the city there are 89 km (55 mi) of marked cycle routes. Get the brochure *Cycling in Linz* from the tourist office. You can rent a bike through **LILO Bahnhof** (⊠ Coulinstrasse 30 ☎ 0732/600703).

ICE-SKATING Linz is an ice-skating city. From late October to early March there's outdoor skating at the city rink. Check with Tourist Information for the times the rink is open. Skating is also available late September to April at the adjoining indoor sports complex, the **Eishalle,** Wednesday 8–12:30, Saturday 2–4:45, and Sunday 9–11:30 and 2:30–5. Hockey and skating competitions are also held in the Eishalle. ⊠ *Untere Donaulände 11* ☎ *0732/340–0663–1.*

EXCURSIONS FROM LINZ

Many travelers find Linz the most practical point of departure for visits to the Mühlviertel and the Gothic and Baroque sights found in the towns of St. Florian, Kremsmünster, and Steyr, although Steyr—a gorgeously Gothic-flavored town once home to the great composer Anton Bruckner—certainly merits an overnight itself. Along the way you'll be dazzled by two masterworks of the Austrian Baroque, the great abbeys of St. Florian's and Stift Kremsmünster. To the west of Linz, south of the Danube, lies the Innviertel, named for the Inn River (which forms the border with Germany before it joins the Danube), a region of broad fields and meadows, and enormous woodland tracts, ideal for cycling, hiking, and riding. To the south, the hilly landscape introduces the foothills of the Austrian Alps.

St. Florian

29 *13 km (8 mi) southeast of Linz.*

St. Florian is best known for the great Augustinian abbey, considered among the finest Baroque buildings in Austria. Composer Anton Bruckner (1824–96) was organist here for 10 years and is buried in the abbey. From Linz, you can drive south through Kleinmünchen and Ebelsberg to St. Florian, or for a more romantic approach try the **Florianer Bahn** (☎ 0732/387778), a resurrected electric interurban tram line, which runs museum streetcars on Sundays and holidays from May to early July, and from mid-August until mid-October, 6 km (4 mi) from Pichling to St. Florian; streetcars depart at 10, 1:30, and 3. At press time (summer 2004), part of the rail tracks were damaged and the Florianer Bahn will be closed for renovations. Check with the Upper Austria tourist office in Linz for information. ✉ *Freistaedterstrasse 119* ☎ *07324/221022* 🖷 *07224/ 727–7701* ⊕ *www.oberoesterreich.at.*

Built to honor the spot on the river Enns where St. Florian was drowned by pagans in 304 (he is still considered the protector against fire and **FodorsChoice** flood by many Austrians), the **Stift St. Florian** (St. Florian Abbey) over ★ the centuries came to comprise one of the most spectacular Baroque showpieces in Austria, landmarked by three gigantic "candle-snuffer" cupolas. In 1686 the Augustinian abbey was built by the Italian architect Carolo Carlone, then finished by Jakob Prandtauer. More of a palace than anything else, it is centered around a mammoth marble **Marmorsaal**—covered with frescoes honoring Prince Eugene of Savoy's defeat of the Turks—and a sumptuous library filled with 140,000 volumes. In this setting of gilt and marble, topped with ceiling frescoes by Bartolomeo Altomonte, an entire school of Austrian historiographers was born in the 19th century. Guided tours of the abbey begin with the magnificent figural gateway which rises up three stories and is covered with symbolic statues. The "Stiegenhaus," or Grand Staircase, leads to the upper floors, which include the **Kaiserzimmer**, a suite of 13 opulent salons (where you can see the "terrifying bed" of Prince Eugene, fantastically adorned with wood-carved figures of captives). The tour includes one of the great masterworks of the Austrian Baroque, Jakob Prandtauer's **Eagle Fountain courtyard,** with its richly sculpted figures. In the over-the-top **abbey church,** where the ornate surroundings are somewhat in contrast to Bruckner's music, the Krismann organ (1770–74) is one of the largest and best of its period and Bruckner used it to become a master organist and composer. Another highlight is the **Altdorfer Gallery,** which contains several masterworks by Albrecht Altdorfer, the leading master of the 16th-century Danube School and ranked with Dürer and Grunewald as one of the greatest northern painters. ✉ *Stiftstrasse 1* ☎ *07224/8902–0* 🖷 *07224/8902–31* ⊕ *www.stift-st-florian.at* 🖾 *€5.30* ⊘ *70-min tour Easter–Oct., daily at 10, 11, 2, 3, and 4.*

Nightlife & the Arts

Summer concerts are held weekends in June and July at the Kremsmünster and St. Florian abbeys; for tickets, contact **Oberösterreichische Stiftskonzerte** (✉ Domgasse 12 ☎ 0732/776127 ⊕ www.stiftskonzerte.at). A series of **concerts** (☎ 0732/221022 🖷 0732/727–7701 ⊕ www.florianer. at) on the Bruckner organ are given in the church of St. Florian during varying summer months. Also look for the St. Florian choir boys' (*Sängerknaben*) annual Christmas concert. For details check their Web site.

Kremsmünster

🟢 *36 km (22½ mi) south of Linz.*

★ The vast Benedictine **Stift Kremsmünster** was established in 777 and remains one of the most important abbeys in Austria. Most travelers arrive here by taking Route 139 (or the train) heading southwest from Linz. Inside the church is the Gothic memorial tomb of Gunther, killed by a wild boar, whose father, Tassilo, duke of Bavaria (and nemesis of Charlemagne), vowed to build the abbey on the site. Centuries later, the initial structures were replaced in the grand Baroque manner, including the extraordinary tower. Magnificent rooms include the Kaisersaal and the frescoed library with more than 100,000 volumes, many of them manuscripts. On one side of the Prälatenhof courtyard are Jakob Prandtauer's elegant fish basins, complete with sculpted saints holding squirming denizens of the deep, and opposite is the Abteitrakt, whose art collection includes the Tassilo Chalice, from about 765. The seven-story observatory (*Sternwarte*) houses an early museum of science. ☎ *07583/5275–151* ⊕ *www. kremsmuenster.at* 🖾 *Rooms and art gallery €4, observatory and tour €4.50* ⊘ *Rooms and art gallery tour (minimum 5 people) Easter–Oct., daily at 10, 11, 2, 3, and 4; Nov.–Easter, Tues.–Sun. at 11 and 2. Observatory tour (minimum 5 people) May–Oct., daily at 10 and 2.*

Schloss Kremsegg has a collection of rare musical instruments, mostly brass, with plans for a woodwind and folk music section in the future. ✉ *Kremseggerstrasse 59* ☎ *07583/52470* 🖷 *07583/6830* 🖾 *€5* ⊘ *Apr.–Oct., Wed.–Mon. 10–5. Open in winter by arrangement.*

★ $$$ ✕ **Gasthof Moser.** North of Kremsmünster on Highway 139 in the village of Neuhofen, the Moser is known throughout the countryside for its good cooking. Built in 1640, it retains a time-stained ambience with its vaulted ceilings, curving, thick white walls, and dark wood. The menu

ranges from old standards like turkey cordon bleu to the innovative can-
nelloni stuffed with *Zanderfilet* (pike perch) on a bed of roast zucchini
and tomatoes. ✉ *Marktplatz 9, A-4501 Neuhofen an der Krems* ☎ *07227/
4229* 🖷 *07227/42294* 🖃 *DC, V* ⏁ *Reservations essential* 🖃 *V* ⊙ *Closed
Mon. and 1st 2 wks of Aug. No dinner Sun., no lunch Tues.* ¶⊙¶ *BP.*

Bad Hall

③① *9 km (5½ mi) southeast of Kremsmünster, 36 km (22 mi) south of Linz.*

Bad Hall is a curious relic from earlier days when "taking the cure" was
in vogue in Europe. It's still a spa and its saline-iodine waters are pre-
scribed for internal and external complaints, but you can also enjoy the
town for its turn-of-the-20th-century frills and houses. Since those on
the cure need amusement between treatments, the town lays on numerous
sports offerings—during warm weather, there are especially excellent
opportunities for golf and tennis—and an operetta festival in summer.

Where to Stay & Eat

$$ ✕ **Forsthof.** Located between Bad Hall and Steyr in the village of Siern-
ing on Highway 122, this bustling, popular restaurant is reminiscent of
a large, venerable farmhouse, with lots of cozy rooms. The kitchen
prides itself on good home-style cooking, and local specialties might in-
clude turkey breast in a paprika sauce or *Pfandl*, a hearty skillet dish of
pork fillet with spinach spätzle and cheese gratiné. ✉ *Neustrasse 29,
A-4522 Sierning* ☎ *07259/23190* 🖷 *07259/2319–66* 🖃 *AE, MC, V*
⊙ *No dinner Sun.*

★ **$$$$** 🏨 **Schlosshotel Feyregg.** A rather grand "castle," this is more of a
palace—a textbook example of Austrian Baroque which splendidly
shimmers in a facade of white pilasters and 18th-century yellow trim.
Once the elegant summer residence of a very rich abbot, Feyregg has
some comfortable, spacious guest rooms that are a tribute to the Bie-
dermeier style. Period knickknacks scattered throughout add to the
overall feeling of being a guest in a treasured home rather than a hotel.
Baths are modern and filled with light. The township's golf course is
within an easy stroll. This is an ideal base for exploring the monaster-
ies in the area. ✉ *A-4540* ☎ *07258/2591* ⊕ *www.schlosshotels.co.at*
🖭 *11 rooms* 🖃 *No credit cards* ¶⊙¶ *BP.*

Steyr

★ ③② *18 km (11 mi) east of Bad Hall, 40 km (25 mi) south of Linz. If you
travel to Steyr from Kremsmünster, follow Route 139 until it joins
Route 122 and take the road another 17 km (10½ mi).*

Steyr is one of Austria's best-kept secrets, a stunning Gothic market
town that watches over the confluence of the Steyr and Enns rivers. Today
the main square is lined with Baroque facades, many with Rococo trim,
all complemented by the castle that sits above. The Bummerlhaus at Num-
ber 32, in its present form dating from 1497, has a late-Gothic look. On
the Enns side, steps and narrow passageways lead down to the river. Across
the River Steyr, St. Michael's church, with its Bohemian cupolas and gable
fresco, presides over the postcard-perfect scene. In the center of town is

the Stadtplatz, lined with arcaded houses, along with a Rococo-era town hall and a Late Gothic "Burger" house. Elsewhere in town are a bevy of lovely Gothic, Baroque, and Rococo churches.

In Steyr you are close to the heart of Bruckner country. He composed his Sixth Symphony in the parish house here, and there is a Bruckner room in the Meserhaus, where he composed his "sonorous music to confound celestial spheres." Schubert also lived here for a time. So many of the houses are worthy of attention that you will need to take your time and explore. Given the quaintness of the town center, you'd hardly guess that in 1894 Steyr had Europe's first electric street lighting.

The **Steyrertalbahn** (☎ 0664/381–2298), a narrow-gauge vintage railroad, wanders 17 km (10½ mi) from Steyr through the countryside from late May to late September and on weekends in December. It also runs on the holidays December 8th and 31st.

The **Museum Industrielle Arbeitswelt** (industrial museum), set in former riverside factories, is a reminder of the era when Steyr was a major center of ironmaking and armaments production; hunting arms are still produced here, but the major output is powerful motors for BMW cars, including those assembled in the United States. ⊠ *Wehrgrabengasse 7* ☎ *07252/77351* ⊕ *www.museum-steyr.at* ⊠ *€4.75* ☉ *Early Mar.–3rd week in Dec., Tues.–Sun. 9–5.*

Where to Stay & Eat

★ **$$$$** ╳ **Rahofer.** You'll have to search for this popular restaurant, which is hidden away at the end of one of the passageways off the main square. Inside it's warm and cozy with dark-wood accents and candlelight. The focus here is Italian, from the Tuscan bread and olives that are brought to your table on your arrival to the selection of fresh pastas and lightly prepared meat and fish dishes. Individual pizzas are baked to perfection with a thin, crispy crust and toppings ranging from arugula and shaved Parmesan to tuna and capers. ⊠ *Stadtplatz 9* ☎ *07252/54606* ▤ *MC, V* ☉ *Closed Sun.–Mon.*

$$–$$$$ ╳▥ **Minichmayr.** From this traditional hotel the view alone—out over the confluence of the Enns and Steyr rivers, up and across to the Schloss Lamberg and the Baroque cupolas of St. Michael's church—will make your stay memorable. And what could be more wonderful than falling asleep while listening to the river outside your window? Some of the bedrooms have been renovated with modern-style Biedermeier furnishings, complementing the Old World charm of the building's exterior and public rooms, while others have traditional cherrywood furniture. Try to get a room on the river side—the front of the hotel overlooks a busy traffic street. The restaurant, with a Secession-style inspired bar, offers classic Austrian cuisine, specializing in fresh fish. ⊠ *Haratzmüllerstrasse 1–3, A-4400* ☎ *07252/53410–0* 🖷 *07252/48202* ⊕ *www.hotel-minichmayr.at* ⇥ *47 rooms* ⌂ *Restaurant, bar, Internet; no a/c* ▤ *AE, DC, MC, V* ❙⦿❙ *BP.*

$$ ╳▥ **Mader/Zu den Drei Rosen.** In this very old family-run hotel with small but pleasant modern rooms you're right on the attractive town square. The restaurant offers solid local and traditional fare, with outdoor dining in a delightful garden area within the ancient courtyard. ⊠ *Stadt-*

platz 36, A-4400 ☎ *07252/53358–0* 🖷 *07252/53358–6* ⊕ *www.mader. at* ⇆ *62 rooms* ᗌ *Restaurant, minibars in some rooms; no a/c* ▤ *AE, DC, MC, V* ▧ *BP.*

off the
beaten
path

WAIDHOFEN AN DER YBBS – Well worth a slight detour from the more traveled routes, this picturesque river town (30 km [18 mi] east of Steyr) developed early as an industrial center, turning Styrian iron ore into swords, knives, sickles, and scythes. These weapons proved successful in the defense against the invading Turks in 1532; marking the decisive moment of victory, the hands on the north side of the town tower clock remain at 12:45. In 1871 Baron Rothschild bought the collapsing castle and assigned Friedrich Schmidt, architect of Vienna's City Hall, to rebuild it in neo-Gothic style. Stroll around the two squares in the Altstadt to see the Gothic and Baroque houses and to the Graben on the edge of the Old City for the delightful Biedermeier houses and churches and chapels.

THE WACHAU:
ALONG THE SOUTH BANK OF THE DANUBE

The gentle countryside south of the Danube and east of Linz is crossed by rivers that rise in the Alps and eventually feed the Danube. Little evidence remains today, in this prosperous country of light industry and agriculture, that the area was heavily fought over in the final days of World War II. From 1945 to 1955 the River Enns marked the border between the western (U.S., British, and French) and eastern (Russian) occupation zones. The great attractions here—and the adjective is entirely appropriate—is a string of Baroque-era abbeys, including the incomparable Stift Melk, set over the Danube.

Enns

❸❸ *20 km (12 mi) southeast of Linz.*

Enns has been continuously settled since at least AD 50; the Romans set up a major encampment shortly after that date. Contemporary Enns is dominated by the 184-foot-high city tower (1565–68) that stands in the town square. A number of Gothic buildings in the center have Renaissance or Baroque facades. Visit the **Basilika St. Laurenz,** built on the foundations of a far earlier church, west of the town center, to view the glass-encased archaeological discoveries. And outside, look for the Baroque carved-wood Pontius Pilate disguised as a Turk, alongside a bound Christ, on the balcony of the old sanctuary. **Guided tours** (☎ 07223/82777) of the town's highlights, starting at the tower, are available daily for a minimum of three persons at 10:30, May–mid-September. The cost is €4 for the 1½-hour tour, and if there are 10 or more people, the price drops to €3.

Where to Stay

$ ▨ **Lauriacum.** You might overlook this plain contemporary building, set as it is among Baroque gems in the center of town, but it's the best place to stay. An effort has been made to make the rooms attractive; some are painted a warm yellow while others have pretty bed throws or cozy quilts. In fine weather, the quiet garden is a welcoming spot. ☒ *Wienerstrasse 5–7, A-4470* ☎ *07223/82315* 🖷 *07223/82332–29* ⊕ *www.lauriacum. at* 🛏 *30 rooms* ⚭ *Restaurant, café, sauna, bar, Internet, minibars; no a/c* ⊟ *MC, V* ⊙ *BP.*

Mauthausen

㉞ *14 km (8½ mi) southeast of Linz, 6 km (4 mi) north of Enns.*

In the midst of all the beauty of the Wachau Valley, horror. Adolf Hitler had the **Mauthausen Konzentrationslager,** the main concentration camp in Austria, built here along the bank of the Danube in the town of the same name. From Linz, follow signs to Enns and Perg, and then to the EHE-MALIGE KZ DENKMAL, the concentration-camp memorial. The pretty town of Mauthausen, set with numerous 15th- and 16th-century buildings, was selected as the site for a concentration camp because of the granite quarries nearby, which would provide material needed for the grandiose buildings projected in Hitler's "Führer cities." The grim, gray fortress was opened in August 1938 for male prisoners (including boys), and the conditions under which they labored were severe even by SS standards. Beginning in the early 1940s, women were also admitted as prisoners. More than 125,000 people lost their lives here before the camp was liberated by the American army in May 1945. Much of the camp is preserved exactly as it was left after the liberation, and it's possible to walk through many of the low, wooden buildings. An impressive new visitors' information center opened in 2003, offering semi-private cubicles with headphones for listening to videotaped testimonies of survivors. The site also includes a small museum and memorials, as well as a bookstore. ☒ *Erinnerungsstrasse 1, A-4310* ☎ *07238/2269* 🖷 *07238/2269–40* ⊕ *www.mauthausen-memorial.at* 🎫 *€2* ⊙ *Open daily 9–5:30.*

Ybbs an der Donau

㉟ *69 km (43 mi) east of Linz.*

Floods and fires have left their mark on Ybbs an der Donau, but many 16th-century houses remain, their courtyards vine-covered and shaded. The parish church of **St. Laurence** has interesting old tombstones, a gorgeous gilt organ, and a Mount of Olives scene with clay figures dating from 1450. To get to Ybbs an der Donau from Waidhofen an der Ybbs, make your way back to the Danube via Routes 31 and 22 east, then take Route 25 north through the beer-brewing town of Wieselburg.

Melk

★ **㊱** *22 km (13 mi) east of Ybbs an der Donau, 18 km (11 mi) west of St. Pölten, 33 km (20¾ mi) southwest of Krems.*

Unquestionably one of the most impressive sights in all Austria, the abbey of Melk is best approached in mid- to late afternoon, when the setting sun ignites the abbey's ornate Baroque yellow facade. As one heads eastward paralleling the Danube, the abbey, shining on its promontory above the river, comes into view. It easily overshadows the town—located along Route 1—but remember that the riverside village of Melk itself is worth exploring. A self-guided tour (in English, from the tourist office) will head you toward the highlights and the best spots from which to photograph the abbey.

Fodor's Choice By any standard, **Stift Melk** (Melk Abbey) is a Baroque-era masterpiece.
★ Part palace, part monastery, part opera-set, Melk is a magnificent vision thanks greatly to the upward-reaching twin towers, capped with Baroque helmets and cradling a 208-foot-high dome, and a roof bristling with Baroque statuary. Symmetry here beyond the towers and dome would be misplaced, and much of the abbey's charm is due to the way the early architects were forced to fit the building to the rocky outcrop that forms its base. Locale for part of Umberto Eco's *Name of the Rose,* once Napoléon's Upper Austria redoubt, erected on the site of an ancient Roman fort, and still a working monastery, the Benedictine abbey has a history that extends back to the 11th century, as it was established in 1089. The glorious building you see today is architect Jakob Prandtauer's reconstruction, completed in 1736, in which some earlier elements are incorporated; two years later a great fire nearly totally destroyed the abbey and it had to be rebuilt. A tour of the building includes the main public rooms: a magnificent library, with more than 90,000 books, nearly 2,000 manuscripts, and a superb ceiling fresco by the master Paul Troger; the **Marmorsaal,** whose windows on three sides enhance the ceiling frescoes; the glorious spiral staircase; and the **Stiftskirche** (abbey church) of Saints Peter and Paul, an exquisite example of the Baroque style. Call to find out if tours in English will be offered on a specific day. The **Stiftsrestaurant** (closed November–April) offers standard fare, but the abbey's excellent wines elevate a simple meal to a lofty experience—particularly on a sunny day on the terrace. ⊠ *Abt Berthold Dietmayr-Strasse 1* ☎ *02752/555–225* 🖷 *02752/555–226* ⊕ *www.stiftmelk.at* 🎟 *€7; with tour €8.60* ☉ *End of Mar.–Apr. and Oct., daily 9–5 (ticket office closes at 4); May–Sept., daily 9–6 (ticket office closes at 5).*

Where to Stay & Eat

★ **$$–$$$** ✕🏨 **Tom's.** The Wallner family has given son Tom full creative control of the kitchen in this Melk landmark, and to show their approval, they even changed the name from Stadt Melk to Tom's. Nestled below the golden abbey in the center of the village square, the high standards of this elegant outpost (whose guest roster includes the Duke and Duchess of Windsor) have been upheld, and the decidedly Biedermeier atmosphere unchanged. The seasonal menu may include zucchini Parmesan lasagne with truffles or fresh grilled crayfish dribbled with butter and lemon. The fried chicken is excellent. Desserts are irresistible, such as chocolate pudding with a Grand Marnier parfait or cheese curd soufflé with homemade pistachio ice cream. Upstairs are 16 (rather plain) bedrooms in the $ category, a good bet if you wish to overnight in magical Melk. ⊠ *Hauptplatz 1, A-3390* ☎ *02752/52475* 🖷 *02752/52475–19* 🛏 *16 rooms* ▤ *AE, DC, MC, V* ☉ *Closed Wed. and variable weeks in winter* ⦿❘ *BP.*

$–$$ 🏨 **Hotel zur Post.** Here in the center of town you're in a typical village hotel with the traditional friendliness of family management. The rooms are nothing fancy, though comfortable, and the restaurant offers solid, standard fare. ⊠ *Linzer Strasse 1, A-3390* ☎ *02752/52345* 🖷 *02752/ 52345–50* 🖘 *27 rooms* ⚴ *Restaurant; no a/c* ▤ *DC, MC, V* ⊘ *Closed Jan.–Feb.* ⦙◉⦙ *BP.*

Schallaburg

③⑦ *6 km (4 mi) south of Melk.*

From Melk, take a road south marked to Mank to arrive at the restored **Schloss Schallaburg** (dating from 1573), a castle featuring an imposing two-story arcaded courtyard that is held to be the area's finest example of Renaissance architecture. Its ornate, warm brown terra-cotta decoration is unusual. The yard once served as a jousting court. Many centuries have left their mark on the castle: inside, the Romanesque living quarters give way to an ornate Gothic chapel. The castle now houses changing special exhibits. ⊠ *3382 Schloss Schallaburg* ☎ *02754/6317* 🖷 *02754/631755* ⊕ *www.schallaburg.at* 🗐 *€7* ⊘ *May–early Nov., Mon.–Fri. 9–5, Sat.–Sun. 9–6 (last admission 1 hr before closing).*

en route To return to the Wachau from Schallaburg, head back toward Melk and take Route 33 along the south bank. This route, attractive any time of year, is spectacular (and thus heavily traveled) in early spring, when apricot and apple trees burst into glorious bloom. Among the palette of photogenic pleasures is **Schönbühel an der Donau,** whose unbelievably picturesque castle, perched on a cliff overlooking the Danube, is unfortunately not open to visitors. Past the village of Aggsbachdorf you'll spot, on a hill to your right, the romantic ruin of 13th-century Aggstein Castle, reportedly the lair of pirates who preyed on river traffic.

Mautern

③⑧ *34 km (21 mi) northeast of Melk, 1 km (½ mi) south of Stein.*

Mautern, opposite Krems, was a Roman encampment mentioned in the tales of the Nibelungs. The old houses and the castle are attractive, but contemporary Mautern is known for one of Austria's top restaurants, in an inn run by Lisl Wagner-Bacher; another culinary landmark, Schickh, near Göttweig Abbey, is also excellent and run by her brother and sister.

Where to Stay & Eat

$$$$ ✕🏠 **Landhaus Bacher.** This is one of Austria's best restaurants, elegant
Fodor'sChoice but entirely lacking in pretension. The innovative style of Lisl Wagner-
★ Bacher, the top female chef in the country, is based on the changing seasons. In autumn, look for pumpkin cream soup and pheasant breast with chestnut ravioli; in winter, scallops with sautéed chicory and pike perch with crispy cabbage lasagne; then in spring, Bärlauch (wild wood garlic) spagettini and tender veal fillet with prosciutto and fresh asparagus; and in summer, locally caught grilled trout, or cornfed chicken with citrus ginger noodles. Dining in the garden in summer enhances the experience, but the dining rooms are very soigné, with library shelves, coun-

try curtains, and a mellow, golden light. For an added treat, stay overnight in an exquisite Laura Ashley–decorated bedroom in the 10-room guest house (in the $$–$$$ category), located on the riverbank opposite Krems. ⊠ *Südtirolerplatz 208* ☎ *02732/82937–0* 🖷 *02732/ 74337* ⊕ *www.landhaus-bacher.at* ♒ *Reservations essential* 🖃 *DC, V* ☉ *Closed Mon.–Tues. and Jan. 7–Feb.* ⦿ *BP.*

Göttweig

③⑨ *4 km (2½ mi) south of Mautern, 7 km (4½ mi) south of Krems.*

★ You're certain to spot the "Austrian Montecassino," **Stift Göttweig** (Göttweig Abbey), as you come along the riverside road: vast and squat like its famous Italian counterpart, this vast Benedictine abbey sits high above the Danube Valley atop a mountain gateway to the Wachau. To reach it, cross the river from Krems in the direction of Mautern and then follow signs to Stift Göttweig. Göttweig's exterior was redone in the mid-1700s in the classical style, which you'll note from the columns, balcony, and relatively plain side towers. Inside, it is a monument to Baroque art, with marvelous ornate decoration against the gold, brown, and blue. The stained-glass windows behind the high altar date from the mid-1400s. The public rooms of the abbey are splendid, particularly the **Kaiserzimmer** (Emperor's Rooms), in which Napoléon stayed in 1809, reached via the elegant Emperor's Staircase. During the summer, the abbey presents concerts. The abbey has rooms for overnight guests, so you might wish to book accordingly. ⊠ *Furth bei Göttweig* ☎ *02732/85581–231* ⊕ *www.stiftgoettweig.or.at* 🎫 *€5, with guided tour €7* ☉ *Mid-Mar.–mid-Nov. daily 10–6 (last admittance at 5); guided tours at 11 and 3; rest of year by appt.*

Where to Eat

★ **$–$$** ✕ **Schickh.** This rambling yellow restaurant, tucked away next to a brook and among lovely old trees below the north side of Göttweig Abbey, is worth looking for. Chef Christian Schickh creates new versions of traditional Austrian dishes while his sister Eva makes sure everything runs smoothly. Seasonal choices might include creamy *Bärlauch* (wild wood garlic) soup, organic Waldviertler duck and homemade dumplings, or delicately seasoned fried chicken. Be sure to save room for the house dessert, *Cremeschnitte,* a light cream pastry. There's a handful of agreeable guest rooms in the $ category available for overnighters. To reach Schickh, cross the river from Krems in the direction of Mautern and Furth bei Göttweig, continuing on a couple of kilometers to the tiny village of Klein Wien. ⊠ *Klein-Wien 2, Furth bei Göttweig* ☎ *02736/7218–0* 🖷 *02736/7218–7* ⊕ *www.schickh.at* ♒ *Reservations essential* 🖃 *MC, V* ☉ *Closed Wed.–Thurs. and mid-Jan.–Mar.*

Tulln

④⓪ *41 km (24½ mi) northeast of St. Pölten, 42 km (26¼ mi) west of Vienna.*

At Tulln you'll spot a number of charming Baroque touches in the attractive main square. There's an **Egon Schiele Museum** to honor the great modern artist (1890–1918), who was born here; the museum showing a selection of his works is in the one-time district prison, with a reconstruction of the cell in which Schiele—accused of producing "pornography"—was locked up in 1912. ⊠ *Donaulände 28* ☎ *02272/64570* ⊕ *www.egonschiele. museum.com* 🖅 *€3.50, more for special exhibits* ۞ *1st 3 wks of Mar. and July 5–Oct., Tues.–Sun. 1–6; end Mar.–July 4, Tues.–Sun. 10–6.*

A former **Minorite cloister** houses the interesting **Römemuseum** (Rome Museum) which recalls the early Roman settlements in the area. Also look inside the well-preserved, late-Baroque (1750) Minorite church next door. ⊠ *Marc-Aurel-Park 1b* ☎ *02272/65922* 🖅 *€3* ۞ *Mar.–Oct., Tues.–Sun. 1–6.*

Where to Stay & Eat

★ **$$–$$$** ✕ **Floh.** Charmingly homey and cozy, this corner Gasthaus is located on the main street of tiny Langelebarn, just a couple of kilometers from Tulln. Josef Floh, the young and creative chef, trained at top restaurants in the Salzkammergut and Tirol before setting up his own establishment. You're in luck if you're here in spring, when it's possible to have a plateful of the outstanding Tullnerfeld asparagus (to connoisseurs, more prized than the Marchfeld asparagus of Burgenland), dressed with local organic melted butter and Parmesan. If you're in the mood for a heartier dish, try the tender, perfectly grilled beef with light, creamy semolina dumplings, the duck breast with lentils, or the delicious fried chicken and potato salad. Austrian wines from the area are reasonably priced. ⊠ *Tullner Strasse 1* ☎ *02272/62809* ⌂ *Reservations essential* ▤ *AE, DC, MC, V* ۞ *Closed Tues.–Wed. and last wk of June, 1st 3 wks of Sept.*

$$$ ✕ **Zur Sonne.** Just a 5-minute walk from the Tulln train station, this upscale Gasthaus is owned by the Sodoma family, who regularly zip down to Italy to get the latest Italian cuisine. Elegant yet unpretentious, Zur Sonne has high ceilings, large windows, and fresh flowers. The seasonally changing menu may include *Saibling* (char) lasagne with garden vegetables, organic pork in a creamy mushroom cabbage sauce with *Erdäpfelpuffer* (hash browns), or saltimbocca of chicken breast with herb risotto. Austrian wines by the glass are very reasonable. Make sure to end your meal with the homemade apple strudel, which comes warm out of the oven. It's a 20-minute train ride from the Heiligenstadt or Franz Josef stations in Vienna. ⊠ *Bahnhofstrasse 48* ☎ *02272/64616* ⌂ *Reservations essential* ▤ *No credit cards* ۞ *Closed Sun.–Mon.*

$–$$ 🏠 **Zur Rossmühle.** From the abundant greenery of the reception area to the table settings in the dining room, you'll find pleasing little touches in this attractively situated hotel on the town square. The rooms are done in grand-old yet brand-new Baroque. Take lunch in the courtyard garden; here, as in the more formal dining room, you'll be offered Austrian standards. ⊠ *Hauptplatz 12–13, A-3430* ☎ *02272/62411* 🖶 *02272/ 62411–33* ⊕ *www.rossmuehle.at* ⇆ *55 rooms* ⌂ *Restaurant, sauna, horseback riding, bar; no a/c* ▤ *AE, DC, MC, V* ۞| *BP.*

Greifenstein

41 *10 km (6½ mi) northeast of Tulln.*

Greifenstein is east of Tulln along Route 14; turn left at St. Andrä-Wördern and stay on bank of the Danube. Atop the hill at Greifenstein, yet another **castle** with spectacular views looks up the Danube and across to Stockerau. Its earliest parts date from 1135, but most of it stems from a thorough but romantic renovation in 1818. The view is worth the climb, even when the castle and inexpensive restaurant are closed. ✉ *Koster-sitzgasse 5* ☎ *02242/32353* ⊕ *www.burggreifenstein.at* 🎫 *€4 for guided tour, 8-person minimum* ☉ *Apr.–Oct., Sat.–Sun. 1–5.*

Klosterneuburg

④② *13 km (8 mi) northwest of Vienna.*

★ The great Augustinian abbey **Stift Klosterneuburg** dominates the town. The structure has undergone many changes since the abbey was established in 1114, most recently in 1892, when Friedrich Schmidt, architect of Vienna's City Hall, added neo-Gothic embellishments to its two identifying towers. Klosterneuburg was unusual in that until 1568 it housed both men's and women's religious orders. In the abbey church, look for the carved-wood choir loft and oratory and the large 17th-century organ. Among Klosterneuburg's treasures are the beautifully enameled 1181 Verdun Altar in the Leopold Chapel, stained-glass windows from the 14th and 15th centuries, Romanesque candelabra from the 12th century, and gorgeous ceiling frescoes in the great marble hall. In an adjacent outbuilding there's a huge wine cask over which people slide; the exercise, called *Fasslrutsch'n,* is indulged in during the Leopoldiweinkost, the wine tasting around St. Leopold's Day, November 15. The **Stiftskeller,** with its atmospheric underground rooms, serves standard Austrian fare and wine bearing the Klosterneuberg label. ✉ *Stiftsplatz 1* ☎ *02243/411-0* ⊕ *www.stift-klosterneuburg.at* 🎫 *€5.50* ☉ *Mon.–Fri. 9–6, Sat.–Sun. 9–5, tours in English Sun. at 1 and 4.*

The **Sammlung Essl** contemporary art museum, somewhat alarmingly resembling a sports center from the outside, was designed by Heinz Tesar to showcase works created after 1945. The permanent collection includes works by such regional artists as Hermann Nitsch and Arnulf Rainer, and changing exhibitions focus on contemporary artists, including Nam June Paik. The emphasis here is on "new," including special evening concerts highlighting various modern composers' work. To get to the Sammlung Essl museum, take the U-4 to Heiligenstadt, then transfer to Bus 239 to Klosterneuberg. ✉ *An der Donau–Au 1* ☎ *02243/370-5015-0* 🖷 *02243/370-5022* ⊕ *www.sammlung-essl.at* 🎫 *€6* ☉ *Tues.–Sun. 10–7, Wed. 10–9.*

off the
beaten
path

KAHLENBERGERDORF – Near Klosterneuburg and just off the road tucked under the Leopoldsberg promontory is the charming small vintners' village of Kahlenbergerdorf, an excellent spot to stop and sample the local wines. You're just outside the Vienna city limits here, which accounts for the crowds (of Viennese, not international tourists) on weekends.

DANUBE VALLEY A TO Z

To research prices, get advice from other travelers, and book travel arrangements, visit www.fodors.com.

AIR TRAVEL

Linz is served mainly by Austrian Airlines, Lufthansa, Swissair, and Tyrolean. Regular flights connect with Vienna, Amsterdam, Berlin, Düsseldorf, Frankfurt, Paris, Stuttgart, and Zürich.

AIRPORTS   The Linz airport is in Hörsching, about 12 km (7½ mi) southwest of the city. Buses run between the airport and the main train station according to flight schedules.

🚹 Airport Information **Linz airport** ☎ 07221/600-0.

BIKE TRAVEL

At train stations along the Danube Valley, you can rent bikes from various concessioners. The best option is to rent from Pedal Power in Vienna. They have a great guidebook in English, "The Danube Bike Trail" for €13 (€20 if mailed to the U.S.). As for taking the bikes on trains: many trains, especially Vienna's Inner City trains, limit the amount of bikes they'll haul, and in summer it's really hard to get a space for your bike. Regional trains are then the best bet, and they'll also stop in Melk and Krems, for instance.

For details on the scenic Danube river route, ask for the folder "Danube Cycle Track" (in English, from Tourist Office of Lower Austria). The brochure "Radfahren" is in German, but lists contact numbers for cycle rentals throughout Austria. You can rent a bike in Linz (⇨ Outdoor Activities and Sports *in* Linz, *above*). You can rent a bike privately in Kremsmünster at Tenniscenter Stadlhuber.

🚹 Bike Maps **Tourist Office of Lower Austria** ☎ 01/53610-6200 🖶 01/53610-6060.
🚹 Bike Rentals **Pedal Power** ✉ Ausstellungsstrasse 3, A-1020 Vienna ☎ 01/729-7234
🖶 01/729-7235 ⊕ www.pedalpower.at. **Tenniscenter Stadlhuber** ☎ 07583/7498-0.

BOAT & FERRY TRAVEL

You can take a day trip from Vienna and explore one of the stops, such as Krems, Dürnstein, or Melk. Boats run from May to late September. There are two boat companies that ply the Danube. For full information on cruises offered by the Blue Danube Schifffahrt/DDSG (Vienna to Dürnstein) and the Brandner Schifffahrt (Krems to Melk), *see* "And the Danube Waltzes On," in the Pleasures & Pastimes section.

Bridges across the river are few along this stretch, so boats provide essential transportation; service is frequent enough that you can cross the river, visit a town, catch a bus or the next boat to the next town, and cross the river farther up- or downstream.

🚹 Boat & Ferry Information **Blue Danube Schifffahrt/DDSG** ✉ Friedrichstrasse 7, A-1043 Vienna ☎ 01/588-800 🖶 01/58880-440 ⊕ www.ddsg-blue-danube.at. **Brandner Schifffahrt** ✉ Ufer 50, A-3313 Wallsee ☎ 07433/2590-21 ⊕ www.brandner.at.

BUS TRAVEL

If you link them together, bus routes will get you to the main points in this region and even to the hilltop castles and monasteries, assuming you have the time. If you coordinate your schedule to arrive at a point by train or boat, you can usually make reasonable bus connections to outlying destinations. The main bus route links Krems and Melk. You can book bus tours in Vienna or Linz by calling central bus information, listed below.
▓ Bus Information **Central bus information** ☎ 01/71101.

CAR RENTALS

Cars can be rented at the airports in Vienna (⇨ Vienna A to Z *in* Chapter 1) or Linz. Linz contacts are listed below.
▓ Major Agencies **Avis** ⊠ Flughafenstrasse 1 ☎ 0732/662881. **Denzel Drive** ⊠ Wienerstrasse 91 ☎ 0732/6000-91. **Hertz** ⊠ Bürgerstrasse 19 ☎ 0732/784841-0.

CAR TRAVEL

A car is certainly the most comfortable way to see this region, as it conveniently enables you to pursue the byways. The main route along the north bank of the Danube is Route 3; along the south bank, there's a choice between the autobahn Route A1 and a collection of lesser but good roads. Roads are good and well marked, and you can switch over to the A1 autobahn, which parallels the general east–west course of the Danube Valley route.

EMERGENCIES

If you need a doctor and speak no German, ask your hotel how best to obtain assistance.
▓ Emergency services **Ambulance** ☎ 144. **Fire** ☎ 122. **Police** ☎ 133.

SPORTS & THE OUTDOORS

CANOING The Danube is fast and tricky, so you're best off sticking to the calmer waters back of the power dams (at Pöchlarn, above Melk, and near Grein). You can also canoe on an arm of the Danube near Ottensheim, about 8 km (5 mi) west of Linz. There are a couple of places to rent canoes, which are listed below.
▓ **Ruderverein Donau** ⊠ Heilhamerweg 2, Linz ☎ 0732/736250. **Ruderverein Ister-Sparkasse** ⊠ Am Winterhafen 19, Linz ☎ 0732/774888.

FISHING In the streams and lakes of the area around Linz, you can fly-cast for rainbow and brook trout and troll for pike and carp. Check with the town tourist offices about licenses and fishing rights for river trolling and fly-casting in Aggsbach-Markt, Dürnstein, Emmersdorf, Grein, Klein-Pöchlarn, Krems, Mautern, Mauthausen, Persenbeug–Gottsdorf, Pöchlarn, Schönbühel/Aggsbachdorf, Spitz, Waidhofen/Ybbs, and Ybbs.

HIKING Local tourist offices have maps and route details of the fabulous trails in the area. For information on the Mühlviertel from Freistadt to Grein, contact the Freistadt tourist office below.

TOURS

Tours out of Vienna take you to Melk and back by bus and boat. For example, see the tour offered by www.viennasightseeingtours.com/EFIRST. htm (click on Danube Valley and then full day tours). These tours usually run about eight hours, with a stop at Dürnstein. Bus tours operate year-round except as noted, but the boat runs only April–October.

🔗 Fees and Schedules **Cityrama Sightseeing** ✉ Börsegasse 1 ☎ 01/534-130 📠 01/534-1328. **Vienna Sightseeing Tours** ✉ Graf Starhemberggasse 25 ☎ 01/712-4683-0 📠 01/714-1141.

TRAIN TRAVEL

Rail lines parallel the north and south banks of the Danube. Fast services from Vienna run as far as Stockerau; beyond that, service is less frequent. The main east–west line from Vienna to Linz closely follows the south bank for much of its route. Fast trains connect German cities via Passau with Linz.

All the larger towns and cities in the region can be reached by train, but the train misses the Wachau Valley along the Danube's south bank. The rail line on the north side of the river clings to the bank in places; service is infrequent. You can combine rail and boat transportation along this route, taking the train upstream and crisscrossing your way back on the river. From Linz, the delightful LILO (Linzer Lokalbahn) interurban line makes the run up to Eferding. A charming narrow-gauge line meanders south to Waidhofen an der Ybbs.

🔗 Train Information **LILO** ☎ 0732/600703 or 0732/707-0145-0. **ÖBB–Österreichisches Bundesbahn** ☎ 05/1717.

TRAVEL AGENCIES

In Linz, there are several leading travel agencies.

🔗 Local Agent Referrals **American Express** ✉ Bürgerstrasse 14 ☎ 0732/669013 📠 0732/655334. **Kuoni** ✉ Hauptplatz 14 ☎ 0732/771301 📠 0732/775338. **Oberösterreichisches Landesreisebüro** ✉ Hauptplatz 9 ☎ 0732/771061-0 📠 0732/771061-49.

VISITOR INFORMATION

For general information on the area, check with the district tourist offices: Lower Austria, Upper Austria, Linz, Mühlviertel, and Wachau. In Linz you can pick up the latest *Guests Magazine* in English as well as German.

Most towns have a local *Fremdenverkehrsamt* (tourist office); these are listed below by town name.

🔗 Tourist Information **Dürnstein** ✉ Rathaus A-3601 ☎ 02711/200. **Grein** ✉ Stadtplatz 7, A-4360 ☎ 07268/7055. **Klosterneuburg** ✉ Rathausplatz1, A-3400 ☎ 02243/34396 ⊕ www.klosterneuburg.net/tourismus. **Krems/Stein** ✉ Undstrasse 6, A-3500 ☎ 02732/82676 📠 02732/70011 ⊕ www.krems.at. **Linz** ✉ Hauptplatz 1, A-4020 Linz ☎ 0732/707-0177-1 📠 0732/772873 ⊕ www.linz.at. **Lower Austria** ✉ Niederösterreich Werbung GmbH, Fischhof 3/3, A-1010 Vienna ☎ 01/53610-6200 📠 01/53610-6060. **Melk** ✉ Babenbergerstrasse 1, A-3390 ☎ 02752/52307-410 📠 02752/52307-490. **Steyr** ✉ Stadtplatz 27, A-4400 ☎ 07252/53229-0 📠 07252/53229-15. **Tulln** ✉ Minoritenplatz 2, A-3430 ☎ 02272/67566 📠 02272/67566-44 ⊕ www.tulln.at. **Upper Austria** ✉ Freistaedter Strasse 119, A-4041 Linz ☎ 0732/221022 📠 0732/727-7701 ⊕ www.oberoesterreich.at. **Wachau** ✉ Schlossgasse 3, A-3620 Spitz an der Donau ☎ 02713/300-6015 📠 02713/300-6030 ⊕ www.wachau.at. **Waidhofen an der Ybbs** ✉ Freisingerberg 2, A-3340 ☎ 07442/511255 📠 07442/511259 ⊕ www.waidhofen.at. **Weissenkirchen** ✉ Donaulände 262, A-3610 ☎ 02715/2600 📠 02715/2600-16 ⊕ www.weissenkirchen-wachau.at.

SALZBURG

5

PONDER THE MYSTERY OF GENIUS
at Mozart's Birthplace ⇨*p.254*

CATCH ALL THE SIGHTS DEVOTED TO
Salzburg's unofficial anthem—
"The Sound of Music" ⇨*p.260*

SAVOR A VIENNESE COFFEE
at the famed Café Tomaselli ⇨*p.276*

HOIST A STEIN TO AULD LANG SYNE
at the glamorous Goldener Hirsch ⇨*p.278*

GO FOR BROKE FOR THE BIG ONE:
a Salzburg Music Festival gala ⇨*p.285*

DANCE UP ALL 1,000 STEPS
to the Fortress Hohensalzburg ⇨*p.262*

SEEK THE SOURCE OF "SILENT NIGHT"
at the chapel in Oberndorf ⇨*p.268*

Updated by
Horst Erwin
Reischenböck

"ALL SALZBURG IS A STAGE," Count Ferdinand Czernin once wrote. "Its beauty, its tradition, its history enshrined in the grey stone of which its buildings are made, its round of music, its crowd of fancy-dressed people, all combine to lift you out of everyday life, to make you forget that somewhere far off, life hides another, drearier, harder, and more unpleasant reality." Shortly after the count's book, *This Salzburg,* was published in 1937, the unpleasant reality arrived; but having survived the Nazis, Salzburg once again became one of Austria's top drawing cards. Art lovers call it the Golden City of High Baroque; historians refer to it as the Florence of the North or the German Rome; and, of course, music lovers know it as the birthplace of one of the world's most beloved composers, Wolfgang Amadeus Mozart (1756–91). If the young Mozart was the boy wonder of 18th-century Europe and Salzburg did him no particular honor in his lifetime, it is making up for it now. Since 1920, the world-famous Salzburger Festspiele (Salzburg Festival), the third oldest on the continent, has honored "Wolferl" with performances of his works by the world's greatest musicians. To see and hear them, celeb-heavy crowds pack the city from the last week in July until the end of August. Whether performed in the festival halls—the Grosses Festspielhaus, the "House for Mozart," and the Felsenreitschule, to name the big three—or outdoors with opulent Baroque volutes and pilasters of Salzburg's architecture as background, Mozart's music serves as the heartbeat of the city. No more so than during the 2006 Mozart Year, when the city will celebrate the 250th birthday of its most famous home boy with a nearly 24/7 year-long party which kicks off on the big B-day itself, January 27.

Ironically, many who come to this golden city of High Baroque may first hear the instantly recognizable strains of music from the film that made Salzburg a household name: from the Mönchsberg to Nonnberg Convent, it's hard to go exploring without hearing someone humming "How Do You Solve a Problem Like Maria?" A popular tourist exercise is to make the town's acquaintance by visiting all the sights featured in that beloved Hollywood extravaganza, *The Sound of Music,* filmed here in 1964. Julie Andrews may wish it wasn't so, but one can hardly imagine taking in the Mirabell Gardens, the Pferdeschwemme fountain, Nonnberg Convent, the Residenzplatz, and all the other filmed locations without imagining Maria and the von Trapp children trilling their hearts out. Oddly enough, just like Mozart, the Trapp family—who escaped the Third Reich by fleeing their beloved country—were little appreciated at home; Austria was the only place on the planet where the film failed, closing after a single week's showing didn't in Vienna and Salzburg. It is said that the Austrian populace at large didn't cotton to a prominent family up-and-running in the face of the Nazis; Whispers persist, however, that if the Austrians made a show of disdaining the anti-Nazi von Trapps, well, that proves. . . . Even now, locals are amazed by *The Sound of Music*'s popularity around the world, but slowly, more and more Austrians are warming up to the film. In fact, it was just in 2005 that Vienna's Volksoper premiered the first Austrian stage production of the Broadway musical, so it may just be a matter of time before the Panorama Sightseeing bus tours of Salzburg's *SoM* sites may be crammed with as many Austrians as Americans.

But whether it is the arias of Mozart or the ditties of Rodgers and Hammerstein, no one can deny music is the element that shapes the life of the city. It is heard everywhere: in churches, castles, palaces, town house courtyards, and, of course, concert halls. During the five weeks of the Salzburger Festspiele, there are as many as ten concerts a day to select from (months in advance, of course—many events are pre-sold out). If the Salzburg Music Festival remains one of the world's most stirring musical events, this is also due to its perfect setting. Salzburg lies on both banks of the Salzach River, at the point where it is pinched between two mountains, the Kapuzinerberg on one side, the Mönchsberg on the other. In broader view are many beautiful Alpine peaks. To these many gifts of Mother Nature, man's contribution is a trove of buildings worthy of such surroundings. Salzburg's rulers pursued construction on a grand scale ever since Wolf-Dietrich von Raitenau—the "Medici prince-archbishop who preached in stone"—began his regime in the latter part of the 16th century. Astonishingly, they all seem to have shared the same artistic bent, with the result that Salzburg's many fine buildings blend into a harmonious whole. Perhaps nowhere else in the world is there so cohesive a flowering of Baroque architecture. That is because Wolf-Dietrich employed nothing but Italian architects. At the age of only 28, he envisioned "his" Salzburg to be the Rome of the Alps, with a town cathedral grander than St. Peter's, a Residenz as splendid as a Roman palace, and his private Mirabell Gardens flaunting the most fashionable styles of Italianate horticulture. This amazing man did not deny himself passion simply because he was a bishop: he honored his mistress with twelve children and a palace of her very own. After he was deposed by the rulers of Bavaria—he was imprisoned (very elegantly, thank you) in the Hohensalzburg fortress—other cultured prince-archbishops took over. Markus Sittikus and Paris Lodron dismissed the Italian artists and commanded the masters of Viennese Baroque, Fischer von Erlach and Lukas von Hildebrandt, to complete Wolf-Dietrich's vision. Today, thanks to these patrons and architects, Salzburg remains a visual pageant of Baroque motifs.

But times change and the Salzburgians with them. Despite its seeming emphasis on past glory, the stop-press news is that this dowager of Old Europe is ready to straighten up and once again lead the vanguard. Museums of contemporary art are springing up as fast as edelweiss across Austria, so it is not surprising to learn that Salzburg is now home to one of its most striking: the Museum der Moderner Salzburg. As if to announce that this Baroque city is virtually leapfrogging from yesterday to tomorrow, the avant-garde showcase opened in 2004 on the very spot where Julie Andrews "do-re-mi"-d with the von Trapp brood: where once the fusty Café Winkler stood atop the Mönchsberg mount, and commanding one of the grandest views of the city, a moderne, cubical structure now glitters as a museum devoted to the latest in cutting-edge art. Celebrating both this new museum and Mozart's 250th birthday, Salzburg is reveling in its passementeried past while it takes a Giant Step Forward.

Numbers in the text correspond to numbers in the margin and on the Exploring Salzburg map.

If you have 1 day

It is the tourist who comes to Salzburg outside of festival season who will have the most time to explore its many fascinating attractions. But even for festival-busy visitors, making the acquaintance of the town is not too difficult, for most of its sights are conveniently located within a comparatively small area. Of course, if you are doing this spectacular city in just one day, there is a flip-book approach to Salzburg 101: take one of those escorted bus tours through the city. However, much of Salzburg's historic city center is for pedestrians only, and the bus doesn't get you close to some of the best sights, so some will prefer to take a walking tour run by city guides every day at 12:15 PM, setting out from the tourist information office, **Information Mozartplatz,** at Mozart square (closed on some Sundays during the off-season).

So if you are joining the army of bipeds exploring the town on foot, start at the **Mozartplatz** ❶, not just to make a pit stop at the main tourist information office, but to sweeten your tour with a few *Salzburger Mozartkugeln* from the nearby chocolate manufacturers Fürst (Brodgasse 13, at Alter Markt, on the square), the creators of these omnipresent candy balls of pistachio-flavored marzipan rolled in nougat cream and dipped in dark chocolate, which bear a miniportrait of Mozart on the wrapper. Flower-bedecked cafés beckon, but this is no time for a coffee—one of the glories of Europe is just a few steps away: the palatial **Residenz** ❹, home to the great Prince-Archbishops and the veritable center of Baroque Salzburg. Nearby is the **Dom** ❺, Salzburg's grand 17th-century cathedral. Across the Domplatz is the Francescan church, the **Franziskanerkirche** ❽ (note that entrance into all Salzburg churches is free). A bit to the south is the Romanesque-turned-Rococo **Stiftkirche St. Peter** ❼, where, under the cliffs, you'll find the famous **Petersfriedhof** ❻—St. Peter's Cemetery, whose wrought-iron grills and Baroque vaults shelter the final resting place of Mozart's sister and much of Old Salzburg. This famed locale was recreated for the escape scene in *The Sound of Music.* After exploring St. Peter's Abbey, you're now ready to take the Festungsbahn cable car (it's just behind the cathedral) up to the **Fortress Hohensalzburg** ❿—the majestic castle atop the Mönchsberg peak that overlooks the city. Enjoy a rest at the Stadt Alm restaurant, or opt for enjoying some picnic provisions in a quiet corner. Descend back to the city via the Mönchsberg express elevators, which will deposit you at Gstättengasse 13. Head over to the **Pferdeschwemme** ⓭—the Baroque horse trough that is a somewhat bewildering tribute to the chevaline race—then over to the **Getreidegasse,** the Old City's main shopping street. Here, posh shops set in pastel-covered townhouses announce their wares through the overhanging wrought-iron scroll signs, which one writer has compared to chandeliers (there is even one for the neighborhood McDonald's). Wander around this venerable merchant's quarter—some of the houses have hidden and enchanting courtyards set with timber-lined balconies—then head to the most famous address in town: No. 9 Getreidegasse—**Mozarts Geburtshaus** ⓱, the birthplace of Mozart. After paying your respects, head over to the nearby and charming **Alter Markt** ⑱ square to welcome twilight with a *Kaffee mit Schlag* (coffee with whipped cream) at its famous Café Tomaselli. Choose from the more than 40 pastries and congratulate yourself: you may not have seen everything in Salzburg, but you've missed few of its top sights.

If you have 3 days

With three days, you can explore the **Altstadt**—the Old City—and the **New Town** as described in the two walking tours below. Try to catch an evening concert—perhaps of Mozart's music—at one of the many music halls in the city (before you arrive in Salzburg, do some advance telephone calls to determine the music schedule of the city for the time you will be there and, if need be, book reservations; if you'll be attending the summer Salzburg Festival, this is a must). For your third day, try one of four options: book a *Sound of Music tour,* then, in the afternoon, relax and take a ride up the **Untersberg**; or opt for a boat trip along the Salzach river south to the 17th-century Hellbrunn Palace (famous for its mischievous water fountains); or try to arrange an excursion to the the picture-book towns of the **Salzkammergut** (*see* Chapter 6). Yet another idea is to walk for about two hours over the Mönchsberg, starting in the south at the **Nonnberg Convent** ⑳ and continuing on to the **Richterhöhe** to enjoy the southwestern area of the city. Above the Siegmundstor, the tunnel through the mountain, there is a nice belvedere to take in a city view. But the most fascinating view is from the terrace in front of the new **Museum der Moderne** ⑯, which you reach after passing the old fortifications from the 15th century. Then, you can either head back to the center of town by using the rock-face elevator or just continue on to the Bräustübl, the large beer cellar at the northern end of the hill for some of the best brews and conviviality in town.

EXPLORING SALZBURG

The Altstadt (Old City)—a very compact area between the jutting outcrop of the Mönchsberg and the Salzach River—is where most of the major sights are concentrated. The cathedral and interconnecting squares surrounding it form what used to be the religious center, around which the major churches and the old archbishops' residence are arranged. The rest of the Old City belonged to the wealthy burghers: the Getreidegasse, the Alter Markt (old market), the town hall, and the tall, plain burghers' houses (like Mozart's Birthplace). The Mönchsberg cliffs emerge unexpectedly behind the Old City, crowned to the east by the Hohensalzburg Fortress. Across the river, in the small area between the cliffs of the Kapuzinerberg and the riverbank, is Steingasse, a narrow medieval street where working people lived. Northwest of the Kapuzinerberg lie Mirabell Palace and its gardens, now an integral part of the city but formerly a country estate on the outskirts of Salzburg.

It's best to begin by exploring the architectural and cultural riches of the Old City, then go on to the fortress and after that cross the river to inspect the other bank. Ideally, you need two days to do it all. An alternative, if you enjoy exploring churches and castles, is to stop after visiting the Rupertinum and go directly up to the fortress, either on foot or by returning through the cemetery to the funicular railway.

About the Restaurants & Hotels

Salzburg has some of the best—and most expensive—restaurants in Austria, so if you happen to walk into one of the Altstadt posheries without a reservation, you may get a sneer worthy of Captain von Trapp. Happily, the city is plentifully supplied with pleasant eateries, offering not only good, solid Austrian food (not for anyone on a diet), but also exceptional Italian dishes and newer-than-now *neue Küche* (nouvelle cuisine) delights. There are certain dining experiences that are quintessentially Salzburgian, including restaurants perched on the town's peaks that offer "food with a view"—in some cases, it's too bad the food isn't up to the view—or rustic inns that offer "Alpine evenings" with entertainment. Favorite dishes are fresh fish caught from the nearby lakes of the Salzkammergut, usually *gebratene* (fried), and that ubiquitous Salzburgian dessert *Salzburger Nockerln*—a snowy meringue of sweetened whisked egg whites with a little bit of flour and sugar.

In the more expensive restaurants the set menus give you an opportunity to sample the chef's best; in less expensive ones they help keep costs down. Note, however, that some restaurants limit the hours during which the set menu is available. Many restaurants are open all day; otherwise, lunch is served from approximately 11 to 2 and dinner from 6 to 10. In more expensive restaurants it's always best to make a reservation. At festival time, most restaurants are open seven days a week and have generally more flexible late dining hours.

The Old City has a wide assortment of hotels and pensions, some in surprising locations and with considerable ambience, but everything has its price and there are few bargains. In high season, and particularly during the festival (July and August), some prices soar over their already high levels and rooms are very difficult to find, so try to reserve at least two months in advance. In fact, during the high season, rate differences may push a hotel into the next-higher price category. If you're looking for something really cheap (less than €50 for a double), clean, and comfortable, stay in a private home, though the good ones are all a little way from downtown. Room rates include taxes and service charges. Many hotels include a breakfast in the room rate—check when booking—but the more expensive hostelries often do not. The tourist information offices don't list private rooms; try calling Eveline Truhlar of **Bob's Special Tours** (☎ 0662/849511–0), who runs a private-accommodations service.

WHAT IT COSTS In euros					
	$$$$	$$$	$$	$	¢
RESTAURANTS	over €22	€18–€22	€13–€17	€7–€12	under €7
HOTELS	over €270	€170–€270	€120–€170	€80–€120	under €80

Restaurant prices are per person for a main course at dinner. Hotel prices are for a standard double room in high season, including taxes and service. Assume that hotels operate on the European Plan (EP, with no meal provided) unless we note that they use the Breakfast Plan (BP), Modified American Plan (MAP, with breakfast and dinner daily, known as "halb pension"), or Full American Plan (FAP, or "voll pension," with three meals a day). Higher prices (inquire when booking) prevail for any meal plans.

The Altstadt: In Mozart's Footsteps

Intent on becoming a patron of the arts, the Prince-Bishop-Archbishop Wolf-Dietrich lavished much of his wealth on rebuilding Salzburg into a beautiful and Baroque city in the late 16th and early 17th centuries. In turn, his grand townscape came to inspire the young Joannes Chrysostomus Wolfgangus Amadeus Theophilus Mozart. It is no surprise that there is no better setting for his music than the town in which he was born. For, in point of fact, growing up in the center of the city and composing minuets already at five years of age, Mozart set lovely Salzburg itself to music. He was perhaps the most purely Austrian of all composers, a singer of the smiling Salzburgian countryside, of the city's gay Baroque and Rococo architecture. So even if you are not lucky enough to snag a ticket to a performance of *The Marriage of Figaro* or *Don Giovanni* in the Grosses Festspielhaus, you can still enjoy his melodies just by strolling through his streets and, as critic Erich Kästner once put it, "seeing a symphony."

With the Mozart Year celebrations coming to a head, Salzburg symbolizes Mozart more than ever. Ever since the 1984 Best Film Oscar-winner *Amadeus* (remember Tom Hulse as "Wolfie"?), the composer has been the 18th-century equivalent of a rock star. Born in Salzburg on January 27, 1756, he crammed a prodigious number of compositions into the 35 short years of his life, many of which he spent in Salzburg (he moved to Vienna in 1781). Indeed, the Altstadt (or Old Town) revels in a bevy of important sights, ranging from his birthplace on the Getreidegasse to the abbey of St. Peter's, where the composer's "Mass in C Minor" was first performed. Beyond the Altstadt—the heart of the Baroque Salzburg familiar to the young prodigy—other Mozart-related sights are included in our second Salzburg tour. As you tour the composer's former haunts, why not listen to Papageno woo Papagena on your Walkman?

A Good Walk

In Salzburg, as anywhere else, if you start from the right departure point you will have a good journey and ultimately arrive at the proper place. For this city, there is no more appropriate center-of-it-all than **Mozartplatz** ❶ ▶, the square named to honor Salzburg's native genius. Get in the mood by noticing, near the statue of Mozart, the strolling street violinists, who usually play a Mozart sonata or two. Walk past the Glockenspiel café into the next square, the Residenzplatz, centered by the 40-foot-high Court Fountain, which is often illuminated at night. Take in the famous **Glockenspiel** ❷ (chances are the tunes it plays will be by you-know-who), set atop the Neubau Palace, now the city's newly renovated **Salzburg Museum** ❸—doors open in January 2006 just in time to kick off the Mozart Year with a major exhibition on the composer. Then cross the plaza to enter the **Residenz** ❹, the opulent Baroque palace of Salzburg's prince-archbishops and Mozart's patrons. From the Residenzplatz, walk through the arches into Domplatz, the city's majestic cathedral square—in August, set out with seats for the annual presentation of Hofmannsthal's play *Jedermann*. The **Dom** ❺ (Salzburg Cathedral) is among the finest Italian-style Baroque struc-

A Lot of Night Music Music in Salzburg is not just *Eine Kleine Nacht-musik*, to mention one of Mozart's most famous compositions (which, incidentally, he composed in Vienna . . .). The city's nightlife is livelier than it is reputed to be. The "in" areas include the "Bermuda Triangle" (Steingasse, Imbergstrasse, and Rudolfskai); young people tend to populate the bars and discos around Gstättengasse. Of course, Salzburg is most renowned for its **Salzburger Festspiele** of music and theater (end of July–August), and most festivalgoers come during this season. Much of Salzburg's very special charm can, however, be best discovered and enjoyed off-season. For instance, real Mozart connoisseurs come to Salzburg for the **Mozart Week** (a 10-day festival held around Mozart's birthday, January 27). And in general, music lovers face an embarrassment of riches in this most musical of cities, ranging from chamber concerts, held in the Marmorsaal (Marble Hall) of the Mirabell Palace, the Goldene Stube (Golden Hall) of the Fortress, or the Gotischer Saal (Gothic Hall) at St. Blasius, to the numerous concerts organized by the International Mozarteum Foundation from October to June in the Grosser Saal (Great Hall) of the Mozarteum and those by the Salzburger Kulturvereinigung in the Grosses Festspielhaus (Large Festival House). Salzburg concerts by the Mozarteum Orchestra and the Camerata Academica are now just as much in demand as the subscription series by the Vienna Philharmonic in the Musikverein in Vienna. The **Landestheater** season runs from September to June and presents operas, operettas, plays, and ballet. No music lover should miss the chance to be enchanted and amazed by the skill and artistry of the world-famous **Salzburg Marionette Theater,** not only performing operas by Mozart, but also goodies by Rossini, Strauss the younger, Offenbach, Humperdinck, and Mendelssohn (who wrote the accompanying music for the troupe's delightful show devoted to William Shakespeare's "A Midsummer Night's Dream."

Bicycling As most Salzburgers know, one of the best and most pleasurable ways of getting around the city and the surrounding countryside is by bicycle. Bikes can be rented (for rental places, *see* Salzburg A to Z, *below*), and local bookstores have maps of the extensive network of cycle paths. The most delightful ride in Salzburg? The **Hellbrunner Allee** from Freisaal to Hellbrunn Palace is a pleasurable run, taking you past Frohnburg Palace and a number of elegant mansions on either side of the tree-lined avenue. The more adventurous can go farther afield, taking the **Salzach cycle path** north to the village of Oberndorf, or south to Golling and Hallein.

Everybody Drink! Salzburg loves beer and has some of the most picturesque Bierkellers in Austria. A top beer paradise is the **Stieglkeller** (✉ Festungsgasse 10 ☎ 0662/842681 ⊕ www.imlauer.com ⊙ May 1–Sept. 30), by the funicular station of the Hohensalzburg tram. The noted local architect Ceconi devised this sprawling place around 1901. The Keller is partly inside the Mönchsberg hill so its cellars guarantee the quality and right temperature of the drinks. The gardens here have chestnut trees and offer a marvelous view above the roofs of the old city—a lovely place to enjoy your *Bauernschmaus* (farmer's dish). The **Sternbräu** (✉ Griesegasse 23 ☎ 0662/842140) is a mammoth Bierkeller, with eight rambling halls festooned with tile stoves, paintings, and wood beams. The chestnut-tree beer garden or the courtyard are divine on hot summer nights. Many travelers head here for the **Sound of Music Dinner Shows**, presented May through September, daily 7:30 to 10 PM. A three-course meal and show costs €40, or you can arrive at 8:15 PM to see the show and just have Apfelstrudel and coffee for €25. On the first Sunday of the month, a *Fruhschoppen*—a traditional Salzburger music fest—is presented at 10:30 PM, or you can enjoy another musical evening, a *Happing*, staged from May to September every Thursday evening at 6.

---

tures in Austria. Walk into the Kapitelplatz through the arches across the square and go through two wrought-iron gateways into **St. Peter's Cemetery** ❻—one of the most historic and beautiful places in Salzburg. Enter the church of **Stiftkirche St. Peter** ❼. Above the main entrance the Latin inscription reads: "I am the door—by me if any man enters here, he shall be saved." If it's nearing lunchtime, be sure to stop at the Stiftskeller St. Peter—so legendary a restaurant that the story has it Mephistopheles met Faust here.

As you leave St. Peter's, look up to the right to see the thin Gothic spire of the **Franziskanerkirche** ❽. Leave the courtyard in this direction, cross the road, and enter around the corner by the main entrance (the side one is closed). It will bring you into the Gothic apse crowned by the ornate red-marble altar designed by Fischer von Erlach. Return back up the Romanesque aisle an exit on Sigmund-Haffner-Gasse. Opposite is the rear entrance to one of Salzburg's galleries of contemporary art, the **Rupertinum** ❾. Turn left around the corner into **Toscaninihof** ❿, the square cut into the dramatic Mönchsberg cliff. The wall bearing the harp-shape organ pipes is part of the famed **Festspielhaus** ⓫. The carved steps going up the Mönchsberg are named for Clemens Holzmeister, architect of the festival halls. If you climb them, you get an intimate view of the Salzburg churches at the level of their spires, and if you climb a little farther to the right, you can look down into the open-air festival hall, the Felsenreitschule, cut into the cliffs. From Hofstallgasse—the main promenade (sometimes floodlit and adorned with flags during the festival) connecting the main festival theaters—you can either walk directly up to Herbert-von-Karajan-Platz or, preferably, walk around by Universitätsplatz to take a look at one of Johann Bernhard Fischer von Erlach's Baroque masterpieces, the **Kollegienkirche** ⓬, or Collegiate Church. In Herbert-von-Karajan-Platz is another point at which building and cliff meet: the **Pferdeschwemme** ⓭, a horse trough decorated with splendid Baroque-era paintings. To the left is the Siegmundstor, the impressive road tunnel blasted through the Mönchsberg in 1764. The arcaded Renaissance court on your left houses the **Spielzeugmuseum** ⓮, a delightful toy museum.

Pass by the tiny church of St. Blasius, built in 1350, and follow the road on through the Gstättentor to the **Mönchsberg elevator** ⓯ for a trip up the hill to a rocky terrace formerly known as the Winkler Terrace,

Salzburg's most famous outlook, now the site of a large "white marble brick" (as critics carp), the **Museum der Moderne** ⑯, or Museum of Modern Art, which includes a restaurant, which opened in October 2004. After descending from the heights, turn left into the short street leading to Museumsplatz where you could explore the Haus der Natur, one of the Europe's finest museums of natural history. Walk back toward the Blasius church, which stands at the beginning of the Old City's major shopping street, **Getreidegasse,** hung with numerous signs depicting little wrought-iron cobblers and bakers (few people could actually read centuries ago). Amid the boutiques and Salzburg's own McDonald's (featuring its own elegant sign) is **Mozarts Geburtshaus** ⑰, the celebrated composer's birthplace. Continue down the street past the Rathaus (town hall), and enter the **Alter Markt** ⑱, the old marketplace, adorned with historic buildings, including the Café Tomaselli (1703) and the Baroque Hofapotheke (prince-archbishop's court apothecary, 1591), still kept as it was back then. Finish up with some "I Was Here" photographs at the marble St. Florian's Fountain, then enjoy a finale back on Mozartplatz.

TIMING The Old City—the left bank of the Salzach River—contains many of the city's top attractions. Other than exploring by horse-drawn cabs (*Fiakers*), available for rental at Residenzplatz, most of your exploring will be done on foot, since this historic section of town bans cars. The center city is compact and cozy, so you can easily cover it in one day. Note that many churches close at 6 PM, so unless you're catching a concert at one of them, be sure to visit them during the daylight hours.

What to See

⑱ **Alter Markt** (Old Market). Right in the heart of the Old City is the Alter Markt, the old marketplace and center of secular life in past centuries. The square is lined with 17th-century middle-class houses, colorfully hued in shades of pink, pale blue, and yellow ocher. Look in at the old royal pharmacy, the **Hofapotheke,** whose incredibly ornate black-and-gold Rococo interior was built in 1760. Inside, you'll sense a curious apothecarial smell, traced to the shelves lined with old pots and jars (labeled in Latin). These are not just for show: this pharmacy is still operating today. You can even have your blood pressure taken—but preferably not after drinking a *Doppelter Einspänner* (black coffee with whipped cream, served in a glass) in the famous Café Tomaselli just opposite. In warm weather, the café's terrace provides a wonderful spot for watching the world go by as you sip a *Mélange* (another coffee specialty, served with frothy milk), or, during the summer months, rest your feet under the shade of the chestnut trees in the Tomaselli garden at the top end of the square. Next to the coffeehouse, you'll find the **smallest house in Salzburg,** now a shop for the *"Salzburger Engerl,"* a little silver putto modelled after a pattern by the Baroque sculptor Meinrad Guggenbichler that has become a traditional souvenir of Salzburg; note the slanting roof decorated with a dragon gargoyle. In the center of the square, surrounded by flower stalls, is the marble **St. Florian's Fountain,** dedicated in 1734 to the patron saint of firefighters.

★ ⑤ **Dom St. Rupert** (St. Rupert's Cathedral). When you walk through the arches leading from Residenzplatz into **Domplatz,** it is easy to see why Max

Alter Markt **18**

Dom St. Rupert . . **5**

Dreifaltigkeits-
kirche **28**

Festspielhaus . . **11**

Fortress
Hohensalzburg . . . **19**

Franziskaner-
kirche **8**

Glockenspiel . . . **2**

Kapuzinerberg
Hill **22**

Kollegienkirche . . **12**

Marionetten-
theater **27**

Mirabellgarten . **24**

Mirabell
Palace **25**

Mönchsberg
elevator **15**

Mozart
Wohnhaus . . . **29**

Mozarteum . . . **26**

Mozartplatz **1**

Mozarts
Geburtshaus . . **17**

Museum der
Moderner **16**

Nonnberg
Convent **20**

Pferdeschwemme . **13**

Residenz **4**

Rupertinum **9**

Salzburg
Museum **3**

St. Peter's
Cemetery **6**

St. Sebastian's
Cemetery **23**

Spielzeug-
museum **14**

Steingasse **21**

Stiftkirche
St. Peter **7**

Toscaninihof . . **10**

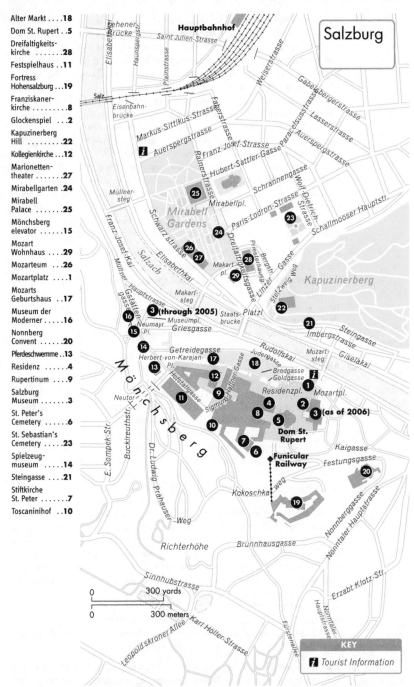

Salzburg

Reinhardt chose it in August of 1920 as the setting for what has become the annual summer production of Hugo von Hofmannsthal's *Jedermann* (*Everyman*). The plaza is a complete, aesthetic concept and one of Salzburg's most beautiful urban set pieces. In the center rises the Virgin's Column, and at one side is the cathedral, considered to be the first early Italian Baroque building north of the Alps, and one of the finest. Its facade is of marble, its towers reach 250 feet into the air, and it holds 10,000 people (standing . . .). There has been a cathedral on this spot since the 8th century, but the present structure dates from the 17th century. The cathedral honors the patron saint of Salzburg, St. Rupert, whose relics lie buried beneath the altar; Rupert founded the town's St. Peter's Church and its Nonnberg Abbey around 700. Archbishop Wolf-Dietrich took advantage of (some say caused) the old Romanesque-Gothic cathedral's destruction by fire in 1598 to demolish the remains and make plans for a huge new structure facing onto the Residenzplatz to reaffirm Salzburg's commitment to the Catholic cause. His successor, Markus Sittikus, and the new court architect, Santino Solari, also ordered to build the city walls protecting Salzburg during the 30-years war started the present cathedral in 1614, which was consecrated with great ceremony in 1628 during the 30-years war. The church's simple sepia-and-white interior, a peaceful counterpoint to the usual Baroque splendor, dates from a later renovation. Mozart's parents, Leopold and Anna-Maria, were married here on November 21, 1747. Mozart was christened, the day after he was born, at the 13th-century font inside this cathedral, where he later served as organist from 1779 to 1781. Some of his compositions, such as the *Coronation Mass,* were written for the cathedral, and many were performed here for the first time. On Sunday and all catholic Holidays, mass is sung here at 10 AM—the most glorious time to experience the cathedral's full splendor. This remains the only house of worship worldwide with no less than five independent fixed organs, which are sometimes played together during special church music concerts. Many of the church's treasures are in a special museum on the premises. ⊠ *Domplatz* ☎ *0662/844189* 🖶 *0662/840442* ⊕ *www. kirchen.net/dommuseum* 🖳 *Museum: €4.50* ⊘ *Early May–late Oct., Mon.–Sat. 10–5, Sun. and holidays 1–6.*

⑪ **Festspielhaus** (Festival Hall Complex). With the world-famous Salzburg Festival as their objective, music lovers head for the Hofstallgasse, the street where the three main festival theaters are located. Arrow-straight and framing a grand view of the Fortress Hohensalzburg, the street takes its name from the court stables once located here. Now, in place of the prancing horses, festivalgoers promenade along Hofstallgasse during the intervals of summer performances, showing off their suntans and elegant attire. The festival complex consists of three theaters. The first is the new **Haus für Mozart** (House for Mozart). This was the former Kleines Festspielhaus, or Small Festival Hall. It will now seat about 1,600 and will be specially used for productions of Mozart's operas. The center ring is occupied by the famous **Grosses Festspielhaus** (Great Festival Hall, 1956–60), leaning against the solid rock of the Mönchsberg and opened in 1960, with a maximum stage width of 104 foot and a seating capacity of more than 2,150. In recent times, the Grosses Festspielhaus, nicknamed the Wagner Stage because of its width (not to mention its headline-making productions of the "Ring of the Nibelungs"), has been the venue for spectacular productions of Modest Mussorgsky's *Boris Godunov* and Richard Strauss's *Der Rosenkavalier*, along with concerts by the world's most famous symphony orchestras. Stage directors are faced with the greatest challenge in the third theater, the **Felsenreitschule** (the Rocky Riding School), the former Summer Riding School, which—hewn out of the rock of the Mönchsberg during the 17th century by architect Fischer von Erlach—offers a setting that is itself more dramatic than anything presented on stage. Here, in the days of the prince-archbishops, the famous Lipizzaner stallions were put through their paces (in the winter, they were moved to Vienna). Max Reinhardt made the first attempt at using the Summer Riding School for Salzburg Festival performances in 1926. With its retractable roof it gives the impression of an open-air theater; the three tiers of arcades cut into the rock of the Mönchsberg linger in the mind of fans of *The Sound of Music* film, for the von Trapps were portrayed as singing "Edelweiss" here in their last Austrian concert (according to Hollywood—in fact, this 1950 Festival farewell by the Trapp Family Singers, conducted by Franz Wasner, actually was given in the Mozarteum and at the cathedral square). The theaters are linked by tunnels (partially in marble and with carpeted floors) to a spacious underground garage in the Mönchsberg. If you want to see the inside of the halls, it's best to go to a performance, but guided tours are given and group tours can be booked on request. ☒ *Hofstallgasse 1* ☎ *0662/ 849097* 🖷 *0662/847835* ⊕ *www.salzburgfestival.at* ☒ *Guided tours: €5* ⊘ *Group tour Jan.–May and Oct.–Dec. 20, daily at 2; June and Sept., daily at 2 and 3:30; July–Aug., daily at 9.30, 2, and 3:30. Advance booking necessary for groups of more than 10 people.*

❽ Franziskanerkirche (Franciscan Church). The graceful, tall spire of the Franciscan Church stands out from all other towers in Salzburg; the church itself encompasses the greatest diversity of architectural styles. There was a church on this spot as early as the 8th century, but it was destroyed by fire. The Romanesque nave of its replacement is still visible, as are other Romanesque features, such as a stone lion set into the steps leading to the pulpit. In the 15th century the choir was rebuilt in Gothic style, then crowned in the 18th century by an ornate red-marble and gilt altar designed by Austria's most famous Baroque architect, Johann Bernhard Fischer von Erlach. Mass—frequently featuring one of Mozart's compositions—is celebrated here on Sunday at 9 AM. ☒ *Franziskanergasse 5* ☎ *0662/843629–0* ☒ *Free* ⊘ *Daily 6:30 AM–7 PM.*

★ Getreidegasse. As for centuries, this today is the main shopping street in the Old City center. According to historians, the historic name means "trade street"—not "grain street," as many people believe. Today it is the address of elegant fashion houses, international shoe chains, and a McDonald's (note its wrought-iron sign—one of many on the street— with classy bronze lettering: like all the other shops, it has conformed with Salzburg's strict Old City conservation laws). Other than coming to shop, crowds flock to this street because at No. 9 they'll find Mozart's birthplace, the **Mozarts Geburtshaus**. Needless to say, in summer the street is as densely packed with people as a corncob with kernels. You can always escape for a while through one of the many arcades—mostly flower-bedecked and opening into delightful little courtyards—that link the Getreidegasse to the river and the Universitätsplatz. At No. 37 you'll find one of the most glamorous hotels in the world, the Goldener Hirsch—just look for its filigree-iron sign showing a leaping stag with gilded antlers. Its interiors are marvels of Salzburgian gemütlichkeit so, if appropriately attired, you may wish to view the lobby and enjoy an aperitif in its gorgeous bar, *the* watering hole of chic Salzburg. The western end of Getreidegasse becomes Judengasse, part of the former Jewish ghetto area, which is also festooned with more of Salzburg's famous wrought-iron signs.

❷ **Glockenspiel** (Carillon). The famous carillon tower is perched on top of the **Residenz Neubau** (New Residence), Prince-Archbishop Wolf-Dietrich's government palace. The carillon is a later addition, brought from the Netherlands in 1696 and finally put in working order in 1702. The 35 bells play classical tunes (usually by Mozart, Carl Maria von Weber, and his teacher in Salzburg, Michael Haydn) at 7 AM, 11 AM, and 6 PM—with charm and ingenuity often making up for the occasional musical inaccuracy. From Easter to October, the bells are immediately followed by a resounding retort from perhaps the oldest mechanical musical instrument in the world, the 200-pipe "Bull" organ housed in the Hohensalzburg Fortress across town. Details about the music selections are listed on a notice board across the square on the corner of the Residenz building. ⊠ *Mozartplatz 1.*

⓬ **Kollegienkirche** (Kollegienkirche, or Collegiate Church). Completed by Fischer von Erlach in 1707, and until its 300th anniversary in restoration too, this church, sometimes called the Universitätskirche, is is one of the purest examples of Baroque architecture in Austria. Unencumbered by Rococo decorations, the modified Greek cross plan has a majestic dignity worthy of Palladio. ⊠ *Universitätsplatz* ☎ *0662/841–327–72* ☉ *Mon.–Sat. 9–7, Sun. 10–7 (winter closing hours approximately 3 hrs earlier).*

⓯ **Mönchsberg Elevator.** Just around the corner from the Pferdeschwemme horse-fountain, at Neumayr Platz, you'll find the Mönchsberg elevator, which carries you up through solid rock not only to the new **Museum der Moderne Kunst** but to wooded paths that are great for walking and gasping—there are spectacular vistas of Salzburg. In summer this can be a marvelous—and quick way—to escape the tiny crowded streets of the Old City. At the top of the Mönchsberg, follow the signs and path south to **Stadt Alm,** a popular café-restaurant open May–mid-October with a magnificent view of the churches and the fortress from its outdoor garden. ⊠ *Gstättengasse 13* ⊠ *Round-trip €2.60, one-way €1.60* ☉ *Open Oct.–May, daily 9–9; June–Sept., daily 9 AM–11 PM.*

❶ **Mozartplatz** (Mozart Square). In the center of the square stands the statue of Wolfgang Amadeus Mozart, a work by sculptor Ludwig Schwanthaler unveiled in 1842 in the presence of the composer's two surviving sons. It was the first sign of public recognition the great composer had received from his hometown since his death in Vienna in 1791. The statue shows a 19th-century stylized view of Mozart, draped in a mantle, holding a page of music and a copybook. A more appropriate bust of the composer, modeled by Viennese sculptor Edmund Heller, is found on the Kapuzinerberg. It contains the inscription *Jung gross, spät erkannt, nie erreicht*—"Great while young, belatedly appreciated, never equaled."

★ ⑰ **Mozarts Geburtshaus** (Mozart's Birthplace). As an adult the great composer preferred Vienna to Salzburg, complaining that audiences in his native city were no more responsive than tables and chairs. Still, home is home, and this was Mozart's—when not on one of his frequent trips abroad—until the age of 17. Mozart was born on the third (in American parlance, the fourth) floor of this tall house, then owned by a family friend, one Johann Lorenz Hagenauer, on January 27, 1756, and the family lived on this floor, when they were not on tour, from 1747 to 1773. As the child prodigy composed many of his first compositions in these rooms, it is fitting and touching to find Mozart's tiny first violin, his clavicord, and a copy of his fortepiano (the original is on view in the Wohnhaus across the river) are on display. For the Mozart Year, special loan exhibitions will also be shown, including original portraits of the family, autograph letters, and manuscripts, all exhibited in cases illuminated by laser to make them easier to read. On the second floor, the day-to-day living and travelling circumstances of his day are the focus of the exhibits, while on the third floor a special annual exhibition is mounted, which normally opens the last week in January and runs until early October. Most of the rooms here are fitted out with modern museum vitrines and there is nothing extant from Mozart's time other than a cupboard on the landing of the fourth floor. Happily, a rear apartment facing Universitätsplatz has been refurbished to look like a "typical Salzburg commoner's apartment of Mozart's day." Like performing monkeys, the five- to seven-year-old Mozart, along with his slightly older sister, were trotted around by their father to entertain the crowned heads of Europe for months at a stretch. Returning from the gilded splendor of royal palaces—not to say the archbishop's residence just across town—to this very modest domicile must have only whetted the young Mozart's taste for grandeur and fine living, which he managed to indulge to the utmost whenever he could afford to do so (not very often—he was a spendthrift). Before leaving this hallowed place, be sure to pay your respects to Joseph Lange's famous unfinished portrait of Mozart, considered the most realistic depiction extant today. ⊠ *Getreidegasse 9* ☎ *0662/844313* ⊕ *www.mozarteum.at* ✉ *€6; combined ticket for Mozart residence and birthplace €9* ☉ *Sept.–June, daily 9–5:30; July–Aug., daily 9–6:30.*

⑯ **Museum der Moderne.** Enjoying one of Salzburg's most famous scenic spots—the Café Winkler terrace (a setting immortalized in *The Sound of Music*—this is where Julie and the kids start warbling "Doe, a deer, a female deer . . . ")—Salzburg's dramatic new museum of modern and contemporary art, the Museum der Moderne, now reposes atop the sheer cliff face of the Mönchsberg. Clad in minimalist white marble, the museum (opened in October 2004) was designed by Friedrich Hoff Zwink

MOZART: MARVEL & MYSTERY

"**M**OZART IS SUNSHINE." So proclaimed the great composer Antonin Dvorak—and how better to sum up the prodigious genius of Wolfgang Amadeus Mozart (January 27, 1756–December 5, 1791)? Listen to his rococo orchestrations, his rose-strewn melodies, and insouciant harmonies, and many listeners seem to experience the same giddiness as happiness. Scientists have found Mozart's music can be so seductive it can cause the heart to pound, bring color to the cheeks, and provide the expansive feeling of being thrilllingly alive. Yet, somehow, Mozart must have sensed how hard it is to recognize happiness, which is often something vaguely desired, its presence frequently not detected until gone. It is this melancholic undertow that makes Mozart modern. So modern, in fact, that he is now the most popular classical composer, having banished the great Beethoven to second place. Shortly after Peter Schaffer's Amadeus won the 1984 Oscar for Best Film—with its portrayal of Mozart as a giggling, foul-mouthed genius—Don Giovanni began to rack up more performances than La Boheme. Frank Sinatra named Mozart his favorite composer; the bewigged face graces countless "Mozartkugeln" chocolates; and Mostly Mozart festivals famously pay him homage. But take a look behind the glare of the spotlights and you'll discover that this blonde, slightly built tuning-fork of a fellow was a quicksilver enigma.

An 18th-century version of Michael Jackson, Mozart was doomed to live as an "eternal child," thanks to the education—nay, exploitation—he suffered at the hands of his father, Leopold. Already a skilled pianist at age three, the musical prodigy was dragged across Europe to perform for empresses and kings. In a life that lasted a mere 35 years, he spent ten on the road—a burden which contributed to making him the first truly European composer. Growing up in Salzburg, the wunderkind, like many a fading Hollywood child star, became less of a wunder as time went by. Prince-Archbishop Hieronymus von Colloredo enjoyed dissing his resident composer by commanding him to produce "table music" with the same, disdainful tone he commanded his chef's dinner orders. Being literally forced to sit with those cooks, Mozart finally rebelled. In March 1781, he set out to conquer Vienna, a dire necessity as he was soon to marry Constanze Weber.

Hated by Mozart's father, Constanze is adored today, since we now know she was Mozart's greatest ally. Highly repressed by stuffy Salzburg, Mozart came to like his humor glandular (he titled one cantata "Kiss My XXX") and his women globular, a bill Constanze adequately filled. She no doubt heartily enjoyed the fruits of his first operatic triumph, the naughty Abduction from the Seraglio (1782): the gilt-trimmed frock coats, the lavishly gemütlich apartment, and the high-stepping horse and carriage. Was this the spendthrift lifestyle of an 18th-century "rock-star"—or was Mozart simply savvy enough to want to one-up the purse-proud Viennese? His next opera, The Marriage of Figaro (1786), to no one's surprise, bombed; Always eager to thumb his nose at authority (paging Dr. Freud), Mozart had adapted a Beaumarchais play so inflammatory, in its depiction of aristos as pawns of their own servants, it soon helped ignite the French Revolution. In revenge, wealthy Viennese gave a cold shoulder to his magisterial Don Giovanni (1787). As he neared the backstretch, Mozart was relegated to composing, for a lowly vaudeville house, the now immortal Magic Flute (1790), and to ghosting a Requiem for a wealthy count. Sadly, his star only began to soar after a tragic, early death. But, in company with fellow starblazers Vincent van Gogh and Marilyn Monroe, we assume he must be enjoying the last laugh.

— Robert I. C. Fisher

of Munich. It has two exhibition levels, which bracket a restaurant with a large terrace—now, as always, *the* place to enjoy the most spectacular view over the city while sipping a coffee. The museum is mounting an impressive calendar of temporary exhibitions of cutting-edge contemporary art. However, its permanent collection features a fine array of paintings and sculptures from the 20th century, ranging from works by Gustav Klimt, Oskar Kokoschka, and Alfred Kubin to important movements like Informel, Fluxus, and Actionism. The contemporary collection is a veritable pantheon of important new Austrian and German artists, including Arnulf Rainer, Maria Lassnig, Hubert Schmalix, Siegfried Anzinger, Erwin Bohatsch, Valie Export, Elke Krystufek, Hermann Nitsch, Rudolf Schwarzkogler, Otto Muehl, and Günter Brus. ⊠ *Mönchsberg 32* ☎ *0662/842220* ⊕ *www.museumdermoderne.at* 🎫 *€8* ⊙ *Tues.–Sun. 10–6, Wed. 10–9.*

⓭ Pferdeschwemme (Horse Pond). If Rome had fountains, so, too, would Wolf-Dietrich's Salzburg. The city is studded with them and none is so odd as this monument to the equine race. You'll find it if you head to the western end of the Hofstallgasse to find Herbert-von-Karajan-Platz (named after Salzburg's second-greatest musical son, maestro Herbert von Karajan, the legendary conductor and music director of the Salzburg Festival for many decades and also founder of its Easter Festival in 1967). On the Mönchsberg side of the square is the Pferdeschwemme—a royal trough where prize horses used to be cleaned and watered, constructed in 1695; as they underwent this ordeal they could delight in the frescoes of their pin-up fillies on the rear wall. The Baroque monument in the middle represents the antique legend of the taming of a horse, Bellerophon and his mount, Pegasus. ⊠ *Herbert-von-Karajan-Platz.*

Rathaus (Town Hall). Where Sigmund-Haffner-Gasse meets the Getreidegasse you will find the Rathaus, a remarkably insignificant building in the Salzburg skyline—apart from its clock, which chimes every quarter hour—no doubt reflecting the historical weakness of the burghers vis-à-vis the Church, whose opulent monuments and churches are evident throughout the city. On the other hand, this structure is a prime example of the Italian influence in Salzburg's architecture, an influence which extends back to the city's merchant class. From their Salzburg perch, they sometimes handled a goodly portion of the Italian goods flowing from Venice to Germany. Originally, this was a family tower (and the only one still remaining here), but it was then sold to the city in 1407. ⊠ *Getreidegasse and Sigmund-Haffner-Gasse.*

★ ❹ Residenz. Situated at the very heart of Baroque Salzburg, the Residenz overlooks the spacious Residenzplatz and its famous fountain. The palace in the present condition was built between 1600 and 1619 as the home of Wolf-Dietrich, the most powerful of Salzburg's prince-archbishops. The *Kaisersaal* (Imperial Hall) and the *Rittersaal* (Knight's Hall), one of the city's most regal concert halls, can be seen along with the rest of the magnificent **State Rooms** on a self-guided tour with headphones. Of particular note are the frescos by Johann Michael Rottmayr and Martino Altomonte depicting the history of Alexander the Great. Upstairs on the third floor is the **Residenzgalerie,** a princely art collection specializing in 17th-century Dutch and Flemish art and 19th-century paintings of Salzburg. On the state room floor, Mozart's opera, *La Finta Semplice*, was premiered in 1769 in the Guard Room. Mozart often did duty here, as, at age 14, he became the first violinist of the court orchestra (in those days, the leader, as there was no conductor). Today the reception rooms of the Residenz are often used for official functions, banquets, and concerts. The palace courtyard has been the lovely setting for Salzburg Festival opera productions since 1956—mostly the lesser-known treasures of Mozart. ⊠ *Residenzplatz 1* ☎ *0662/8042–2690, 0662/840451 art collection* ⊕ *www.residenzgalerie.at/* ⊠ *€7.30 for both museums; art collection only: €5* ⊘ *Daily 10–5, closed 2 wks before Easter. Tours by arrangement. Art collection: daily 10–5, closed early Feb.–mid-Mar. and Wed., Oct.–Mar.*

❾ **Rupertinum.** If you are interested in 20th-century art, don't miss the chance to see the outstanding permanent collection of paintings and graphic art on display in this gallery, now part and parcel of Salzburg's new **Museum der Moderne Salzburg** (which you can spot, shining in white marble atop the Mönchsberg hill, from the Rupertinum's main entrance. ⊠ *Wiener-Philharmoniker-Gasse 9* ☎ *0662/8042–2336* ⊕ *www. rupertinum.at* ⊠ *€9* ⊘ *Sept.–mid-July, Tues., Thurs.–Sun. 10–5, Wed. 10–9; mid-July–Aug., Thurs.–Tues. 10–6, Wed. 10–9.*

❸ **Salzburg Museum** (Neugebäude). The biggest "gift" to Mozart will be
FodorśChoice   opened one day shy of his 250th birthday, when, on January 26, 2006,
★   Salzburg's mammoth 17th-century **Residenz Neubau** (New Residence) will welcome visitors after a year-long renovation to an exhibition entitled "Viva! Mozart." The setting will be splendid, as this building was Prince-Archbishop Wolf-Dietrich's "overflow" palace (he couldn't fit his entire archiepiscopal court into the main Residenz across the plaza). As such, it features 10 state reception rooms that were among the first attempts at a *stil Renaissance* in the North. Under their sumptuous stucco-ceilings, the Mozart homage will unfold in an interactive fashion: in the former dancing hall, visitors will be able to learn historic gavottes, in another, recipes of Mozart's time will be offered. Most of the display will be devoted to Mozart's music, with exhibitions on loan from around the world. All will be overseen by the guests of honor—Mozart's "virtual" family and friends (using state-of-the-art multimedia presentations). This "birthday party" will run through July 1, 2007. In other wings of the building, you can romp through Salzburg history thanks to the collections of the former Carolino-Augusteum Museum. Displays include Hallstatt Age relics, remains of the town's ancient Roman ruins, the famous Celtic bronze flagon found earlier this century on the Dürrnberg near Hallein (15 km [10 mi] south of Salzburg), and an outstanding collection of old musical instruments. Art lovers will the Old Masters paintings, which range from Gothic altarpieces to wonderful "view" paintings of 18th- and 19th-century Salzburg. Pride of place will be given to the new installation of the spectacular **Sattler Panorama**, one of the few remaining 360° paintings in the world, which shows the city of Salzburg in the early 19th century. Also here is the original composition of "Silent Night," composed by Franz Gruber and Josef Mohr in nearby Obern-

dorf in 1818. A new exhibition space below the interior courtyard and restaurant will hold temporary shows. ✉ *Museumsplatz 1 (until end of 2005); Mozartplatz 1 (2006 on)* ☏ *0662/620808-200* 🖨 *0662/620808-220* ⊕ *www.smca.at* 💳 *€7* ⊘ *Mon.–Wed. and Fri.–Sun. 9–5, Thurs. 9–8.*

★ **❼ Stiftkirche St. Peter** (Collegiate Church of St. Peter). The most sumptuous church in Salzburg, St. Peter's is where Mozart's famed *Mass in C Minor* premiered in 1783, with his wife, Constanze, singing the lead soprano role. Wolfgang often directed orchestra and choir here, and also played its organ. During every season of the city's summer music festival in August the *Mass in C Minor* is performed here during a special church music concert. For a long time his *Requiem* was also played every year on the anniversary of his death (December 5): now the annual performance has been moved into the Grosser Saal at the Mozarteum across the river. Originally a Romanesque basilica, the front portal dates from 1245. Inside, the low-ceilinged aisles are charmingly painted in Rococo candy-box style. The porch has beautiful Romanesque vaulted arches from the original structure built in the 12th century; the interior was decorated in the characteristically voluptuous late-Baroque style when additions were made in the 1770s. Note the side chapel by the entrance, with the unusual crèche portraying the Flight into Egypt and the Massacre of the Innocents. Behind the Rupert altar is the "Felsengrab," a rockface tomb where St. Rupert himself may be buried. To go from the sacred to the profane, head for the abbey's legendary Weinkeller restaurant, adjacent to the church. ✉ *St. Peter Bezirk* ☏ *0662/844578-0* 💳 *Free* ⊘ *Apr.–Sept., daily 6:30 AM–7 PM; Oct.–Mar., daily 6:30 AM–6 PM.*

❻ St. Peter's Cemetery. The eerie but intimate Petersfriedhof, or St. Peter's Cemetery, is the oldest Christian graveyard in Salzburg, in the present condition dating back to 1627. Enclosed on three sides by elegant wrought-iron grilles, Baroque arcades contain chapels belonging to Salzburg's old patrician families. The graveyard is far from mournful: the individual graves are tended with loving care, decorated with candles, fir branches, and flowers—especially pansies (because their name means "thoughts"). In Crypt XXXI is the grave of Santino Solari, architect of the cathedral; in XXXIX that of Sigmund Haffner, a patron for whom Mozart composed a symphony and named a serenade. The final communal crypt LIV (by the so-called "catacombs") contains the body of Mozart's sister, Nannerl, and the torso of Joseph Haydn's younger brother, Michael (his head is in an urn stored in St. Peter's). The cemetery is in the shadow of the Monchsberg mount; note the early Christian tombs carved in the rockface. ✉ *St. Peter Bezirk* ☏ *0662/844578-0* ⊘ *Open daily, dawn to dusk.*

☾ **❹ Spielzeugmuseum** (Toy Museum). On a rainy day this is a delightful diversion for both young and old, with a collection of dolls, teddy bears, model railways, and wooden sailing ships. At 3 o'clock on Tuesdays, Wednesdays, and the first Friday of the month, special Punch and Judy–style puppet shows are presented. Performance days change in the summer, so call ahead. ✉ *Bürgerspitalplatz 2* ☏ *0662/620808-300* ⊕ *www.smca.at* 💳 *€2.70* ⊘ *Daily 9–5.*

⑩ Toscaninihof (Arturo Toscanini Courtyard). The famous Italian maestro Arturo Toscanini conducted some of the Salzburg Festival's most legendary performances during the 1930s. Throughout the summer months the courtyard of his former festival residence is a hive of activity, with sets for the stage of the "House for Mozart" being brought in through the massive iron folding gates.

Wiener Philharmoniker-Gasse. Leading into Max-Reinhardt-Platz at the head of the grand Hofstallgasse, this street (once known as Marktgasse, or Market Street) blooms with an open-air food market every Saturday morning; note that there is a fruit and vegetable market on Universitätsplatz every day except Sunday and holidays. The street was renamed after the world-famous Vienna Philharmonic Orchestra in recognition of the unique contribution it has made annually to the Salzburg Festival, playing for most opera productions and for the majority of orchestral concerts.

Across the River Salzach: From the Fortress to the New Town

According to a popular saying in Salzburg, "If you can see the fortress, it's just about to rain; if you can't see it, it's already raining." Fortunately there are plenty of days when spectacular views can be had of Salzburg and the surrounding countryside from the top of this castle. Looking across the River Salzach to the Neustadt (New Town) area of historic Salzburg, you can pick out the Mirabell Palace and Gardens, the Landestheater, the Mozart Residence and the Mozarteum, the Church of the Holy Trinity, and the Kapuzinerkloster perched atop the Kapuzinerberg. Ranging from the "acropolis" of the city—the medieval Fortress Hohensalzburg—to the celebrated Salzburg Marionette Theater, this part of Salzburg encapsulates the city's charm. If you want to see the most delightful Mozart landmark in this section of town, the Zauberflötenhäuschen—the mouthful used to describe the little summerhouse where he finished composing *The Magic Flute*—it can be viewed when concerts are scheduled in the adjacent Mozarteum.

A Good Walk

Start with Salzburg's number one sight—especially the case at night, when it is spectacularly spotlit—the famed **Fortress Hohensalzburg ⑲** ▶, the 11th-century castle that dominates the town. Take the Mönchsberg elevator or the Festungsbahn cable car on Festungsgasse, located behind the cathedral near St. Peter's Cemetery. If it's not running, you can walk up the zigzag path that begins a little farther up Festungsgasse; it's steep in parts but gives a better impression of the fortress's majestic nature. Once you've explored this, the largest medieval fortress in Central Europe, head back to the footpath, but instead of taking the steps back into town, turn right toward the **Nonnberg Convent ⑳**. Explore the church—the real Maria von Trapp almost found her calling here—then return along the path to the first set of steps, take them down them into Kaigasse, and continue on to Mozartplatz. From here you can cross the Salzach River over the oldest extant footbridge in the city, Mozartsteg. Cross the road and walk west a minute or two along Imbergstrasse until you see a bookstore on the corner. Here a little street runs into **Steingasse ㉑**—a picturesque

"OH, THE HILLS ARE ALIVE . . ."

FEW SALZBURGERS WOULD PUBLICLY ADMIT IT, *but* The Sound of Music, Hollywood's interpretation of the trials and joys of the local Trapp family, has become their city's most eminent emissary when it comes to international promotion. The year after the movie's release, international tourism to Salzburg jumped 20%, and soon The Sound of Music was a Salzburg attraction. The **Sternbräu Dinner Theater** (✉ *Griesgasse 23* ☎ *0662/826617*) offers a dinner show featuring those unforgettable songs from the movie, as well as traditional folksongs from Salzburg and a medley of Austrian operettas. The cost of the dinner show is €43; without dinner it's €31.

Perhaps the most important Sound spin-offs are the **tours** offered by several companies (for a number of them, see Guided Tours in *Salzburg A to Z, below*). Besides showing you some of the film's locations (usually very briefly), these four-hour rides have the advantage of giving a very concise tour of the city. The buses generally leave from Mirabellplatz; lumber by the "Do-Re-Mi" staircase at the edge of the beautifully manicured Mirabell Gardens; pass by the hardly visible Aigen train station, where in reality the Trapps caught the escape train; and then head south to Schloss Anif. This 16th-century water castle, which had a cameo appearance in the opening scenes of the film, is now in private hands and not open to the public.

First official stop for a leg-stretcher is at the gazebo in the manicured park of Schloss Hellbrunn at the southern end of the city. Originally built in the gardens of Leopoldskron Palace, it was brought out here to give the chance for taking pictures. This is where Liesl von Trapp sings "I Am Sixteen Going on Seventeen" and where Maria and the Baron woo and coo

"Something Good." The simple little structure is the most coveted prize of photographers. The bus then drives by another private palace with limited visiting rights, Schloss Leopoldskron. The estate's magical water-gate terrace, adorned with rearing horse sculptures and "site" of so many memorable scenes in the movie, was re-created elsewhere on the lake for the actual filming; its balcony, however, was really used for the scene where Maria and Baron von Trapp dance during the ball. The bus continues on to Nonnberg Convent at the foot of the daunting Hohensalzburg fortress, then leaves the city limits for the luscious landscape of the Salzkammergut. These are the hills "alive with music," where Julie Andrews prances about in the opening scenes. You get a chance for a meditative walk along the shore of the Wolfgangsee in St. Gilgen before the bus heads for the pretty town of Mondsee, where, in the movie, Maria and Georg von Trapp were married at the twin-turreted Michaelerkirche.

Tour guides are well trained and often have a sense of humor, with which they gently debunk myths about the movie. Did you know, for example, that Switzerland was "moved" 160 km (100 mi) eastward so the family could hike over the mountains to freedom (while singing "Climb Every Mountain")? It all goes to show that in Hollywood, as in Salzburg and its magical environs, almost anything is possible.

medieval street, and the old Roman street coming into from the south. After exploring this "time machine," walk through the Steintor gate, past the chapel of St. Johann am Imberg to the Hettwer Bastion on the **Kapuzinerberg Hill** ㉒ for another great vista of the city.

Continue up the path to the Kapuziner-Kloster. From here, follow the winding road down past the stations of the cross. Turn right at the bottom of the road into Linzergasse, the New Town's answer to the Getreidegasse. Continue up this street to St. Sebastian's Church on the left. An archway will lead you into the tranquil **St. Sebastian's Cemetery** ㉓— if it looks somewhat familiar that's because it inspired the scene at the end of *The Sound of Music,* where the von Trapps are nearly captured. When you leave the cemetery, walk north through a passageway until you reach Paris-Lodron-Strasse. To the left as you walk west down this street is the Loreto Church. At Mirabellplatz, cross the road to the **Mirabell Gardens** ㉔—the Pegasus Fountain (remember "Do-Re-Mi"?) and the Dwarfs' Garden are highlights here.

Take in Prince-Archbishop Wolf-Dietrich's private Xanadu, the adjacent **Mirabell Palace** ㉕ and its noted 18th-century Angel Staircase. Turn left out of the garden park onto busy Schwarzstrasse. Along this road you will find the famous center of Mozart studies, the **Mozarteum** ㉖, whose Great Hall is often the venue of chamber concerts (during which you can view the "Magic Flute" House in the nearby Bastionsgarten). Next door is the **Marionettentheater** ㉗—home to those marionettes known around the world. Turn left at the corner, around the Landestheater, and continue onto Makartplatz, dominated at the far end by Fischer von Erlach's **Dreifaltigkeitskirche** ㉘. Across from the Hotel Bristol is the second-most famous Mozart residence in the city, the **Mozart Wohnhaus** ㉙, where you can complete your homage to the city's hometown deity. Just to its right is the house where another famous Salzburger, the physicist Christian Doppler, was born in 1803.

TIMING Allow half a day for the fortress, to explore it fully both inside and out. If you don't plan an intermission at one of the restaurants on the Mönchsberg, you can stock up on provisions at Nordsee (next door to Mozart's Birthplace) or Fasties (Pfeifergasse 3, near the Kajetanerplatz). Call the Mozarteum to see if there will be evening recitals in their two concert halls; hearing the *Haffner* or another of Mozart's symphonies could be a wonderfully fitting conclusion to your day.

Sights to See

㉘ **Dreifaltigkeitskirche** (Church of the Holy Trinity). The Makartplatz—named after Hans von Makart, the most famous Austrian painter of the mid-19th-century—is dominated at the top (east) end by Fischer von Erlach's first architectural work in Salzburg, built 1694–1702. It was modeled on a church by Borromini in Rome and prefigures von Erlach's Karlskirche in Vienna. Dominated by a lofty, oval-shape dome—which showcases a painting by Michael Rottmayr—this church was the result of the archbishop's concern that Salzburg's new town was developing in an overly haphazard manner. The church interior is small but perfectly proportioned, surmounted by its dome, whose trompe-l'oeil fresco seems to open up the church to the sky above. ✉ *Dreifaltigkeitsgasse 14* ☎ *0662/877495* ✆ *Mon.–Sat. 6:30–6:30, Sun. 8–6:30.*

Festungsbahn (funicular railway). This is the easy way up to Fortress Hohensalzburg; it's located behind St. Peter's Cemetery. ✉ *Festungsgasse 4* ☎ *0662/842682* ⊕ *www.festungsbahn.at* ✑ *Round-trip including the entrance fee to the bastions of the fortress €8.50, one-way down €3.70* ✆ *Every 10 min Oct.–Mar., daily 9–5; May–Sept., daily 9–9.*

★ ⑲ **Fortress Hohensalzburg.** Founded in 1077, the Hohensalzburg is Salzburg's acropolis and the largest preserved medieval fortress in Central Europe. Brooding over the city from atop the Festungsberg, it was originally founded by Salzburg's Archbishop Gebhard, who had supported the pope in the investiture controversy against the Holy Roman Emperor. Over the centuries, the archbishops gradually enlarged the castle, using it originally only sometimes as a residence, then as a siege-proof haven against invaders and their own rebellious subjects. The exterior may look grim, but inside there are lavish state rooms, such as the glittering **Golden Room,** the **Burgmuseum**—a collection of medieval art—and the **Rainer's Museum,** with its brutish arms and armor. Politics and Church are in full force here: there's a torture chamber not far from the exquisite late-Gothic **St. George's Chapel** (although, in fact, the implements on view came from another castle and were not used here). The 200-pipe organ from the beginning of the 16th century, played during the warmer months daily after the carillon in the Neugebäude, is best to listen from a respectful distance, as it is not called the Bull without reason. Everyone will want to climb up the 100 tiny steps to the **Reckturm,** a grand lookout post with a sweeping view of Salzburg and the mountains. Remember that visitor lines to the fortress can be long, so try to come early. Children will love coming here, especially as some rooms of the castle are now given over to a special exhibitions, the **Welt der Marionetten,** which offers a fascinating view into the world of marionettes—a great preview of the treats in store at the nearby Marionettentheater.

You can either take the funicular railway, the more-than-110-year-old **Festungsbahn,** up to the fortress (advisable with young children) or walk up the zigzag path that begins just beyond the Stieglkeller on Festungsgasse. Note that you don't need a ticket to walk down the footpath. ✉ *Mönchsberg 34* ☎ *0662/842430–11* ⊕ *www.salzburg-burgen.at* ✑ *Fortress €3.60; apartments €3.60; marionette museum €3* ✆ *Mid-Mar.–mid-June, daily 9–6; mid-June–mid-Sept., daily 8:30–8; mid-Sept.–mid-Mar., daily 9–5; Marionette museum, Mar. 1–Dec. 31, daily 10–5.*

㉒ **Kapuzinerberg Hill.** Directly opposite the Mönchsberg on the other side of the river, Kapuzinerberg Hill is crowned by several interesting sights. By ascending a stone staircase near Steingasse 9 you can start your climb up the peak. At the top of the first flight of steps is a tiny chapel, **St. Johann am Imberg,** built in 1681. Farther on are a signpost and gate to the **Hettwer Bastion,** part of the old city walls that is one of the most spectacular viewpoints in Salzburg. At the summit is the gold-beige **Kapuzinerkloster** (Capuchin Monastery), originally a fortification built to protect the one bridge crossing the river, which dates from the time of

Prince-Archbishop Wolf-Dietrich. It was restored for the 1988 visit by Pope John Paul II. The road downward—note the Stations of the Cross along the path—is called Stefan Zweig Weg, after the great Austrian writer who rented the **Paschingerschlössl** house (on the Kapuzinerberg to the left of the monastery) until 1935, when he left Austria after the Nazis had murdered chancellor Dollfuss. As one of Austria's leading critics and esthetes, his residence became one of the cultural centers of Europe.

★ ☾ ㉗ **Marionettentheater** (Marionette Theater). The Salzburger Marionetten-theeater is both the world's greatest marionette theater and—surprise!—a sublime theatrical experience. Many critics have noted that viewers quickly forget the strings controlling the puppets, which assume lifelike dimensions and provide a very real dramatic experience. The Marionettentheater is identified above all with Mozart's operas, which seem particularly suited to the skilled puppetry; a delightful production of *Così fan tutte* captures the humor of the work better than most stage versions. The theater itself is a Rococo concoction. The company is famous for its world tours but is usually in Salzburg around Christmas, during the late-January Mozart Week, at Easter, and from May to September (schedule subject to change). ⊠ *Schwarzstrasse 24* ☎ *0662/872406–0* 🖷 *0662/882141* ⊕ *www.marionetten.at* 🎫 *€18–€35* ☾ *Box office Mon.–Sat. 9–1 and 2 hrs before performance; Salzburg season May–Sept., Christmas, Mozart Week (Jan.), Easter.*

☾ ㉔ **Mirabellgarten** (Mirabell Gardens). While there are at least four en-
FodorśChoice trances to the Mirabell Gardens—from the Makartplatz (framed by the
★ statues of the Roman gods), the Schwarzstrasse, and the Rainerstrasse—you'll want to enter from the Rainerstrasse and head for the Rosenhügel (Rosebush Hill): you'll arrive at the top of the steps where Julie Andrews and her seven charges showed off their singing ability in *The Sound of Music*. This is also an ideal vantage point from which to admire the formal gardens and one of the best views of Salzburg, as it shows how harmoniously architects of the Baroque period laid out the city. The center of the gardens—one of Europe's most beautiful parks, partly designed by Fischer von Erlach as the grand frame for the Mirabell Palace—is dominated by four large groups of statues representing the ancient elements of water, fire, air, and earth, and designed by Ottavio Mosto, who came to live in Salzburg from Padua. A bronze version of the horse Pegasus stands in front of the south facade of the palace in the center of a circular water basin. The most famous part of the Mirabell Gardens is the **Zwerglgarten** (Dwarfs' Garden), which can be found opposite the Pegasus fountain. Here you'll find 12 statues of "Danubian" dwarves sculpted in marble—the real-life models for which were presented to the bishop by the landgrave of Göttweig. Prince-Archbishop Franz Anton von Harrach had the stone figures made for a kind of stone theater below. The **Heckentheater** (Hedge Theater), an enchanting natural stage setting that dates from 1700, will once again host chamber operas (like Mozart's *Bastien und Bastienne*) during the 2006 Mozart year. The Mirabell Gardens are open daily 7 AM–8 PM. Art lovers will make a beeline for the **Barockmuseum** (⊠ Orangeriegarten ☎ 0662/877432), beside the Orangery of the Mirabell Gardens. It houses a collection of

late-17th- and 18th-century paintings, sketches, and models illustrating the extravagant vision of life of the Baroque era—the signature style of Salzburg. Works by Giordano, Bernini, and Rottmayr are the collection's highlights. The museum is open Tuesday to Saturday, 9 to noon and 2 to 5, and Sunday and holidays 10 to 1; admission is €3.

㉕ Mirabell Palace. The "Taj Mahal of Salzburg," Schloss Mirabell was built in 1606 by the immensely wealthy and powerful Prince-Archbishop Wolf-Dietrich for his mistress, Salomé Alt, and their 15 children: It was originally called Altenau in her honor. Such was the palace's beauty that it was taken over by succeeding prince-archbishops, including Markus Sittikus, Paris Lodron (who renamed the estate in honor of *his* mistress), and finally, Franz Anton von Harrach, who brought in Lukas von Hildebrandt to Baroque-ize the place in 1727. Unfortunately, a disastrous fire hit in 1818. Happily, three of the most spectacular set-pieces of the palace—the Chapel, the Marble Hall, and the Angel Staircase—survived. The Marble Hall is nowadays used for civil wedding ceremonies and is regarded as the most beautiful registry office in the world. Restored in 1999, its marble floor in strongly contrasting colors and walls of stucco and marble ornamented with elegant gilt scrollwork look more splendid than ever. The young Mozart and his sister gave concerts here, and he also composed *Tafelmusik* (Table Music) to accompany the prince's meals. It is only fitting that candlelit chamber concerts are now offered in this grand room. Beside the chapel in the north-east-corner the only other part of the palace to survive the fire was the magnificent marble Angel Staircase, laid out by von Hildebrandt, with sculptures by Georg Rafael Donner. The staircase is romantically draped with white marble putti, whose faces and gestures reflect a multitude of emotions, from questioning innocence to jeering mockery. The very first putti genuflects in an old Turkish greeting (a reminder of the Siege of Vienna in 1683). Outdoor concerts are held at the palace and gardens May though August, Sunday mornings at 10:30 and Wednesday evenings at 8:30. ☒ *Off Makartplatz* ☎ *0662/889–87–330* ☜ *Free* ☉ *Weekdays 8–6.*

Mozart Audio and Video Museum. In the same building as the Mozart Wohnhaus (Residence) is the Mozart Audio and Video Museum, an archive of thousands of Mozart recordings as well as films and video productions, all of which can be listened to or viewed on request. ☒ *Makartplatz 8* ☎ *0662/883454* ⊕ *www.mozarteum.at/seiten/mtfset.htm* ☜ *Free* ☉ *Mon., Tues., and Fri. 9–1, Wed. and Thurs. 1–5.*

㉙ Mozart Wohnhaus (Mozart Residence). The Mozart family moved from their cramped quarters in Getreidegasse to this house on the Hannibal Platz, as it was then known, in 1773. Wolfgang Amadeus Mozart lived here until 1780, his sister Nannerl stayed here until she married in 1784, and their father Leopold lived here until his death in 1787. The house is accordingly referred to as the Mozart Residence, signifying that it was not only Wolfgang who lived here. During the first Allied bomb attack on Salzburg in October 1944, the house was partially destroyed, but was reconstructed in 1996. Mozart composed the "Salzburg Symphonies" here, as well as all five violin concertos, church music and some sonatas, and parts of his early operatic masterpieces, including *Idome-*

neo. Besides an interesting collection of musical instruments (for example, his own pianoforte), among the exhibits on display are books from Leopold Mozart's library. Autograph manuscripts and letters can be viewed, by prior arrangement only, in the cellar vaults. One room offers a multi-media-show and wall-size map with more personal details about Mozart like his numerous travels across Europe. Another salon has been decorated in the domestic decor of Mozart's day. ⊠ *Makartplatz 8* ☎ *0662/874227–40* 🖷 *0662/872924* ⊕ *www.mozarteum.at* 🖃 *Mozart residence €6, combined ticket for Mozart residence and birthplace €9* ☉ *Sept.–June, daily 9–5:30; July–Aug., daily 9–6:30.*

㉖ Mozarteum. Two institutions share the address in this building finished just before World War I here—the International Mozarteum Foundation, set up in 1870, and the University of Music and Performing Arts, founded in 1880. Scholars come here to research in the **Bibliotheca Mozartiana,** the world's largest Mozart library. The Mozarteum also organizes the annual Mozart Week festival in January. Many important concerts are offered from October to June in its two recital halls, the Grosser Saal (Great Hall) and the Wiener Saal (Vienna Hall).

Behind the Mozarteum, sheltered by the trees of the Bastiongarten, is the famous **Zauberflötenhäuschen**—the little summerhouse where Mozart finished composing *The Magic Flute* in Vienna, with the encouragement of his frantic librettist, Emanuel Schikaneder, who finally wound up locking the composer inside to force him to complete his work. The house was donated to the Mozarteum by Prince Starhemberg. It is much restored: back in the 19th century, the faithful used to visit it and snatch shingles off its roof. The house can generally be only viewed when concerts are offered in the adjacent Grosser Saal. ⊠ *Schwarzstrasse 26* ☎ *0662/88940–21* ⊕ *www.mozarteum.at* ☉ *Summerhouse: only during Grosser Saal concerts.*

㉑ Nonnberg Convent. Just below the south side of the Fortress Hohensalzburg—and best visited in tandem with it—the Stift Nonnberg was founded right after 700 by St. Rupert, and his niece St. Erentrudis was the first abbess (in the archway a late-Gothic statue of Erentrudis welcomes the visitor). Note, just below the steeple, some of the oldest frescos in Austria, painted in the Byzantine style during the 10th century). It is more famous these days as "Maria's convent"—both the one in *The Sound of Music* and that of the real Maria. She returned to marry her Captain von Trapp here in the Gothic church (as it turns out, no filming was done here—"Nonnberg" was recreated in the film studios of Salzburg-Parsch). Each evening in May at 7, the nuns sing a 15-minute service called Maiandacht in the old Gregorian chant. Their beautiful voices can be heard also at the 11 PM mass on December 24. Parts of the private quarters for the nuns, which include some lovely, intricate woodcarving, can be seen by prior arrangement. ⊠ *Nonnberggasse 2* ☎ *0662/841607–0* ☉ *Fall–spring, daily 7–5; summer, daily 7–7.*

★ **㉓ St. Sebastian's Cemetery.** Memorably recreated for the escape scene in *The Sound of Music* on a Hollywood soundstage, final resting place for many members of the Mozart family, and situated in the shadows of St. Sebastian's Church, the Friedhof St. Sebastian is one of the most peace-

CloseUp
HAPPY 250TH BIRTHDAY, WOLFERL!

THE MOZART YEAR 2006 *birthday celebrations in the composer's home town get a build-up to the big B-day, January 27, 2006, when the annual Salzburg Mozart Week (Mozartwoche) opens on January 20th—there are so many star-studded concerts scheduled it runs a full two weeks at the Grosses Festspielhaus and the Mozarteum theaters (⊕ www. mozarteum.at). On Wolfgang Amadeus Mozart's 250th birthday itself, the city becomes an immense concert stage, with the composer's music to flood out from regal squares and courtyards; on the same day, the city's Mozart instititions to unveil their birthday exhibitions, including the biggest, "Viva Mozart!", at the Salzburg Museum in the Neue Residenz on Mozartplatz (where a special Mozart Corner booth will be found all year long). Holy of holies, Mozart's Birthplace (⊕ www.mozarteum.at), will introduce special guided tours that even include a mini-piano recital. By summer, most of the civilized world will be heading to the famous Salzburger Festspiele (⊕ www. salzburgfestival.at), end-July to end-August, during which all of the composer's 22 operas will be presented in the three Festspielhäuser theaters. The Grosses Festspielhaus and the Mozarteum theaters will also be hosting special "Best of Mozart" concerts (⊕ www.salzburgticket. com) on thirty weekends from February 18 to November 18. All of Mozart's masses, including the Missa brevis and the Coronation mass, will be presented on Sunday mornings from January through December.*

For pure birthday sparkle, book the Mozart Gala Banquets, held in the gilded Baroque staterooms of Salzburg's Residenz (where Mozart often conducted "dinner music"). Concert-banquets, these are mounted by the Konzerthüro Salzburg Special (offered February 10; May 6, 13,

20, 27; June 3, 10, 17, 24; July 1, 8, 15; August 5, 12; and September 2, 9, 16). Or repair to the Residenz for its series of mid-day recitals, the Mozart Matineès, running from late July to late August. Other historic surrounds where you can raise a glass of champagne in Wolfie's honor? At the Fortress Hohensalzburg, the Salzburger Festungkonzerte (⊕ www.mozartfestival. at) will host concerts, often offered in tandem with candlelit dinners, in its Prince's Chamber. Weekly Mozart dinner-concerts—replete with bewigged musicians—will be presented in the beautiful Baroque Hall of the Stiftskeller St. Peter (⊕ www.mozart-serenaden.com), while the Salzburger Schlosskonzerte will be presenting many Mozart concerts in the spectacular Marble Hall of the Mirabell palace (⊕ www.salzburger. schlosskonzerte.at).

If you want a kid-friendly Mozart experience, head over to the Salzburger Marionettentheater (⊕ www.marionetten. at) for its enchanting (and nicely shortened) Mozart opera shows or its special Mozart Year one-hour "Best of" show (every Friday from May through September at 2 PM). During the autumn, catch the three-week-long festival of Mozartian sacred music, from October 22 to November 12, at the city's leading churches. To bring the gala year to a close, on December 3 and 4, a wide range of memorial concerts will be mounted, with the anniversary of his death on December 5 marked by a performance of his Requiem at the Mozarteum's Grosser Saal theater (⊕ www.mozarteum. at). For a complete rundown on all the hundreds of Salzburg events and concerts for the Mozart Year, log on to (⊕ www. mozart2006.net/downloads/en/MSM_e 150904.pdf)

ful spots in Salzburg. Prince-Archbishop Wolf-Dietrich commissioned the cemetery in 1600 to replace the old cathedral graveyard, which he planned to demolish. It was built in the style of an Italian *campo santo*, (sacred field) with arcades on four sides, and in the center of the square he had the Gabriel Chapel, an unusual, brightly tiled Mannerist mausoleum built for himself, in which he was interred in 1617 (now closed for visitors). Several famous people are buried in this cemetery, including the medical doctor and philosopher Theophrastus Paracelsus, who settled in Salzburg in the early 16th century (his grave is by the church door). Around the chapel are the graves of eight members of Mozart's family, including his wife, Constanze, his father, Leopold, and Genoveva Weber, the aunt of Constanze and the mother of Carl Maria von Weber (by the central path leading to the mausoleum). If the gate is closed, try going through the church, or enter through the back entrance around the corner in the courtyard. ⊠ *Linzergasse* ⊙ *Daily 9 AM–6 PM.*

㉑ Steingasse. This narrow medieval street, walled in on one side by the bare cliffs of the Kapuzinerberg, was originally the ancient Roman entrance into the city from the south. The houses stood along the riverfront before the Salzach was regulated. Nowadays it's a fascinating mixture of artists' workshops, antiques shops, and trendy nightclubs, but with its tall houses the street still manages to convey an idea of how life used to be in the Middle Ages. The **Steintor** marks the entrance to the oldest section of the street; here on summer afternoons the light can be particularly striking. House No. 23 on the right still has deep, slanted peep-windows for guarding the gate.

Short Side Trips from Salzburg

Gaisberg and Untersberg. Adventurous people might like to ascend two of Salzburg's "house mountains" (so-called because they are so close to the city settlements). You can take the bus to the summit of the Gaisberg, where you'll be rewarded with a spectacular panoramic view of the Alps and the Alpine foreland. In summer Dr. Richard/Albus bus (☎ 0662/424–000–0) leaves from Mirabellplatz at 10, 12, 2, and 5:15, and the journey takes about half an hour. The Untersberg is the mountain Captain von Trapp and Maria climbed as they escaped the Nazis in *The Sound of Music.* In the film they were supposedly fleeing to Switzerland; in reality, the climb up the Untersberg would have brought them almost to the doorstep of Hitler's retreat at the Eagle's Nest above Berchtesgaden (!). A cable car from St. Leonhard (about 13 km [8 mi] south of Salzburg) takes you up 6,020 feet right to the top of the Untersberg, giving you a breathtaking view. In winter you can ski down (you arrive in the village of Fürstenbrunn and taxis or buses take you back to St. Leonhard); in summer there are a number of hiking routes from the summit. ⊠ *Untersbergbahn* ☎06246/72477 ⊕*www.untersberg.net* ⊠ *Round-trip €17* ⊙ *Mid-Dec.–Feb., daily 10–4; Mar.–June and Oct., daily 9–5; July–Sept., daily 8:30–5:30.*

Hallein. The second largest town of the region, 15 km (10 mi) south of Salzburg, Hallein was once famed for its caves of "white gold"—salt. Centuries ago, salt was often used as payment; it was converted into hard cash to finance the construction of Salzburg's Baroque monuments by the prince-archbishops. It was especially prized because it was used to smoke (or salt) meat and preserve it long before the days of refrigerators. "Hall" is the old Celtic word for salt and this treasure was mined in the neighboring Dürrnberg mountain. To learn all about Hallein, head to the **Keltenmuseum** (Museum of the Celts) (✉ Pflegerplatz 5 ☎ 06245/80783 ☜ €4), where over 30 rooms explore the history of the region's Celtic settlements (before the birth of Christ). In the three staterooms, more than 70 oil paintings show the working conditions of the salt mines and the salina. You can get to Hallein by regular bus system, by car along the B159 Salzachtal-Bundesstrasse, or by bicycle along the River Salzach. Once in Hallein, you can pay your respects to Franz Gruber, the composer of "Silent Night, Holy Night," who lies in the only grave still extant next to the town's parish church.

Oberndorf. This little village 21 km (13 mi) north of Salzburg has just one claim to fame: it was here on Christmas Eve, 1818, that the world famous Christmas Carol "Silent Night, Holy Night", composed by the organist and schoolteacher Franz Gruber to a lyric by the local priest, Josef Mohr, was sung for the first time. The church was demolished and replaced in 1937 by a tiny commemorative chapel containing a copy of the original composition (the original is in the Museum Salzburg), stained-glass windows depicting Gruber and Mohr, and a Nativity scene. About a 10-minute walk from the village center along the riverbank, the local **Heimatmuseum** (✉ Stille-Nacht-Platz 7 ☎ 06272/4422–0), opposite the chapel, documents the history of the carol. The museum is open daily 9–noon and 1–5; admission is €2.50. You can get to Oberndorf by the local train (opposite the main train station), by car along the B156 Lamprechtshausener Bundesstrasse, or by bicycle along the River Salzach.

☺ **Schloss Hellbrunn** (Hellbrunn Palace). Just 6½ km (4 mi) south of
Fodor's Choice Salzburg, the Lustschloss Hellbrunn was the prince-archbishops' plea-
★ sure palace. It was built early in the 17th century by Santino Solari for Markus Sittikus, after the latter had imprisoned his uncle, Wolf-Dietrich, in the fortress. The castle has some fascinating rooms, including an octagonal music room and a banquet hall with a trompe-l'oeil ceiling. From the magnificent gardens and tree-lined avenues to the silent ponds, Hellbrunn Park is often described as a jewel of landscape architecture. It became famous far and wide because of its **Wasserspiele,** or trick fountains: in the formal gardens, a beautiful example of the Mannerism stile including a later-added outstanding mechanical theater, some of the exotic and humorous fountains spurt water from strange places at unexpected times—you will probably get doused (bring a raincoat). A visit to the gardens is highly recommended: nowhere else can you experience so completely the realm of fantasy that the grand Salzburg archbishops indulged in. The **Monatsschlösschen,** the old hunting lodge (built in one month), contains an excellent folklore museum. Following the path over the hill you find the **Steintheater** (Stone Theater), an old quarry made into the earliest open-air opera stage north of the Alps. The former palace deer park has become a **zoo** featuring

free-flying vultures and Alpine animals that largely roam unhindered. You can get to Hellbrunn by Bus 5, by car on Route 159, or by bike or on foot along the beautiful Hellbrunner Allee past several 17th-century mansions. The restaurant in the castle courtyard serves good food. On the estate grounds is the little gazebo filmed in *The Sound of Music* ("I am 16 . . . ")—the doors are now locked because a person once tried to repeat the movie's dance steps, leaping from bench to bench, and managed to fall and break a hip. ✉ *Fürstenweg 37, Hellbrunn* ☎ *0662/ 820372* ⊕ *www.hellbrunn.at* 🖂 *Tour of palace and water gardens €7.50* ⊙ *Apr. and Oct., daily 9–4:30; May–Sept., daily 9–5:30; evening tours July–Aug., daily on the hr 6–10.*

Schloss Frohnburg (Frohnburg Palace). Only walkers and bikers can pass by this charming little yellow building from the 17th century set along the Hellbrunner Allee, the old road that leads out to the Schloss Hellbrunn at the southern end of the city. Producer Robert Wise chose it as the front of Baron van Trapp's house in *The Sound of Music*—from here they set out on their first attempt to escape. The house belongs to the University of Music and Performing Arts "Mozarteum" (closed to public) and contains the **Orff Institute**, named after the great Bavarian composer Carl Orff. He developed the "Orff Schoolwork," a special musical training method for children, which has its central headquarters here. Maria von Trapp would undoubtedly approve.

★ **Schloss Leopoldskron** (Leopold's Crown Palace). One of Salzburg's most glamorous pleasure palaces, this lakeside villa earned Hollywood immortality when it was used as the "back" of Baron von Trapp's house in *The Sound of Music*. The front was that of Schloss Frohnburg, across the lake. While the enchanting water terrace—framed by the winged horses (remember?)—was recreated elsewhere on the lake for many of the villa scenes, several shots did utilize this stepped lakeside garden, which, in fact, still exists in all its splendor. A gorgeous example of Austrian Rococo, the house itself dates back to the first half of the 18th century and was built for Archbishop Stuart (who, in 1731, had 20,000 evicted from catholic Salzburg—many wound up in the U.S.). Count Firmian—who often supplied the Mozart family with money for their concert tours through Europe—then used the house for his vast art collection. Finally, it became the summer residence of Max Reinhardt, one of the founders of the Salzburg Festival, in 1937. Only the fixed decoration of the Venetian Room and the copy of the St. Gallen monastery library still remain in situ. The house is now owned by the "Salzburg Seminar in American Studies" which uses it for high-end conferences only and does not open it to visitors. There is also no bus service through Leopoldskronstrasse, so you need to hike around the Nonnberg hill for some distance to get to the house. Happily, once you get to Leopoldskron, there is a pool set to the side of the palace where you can enjoy an appropriate vista of the house right out of *The Sound of Music*. With the Fortress Honhensalzburg looming in the distance, you'll want to have your Nikon handy. Note that the tree-lined road where Julie Andrews gets off the Albus bus to get to the von Trapp home can be found a short way from the Schloss.

WHERE TO EAT

Many restaurants favor the *neue Küche*—a lighter version of the somewhat heavier traditional specialties of Austrian cooking, but with more substance than nouvelle cuisine. The only truly indigenous Salzburg dish is *Salzburger Nockerln,* a snowy meringue of sweetened whisked egg, but the Salzburgers have a wonderful way with fish—often a fresh catch from the nearby lakes of the Salzkammergut. Some of the most distinctive places in town are the fabled hotel restaurants, such as those of the Goldener Hirsch and the Schloss Mönchstein, or the "Ratsherrenkeller" of the Hotel Elefant; see our hotel reviews for details. The newest spot in town, M32—the restaurant of the Museum der Moderne Salzburg—was not open at press-time, but the decor will be formidably mod-minimalist (concrete walls and animal horns) and there are high hopes for an adventurous menu. Also in the news is the legendary Café Glockenspiel, the most popular café on Mozartplatz. It is now undergoing renovation and will reopen as a pricey restaurant in 2005. For fast food, Salzburgers love their broiled-sausages street-stands. Some say the most delicious are to be found at the Balkan Grill at Getreidegasse 33 (its recipe for spicy Bosna sausage has always been a secret).

★ $$$$ ✕ **Gasthof Hohlwegwirt.** It's worth a detour on the way to Hallein along the B159 Salzachtal-Bundesstrasse about 10 km (6 mi) south of Salzburg to dine at this inviting inn, run by the same family for more than 130 years. Visitors to the summer music festival may find a hard time landing a table since there are so many local regulars, all here to enjoy the suburban cooking, the wine cellar filled with more than 100 different vintages, and the unmistakable atmosphere of this *stil Salzburg* house with its four nicely decorated salons. Chef Ernst Kronreif uses recipes from his legendary mother, Ida: spring for the delicious *Butternockerlsuppe* (soup-broth with buttered dumplings), the *Kalbsbries* (calf's sweetbreads), or the *Salzburger Bierfleisch* (beef boiled in beer)—all Salzburgian classics and yet always so up-to-date. Upstairs are some delightfully gemütlich guest rooms. ⊠ *Salzachtal-Bundesstrasse Nord 62, A-5400 Hallein-Taxach* ☎ *06245/82415–0* 🖷 *06245/8241572* ⊕ *www. hallo-hallein.at/page/hohlwegwirt.html* ⌦ *Reservations essential* ☉ *Closed Mon., except during Summer Festival* ☰ MC, V.

★ $$$$ ✕ **Pfefferschiff.** The "Pepper Ship" is one of the most acclaimed restaurants in Salzburg—or, actually, 3 km (2 mi) northeast of the center. It's in a pretty, renovated rectory, dated 1640, adjacent to a pink-and-cream chapel. Klaus Fleishhaker, an award-winning chef, and his German wife Petra make your table feel pampered in the country-chic atmosphere, nicely adorned with polished wooden floors, antique hutches, and tabletops laden with fine bone china and Paloma Picasso silverware. The menu changes seasonally. A taxi is the least stressful way of getting here, but if you have your own car, drive along the north edge of the Kapuzinerberg toward Hallwang and then Söllheim. ⊠ *Söllheim 3, A-5300 Hallwang* ☎ *0662/661242* ⌦ *Reservations essential* ☰ AE.

$$$–$$$$ ✕ **Pan e Vin.** This tiny trattoria has only a handful of tables, and they're hard to obtain, since the Italian specialities on tap are top-flight. Burnt

sienna walls are lined with wine bottles, colorful ceramic plates, and Italian dry stuffs, and the chef cooks in full view. The upstairs restaurant of the same name has a more extensive menu, but it's also much more expensive. ⊠ *Gstättengasse 1* ☎ *0662/844666* 🖷 *0662/844666–15* 🖃 *AE, DC, MC, V* ⌒ *Reservations essential* ⊙ *Closed Sun.–Mon.*

$$–$$$$
Fodor$Choice
★

✕ **Stiftskeller St. Peter.** Legends swirl about the famous "St. Peter's Beer Cellar." Locals claim that Mephistopheles met Faust here, other say Charlemagne dined here, and some believe Columbus enjoyed a glass of its famous Salzburg Stiegl beer just before he set sail for America in 1492. But there is no debating the fact that this place—first mentioned in a document dating back to 803—is Austria's oldest restaurant, part of the famous abbey whose Benedictine monks were Christianity's first ambassadors in these formerly pagan parts. If this is Europe's oldest Gasthaus, it still remains one of the most dazzling dining experiences in Salzburg. Choose between the fairly elegant, dark-wood-paneled Prälatenzimmer (Prelates' Room) or one of several less formal banqueting rooms. On hot summer days, the dramatic gray-stone courtyard is a favorite for drinking a glass of wine or a glass of that noted beer, accompanied by fingerlickingly good morsels of fried Wiener Schnitzel. Along with other Austrian standards, you can dine on fish caught in local rivers and lakes, and, of course, Salzburger Nockerl. For the full St. Peter splendor and to get in on the Mozart festivities, attend a candlelit Mozart Dinner Concert (€45, plus drinks) in the abbey's beautiful Baroque Hall—a dazzling white-and-blue chandeliered wonder. Almost every evening during 2005 and 2006 at 8 PM, you'll be able to enjoy 18th-century delectables along with tunes by the Wolfgang played by musicians in historic costume. Dessert will be "Mozart's Secret Sweet." ⊠ *St. Peter Bezirk 4* ☎ *0662/841268–0, Mozart dinner: 0662/828695–0* ⊕ *www.stiftskellerstpeter.at; Mozart dinner: www.mozartdinnerconcert. com* 🖃 *AE, DC, MC, V.*

$$$ ✕ **Perkeo.** Small and modern with minimalist decor, close-set tables, and an open kitchen, this upscale establishment across the river from the Altstadt is one of the city's standard bearers for future-forward cuisine. Specialities of the house include crepes stuffed with braised oxtail and red-wine shallots or *Seeteufel* (monkfish) with thistle and spinach on a bed of buttery noodles. Wines by the glass are priced at the high end. The wine list by the bottle confusingly lists the cheaper "take-out" prices—make sure of the price before ordering. ⊠ *Priesterhausgasse 20* ☎ *0662/870899* ⌒ *Reservations essential* 🖃 *No credit cards* ⊙ *Closed weekends.*

★ **$$–$$$** ✕ **Blaue Gans.** In a 500-year-old building with vaulted ceilings and windows looking out onto the bustling Getreidegasse, this formerly old-style restaurant in the Blaue Gans hotel has been revamped to showcase a more innovative style of Austrian cooking. There are always vegetarian choices, too. Service is top-notch, the *Wolfsbarsch* (perch) comes with a cilantro-chili cream sauce, and you can peer through a glass floor to study an old mystic cellar—this, as it turns out, was the site of the oldest inn in Salzburg. ⊠ *Getreidegasse 41–43* ☎ *0662/842491–0* 🖃 *AE, DC, MC, V* ⊙ *Closed Tues.*

$$–$$$ ✕ **Mundenhamer.** Set next to the Mirabell Palace, this old-fashioned restaurant is masterminded by chef Ernst Breitschopf. He knows the reper-

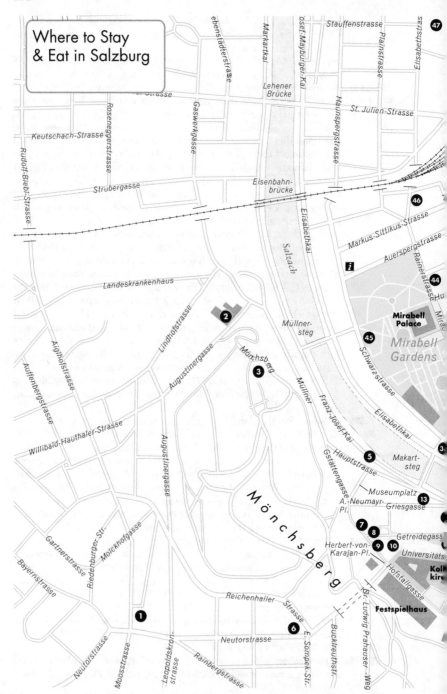

Where to Stay
& Eat in Salzburg

Restaurants ▼

Ährlich .35
Augustinerbräu 2
Blaue Gans 9
Café Sacher 33
Café Tomaselli 17
Coco Lezzone 5
Daxlueg 47
Die Weisse 42
Gablerbräu 27
Gasthof Hohlwegwirt 25
Fabrizi Espresso 11
K&K am Waagplatz 20
Krimpelstätter 4
Kuglhof 1
Mundenhamer 44
Pan e Vino 8
Perkeo 31
Pfefferschiff 38
Ristorante Pizzeria al Sole 7
Stiftskeller St. Peter 16
Wilder Mann 13
Zipfer Bierhaus 14
Zum Eulenspiegel 12
Zum Fidelen Affen 29
Zum Mohren 19

Hotels ▼

Altstadt Radisson SAS 18
Am Dom 21
Amadeus 34
Auersperg 43
Bergland 41
Bristol 32
Blaue Gans 9
Cordial Theaterhotel 37
Elefant 15
Gersberg Alm 40
Goldener Hirsch 10
Kasererbräu 23
Neutor 6
NH Salzburg 36
Pension Wolf 22
Rosenvilla 26
Sacher Salzburg 33
Schloss Mönchstein 3
Schwarzes Rössl 28
Sheraton Salzburg 45
Stadtkrug 30
Stieglbräu/Imlauer 46
Turnerwiit 39
Weisse Taube 24
Wolf-Dietrich 35

toire of good old Upper Austrian dishes inside out. So just come here and feast: an *Innviertler* raw ham with horseradish, dark bread, and butter; a garlic soup with bread croutons; a roast pork chop served in a pan with bread dumplings and warm bacon-cabbage salad; homemade spätzle with braised white cabbage and bacon; a *Salzburger Schnitzel* (scallop of veal filled with minced mushrooms and ham) with buttered finger dumplings. Dessert? Who can resist the *Mohr im Hemd* ("Moorin-a-shirt"), the warm chocolate cake garnished with fruits, chocolate sauce, vanilla ice-cream, and whipped cream? Only problem? You may not be able to move after your last bite. ⊠ *Rainerstrasse 2* ☎0662/875693 ▤ *AE, DC, MC, V* ◷ *Closed Sun.*

★ **$$–$$$** ✕ **Zum Eulenspiegel.** What has Till Eulenspiegel, the 14th-century jester from Germany's Braunschweig, to do with Salzburg? Not much, but when Hans Grassl opened this restaurant in 1950 (set just across the way from Mozart's birthplace), he saw the surrounding medieval townscape—the old town wall, the "little gate," and its historic 1414 'Griess rooms—and decided to go for it. This inn actually was first mentioned In 1713 and, today, spiffily restored, it allures with rustic wooden furniture, old folio volumes, antique weapons, and open firesides. Tables gleaming with white linen are set in wonderful nooks and crannies reached by odd staircases and charming salons, like the tiny "women's apartment," offer delightful views over the city and river. The unique setting is matched by the delicious food. Try the potato goulash with chunks of sausage and beef in a creamy paprika sauce, or the house specialty, fish stew Provençal. These are served at lunch, or all day in the bar downstairs. A final plus: the staff speaks English. ⊠ *Hagenauerplatz 2* ☎ *0662/843180–0* ◮ *Reservations essential* ▤ *AE, DC, MC, V* ◷ *Closed Sun., except during festival and Jan.–mid-Mar.*

$$–$$$ ✕ **Zum Mohren.** Good food, a central location by the river, a friendly welcome, attentive service, and reasonable prices have made Zum Mohren very popular with both Salzburgers and tourists. The restaurant is in the cellar of a 15th-century house, with cozy lighting, polished copper pots adorning the walls, and a vaulted Gothic room. The menu is imaginative, featuring such dishes as *Zanderfilet* (pike perch) in an herb-cheese crust with potato leek ragout. There's also a good vegetarian selection. ⊠ *Judengasse 9/Rudolfskai 20* ☎ *0662/842387* ▤ *AE, MC, V.*

$–$$$ ✕ **Café Sacher.** Red velvet banquettes, sparkling chandeliers, and lots of gilt mark this famous gathering place, a favorite of well-heeled Salzburgers and an outpost of the celebrated Vienna landmark. It's a perfect choice for a leisurely afternoon pastry (especially the famous chocolate Sachertorte) and coffee—and of course the coffee is second to none. Full meals are also served and they offer a no-smoking room, too. (Pastries and coffee are in the $ category.) ⊠ *Schwarzstrasse 5–7* ☎ *0662/889770* ▤ *AE, DC, MC, V.*

$$ ✕ **Ährlich.** Just because this restaurant is all-organic doesn't mean it isn't fun. The dining room has a country casual ambience with cozy booths. ⊠ *Wolf-Dietrich-Strasse 7* ☎0662/871275 ▤ *AE, DC, MC, V* ◷ *Closed Sun. No lunch.*

$$ ✕ **Coco Lezzone.** You'll always find a lively crowd at this popular spot on the quay on the Altstadt side of the river. Spacious with a contemporary, informal dining room, it can be a bit noisy at night. The menu changes with the seasons. ⊠ *Franz-Josef-Kai 7* ☎ *0662/846735* ⊟ *No credit cards* ⊙ *Closed Sun. No lunch Sat.*

★ $$ ✕ **Die Weisse** This *Weissbierbrauerei* occupies one of Salzburg's most historic breweries and many locals consider it to be their ultimate private retreat (so much so that from Wednesday through Saturday, it's best to make a reservation). The beer garden really hits the spot on a hot summer day but, year long, you can delight in traditional Bavarian goodies (veal sausages with sweet mustard!) as well as the usual array of tempting Salzburg delights. ⊠ *Rupertgasse 10* ☎ *0662/8722460* ⊟ *MC, V* ⊙ *Closed Sun.*

★ $$ ✕ **Daxlueg.** If you really want to enjoy "food-with-a-view," drive 3 km (2 mi) north along the B1 Linzer Bundesstrasse to Mayrwies and turn right up through the woods. Here, you can take in a Cineramic view of Salzburg from the mountainside perch of this former *Rupertialm* (St. Rupert's pasture), a famous scenic lookout even in Mozart's time. Owned by St. Peter's monastery and now nicely renovated, this restaurant allures with the romantic charm of an alpine chalet. Seasonal specialities of the region top the bill: not only venison and fried trout but heavenly garnishes—cress, elder blossoms, herbs from the meadows, raspberries, blueberries, *Schwammerl* (mushrooms) fresh out of the forest, cheese from goat and sheep. Ah, Salzburg! ⊠ *Daxluegstrasse 5, A-5300 Hallwang* ☎ *0662/665800* ⊟ *AE, DC, MC, V.*

$$ ✕ **Gablerbräu.** You like it quick and good? Many like to stop here for a fast bite, but you should ponder the historic vibes, too. In this old inn Richard Mayr—a famous star of Vienna's State Opera House (he was the first to record Baron Ochs in Strauss's *Der Rosenkavalier*)—was born. He later became one of the organizers of the famous Salzburg music festival. After studying the parlor of Mayr's parents—a dark, wood-carved, neo-Gothic interior of the end of the 19th century—head for a table and settle down to "hot breads and cold beer": a selection of beers from different provinces along with a large variety of sandwiches for any taste. There is also a self-service salad buffet. Other treats on the menu are Northern Italian (in former days, of course, Austrian), including the polenta croquets with ratatouille and Gorgonzola cream sauce or the homemade linguine with courgettes in tomato sauce—best paired with a glass of white or red wine from Guttmann's cellars. ⊠ *Linzergasse 9* ☎ *0662/88965* ⊟ *AE, DC, MC, V.*

$$ ✕ **K&K am Waagplatz.** This old house was once the domicile of the Freysauff family, who once counted among their close friend Leopold Mozart, the composer's father. Its cellar, the downstairs section of the restaurant, is still called the Freysauff (but don't be misled—this translates into "free drinks"!). The restaurant is particularly pleasant, with white linen tablecloths, candles, and flowers, and windows opening onto the street. Menu selections consist of locally caught fish, delicious chicken-breast medaillons, lentil salad with strips of goose breast, and traditional Austrian dishes and game in season. Service is friendly. ⊠ *Waagplatz 2* ☎ *0662/842156* ⊟ *AE, DC, MC, V.*

★ $$ ✕ **Kuglhof.** In Maxglan, a famous "farmer's village" of Austria, now part of the city tucked behind the Mönchsberg and next to the Stiegl brewery (best, therefore, reached by taxi), Alexander Hawranek perfects Old-Austrian specialities by giving them a nouvelle touch. The setting is your archetypal black-shuttered, yellow-hued, begonia-bedecked Salzburgian farmhouse, oh-so-cozily set with a tile oven, mounted antlers, embroidered curtains, and tons of yummy gemütlichkeit. The menu is seasonal, so you might not be able to enjoy the signature *Beuschl* (calf's lights) with dumplings. Best best for dessert is the *Apfelschmarrn*, sliced pancake with apples. In the summer, opt for a table out in the shady garden. ⊠ *Kuglhofstrasse 13* ☎ *0662/832626* ⊕ *www. kuglhof.at* ⊟ *AE, DC, MC, V.*

$–$$ ✕ **Café Tomaselli.** Not many years after the attacking Turks fled Vienna,
Fodor'sChoice leaving behind tons of coffee beans, this inn opened its doors in 1705
★ as an example of that new-fangled thing, a "Wiener Kaffeehaus" (Vienna coffeehouse). It was an immediate hit. Enjoying its more than 14 types of coffee was none other than Mozart's beloved, Konstanze, who often dropped in as her house was just next door. The Tomasellis set up shop here in 1753, became noted as "chocolatmachers," and are still running the place. You'll want to feast on the famous "Tomaselliums Café" (mocca, Mozart liqueur, and whipped cream) and the large selection of excellent homemade cakes, tarts, and strudels. Inside, the decor is marble, wood, and walls of 18th-century portraits. In the summer, however, the best seats are on the terrace and at the pretty "Tomsalli-Kiosk" on the square. ⊠ *Alter Markt 9* ☎ *0662/844488–0* ⊕ *www. tomaselli.at* ⊟ *No credit cards.*

$–$$ ✕ **Fabrizi Espresso.** Named after the former Italian owner of this historic house (note the beautiful small archway passage), this is a top spot for tasting *Marzemino*, the red wine Don Giovanni drinks in Mozart's opera. But there are plenty of other goodies here: some of the best Italian coffees in the city; outstanding Austrian *Apfel- oder Topfenstrudel* (apple or cheese pie—worth any money, but not expensive); excellent Prosecco Italian sparkling wine; various salads; and a fine Wiener Schnitzel. ⊠ *Getreidegasse 21* ☎ *0662/845914* ⊟ *No credit cards* ⊙ *Closed Sun. Oct.–Easter.*

★ $ ✕ **Krimpelstätter.** About a 15-minute walk downriver from the Altstadt in the Müllner neighborhood, this is one of the top spots where the artists of the Summer Festival like to celebrate after their premieres. Everyone enjoys the traditional Salzburg cooking: seasonal and delicious *Bärlauch* (wild wood garlic) soup, or the potato goulash with chunks of country ham, or the homemade pork sausage with dumplings, or the *Zanderfilet* (pike perch). Happily, all this is served up in a delicious, centuries-old building, with fetching accents provided by vaulted ceilings, leaded-glass windows, and homespun tablecloths. Augustiner beer (from the monastery next door) is fresh on tap, and there's a big shady garden for dining in summer. ⊠ *Müllner Hauptstrasse 31* ☎ *0662/432274* ⌂ *Reservations essential* ⊟ *No credit cards* ⊙ *Closed Sun.–Mon., Sept.–Apr.; Mon., May–Aug.*

$ ✕ **Wilder Mann.** "After a certain time all men become wild." So goes a famous Salzburg saying, perhaps coined after someone drank too much of the local "liquid bread"—Stiegl beer. In fact, when this inn opened its doors in 1884 it became one of the most important burgher houses in the Altstadt. Today, it offers a true time-stained ambience of an old Salzburg *Gasthaus,* right down to the wooden chairs that generations of locals have sat on and the enormous plates of *Bauernschmaus* (farmer's dish) overflowing with veal, pork, sausage, sour cabbage, and dumplings. ⊠ *Getreidegasse 20* ☎ *0662/841787* ⊟ *No credit cards* ⊘ *Closed Sun.*

$ ✕ **Zipfer Bierhaus.** Arched ceilings, brick floors, flowered curtains, and wooden banquettes provide the right setting for good, standard local fare such as roast pork and dumplings. This is one of Salzburg's oldest Gasthäuser; look down the ancient cistern in the passageway connecting the two main rooms and try the different taste of the beer from Upper Austria. ⊠ *Sigmund-Haffner-Gasse 12/Universitätsplatz 19* ☎ *0662/840745* ⊟ *No credit cards* ⊘ *Closed Sun.*

★ $ ✕ **Zum Fidelen Affen.** The name means "At the Faithful Ape," which explains the ape motifs in this popular Gasthaus dominated by a round copper-plated bar and stone pillars under a vaulted ceiling. Besides the beer on tap, the kitchen offers tasty Austrian dishes, such as *Schlutzkrapfen,* cheese ravioli with a light topping of chopped fresh tomatoes, or a big salad with strips of fried chicken. It's always crowded, so be sure to arrive early or book ahead. ⊠ *Priesterhausgasse 8* ☎ *0662/877361* ⌂ *Reservations essential* ⊟ *DC, MC, V* ⊘ *Closed Sun. No lunch.*

★ ¢–$ ✕ **Augustinerbräu.** One of the largest beer cellars in Europe and Salzburg's homegrown version of a Munich beer house, the celebrated Augustinerbräu is located at the north end of the Mönchsberg next to St. Augustine's church. You can even bring your own food—a relic of the old tradition that forbade breweries from serving meals in order to protect the status of restaurants. Pick up a stone jug of strong, frothy Augustiner beer and sit in the gardens or at a dark-wood table in one of the large refectory halls. Shops in the huge monastery complex sell a vast array of salads, breads, and pastries, as well as sausage and spit-roasted chicken. If you don't feel up to cold beer, there's an old copper beer warmer in the main hall. During Advent and Lent a special beer is offered, with the blessing of past popes, one of whom commented, "drinking does not interrupt fasting." ⊠ *Augustinergasse 4* ☎ *0662/431246* ⊟ *No credit cards* ⊘ *Weekdays 3–11, weekends 2:30–11.*

¢–$ ✕ **Ristorante Pizzeria al Sole.** Next to the Mönchsberg elevator you sit in this Italian restaurant upstairs in a pretty room lined with Venetian prints or in the more casual downstairs area. Choose from an impressive menu of scrumptious thin-crust pizzas. Pasta dishes are numerous and delicious, and may include tagliatelle with grilled shrimp or penne with tuna and capers. ⊠ *Gstättengasse 15* ☎ *0662/843284* ⊟ *AE, DC, MC, V.*

WHERE TO STAY

It is difficult for a Salzburg hotel not to have a good location—you can find a room with a stunning view over the Kapuzinerberg or Gaisberg or one that simply overlooks a lovely Old City street. However, it is possible. The fact is that Salzburg is not a tiny town and you can spend a half hour walking from one end of town to the other. Clearly, it is best to be located near the historic city center. It is about a mile from the railway station to historic Zentrum (center), right around the main bridge of the Staatsbrücke. Many hostelries are charmingly decorated in *Bauernstil*—the rustic look of Old Austria, with the ultimate in peasant-luxe found at the world-famous Hotel Goldener Hirsch. Note that many hotels in the Old City have to be accessed on foot, as cars are not permitted on many streets. If you have a car, of course, you may opt to do what many do—find a hotel or converted castle on the outskirts of the city. Needless to say, if you're planning to come at festival time you must book as early as possible. If you don't have a reservation, go to one of the tourist information offices or the accommodations service (*Zimmernachweis*) on the main platform of the railway station. Prices are highest during the festival weeks, and drop considerably in between.

★ $$$$ 🏨 **Altstadt Radisson SAS.** Venerable is the word to describe this current outpost of the Radisson group: after its founding in 1372 it was a brewery for centuries, then soon became one of the city's first inns, and has been a luxury hotel since 1992. The exterior is an Old City charmer, done up in buff pink, white trim, sash windows, and iron lanterns. Inside, much has been renovated to within a inch of its life, but historic stone arches and a super-tasteful assortment of antiques adorn many rooms, so the ambience allures. On one side, rooms overlook the river and the picturesque Capuchin cloister atop the hill opposite; on the other, upper rooms sneak a peek at the fortress. Despite smaller windows and original beamed ceilings, rooms are light and spacious and most are furnished with reproduction antiques and traditional accents. The Symphonie Restaurant is elegance personified, with royal-blue and gold hues ashimmer under Rococo chandeliers. Added bonuses are the central yet quiet location and generous buffet breakfast. ⊠ *Judengasse 15/Rudolfskai 28, A-5020* ☎ *0662/848571–0* 🖷 *0662/848–5716* ⊕ *www.austria-trend.at/ass* 🗺 *42 rooms, 20 suites* ⌂ *Restaurant, bar* ⊟ *AE, DC, MC, V* ⫶⊙⫶ *BP.*

$$$$ 🏨 **Goldener Hirsch.** Picasso and Pavarotti, Rothschilds and Gettys, Tay-
Fodor's Choice   lor and Burton, Sayn-Wittgensteins and Queen Elizabeth—all have
★   made the "Golden Stag" their Salzburg home-away-from-home. You, too, will want to experience its unique champagne gemütlickeit, patrician pampering, and adorable decor, if not with a stay, then with a meal. The location is tops—just down the street from Mozart's Birthplace and steps from the Festspielhaus. This means crowds, but double-paned windows ensure you won't hear a thing once you enter the special, private world here. Inside it offers a delightfully rustic look with woodwork, peasant-luxe furniture, medieval statues, and some of the lowest ceilings in town; the stag motif is even on lamp shades, which were hand-painted by an Austrian countess. The hotel actually comprises four separate town houses, all connected in a welter of staircases and elevators. As a historic treasure expect some rooms to have snug (yet cozy) dimensions (in fact, some readers have written in alarm about some far-flung rooms tucked under the eaves—still, other "distant" chambers, such as those in the Kupferschmied Haus annex across the street, are prized since they are far from the fracas of this extremely popular place). There are two restaurants: the hotel's very regal dining room and its smaller bistro-brother, "s'Herzl." The latter is set on the pretty Sigmundsplatz, next to the hotel, and big stars and locals love its cozy, gemütlichkeit

timbered look. To go beyond yum to yum-yum, be sure to get the house speciality, *Nürnberger Bratwürstl* (half a dozen little roasted Nürnberg sausages served with sauerkraut and served on pewter heart-shaped plates). During festival time, tables for aprés-performance dinners in the main restaurant are impossible to come by, having been booked eight months in advance, so why not try to rub elbows with *le tout Salzburg* in the hotel bar, probably the world's most beautifully decorated *Bauernstil* room. Long run by Count Johannes Walderdorff, the hotel has now been taken over by a luxury chain, so some high-rollers are complaining that the hotel is not what it used to be (but what is?). The expensive breakfast is not included in the room price. ⊠ *Getreidegasse 37, A-5020* ☎ *0662/8084–0* 🖷 *0662/848511–845* ⊕ *www.goldenerhirsch.com* ↪*69 rooms* ⌂ *2 restaurants, minibars, bar, Internet, parking (fee)* ▤ *AE, DC, MC, V* ⦿ *EP.*

★ **$$$$** ⊞ **Sacher Salzburg.** Formerly famous as the Österreichischer Hof, this mammoth hotel on the bank of the Salzach River has attracted guests from the Beatles and the Rolling Stones to Hillary and Chelsea Clinton. A great fave of the Salzburg Festival crowd, it's owned by the Gürtler family, who also own the famous Hotel Sacher in Vienna. The staff has recently taken the monocle out of its eye, so even if you don't have a Vuitton steamer trunk, you'll probably feel welcome here. The main atrium is a symphony in marble, while the grand staircase still looks like the Empress Sissi could make a dazzling entrance amidst its ferns. Upstairs, guest rooms are so lovely there is a danger you won't want to leave to explore the city (especially if you get one with picture-perfect views of the Old City). Each is different, but all are exquisitely decorated. Room prices include a delicious buffet breakfast, including Sekt (Austrian sparkling wine). In nice weather tables are set outside on the terrace where you can enjoy a salad or hamburger (called a "Salzburger") for lunch while gazing across at the fortress. Restaurants include haute, tavern, and the Salzburg outpost of Vienna's fabled Café Sacher—enjoy your slice of Sachertorte at the latter. ⊠ *Schwarzstrasse 5–7, A-5020* ☎ *0662/ 88977* 🖷 *0662/88977–14* ⊕ *www.sacher.com* ↪ *119 rooms* ⌂ *5 restaurants, minibars, sauna, gym, bar, Internet, meeting rooms, parking (fee)* ▤ *AE, DC, MC, V* ⦿ *BP.*

★ **$$$$** ⊞ **Schloss Mönchstein.** After extensive renovations in 2004, this fairy-tale and palatial mountain retreat has become even more magical. With gardens and hiking trails, yet just minutes from the city center, it's little wonder the 19th-century naturalist Alexander von Humboldt called this a "small piece of paradise." Catherine of Russia and the Duchess of Liechtenstein are just two of the notables who have stayed at this gable-roofed, tower-studded mansion. Inside, a series of lovely, luxurious rooms are hung with tapestries and adorned with painted chests and Old Master daubs; some salons have views of the woods and Salzburg in the distance. Service is pleasant and discreet, and the Paris Lodron restaurant is the epitome of Old World elegance (for hotel guests only)—a terrace is set with tables for great food-with-a-view under the ivy-covered walls. For those in love, the maximum treat might be a dinner in "the tiniest restaurant in the world"—a tower aerie set with banquettes and with windows offering fetching views (dinner is €109—do book in advance). Suites are ravishing here. The castle has its own wedding chapel, which is particularly popular with American and Japanese couples. Getting in and out of town calls for a car or taxi, unless you are willing to negotiate steps or take the nearby Mönchsberg elevator, which is about an eight-minute walk away. ⊠ *Mönchsberg 26, A-5020* 🖀 *0662/ 848555-0* 🖶 *0662/848559* ⊕ *www.monchstein.com* ⤺ *23 rooms* ♨ *Restaurant, café, minibars, tennis court, bar, free parking* ⊟ *AE, DC, MC, V* ⊺⊙⊺ *BP.*

$$$$ ⊡ **Sheraton Salzburg.** With the lovely Mirabell park and gardens virtually at its back door, this beige, modern hotel tastefully blends in with the Belle Epoque buildings that surround it. Rooms are spacious and soothing in tone with contemporary furniture, and contain all the little extras and then some. Try to get a room facing the gardens. The buffet breakfast is outstanding—enough to keep you going all day. The house café, with attractive garden seating, bakes all its tempting pastries and strudels on the premises. It's about a 10-minute walk from the Altstadt across the river. ⊠ *Auerspergstrasse 4, A-5020* 🖀 *0662/889990* 🖶 *0662/ 881776* ⊕ *www.sheraton.at* ⤺ *163 rooms* ♨ *2 restaurants, café, minibars, gym, sauna, bar, Internet, parking (fee), no-smoking floor* ⊟ *AE, DC, MC, V* ⊺⊙⊺ *BP.*

★ **$$$–$$$$** ⊡ **Bristol.** Just across the river from the Altstadt next to the Mirabell Gardens, this grand, pale yellow palace-hotel dating from 1892 as "electric hotel" (connected with the first power station in the city) has hosted, in turn, Franz Josef I, Freud, and the cast of *The Sound of Music.* The sunny lobby showcases a huge ancient tapestry along one wall and works by the Salzburg-born painter Hans von Makart, and the Pianobar contains framed black and white photos of prominent guests (including Max, the Captain, and Liesl from the film cast). No two rooms are alike, but all have impressive fabrics, chandeliers, and marble baths (some have inner doors with their original etched glass). A few rooms are done in a whimsical Napoleonic-style with tented ceilings. The classy rooftop suite, known simply as "The View," has arguably the most stupendous views in the entire city. ⊠ *Makartplatz 4, A-5020* 🖀 *0662/ 873557* 🖶 *0662/873557-6* ⊕ *www.bristol-salzburg.at* ⤺ *60 rooms* ♨ *Restaurant, minibars, bar, Internet, parking (fee)* ⊟ *AE, DC, MC, V* ⊙ *Closed Feb.–Mar.* ⊺⊙⊺ *BP.*

$$$ ⊡ **Blaue Gans.** "The Blue Goose" has always been a popular option— its location on the main shopping drag of Getriedegasse, within sight of the Festival theaters, Mozart's Birthplace, and the Pferdeschwemme fountain, is tops. Clearly, in light of its 400-year-old pedigree, it has one foot in Old World charm and still retains its ancient wood beams, winding corridors, and low archways. But in 2002, it took one giant step into the future when it was became the first "art hotel" in Salzburg, thanks to the efforts of such local artists Erich Shobesberger, Christian Ecker, and Waldemar Kufner, whose avant-garde works now adorn its walls. Upstairs, the guest rooms are spacious and have contemporary furnishings, whitewashed walls with cheeky framed posters and cheerful curtains; a few have skylights. The popular restaurant is a bright and festive place, with lively contemporary art on the walls and nouvelle Austrian delights on your dishes. Now that Salzburg's profile in the modern art world has expanded considerably with the opening of its new Museum der Moderne Salzburg, artists and curators will undoubtedly be touching down here, so be sure to make reservations well in advance. ⊠ *Getreidegasse 43, A-5020* 🏨 *0662/842491–0* ⊕ *www.blauegans. at* 🖥 *40 rooms* ⚅ *Restaurant, minibars, bar, Internet, parking (fee); no a/c in some rooms* ▤ *AE, DC, MC, V* ⏍ *BP.*

$$$ 🏨 **Stieglbräu/Imlauer.** Midway between the train station and the Mirabell Gardens this interesting option is named after a noted Salzburg brewery. Modernized in 2004, it now features comfortably equipped rooms that come with individually adjustable air-conditioners and sound-proof windows. Just hop on the No. 1 bus to take you to the city center. The hotel has some leafy gardens and serves up the old fashioned treats the beer coachmen of yore liked, such as *Liptauer* (hot spiced cheese served with radish, bacon, cold pork, sausages, butter, and bread, along with a mug of the fresh beer on tap. ⊠ *Rainerstrasse 12–14, A-5020* 🏨 *0662/ 88992* 🖨 *0662/8899271* ⊕ *www.imlauer.com* 🖥 *99 rooms* ⚅ *Restaurant, a/c, free parking* ▤ *AE, DC, MC, V* ⏍ *BP.*

$$-$$$ 🏨 **Auersperg.** Would you like to start your mornings with a stroll by a pool flowered with water lilies? You'll find this green oasis between the two buildings which comprise the Auersperg—the hotel, built in 1892 by the noted Italian architect Ceconi and its neighboring "villa." The lobby welcomes you with Biedermeier antiques, while upstairs, the guest rooms are decorated in a suave and soigne manner, with mostly modern pieces accented with classic ornaments. A rich breakfast buffet and the use of the roof sauna and a steam-bath are included. Outside the door and it takes but five minutes to walk to the historic section. A big plus: just around the corner is that Salzburg treasure of a restaurant/beer garden, Die Weisse. ⊠ *Auerspergstrasse 61, A-5020* 🏨 *0662/ 88944* 🖨 *0662/889–4455* ⊕ *www.auersperg.at* 🖥 *51 rooms* ⚅ *Sauna, steam-bath, free parking, Internet; no a/c* ▤ *AE, DC, MC, V* ⏍ *BP.*

$$-$$$ 🏨 **Elefant.** An old-time favorite, this hotel was once graced by the real Maria von Trapp (her personal check, written when she stayed here in 1981, is set under glass at the reception desk). But we mean really old: this 700-year-old house began life as an inn run by Salzburg citizen Hans Goldeisen, provisioner to Duke Ernst, and host to the likes of Maximilian II, who on his way from Spain via Italy to Vienna was accompanied by his new pet, an Indian elephant named Soliman. That's also the reason why guests are welcomed by the sight of an elephant sculpture in the lobby. Most of the decor is decidedly less exotic: A renovation finished in 2002 reduced the number of guest rooms in order to make each one more spacious and added air-conditioning to all of them. Some rooms are alluring, with pale yellow striped wallpaper, blue accents, and antique-style furniture, but others are much more generic. In fact, much of the local color has disappeared since the Elephant was rounded up by Best Western. For real history, repair to the hotel's "Ratsherrenkeller," one of Salzburg's most famous wine cellars in the 17th century. Today, it is the restaurant Bruno and offers alluring candlelit dinners. Cars can be parked in the Altstadt Garage. ⊠ *Sigmund-Haffner-Gasse 4, A-5020* 🏨 *0662/ 843397* 🖨 *0662/840109–28* ⊕ *www.elefant.at* 🖥 *31 rooms* ⚅ *Restaurant, minibars, Internet, parking (fee)* ▤ *AE, DC, MC, V* ⏍ *BP.*

$$–$$$ 🏨 **Rosenvilla.** A haven of peace and tranquillity, this upscale bed-and-breakfast is across the Salzach River from the Altstadt. Through an arbored garden gate, you enter the pretty suburban villa. Guest rooms, all designed with taste, are a seductive mixture of contemporary, French Empire, and Biedermeier accents, with pretty fabrics and lots of light. Some have balconies overlooking the soothing feng shui garden with its expanse of velvet green lawn, tiled pathways, and a little pond with ducks. A special three-day offer includes dinner at the owners' top-ranked restaurant, the important Pfefferschiff, which is a great value. The Rosenvilla is a 15-minute walk from the center, or you can take Bus 7, which normally runs every 10 minutes. ⊠ *Höfelgasse 4, A-5020* 🕾 *0662/621765* 🖷 *0662/6252308* ⊕ *www.rosenvilla.sbg.at* 🖙 *14 rooms* ♻ *Free parking; no a/c* ⊟ *AE, DC, MC, V* ¶◎¶ *BP.*

$$ 🏨 **Amadeus.** There isn't much here to clue you into why the hotel has adopted Mozart's second name, but dig a bit. You'll learn that this 500-year-old, rather ramshackle-y yet charming house is not far from the St. Sebastian church and cemetery, where many members of his family are booked for an eternal stay. The hotel site was once home to one of Salzburg's communal baths. Back in Wolfgang's time, there was no running water in houses, so travelers—especially those arriving through the nearby Linz Gate—would immediately repair to this official bath after their long trip along dusty roads. Today, travelers still make a bee line here. The guest rooms are each decorated differently, with several featuring charming wood armoires and beds, others in a calm and modern fashion. Downstairs, greet the day in one of the cutest breakfast nooks in Salzburg, festively done up in alpine red, white, and green (the large breakfast buffet is included in the room rate as well as afternoon coffee and tea). But if you have a problem with Salzburg's incessantly ringing church bells, beware—there is a church next door and its bell goes off every quarter hour. It stops at 11 PM but will prove a rather loud alarm clock at 5 AM. ⊠ *Linzergasse 43–45, A-5020* 🕾 *0662/871401* 🖷 *0662/876163-7* ⊕ *www.hotelamadeus.at* 🖙 *23 rooms* ♻ *No a/c* ⊟ *AE, DC, MC, V* ¶◎¶ *BP.*

★ $$ 🏨 **Gersberg Alm.** A picture-perfect Alpine chalet on the lofty perch of the Gersberg high above Salzburg, this Romantic Hotel is less than 15 minutes by car from the center of the city. Inside it has all the warmth and rustic coziness you would expect in a country house; indeed, it originally was a 19th-century farmhouse. Guest rooms are pleasantly decorated with contemporary furniture and have wooden balconies overlooking the mountain scenery. The house restaurant is excellent—top choices include ravioli stuffed with spinach in a tomato-butter sauce, or lightly fried pike perch in a tomato-olive crust with pesto spaghetti. Be sure to try the warm apricot fritters for dessert. The wine list has an outstanding selection of Austrian wines. ⊠ *Gersberg 37, A-5020* 🕾 *0662/641257* 🖷 *0662/644248* ⊕ *www.gersbergalm.at* 🖙 *43 rooms* ♻ *Restaurant, minibars, pool, sauna, free parking; no a/c* ⊟ *AE, DC, MC, V* ¶◎¶ *BP.*

$$ 🏨 **Kasererbräu.** Standing on the site of an ancient Roman temple and just a few blocks from Salzburg's grand cathedral, this hotel offers a variety of tastes in design, resulting in a compatible mixture of folkloric

kitsch and sleek elegance. The public rooms are decorated with antiques and Oriental carpets; some of the guest rooms have sleigh beds or pretty carved and handpainted headboards, although others are more plainly decorated. Apart from the friendly staff, the hotel has two big advantages: set in the Old City, it's close to everything and has pleasant sauna and steam-bath facilities included in the price. ⊠ *Kaigasse 33, A-5020* ☎ *0662/842445–0* 🖷 *0662/84244551* ⊕ *www.kasererbraeu.at* ➾ *43 rooms* ⏶ *Sauna, Internet, parking (fee); no a/c* ⊟ *AE, DC, MC, V* ☾ *Closed early Feb.–mid-Mar.* ❙◯❙ *BP.*

$$ **NH Salzburg.** While a modern construction, this is a very pretty building, with Art Nouveau awnings, Secession-style sash windows, and white stone trim. Inside all is sleek and comfy. The location is nice—you're only around the corner from the shopping street leading to the Salzach river or five minutes away from the beautiful Mirabell Gardens. There is a rich buffet-style breakfast and the restaurant has a garden terrace. ⊠ *Franz-Josef-Strasse 26, A-5020* ☎ *0662/8820410* 🖷 *0662/ 874240* ⊕ *www.nh-hotels.com* ➾ *140 rooms* ⏶ *Restaurant, bar, garage, Internet; no a/c* ⊟ *AE, DC, MC, V* ❙◯❙ *BP.*

$$ 🖭 **Neutor.** Only a two-minute walk from the Old City and next to the historic tunnel that plows through the Mönchsberg, this modern but classy option is divided between two buildings on opposite sides of the street. The decor is bright and shiny—a real blessing on a gray, rainy day—and all rooms are equipped with modern technology. Children ages six and under are free, from 7–12 they get a 50 percent reduction for the third bed in the parent's room. ⊠ *Neutorstrasse 8, A-5020* ☎ *0662/ 844154–0* 🖷 *0662/84415416* ⊕ *www.schwaerzler-hotels.com* ➾ *89 rooms* ⏶ *Restaurant, bar, parking; no a/c* ⊟ *AE, DC, MC, V* ❙◯❙ *BP.*

$$ 🖭 **Pension Wolf.** The embodiment of Austrian gemütlichkeit, just off Mozartplatz, the small, family-owned, in-the-center-of-everything Wolf offers spotlessly clean and cozy rooms in a rustic 1429 building. Rooms are idiosyncratically arranged on several upper floors, connected by narrow, winding stairs, and are decorated with a pleasing Salzburg mix of rag rugs and rural furniture. This is very popular so be sure to book far in advance. ⊠ *Kaigasse 7, A-5020* ☎ *0662/843453–0* 🖷 *0662/842423–4* ⊕ *www.hotelwolf.com* ➾ *12 rooms* ⏶ *Sauna, parking (fee); no a/c* ⊟ *AE* ☾ *Closed early Feb.–early Mar.* ❙◯❙ *BP.*

$$ 🖭 **Stadtkrug.** Snuggled under the monument-studded Kapuzinerberg and just a two-minute walk from the bridge leading to the center of the Alt Stadt, the Stadtkrug (dated 1353) hits an idyllic, romantic, and quiet vibe, thanks to its mountainside setting. A traditional-style wrought-iron sign greets you, the lobby tinkles with chandeliers, and the main floor restaurant is your archetypal, white, classic, vaulted Salzburg sanctorum. Upstairs, you can find a charming atmosphere, even if some of the rustic furnished rooms are tiny. Head up to the roof to enjoy a restaurant that is terraced into the mountainside and set with statues, potted begonias, echoes of Italy, and lovely views. ⊠ *Linzergasse 20, A-5020* ☎ *0662/873545–0* 🖷 *0662/87353454* ⊕ *www.stadtkrug.at* ➾ *34 rooms* ⏶ *2 restaurants; no a/c* ⊟ *AE, DC, MC, V* ❙◯❙ *BP.*

$$ 🖭 **Weisse Taube.** In the heart of the pedestrian-area of the Alt Stadt, the centuries-old "White Dove" is around the corner from Mozartplatz, the

Residenz and just a block from the cathedral. Comfortably renovated into a hotel—now family-run for four generations—this 14th-century Bürgerhaus (citizen's house) has been traditionally restored, but some time-burnished touches remain: uneven floors, ancient stone archways, and wood-beam ceilings. Guest rooms are simply furnished, with dark-wood accents. Several no-smoking rooms are available, and the main section of the breakfast room is also no-smoking. The staff is most friendly. ⊠ *Kaigasse 9, A-5020* ☎ *0662/842404* 🖷 *0662/841783* ⊕ *www. weissetaube.at* ⤳ *33 rooms* ⌂ *Bar, Internet, parking (fee), no-smoking rooms; no a/c* ⊟ *AE, DC, MC, V* ⊘ *Closed 2 wks in Jan.* ⊺◯⊺ *BP.*

★ $$ 🎦 **Wolf-Dietrich.** Guest rooms in this small, family-owned hotel across the river from the Altstadt are elegantly decorated (some with Laura Ashley fabrics) and have extra amenities, such as VCRs (they stock *The Sound of Music*) and attractive sitting areas. Those in the back look out over the looming Gaisberg and the cemetery of St. Sebastian. The staff is warm and helpful. ⊠ *Wolf-Dietrich-Strasse 7, A-5020* ☎ *0662/871275* 🖷 *0662/882320* ⊕ *www.salzburg-hotel.at* ⤳ *32 rooms* ⌂ *Restaurant, indoor pool, Internet, parking (fee); no a/c* ⊟ *AE, DC, MC, V* ⊺◯⊺ *BP.*

$ 🎦 **Bergland.** Just about a 10-minute walk from the train station, this cheerful, pleasant, family-owned pension offers modern, comfortable rooms with breakfast included in the price. The sitting room includes an English library. ⊠ *Rupertgasse 15, A-5020* ☎ *0662/872318* 🖷 *0662/ 872318-8* ⊕ *www.berglandhotel.at* ⤳ *17 rooms with bath* ⌂ *Sauna, free parking; no a/c, no smoking* ⊟ *AE, DC, MC, V* ⊘ *Closed Nov.–Christmas* ⊺◯⊺ *BP.*

$ 🎦 **Cordial Theaterhotel.** Music lovers will enjoy studying the myriad production posters and photographs of famous artists that festoon the lobby here. Part of a classy chain, this is a modern option, with very comfy guest rooms. The location is about a 10-minute walk from the city center, as are the auditoriums on both sides of the Salzach River. The room rate includes the buffet-breakfast. ⊠ *Schallmooser Hauptstrasse 13, A-5020* ☎ *0662/881681-0* 🖷 *0662/88168692* ⊕ *www. theaterhotel-salzburg.at* ⤳ *58 rooms with shower, 10 apartments with bath* ⌂ *Bar, café, sauna, solarium; no a/c* ⊟ *AE, DC, MC, V* ⊺◯⊺ *BP.*

$ 🎦 **Turnerwirt.** Located in the former farmer's village of Gnigl, part of Salzburg's outskirts, this is a quaint complex of buildings. The most charming is the small "Villa," an adorable mansion fitted out with begonia-hung windows, red storybook roof, and fairytale turret. Out front is the massive *gasthaus*—an alpine roof and its name picked out in Gothic lettering on the front makes the building look on sabbatical from an Albrecht Dürer engraving. Renovated in 2000, both offer a friendly family-owned atmosphere and guest rooms are decorated in a traditional and pleasing style. The largest suites have three and four bedrooms. To get to Salzburg's center city, just hop on the No. 4 bus for a 10-minute ride. By car, the Turnewirt can be reached from Salzburg by taking the motorway and exiting after 2 mi (1 km) at Salzburg Nord or Wallersee. ⊠ *Linzer Bundesstrasse 54, A-5020* ☎ *0662/640630* 🖷 *0662/6406–3077* ⊕ *www. turnerwirt.at* ⤳ *62 rooms* ⌂ *Parking; no a/c* ⊟ *AE, DC, MC, V* ⊺◯⊺ *BP.*

¢–$ 🎦 **Am Dom.** Tucked away on a tiny street near Residenzplatz, this small pension in a 14th-century building offers simply furnished, rustic-style rooms, some with oak-beamed ceilings. Note the beautiful hand-carved Renaissance reception desk. The selling point here is the great location in the heart of the Altstadt. ⊠ *Goldgasse 17, A-5020* ☎ *0662/842765* 🖷 *0662/842765–55* ⊕ *www.amdom.at* 🛏 *15 rooms* 🛆 *No a/c, no room TVs* 🖃 *AE, DC, MC, V* ⊘ *Closed 2 wks in Feb.* ⦿ *BP.*

¢ 🍴 **Schwarzes Rössl.** Once a favorite with Salzburg regulars, this traditional Gasthof now serves as student quarters for most of the year but is well worth booking when available. Rooms are fresh and immaculate, if not charming, and the location is excellent—close to the nighttime action. ⊠ *Priesterhausgasse 6, A-5020* ☎ *0662/874426* 🖷 *01/401–76–20* 🛏 *51 rooms, 4 with bath* 🛆 *No a/c* 🖃 *AE, DC, MC, V* ⊘ *Closed Oct.–June* ⦿ *BP.*

NIGHTLIFE & THE ARTS

The Arts

The Salzburg Music Festival

Any office of the Salzburg Tourist Office and most hotel concierge desks can provide schedules for all the arts performances held year-round in Salzburg, and you can find listings in the daily newspaper, *Salzburger Nachrichten.* The biggest event on the calendar—as it has been since it was first organized by composer Richard Strauss, producer Max Reinhardt, and playwright Hugo von Hofmannsthal in 1920—is the world-famous **Salzburger Festspiele** (⊠ Hofstallgasse 1, A-5020 Salzburg ☎ 0662/8045–500 for summer festival, 0662/8045–361 for Easter festival 🖷 0662/8045–555 for summer festival, 0662/8045–790 for Easter festival ⊕ www.salzburgfestival.at). The main summer festival is usually scheduled for the last week of July through the end of August; the actual dates for 2005 are July 25 through August 31; the dates for 2006, the Mozart Year, should correspond approximately. In addition, the festival also presents two other major annual events: the Easter Festival (early April), and the Pentecost Baroque Festival (late May).

The most star-studded events—featuring the top opera stars and conductors such as Riccardo Muti, Claudio Abbado, and Nikolaus Harnoncourt—have tickets ranging from €22 to €340; for this glamorous events, first-nighters still pull out all the stops—summer furs, Dior dresses, and white-ties stud the more expensive sections of the theaters. Other performances can run from €8 to €190, with still lesser prices on tap for events outside the main festival halls, the **Grosses Festspielhaus** (Great Festival Hall) and the **Haus für Mozart** (House for Mozart, a new renovation of the former Small Festival Hall), located shoulder to shoulder on the grand promenade of Hofstallgasse. This street offers one of the most festive settings for a music festival and is especially dazzling at night, thanks to the floodlit Fortress Hohensalzburg which hovers on its hilltop above the theater promenade. Set behind the court stables first constructed by Wolf Dietrich in 1607, the Festspielhäser (festival halls) auditoria are modern constructions—the Grosses Haus was built in 1960 with 2,300 seats—but are actually "prehistoric," being dug out of the bedrock of the Mönchsberg mountain. Also hewn into the mountainside are vast parking lots that can be used by theatergoers. There are glittering concerts and operas performed at many other theaters in the city. You can catch Mozart concertos in the 18th-century splendor of two magnificent state rooms the composer himself once conducted in: the Rittersaal of the Residenz (⇨ above) and the Marble Hall of the Mirabell Palace (⇨ below). Delightful Mozart productions are offered by the Salzburger Marionetten Theater (⇨ below). In addition, many important concerts are offered in the two auditoria of the Mozarteum (⇨ below).

Note that you *must* order your tickets as early as possible, therefore make your decisions as soon as the program comes out end of every year—many major performances are sold out two or three months in advance, as hordes descend on the city to enjoy staged opera spectacles, symphonic concerts by the Vienna Philharmonic and other great troupes, recitals, church oratorios, and special evenings at the Mozarteum year after year. Tickets can be purchased directly at the box office, at your hotel, or, most conveniently, at the festival Web site listed above. Next to the main tourist office is a box office where you can get tickets for Great Festival Hall concerts Monday through Friday, 8 to 6: **Salzburger Kulturvereinigung** (⊠ Waagplatz 1A ☎ 0662/845346). The following agencies also sell tickets: **Salzburg Ticket Service** (⊠ Mozartplatz 5 ☎ 0662/840310 🖷 0662/842476). **Polzer** (⊠ Residenzplatz 3 ☎ 0662/846500 🖷 0662/840150). **American Express** (⊠ Mozartplatz 5 ☎ 0662/8080–0 🖷 0662/8080–9).

Music

There is no shortage of concerts in this most musical of cities. Customarily, the Salzburg Festival headlines the Vienna Philharmonic, but other orchestras can be expected to take leading roles as well. Year-round, there are also the Palace-Residenz Concerts, the Fortress Concerts, while in the summer, there are Mozart Serenades in the Gothic Room at St. Blase's Church. In addition, there are the Easter Festival, the Pentecost Baroque Festival, Mozart Week (late January), and the Salzburg Cultural Days (October). Mozart Week is always special; in recent seasons, Nikolaus Harnoncourt, Zubin Mehta, and Sir Charles Mackerras have conducted the Vienna Philharmonic, while Sir Neville Marriner, Daniel Harding, and Sir Roger Norrington were in charge with other orchestras.

Fodor's Choice ★ The **Salzburger Schlosskonzerte** (⊠ Theatergasse 2 ☎ 0662/848586 ⊕ www.salzburger.schlosskonzerte.at €26–€35) presents concerts in the the palatial **Residenz** on Residenzplatz as well as at the Mirabell Palace. In the Residenz, recitals are performed in the magnificent Rittersaal and the Konferenzzimmer (Conference Room), where Mozart premiered some of his works. The grand courtyard sometimes hosts operas put on by the Summer Festival. Over at the **Mirabell Palace**, where Mozart also performed, recitals are presented in the legendary Marmorsaal (Marble Hall).

The **Salzburger Festungskonzerte** (⊠ Fortress Hohensalzburg ☎ 0662/825858 ⊕ www.mozartfestival.at €29–€36) are presented in the grand

Prince's Chamber at Festung Hohensalzburg. Concerts often include works by Mozart. A special candlelight dinner and concert ticket–combo is often offered.

Organizer of the important Mozart Week held every January, the **Mozarteum** (✉ Schwarzstrasse 26 ☎ 0662/88940–21 ⊕ www.mozarteum.at) center is open to scholars only. However, thousands flock here for its packed, calendar of important concerts. The two main concert rooms are located in the main facility on Schwarzstrasse. Located at Mirabellplatz 1, the Mozarteum's new building, in construction until 2006, will include the Great Studio and the Leopold-Mozart-Hall.

Opera

The great opera event of the year is, of course, the **Salzburger Festspiele** (✉ Hofstallgasse 1, A-5020 Salzburg ☎ 0662/8045–500 🖷 0662/ 8045–555 ⊕ www.salzburgfestival.at). The Salzburg Festival annually mounts a full calendar of operas (for example, just half of the schedule for 2004 included Henry Purcell's *King Arthur,* Mozart's *Die Entführung aus dem Serail [The Abduction from the Seraglio],* and *Così fan tutte,* Richard Strauss's *Der Rosenkavalier,* Erich Wolfgang Korngold's *Die tote Stadt [The Dead City],* and Vincenzo Bellini's *I Capuleti e i Montecchi*). These performances are held in the Grosses Festspielhaus (Great Festival Hall), the Haus für Mozart (House for Mozart), the Landestheater, the Felsenreitschule, the Mozarteum, and numerous other smaller venues, where lieder recitals and chamber works predominate. Prices range from €8 to €340. The season at the **Landestheater** (✉ Schwarzstrasse 22 ☎ 0662/871512–21 🖷 0662/871512–70 ⊕ www.theater.co.at) runs from September to June. New productions in 2005 will include Verdi's *Falstaff,* Franz Lehár's *Die lustige Witwe (The Merry Widow),* Andrew Lloyd Webber's *Jesus Christ Superstar,* and Britten's *The Turn of the Screw.* You may place ticket orders by telephone Monday and Saturday 10–2, Tuesday–Friday 10–5.

Fodor'sChoice ★ The delightful, acclaimed **Salzburger Marionettentheater** (✉ Schwarzstrasse 24 ☎ 0662/872406–0 🖷 0662/882141) is also devoted to opera, with a particularly renowned production of *Così fan tutte* to its credit, and gives performances during the first week of January, during Mozart Week (late January), from May through September, and December 25 through January 7th. Tickets usually range from €18 to €35. The box office is open Monday through Saturday 9–1 and two hours before the performance.

Theater

The **Jedermann** ("Everyman") morality play, written by Hugo von Hofmannsthal, is famously performed annually (in German) in the forecourt of the **city cathedral** (🏛 Salzburger Festspiele, Postfach 140 ☎ 0662/ 8045–500 🖷 0662/8045–555 ⊕ www.salzburgfestival.at). This is a spine-tingling presentation and few of the thousands packing the plaza are not moved at the moment at the height of the banquet when the voice of Death—"Jedermann—Jedermann—Jed-er-*mann*"—is heard from the Franziskanerkirche tower, then followed with echoes of voices from other steeples and from atop the Fortress Hohensalzburg. As the sun sets, the doors of the great cathedral hover open and the sounds of its organ announce the salvation of Everyman's soul.

SHOPPING

For a small city, Salzburg has a wide spectrum of stores. The specialties are traditional clothing, like lederhosen and loden coats, jewelry, glassware, handicrafts, confectionary, dolls in native costume, Christmas decorations, sports equipment, and silk flowers. A *Gewürzsträussl* is a bundle of whole spices bunched and arranged to look like a bouquet of flowers (try the markets on Universitätsplatz). This old tradition goes back to the time when only a few rooms could be heated and, therefore, humans and their farm animals would often cohabitate on the coldest days. You can imagine how lovely the aromas must have been—so this spicy room-freshener was invented. At Christmas there is a special Advent market on the Domplatz offering regional decorations, held from the week before the first Advent-Sunday until December 24, daily from 9 AM to 8 PM. Stores are generally open weekdays 9–6 and Saturday 9–5. Many stores stay open until 5 on the first Saturday of the month and on Saturday during the festival and before Christmas. Some supermarkets stay open until 7:30 on Thursday or Friday. Only shops in the railway station, the airport, and near the general hospital are open on Sunday.

Shopping Streets

The most fashionable specialty stores and gift shops are to be found along Getreidegasse and Judengasse and around Residenzplatz. Linzergasse, across the river, is less crowded and good for more practical items. There are also interesting antiques shops and jewelry workshops in the medieval buildings along Steingasse and on Goldgasse.

Specialty Stores

Antiques

Ilse Guggenberger (⊠ Brodgasse 11 ☎ 0662/843184) is the place to browse for original Austrian country antiques. **Marianne Reuter** (⊠ Gstättengasse 9 ☎ 0662/842136) offers a fine selection of porcelain and 18th-century furniture. **Schöppl** (⊠ Gstättengasse 5 ☎ 0662/842154) has old desks, hutches, and some jewelry. For an amazing assortment of secondhand curiosities, try **Trödlerstube** (⊠ Linzergasse 50 ☎ 0662/871453). **Internationale Messe für Kunst und Antiquitäten** (⊠ Residenzplatz 1 ☎ 0662/8042–2690) is the annual antiques fair that takes place from Palm Sunday to Easter Monday in the state rooms of Salzburg's Residenz.

Confectionary

If you're looking for the kind of *Mozartkugeln* (chocolate marzipan confections) you can't buy at home, try the store that claims to have invented in 1890 them: **Konditorei Fürst** (⊠ Brodgasse 13 ☎ 0662/843759–0), that's where they are still produced by hand after the original recipe this family never gave away. **Konditorei Schatz** (⊠ Getreidegasse 3, Schatz passageway ☎ 0662/842792) is a top mecca for Mozartkugeln and other delectable goodies.

Crafts

Fritz Kreis (⊠ Sigmund-Haffner-Gasse 14 ☎ 0662/841768) sells ceramics, wood carvings, handmade glass objects, and so on. **Salzburger
Heimatwerk** (⊠ Residenzplatz 9 ☎ 0662/844110–0) has clothing, fabrics, ceramics, and local handicrafts at good prices. **Christmas in Salzburg**
(⊠ Judengasse 10 ☎ 0662/846784) has rooms of gorgeous Christmas-
tree decorations, some hand-painted and hand-carved. **Gehmacher**
(⊠ Alter Markt 2 ☎ 0662/845506–0) offers whimsical home-decora-
tion items.

Traditional Clothing

Dschulnigg (⊠ Griesgasse 8/corner of Münzgasse ☎ 0662/842376–0) is
a favorite among Salzburgers for lederhosen, dirndls, and *Trachten,* the
typical Austrian costume with white blouse, print skirt, and apron. For
a wide selection of leather goods, some made to order, try **Jahn-Markl**
(⊠ Residenzplatz 3 ☎ 0662/842610). **Lanz** (⊠ Schwarzstrasse 4 ☎ 0662/
874272) sells a good selection of long dirndls, silk costumes, and loden
coats. **Madl am Grünmarkt** (⊠ Universitätsplatz 12 ☎ 0662/845457)
has more flair and elegance in its traditional designs.

SALZBURG A TO Z

*To research prices, get advice from other travelers, and book travel ar-
rangements, visit www.fodors.com.*

AIR TRAVEL TO & FROM SALZBURG

There are direct flights from London and other European cities to
Salzburg, but not from the United States. Americans can fly to Munich
and take the 90-minute train ride to Salzburg.

AIRPORTS & TRANSFERS

Salzburg Airport, 4 km (2½ mi) west of the city center, is Austria's second-largest international airport.

🏢 Airport Information **Salzburg Airport** ⊠ Innsbrucker Bundesstrasse 96 ☎ 0662/
8580.

TRANSFERS If you fly to Munich, you can take the 90-minute train ride to Salzburg.
Alternatively, you can take a transfer bus from or to the Munich airport: contact Salzburger Mietwagenservice for details. Taxis are the easiest way to get downtown from the Salzburg airport; the ride costs around
€13–€14 and takes about 20 minutes. City Bus No. 2, which makes a
stop by the airport every 15 minutes, runs down to Salzburg's train station (about 20 minutes), where you can change to Bus No. 3 or 5 for
the city center.

🏢 Taxis & Shuttles **Salzburger Mietwagenservice** ⊠ Ignaz-Harrer-Strasse 79a
☎ 0622/8161–0 🖶 0622/436324.

BIKE TRAVEL

Salzburg is fast developing a network of bike paths as part of its effort
to reduce car traffic in the city. A detailed bicycle map with suggested
tours (AS89) will help you get around. You can rent a bike by the day
or the week from Shake & Snack. Also check Veloclub Salzburger

Fahrradclub. It's best to call and reserve in advance; you will need to leave your passport or a deposit.

Just in time for the Mozart Year, a new **Mozart Radweg** (bicycle route) has been created by the Salzburg Land Tourist Office together with some travel agents so cyclists and music-lovers can follow his path around Salzburg and through the lake districts of Austria and Bavaria. All told, the itinerary can take 13 days and runs 410 km (255 mi), but shorter versions are custom-tailored by various outfitters in the region. For instance, there is an eight-day tour heading west to Bavaria, arranged by Austria Radreisen (⊠ Joseph-Haydn-Strasse 8, A-4780 Schärding ☎ 07712/5511–0 ⊕ www.austria-radreisen.at). Heading east for five days is a planned itinerary mapped out by Oberösterreich Touristik (⊠ Freistädter Strasse 49, A-4041 Linz ☎ 0732/663024–0 ⊕ www.touristik.at ⊕ www.mozartradweg.com).

🚲 Bike Rentals **Shake & Snack** ⊠ Kajetanerplatz 3–4 ☎ 0662/848168. Next to the train station is **Top Bike** ⊠ Rainerstrasse/Café Intertreff ☎ 06272/4656 or 0676/476–7259. **Veloclub Salzburger Fahrradclub** ⊠ Franz-Josef-Strasse 23 ☎ 0662/882-7880.

BUS TRAVEL WITHIN SALZBURG
Single tickets bought from the driver cost €1.80. Special multiple-use tickets, available at tobacconists (*Tabak-Trafik*), ticket offices, and tourist offices, are much cheaper. You can buy five single tickets for €1.60 each (not available at tourist offices), a single 24-hour ticket for €3.40.

🚌 Bus Information **Salzburger Verkehrsverbund (Main ticket office)** ⊠ Schrannengasse 4 ☎ 0662/44801500.

CAR TRAVEL
The fastest routes to Salzburg are the autobahns. From Vienna (320 km [198 mi]), take A1; from Munich (150 km [93 mi]), A8 (in Germany it's also E11); from Italy, A10.

RULES OF THE ROAD The only advantage to having a car in Salzburg is that you can get out of the city for short excursions or for cheaper accommodations. The Old City on both sides of the river is a pedestrian zone (except for taxis), and the rest of the city, with its narrow, one-way streets, is a driver's nightmare. A park-and-ride system covering the major freeway exits is being developed, and there are several underground garages throughout the city.

CONSULATES
The U.K. consulate is open weekdays 9–11:30. The U.S. consulate is open Monday, Wednesday, and Friday 9–noon.

🏛 United Kingdom ⊠ Alter Markt 4 ☎ 0662/848133 🖷 0662/845563.
🏛 United States ⊠ Alter Markt 1/3 ☎ 0662/848776 🖷 0662/849777.

EMERGENCIES
If you need a doctor or dentist, call the Ärztekammer für Salzburg. For emergency service on weekends and holidays, call the Ärzte-Bereitschaftsdienst Salzburg-Stadt. The main hospital is the St. Johannsspital-Landeskrankenanstalten, located just past the Augustinian Monastery heading out of town. For medical emergencies or an ambulance, dial 144.

In general, pharmacies are open weekdays 8–12:30 and 2:30–6, Saturday 8–noon. When they're closed, the name and location of a pharmacy that's open are posted on the door.

⚑ Doctors & Dentists **Ärztekammer für Salzburg** ⊠ Bergstrasse 4 ☎ 0662/871327–0. **Ärzte-Bereitschaftsdienst Salzburg-Stadt** ⊠ Dr.-Karl-Renner-Strasse 7 ☎ 0662/141. ⚑ Emergency Services **Ambulance** ☎ 144. **Fire** ☎ 122. **Police** ☎ 133. ⚑ Hospitals **St. Johannsspital-Landeskrankenanstalten** ⊠ Müllner Hauptstrasse 48 ☎ 0662/44820.

MONEY MATTERS

CURRENCY EXCHANGE Banks are open from Monday to Friday 8:30–12:30 and 2–4:30, American Express offices from Monday to Friday 9–5:30, Saturday 9 to noon. You can change money at the railway station daily 7:30 AM–8:30 PM.

TAXIS

There are taxi stands all over the city; for a radio cab, call the number listed below. Taxi fares start at €3, Sundays and holidays, €3.50; a special offer is the bus-taxi running between 11:30 and 1:30 at night, which has routes through the city and into the neighboring villages—the fare is €3.70. Limousines can be hired for €200 to €245 per hour (three-hour minimum) from Salzburg Panorama Tours. They also offer a private "Sound of Music" limousine tour for €265.

⚑ Taxi Information **Radio Cab** ☎ 0662/8111. **Salzburg Panorama Tours** ☎ 0662/883211–0 🖷 0662/871628 ⊕ www.panoramatours.com.

TOURS

Because the Old City is largely a pedestrian zone, bus tours do little more than take you past the major sights. You would do better seeing the city on foot unless your time is really limited.

BOAT TOURS For a magically different vantage point, take a round-trip boat ride along the relentlessly scenic Salzach River, departing at the Markartsteg in the Altstadt, from April until October. The boat journeys as far south as Hellbrunn Palace (depending on the the water level). In June, July, and August you can also take the cruise as you enjoy a Candlelight Dinner—the real dessert is a floodlit view of Salzburg!

⚑ Fees & Schedules **Salzburger Festungskonzerte GmbH** ⊠ Anton-Adlgasser-Wegasse 22 ☎ 0662/825769–12 🖷 0662/825859 ⊕ www.salzburgschifffahrt.at

BUS TOURS American Express is one of several companies that offer day bus trips from Vienna to Salzburg. Vienna Sightseeing Tours runs one-day bus trips in winter on Tuesday and Saturday to Salzburg from Vienna, and in summer on Tuesday, Thursday, Saturday, and Sunday. The €100 fare includes a tour of the city, but not lunch. Cityrama Sightseeing offers a schedule similar to Vienna Sightseeing Tours.

Several local companies conduct 1½- to 2-hour city tours. The desk clerks at most hotels will book for you and arrange hotel pickup. Depending on the number of people, the tour will be in either a bus or a minibus; if it's the former, a short walking tour is included, since large buses can't enter the Old City. Tours briefly cover the major sights in Salzburg, including Mozart's Birthplace, the festival halls, the major squares, the churches, and the palaces at Hellbrunn and Leopoldskron. Bob's Special Tours is well known to American visitors—the company offers a 10% discount to Fodor's readers who book directly with them without help from their hotel. Salzburg Panorama Tours and Albus/Salzburg Sightseeing Tours offer similar tours.

🔢 Fees & Schedules **Albus/Salzburg Sightseeing Tours** ✉ Am Mirabellplatz 2, Salzburg ☎ 0662/881616 🖷 0662/878776 ⊕ www.welcome-salzburg.at. **American Express** ✉ Kärntnerstrasse 21–23, A-1010 Vienna ☎ 01/515-400 🖷 01/515-4070. **Bob's Special Tours** ✉ Rudolfskai 38, Salzburg ☎ 0662/849511-0 🖷 0662/849512. **Cityrama Sightseeing** ✉ Börsegasse 1, A-1010 Vienna ☎ 01/534-130 🖷 01/534-13-16. **Salzburg Panorama Tours** ✉ Schrannengasse 2/2, Salzburg ☎ 0662/883211-0 🖷 0662/871618 ⊕ www.panoramatours.com. **Vienna Sightseeing Tours** ✉ Stelzhammergasse 4/11, A-1030 Vienna ☎ 01/712-4683-0 🖷 01/714-1141.

SPECIAL-
INTEREST TOURS

The *Sound of Music* tour—for the complete scoop, see this chapter's Close-Up box—has been a staple of visits to Salzburg for the past 20 years and is still a special experience. All tour operators conduct one. The bus company actually featured in the film, Albus/Salzburg Sightseeing Tours offers a 4-hour bus tour departing daily, which includes such sights as Anif Castle, Mondsee Church, and the little summer house in the gardens of Hellbrunn. Some travelers say the most personal approach to Maria's Salzburg is found with Bob's Special Tours. One of the most popular is the tour offered by Salzburg Panorama (for contact information for this bus lines, *see* Bus Tours, *above*).

WALKING TOURS

The tourist office's folder "Salzburg—The Art of Taking It All In at a Glance" describes a self-guided one-day walking tour that's marked on a map. Salzburg's official licensed guides offer a one-hour-walking tour through the Old City every day at 12:15, which starts in front of the Information Mozartplatz (€8—owners of the Salzburg Card get a reduced fee).

TRAIN TRAVEL

You can get to Salzburg by rail from most European cities, arriving at Salzburg Hauptbahnhof, a 20-minute walk from the center of town in the direction of Mirabellplatz. A taxi to the center of town should take about 10 minutes and cost €9. Train information is available through the number listed below; don't be put off by the recorded message in German—eventually, you will be put through to a real person who should be able to speak English. You can buy tickets at any travel agency or at the station. The bus station and the suburban railroad station are at the square in front.

🔢 Train Information **Salzburg Hauptbahnhof** ✉ Südtirolerplatz ☎ 05/1717.

TRANSPORTATION AROUND SALZBURG

The Old City, composed of several interconnecting squares and narrow streets, is best seen on foot. An excellent bus service covers the rest of the city. A tourist map (available from tourist offices in Mozartplatz and the train station) shows all bus routes and stops; there's also a color-coded graphic public-transport-network map, so you should have no problem getting around. Virtually all buses and trolleybuses (O-Bus) run via Mirabellplatz and/or Hanuschplatz.

One of the most delightful ways to tour Salzburg is by horse-drawn carriage. Most of Salzburg's fiakers are stationed in Residenzplatz, and cost €33 per fiaker (up to 4 people) for 20 minutes, €66 for 50 minutes. During the Christmas season, large, decorated horse-drawn carts take people around the Christmas markets.

Fiakers ☎ 0662/844772.

TRAVEL AGENCIES

American Express is next to the tourist office at Mozartplatz 5–7. Columbus is near the Mönchsberg in the Old City.

Local Agent Referrals **American Express** ☎ 0662/8080-0 🖷 0662/8080-9. **Columbus** ✉ Griesgasse 2 ☎ 0662/842755-0 🖷 0662/842755-5.

VISITOR INFORMATION

The Salzburg City Tourist Office handles written and telephone requests for information. You can get maps, brochures, and information in person from Information Mozartplatz in the center of the Old City. The railway station also has a tourist office.

Don't forget to consider purchasing the Salzburg Card. SalzburgKarten are good for 24, 48, or 72 hours at €19–€34, respectively, and allow no-charge entry to most museums and sights, use of public transport, and special discount offers. Children under 15 pay half.

All the major highways into town have their own well-marked information centers. The Salzburg-Mitte center is open April–October, daily 9–7, and November–March, Monday–Saturday 11–5; the Salzburg-Süd, April–October, daily 9–7; and the Salzburg-Nord Kasern service facility is open June–mid-September, daily 9–7.

Tourist Information **Information Mozartplatz** ✉ Mozartplatz 5. **Railway Station tourist office** ✉ Platform 2A ☎ 0662/88987-330. **Salzburg City Tourist Office** ✉ Auerspergstrasse 6, A-5024 Salzburg ☎ 0662/88987-0 🖷 0662/88987-435 ⊕ www.salzburginfo.at. **Salzburg-Süd** ✉ Park & Ride-Parkplatz, Alpensiedlung-Süd, Alpenstrasse 67 ☎ 0662/88987-360.

SALZKAMMERGUT

6

UNWIND IN A DRIFTING PADDLEBOAT
to the operetta town of St. Wolfgang ⇨ *p.306*

**SEE WHERE MARIA MARRIED
CAPTAIN VON TRAPP**
at Mondsee's golden-hued church ⇨ *p.302*

MARVEL AT MASSIFS MAJESTICALLY SET
above the mirroring lakes of Gosau ⇨ *p.316*

COUNT THE MANY BRANCHES
of Mozart's family tree in St. Gilgen ⇨ *p.305*

CELEBRATE EMPEROR FRANZ JOSEF
at his Kaiservilla in Bad Ischl ⇨ *p.309*

SIGN IN FOR POSTERITY
at the legendary Schloss Fuschl hotel ⇨ *p.304*

GET A FERRY VIEW
of lakeside Hallstatt ⇨ *p.318*

Updated by
Horst Erwin
Reischenböck

REMEMBER THE EXQUISITE OPENING SCENES of *The Sound of Music*? Castles reflected in water, mountains veiled by a scattering of downy clouds, flower-strewn valleys dotted with cool blue lakes: a view of Austria as dreamed up by a team of Hollywood's special-effects geniuses—so many thought. But, no, those scenes were filmed right here, in Austria's fabled Salzkammergut region, not so far from where the Trapp children "Do-Re-Mi"-ed in the city of Salzburg. As you travel through this area you'll reach heights both physical and spiritual. From the Schafberg, above the village of St. Wolfgang, you can see just about every lake in the entire region, and in the pilgrimage church below, Michael Pacher's great, 15th-century winged altar rises like a prayer. So ready your camera, dust off your supply of *wunderschöns*, and prepare for enchantment as you head into this compact quarter of Austria. The Lake District of Upper Austria, centered on the region called the Salzkammergut (literally, "salt estates"), presents the traveler with many such sights: soaring mountains and needlelike peaks; a glittering necklace of turquoise lakes; forested valleys that are populated with the *Rehe* (roe deer) immortalized by Felix Salten in *Bambi*—this is Austria at its most lush and verdant. Some of these lakes, like the Hallstätter See and Gosauer See, remain quite unspoiled, partly because the mountains act as a buffer from busier, more accessible sections of the country. Another—historic—reason relates to the presence of the salt mines, which date back to the Celtic era; with salt so common and cheap nowadays, many forget it was once a luxury item mined under strict government monopoly. The Salzkammergut was closed to the casually curious for centuries, opening up only after Emperor Franz Josef I made Bad Ischl—one of the area's leading spa towns (even then, studded with *salt*-water swimming pools)—his official summer residence in 1854 and turned it into the "drawing room" of the Lake District. Lured by idyllic landscapes and a taste for cosmopolitanism, a host of prominent people from crowned heads and their ministers to artists of every stamp soon flocked regularly to the Salzkammergut. Its salt-inspired isolation was ended.

To the west of Bad Ischl are the best known of all the Salzkammergut's 76 lakes—the Wolfgangsee, the Mondsee, and the Attersee (*See* is German for "lake"). Not far beyond these lakes lies one of Austria's loveliest spots, Gosau am Dachstein. Here the three Gosau lakes are backdropped by a spectacular sight that acts as a landmark for many leagues: the Dachstein peak. Baron Alexander von Humboldt, the 19th-century naturalist and traveler, called Gosau am Dachstein one of the most beautiful spots in the world, and few persons at that time had seen more of the world than he. It is not surprising that Gosau inspired Richard Wagner while he was writing *Parsifal;* even today, Gosau remains a world's end, a place where people are content simply to drink in the view. Another scenic wonder is the storybook village of Hallstatt, huddled between mountain and lake. It is believed to be the oldest community in Austria and it has been such an important source of relics of the pre-Christian Celtic period that this age is known as the Hallstatt epoch.

The region truly comes into its own during the summer, when vacationers head for the lakes, streams, meadows, and woods, for boating, fishing, swimming (remember: the taller the lakeside peak, the colder the water), and those stimulating pine-needle baths. A favorite passion for Austrians is *das Wandern,* or hiking. The Lake District has many miles of marked trails, with lovely stretches around Bad Ischl—with more than 100 km (62 mi) of trails alone; the Attersee area, which has one great 35-km (22-mi) course that takes about 7½ hours to complete; the mountains in the Hallstatt and Altaussee/Bad Aussee areas; and Bad Aussee, with more than 150 km (93 mi) of trails. Cycling, a growing sport, offers a fine way to see miles of landscape at a human pace while also taking care of your fitness requirements. In winter, many come to the region to ski in the mountains of Salzburg Province and Styria. Within this pastoral perfection, you can stay in age-old *Schloss* hotels or modern villas, dine in fine restaurants, and shop for the linens and ceramics, wood carvings, and painted glass of the region.

Exploring the Salzkammegut

Whether you start out from Salzburg or set up a base in Bad Ischl—the heart of the Lake District—it's best to take in the beauties of the Salzkammergut in perhaps two separate courses: first around the Mondsee, the Wolfgangsee, and Bad Ischl; then southwest to Gosau am Dachstein, back to the Hallstätter See, and east to Bad Aussee and the Altausseer See, returning via the Pötschen mountain pass.

Numbers in the text correspond to numbers in the margin and on the Salzkammergut/Lake District map.

About the Restaurants & Hotels

Fresh, local lake fish is on nearly every menu in the area, so take advantage of the bounty. The lakes and streams are home to several types of fish, notably trout, carp, and perch. They are prepared in numerous ways, from plain breaded (*gebacken*), to smoked and served with *Kren* (horseradish), to fried in butter (*gebraten*). Look for *Reinanke,* a mild whitefish straight from the Hallstättersee. Sometimes at country fairs you will find someone charcoaling fresh trout wrapped in aluminum foil with herbs and butter: it's worth every euro. *Knödel*—bread or potato dumplings usually filled with either meat or jam—are a tasty specialty. Desserts are doughy as well, though *Salzburger Nockerl,* a sabayon-based soufflé worthy of the gods, consist mainly of sugar, beaten egg whites, and air. And finally, keep an eye out for seasonal specialties: in summer, restaurants often serve chanterelle mushrooms (*Eierschwammerl*) with pasta, and in October it's time for delicious venison and game during the *Wildwochen* (game weeks). Culinary shrines are to be found around Mondsee. However, in many of the towns of the Salzkammergut you'll find country inns with dining rooms but few independent restaurants, other than the occasional, very simple *Gasthäuser.*

In the grand old days, the aristocratic families of the region would welcome paying guests at their charming castles. Today most of those castles have been, if you will, degentrified: they are now schools or very fine hotels. But you needn't stay in a castle to enjoy the Salzkammergut—there are also luxurious lakeside resorts, small country inns,

6

If you have
4 days

Setting out early from Salzburg or Vienna, head to the core of the Lake District, 🚗 **Bad Ischl** ⑤. Franz Lehár—the composer of so many operettas that glorified the region—had a vacation villa here, where he could rub elbows with other notables as eager as he was to holiday in Franz Josef's favorite getaway. After exploring the emperor's villa, a majestic manor in the warm "imperial" yellow so typical of Austria, created for his empress, Elisabeth—the immortal "Sisi"—stop in at Zauner (just as Franz Josef did) for some of the best pastry in Europe. Delicious, but beware: *two* to a person will be plenty. After a day taking in this history-rich spa—today it is one of the best equipped in Austria—enjoy an overnight and the next morning head south on Route 145 toward Hallstatt. After Bad Goisern bear right past Au, then turn right over the bridge to cross the River Traun into Steeg (don't worry about the factory smokestack—it's an isolated affair in these parts). Twenty-nine kilometers (18 mi) from Bad Ischl you'll come to a junction with Route 166. Here you should turn right into the ravine of the Gosaubach river. After heading through very scenic territory framed by steep wooded slopes for some 32 km (20 mi), you'll reach 🚗 **Gosau am Dachstein** ⑧, which spreads out over a comfortable north–south valley, at the end of which lie the famous Gosau lakes. You have now reached one of Austria's most beautiful spots. There are three lakes here, several miles apart from each other and all framed by the craggy heights of the Dachstein range. After taking in the views, spend the night in the village and awaken to a dazzling dawn glistening over the snow-swept Bischofsmütze peak.

On your third morning, head back to Route 145 and south to 🚗 **Hallstatt** ⑨, which, in addition to being called the "world's prettiest lakeside village," is also the oldest settlement in Austria. After spending quality time with your Nikon (do your photography in the morning when the village is nicely lit), check out two natural wonders: the salt mines above Hallstatt (accessible by funicular or by a good one-hour walk) and, continuing around the southern end of the lake for 5 km (3 mi), the **Dachstein Ice Caves** ⑩ at Obertraun. On your fourth morning, leave Upper Austria and head for 🚗 **Bad Aussee** ⑪ along the romantic old road that follows the Traun River. It is still in part covered with hand-hewn paving stones and has at one point an impressive gradient of 23% (sometimes closed in winter). After exploring the town's picturesque 15th- and 16th-century architecture, you should still have time for a stroll around neighboring **Altaussee** ⑬, whose romantic landscape has inspired many artists and poets. Return to Bad Aussee, then catch Route 145 north across the Pötschen pass to Bad Ischl, enjoying spectacular vistas along the way back.

If you have
7 days

If you have a more leisurely schedule, you'll want to explore more of the Lake District, while still encompassing the itinerary outlined above. Start off by taking Route B158 from Salzburg, making a detour left toward Thalgau. After 5 km (3 mi) you'll reach Thalgau, and then a little farther on, the lake, where you'll go left to Route B154 and 🚗 **Mondsee** ①, the gateway to the Salzkammergut. (You can also take the A1 Autobahn in the direction of Vienna, exiting at Mondsee.) Stroll along the charming Marktplatz square full of lively cafés and restaurants, and the impressive Michaelerkirche parish church, where Maria married Captain von Trapp in *The Sound of Music*. Back on Route 158, head for **Fuschl** ❷ and the famous Hotel Schloss Fuschl, overlooking the western tip of the Fuschlsee, a former summer address of the prince-archbishops of Salzburg in the 16th century. This is an ideal spot for lunch (be sure to make reservations), as the dining room and terrace have grand vistas. Then it's back to Route 158 again, where a stop is in order for your trip's second night at 🏨 **St. Gilgen** ❸. The town gets very crowded in summer, especially along the shore, which is lined with ice-cream parlors and souvenir shops. But the little house near the dock on Ischler Strasse where Mozart's mother was born and his sister later lived should be spotlighted on your itinerary. From St. Gilgen head south on your third morning on Route 158, bearing left toward Strobl, then left again to drive along the eastern shore of the Abersee (the old name of the lake). The road bypasses the bulge of the lake, which consists mainly of campsites and very crowded beaches (one of which offers a beautiful view of St. Wolfgang). 🏨 **St. Wolfgang** ❹ is a town that all but clicks your camera shutter for you. For centuries it quietly harbored one of Austria's great art treasures, the great altarpiece by the late-Gothic wood-carver Michael Pacher, in the parish church. However, it was the inn near the dock—now Hotel Weisses Rössl (White Horse)—that spread the little Alpine town's fame (and made its fortune): it became the subject of a very popular operetta, *Im Weissen Rössl*, composed for the most part by Ralph Benatzky and premiered in Berlin in 1930. After an enchanting steamer trip on the lake, enjoy the popular excursion by rack rail to the top of the nearby Schafberg mountain; then return to St. Wolfgang for a dinner of trout *blau* (steamed) and an overnight stay. On your fourth morning, backtrack to Strobl and then follow signs for Bad Ischl to join Route 158. 🏨 **Bad Ischl** ❺ is the unofficial "capital" of the region and was Emperor Franz Josef's old stomping ground. Have lunch at one of the excellent recommended restaurants, then take in some of the town's sights. Bad Ischl is the departure point for 🏨 **Gosau am Dachstein** ❽, as outlined above in the 4-day itinerary. After spending a day at Gosau, head south to 🏨 **Hallstatt** ❾ and then move on to explore the splendors of Altausseerland in 🏨 **Bad Aussee** ⓫ and **Altaussee** ⓭. After Hallstatt, return to Bad Ischl and go west to Salzburg. However, if Vienna is your destination, go for an alternate finale to your trip and take Route B145 north to 🏨 **Gmunden** ❻, at the top of the Traunsee. This is one of the prettiest drives in the Salzkammergut, taking you past many little lakeside villages, most notably tiny Traunkirchen, dramatically perched on a peninsula with a former Benedictine nunnery. In Gmunden take time to shop for local ceramics, board the steam-wheeler *Gisela* for a boat tour, or ride the cable car to the top of the Grünberg. Spend the night in Gmunden or continue north a short distance to the A1 autobahn, which will take you to Vienna or Salzburg, which you can reach too by driving over the mountain to the Attersee and via Mondsee.

---

even guest houses without private baths; in some places, the *Herr Wirt*, his smiling wife, and his grown-up children will do everything to make you feel comfortable. Although this chapter's hotel reviews cover the best in every category, note that nearly every village, however small, also has a Gasthaus or village inn. Many hotels offer half-board, with din-

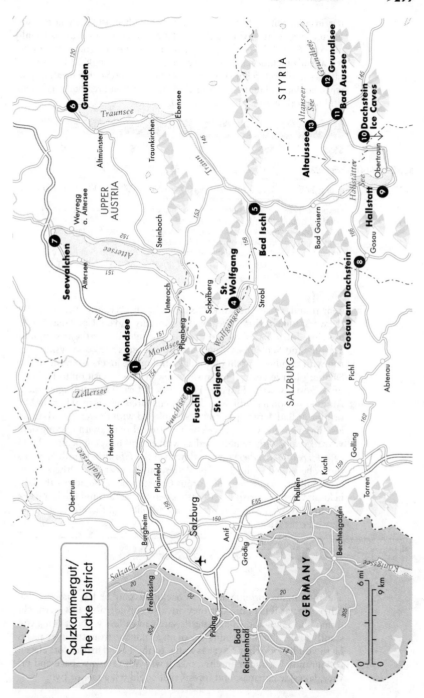

**Salzkammergut/
The Lake District**

STYRIA

UPPER AUSTRIA

SALZBURG

GERMANY

6 Gmunden
Traunsee

12 Grundlsee
Grundlsee

11 Bad Aussee

13 Altaussee
Altausseer See

10 Dachstein
Ice Caves

9 Hallstatt
Hallstätter See
Obertraun

7 Seewalchen
Attersee

5 Bad Ischl

8 Gosau am Dachstein

1 Mondsee
Mondsee

3 St. Gilgen

4 St. Wolfgang
Wolfgangsee

2 Fuschl

Salzburg

Ebensee
Traunkirchen
Altmünster
Weyregg a. Attersee
Steinbach
Unterach
Attersee
Schafberg
Strobl
Bad Goisern
Gosau
Pichl
Abtenau
Golling
Kuchl
Hallein
Anif
Grödig
Berchtesgaden
Torren
Zellersee
Fuschlsee
Plomberg
Scharfling
Henndorf
Plainfeld
Obertrum
Burgheim
Freilassing
Pidhag
Bad Reichenhall
Wallersee
Königssee

6 mi

9 km

ner in addition to buffet breakfast (although most $$$$ hotels will often charge extra for breakfast). The half-board room rate is usually an extra €15–€30 per person. Occasionally quoted room rates for hotels already include half-board accommodations, though a "discounted" rate is usually offered if you prefer not to take the evening meal. Inquire when booking. Happily, these hotels do not put their breathtakingly beautiful natural surroundings on the bill.

WHAT IT COSTS In euros				
$$$$	**$$$**	**$$**	**$**	**¢**
RESTAURANTS over €22	€18–€22	€13–€17	€7–€12	under €7
HOTELS over €175	€135–€175	€100–€135	€70–€100	under €70

Restaurant prices are per person for a main course at dinner. Hotel prices are for a standard double room in high season, including taxes and service. Assume that hotels operate on the European Plan (EP, with no meal provided) unless we note that they use the Breakfast Plan (BP), Modified American Plan (MAP, with breakfast and dinner daily, known as "halb pension"), or Full American Plan (FAP, or "voll pension," with three meals a day). Higher prices (inquire when booking) prevail for any meal plans.

Timing

Year-round, vacationers flock to the Lake District; however, late fall is the worst time to visit the region, for it is rainy and cold, and many sights are closed or operate on a restricted schedule. By far the best months are July and September. August, of course, sees the countryside overrun with families on school holidays and music lovers from the nearby Salzburg Music Festival (even so, who can resist a visit on to Bad Ischl on August 18, when Emperor Franz Josef's birthday is still celebrated). Another seasonal highlight is the annual Narcissus Festival held in May or June at Bad Aussee (the town is blanketed with flowers). Bad Aussee also has a special Carnival celebration (in February, with varying dates year to year), with men dressed as women and banging drums (the so-called *Trommelweiber*) on one day, then the *Flinserln* parading in costumes bedecked with silvery paillettes, on the next day. Others like to visit Hallstatt for its annual Corpus Christi procession across the lake, held on Corpus Christi day (weather permitting, around the last weekend in May, or the Sunday after)—a Catholic, and therefore, state holiday all over Austria.

ON THE ROAD TO ST. WOLFGANG & BAD ISCHL

The mountains forming Austria's backbone may be less majestic than other Alps at this point, but they are also considerably less stern; glittering blue lakes and villages nestle safely in valleys without being constantly under the threatening eye of an avalanche from the huge peaks. Here you'll find what travelers come to the Lake District for: elegant restaurants, Baroque churches, meadows with getaway space and privacy, lakeside cabanas, and forests that could tell a tale or two.

6

The Most Beautiful?

Whatever town or valley you pick, you'll have a battle on your hands insisting that your favorite spot in the Salzkammergut is the (only/best/unique) place in the region. The *whole* Salzkammergut is undeniably beautiful. As you explore the region, you'll note that if Austria were rated on a beauty-measuring gauge, the needle would fly off the scale in the Lake District. Travelling alongside the Hallstätter See to the lakeside village of Hallstatt, you will think you have made a magical detour into Norway: the lake, surrounded by towering peaks, almost looks like a fjord. The Dachstein massif—crowned in snowy ermine and reflected in the gorgeous Gosau lakes—puts Chamonix's Aiguilles to shame. Traveling through this region makes you feel like a judge in Mother Nature's own beauty contest. In this area, however, beauty is not only skin deep. Many of the most amazing sights lie below the surface of the earth, such as the Hallstatt salt mines or the Dachstein ice caves. Indeed, it would be difficult to imagine a more impressive spectacle than these ice caverns, of which the largest is more than 20 mi long.

Music in the Air

For nearly two centuries, the Salzkammergut lake district has been a wellspring of inspiration to great artists and composers. Richard Strauss, Gustav Klimt, and Franz Léhar are just a few of the great names who ventured here to holiday and, as souvenirs of their trips, left behind immortal symphonies and paintings. Today, you can follow a "Via Artis" in Bad Aussee to view different locales that inspired many artists. As it turns out, these great figures only discovered this region in the 19th century, after the French philosopher Jean Jacques Rousseau had preached "Back to nature!," the Romantic movement of the 19th century made tourism fashionable, and it was opened for the first time to visitors (previously, the "salt-mine" region was a private preserve of the Habsburgs). All this explains why Mozart, in the 18th-century never traveled from Salzburg to the Lake District village of St. Gilgen, where his mother was born.

But, following the example of Emperor Franz Josef and other royals, painters and poets soon began flocking to this region to enjoy the "simple life." The region's spas also attracted aristos by the boatload. Archduke Rudolf—brother of the emperor and pupil of Beethoven (for whom the composer wrote his *Missa solemnis*)—was the first Habsburg to enjoy the cure in Bad Ischl. The sensitive souls of the composers of the Romantic era were highly attracted by the beauty of the landscape. Little wonder that listeners can hear its reflection in the music written here: drive along the Attersee and listen to the *Scherzo*-movement of Gustav Mahler's Third Symphony and you'll know where its cuckoo-theme and wistful posthorn come from. Then when the Salzburg Music Festival hit its stride in the 1930s, many of the great musicians involved—such as Hugo von Hofmannsthal and Richard Strauss—liked to escape to summer houses in the hills after performing in town. Just like Johannes Brahms used to walk over a meadow on a sunny day or through a silent forest, or climb a mountain to renew mind and spirit, they follow his example and footsteps. So should you.

Mondsee

➊ *35½ km (22 mi) east of Salzburg, 100 km (62 mi) southwest of Linz.*

Mondsee is the gateway to the Salzkammergut for many tourists and Salzburgers alike. *Mondsee* means "Moon Lake," a name whose origins are the subject of some debate. Some say this body of water (11 km [7 mi] long and 2 km [1 mi] wide), which vaguely resembles a crescent moon, was named after a prehistoric lunar deity, although the Mondsee Monastery had its own story about a Bavarian duke being saved from falling into the lake water by a full moon that showed him a safe passage, after which he vowed to found a monastery. The water is warmer than that of any of the other high-altitude lakes, which makes it a good place for swimming, sailing, and windsurfing (head to the tourist office at Dr-Müller-Strasse 4, near the town bus stop, for all the info). In addition, Mondsee has some of the best dining the Salzkammergut has to offer.

Most travelers first head for the town square, adorned with pretty, somewhat gaudily colored houses, to visit the marvelous Baroque twin-towered **Michaelerkirche** (St. Michael's), built in 1470, with a famous twin-towering facade dating from the 18th century. This is the second-largest church in Upper Austria, thanks to the fact that it was originally part of a powerful Benedictine monastery—the *monasterium altissimum* (the Most High)—founded in the 8th century, closed in 1791. It holds a special place in the hearts of many travelers who remember it as the church in which Maria finally wed her Captain von Trapp in *The Sound of Music* (years later, Julie Andrews featured it in her *Sound of Christmas* television special). Inside, the vast apse and altar draw all eyes, but don't overlook the gilded Baroque side-altars decorated by Meinrad Guggenbichler (1649–1723), a famed Swiss sculptor, said to have used his own children as models for the little angels festooning the Corpus Christi Altar (halfway down the nave on the left side). Today, the monastery building is the site of the "Mondseetage" (⊕ www.mondseetage.com), an annual chamber music festival held during the first week in September. The monastery complex also houses a small museum, with sculptures ranging from prehistoric finds to Guggenbichler models.

Set on a hillock behind St. Michael's is a primitive **Rauchhaus.** Dating from 1420, this farmhouse is a rare extant example of a medieval "smoke house," in which smoke from the fireplace was directed up to the threshing floor above in order to dry corn and meats. A family resided in this dwelling as late as 1950 and it gives a fascinating relic of peasant life. ▨ €2.20 ⊙ *May–Aug., Tues.–Sun. 10–6; Sept., Tues.–Sun. 10–5; Oct., weekends 10–5.*

Where to Stay & Eat

★ **$$$–$$$$** ╳▨ **Schloss Mondsee.** Adjacent to the golden-hued church where Maria married Captain von Trapp in *The Sound of Music,* this former monastery opened as a hotel in 2001. The centuries-old complex is yellow hued and white trimmed, with a lovely garden courtyard; the accent notes of the sleekly renovated interiors are plate-glass windows and scrubbed monastic stone. Guest rooms are large, ultramodern, comfortable if a bit spartan, and most are duplexes, complete with living room, bedroom, and kitchenette. Chances are you won't be using the latter too often, as the hotel has two excellent restaurants, the casual Gewölbe and the intimate, but ambitious, Monchsküche. Menu delights may include beef carpaccio with shaved Parmesan and pesto, pork medallions with zucchini spaghetti, or grilled *Saiblingsfilet* (char) on a bed of sautéed spinach. In summer, tables are set outside in the pretty Blumenhof courtyard. ⊠ *A-5310 Mondsee* ☎ *06232/5001* 🖷 *06232/5001–22* ⊕ *www.schlossmondsee.at* ↩*67 rooms* ♧*2 restaurants, kitchenettes, indoor pool, gym, bar, Internet, free parking; no a/c* ☰ *AE, DC, MC, V* ¶⊙¶ *BP, MAP.*

$$$ Seehotel Königshof. Sparking with festivity, this massive, five-story "chalet" puts you in a resort mood with one look at its lime-green facade studded with lakeside balconies. Set at the northeast shore of the Mondsee, it comes with its own beach. Inside, guest rooms are spacious enough to have separated living and sleeping areas. A rich breakfast buffet and the use of sauna and steam-baths are included in the room rate. The restaurant is known for its light and slightly Asian-styled cuisine and offers hotel guests changing 3-course menus for an extra €20. ⊠ *A-5310 Mondsee* ☎*06232/5627* 🖷*0632/562755* ⊕*www.koenigshof.at* ↩ *19 rooms* ♧ *Restaurant, sauna, steam-bath, free parking; no a/c* ☰ *AE, DC, MC, V* ¶⊙¶ *MAP, FAP.*

$$–$$$ Seegasthof-Hotel Lackner. Only a 10-minute walk west from the center of Mondsee village, this flower-bedecked modern inn glows in ochre-hued stone, putting you in mind of a Tuscany villa. Inside, faux-Romanesque columns, terra-cotta walls, and enchanting lake views also allure. The range of rooms is wide here, but whether you go for simple and standard or a larger suite, always opt for a room with a balcony overlooking the lake. After enjoying the natural beach, head back to enjoy the critically praised cuisine cooked up by owner, Martin Lackner. His signature tomato soup, spaghetti with rabbit ragout, or dessert of cheese-dumplings with plums can all be enjoyed with a noted selection of Austrian wines. ⊠ *Mondseestrasse 1, A-5310 Mondsee* ☎ *06232/2359–0* 🖷 *06232/235950* ⊕ *www.hotel-ami.de* ↩ *16 rooms* ♧ *Restaurant, free parking; no a/c* ☰ *AE, DC, MC, V* ¶⊙¶ *MAP.*

★ $ Gasthof Drachenwand. "Preserve the old, discover the new" is the motto of the Eder family and that is certainly true at this lovely, off-the-beaten-track inn—a traditional *gästhof* chalet, complete with Tyrolean hipped roof and a facade dotted with hunter-green shutters. Set next to a small Baroque church and a former stop of the old *Salzkammergutlokalbahn* local railway (not defunct), the inn enjoys a scenic backdrop: the "Dragon Wall," a soaring limestone rock cliff west of the Mondsee lake. Inside, the inn's rooms have been sleekly and sophisticatedly renovated, yet rustic local furniture provides great charm. A five-minute walk from the hotel's shady garden will get you to the lakeside beach. The restaurant is supplied by local farmers and doesn't take credit cards—but who cares? The menu is very reasonably priced. ⊠ *St. Lorenz 32, A-5310 St. Lorenz/Mondsee* ☎ *06232/4417* 🖷 *06232/3356–10* ⊕ *www.drachenwand.at* ↩ *7 rooms* ♧ *Restaurant; no a/c* ☉ *Restaurant closed*

Mon.–Tues. during Oct.–Apr. and Mon. during May–Sept. ⊟ *AE, DC, MC, V* ¶◎¶ *MAP.*

Fuschl

❷ *20 km (12 mi) south of Mondsee, 30½ km (19 mi) east of Salzburg.*

Fuschl is so close to Salzburg that many attendees of the Salzburger Festspiele choose to stay in a hotel here, enjoying urban comforts while getting to savor rural pleasures at the same time. Located on Route 158, the town is on the Fuschlsee—a gem of a very clear small (only 2 mi long) deep lake, whose bluish-green water is ideal for swimming and wind-surfing—surrounded by a nature preserve once the hunting domain of Emperor Franz Josef himself. There's not much to do in Fuschl, the beaches being very limited in number, though those willing to hike can reach an extremely narrow strip on the northern shore that is especially popular with nudists. The town is noted for its many good places to eat and spend the night, including Schloss Fuschl, one of the finest establishments in the Salzkammergut.

Where to Stay & Eat

$$$$ ✕ **Brunnwirt.** You'll have to knock to be admitted, but once inside, you'll find elegantly set tables in this atmospheric 15th-century house. Frau Brandstätter presides over a kitchen that turns out good-sized portions of excellent Austrian and regional dishes. You might be offered game (in season) or roast lamb, always prepared with a light touch. Fish fresh from the lake is a regular specialty. ⊠ *Brunn 8* ☎ *06226/8236* 🖷 *06226/8236* ⚲ *Reservations essential* ⊟ *AE, DC, MC, V* ☾ *Closed Mon. No lunch except Sun. and during Salzburg Festival wks.*

$$$$ ✕▦ **Schloss Fuschl.** Once one of the most legendary hotels in Europe—guests with names like Roosevelt and Nehru were common—this dramatic 15th-century tower-like castle enjoys a spectacular, mountain-ringed perch atop a promontory over the Fuschlsee. Sixteen kilometers (10 mi) from Salzburg, this former hunting lodge for the Salzburg prince-archbishops quickly became a top address for posh festivalgoers. The main structure remains imposingly fortresslike, but warmed up with quaint red-and-white shutters. Inside, finely frescoed ceilings, intriguing passageways lined with antique furniture, and a sumptuously outfitted restaurant make a haute Alpine splash. Guest rooms vary in size from the baronial to the surprisingly small. The suites and superior rooms are regally splendid, and though the standard rooms are more modern, most have spectacular views of the lake. In fine weather, dining is outdoors on the magically beautiful stone terrace—whether a guest or not, be sure to splurge on a meal here. Opt for the trout caught in the lake (which is unpolluted by motorboats) and then delicately smoked in the smokehouse on the premises. The hotel presides over an 85-acre estate, replete with 9-hole golf course, sailing, and a gorgeous private beach and pier. Closed for a major renovation by the Sheraton chain during 2004, the hotel will reopen in mid-2005. Until then, the Arabella Sheraton Hotel Jagdhof, on a mountain side overlooking the schloss, is a newly built Lake District xanadu, rippling with spas, restaurants, 130 rooms, and any number of modern amenities, although set in a centuries-

FodorsChoice
★

old country manor. ⊠ *A-5322 Hof bei Salzburg* ☎ *06229/2253–0* 🖷 *06229/2253–531* ⊕ *www.arabellasheraton.com* ➥ *Castle 84 rooms, hotel 143 rooms* ⌂ *Restaurant, minibars, pool, Internet; no a/c* 🖃 *AE, DC, MC, V* |◎| *MAP.*

St. Gilgen

❸ *10 km (6 mi) south of Fuschl, 34 km (21 mi) east of Salzburg.*

Though its modest charms tend to be overshadowed by neighboring St. Wolfgang, St. Gilgen has a pretty main square, a nice beach (the northernmost strand on the Wolfgangsee), and an impressive musical pedigree. A Mozart fountain in the town square commemorates the fact that Mozart's mother, Anna Pertl, was born here on December 25, 1720. Later, his sister Nannerl resided in the same house when she married a town magistrate, Baron Baptist von Berchtold zu Sonnenberg. Their house, the **Mozart-Gedenkstätte St. Gilgen,** stands near the dock and has a room devoted to the town's Mozart legacy, with documents and copies of objects from the Mozart museums in Salzburg. After exploring the small town—more than Mozart himself ever did, since he never came here—you can see its small Baroque parish church (where Mozart's grandparents and sister married and his mother was baptized), then take the Zwölferhornbahn cable car (next to the bus station) up to the summit of the majestic Zwölferhorn peak. ⊠ *Mozart Museum: Ischler Strasse 15* ☎ *0662/844313–78* ⊕ *www.mozarteum.at* ☉ *June–Sept., Tues.–Sun. 10–12 and 2–6* 🎫 *€1.*

Where to Stay & Eat

★ **$$$-$$$$** ✕**Timbale.** Cozy and cheerful, Timbale is one of the premier restaurants in the Salzkammergut, known far and wide for regional specialties done just so. The taste treats start with the corn, whole wheat, and French breads baked on the premises, and dazzle on to the *Stubenküken* (chicken breast) stuffed with a cheese soufflé and wild mushrooms, or the *Kalbsrücken* (veal) with risotto and grilled shallots. Your eyes, as well as your stomach, will be happy—the crocheted red flower petals on periwinkle-blue tablecloths make everyone smile. ⊠ *Salzburgerstrasse 2, A-5340* ☎🖷 *06227/7587* ⌂ *Reservations essential* 🖃 *No credit cards* ☉ *Closed all day Thurs., Fri. lunch, and Aug.*

★ **$-$$** ✕🛏 **Hotel Gasthof zur Post.** An inn since 1415, the family-owned Post is one of the most attractive houses in town, a former domicile of Mozart's grandfather. A beautiful old sprucewood staircase leads to spacious rooms with contemporary furniture and stunning views of the village and the Wolfgangsee (most rooms have balconies). Owner Norbert Leitner is also a top chef—his seasonal menus might include a salad of wild greens with duck breast, spinach and garlic soup with slivers of smoked freshwater salmon, and *Tafelspitz* (boiled beef). On Friday evenings from September to mid-November, the restaurant offers live folk music. Be sure to have a glass of wine in the Vinothek, with its original 12th-century entrance. And get to know the secret behind the old hunting-scene fresco in the main parlor (with hidden motifs symbolizing "hunted" Lutherans). ⊠ *Mozartplatz 8, A-5340* ☎ *06227/2157* 🖷 *06227/2157–600* ⊕ *www.gasthofzurpost.at* ➥ *18 rooms* ⌂ *Restau-*

rant, sauna; no a/c ☰ *AE, DC, MC, V* ⊘ *Closed 1 month (variable) in winter. Restaurant closed Wed.–Thurs., Nov.–Apr.* ¶◯| *MAP.*

$$$–$$$$ 🏨 **Parkhotel Billroth.** Theodor Billroth was a member of the famous Viennese medical school, a surgeon who specialized in stomach ailments. Like many doctors, he was musically talented, playing violin and viola and becoming president of Vienna's famous Gesellschaft der Musikfreunde (Society of Music Friends) in Vienna: its chorus master Johannes Brahms often came to see his friend at this summer residence. After Billroth's death, his house was replaced by this elegant villa, decorated in 19th-century style, set in a huge park 10 minutes from the town center but close to the lake. The house is pleasantly worn at the edges yet spaciously arranged and luxuriously appointed, with a fine dining room. Sun terraces are particularly inviting. ⊠ *Billrothstrasse 2, A-5340* ☎ *06227/ 2217* 🖷 *06227/2218–25* 🛏 *44 rooms* ⚬ *Restaurant, tennis court, massage, sauna, beach, boating, bar; no a/c* ☰ *MC, V* ⊘ *Closed mid-Dec.–mid-Jan.* ¶◯| *MAP.*

★ $–$$$ 🏨 **Fürberg.** If you drive down from Winkl to the northeastern corner of Wolfgangsee lake (not far from a famous pilgrimage route used to get to St. Wolfgang), you'll leave the crowds of St. Wolfgang far behind and immerse yourself in the peace and scenic splendors of the mountains. To savor it all, this old inn in the typical Salzkammergut-style offers a perfect perch. Flower-decorated balconies and bathing jetties, most comfortable guest rooms (all non-smoking) in elegant dark-brown woods, an excellent breakfast buffet, and the elegant Stüberl restaurant (with a finely carved wooded ceiling) are some of the allures here. Fishing is possible, the use of rowing boats free, and the kitchen may even do the honors in cooking up your afternoon haul. ⊠ *A-5340* ☎ *06227/ 2385–0* 🖷 *06227/238535* ⊕ *www.fuerberg.at* 🛏 *25 rooms* ⚬ *Fishing, bicycles; no a/c* ☰ *AE, DC, MC, V* ¶◯| *MAP, FAP.*

Outdoor Activities and Sports

SKIING **Zwölferhorn,** to be reached via cable car, (⊠ St. Gilgen, A-5340 ☎ 06227/ 2348 🖷 06227/72679 🎫 Cable car round trip €17, one way €12 ⊘ 9–5, July / Aug. 9–6) has two runs totaling 10 km (7 mi) for ski experts, and offers a ski school.

St. Wolfgang

④ *19 km (12 mi) east of St. Gilgen, 50 km (31 mi) east of Salzburg.*

Fodor'sChoice
★

A delightful way to enter the picture-book town of St. Wolfgang is to leave your car at Strobl, at the southern end of the Wolfgangsee, and take one of the steamers that ply the waters of the lake. Strobl itself is a delightful village, but not as fashionable as St. Wolfgang; if you prefer a quiet vacation base, this may be its attraction for you. Between St. Wolfgang and Strobl, the Wolfgangsee still retains its old name of "Abersee." One of the earliest paddleboats on the lake is still in service, a genuine 1873 steamer called the *Kaiser Franz Josef.* Service is regular from May to mid-October. The view of the town against the dramatic mountain backdrop is one you'll see again and again on posters and postcards. If you decide to drive all the way to town, be prepared for a crowd.

Unless your hotel offers parking, you'll have to park on the fringes of town and walk a short distance, as the center is a pedestrian-only zone.

The town has everything: swimming and hiking in summer, cross-country skiing in winter, and natural feasts for the eye at every turn. Here you will find yourself in the Austria of operetta. Indeed, St. Wolfgang became known around the world thanks to the inn called the **Weisses Rössl**, which was built right next to the landing stage in 1878. It featured prominently in a late-19th-century play that achieved fame as an operetta by Ralph Benatzky in 1930. Ironically, the two original playwrights, Gustav Kadelburg and Oskar Blumenthal, had another, now destroyed, Weisses Rössl (along the road from Bad Ischl to Hallstatt) in mind. In the years following World War II both the composers Samuel Barber and Gian Carlo Menotti spent summer vacations here, too.

You shouldn't miss seeing Michael Pacher's great altarpiece in the 15th-century **Wallfahrtskirche** (pilgrimage church), one of the finest examples of late-Gothic wood carving to be found anywhere. This 36-foot masterpiece took 10 years (1471–81) to complete. As a winged altar, its paintings and carvings were used as *Armenbibel* (a bible for the poor)—illustrations for those who couldn't read or write. The coronation of the Virgin Mary is depicted in detail so exact that you can see the stitches in her garments. Gesturing, she invites the onlooker to pray and is surrounded by various saints, including the local patron, bishop St. Wolfgang from Regensburg in Bavaria. Since the 15th century his namesake town has been a place of pilgrimage. Pacher set his painted scenes in landscapes inspired by his homeland, South Tirol (now Italy). You're in luck if you're at the church on a sunny day, when sunlight off the nearby lake dances on the ceiling in brilliant reflections through the stained-glass windows. ☉ *May–Sept., daily 9–5; Oct.–Apr., daily 10–4; altar closed to view during Lent.*

off the beaten path

SCHAFBERG – –From May to mid-October the rack railway trip from St. Wolfgang to the 5,800-foot peak of the Schafberg offers a great chance to survey the surrounding countryside from what is acclaimed as the "belvedere of the Salzkammergut lakes." On a clear day you can almost see forever—at least as far as the Lattengebirge mountain range west of Salzburg. Figure on crowds, so reserve in advance or start out early. The train—itself a curiosity dating from 1893—departs hourly early May to early July; from the second week in July until early September, daily from 8:25 AM to 7:55 PM; early September to late October, daily from 9:55 AM to 2:55 PM. The train (☎ 06138/2232 🖷 06138/2232–12) does not run in bad weather. Allow at least a good half day for the outing, which costs €22.

Where to Stay & Eat

$$$$
Fodor'sChoice
★

✕🏨 **Landhaus zu Appesbach.** Very secluded and quiet and offering excellent service, this old ivy-covered manor hotel set away from the hubbub of the village is the place to get away from it all while at the same time enjoying the activities of the region. Public salons are charmingly furnished with Biedermeier pieces, while guest rooms are a mixture of country antiques and modern pieces, with grand overtones. Some have large balconies overlooking the lake. Both the Duke of Windsor and writer Thomas Mann once enjoyed respites here. The hotel has its own restaurant, for guests only, though it isn't at all stuffy. The menu is seasonal, but a staple is the fantastic antipasti buffet. Half pension is included in the room price, or you can opt for a reduction without. ⊠ *A-5360 St. Wolfgang am See* ☎ *06138/2209* ⊟ *06138/2209–14* ⊕ *www.appesbach. com* ➥ *26 rooms* ⚭ *Restaurant, minibars, tennis court, sauna, steam room, beach, dock; no a/c* ⊟ *AE, DC, MC, V* ⊗ *Closed varying wks in Nov. and last 3 wks of Jan.* |◎| *MAP.*

★ **$$$–$$$$** ✕⬚ **Weisses Rössl.** The "White Horse" has been featured in films and theater over the years, thanks to the famous operetta set here. Part of the Romantik Hotel group, it has been family-owned since the 1800s. Much of the hotel was extensively renovated in the rickety 1960s, but most guest rooms are still full of country charm, with pretty chintz fabrics and quaint furniture, and many have a balcony with a lake view. Baths are luxurious, complete with controls to set the exact water temperature you desire. The buffet breakfast is outstanding. An added attraction is the outdoor pool, situated directly on the lake and heated to a constant 86 degrees year-round. The dining terraces, built to float over the water, are enchanting, where you can enjoy the noted leek cream soup with scampi, *Forelle Müllerin* (trout "miller's daughter" simply fried in butter), or corn-fed chicken in a rosemary gravy. The hotel is world famous, so book well in advance, especially for the summer. ⊠ *Markt 74, A-5360* ☎ *06138/2306–0* ⊟ *06138/2306–41* ⊕ *www.weissesroessl. at* ➥ *72 rooms* ⚭ *2 restaurants, minibars, tennis court, indoor and outdoor pool, lake, sauna, windsurfing, boating, bar, Internet; no a/c* ⊟ *AE, DC, MC, V* ⊗ *Closed Nov.–mid-Dec.* |◎| *MAP.*

★ **$$** ⬚ **Cortisen am See.** A large châlet-style structure, with a glowing yellow facade, "At the Court" has become one of St. Wolfgang's most stylish and comfortable hotels. It has a lakeside perch, of course, replete with its own beach, rowing boats, terrace dining, and plenty of mountain bikes. Inside, all is gemütlichkeit nouvelle—chintz fabrics, tin-wrought lanterns, Swedish woods, sash windows, and exquisitely designed guest rooms make this a Lake District xanadu. The restaurant sparkles with a mix of 19th-century fabrics and gleaming white trim. The menu is mighty spiffy and owner Roland Ballner is proud to offer not only the largest wine selection in the area but also its most exotic cigar collection. ⊠ *Markt 15, A-5360* ☎ *06138/ 2376–0* ⊟ *06138/236744* ⊕ *www.cortisen.at* ➥ *36 rooms* ⚭ *Restaurant, bar, sauna, steam-bath, gym; no a/c* ⊟ *AE, DC, MC, V* |◎| *MAP.*

¢ ⬚ **Gasthof Zimmerbräu.** This pretty, pleasant budget Gasthof is four centuries old and was once a brewery, though for the last hundred years it has been an inn run by the Scharf family. Centrally located, the Zimmerbräu is not near the lake but does maintain its own bathing cabana by the water. The decor is appealingly rustic in some rooms, contemporary in others, but all rooms have balconies, and there is a lovely sitting room with Biedermeier furnishings on the first floor. Half pension is offered in the summer season only. ⊠ *Im Stöck 85, A-5360* ☎ *06138/ 2204* ⊟ *06138/2204–45* ⊕ *www.zimmerbraeu.com* ➥ *25 rooms* ⚭ *Restaurant, bar; no a/c* ⊟ *MC, V* ⊗ *Closed Nov.–Dec. 26* |◎| *MAP.*

Nightlife & the Arts

Free brass-band concerts are held on the Marktplatz in St. Wolfgang every Saturday evening at 8:30 in May, and on both Wednesday and Saturday at 8:30 PM from June to September. Folk events are usually well publicized with posters (if you are lucky, even Benatzky's operetta *Im Weissen Rössl* might be on schedule). Not far from St. Wolfgang, the town of Strobl holds a Day of Popular Music and Tradition in early July—"popular" meaning brass band, and "tradition" being local costume. Check with the regional tourist office for details.

Bad Ischl

❺ *56 km (35 mi) east of Salzburg, 16 km (10 mi) southeast of St. Wolfgang.*

Many travelers used to think of Bad Ischl primarily as the town where Zauner's pastry shop is located, to which connoisseurs drove miles for the sake of a cup of coffee and a slice of *Guglhupf,* a lemon sponge cake studded with raisins and nuts. Pastry continues to be the best-known drawing card of a community that symbolizes, more than any other place except Vienna itself, the Old Austria of resplendent uniforms and balls and waltzes and operettas. Although the center is built up, the town is charmingly laid out on a peninsula between the Rivers Traun and Ischl, whose amazing waters still run crystal clear. Bad Ischl was the place where Emperor Franz Josef chose to establish his summer court: when he died in 1916 at an age of 85, he had spent 82 summers in Ischl (the story goes that his mother, Sophie, had stayed at the spa in 1829 at the time of his conception, thereby earning the ruler his nickname, the "saltprince"). And it was also here that Franz Josef met and fell in love with his future empress, the troubled Sisi, though his mother had intended him for Sisi's elder sister. Today, you can enjoy the same sort of pastries *mit Schlag* (whipped cream) that the emperor loved. Afterward, you can hasten off to the town's modern spa, one of the best-known in Austria. The town initially grew up around the curative mineral salt springs. One of the town's main landmarks is the classic 19th-century *Kurhaus* (spa building), which is now a theater for operetta festivals (note the monuments to Lehár and Kálman in the adjoining park), and is home to the town's Kurorchestra (spa orchestra), which can also be found at various venues around town, including the Esplanade. Nearby are buildings from the 1860s which still offer spa treatments.

You'll want to stroll along the shaded **Esplanade,** where the pampered and privileged of the 19th century loved to take their constitutionals, usually after a quick stop at the **Trinkhalle,** a spa pavilion in high 19th-century Austrian style, still in the middle of town on Ferdinand-Auböck-Platz.

In Bad Ischl the quickest way to travel back in time to the gilded 1880s ★ is to head for the mammoth **Kaiservilla,** the imperial-yellow (signifying wealth and power) residence, which looks rather like a miniature Schönbrunn: its ground plan forms an "E" to honor the empress Elisabeth. Archduke Markus Salvator von Habsburg-Lothringen, great-grandson of Franz Josef I, still lives here, but you can tour parts of the building to see the ornate reception rooms and the surprisingly modest residential quarters (through which sometimes even the archduke guides guests with what can only be described as a very courtly kind of humor). It was at this villa that the emperor signed the declaration of war against Serbia, which officially marked the start of World War I. The villa is filled with Habsburg and family mementos, none more moving than the cushion on which the head of Empress Elisabeth rested after she was stabbed by an Italian assassin in 1898, which is on view in the villa's chapel. ⊠ *Kaiserpark* ☎ *06132/23241* ⊕ *www.kaiservilla.at* ⊠ *Grounds €3.50; combined ticket, including tour of villa, €9.50* ☉ *Easter, Apr. weekends, and May–mid-Oct., daily 9:30–4:45.*

Don't overlook the small but elegant "marble palace" built near the Kaiservilla for Empress Elisabeth, who used it as a teahouse; this now houses a **photography museum.** (The marriage between Franz Josef and Elisabeth was not an especially happy one; a number of houses bearing women's names in Bad Ischl are said to have been quietly given by the emperor to his various lady friends (most prominently, Villa Schratt— *see* Dining and Lodging, *below*—given to Katharina Schratt, the emperor's nearly official mistress). You'll first need to purchase a ticket to the museum to enter the park grounds. ⊠ *Kaiserpark* ☎ *06132/24422* ⊠ *€1.50* ☉ *Apr.–Oct., daily 9:30–5.*

Fascinating is the only word to describe the **Museum der Stadt Ischl,** which occupies the circa 1880 Hotel Austria—the favored summer address for archduke Franz Karl and his wife Sophie (from 1834 on). More momentously, the young Franz Josef got engaged to his beloved Elisabeth here in 1853. After taking in the gardens (with their Brahms monument), explore the various exhibits, which deal with the region's salt, royal, and folk histories. Note the display of national folk costumes, which the emperor made presentable even for his court aristos by wearing them while hunting. From December until the beginning of February, the museum shows off its famous *Kalss Krippe,* an enormous mechanical Christmas crêche. Dating from 1838, it has about 300 figures. The townsfolk of Ischl, in fact, are famous for their Christmas "cribs" and you can see many of them in tours of private houses opened for visits after Christmas until January 6th. ⊠ *Esplanade 10* ☎ *06132/30114* ⊕ *www.stadtmuseum.at* ⊠ *€4.20* ☉ *Jan.–Mar., Fri.–Sun. 12–5; Apr.–Oct. and Dec., Sun.–Tues. and Thurs.–Sat. 10–5, Wed. 2–7.*

In the center of town, **St. Nikolaus** parish church graces Ferdinand-Auböck-Platz. It dates back to the middle ages but was enlarged to its present size during Maria Theresa's time in the 1750s. The decoration inside is in the typically gloomy style of Franz Josef's days (note the emperor's family portrayed to the left above the high altar). Anton Bruckner used to play on the old church organ.

A steady stream of composers followed the aristocracy and the court to Bad Ischl. Anton Bruckner, Johannes Brahms (who composed his famous *Lullaby* here as well as many of his late works), Johann Strauss the Younger, Carl Michael Ziehrer, Oscar Straus, and Anton Webern all spent summers here, but it was the Hungarian born Franz Lehár, composer of *The Merry Widow,* who left the most lasting musical impression—today, Bad Ischl's summer operetta festival (*see* Music *in* Nightlife and the Arts, *below*) always includes one Lehár work. With the royalties he received from his operettas, he was able to afford his own vacation villa from 1912 on. Previously, he rented the Rosenvilla, set between the trees to the left of the Kongresshaus (a house in which Giacomo Meyerbeer composed parts of his opera *Le Prophete*). He finally settled into the sumptuous **Villa Lehár**, in which he lived from 1912 to his death in 1948. Now a museum, it contains a number of the composer's fin-de-siècle period salons, which can be viewed on guided tours. ⊠ *Lehárkai 8* ☎ *06132/26992* 🖃 *€4.50* ◷ *May–Sept., daily 9–noon and 2–5.*

Bad Ischl is accessed easily via various routes. From St. Wolfgang, backtrack south to Strobl and head eastward on Route 158. To get to the town directly from Salzburg, take the A1 to Mondsee, then Routes 151 and 158 along the Wolfgangsee and the Mondsee. There are many buses that depart hourly from Salzburg's main railway station; you can also travel by train via the junction of Attnang-Puchheim or Stainach-Irdning (several transfers are required)—a longer journey than the bus ride, which is usually 90 minutes. There are also many regular bus and train connections between Gmunden and Bad Ischl.

Where to Stay & Eat

$–$$ ✕ **Rettenbachmühle.** A shady walk of about 20 minutes east from Bad Ischl's town center follows a brook and deposits you at this former farmhouse, once thought to be the supplier of eggs and milk for the imperial breakfast table (a nice story, though probably not true). The Vierthaler family, the present owners, swear, however, that this was the very locale where the *Kaiserschmarrn* was born. The name literally translates to "emperor's nonsense," but many consider it to be the most delicious dessert in Austria—a raisin-studded pancake covered with powdered sugar. It makes for a lovely time to stop here to enjoy this treat along with an afternoon coffee. ⊠ *Hinterstein 6* ☎ *06132/23586* ◷ *Closed Mon.–Tues.*

★ **$–$$** ✕ **Weinhaus Attwenger.** Once the summer residence of composer Anton Bruckner (who journeyed here to be the emperor's organist in the town parish church), this turn-of-the-19th-century gingerbread villa is set in a shady garden overlooking a river, with the Villa Lehár perched just next doors. The tranquil garden is ideal for summer dining, and inside the house the cozy, wood-paneled rooms are decorated with antique country knickknacks. Order the crispy duck in a honey-ginger sauce or the basket of country-fried chicken, or ask for seasonal recommendations; the fish and game dishes are particularly good. ⊠ *Lehárkai 12* ☎☎ *06132/ 23327* 🖃 *No credit cards* ◷ *Closed Wed.–Thurs. and 2 wks in Mar.*

★ **¢–$** ✕ **Café Zauner.** If you haven't been to Zauner, you've missed a true highlight of Bad Ischl. There are two locations, one on the Esplanade overlooking the River Traun (open only in summer) and the other a few blocks away on Pfarrgasse. The desserts—particularly the house creation, *Zaunerstollen,* a chocolate-covered confection of sugar, hazelnuts, and nougat—have made this one of Austria's best-known pastry shops. Emperor Franz Josef used to visit every day for a Guglhupf, a lemon sponge cake. ⊠ *Pfarrgasse 7* ☎ *06132/23522* ⊕ *www.zauner.at* 🖃 *MC* ◷ *Closed Tues.*

$$-$$$$ ✕▦ **Villa Schratt.** About a mile outside of Bad Ischl on the road to
Fodor'sChoice Salzburg is this enchanting, secluded villa, fabled retreat of the actress
★ Katharina Schratt. "Kati"—star of Vienna's k.k. Hofburgtheater (the Im-
perial and Royal court theater)—was Emperor Franz Josef's mistress in
his later years and almost every summer morning, the emperor would
stroll over here for his breakfast. Over the course of their time together,
most of European royalty dropped in for a visit. Nowadays the Villa Schratt
is one of the best places to dine in the area. Choose between two dining
rooms—one with a *Jugendstil* slant, the other, country-style with chintz
curtains, a ceramic stove, and a hutch displaying homemade jams. Try
the *Zanderfilet* (pike perch) on a bed of delicate beets soaked in port wine,
or beef tenderloin strips with oyster mushrooms in a cream sauce. For
dessert, order the traditional Guglhupf sponge cake, Franz Josef's favorite—
it even comes warm out of the oven. Upstairs are four lovely, antiques-
filled bedrooms for overnighters. ⊠ *Steinbruch 43, A-4820* ☎ *Restaurant
06132/27647, rooms 06132/23535* 🖷 *06132/27647–4* ⊕ *www.tiscover.
com/villa.schratt* ⌕ *Reservations essential* 🛏 *2 rooms* ⊟ *AE, MC*
☉ *Closed Tues., Wed., early–mid-Nov., and varying wks in spring* � *BP.*

$ ▦ **Goldener Ochs.** The "Golden Ox" is in a superb location in the
town center, with the sparkling River Traun just a few steps away. Rooms
are modern with blond-wood furniture; some have balconies, and there
are a few large rooms designed for families. The kitchen prides itself
on its health-oriented cooking. ⊠ *Grazerstrasse 4, A-4820* ☎ *06132/
235290* 🖷 *06132/235293* ⊕ *www.tiscover.com/goldener-ochs* 🛏 *48
rooms* ⌕ *Restaurant, gym, sauna, Internet; no a/c* ⊟ *AE, DC, MC, V*
⑩ *MAP, FAB.*

Nightlife & the Arts
The main musical events of the year in the Salzkammergut are the July
and August operetta festivals held in Bad Ischl. In addition, performances
of at least two operettas (*The Merry Widow* is a favorite standard) take
place every season in the **Kongress and Theaterhaus** (☎ 06132/23420),
where tickets are sold. For early booking, contact the **Operrettengemeinde**
(⊠ Kurhausstrassse 8, A-4820 Bad Ischl ☎ 06132/23839 🖷 06132/
23839–39).

Gmunden

❻ *76 km (47 mi) northeast of Salzburg, 40 km (25 mi) southwest of Linz,
32 km (20 mi) northeast of Bad Ischl.*

Gmunden, at the top of the Traunsee, is an attractive town to stroll about
in. The tree-lined promenade along the lake is reminiscent of past days
of the idle aristocracy and artistic greats—the composers Franz Schu-
bert, Johannes Brahms, Béla Bartók, Arnold Schoenberg, Erich Wolf-
gang Korngold, and the Duke of Württemberg were just some who strolled
under the chestnut trees. The gloriously ornate, arcaded yellow-and-white
town hall, with its corner towers topped by onion domes, can't be over-
looked; it houses a famous carillon, with bells fashioned not from the
local clay but from fabled Meissen porcelain (which gives a better
sound) decorated in the Gmunden style. Head to the upper town and
take in the parish church on Pfarrhofgasse. It has a beautiful high altar

dedicated to the Three Holy Kings. You can easily walk to the **Strandbad,** the swimming area, from the center of town. The beaches are good, and you can sail, water ski, or windsurf.

Be sure to head out to the town's historic castles: the "lake" castle, **Schloss Orth,** on a peninsula known as Toskana, was originally built in the 15th century. It was once owned by Archduke Johann, who gave up his title after marrying an actress and thereafter called himself Orth. He disappeared with the casket supposedly holding the secret of the Mayerling tragedy after the death of Emperor Franz Josef's son Rudolf. The **Landschloss** on the shore is a simple 17th-century affair now operating as a government school of forestry; you can visit the courtyard, with its coats of arms and Rococo fountain, daily 8 AM–dusk.

Music lovers will enjoy the Brahms memorial collection—the world's largest—on display in the **Stadtmuseum** (City Museum) at the town Kammerhof. Other exhibitions are devoted to the town's history and the region's salt and mineral resources. ✉ *Kammerhofgasse 8* 📞📞 *07612/ 794420* ☉ *May–Oct. and Dec.–Jan., Mon.–Sat. 10–noon and 2–5, Sun. 10–noon* 💶 *€4.*

★ From Gmunden, take a lake trip on the **Gisela,** built in 1872, the oldest coal-fired steam side-wheeler running anywhere. It carried Emperor Franz Josef in the last century and is now restored. For departure times, check with **Traunseeschiffahrt Eder** (📞 07612/66700 ⊕ www. traunseeschifffahrt.at).The boat route crisscrosses the whole 12-km (7-mi) length of the lake.

From beyond the railroad station, a 12-minute cable-car ride brings you to the top of the **Grünberg.** From here you will have a superb view over the Traunsee, with the Dachstein glacier forming the backdrop in the south. In the winter, there are good ski runs here. ✉ *Freygasse 4* 📞 *07612/64977–0* 💶 *Round-trip €10, one-way €7* ☉ *Apr.–June and Sept., daily 9–5; July–Aug., daily 9–6; Oct., daily 9–4:30.*

To get to Bad Ischl from Gmunden, take Route 145 along the western shore of the Traunsee—note the Traunstein, Hochkogel, and Erlakogel peaks on the eastern side, the latter nicknamed *die schlafende Griechin* ("the slumbering Greek girl")—and then along the Traun River. At **Ebensee** is the chance to enjoy the overwhelming karst scenery of the limestone alps from above by using the cable car up the Feuerkogel mountain (✉ Rudolf -Ipplisch-Platz 4 📞 06133/5219 ☉ May 15–Oct. 10, daily 💶 €16). You can also take a train to Gmunden via Attnang-Puchheim from Salzburg, or from the main station in Linz.

off the beaten path

TRAUNKIRCHEN – About 4½ km (3 mi) north of Ebensee on Route 145 you'll come to Traunkirchen, a little village where Arnold Schoenberg invented his 12-tone method of composition; stop for a look at the famous "fishermen's pulpit" in the parish church next to a convent founded by the nuns from Nonnberg in Salzburg. This 17th-century Baroque marvel, carved from wood and burnished with silver and gold, portrays the astonished fishermen of the Sea of Galilee pulling in their suddenly full nets at Jesus' direction.

Where to Stay & Eat

$$$ ✕🏨 **Schloss Freisitz Hotel Roith.** Crowning the eastern shores of the Traunsee, this landmark "schloss" draws all eyes, thanks to its flapping flag atop its white turret, its *mittel-europisch* baroque pediments, and expansive "hunting lodge" facade. Gracing a castle site from 1550, it was renovated in 1887 by Gustav Faber. In 1964 the mansion became a hotel and now anyone can experience the 19th-century luxe that the famous German pencil maker once enjoyed—Oriental carpets, art nouveau furniture, and those breathtaking vistas down to the lake. The breakfast buffet is almost as beautiful. ✉ *Traunsteinstrasse 87, A-4810* ☎ *07612/64905* 🖷 *07612/649–0517* ⊕ *www.schlosshotel.at* 🛏 *14 rooms* ⚴ *Restaurant, sauna, steam-bath, gym* ▭ *AE, DC, MC, V* ⊚❘ *EP.*

$$ ✕🏨 **Grünberg am See.** This sprawling, multilevel chalet hotel makes a pretty picture along the lakeshore opposite Gmunden's city center. Rooms are spacious with contemporary blond-wood furniture, and many have balconies with stunning views. The popular restaurant serves good local cuisine, emphasizing fish fresh from the lake. The hotel offers superb sports opportunities, from hiking to cycling to swimming. Half pension plans are offered for a stay of three days or more. ✉ *Traunsteinstrasse 109, A-4810* ☎ *07612/777–00* 🖷 *07612/77700–33* ⊕ *www.gruenberg.at* 🛏 *30 rooms* ⚴ *Restaurant, beach, bicycles, hiking, bar; no a/c* ▭ *AE, DC, MC, V* ⊘ *Closed 2 wks. in Feb.* ⊚❘ *MAP.*

$$ 🏨 **Hois'n Wirt.** This large, modern-chalet complex enjoys a swooningly idyllic Traunsee setting. Now run by the fourth generation of the Schallmeiner family, it is geared to please. The restaurant has a glittering glass window wall overlooking the lakeside view, the kitchen uses the lake as its larder, cooking up some of the best trout and Reinanke around, and guest rooms are pretty, light-filled, and casual-modern, with balconies overlooking the lakeside beach. Many guests check in and then immediately dive in. In a house not far away from the hotel, Arnold Schoenberg composed some of his most famous string quartets. ✉ *Traunsteinstrasse 277, A-4810* ☎ *07612/77333* 🖷 *07612/773–3395* ⊕ *www.hoisnwirt.at/hoisnwirt* 🛏 *16 rooms* ⚴ *Beach; no a/c* ▭ *AE, DC, MC, V* ⊚❘ *MAP, FAP.*

$ 🏨 **Seehotel Schwan.** On the edge of the lake in the center of town, this grand old hotel is part of the Best Western chain. Rooms are standard, but the views make up for what they might be lacking in character. The restaurant, with huge windows overlooking the lake, has a creative menu with lots of fresh fish offerings. ✉ *Rathausplatz 8, A-4810* ☎ *07612/63391–0* 🖷 *07612/63391–8* 🛏 *30 rooms* ⚴ *Restaurant, bar; no a/c* ▭ *AE, DC, MC, V* ⊚❘ *MAP, FAP.*

Shopping

Among the many souvenirs and handicrafts you'll find in Salzkammergut shops, the most famous are the handcrafted ceramics of Gmunden. The green-trimmed, white country ceramics are decorated with blue, yellow, green, and white patterns, including the celebrated 16th-century *Grüngeflammte* design, solid horizontal green stripes on a white background. You'll find them at **Gmundner Keramik** (✉ Keramikstrasse 24 ☎ 07612/786–0).

Seewalchen

❼ *19 km (12 mi) west of Gmunden, 57 km (35 mi) northeast of Salzburg.*

Heading northwest from Gmunden it is easy to reach the Attersee, whose length of 21 km (13 mi) makes it the largest lake in the Salzkammergut and the second largest in Austria. Here in Seewalchen and other Attersee lake towns you can attend the Attersee Klassik, a music festival held mainly in village churches, from the end of July until end of August. Along the Attersee, between Seewalchen and Steinbach, there are 19 locations that inspired the great Secessionist painter Gustav Klimt. From 1900 until two years before his death in 1918 he often holidayed in this area and, as a result, used its landscape motifs in more than fifty of his paintings. From May to September, special guided tours (via foot, bus, or ferry) are given by the regional tourist office to show the areas he immortalized along a route running some 45 km (28 mi). For details contact the Tourismusverband Attersee (✉ Hauptstrasse 1, A-4861 Schörfling ☎ 07662/2578 🖷 07662/2360 ⊕ www.attersee. at). In Seewalchen itself, Klimt often stayed at the Villa Paulick, along the Seepromenade. Don't fail to stop in on the village's noted Konditorei Rohringer, an excellent pastry shop famous for its cookies.

From Seewalchen, head south along the road lining the eastern shore of the Attersee and go to **Steinbach**, another "genius loci" for an Austrian cultural giant, in this case, Gustav Mahler, the so named "Summer composer," who wrote some of his *Wunderhorn-Lieder*, the 2nd–6th movements of his Second Symphony, and his entire Third Symphony during four holidays here from 1893 on. Music lovers make a bee line for the composer's *Komponierhäuschen*, the little wooden hut he had built to work undisturbed in total isolation next to the lake (it figures prominently in Ken Russell's film about the composer). Head for the Gasthof Föttinger (☎ 07663/8100) to get the key for the hut (don't forget to lock the door afterwards and bring the key back). Mahler's pupil, Bruno Walter, the great conductor, visited him here and was overwhelmed with the beauty of the landscape. Mahler only grumbled, "You don't have to pay attention to it—I composed it already!"

Where to Stay & Eat

$$$–$$$$ ✕🏨 **Residenz Häupl.** On the prettiest side of the Attersee, this inn has roots going back to 1831 (the seventh generation of the same family is running it) but has received a spiffy renovation. This is a sports valhalla, with its own golf course, sailing on a 400 hp-powerboat, tennis, mountain biking, beach facility, rafting on the Traun river, and Nordic walking. Inside, guest rooms are charmingly elegant, most of them with balconies and lush views. Best of all, the restaurant is so good it is a member of the celebrated culinary society, the Châine des Rotisseurs. ✉ *Hauptstrasse 20, A-4863 Seewalchen* ☎ *07662/6363* 🖷 *07662/ 636363* ⊕ *www.residenz-haeupl.at* ➳ *33 rooms* △ *Restaurant, sauna, golf, tennis court; no a/c* ⊟ *AE, DC, MC, V* ⑩ *MAP, FAP.*

GOSAU, HALLSTATT & BAD AUSSEE

It is hard to imagine anything prettier than this region of the Salzkammergut, which takes you into the very heart of the Lake District. The great highlight is Gosau am Dachstein—a beauty spot that even the least impressionable find hard to forget. But there are other notable sights, including Hallstatt, the Dachstein Ice Caves, and the spa of Altaussee. Lording over the region is the Dachstein range itself—the backbone of Upper Austria, Styria, Land Salzburg, and a true monarch of all it surveys.

Gosau am Dachstein

8 *10 km (6 mi) west of the Hallstättersee.*

Fodor'sChoice
★

Lovers of scenic beauty should not leave the Hallstatt region without taking in Gosau am Dachstein, considered the most beautiful spot in Austria by 19th-century travelers but unaccountably often overlooked today. This lovely spot is 10 km (6 mi) west of the Hallstätter See, just before the Geschütt Pass: you travel either by bus (eight daily from Bad Ischl to Gosau) or car. The village makes a good lunch stop and, with its many *Gasthöfe* and pensions, could be a base for your excursion. Instead of driving, it's worth to take a serious walk (about 2½ hours, depending on your speed), departing from the tourist information office not far from the crossroads known as the Gosaumühle. Passing by churches the road follows the valley over the meadows. From Gosauschmied Café on, it's a romantic way through the forest to the first Gosau lake, the Vorderer Gosausee (the "Front Gosau Lake"), which is the crown jewel, located some 8 km (5 mi) to the south of the village itself. Beyond a sparkling, almost fjordlike basin of water rises the amazing Dachstein massif, majestically reflected in the lake's mirrorlike surface. Other than a restaurant and a gamekeeper's hut, the lake is undefiled by man-made structures. At the right hour—well before 2:30 PM, when, due to the steepness of the mountain slopes, the sun is already withdrawing—the view is superb. Unfortunately, the lake can get shallow during summer months. Following the path around this lake will clarify some of the greatest passages in Richard Wagner's *Parsifal*, which were composed with these vistas in mind. Then you may choose to endure the stiff walk to the other two lakes set behind the first lake and not as spectacularly located (in fact, the third is used by an electric power station and therefore is not always full of water, yet it remains the closest place to see the glittering Dachstein glacier). Hiking to these latter two lakes will take about two hours. You can also take a cable car up to the Gablonzer Hütte on the Zwieselalm (you might consider skiing on the Gosau glacier); or tackle the three-hour hike up to the summit of the Grosser Donnerkogel. At day's end, head back for Gosau village, settle in at one of the many Gasthöfe (reserve ahead) overhung with wild gooseberry and rosebushes (or stay at one of Gosau's charming *Privatzimmer* accommodations). Cap the day off with a dinner of fried *Schwarzrenterl*, a delicious regional lake fish. To get to Gosau, travel north or south on Route 145, turning off at the junction with Route

166, and travel 36 km (20 mi) east through the ravine of the Gosaubach river.

Where to Stay & Eat

★ **$$$** ✕⊞ **Hotel Koller.** One of the most charming hotels in Gosau, the Koller was originally the home of famed industrialist Moriz Faber. With peaked gables and weather vanes, the Koller has a fairy-tale aura when seen from its pretty park. Inside are an open fireplace and warm woodwork; guest rooms—many offering breathtaking views—have blond-wood furniture and cheerful curtains. Try to get a room in the main house. Special highlights are the tavern's gala dinners, featuring regional barbecued specialties and health foods supplied fresh by the farmers of Gosau. Half board is required and included in the room price. ⊠ *A-4824 Gosau am Dachstein* ☎ *06136/8841* 📠 *06136/884150* ⊕ *www.hotel-koller.com* 🛏 *17 rooms* ⚐ *2 restaurants, pool, sauna, steam room, bar, playground; no a/c* ☰ *V* ☉ *Closed Nov. and also for 1 month around Easter (dates vary)* ⟐ *MAP.*

¢–$ ✕⊞ **Kirchenwirt.** Snuggly adjacent to Gosau's pretty parish church, this inn is evidence of the venerable tradition of locating town restaurants next to houses of worship (on Sundays, all the farmers would attend the service and afterwards chow down at the nearest table to discuss what happened during the past week). Mentioned back in the town records as early as 1596, the inn here has now been much restored and built up in typical modern alpine decor—woodwork, mounted antlers, hunter greens, bright reds. The current hosts, the Peham family are proud of their restaurant and its rich breakfast buffet. Best bets for other meals include the broth with strudel of minced meat, or the homemade noodles with cheese and white cabbage salad, or the plums with vanilla ice cream and whipped cream. A nice touch: guests here can use the village's indoor swimming pool for free. In August, the inn hosts some festive concerts of traditional Trachtenmusikkapelle, with a brass bank dressed in folkloric costume. The inn is open year-round so you can enjoy Gosau in all its snowy splendor. ⊠ *Gosau 2, A-4824* ☎ *06136/8196* 📠 *06136/819615* ⊕ *www.kirchenwirt-peham.at* 🛏 *22 rooms* ⚐ *Restaurant, no a/c* ☰ *MC* ⟐ *HP.*

$$$ ⊞ **Sommerhof.** In the center of the extended village of Gosau, this large, modern resort hotel is surrounded by blooming alpine meadows in the summer, while in winter it makes a great perch for skiers heading to Dachstein West, the largest ski region in the province of Salzburg (some 50 lifts and some 140 km [87 mi] of ski runs). The yellow- and green-hued châlet is lined with "Rapunzel" balconies, the guest rooms are modern-traditional in decor and very comfy, and the grounds are rife with facilities for children, including a Mini Club playground and a *Kaiserbad* (emperor's bath) with heated water. Hikers, skiers, and families will love this hotel. At night, the Vinothek and the Café-Bar come into their own. ⊠ *Gosau 25, A-4824* ☎ *06136/8258* 📠 *06136/825850* ⊕ *www. sommerhof.at* 🛏 *48 rooms* ⚐ *Café, sauna, whirlpool; no a/c* ☰ *No credit cards* ⟐ *MAP, FAP.*

Hallstatt

❾ *89 km (55 mi) southeast of Salzburg, 19 km (12 mi) south of Bad Ischl.*

Fodor'sChoice
★

As if rising from Swan Lake itself, the town of Hallstatt is the subject of thousands of travel posters. "The world's prettiest lakeside village" perches precariously on the lakeside on what seems the smallest of toe-holds, one that nevertheless prevents it from tumbling into the dark waters of the Hallstättersee. Down from the steep mountainside above it crashes the Mühlbach waterfall, a sight that can keep one riveted for hours. Today, as back when—Emperor Franz Josef and his Elisabeth took an excursion here on the day of their engagement—the town is a magnet for tourists and, as such, a bit too modernized, especially considering that Hallstatt is believed to be the oldest community in Austria. More than a thousand graves of prehistoric men have been found here, and it has been such an important source of relics of the Celtic period that this age is known as the Hallstatt epoch.

Arriving in Hallstatt is a scenic spectacular if you come by train. The Hallstatt railroad station is on the opposite side of the lake; when you arrive by train, a boat, the *Hemetsberger* (✉ Hallstättersee-Schiffahrt ☎ 06134/8228 ⊕ www.hallstatt.net/schiffahrt), will take you across Hallstättersee to the town, leaving every hour. This is widely celebrated as the most beautiful way to arrive, because it is the only chance to see the entire village arrayed across the lakefront. If you miss out on arriving by ferry, you can also opt for a boat tour around the lake via Obertraun, available May–September daily at 1, 2, and 3; July–August also at 11 and 4:15. Boat tours around the lake via Steeg, July–August daily at 10:30, 1:30, and 3:30. Embark via train for Hallstatt from Bad Ischl or via the Stainach-Irdning junction. From Bad Ischl, you can also take a half-hour bus ride to Hallstatt. To get to Hallstatt from Bad Ischl via car, head south on Route 145 to Bad Goisern (which also has curative mineral springs but never achieved the cachet of Bad Ischl). Just south of town, watch for signs for the turnoff to the Hallstättersee. Since the lake is squeezed between two sharply rising mountain ranges, the road parallels the shore, with spectacular views.

★ The Hallstatt market square, now a pedestrian area, is bordered by colorful 16th-century houses. Be sure to visit the **Michaelerkirche** (parish church of St. Michael's) which is picturesquely sited near the lake. Within the 16th-century Gothic church you'll find a beautiful winged altar, which opens to reveal nine 15th-century paintings. The charnel house beside the church is a rather morbid but regularly visited spot. Because there was little space to bury the dead over the centuries in Hallstatt, the custom developed of digging up the bodies after 12 or 15 years, piling the bones in the sun, and painting the skulls. Ivy and oak-leaf wreaths were used for the men, Alpine flowers for the women, plus names, dates, and often the cause of death. The myriad bones and skulls are now on view in the *karner* (charnel house). The cemetery, adorned with traditional Alpine crosses and memorial, has a stunning setting overlooking the lake. The vistas are spectacular and people love to feed the fish by the shore. Each year, at the end of May, the summer season kicks off with the Fronleichnahm (Corpus Christi) procession, which concludes with hundreds of boats out on the lake

Most of the early relics of the Hallstatt era are in Vienna (including the greatest Iron Age totem of them all, the Venus of Willendorf, now a treasure of Vienna's Naturhistorisches Museum), but some are here in the **World Heritage Museum,** the former Prähistorische Museum. ⊠ *Seestrasse 56* ☎ *06134/828015* ⊕ *www.museum-hallstatt.at* ☞ *€7* ⊙ *Nov.–Mar., Tues.–Sun. 11–3; Apr. and Oct., daily 10–4; May–Sept., daily 9–6.*

A peek into the Celtic past is offered at the Zentrasport Janu shop. A decade ago, its intention to put a new heating system in the cellar unexpectedly turned into a **historical excavation** when workmen found the remains of a Celtic dwelling, now open to visitors. ⊠ *Seestrasse 50* ☎ *06134/8298* ☞ *Free* ⊙ *Mon.–Sat. 8–6.*

Salt has been mined in this area for at least 4,500 years, and the Hallstatt mines of the Salzberg (not "burg") mountain are the oldest in the world. These "show-mines" are known as the **Schaubergwerk** and are set in the Salzbergtal valley, accessed either by paths from the village cemetery or, much more conveniently, via a funicular railway that leaves from the southern end of the village. From the railway, a 10-minute walk takes you to a small-scaled miner's train (tall people, beware) which heads deep into the mountain. Inside, you can famously slide down the wooden chutes once used by the miners (watch out, or you'll get a bad case of "hot pants") all the way down to an artificial subterranean lake, once used to dissolve the rock salt. At the entrance to the mines you'll find an Iron Age cemetery and a restaurant. ⊠ *Salzberg* ☎ *06132/200–2490* ⊕ *www.salzwelten. at* ☞ *Funicular railway round-trip €7.90, one-way €4.70; mine and tour €14.50, combination cable car and salt mines €19.90* ⊙ *Late Apr.–late Sept., daily 9–4:30; late Sept.–Oct. 27, daily 9:30–3.*

Where to Stay & Eat

$$$ ✕▥ **Grüner Baum.** Glowing with a daffodil-yellow facade, sitting directly on the shore of the lake, and at the foot of a picture-perfect square, this traditional inn is one of Hallstatt's best. Dating from 1760, it was the house of the most important salt trader in town. Today, its renovated interiors are friendly and homey; family pets sit near the reception desk on 19th-century armchairs offering a special welcome. Rooms are simply furnished and are slowly being renovated; try to get one with a balcony facing the lake. ⊠ *Marktplatz 104, A-4830* ☎ *06134/8263* 🖷 *06134/8420* ⇱ *20 rooms* ⬩ *Restaurant, some minibars, lake, boating, bar, Internet; no a/c, no room phones, no TV in some rooms* ☰ *AE, DC, MC, V* ⊙ *Closed late Oct.–Apr.* ⦿ *MAP.*

$–$$ ✕▥ **Gasthof Zauner.** Crammed into a medieval bend in the street, this towering, multistoried, flower-bedecked chalet is set just a few steps up the hill from the front entrance of the Grüner Baum. Inside, the decor tends toward alpine woodwork. Charming, rustic guest rooms have beds with carved headboards and balconies overlooking the village and lake (the higher up you are, the better your view here). Atop the hotel is its well-known restaurant, famed for its regional dishes of lake fish and forest game—try the light cheese soup followed by the delicious grilled

Reinanke, a mild, local lake fish—and adored for its wood-paneled, ivy-hung center salon, which offers the quintessence of Hallstatt ambience. ⊠ *Marktplatz, A-4830* ☎ *06134/8246* 🖷 *06134/8246–8* ⊕ *www.zauner.hallstatt.net* ⤙ *12 rooms* ⚭ *Restaurant; no a/c* ▤ *DC, MC, V* ⊙ *Closed mid-Nov.–mid-Dec.* ⥾ *MAP.*

$ ✕▥ **Bräugasthof.** With an idyllic lakeside perch, this former 16th-cen-
Fodor'sChoice tury brewery, or Bräugasthof, offers distinctive charm. Outside is a
★ pretty terrace set with trees and umbrellaed tables. Beyond the beer-hall restaurant (open May to October), you'll find Hallstatt *gemütlichkeit* in excelsis—cozy nooked rooms, lead-glass windows, Tyrolean armoires, tapestried chairs, coved hallways, antique chandeliers. Upstairs, the guest rooms are fetching in their simplicity and give a taste of the "pension"-style rooms so prevalent in Hallstatt (the tourist office can often place visitors for overnights in actual homes in the village); most have wooden balconies. The Lobisser family are your hosts and can tell you all about the brewery's connection to Emperor Maximilian I. ⊠ *Seestrasse 120, A-4830* ☎ *06134/8221* 🖷 *06134/82214* ⊕ *www.brauhaus-lobisser. com* ⤙ *8 rooms* ⚭ *Restaurant; no a/c* ▤ *MC, V* ⊙ *Restaurant closed mid-Oct.–Easter* ⥾ *BP.*

Sports & Outdoor Activities

BOATING The lakes of the Salzkammergut are excellent for **canoeing** because most prohibit or limit powerboats. Try canoeing on the Hallstätter See. For information, contact **Alois Zopf** (⊠ Hauptstrasse 237, Bad Goisern ☎ 06135/8254 🖷 06135/7409). For white-water **kayaking** on the Traun River, call **Fritz Schiefermeyer** (☎ 06134/8338).

HIKING There are many great hiking paths around Hallstatt; contact the local tourist office for information about the path along the Echerntal to Waldbachstrub past pleasant waterfalls, or the climb to the Tiergartenhütte, continuing on to the Wiesberghaus and, two hours beyond, the Simony-Hütte, spectacularly poised at the foot of the Dachstein glacier. From here, mountain climbers begin the ascent of the Hoher Dachstein, the tallest peak of the Dachstein massif.

Dachstein Ice Caves

5 km (3 mi) east of Hallstatt.

★ ❿ Many travelers to Hallstatt make an excursion to one of the most impressive sights of the eastern Alps, the **Dachstein Ice Caves.** From Hallstatt, take the scenic road around the bottom of the lake to Obertraun; then follow the signs to the cable car, the *Dachsteinseilbahn,* which will ferry you up the mountain (you can hike all the way up to the caves, if you prefer). From the cable-car landing, a 15-minute hike up takes you to the entrance (follow signs to DACHSTEINEISHÖHLE) of the vast ice caverns, many of which are hundreds of years old and aglitter with ice stalactites and stalagmites, illuminated by an eerie light. The most famous sights are the **Rieseneishöhle** (Giant Ice Cave) and the **Mammuthöhle** (Mammoth Cave), but there are other caves and assorted frozen waterfalls. The cave entrance is at about 6,500 feet, still well below the 9,750-foot Dachstein peak farther south. Be sure to wear warm, weatherproof clothing and good shoes; inside the caves it is very cold, and outside, the slopes can be swept by chilling winds. ☎ *06134/8208* ⊕ *www.oberoesterreich.at/obertraun* ⌀ *Cable car round-trip €13.40, Giant Ice Cave €8.20, Mammoth Cave €8.20, combined ticket for both caves €12.70* ◷ *Mammoth Cave: late May–late Oct., daily 9:30–3; Giant Ice Cave: May 1–Oct. 15, daily 9:30–4, cable car: late May–Oct.*

Bad Aussee

⓫ *81 km (50 mi) southeast of Salzburg, 24 km (15 mi) west of Hallstatt.*

Following the bumpy old road westward (often closed in winter) from Hallstatt, you'll find yourself in company with the railroad and the Traun River (watch out for the precipitous 23% gradient at one point) and entering a region dotted with small lakes. The heart of this region is Bad Aussee, a great lure in the summertime, for the town's towering mountains and glacier-fed lake keep the area cool. Even in midsummer the waters of the lake are so cold that the presence of the municipal swimming pool is easy to account for. In the town, several miles from the lake, salt and mineral springs have been developed into a modern spa complex, yet the town retains much of its 15th- and 16th-century character in the narrow streets and older buildings, particularly in the upper reaches. To see its quaintest corners, head for Chumeckyplatz, lined with centuries-old houses. Here you will also find the town **Heimatmuseum**, set in a Gothic Kammerhof, renovated in early 2005; inside are exhibits on regional costume and the 18th-century landscape frescoes of the Kaiserssal room. ✉ *Hauptstrasse 48.*

The 1827 marriage of Archduke Johann (notoriously nicknamed the "father of Styria"—at last count, he had 1,200 descendants) to Anna Plochl, the daughter of the local postmaster, brought attention and a burst of new construction, including some lovely 19th-century villas. Of special note is the little late-Gothic hospital church, with its 16th-century frescoes. In the mid-19th century, musicians flocked here to relax and compose. Nikolaus Lenau worked on his version of *Faust* here, Mahler began his Fourth Symphony in 1899, and right after the turn of the century, Hugo von Hofmannsthal wrote his famous *Jedermann* play as well as the beloved libretti for Richard Strauss's operas, *Der Rosenkavalier* and *Ariadne auf Naxos.* You can walk along a special marked 8-mi-long *Via Artis* here and in Altaussee to see all the different locales that gave their inspiration to such famed creative souls. Aussee is a good base for hiking in the surrounding countryside in summer and for excellent skiing in winter. Many travelers come to Bad Aussee via the train from Salzburg, making a connection southward at the Attnang–Puchheim junction.

Where to Stay & Eat

¢ ✗ **Lewandofsky.** This popular café in the center of town is *the* place to meet, especially in summer when tables are spread under the chestnut trees overlooking the main square. Choose from tempting pastries (marzipan-topped gingerbread!) to go along with the excellent coffee. ✉ *Kurhausplatz 144* ☎ *03622/53205* ▭ *No credit cards* ◷ *Mon.–Sat. 8–8, Sun. 10–8.*

$$$$ ╳🖪 **Erzherzog Johann.** A festively golden yellow facade identifies this traditional house, which, though in the center of town, is quiet. A direct passageway connects the hotel to a spa next door, with a heated Olympic-size swimming pool and cure facilities. The hotel rooms are large and contemporary in style, and all have balconies. Extras include complimentary coffee and cake in the afternoon and a van that fetches guests at the train station free of charge. The elegant restaurant serves the best creative cooking in the area; look for poached salmon and wild rice or baby lamb with potato strudel. ⌧ *Kurhausplatz 62, A-8990* ☏ *03622/52507* 🖷 *03622/52507–680* ⊕ *www.erzherzogjohann.net* ⇗ *62 rooms* ♢ *Restaurant, minibars, indoor pool, gym, sauna, spa, bar, Internet; no a/c* ⊟ *AE, DC, MC, V* ☉ *Closed late Nov.–mid-Dec.* ¡◎¡ *MAP, FAP.*

★ **$** 🖪 **Villa Kristina.** In a lovely wooded park, this adorably charming 19th-century hotel comes replete with Tyrolean wood balconies, regional antiques, antlers, and trophies; its guest rooms are appropriately outfitted with older furniture. ⌧ *Altausseer Strasse 54, A-8990* ☏ *03622/52017* 🖷 *03622/52017* ⊕ *www.villakristina.at/kontakt1.htm* ⇗ *12 rooms* ♢ *Restaurant; no a/c* ⊟ *AE, DC, MC, V* ☉ *Closed Nov. and Apr.* ¡◎¡ *MAP.*

Grundlsee

⑫ *8 km (5 mi) west of Bad Aussee.*

From Bad Aussee journey into deepest, darkest Salzkammergut with a trip to the Styrian end of the region. Head to the Grundlsee, a small, scenically charming lake and take, from its eastern end, a walk of 15 minutes to arrive at nearly hidden, even smaller Toplitzsee. Legend has it that the Nazis loaded it up with their golden plunder. Diver teams of the Allied forces, however, came up empty. The journey's end feel of the area beckoned to various aristos and musicians, most famously Richard Strauss, who often spent holidays here.

Where to Stay & Eat

★ **¢–$** ╳🖪 **Gasthof Ladner.** Located 3 km (2 mi) east of Grundlsee village, this is one of the oldest family-owned inns and cafés in Austria: Empress Maria Theresa herself ordained its opening back in 1745 and other Austrian royals later made merry here. The great composer Richard Strauss often came for a visit and ultimately immortalized this inn in the "Ball at Ladner" scene in his (not his last!) opera, *Intermezzo.* For all its pedigree, the inn itself is unpretentious and rather modest. Enjoy the rustic furnished rooms with the view of the lake from the balconies. When dining (of course, the local *Saibling* charr or trout with parsley potatoes), be sure to sit in the old dark and wooden Erzherzog Johann Stube. You can channel the spirit of the room, in which Archduke Johann famously met his beloved Anna for the first time. ⌧ *Gössl 1, A-8993 Grundlsee* ☏ *03622/8211* 🖷 *03622/82114* ⊕ *http://members.eunet.at/ladner/* ⇗ *10 rooms* ♢ *Restaurant; no a/c* ⊟ *AE, MC, V* ¡◎¡ *MAP.*

Altaussee

⓭ *4 km (2½ mi) north of Bad Aussee.*

Taking a fairly steep road from Bad Aussee, you'll find Altaussee tucked away at the end of a lake cradled by gentle mountains. This is one of the most magical spots of the Salzkammergut. Over the years it attracted so many fine musicians and writers who came for inspiration (Johannes Brahms, Arthur Schnitzler, and Hugo von Hofmannsthal, to name just a few) that author Alex Storm famously called the lake "an inkwell into which we all dip our quills." Or, as Austrian poet Friedrich Torberg put it: "Who ever comes to Altaussee does not want to go anywhere else, and if he would, he couldn't. Altaussee is a crowning conclusion. The mountains not only lie around the lake, they surround and protect it. Like a fortress, they make you feel cozy and secure."

During the war, Nazi leaders were ordered to store stolen art in underground caverns near Altaussee. In their hurry to get the job done, they skipped a few details; one story has it that a famous painting from Vienna, possibly a Rubens or a Rembrandt, was overlooked and spent the remaining war years on the porch of a house near the entrance to the mines. At the end of the war, Allied forces were directed to the mines by the local populace, and, once unsealed, the caverns released a trove unlikely to be assembled in one place ever again.

The town is completely unspoiled, perfect for those who simply want an Alpine idyll: to do nothing, hike in the meadows, climb the slopes, or row on the lake. The end of May to the beginning of June is perhaps the best time to visit; the field flowers have burst forth and Bad Aussee holds its famous Narcissus Festival, which includes a procession to Altaussee.

Salt is still dug in the nearby Sandling Mountain, and the **mines** are open to visitors. Check with the tourist office or phone for details of guided tours. ☎ *06132/200–2551 or 0664/1034185* ✉ *€11.50* ☉ *Late Apr.–late Sept., daily 10–4; late Sept.–late Oct., daily 10–2.*

If time allows and you feel fit enough, do the approximately 2½-hour walk up the **Loser Mountain** that begins at the end of Altaussee (follow the colored marks and occasional signs), where at the top of the Panorama Strasse you can rest and refuel at your choice of two restaurants: the cafeteria-style Loser-Berg (at the very top of the mountain) or the Loserhütte. Richard Strauss also walked up the Loser, which is said to have inspired his great *Alpensinfonie* (Alpine Symphony). A much easier way to reach the top of the Panorama Strasse is to drive, but you pay for the privilege—€6.70 for your car with two persons.

Where to Stay & Eat

¢ ✕⌂ **Loserhütte.** A short walk down a well-marked path just before the crest of Loser Mountain leads to this chalet restaurant with a wraparound terrace affording panoramic views of the surrounding mountains and the sparkling lake below. Dishes are local and hearty, such as the *Pfandl,* a mixture of home-fried potatoes, pork, and cheese served in a blackened skillet. Don't confuse this restaurant with the Loser-Berg cafeteria, which is a little bit farther up the mountain. The Loserhütte also has seven simply furnished bedrooms for overnighters on the floor above. ⊠ *Fischerndorf 80, A-8992* ☎☎ *03622/71202* ☜ *7 rooms* ⛄ *Restaurant, hiking; no a/c* ☰ *No credit cards* ⊗ *Closed Nov.–mid-Dec. and late Apr.–mid-May* ⍥ *MAP, FAP.*

$$ ⊞ **Herrenhaus Hubertushof.** This stunning former hunting lodge with green shutters is perched on a hillside high above the town. Run by its indomitable owner, Countess Strasoldo, it is a treasure of a home, with gleaming Biedermeier and Rococo antiques, wood-beamed ceilings, and brass chandeliers. Bedrooms are either country rustic with carved cedar headboards or furnished with elegant, faux French provincial pieces. Breakfast is served on the terrace overlooking the lake and surrounding mountains. To reach the Hubertushof, turn off the main road in Altaussee at the Hotel Tyrol and go straight, continuing to your right at the fork. ⊠ *Puchen 86, A-8992* ☎ *03622/71280* 🖷 *06322/71280–80* ⊕ *www.herrenhaus-hubertushof.at* ☜ *9 rooms* ⛄ *Hiking, bar; no a/c* ☰ *MC, V* ⊗ *Closed mid-Oct.–Dec. 26, Jan. 10–31, and varying wks Mar.–May 14* ⍥ *BP.*

> **en route** To get back to Bad Ischl, your best bet is to return to Bad Aussee and then take Route 145 north. It's only 28 km (18 mi), but a great deal of this consists of precipitous ups and downs, the highest point being at 3,200 feet before you head down through the Pötschen Pass. Not surprisingly, the views are spectacular; don't miss the lookout point at a hairpin turn at Unter, far above the Hallstätter See.

SALZKAMMERGUT A TO Z

To research prices, get advice from other travelers, and book travel arrangements, visit www.fodors.com.

AIR TRAVEL

The Lake District is closer to Salzburg than to Linz, but ground transportation is such that there is little preference for one departure point over the other. The Salzburg airport is about 53 km (33 mi) from Bad Ischl, heart of the Salzkammergut; the Linz airport (Hörsching) is about 75 km (47 mi). Both cities have good connections to European destinations but no flights to or from North America. A number of charter lines fly into Salzburg, including some from the United Kingdom.

BIKE TRAVEL

Much of the Salzkammergut is rather hilly if you are just a casual cyclist, but you'll find reasonably good cycling country around the lakes, including the Wolfgangsee (though Route 158 can become quite noisy and fume-filled). Sports shops throughout the area rent bikes; local tourist offices can point you to the right place. You can cycle the 14 km (9 mi) from St. Wolfgang to Bad Ischl on back roads.

BUS TRAVEL

Rail service is fairly good, but won't get you off the beaten path. Where the trains don't go, the post office or railway buses do, so if you allow enough time, you can cover virtually all the area by public transportation. Check at tourist offices and at railroad stations in the Salzkammergut and in Linz for the availability of the "Salzkammergut Ticket" (€4.90), good for a 30% reduction on rail travel, boat trips, mountain and cable railways, cave tours, salt mines, and scenic roads. It's valid from May to October.

The main bus routes through the region are: Bad Aussee, to Gründlsee; Bad Ischl, to Gosau, Hallstatt, Salzburg, and St. Wolfgang; Mondsee, to St. Gilgen and Salzburg; St. Gilgen, to Mondsee; Salzburg, to Bad Ischl, Mondsee, St. Gilgen, and Strobl.

🚍 Bus Information **Zentrale Busauskunft** ☎ 05/1717-3 ⊕ www.oebb.at.

CAR TRAVEL

Driving is by far the easiest and most convenient way to reach the Lake District; traffic is excessive only on weekends (although it can be slow on some narrow lakeside stretches). From Salzburg you can take Route 158 east to Fuschl, St. Gilgen, and Bad Ischl or the A1 autobahn to Mondsee. Coming from Vienna or Linz, the A1 passes through the northern part of the Salzkammergut; get off at the Steyermühl exit or the Regau exit and head south on Route 144/145 to Gmunden, Bad Ischl, Bad Goisern, and Bad Aussee. From the Seewalchen exit, take Route 152 down the east side of the Attersee, instead of the far less scenic Route 151 down the west side. Remember: gasoline is expensive in Austria.

EMERGENCY SERVICES Call 120 for the automobile club ÖAMTC.

EMERGENCIES

If you need a doctor and speak no German, ask your hotel how best to obtain assistance.

🚑 Emergency services **Ambulance** ☎ 144. **Fire** ☎ 122. **Medical Service–St. Johannsspital-Landeskrankenanstalten** ⊠ Müllner Hauptstrasse 48, Salzburg ☎ 0662/44820. **Police** ☎ 133.

SPORTS & OUTDOOR ACTIVITIES

CANOEING Intersport Steinkogler and Pro-Travel are two helpful firms for canoers in the Salzkammergut region.

🚩**Intersport Steinkogler** ⊠ Salzburger Strasse 3, Bad Ischl ☎ 06132/23655. **Pro-Travel** ⊠ Pilgerstrasse 152, St. Wolfgang ☎ 06138/2525 🖷 06138/3054.

FISHING The Salzkammergut is superb fishing country, whether casting or trolling—the main season runs June–September—but you will need a license. Many townships have their own licensing offices. A number of hotels in the Altaussee–Bad Aussee area have packages that combine a week's stay with the fishing license; contact Steirischer Tourismus for details and booking.

🎣**Attersee** Matthäus Hollerweger ⊠ Esso station, Nussdorf ☎ 07666/8063-15. **Bad Ischl** Ischler Waffen, Manfred Zeitler ⊠ Schröpferplatz 4 ☎ 06132/23351. **Ebensee** ⊠ Langbathsee 1, Baier/Landgasthof in der Kreh ☎ 06133/6235 🖷 06133/520852. **Family Faber** ⊠ Thalgaustrasse 27, Mondsee ☎ 06232/4238. **Gasthof Steinmaurer**

✉ Traunsteinstrasse 23, Gmunden ☎ 07612/704888. **Hallstatt** Zentrasport Janu ✉ Seestrasse 50 ☎ 06134/8298-0. **Radsport Hofer** ✉ Herzog-Odilo-Strasse 52, Mondsee ☎ 06232/3121. **Sportsware Höller** ✉ Kammerhofg. 6, Gmunden ☎ 07612/64222. **Steirischer Tourismus** ✉ St. Peter-Hauptstrasse 243, A-8042 Graz ☎ 0316/4003-0 🖨 0316/4003-1. **St. Wolfgang** Fischerhaus Höplinger ✉ Dr.-Rais-Promenade 79 ☎ 06138/2241.

SKIING   The Salzkammergut offers challenging runs for experts and gentle slopes for novices. The main ski center is in St. Gilgen. Great cross-country trails can be found in Fuschl and Strobl. There's a 15-km (9-mi) high-altitude trail in Postalm. In the Ausseerland region you'll find powder-perfect skiing lessons in Altaussee at the Helmut Kaiss Ski School.

🎿 **Fuschl and Strobl** ✉ Fuschl am See, A-5330 ☎ 06226/8250 🖨 06226/8650. **Helmut Kaiss Ski School** ✉ Altaussee, A-8992 ☎ 03622/71310 🖨 03622/71701. **St. Gilgen** ✉ Gilgen, A-5340 ☎ 06227/2348 🖨 06227/72679.

WATER SPORTS   There's every kind of water sport in the Salzkammergut, from windsurfing to sailing. You can water-ski at Strobl and St. Wolfgang on the Wolfgangsee and at most towns on the Attersee and Traunsee. At Ebensee, check with Diving School Gigl, which also offers skin diving. In Gmunden, contact the Wasserskischule. You can explore the mysterious depths of the Hallstätter See by scuba diving with Tauchschule und Bergefirma Zauner.

🎿 **Diving School Gigl** ✉ Strandbadstrasse 12 ☎ 06133/6381 🖨 06133/6386. **Tauchschule und Bergefirma Zauner** ✉ Markt 113 ☎ 06134/8286. **Wasserskischule** ✉ Traunsteinstrasse ☎ 07612/63602.

TOURS

BUS TOURS   Day-long tours of the Salzkammergut, offered by Dr. Richard/Albus/Salzburg Sightseeing Tours and Salzburg Panorama Tours, whisk you all too quickly from Salzburg to St. Gilgen, St. Wolfgang, and Mondsee. Full-day tours to Salzburg from Vienna pass through Gmunden and the Traunsee, Bad Ischl, the Wolfgangsee, St. Gilgen, and Fuschlsee, but you can't see much from a bus window.

🎿 Fees & Schedules **Dr. Richard/Albus/Salzburg Sightseeing Tours** ✉ Mirabellplatz 2, A-5020 Salzburg ☎ 0662/881616 🖨 0662/878776. **Cityrama Sightseeing** ✉ Börsengasse 1, A-1010 Vienna ☎ 01/534-13-0 🖨 01/534-1328. **Salzburg Panorama Tours** ✉ Schrannengasse 2/2, A-5020 Salzburg ☎ 0662/883211 🖨 0662/871628. **Vienna Sightseeing Tours** ✉ Stelzhammergasse 4/11, A-1031 Vienna ☎ 01/712-4683-0 🖨 01/714-1141.

TRAIN TRAVEL

The geography of the area means that rail lines run mainly north–south. Trains run from Vöcklabruck to Seewalchen at the top end of the Attersee and from Attnang-Puchheim to Gmunden, Bad Ischl, Hallstatt, Bad Aussee, and beyond. Both starting points are on the main east–west line between Salzburg and Linz.

🎿 Train Information **ÖBB–Österreichisches Bundesbahn** ☎ 05/1717 ⊕ www.oebb.at.

VISITOR INFORMATION

Most towns in the Salzkammergut have their own *Fremdenverkehrsamt* (tourist office), which are listed below by town name. The main tourist offices for the provinces and regions covered in this chapter are Salzkammergut/Salzburger Land, Styria, Tourismusverband Ausseerland, and Upper Austria. Styria, Upper Austria, and Salzburg Province all comprise the backbone of the Dachstein range.

Tourist Information Altaussee ✉ Fischerndorf 44, A-8992 ☎ 03622/71643 🖷 03622/716437 ⊕ www.ausseerland.at. **Bad Aussee** ✉ Bahnhofstrasse 138 (entrance on Pratergasse), A-8990 ☎ 03622/52323 🖷 03622/52323−4 ⊕ www.badaussee.at. **Bad Ischl** ✉ Bahnhofstrasse 6, A-4820 ☎ 06132/277570 🖷 06132/27757−77 ⊕ www.badischl.at. **Gmunden** ✉ Am Graben 2, A-4810 ☎ 07612/64305 🖷 07612/71410 ⊕ www.oberoesterreich.at/gmunden. **Gosau am Dachstein** ✉ Tourismusverband Gosau, A-4824 ☎ 06136/8295 🖷 06136/8255 ⊕ www.gosau.at. **Hallstatt** ✉ Seestrasse 169, A-4830 ☎ 06134/8208 🖷 06134/8352 ⊕ www.oberoesterreich.at/hallstatt. **Mondsee** ✉ Dr.-Franz-Müller-Strasse 3, A-5310 ☎ 06232/2270 🖷 06232/4470 ⊕ www.mondsee.org. **St. Gilgen** ✉ Mozartplatz 1, A-5340 ☎ 06227/2348 🖷 06227/7267−9 ⊕ www.wolfgangsee.at. **St. Wolfgang** ✉ Au 140, A-5360 ☎ 06138/8003 🖷 06138/8003−81 ⊕ www.wolfgangsee.at. **Salzkammergut/Salzburger Land** ✉ Wirerstrasse 10, A-4820 Bad Ischl ☎ 06132/26909−0 🖷 06132/26909−14 ⊕ www.salzkammergut.at. **Tourismusverband Ausseerland** ✉ Chlumeckyplatz 44, A-8890 Bad Aussee ☎ 03622/54040−0 🖷 03622/540407 ⊕ www.ausseerland.at. **Upper Austria** ✉ Schillerstrasse 50, A-4010 Linz ☎ 0732/6002−219 🖷 0732/600220 ⊕ www.oberoesterreich.at.

CARINTHIA

7

SEE CARINTHIA'S "RIVIERA" REGION
from grandly restored cruiser
S.S. Thalia ⇨*p.332*

CHECK OUT THE CRAGGY VIEWS
from Disney's "Snow White"
Hochosterwitz castle ⇨*p.351*

PREPARE TO RAVE ABOUT
Brahms' fave, the Schloss Leonstain hotel ⇨*p.340*

DIP INTO A SPA BATH
in the-cure's-the-thing Warmbad Villach ⇨*p.347*

WANDER THROUGH STONE CHURCHES
and medieval marvels
in storybook Friesach ⇨*p.350*

SUPERPLUSH YOUR STAY
with an overnight at the Palais Porcia ⇨*p.338*

ENJOY EVERY STYLE OF MUSIC
at Ossiach's Carinthian Summer Festival ⇨*p.347*

Updated by
Bonnie Dodson

WHEN MANY PEOPLE THINK OF AUSTRIA, they imagine the superb, mountainous terrain of Tirol with its snowy peaks and powdery slopes perfect for skiing and dotted with storybook Alpine chalets clustered around a village church. Of course, the heavily touristed cities of Salzburg and Vienna also come to mind. But there is another, less well known part of Austria which beckons with its own set of spectacular mountain ranges, abundant forests, and some of the most gorgeous, glass-clear resort lakes in all Europe. This is the southern province of Carinthia—Kärnten to the Austrians—located directly above Italy and Slovenia.

To give an idea of the terrain, Carinthia is protected in the northwest by the vast Hohe Tauern range and the impossibly high and mighty Grossglockner. Along its northern borders are the bulky Nockberge and the massive crests of the Noric mountain range, and to the east are the grassy meadows on the slopes of the Saualpe and Koralpe. Completing the circle in the south and bordering Slovenia and Italy, are the steep, craggy Karawanken mountains and Carnic Alps. Lying serenely in the valleys between these rocky mountains is the long, meandering Drau River and more than 100 lakes, including the most well-known and largest, the Wörther See, as well as the Ossiacher See and Faaker See. Because of its close proximity to Italy and the bulwark of mountains that protect it from the cold winds of the north, the Carinthian climate is milder than the rest of Austria, and it also boasts more sunshine. Consequently, the lakes maintain an average summer temperature of between 75 and 82 degrees Fahrenheit.

In addition to all this, ancient castles, intact or in partial ruin, are perched on jutting crags or nestled in valleys, with several of them the scene of summer outdoor concerts. There are also fine ski resorts, assorted medieval strongholds, and art-filled churches. It's no wonder Carinthia is one of the top tourist destinations for Italians, Germans, and Swiss, and with an ever-growing number coming from Britain, it's easy to predict it won't be unknown to Americans for long.

Art lovers will immediately head to such architectural landmarks as the Romanesque Gurk Cathedral, a host of Baroque town halls, and the medieval fantasy of the 9th-century castle of Hochosterwitz. You would not be at all surprised if a dragon rose from a puff of smoke above its ramparts, or to see troubadours warbling at its entrance. Most delightfully, there is also the gaiety bubbling up in such waterside resorts as Maria Wörth and Velden, set within the spectacular pleasure-land that is the "Austrian Riviera." As the province's summer season is custom-tailored for bicycling, fishing, hiking, and water sports, reservations for the resort towns need to be booked well in advance. Carinthia is a multiethnic area, whose three nationalities—Austrian (German), Slovenian, and Italian—are gradually developing pride in their shared roots. Since post–World War I days, when parts of Carinthia were almost given away to the new Yugoslav state, the spirit in the land has changed. It seems the more Europe grows together, the more a sense of solidarity and regional identity deepens. Klagenfurt is the official seat of the government, but over the course of time Villach, an equally attractive small city, has emerged as the "secret" capital, especially when the spirit of

Carnival captivates Austria; the Villach Carnival reigns supreme in the week before Lent. Its costume parades, floats, parodies, and cabarets are now televised annually for international viewing. Another popular event is the Carinthian Summer Festival, held in Villach and Ossiach and in various other spots in the region during July and August.

Exploring Carinthia

Reputedly founded by the fairy goddess Fata Morgana as a retreat from her main Italian haunting grounds, just across the border, Carinthia is landmarked by its two main cities, Klagenfurt, the regional capital, and Villach, the main transport hub to the eastern Alps. But venture off the main byways and you'll sense that much of the Carinthian countryside seems so hidden away you won't find it on maps. If you approach Carinthia from Vienna not by the official A2 autobahn that passes through Graz but on Route 83 from the Murtal in the north, passing through Bad Einöd and Friesach, you will be taking one of the main gateways into Carinthia. The broad, open countryside you cross from there leads you to the region's main mecca for sun worshippers, the Wörther See. But if you approach the province from any other direction, you will get a very different impression—that of an area walled in by towering mountains, surmountable only through a few, mostly high passes, notably the Turracher Höhe pass, a scenic glory, which is found along Route 95 or the A10 autobahn, which snakes from Salzburg through tunnels under the Tauern mountains. Whichever route you take—for the shortest itinerary, tackle the Austrian Riviera; for a longer stay, Villach makes a good base—your ultimate Carinthian destination will deliver a host of rewards. Begin with the region around Klagenfurt and the adjacent Austrian Riviera lake district. Then take off for Villach and the storybook Gurktal district.

About the Restaurants & Hotels

Thanks to the region's many lakes and rivers, this is above all fish country: carp, pike, perch, eel, bream, crawfish (in a rather short season), and, best of all, a large variety of trout. Austrian brook trout and rainbow trout are delicious. The most popular way of serving them is "blue," the whole fish simmered in a court bouillon and served with drawn butter. Or try it *Müllerin*—sautéed in butter until a crisp brown. In summer, try cold smoked trout with lemon or horseradish as a delicate hors d'oeuvre. Carinthia's basically peasant tradition, however, is also reflected in its culinary specialties, such as *Kärntner Käsnudeln* (giant ravioli stuffed with a ricotta-like local cheese and a whisper of mint), *Sterz* (polenta served either sweet or salty), and *Hauswürste* (smoked or air-cured hams and sausages, available at butcher shops). Through much of Carinthia you'll discover that, other than simple Gasthäuser, pizzerias, and the ubiquitous Chinese restaurants, most dining spots are not independent establishments, but belong to country inns.

Accommodations range from luxurious lakeside resorts to small country inns, and even include guest houses without private baths. Summers are never too hot, and it cools off delightfully at night, which means that most hotels are not equipped with air-conditioning.

Carinthia could quite rightly be designated "Extract of Austria," since it contains a greater concentration of Austria's charms than any of the country's other provinces. Many routine-fatigued Viennese spend hours dreaming of its Austrian Riviera, where waterside gaiety emanates from such resorts as Maria Wörth and Velden; the richly scenic cities of Klagenfurt and Villach beckon; and luminous art treasures await, such as Gurk's great Romanesque cathedral and the iconic model for the Gothic castle in Walt Disney's *Snow White*, Hochosterwitz Castle.

Numbers in the text correspond to numbers in the margin and on the Carinthia map.

If you have 3 days

If time is limited, head to the Austrian Riviera, the perfect balm for travelers who wish simply to sun and soak. Start off with a visit to the provincial capital **Klagenfurt** ❶ before heading out to the most popular lake, the Wörther See. You can make stops along the way at resorts such as **Krumpendorf** ❷ and **Pörtschach** ❸, before spending the night and next day in ☒ **Maria Wörth** ❹, with its postcard-perfect spired chapel overlooking the lake. For the next night, head to chic ☒ **Velden** ❺. On your final day, take in the idyllic town of Maria Gail and **Egg am Faaker See** ❻.

If you have 7 days

If you plan on a week's worth of wonders, on your third day continue west into ☒ **Villach** ❼—one of Carinthia's most historic cities—for your next overnight. Start your visit in this town nestled on the banks of the Drau River by wandering through the meandering lanes of the Altstadt (Old Town). Spend the night in the city or head for the nearby spa of **Warmbad Villach** ❽, where you can relax with a massage or soak in the soothing hot springs and then check out the imposing ruins of Landskron Castle. Spend your fourth day enjoying the resort town of ☒ **Ossiach** ❾ and its 11th-century monastery, where the sounds of music waft softly through summer nights during the annual music festival. After your overnight, your fifth day is packed, so get an early start on the day's full schedule of sightseeing attractions, including the medieval city of **Feldkirchen** ❿; the massive Romanesque cathedral at **Gurk** ⓫; and a stop in **Strassburg** ⓬, formerly the seat of the bishopric. On your fifth night pull into ☒ **Friesach** ⓭, where it's easy to imagine lords and ladies descended from the Middle Ages living in this village. On the sixth day discover **St. Veit an der Glan** ⓯, Carinthia's capital until the 16th century; then move on to the amazing castle-fortress of **Hochosterwitz** ⓮. For your last evening and day, return to ☒ **Klagenfurt** ❶.

Some hotels offer half-board, which includes dinner in addition to buffet breakfast (although most $$$$ hotels will charge extra for breakfast). The half-board room rate is usually an extra €15–€30 per person. Occasionally quoted room rates for hotels already include half-board accommodations, though a "discounted" rate is usually available if you prefer not to take the evening meal. Inquire when booking.

WHAT IT COSTS In euros					
	$$$$	$$$	$$	$	¢
RESTAURANTS	over €22	€18–€22	€13–€17	€7–€12	under €7
HOTELS	over €175	€135–€175	€100–€135	€70–€100	under €70

Restaurant prices are per person for a main course at dinner. Hotel prices are for a standard double room in high season, including taxes and service. Assume that hotels operate on the European Plan (EP, with no meal provided) unless we note that they use the Breakfast Plan (BP), Modified American Plan (MAP, with breakfast and dinner daily, known as "halb pension"), or Full American Plan (FAP, or "voll pension," with three meals a day). Higher prices (inquire when booking) prevail for any meal plans.

Timing

To see the province in its best festive dress of blue and emerald lakes framed by wooded hills and rocky peaks, and also do some swimming, come between mid-May and early October. Early spring, when the colors are purest and the crowds not yet in evidence, and fall, are perhaps the best times for quiet sightseeing.

KLAGENFURT & THE SOUTHERN LAKES

Because of the resorts, the elegant people, the cultural events, and the emphasis on dawn-to-dawn indulgences, the region surrounding Carinthia's pleasure lakes vies with the Salzkammergut for the nickname "Austria's Riviera." They have become tourist draws because of one reason: they are flat-out beautiful. The most popular of the Fünf Schwesterseen (Five Sister Lakes) is certainly the central lake, the Wörther See, sprinkled with such resorts as Krumpendorf, Velden, and Maria Wörth—at one time called the quietest village in all Austria but subsequently overrun by hordes of tourists. The Wörther See is 17 km (10½ mi) long and the warmest of Carinthia's large lakes; people swim here as early as May. A great way to see the lake is from one of the boats that cruise from end to end, making frequent stops along the way; try to book passage on the S.S. *Thalia,* built in 1908 and now beautifully restored. You can follow the north shore to Velden by way of Pörtschach, or swing south and take the less traveled scenic route; in any case, you should visit picturesque Maria Wörth on the south shore. For schedule information and details, check with the Wörthersee Erlebnis Schifffahrt (⊕ www. woerthersee.com) or the Villach tourist office.

Klagenfurt

★ ❶ *329 km (192 mi) southwest of Vienna, 209 km (130 mi) southeast of Salzburg.*

Klagenfurt became the provincial capital in 1518, so most of the delightful sights you can see date from the 16th century or later. However, the Klagenfurt of today is pulsing with newfound excitement, having become a virtual hotbed of design, with a group of attention-getting Carinthian architects breathing new life into old buildings. The town is also an excellent base for excursions to the rest of Carinthia. In the city center you

Lakeside Elegance Set just miles away from Italy, studded with picture-book lakes, and adorned with some of Austria's most elegant and enchanting resort hotels, the southern lake region of Carinthia easily gives the famous Salzkammergut lake district a run for its money. One of the peaks of Austrian *dolce far niente* is reclining on your chaise longue on a flower-bedecked bathing pier at one of the soigne castle-hotels of Pörtschach, Velden, or Maria Wörth. For comfort and smartness, these hotels lack for nothing and make the most alluring retreats—even on a wet day.

7

Hiking Like the rest of the country, the hills and mountains scattered across Carinthia have a wealth of hiking opportunities (bookstores in your resort will have hiking maps of the area). There is a network of footpaths comprising more than 625 mi and ranging from gentle to strenuous. There are even several "geo-trails" which offer glimpses of fossilized shells from the time when a primeval sea covered the area. Most tourist regions have marked trails and local hiking maps, called (*Wanderkarte*), including treks to the many castle ruins which dot the landscape, and more leisurely strolls on well-marked lakeside paths. If you are planning high-altitude hiking, remember that cable cars tend to be closed for repairs out of season. Always take protection against the rain, an extra layer of clothing, and tell your hotel desk where you are going. A nice surprise: rain in the valleys may give way to sunshine above 3,000 feet.

Water Sports In winter, Austrians love to ski; in summer, they take to sail-skiing—just one of the many reasons they flock to the Carinthian lakes during warm weather. The Austrian Riviera resorts are a paradise for water sports—from windsurfing to sailing—with lakes that have public beaches and water pure enough to drink. Swimmers delight in the late summer water temperatures, which can reach 25°C (75°F)—due to the existence of subterranean thermal springs. Most beaches also have wading or supervised areas for small children. To avoid the crowds, book at a hotel that has its own private beach—most do.

Let It Snow Winter brings a lot of sunshine with the snow, and sporting Austrians—from nursery-schoolers up to professionals—flock to Carinthia. If you want to attend ice surfing classes, you can head to Feld am See for a weekend of instruction. If you don't want to give up tennis just because it's winter, then you can strap on your skates and play ice tennis. If this isn't challenging enough, ice climbing in the Liesertal and Maltatal valleys, where ice is guaranteed until mid-March, is always an option. Compared to the chic skiing destinations of St. Anton and Kitzbühel, Carinthia offers good terrain and facilities with much lower prices. The skiing season in the mountain area lasts from December to March, although high up in the Hohe Tauern it extends to late spring and even early June, for the Grossglockner glacier ski racing. Carinthia has slopes of all degrees of difficulty, from the gentler ones for novices to the seriously challenging for the experienced Alpine skier—since the mighty Grossglockner backs into the region, some ski runs even feature vertical drops of over 4,000 feet. When the altitude gets this high, the slopes are treeless. For more scenic

runs, head for Villach and its environs, particularly the slopes of the Kanzel-
höhe, which feature marvelous views of the Karawanken range. There are at
least 20 ski towns in Carinthia. To determine which is best for you, contact the
Austrian Tourist Board. Whether raw beginner or downhill racer, chances are
you will ski down slopes of unforgettable loveliness.

can hardly overlook the *Lindwurm*, Klagenfurt's emblematic dragon with
a curled tail beside a tower, which adorns the fountain on Neuer Platz
(New Square). Legend has it that the town was founded on the spot where
the beast was destroyed by resident peasants back in the days of yore
(but the notion of Klagenfurt's dragon became more intriguing when
the fossilized cranium of a prehistoric rhinoceros was found nearby).
Through the Kramergasse you reach the longish **Alter Platz,** the city's
oldest square and the center of a pleasant pedestrian area with tiny streets
and alleys. South of Neuer Platz (take Karfreitstrasse and turn left on
Lidmansky-Gasse) is the **Domkirche** (cathedral), completed as a Protestant church in 1591, given over to the Jesuits and reconsecrated in
1604, and finally declared a cathedral in 1787. The 18th-century side-
altar painting of St. Ignatius by Paul Troger, the great Viennese Rococo
painter and teacher, is a fine example of the qualities of transparency
and light he introduced to painting.

North of Neuer Platz (go along Kramergasse for two blocks, then angle
left to the Pfarrplatz), is the parish church of **St. Egyd,** with its eye-catching totem-pole bronze carving by Austrian avant-garde artist Ernst
Fuchs in the second chapel on the right. In the next chapel is the crypt
of Julian Green (1900–98), the noted French-born American novelist
whose works include *The Closed Garden* and *The Other One*. On a visit
to Klagenfurt several years before his death for the production of one
of his plays, he perceived the city as a sanctuary of peace in the world
and decided he wanted to be buried here.

One of the most notable sights of the city is the **Landhaus** (district government headquarters), with its towers and court with arcaded stairways.
It was completed in 1591, and at the time formed a corner of the city
wall. The only interior on view is the dramatic **Grosser Wappensaal** (Great
Hall of Coats of Arms), which contains 665 coats of arms of Carinthia's
landed gentry and a stirring rendition of the Fürstenstein investiture ceremony portrayed by Fromiller, the most important Carinthian painter
of the Baroque period. ✉ *Alter Platz* ☎ *0463/57757* ⊕ *www.*
landesmuseum-ktn.at ✆ *€4* ⊙ *Apr.–Oct., daily 9–5.*

From Klagenfurt, bypass the autobahn and instead take Villacher Strasse
(Route 83) to the Wörther See, Austria's great summer-resort area.
↻ You'll pass by the entrancing **Minimundus** park, literally "miniature
world," with more than 175 1:25 scale models of such structures as the
White House, Independence Hall, the Eiffel Tower, and the Gur-Emir
Mausoleum from Samarkand (Uzbekistan). ✉ *Villacher Strasse 241*
☎ *0463/21194* 🖷 *0463/21194–60* ⊕ *www.minimundus.at* ✆ *€11*
⊙ *Apr. and Oct., daily 9–5; May, June, and Sept., daily 9–6; July–Aug.,*
daily 9–9 PM.

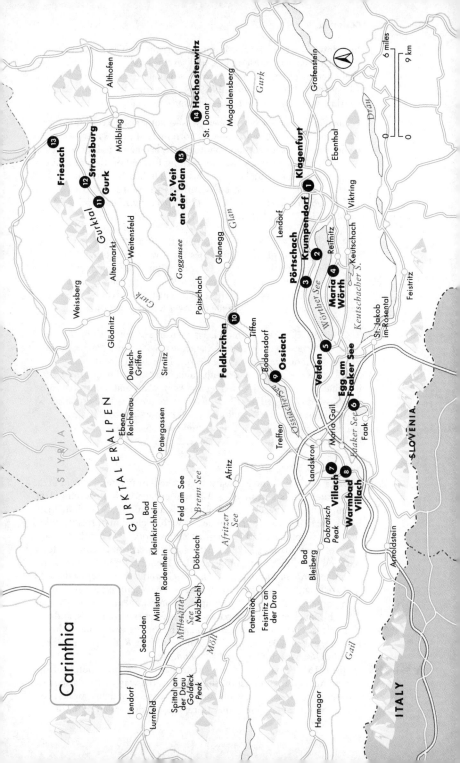

Just down the road from Minimundus is the **Reptilien Zoo,** featuring crocodiles, cobras, rattlesnakes, and several kinds of hairy spiders, as well as colorful fish from the nearby Wörther See. ⊠ *Villacher Strasse 237* ☎ *0463/23425* 🖷 *0463/23425–14* ⊕ *www.reptilienzoo.at* 🖾 *€8.50* ⊙ *May–Oct., daily 8–6; Dec.–Apr., daily 9–5; closed Nov.*

Located in the house where Robert Musil—author of the celebrated novel *The Man Without Qualities*—was born in 1880, the **Robert Musil Museum** displays documents and photographs belonging to him, as well as first editions of his work. Musil's writing focused on the cultural disintegration and spiritual crisis of his day. He fled Nazi-occupied Austria in the 1930s and died penniless in Switzerland in 1942. ⊠ *Bahnhofstrasse 50* ☎ *0463/501429* ⊕ *www.musilmuseum.at* 🖾 *Free* ⊙ *Mon.–Fri. 10–5, Sat. 10–2.*

off the beaten path

PYRAMIDENKOGEL – On the shore of the Keutschacher See, about 8 km (5 mi) west of Klagenfurt, lies the town of Keutschach, with the Romanesque church of St. George, a Baroque castle, and an 800-year-old linden tree. A winding 5-km (3-mi) road ascends to the observation tower atop the 2,790-foot Pyramidenkogel; from here on a clear day you can see out over half of Carinthia.

KLOPEINERSEE – The warmest lake in Austria (if not in all Europe) is about a 30-minute drive east of Klagenfurt. With water temperatures averaging 28 degrees Celsius (82 degrees Fahrenheit) from spring to fall, it's a popular spot for sunbathing. Surrounded by gentle mountains, the lake is 1½ mi long and ½ mi wide, and motorboats are not allowed. To reach the Klopeinersee, take the west Völkermarkt/Tainach exit from the A2 autobahn and follow signs to the lake. For information on lakeside hotels and pensions, contact Klopeinersee Tourismus.

Where to Stay & Eat

$$$$ ✕ **Dolce Vita.** Small and exclusive, this tucked-away establishment in the city center offers cutting-edge Austrian cuisine with an Italian slant. Though the tiny peach-walled interior is appealing, the secluded garden is the real draw. Your meal begins with a selection of freshly baked breads and spreads, and perhaps an *amuse bouche* of a colorful sampling of soups arranged like an artist's palette: saffron potato, white asparagus, cucumber basil, and gazpacho. Frequent offerings include the Venetian *sarde in saor* (sardines in a sweet and sour sauce) or the silky tagliatelle with prosciutto and asparagus. The restaurant is a stickler for using organic products, so fish appears on the menu only if it's wild. Look for chicken breast prepared with sage, cherry tomatoes, and zucchini blossoms or the milk-fed veal, and be sure to save room for homemade ice cream. ⊠ *Heuplatz 2* ☎ *0463/55499* 🕭 *Reservations essential* 🚍 *AE, DC, MC, V* ⊙ *Closed Sat.–Sun.*

★ **$$$–$$$$** ✕ **Bistro 151.** A haunted-house chandelier on the front porch of this sprawling, cottage-like establishment leads the way to 1930s-style salons with crimson accent walls, sofas, gilt sconces, naughty modern art, petite low-lit table lamps, and a fireplace (with a video monitor of a fire playing). The clientele is a mixture of families and trendsetters, and everybody is here to have a good time. Best bets include the seasonal cream of asparagus soup with a generous amount of crayfish, the butter knife–tender filet mignon, and the delicate duck ravioli. The bistro is located five minutes by car outside of town along the way to the Wörthersee. ✉ *Viktring* ☎ *0463/281653* ⌕ *Reservations essential* ▤ *MC, V* ☉ *Closed Sun.*

★ **$$$–$$$$** ✕ **Maria Loretto.** Gorgeous is the word to describe this spot's perch, which offers a view over the Wörther See and makes a fitting backdrop for some of the area's best seafood. This former villa offers several charmingly rustic dining rooms, or you can sit outdoors on the wraparound terrace overlooking the lake. Don't miss the appetizer of delicate trout caviar and smoked salmon on crispy toast points, then try the grilled calamari or *Seeteufel* medallions (monkfish drizzled with garlic butter). You'll probably need a taxi to get here. ✉ *Lorettoweg 54* ☎ *0463/24465* ⌕ *Reservations essential* ▤ *V* ☉ *Closed Jan.–Feb.; Tues. during Mar.–Apr. and Oct.–Dec.*

$$$ ✕ **Oscar.** This bustling, modern restaurant with floor-to-ceiling windows, crimson glass chandeliers, and close-set tables mainly offers innovative Italian dishes, and portions are large. Start with spinach crepes in a light cheese sauce or mushroom risotto with chicory, then move on to pork medallions stuffed with local cheese in a sage sauce with vegetables. Pizza is also tempting. For dessert try the creamy coconut tiramisu. ✉ *St. Veiter Ring 43* ☎ *0463/5001–77* ▤ *0463/507517* ▤ *AE, DC, MC, V* ☉ *Closed Sun.*

$ ✕ **Hamat'le.** Like a little farmhouse in the center of the city, this homey establishment just off the Villacher Ring is the place to go for Kärntner Käsnudeln, a Carinthian specialty of large, round ravioli. They're light as a feather and delicated stuffed with your choice of spinach, cheese, or minced beef. Schnitzels and other Austrian specialties are also featured. ✉ *Linsengasse 1* ☎ *0463/555700* ▤ *0463/555704* ▤ *AE, DC, MC, V* ☉ *Closed Mon.*

$$$$ ✕▥ **Das Salzamt Palais Hotel Landhaus.** Dating from the Renaissance, this majestic palace in the city center was known as the Salzamt—the town salt tax office—from the late 18th century until 1935. Now a trendy new hotel in the pedestrian quarter, its guest rooms are lushly decorated with deep, comfortable chairs and sofas, red or blue and cream bedskirts, fluffy duvets, stuffed headboards that invite you to sit up in bed and read, and floral window shades flanked by long, elegantly striped curtains. Some rooms are whimsically regal, with fun red and gilt over-the-top furniture decorated with portraits and leopard-skin hearts. The house restaurant is in the massive, light-filled atrium and features Continental cuisine. ✉ *Landhaushof 3, A-9020* ☎ *0463/590959* ▤ *0463/590–9590–9* ⊕ *www.landhaushof.at* ⇌ *27 rooms* ⌂ *Restaurant, bar, Internet, minibars* ▤ *AE, DC, MC, V* ¶◎¶ *BP.*

★ **$$$–$$$$** ✕▥ **Sandwirth.** A thriving hotel for more than a century, the Sandwirth was *the* watering hole of Klagenfurt society, with guests that included European luminaries Eugene Ionesco, Maria Schell, and Curt Jürgens, until it fell on hard times by the last decade. Enter an ambitious private buyer, a Carinthian architect, and local artisans who together came to revamp the interior while retaining the 19th-century yellow facade. The result is a harmonious blending of styles, with eye-catching design details. Guest rooms are subtly elegant and modern, with beige and cream accents, while the baths have unique beveled tiles. An added plus here is free pay-TV. Be sure to have the house's signature hazelnut pudding in the café's "library," once again the most popular rendezvous place in town. ⊠ *Pernhartgasse 9, A-9020* ☎ *0463/56209* 🖷 *0463/514322* ⊕ *www.sandwirth.at* ↩ *51 rooms* ♨ *Restaurant, café, sauna, Internet, free parking; no minibars, no a/c* ☰ *AE, DC, MC, V* ¶○¶ *BP.*

$ ╳☷ **Schlosshotel Wörthersee.** At the end of the lake and on its own
Fodor'sChoice beach, this gorgeous pale-yellow mansion with soaring red mansard roof,
★ flower-bedecked balconies, storybook woodwork, and Rapunzel towers will immediately conjure up "holiday" to you. Despite an exterior redolent of the era of grand hotels, the guest rooms are plainly furnished in traditional-modern style, but you can't really expect more at these extremely reasonable room rates; of course, preferred rooms overlook the lake. The restaurant serves hearty local cuisine in the atmosphere of an informal heuriger. The hotel is open year-round and offers a dazzling parade of sports facilities, both summer and winter. ⊠ *Villacher Strasse 338, A-9010* ☎ *0463/21158–0* 🖷 *0463/21158–8* ⊕ *www. schloss-hotel.at* ↩ *35 rooms* ♨ *Restaurant, café, sauna, beach, bicycles, bar; no a/c* ☰ *MC, V* ¶○¶ *BP, MAP.*

$$–$$$$ ☷ **Palais Porcia.** Once the town palace of the Italian princes of Porcia,
Fodor'sChoice this intimate 18th-century hotel still holds the most coveted address in
★ the very center of Klagenfurt. To say the guest rooms are opulently decorated is to beggar the Baroque and Biedermeier antiques, the superplush Genoese brocaded wallpaper, the ornate velvet sofas, the Italian marbles, and the museum-worthy paintings. Adjacent to the reception area is the bar with overstuffed chairs and sofas and an intricately carved Renaissance mahogany bar. Some of the guest rooms are astounding—even former guest Bavarian King Ludwig II himself would have cottoned to the all-out splendor of the Himmelbett (Heaven's Bed) Room, with its enormous oak fourposter bed hung with red velvet trimming. He wouldn't have minded the breakfast served up in the Louis XIV salon, either. For more sedate, but still entrancingly luxe and historic surrounds, book the Blue or Rose room, also swooningly done in posh 19th-century style. ⊠ *Neuerplatz 13, A-9020* ☎ *0463/511590* 🖷 *0463/511590–30* ⊕ *www. hotel-palais-porcia.com* ↩ *35 rooms* ♨ *Minibars, sauna, bar, Internet, parking (fee); no a/c* ☰ *AE, DC, MC, V* ¶○¶ *BP.*

$–$$$ ☷ **Moser-Verdino.** With a facade of dusky rose and wrought-iron balconies, this centrally located hotel has been around for more than a century. Rooms are spacious with soothing tones, imitation Jugendstil accents, pretty drapes with matching bedskirts, and evocative castle prints on the walls. The staff is exceptionally warm and helpful. The café is nearly always full and is a good spot for a snack. ⊠ *Domgasse 2, A-9020* ☎ *0463/57878* 🖷 *0463/516765* ⊕ *www.arcotel.cc* ↩ *71 rooms* ♨ *Café, sauna, bar, parking (fee); no a/c* ☰ *AE, DC, MC, V* ¶○¶ *BP.*

Nightlife & the Arts

Operas and operettas are performed year-round at the Stadttheater in Klagenfurt, a pretty Art Nouveau building designed by the famous theater architects Helmer and Fellner of Vienna and completed in 1910. The schedule here often showcases overlooked jewels—in 2004 Vincenzo Bellini's *Norma* and Giacomo Puccini's *Turandot* were the main productions. For details and tickets, contact **Stadttheater Klagenfurt** (⊠ Theaterplatz 4, A-9020 ☎ 0463/54064 ⊕ www.stadttheater-klagenfurt.at). The box office is open Mon.–Sat. 9–1 and 2–6. If musicals like the *Rocky Horror Picture Show, Evita,* and *Falco Meets Amadeus* are your thing, you won't want to miss the summertime entertainment offered at the **Wörtherseebühne** (Lake Wörth Stage), which is built right on the lake. Seats range in price from €15–€100. For information and ticket purchasing, contact (☎ 0463/507356 or 0463/507355 ☐ 0463/507-3554–0 ⊕ www.woertherseebuehne.com and www.woertherseefestspiele.com).

For a true after-hours scene in Klagenfurt, head for the Pfarrplatz-Herrengasse area, where you'll find a number of intimate bars and cafés. In the Old City, the Klagenfurt young crowd gathers at the **Augustiner Bierhaus** (⊠ Pfarrhofgasse 2 ☎ 0463/513992). It is closed Sunday. For some of the most stylish drinks in town, visit the discreetly marked **Palais Egger Helldorff** (⊠ Herrengasse 12), once the palace where Napoléon camped out during the French occupation in 1797 and housing within its courtyard two hip bars and a trendy Mexican restaurant.

The Outdoors

BICYCLING You can rent bicycles at the **Klagenfurt tourist office** (☎ 0463/537–2223). Many bikers enjoy excursions to the nearby Wörther See.

Krumpendorf

❷ *10 km (6 mi) west of Klagenfurt.*

The first town on the north side of the Wörther See is less chic and less pretentious than the other resorts, but pleasant all the same. The resort's water sports and down-home feel appeal to families, particularly those seeking to escape the higher prices and singles invasions of other areas.

Where to Stay

$ **Schloss Hallegg.** Just east of Krumpendorf, a small road heads north about 3 km (2 mi) to this imposingly stolid and thoroughly Teutonic early-13th-century castle tucked away on the edge of a nature preserve above the lake. Now adapted as a hotel, it has rooms that are spacious and comfortable. You'll get breakfast only, but there is a choice of restaurants in town. There's a small lake for swimming and fishing, and ample grounds for hunting and riding. If you want to get fully Feudal about things, check out the castle's medieval-style wedding receptions. ⊠ *Hallegger Strasse 131, A-9201* ☎ *0463/49311–0* ☐ *0463/49311–8* ⊕ *www.schloss-hallegg.at* ⇱ *15 rooms* △ *Tennis court, lake, fishing, horseback riding; no a/c, no room TVs* ☐ *MC, V* ⊘ *Closed early Oct.–mid-May* ⦿⧉ *BP.*

Pörtschach

★ **❸** *6 km (4 mi) west of Krumpendorf.*

Midway along the gorgeously idyllic Wörther See is Pörtschach, known as the Hamptons of Austria because of its posh, relaxed elegance. Here, the water is often warm enough for swimming as early as May, early indeed for an Alpine region. You'll find dozens of places to stay and even more things to do under the stars: the nightlife here is as varied as the daytime activities. Elegant villas and lakeside promenades line the peninsula, which is abloom with flowers and verdant foliage during the summer months.

Where to Stay & Eat

$$$ ✕ **Rainer's.** Make your way through the bar upstairs to Pörtschach's favored dinner restaurant, which has a rather New Orleans look on the outside. The most desirable tables are on the balcony, although the two inside rooms have an intimacy of their own. Food choices include Kärntner *Almsochsen* (roast ox from free-range Alpine herds), with vegetable risotto, roasted *Reinankenfilet* (a local white fish) from the Millstätter lake with creamy arugula potato salad or a grilled beef tower crowned with fried jumbo shrimp. ⊠ *Monte-Carlo-Platz 1* ☎ *04272/3046* 🖷 *0427/3072* ☰ *AE, MC, V* ☉ *Closed mid-Sept.–mid-May. No lunch.*

★ **$$$$** ✕▨ **Schloss Seefels.** On a gorgeous spot along the banks of the Wörther See about a mile outside of Pörtschach, this grand resort welcomes you with a front porte-cochere in Austrian Baroque–style. But the formality stops as soon as you walk around to the backside of the hotel to find a rambling lakeside manor with green shutters, wrought-iron balconies, elegant sash windows, lots of stone balconies, terraces, and jetties, all shadowed by a pretty pepper-pot tower, part of the original estate (built here in the mid-19th century by the inventor of the Austrian picture postcard). Guest rooms are done in calming beige and cream, with light-toned French provincial-style furniture. The best rooms are the junior suites, which, though not large, have wraparound terraces, cozy sitting rooms, and snug, odd-angled bedrooms. The grand suites are a bit pompous. The grounds are full of little private nooks with heated whirlpools looking out over the lake, or covered loggias with stone pillars, terra-cotta tubs of blooming flowers, spectacular views, and naturally, comfortable lounge chairs. The outdoor pool is situated directly on the lake and is heated year-round, and for those who like to golf, the hotel will ferry you by motorboat to the golf course. ⊠ *Töschling 1, A-9210* ☎ *04272/ 2377* 🖷 *04272/3704* ⊕ *www.seefels.com* ✍ *71 rooms* ♨ *4 restaurants, bar, pool, fitness center, tennis courts, massage, Internet, minibars; no a/c* ☰ *AE, DC, MC, V* ☉ *Possibly closed in Nov.* ▯⃝▮ *BP, MAP.*

$$$–$$$$ ✕▨ **Schloss Leonstain.** The great composer Johannes Brahms knew a thing
FodorśChoice or two about beauty, so it is little wonder he raved about his stay at this
★ magisterially charming retreat. Set in an appealing white stucco 500-year-old manor house, replete with Bohemian cupola, Tyrolean red-and-white doors, and one of the most enchanting Renaissance courtyards in all Austria, this hotel also enjoys a secluded situation despite its address along the main street of Pörtschach. In summer, the courtyard terrace is set with dining tables, a pool, and its half-timber walls, ancient linden trees, and grapevine-covered walls make for a storybook setting for some of the chicest parties around. Needless to say, the restaurant is among the best in the region and is well worth a visit on its own—the hotel offers a wide array of pension plans so avail yourself. Breakfast, served on pretty pear-patterned Limoges porcelain, is very good.

Guest rooms can be super-pretty—adorned with Tyrolean painted beds, for instance—or plain but sweetly gemütlich. No one will want to miss the lakeside pier—pure alpine bliss. It's not surprising to learn that Brahms was inspired to write his Second Symphony here. ⊠ *Leonstainerstrasse 1, A-9210* ☎ *04272/2816–0* 🖷 *04272/2823* ⊕ *www. hotel-leonstain.at* 🖙 *33 rooms* 🖒 *Restaurant, golf course, tennis court, lake, sauna, boating, Internet; no a/c* ▤ *AE, DC, MC, V* ☯ *Closed early Oct.–early May* ⦿❘ *BP, MAP.*

$$ ✕▦ **Strandhotel Europa.** This modern hotel, uninspiring on the outside, stands directly on the water. Rooms are agreeably furnished with warm tones and plaid curtains. Ask for a room on the water and enjoy a view of the sunniest corner of the lake. The view is also wonderful from the restaurant. ⊠ *Augustenstrasse 24, A-9210* ☎ *04272/2244* 🖷 *04272/ 2298* 🖙 *47 rooms* 🖒 *Restaurant, golf course, tennis court, lake, boating, bicycles; no a/c* ▤ *No credit cards* ☯ *Closed mid-Oct.–Mar.* ⦿❘ *BP, MAP.*

★ **$$$$** ▦ **Seehotel Porcia.** Although top-heavy with a faux-mansard roof, this red-hued lakeside villa strikes the right note when it comes to enjoying a lakeside holiday. With its lake terraces, green lawns, private beach, boat landings, and some of the lushest guest rooms around, this exclusive charmer is worth the five-minute walk from the center of Pörtschach. Most guest rooms have an Old World charm but three are spectacular— the Versace Room, done up like a 19th-century jewel with Versace fabrics, swags and tassels, and Empire-style antiques; the Blue Room, with court portraits, gilt chandeliers, and frosty Dresden blue walls; the Lachs Zimmer, with gilded Biedermeier hues and brocaded sofas. Most face the lake and have spectacular views. No matter if your room doesn't view the lake, as there are any number of public terraces and lawns set with chaise longues just ready to help you while away the afternoon. ⊠ *Hauptstrasse 231, A-9210* ☎ *04272/2087* 🖷 *04272/2087–87* ⊕ *www.hotel-palais-porcia.com* 🖙 *13 apartments* 🖒 *Indoor pool, gym, massage, sauna, beach, boating, fishing, bar; no pets* ▤ *AE, DC, MC, V* ⦿❘ *BP.*

Sports & Outdoor Activities

WATER SPORTS Pörtschach is a center of activity for windsurfing, parasailing, and sailing. Check **Herbert Schweiger** (⊠ 10-Oktober-Strasse 33 ☎ 04272/ 2655). Several hotels on the Wörther See offer sailing and water-sports packages.

Maria Wörth

★ ❹ *10 km (6 mi) west of Klagenfurt.*

Using one of the ferries that ply the Wöther See lake, you can head across the waters from Pörtschach to the most beauteous spot along the lake shores, the village of Maria Wörth (note that these ferries operate only from May through September, and cars are not allowed on them; as the lake is 1.5 km (1 mi) wide and 17 km (10½ mi) long, it's not far to drive around). The spire of Maria Wörth's parish church reflected in the waters of the Wörther See is one of Austria's most photographed sights. This unpretentious little town is situated on a wooded peninsula jutting out toward the center of the lake and is almost entirely surrounded by water. It actually has two notable churches, both dating from the 12th century. The smaller **Rosenkranzkirche** (Rosary church) in the town itself is basically Romanesque with later Gothic additions. The interior has a Romanesque choir with fragments of 12th-century frescoes of the apostles, a stained-glass Madonna window from 1420, and Gothic carved-wood figures. The larger **Pfarrkirche** (parish church), despite its Romanesque portal, is mainly Gothic, with a Baroque interior, revealing all the "wrinkles" acquired since the days of its appearance in the 9th century. Skulls and bones can still be seen in the round Romanesque charnel house in the cemetery.

Where to Stay

★ **$$$$** ✕▢ **Aenea.** This modernistic Xanadu offers an eye-popping change of pace from the usual "rustic" resort look. Stylish enough even to convert old-fashioned types to the minimalist way, this five-story stone and glass (well, mostly glass) pavilion prides itself on having no "preordained hotel rhythm"—everything is designed to sooth and pamper its guests, down to the placement of two four-poster beds in the outdoor "loungerie" (so you can really lounge around). Setting the style are the lobby and bar, adorned with Mies-van-der-Rohe-style black leather chairs, accent walls of gleaming red, and plate-glass windows with Cinerama-worthy views of the south side of the Wörthersee. Set in Reifnitz, about 2 miles from Maria Wörth, Aenea (pronounced Ah-en-ay-ah) opened in 2003. The simplistic yet oh-so-comfortable suites (no double rooms) are done by Italian designer Rodolfo Dordoni in cool white with bold, dark fabric accents, and also feature fabulous Philippe Starck bathrooms. Each suite has a nice-sized terrace with great lake views. Only breakfast is included in the room rate, but the weather-proof terrace is the perfect place to dine on Carinthian specialties and just-caught fish while watching sailboats cross the lake at dusk. All this luxury, of course, carries a price. But it may be worth it—spend a week here and you may never need to take a Valium again. ⊠ *Wörthersee Süduferstrasse 86, A-9081 Reifinitz* ☎ *04273/26220* 🖷 *04273/26220–20* ⊕ *www.aenea.at* 🛏 *15 suites* ⌂ *Restaurant, 2 bars, tennis court, indoor pool, sauna, massage, Internet; no a/c* ⊟ *AE, DC, MC, V* ⊘ *Closed Nov. until sometime in Mar.* ⍑⊙⍥ *BP.*

$$$–$$$$ ✕▢ **Astoria.** This massive, comfortable villa on the lake is just 2 km (1 mi) from the 18-hole, par-71 Kärntner Golf Club course at Dellach; the hotel offers golf-holiday packages. The rooms are attractively furnished; those overlooking the lake are preferred. Note that the room price includes half board. ⊠ *A-9082* ☎ *04273/2279* 🖷 *04273/2279–80* 🛏 *45 rooms* ⌂ *Restaurant, tennis court, indoor pool, sauna; no a/c* ⊟ *MC, V* ⊘ *Closed mid-Sept.–Apr.* ⍑⊙⍥ *BP, MAP.*

Velden

❺ *8 km (5 mi) west of Maria Wörth.*

Velden, the largest resort on the lake, is perched at the west end of the Wörther See. The atmosphere here strives to retain its international chic—classy and lively—and the summer carnival in August adds to the action. The fact that a casino has settled here says a lot about Velden, which otherwise has very little in the way of sights. The town's most famous beauty spot is the lakeside promenade, accented by turn-of-the-century lamps and mansions. However, if you're looking for a tranquil holiday, Velden may be too exuberant. The town gets pricey in the July–August main season. The **casino** in the center of Velden is a focal point of the evening, but you must be 18 or over. Along with the gambling tables and slot machines, the complex contains a disco, bars, and a restaurant, whose terrace overlooks the lake. You'll need your passport to enter the casino. ⊠ *Am Corso 17* ☎ *04274/2064* 🖷 *04274/2064–111* 🏛 *Jacket required, but not tie* ☉ *Daily 12 noon–3 or 4* AM.

Where to Stay & Eat

$$$$ ✕ **Casino-Restaurant.** If you're looking for fine cuisine plus a view, this place offers a wondrous vista over the lake. The cuisine ranges from international to regional and seasonal specialties. Keep an eye out for chanterelles in summer and venison at the end of September. The casino complex is limited to those 18 and over, and you'll need your passport for identification. ⊠ *Am Corso 17* ☎ *04274/2948* 🝙 *AE, DC, MC, V.*

★ **$$$$** ✕🖾 **Hubertushof.** Comprised of two houses, the Seevilla (Lake Villa) and Garden Villa, the Hubertushof is owned by the second generation of the Kenney family to live in Austria. (Herr Kenney's father was stationed in Velden during the British occupation of Carinthia after WWII and settled down with a local girl.) The vaguely Secession-style Lake Villa has a superb location with a lawn sloping down to the water and a front entrance next to the casino on the main street. Frau Kenney scours estate sales and travels frequently to London and Italy to get furniture pieces and fabrics for the pleasingly decorated, sunny rooms, which feature art by Austrian artists, eclectic antiques, and beige earth tones or beachy shades of hot pink and mint green. Rooms either have a garden or lake view and most have balconies. The bistro offers excellent fare, including chicken Caesar salad, grilled *Branzino* (loup de mer), and the ubiquitous *Kärntner Kasnudeln* (cheese-filled ravioli) with browned butter and a sprinkle of mint. Breakfast is served on the garden patio. ⊠ *Europaplatz 1, A-9220* ☎ *04274/2676–0* 🖷 *04274/2657–60* ⊕ *www. tiscover.com/hubertushof.velden* ⟿ *45 rooms* ⚲ *2 restaurants, café, mini-bars, indoor pool, gym, sauna, boating; no a/c* 🝙 *AE, DC, MC, V* ☉ *Closed mid-Oct.–mid-Apr.* ⵏ❙ *BP, MAP.*

$$$$ 🖾 **Seeschlössl Velden.** In a nature park by a secluded edge of the lake, this glowingly yellow *fin de siècle* villa with green shutters is on the outskirts of Velden, though still within walking distance to all the action. More like a luxurious vacation home from a bygone age than a hotel, the public rooms are furnished with polished Biedermeier antiques and Oriental carpets. The only sound you'll hear is the gentle lapping of water and the ticking of the grandfather clock. Rooms, some of which have a loft for sleeping, are contemporary in style, with gleaming wooden floors and cool white sofas and chairs. A few have terraces overlooking the lake, but all have gorgeous views. ⊠ *Klagenfurterstrasse 34, A-9220* ☎ *04274/2824* 🖷 *04274/2824–44* ⊕ *www.schlosshotels.co.at* ⟿ *14 rooms* ⚲ *Boating; no a/c* 🝙 *V* ☉ *Closed Nov.–mid-Mar.* ⵏ❙ *BP.*

Sports

WATER SPORTS Velden is another good site for windsurfing, parasurfing, and sailing. Rentals are available at **Segel-und-Surfschule Wörthersee/Berger** (⊠ Seecorso 40/Faagasse 15 ☎ 0664/420–2118).

> **off the beaten path**

MARIA GAIL – The Romanesque parish church here has an unusually fine 14th-century Gothic winged triptych altarpiece. To get to Maria Gail, 15 km (9 mi) west of Velden, take Villacher Strasse, Route 83, out of Velden. If you're heading on to Faaker See, you'll pass, several miles beyond Maria Gail, one of the most famous roadside shrines in Austria: framed by lake and mountain, this *Manterl* is a great photo op.

Egg am Faaker See

⑥ *4 km (2½ mi) east of Maria Gail.*

With turquoise-green waters that seem almost Mediterranean, the Faaker See presents an idyllic setting for swimming and boating. Boating aficionados take to the lake in droves, with a rainbow of sails skimming across the horizon (motorboats are not allowed); even so, the round lake—with its tiny island in the middle—remains less crowded than other resort areas here. Watching over all is the mighty pyramid of the Mittagskogel of the Karawanken range.

Where to Stay & Eat

★ $$$ ✕▦ **Karnerhof.** Blessed with one of the most spectacular lake views in Carinthia, this huge chalet with a long, low extension is in a quiet park, with the Karawanken mountains and Mittagskogel peak serving as a scenic backdrop. Overnighters will enjoy the attractive rustic rooms, but there's also the excellent Götzelstube restaurant—so even if you can't stay here, why not stop for lunch on the terrace and admire the view while dining on *Eierschwammerl* (chanterelle) ravioli with crayfish or grilled *Rotbarbenfilet,* a local freshwater fish. ⊠ *Karnerhofweg 10, A-9580* ☎ *04254/2188* 🖷 *04254/3650* ⊕ *www.karnerhof.com* 🛏 *98 rooms* ঌ *Restaurant, café, tennis court, indoor-outdoor pool, gym, sauna, beach; no a/c* ▤ *AE, DC, MC, V* ☉ *Closed Jan.–Feb. and possibly other winter months* ⦿ *BP, MAP.*

$$ ✕▦ **Tschebull.** Cars begin filling the parking lot before mealtimes at this popular spot near the Faaker See, which can claim fellow Carinthian Wolfgang Puck as a guest whenever he's in the area. You won't find a lake view here—people come for the food, served in a large sunny hall looking out over the rolling hills or in an intimate room with mullioned windows and stag antlers on the walls. The crispy duck comes with home-made dumplings, baked apple and steamed vegetables, and tender, juicy pork from the owner's farm is served with a mound of buttery green beans and golden fried Rösti. Tschebull also offers double rooms for overnighters. ⊠ *Egger Seeuferstrasse 26, A-9580* ☎ *04254/2191* 🖷 *04254/2191–37* ⊕ *www.tiscover.at/gasthoftschebull* 🛏 *16 rooms* ঌ *Restaurant; no minibars, no a/c* ▤ *MC, V* ☉ *Hotel closed Jan. 15–Easter* ⦿ *BP, MAP.*

THE GURKTAL REGION

Storybook names, such as Tannhäuser, Snow White, and the Holy Hemma, are encountered throughout the Gurktal region of Carinthia. The region is populated with medieval strongholds, idyllic lakes, and towns reeking with charm down to the last cobblestone.

Villach

❼ *50 km (30 mi) west of Klagenfurt.*

Carinthia's "other" capital (Klagenfurt is the official one) sits astride the Drau River. The Romans may have been the first to bridge the river here to establish the settlement of Bilachium, from which the present name Villach is derived. The city is compact, with narrow, twisting lanes (restricted to pedestrians) winding through the Old City south of the river. Small, attractive shops are tucked into arcaded buildings, and each corner turned brings a fresh and surprising perspective. Renaissance houses surround the main square, which has a Baroque column honoring the Trinity. The 16th-century alchemist and physician Theophrastus Bombastus Hohenheim—better known as Paracelsus, the inventor of homeopathic medicine—lived at Hauptplatz 14; his father was the town physician.

The late-Gothic 14th-century **St. Jacob** (St. James's) was Protestant during the mid-1500s, making it Austria's first Protestant church. Its marble pulpit dates from 1555; the ornate Baroque high altar contrasts grandly with the Gothic crucifix. If the stair entry is open and you don't mind the rather steep climb, the view from the 310-foot tower is marvelous. Near the river, at the intersection of Ossiacher Zeile and Peraustrasse, the pinkish **Heiligenkreuz** (Holy Cross Church), with two towers and a cupola, is a splendid example of fully integrated Baroque. A good time to visit Villach is around August 1, when the townspeople and folks from surrounding villages don traditional clothes and celebrate *Kirtag*—the traditional feast day of each town's patron saint—with music, folk dancing, and general merrymaking.

In summer, a particularly lovely way to explore the Drau River from Villach is to take a cruise on the **MS** *Landskron*; watching the sun set over the mountains while you dine on board makes for a memorable evening. For schedules and details, check with the tourist office or **Drau-Schifffahrt** (✉ Wirthstrasse 21b ☎ 04242/58071 🖷 04242/58072 ⊕ www. schifffahrt.at/drau).

off the beaten path

LANDSKRON – This ruined castle, which has spectacular views over Villach, the Ossiacher See, and the Karawanken mountain range to the south, makes for an interesting stopping point. The original castle here dated from 1351 and was destroyed by fire in 1861; since then, sections have been rebuilt. It is also a keep for birds of prey, which are trained for shows. To get here, take Route 83 about 4 km (2½ mi) northeast of Villach. There is a small fee, about €2, to drive your car up the road. From September to June you can drive up without paying the fee if you leave before 10 AM or after 4:30 PM.

Where to Stay & Eat

$$–$$$ ✕ **Postillion.** Housed in the Hotel Post, the Postillion is known among locals as the best restaurant in town (in fact, this is where culinary giant Wolfgang Puck got his start—he worked here briefly as an apprentice chef before heading to Los Angeles to open his famed restaurant, Spago). Dine in country-casual comfort on wild duck carpaccio followed by Kärtner Käsnudeln, that favorite Carinthian specialty of large, round ravioli stuffed with cheese. Vegetables and herbs are straight from the bountiful hotel garden. In summer, tables are set outdoors in the Orangerie, where wild roses and ivy climb the courtyard walls. ⊠ *Hauptplatz 26* ☎ *04242/26101–0* 🖷 *04242/26101–420* ⚲ *Reservations essential* 🚍 *AE, DC, MC, V.*

★ **$$** ✕🖃 **Hotel Post.** This beautifully adapted Renaissance palace, which dates from 1500, is in the pedestrian zone in the heart of the Old City. Over the centuries the house has played host to royalty, including Empress Maria Theresia way back in the 1700s. Architects have cleverly created an elegant, stylish hotel while preserving the building's Old World features, most notably the arcaded inner court. Rooms are attractively furnished with polished mahogany and lovely fabrics, some in tones of pale apricot and mauve; a few have balconies overlooking the pretty courtyard. ⊠ *Hauptplatz 26, A-9500* ☎ *04242/26101–0* 🖷 *04242/26101–420* ⊕ *www.romantik-hotel.com* 🛏 *77 rooms* ⚲ *Restaurant, minibars, gym, sauna, bar, free parking; no a/c* 🚍 *AE, DC, MC, V* 🍴 *BP, MAP.*

$–$$ ✕🖃 **Hotel Mosser.** You won't be able to miss the Hotel Mosser; it's right in the center of town, with a peach exterior and faded orange and green candy-stripe columns. The furnishings are a bit nondescript, but the rooms tend to be spacious; ask for one facing the courtyard to avoid the noise from the street below. ⊠ *Bahnhofstrasse 9, A-9500* ☎ *04242/24115* 🖷 *04242/24115–222* 🛏 *29 rooms* ⚲ *Café; no a/c* 🚍 *AE, DC, MC, V* 🍴 *BP, MAP.*

Outdoor Activities

HIKING Southwest of Villach, the extremely scenic 16-km (10-mi) Villach Alpine highway climbs the mountain ridge to about 5,000 feet. From there, a lift gets you up to Hohenrain; then you can hike the marked trail—or take the train—up to the peak of the **Dobratsch,** towering 7,040 feet into the clouds and providing a spectacular view. Close to parking lot 6, at 4,875 feet, is an Alpine botanical garden, which is open mid-June–August, daily 9–6. The cost is €3.50 per person. The 11 parking and outlook points along the highway offer great panoramas.

Warmbad Villach

❽ *3 km (2 mi) southwest of Villach.*

On the southern outskirts of Villach lies Warmbad Villach, its name reflecting the hot springs of radioactive water, believed to combat aging, among other unwelcome visitations. This remains one of the classic spas of Carinthia—one discovered by the Romans—and people come to enjoy its thermal springs and swimming pools for various rheumatic ailments. Many hotels have been built around the *Kurpark,* the wooded grounds of the spa.

Where to Stay & Eat

★ **$$$$** ✕⌨ **Warmbaderhof.** With a tranquil park and a comfortable, meandering house seducing you into relaxation, the cure's the thing here. Rooms are elegantly appointed, with subtle tones, soft carpets, contemporary furnishings, and state-of-the-art baths. Most have nice-sized terraces. Ask for one overlooking "Napoléon's Meadow," where Napoléon's troops once encamped. The very fine Bürgerstube restaurant offers regional and national specialties, and the twice-weekly buffets are extravagant. Half pension in the Bürgerstube is included in the room price. Das Kleine Restaurant, with windows looking out over the woods, changes its offerings with the seasons—in warm weather, many take to the tables on the terrace. ⊠ *Kadischenallee 22–24, A-9504* ☎ *04242/3001-0* 🖷 *04242/ 3001-80* ⊕ *www.warmbad.at* ⤴ *114 rooms* ♨ *2 restaurants, indoor-outdoor pool, gym, sauna, hiking, horseback riding, bar, Internet* 🖃 *AE, DC, MC, V* ⦿ *BP, MAP.*

$$$ ⌨ **Karawankenhof.** The larger rooms in this hotel will appeal to those who want to take the cure or to use this as a base for further excursions in Carinthia. Children are particularly welcome. An underground passageway leads to the spa, with its water slide and pools. The glassed-in terrace restaurant is a delight, but the kitchen, alas, does not quite live up to the decor. The room price includes half board. ⊠ *Kadischenallee 25–27, A-9504* ☎ *04242/3002-0* 🖷 *04242/3002-61* ⊕ *www.warmbad. at* ⤴ *80 rooms, 8 apartments* ♨ *2 restaurants, indoor-outdoor pool, gym, sauna, bar, no-smoking rooms; no a/c* 🖃 *AE, DC, V* ⦿ *BP, MAP.*

Ossiach

★ ❾ *19 km (12 mi) northeast of Warmbad Villach via Rte. 83.*

The resort town of Ossiach is now the center of the Carinthian Summer Festival and is afflicted with wall-to-wall tourists during the high season. The festival, which since its launch in 1969 has expanded to include use of the Congress Center in Villach, covers all styles of music from Baroque to modern, from Gershwin to klezmer. There are also other attractions, including what was originally an 11th-century **monastery**, a typical square building around an inner court, with a chapel at the side, all fetchingly set not far from the water. The chapel, despite its stern, conservative exterior, is wonderfully Baroque. The monastery was razed by the Turks in 1484 and promptly rebuilt, though Baroque renovations have left it with its current look. Legend has it that in the 11th century the Polish king Boleslaw II lived incognito in the monastery for eight years, pretending to be mute, in penance for murdering the bishop of Kraków. A tombstone and a fresco on the church wall facing the cemetery commemorate the tale.

Where to Stay & Eat

$$ ✕ **Stiftsschmiede.** Just to the left of Stift Ossiach (Ossiach monastery), this pretty chalet restaurant serves some of the freshest fish you're likely to find in Austria. Caught right in their own fish pond, the rainbow trout and *Saibling* (char) are grilled or breaded and fried, making a memorable meal, especially if the weather is fine and you're sitting on the terrace overlooking the lake. ⊠ *A-9570* ☎ *04243/45554* ▤ *No credit cards* ⊘ *Closed Sun.–Mon., Sept.–June; Sun., July–Aug. No lunch.*

$ ▥ **Stiftshotel Ossiach.** Occupying one wing of a former monastery dating from the 1620s, this spruced-up hotel offers spacious, high-ceilinged guest rooms with reproduction period furnishings. Somehow they still seem a trifle monastic. The hotel faces the lake and is within walking distance of the main part of town. ⊠ *A-9570* ☎ *04243/8664–0* 📠 *0222/ 8664–8* ⌨ *16 rooms* ⌕ *Restaurant, beach; no a/c* ▤ *MC, V* ⊘ *Closed mid-Sept.–early May* ◯ *BP, MAP.*

Nightlife & the Arts

Even though Ossiach is a small town (with a population of less than a thousand), it hosts an internationally renowned music event, the **Carinthischer Sommer** (Carinthian Summer Festival), which has attracted many notable musicians, including the late Leonard Bernstein, the Collegium Musicum Pragense, and soloists from the London Symphony Orchestra. It is held in July and August and emphasizes 20th-century composition; however, along with Benjamin Britten's opera *The Prodigal Son* you might also hear some Mozart and Vivaldi, plus a little jazz and pop. Chamber concerts are all the more attractive for being presented in the Baroque chapel or the monastery in Ossiach. For a schedule or tickets, contact Carinthischer Sommer, through **late May** (⊠ Gumpendorfer Strasse 76, A-1060 Vienna ☎ 01/596–8198 📠 01/597–1236 ⊕ www. carinthischersommer.at) or after **early June** (⊠ Stift Ossiach, A-9570 Ossiach ☎ 04243/2510 📠 04243/2353 ⊕ www.carinthischersommer.at).

In resort centers like Ossiach you'll find regular evenings of folk music and dancing, some of them organized by the hotels. The local tourist offices will have details, and notices are often posted around the area.

Outdoor Activities

BICYCLING The area around the Ossiacher See is excellent for cycling, and many of the main roads have parallel cycling paths. Rental bicycles are in great demand throughout this area, so reserve in advance. **Feriendorf Ossiach** (⊠ Alt-Ossiach 37, A-9570 Ossiach ☎ 04243/2202). **Bike Paradies** (⊠ Niederdorf 1, A-9521 Treffen ☎ 04248/3833).

Feldkirchen

🔟 *6 km (4 mi) northeast of Ossiach.*

Feldkirchen is a modest little town that hides well the fact that it is one of Carinthia's oldest communities, having been officially mentioned in a document dating from 888. Some relics of the ancient medieval wall that once surrounded Feldkirchen remain in indistinct form; otherwise the town has a pleasant provincial Baroque look, with pastel facades and a shady central square with a fountain dribbling in the middle and a few cafés and Italian ice-cream parlors occupying space on the sidewalks. The relief of the Virgin Mary over the old pharmacy (*Apotheke*) is the only eye-catcher here. At the north end of town (Kirchgasse) is the parish church, in early Romanesque style with a Gothic choir and

Baroque trim. In addition, the town has some Biedermeier-style houses. Though small, Feldkirchen is an important crossroads: one road (Route 93) goes to Gurk, another (Route 94) heads to St. Veit an der Glan, and yet another (Route 95) traverses the remote Nock Mountains up to the Turracher Höhe, a high pass between Carinthia and Styria with a dangerous 23% gradient, a mountain summer resort, and a fine skiing center on a pretty lake.

en route   Heading north along Route 93 out of Feldkirchen are myriad small roads leading to colorful villages. **Goggau** has a small but charming lake. **Sirnitz** (☎ 04279/303 🖷 04279/3034) has an interesting little castle called Schloss Albeck, with a fine restaurant, Saturday evening concerts at 6, and Sunday morning concerts at 11, and an atelier selling clothing made of hand-spun linen. At **Deutsch-Griffen**, with a picturesque fortified church accessed by a long covered staircase, an easy hike up the Meisenberg takes you through Carinthia's first bird sanctuary, an initiative by Gottfried Topf, a retired German businessman who moved to the village permanently in 1990. In **Glödnitz** a road leads up to Flattnitz, a solitary but very beautiful spot with a little skiing and a few isolated houses.

Gurk

⓫ *34 km (21 mi) northeast of Feldkirchen.*

Gurk's claim to fame is its massive Romanesque **Dom** (cathedral) surmounted by two onion cupolas and considered the most famous religious landmark in Carinthia. It was founded in the 11th century by Hemma, Countess of Zeltschach, who after losing her two sons and husband decided to turn to religious works. She had two oxen tied before a cart and let them walk until they stopped on their own. At that spot she founded a cloister and gave all her belongings to the church for building a cathedral. She did not live to see Gurk become a bishopric (in 1072). Construction on the cathedral itself began in 1040 and ended in 1200. Hemma wasn't canonized until 1938. Her tomb is in the crypt, whose ceiling, and hence the cathedral itself, is supported by 100 marble pillars. The Hemma-Stein, a small green-slate chair from which she personally supervised construction, is also there and alleged to bring fertility to barren women. In the church itself, the high altar is one of the most important examples of early Baroque in Austria. Note the *Pietà* by George Rafael Donner, who is sometimes called the Austrian Michelangelo. The 900-square-foot Lenten altar cloth of 1458 shows 99 scenes from the Old and New Testaments—a beautiful example of a *Biblia Pauperum*, a "poor man's Bible" meant to teach the Scriptures to those who could not read. It is displayed from Ash Wednesday to Good Friday. Make sure to visit the bishop's chapel, which features rare late-Romanesque and Gothic frescoes, among the oldest in Europe and in perfect condition (the guidebook in English is helpful). At the end of August and in early September a concert series is held in the cathedral. Tours are restricted by church services, but in summer four tour guides are available, with tours usually scheduled for 10,

1:30, and 3 (though tours can be arranged just about any time), with longer tours including the bishop's chapel. ☎ 04266/8236–0 🖷 04266/8236–16 ✎ *Short tour including crypt €2.60; long tour €7.50* ☉ *Daily 9–6; in winter, daily 9–5.*

☾ The **Zwergenpark** is a vast natural preserve filled with amusing garden statuary, consisting largely of typically Austrian-German garden gnomes; children can traverse the park via a miniature railway. ☎ 04266/1877 ✎ *€5* ☉ *Early May–late June and Sept. 1–15, daily 11–4; late June–Aug., daily 11–6.*

Strassburg

⑫ *3 km (2 mi) northeast of Gurk.*

The seat of the Gurk bishopric until 1787, Strassburg is dominated by the now-restored episcopal palace, which houses small museums covering the history of the valley and of the diocese. The Gothic parish church, one of the most beautiful in Carinthia, has stained-glass windows dating from 1340. Also of note is the Heilig-Geist-Spital Church, constructed in the 13th century.

Outside Strassburg, at the intersection of Route 93 and Route 83/E7, you'll see the 18th-century **Schloss Pöckstein,** belonging to the Carinthian bishops. In the distance off to the left you'll notice a castle on a hilltop, which you can see close-up by turning left at Mölbling on a road marked "Treibach/Althofen." The castle is actually in Ober Markt, an unusually picturesque town with 15th-century decorated houses.

Across the highway from the Pöckstein Castle is the northern terminus ☾ of a small narrow-gauge railway, the **Gurkthaler Museumbahn.** Under steam power, the train meanders for 30 minutes down to Treibach on weekends and holidays from late June to mid-September. For an additional contribution you can ride in the locomotive alongside the engineer. ☎ 04262/4783 ⊕ *www.gurkthalbahn.at* ✎ *Round-trip €5* ☉ *Check Web site for departure times.*

Friesach

★ **⑬** *16 km (9 mi) northeast of Strassburg via Rte. 83/E7.*

The oldest settlement in Carinthia, romantic Friesach is great for wandering. You'll immediately find the **Hauptplatz** (main square), with its old town hall and pretty, multi-colored pastel facades, and as you stroll you'll discover aspects of the medieval-era town: beautiful stone houses, the double wall and the towers, gates, and water-filled moat. Among the medieval tournaments of gallantry that took place here, 600 knights participated in a famous one of May 1224; the Styrian minnesinger Ulrich von Liechtenstein, who appeared dressed and equipped all in green, alone broke 53 of his adversaries' lances. Look into the churches. The 12th-century Romanesque **Stadtpfarrkirche** (parish church) on Wiener Strasse has some excellent stained glass in the choir. The 13th-century church in the **Dominican monastery** north of the moat was the first of its order in Austria. If you believe that Tannhäuser was a creation of Wagner's imagination, you will be surprised to learn that descendants of his family were Salzburg administrators in Friesach; a **Tannhäuser Chapel** was erected in 1509 in this church, with a red-marble tomb of Deputy Dean Balthasar Tannhäuser added after his death, in 1516. From a footpath at the upper end of the main square, take a steep 20-minute climb up to the impressive remains of **Schloss Petersberg** to see 12th- and 13th-century frescoes and a museum housed on several floors of the tower, with examples of late Gothic metal working and hunting rifles. There is also a well-preserved Kammerklavier. Friesach has many more medieval marvels: be sure to stop in at the tourist office for information on all of them.

Where to Stay

$ ✕▦ **Metnitztalerhof.** This delightful hotel has overlooked Friesach's medieval town square for more than 400 years. Rooms are furnished with country charm, from the rich, dark-wood pieces to the floral fabrics covering chairs, curtains, and beds. The best rooms have balconies and overlook the spectacular castle ruins. Other rooms face the town square and are not worth the price. The hotel also hosts gatherings, from wine tastings in its 12th-century wine cellar to medieval-style feasts. A nice extra is free access to the Internet. ✉ *Hauptplatz 11, A-9360* ☎ *04268/ 25100* 🖷 *04268/2510–54* ⊕ *www.metnitztalerhof.at* ⌑ *27 rooms* ♨ *Restaurant; no a/c* ▤ *AE, DC, MC, V* ☉ *Closed 2 wks in Nov.* ¶◎¶ *BP, MAP.*

¢ ✕▦ **Friesacherhof.** Incorporated into a centuries-old building on the main square, this comfortable hotel has rather plain rooms; those in front look out over the square and the Renaissance fountain and can be somewhat noisy. The rooms on the first floor are the nicest. Bathrooms are relics of the 1970s, but some have a separate tub and shower. ✉ *Hauptplatz 4, A-9360* ☎ *04268/2123–0* 🖷 *04268/2123–15* ⊕ *www. friesacherhof.at* ⌑ *20 rooms* ♨ *Restaurant, café; no a/c* ▤ *AE, DC, MC, V* ¶◎¶ *BP (MAP available for stays of 3 days).*

Nightlife & the Arts

From late June to mid-August there is open-air theater, performed in German, at the outdoor stage at Schloss Petersburg in Friesach. Check with the local tourist office for details and tickets.

Hochosterwitz

⑭ *31 km (19 mi) south of Friesach.*

☾ The dramatic 13th-century castle of **Hochosterwitz** crowns the top of a
FodorśChoice steep, isolated outcropping, looking as if it has just emerged from the
★ pages of a fairy tale. You can hardly ignore the Disneyland effect, and in fact, this was the inspiration for Walt Disney's *Snow White* castle. Disney and his staff stayed here for many weeks studying it, and you will find Walt's fantasy to be nearly fact. The castle was first mentioned in 860, and after a tumultuous few centuries ended up in the possession of the counts of Khevenhüller (1571), and has remained ever since. It was in this castle that the besieged "Pocket-Mouthed Meg"—Margarethe Maultasch, the original of Feuchtwanger's *Ugly Duchess*—

slaughtered the last ox of the starving garrison and dropped it onto the heads of the attacking Tyrolese. The stratagem succeeded, and, dispirited by such apparent proof of abundant supplies, the Tyrolese abandoned the siege. The most recent fortifications were added in the late 1500s against invading Turks; each of the 14 towered gates is a small fortress unto itself. Inside, there's an impressive collection of armor and weaponry plus a café-restaurant in the inner courtyard. There's an elevator (accommodating wheelchairs), which costs €3 from a point near the parking-lot ticket office. The hike up the rather steep path to Hochosterwitz, of course, adds to the drama. It's easy to envision yourself as some sort of transplanted knight trying to take the fortress. Your reward at the summit is spectacular vistas from every vantage point. Get to the castle on the back road from Treibach or via Route 83/E7. ⊠ *Laundsdorf-Hochosterwitz* ☎ *04213/2010 or 04213/2020* 🖶 *04213/ 202016* ⊕ *www.burg-hochosterwitz.or.at* 🎫 *€7* ⊙ *Apr. and Oct., daily 9–5; May–Sept., daily 8–6.*

St. Veit an der Glan

⑮ *10 km (6 mi) west of Hochosterwitz via Rte. 82.*

The capital of Carinthia until 1518, this old ducal city remains largely unchanged, with the town hall's Baroque facade and ancient patrician houses forming the main square. Be sure to walk into the arcaded Renaissance courtyard of the **Rathaus** (Town Hall), overflowing with flowers in summer; the main state rooms can be seen on guided tours. The 12th-century Romanesque **Pfarrkirche** (parish church) was later given Gothic overtones; note the attractive entry. The ducal palace, **Schloss St. Veit,** at the north end of town, now houses a small medieval collection; the building itself has a marvelous arcaded stairway in the courtyard.

Where to Stay & Eat

★ **$$$$** ✕ **Pukelsheim.** Despite its enlargement, this restaurant continues to be crowded—which testifies to its good reputation. You'll find regional specialties such as the ravioli-like Kärtner Käsnudeln, *Seeteufel* (monkfish) with olives, or stuffed roast chicken. The chef's recommendations are invariably justified. Pukelsheim is best known for its desserts: superb cakes and pies made with fruit in season. ⊠ *Erlgasse 11* ☎ *04212/2473* 🖶 *AE, DC, MC, V* ⊙ *Closed Sun.–Mon.*

$$ 🏨 **Ernst Fuchs Palast.** The twelve signs of the zodiac are the theme of this eye-popping hotel designed by Austrian avant-garde artist Ernst Fuchs. The exterior brings to mind a huge, psychedelic candy cane, but rooms are much less startling and are decorated with subdued, pastel fabrics and faux Jugendstil furniture. If you give them your birth date, they'll choose a room for you that is most compatible with your zodiac sign. The hotel caused a lot of controversy when it was built in 1998, with many citizens believing it belonged in Las Vegas, not St. Veit—still many can't resist staying at this sure-fire conversation piece. ⊠ *Prof.-Ernst-Fuchs-Platz 1, A-9300* ☎ *04212/4660–0* 🖶 *04212/4660–660* ⊕ *www.fuchspalast.com* 🛏 *60 rooms* ♿ *Restaurant, bar, Internet, minibars* 🖶 *AE, DC, MC, V* ⧖ *BP, MAP.*

CARINTHIA A TO Z

To research prices, get advice from other travelers, and book travel arrangements, visit www.fodors.com.

AIRPORTS

Carinthia is served—mainly by Austrian Airlines and its subsidiary Tyrolean Airways—through the Klagenfurt–Wörther See airport, just northeast of Klagenfurt. Several flights daily connect the provincial capital with Vienna. In summer, service is also available from Zürich, Rome, and Frankfurt. Also, look for cheap flights on Ryan Air from London.

🛈 Airport Information **Klagenfurt–Wörther See airport** ☎ 0463/41500.

BIKE TRAVEL

Rental bicycles are in great demand throughout this area, so reserve in advance. The area around the Ossiacher See is excellent for cycling, as are the larger resort towns around the Wörther See along the Austrian Riviera. North of Villach, the area around the Millstätter See is about the only one good for cycling.

🛈 Bike Rentals **AGIP gas station/Velden** ✉ Villacherstrasse 55 ☎ 04274/2482. **Central bike reservations/Pörstschach** ☎ 04272/3620-81 ⊕ www.kaernten-radreisen.at. **Faak am See Bike Center** ✉ Egg am See 80 ☎ 04254/4224. **Impulse Radverleih Klagenfurt** ☎ 0463/516310. Bus Travel

As in all of Austria, post office or railway (*Bundesbahn*) buses go virtually everywhere, but you'll have to allow plenty of time and coordinate schedules carefully so as not to get stranded in some remote location. Call the number listed below for information on schedules.

🛈 Bus Information **Bus Schedules** ☎ 01/93000 or 04242/1717.

CAR TRAVEL

The most direct route from Vienna is via the Semmering mountain pass through Styria, entering Carinthia on Route 83 just above Friesach and going on to Klagenfurt. From Salzburg, the A10 autobahn tunnels beneath the Tauern range and the Katschberghöhe to make a dramatic entry into Carinthia, although the parallel Route 99, which runs "over the top," is the more scenic route. The Tauern tunnel costs €9.50 and the vignette for the Katschberghöhe is €7.60. A pretty alternative here that leads you straight into the Nock Mountains or Gurk Valley is to leave the A10 at St. Michael after the Tauern Tunnel, head toward Tamsweg, and then take Route 97 through the Mur Valley; at Predlitz the pass road begins its climb over the steep Turracherhöhe into the Nock Mountains. The fork-off to Flattnitz, the most scenic way into the Gurk Valley, is at Stadl. Several mountain roads cross over from Italy, but the most traveled is Route 83 from Tarvisio.

ROAD CONDITIONS Highways in Carinthia are good, although you can hit some stretches as steep as the 23% gradient on the Turracher Pass road (Route 95), for example. Hauling trailers is not recommended (or is forbidden). The north–south passes are kept open in winter as far as possible, but the tunnels under the Tauern and Katschberg mountains ensure that Route A10 is now passable all year.

SKIING

Carinthia offers some great areas for skiing. The Gerlitzenalpe is between Feldkirchen and Villach. A more family-oriented ski resort is Kleinkirchheim. The Schleppe Fun Park offers beginners' slopes and a ski school.

Gerlitzenalpe ✉ Töbringerstrasse 1, A-9523 Villach ☎ 04242/42000 🖶 04242/42000-42 ⊕www.dalachtdasherz.at. **Schleppe Fun Park** ✉A-9020 Klagenfurt ☎0463/410081-4. **Turracherhöhe** ✉ A-9565 ☎ 04275/8392 🖶 04275/8392-10 ⊕ www.turracherhoehe.at.

TRAIN TRAVEL

The main rail line south from Vienna parallels Route 83, entering Carinthia north of Friesach and continuing on to Klagenfurt and Villach. From Salzburg, a line runs south, tunneling under the Tauern mountains and then tracing the Möll and Drau river valleys to Villach. A line from Italy comes into the Drau Valley from Lienz in East Tirol. The main line north from Udine in Italy runs through Tarvisio and up to Villach; other rail lines tie Slovenia with Klagenfurt.

Train Information **ÖBB–Österreichisches Bundesbahn** ☎ 05/1717.

TRANSPORTATION AROUND CARINTHIA

Most of Carinthia's attractive central basin is bypassed by the rail routes. Though you can get into and through Carinthia fairly easily by train, to see the inner province you'll need to rely on a car or the network of buses.

VISITOR INFORMATION

The official tourist office for the province is Kärnten Werbung in Velden. The leading regional *Fremdenverkehrsämter* (tourist offices) are listed below by town name.

The Kärnten Card costs €32, lasts for any two consecutive weeks, and allows you free access to over 100 museums and other sites of interest. Inquire at a local tourist office or call the Carinthia hotline.

Tourist Information **Friesach** ✉ Hauptplatz 1, A-9360 ☎ 04268/4300 🖶 04268/4280 ⊕www.friesach.at. **Kärntner (Carinthia) Tourismus** ✉Casinoplatz 1, A-9220 Velden ☎ 0463/3000 🖶 04274/521-0050 ⊕ www.kaernten.at. **Klagenfurt** ✉ Neuerplatz 1, A-9010 ☎ 0463/537-2223 🖶 0463/537-6218 ⊕ www.info.klagenfurt.at. **Klopeinersee** ✉ Schulstrasse 10, A-9122 ☎ 00800/847-2683-7. **Maria Wörth/Reifnitz** ✉ Seepromenade 5, A-9081 ☎ 04273/2240-0 🖶 04273/3703. **Ossiach Lake area** ✉ Ossiach 8, A-9570 ☎ 04243/497 🖶 04243/8763 ⊕ www.ossiach.at. **Pörtschach** ✉ Hauptstrasse 153, A-9210 ☎ 04272/2354 🖶 04272/3770 ⊕ www.poertschach.at. **Velden** ✉ Villacherstrasse 19 ☎ 04274/2103-0 🖶 04274/2103-50 ⊕ www.velden.at. **Villach** ✉ Rathausplatz 1, A-9500 ☎ 04242/205-2900 🖶 04242/205-2999 ⊕ www.villach.at.

EASTERN ALPS

8

WARM UP FOR THE ICE CAVES
of the fantastic Eisriesenwelt complex ⇨*p.386*

SNAP YOUR OWN POSTCARDS
from the alpine nirvana of Heiligenblut ⇨*p.368*

BREATHE THE "HEALING MINE"
at the Bad Gadstein spa ⇨*p.376*

CATCH A LIVE FALCONRY SHOW
at the fortress of Burg Hohenwerfen ⇨*p.385*

DINE ON INSPIRED REGIONAL FARE
at the culinary shrine of Obauer ⇨*p.386*

SMELL THE EDELWEISS
while navigating the twisty turns of mountaintop
Grossglockner Pass ⇨*p.370*

FOLLOW THE GEO-TRAIL
at the earth's birthplace, Hermagor ⇨*p.362*

Updated by
Lee Hogan

YOU CAN GET INTO SERIOUS TROUBLE by deciding where to go in Austria on the basis of the alluring photographs found in books and travel brochures. Pictures can be misleading—and, using the sheer joy of nature's (and some of mankind's) creative magnificence as a measure, they sometimes end up endorsing a whole country. One place that truly lives up to its pictures is Heiligenblut. One of the most photographed places in the country, it remains Austria's most picturesque Alpine village. With the majestic Grossglockner—Austria's highest mountain—for a backdrop, the town cradles the pilgrimage church of St. Vincent. Though most every Austrian hamlet has a church, or two, nowhere else does a steeple seem to find such affirmation amid soaring peaks.

While this little town is a visual treat, the whole Eastern Alps region is dramatic countryside, with breathtaking scenery and great winter sports equal to those in Switzerland. Here majestic peaks, many well over 9,750 feet, soar above slow-moving glaciers that give way to sweeping Alpine meadows ablaze with wildflowers in spring and summer. Long, broad valleys (many names have the suffix -au, meaning "water-meadow") are basins of rivers that cross the region between mountain ranges, sometimes meandering, sometimes plunging. The land is full of ice caves and salt mines, deep gorges, and hot springs. Today most tourism is concentrated in relatively few towns, but wherever you go, you'll find good lodging, solid local food, and friendly folk; it is countryside to drive and hike and ski through, where people live simply, close to the land.

Western Carinthia and East Tirol are dotted with quaint villages that have charming churches, lovely mountain scenery, and access to plenty of outdoor action—from hiking and fishing in summer to skiing in winter. Across the southern tier, a series of scenic routes passes from Carinthia to that political anomaly Osttirol (East Tirol). In 1918, after World War I, South Tirol was ceded to Italy, completely cutting East Tirol off from the rest of Tirol and the administrative capital in Innsbruck. The mountains along the Italian border and those of the Hohe Tauern, to the north, also isolate East Tirol, which has consequently been neglected by tourists.

This chapter starts out from Villach, in Carinthia, and travels to Lienz, in East Tirol, then into the Defereggental, north to Matrei, and back to Lienz. The next itinerary takes you from Heiligenblut over the Grossglockner mountain pass (in summer only), through Salzburg Province to charming Zell am See and beyond. The route then heads east along the Salzach river valley from Zell am See, with a side trip to Bad Gastein, then on to Radstadt and Schladming, just over into Styria. Finally, it takes in the magnificent Dachstein mountain complex and retraces its steps to go up through the Salzburg Dolomite range, ending about 40 km (25 mi) from Salzburg. You can do it all in a rather full three days, or you could take a leisurely week, which allows time to explore the smaller towns and byways.

Exploring the Eastern Alps

Austria's Eastern Alps straddle four different provinces: Carinthia, East Tirol, Salzburg, and Styria. Imposing mountain ranges ripple through

It's easy to feel on top of the world, which you almost literally are, if you take the Grossglockner High Alpine Highway—the most thrilling pass over the Alps. Nestled in a nearby valley is Heiligenblut, a town commemorated in a thousand picture postcards. Everywhere, breathtaking Alpine vistas and centuries-old castles dot the landscape. For many travelers the Eastern Alps, concentrated around the Grossglockner peak, represent not only the most fascinating part of Austria's mountainous land-scape, but its most unspoiled region as well.

Numbers in the text correspond to numbers in the margin and on the Eastern Alps map.

8

If you have
3 days

Start in the charming villages of **Hermagor** ❶ and **Kötschach–Mauthen** ❷, stopping off at the Geo-Trail, which traces 50 million years of geological his-tory. Then spend the afternoon exploring the East Tirolean capital of 📷 **Lienz** ❸. Castle ruins, churches, and more spectacular landscapes are in store on your second day as you visit **St. Jakob in Defereggen** ❹ and **Matrei in Osttirol** ❺ before returning to Lienz. On your final day, crown your trip with a visit to that Alpine jewel **Heiligenblut** ❼, making stops at **Döllach–Grosskirchheim** ❻ and elsewhere along the imposing **Grossglockner Highway** ❽.

If you have
5 days

Begin your trip in East Tirol's capital, **Lienz** ❸, before heading to picture-perfect 📷 **Heiligenblut** ❼. As long as it's not wintertime, your second day can be spent taking the scenic **Grossglockner Highway** ❽ through the Hohe Tauern National Park to the lake resort of 📷 **Zell am See** ❾. In winter, you'll have to use the Felbertauern tunnel route, which runs between Mittersill and Matrei in East Tirol. On day three, make a day trip to the mountain resorts of **Saalbach–Hinterglemm** ❿ and **Saalfelden** ⓫, and descend into the depths with a tour of the **Lamprechtshöhle** (cave). On your fourth day, travel to 📷 **Bad Gastein** ⓬ and "take the cure." Then use your last day to visit the Domkirche (cathedral) in **St. Johann im Pongau** ⓮ and the **Liechtensteinklamm** ⓭, the deepest, most dramatic gorge in the Eastern Alps.

If you have
7 days

With a week at your disposal, you can see even more of the charming Alpine towns that dot the awesome landscape. Explore **Lienz** ❸ and the lovely town of 📷 **Heiligenblut** ❼ on your first day. Then take on the twists and turns of the **Grossglockner Highway** ❽ before lingering by the lake at the resort town of 📷 **Zell am See** ❾. On your third day, see the spectacular **Liechtensteinklamm** ⓭ gorge, and then overnight in 📷 **St. Johann im Pongau** ⓮. Villages seemingly unchanged by the years are on the agenda for the fourth day, with visits to the charming town of **Altenmarkt** ⓯, the medieval haven of **Radstadt** ⓰, and the former silver-mining town of 📷 **Schladming** ⓱. A cable car will whisk you to the top of the Hunerkogel the next day during a stop at **Ramsau am Dachstein** ⓲, and then it's on to the resort town of 📷 **Filzmoos** ⓳. On your sixth day, make an excursion to the dramatic underworld of the **Eisriesenwelt** ice caves near 📷 **Werfen** ㉑, winding up your journey with a trip to the magnificent medieval castle, where birds of prey still swoop over the imposing fortress, and a final evening culinary blow-out at Obauer, one of the finest restaurants in Austria.

the region, isolating Alpine villages whose picture-postcard perfection has remained unspoiled through the centuries. The mountainous terrain makes some backtracking necessary if you're interested in visiting the entire area, but driving through the spectacular scenery is part of the appeal of touring the region.

About the Restaurants & Hotels

While this region contains fine restaurants—in fact, two of the country's top dozen dining establishments are here—most of the dining in the small towns of the Eastern Alps will take place in *Gasthöfe*/*Gasthäuser* (country hotels/inns), where the dining rooms are not necessarily separate restaurants. Note that in many cases such inns are closed in the off season, particularly November and possibly April or May.

When you think of Alpine hotels, you probably think of chalet-style inns with flower-decked balconies and overhanging eaves. Not surprisingly, that's mainly what you find in the Eastern Alps, though the range runs from family-run country inns to professionally managed resorts. This part of Austria is relatively inexpensive, except for the top resort towns of Saalbach–Hinterglemm, Bad Gastein, and Zell am See. Even there, however, cheaper accommodations are available outside the center of town or in pensions.

Note that room rates include taxes and service and almost always breakfast, except in the most expensive hotels, and one other meal, which is usually dinner. *Halb Pension* (half board), as this plan is called, is de rigueur in most lodgings. However, most will offer a breakfast buffet–only rate if requested. Most hotels offer in-room phones and TVs. A few of the smaller hotels still take no credit cards. In the prominent resorts, summer prices are often as much as 50% lower than during the ski season.

WHAT IT COSTS In euros				
	$$$$	**$$$**	**$$**	**$**	**¢**
RESTAURANTS	over €22	€18–€22	€13–€17	€7–€12	under €7
HOTELS	over €175	€135–€175	€100–€135	€70–€100	under €70

Restaurant prices are per person for a main course at dinner. Hotel prices are for a standard double room in high season, including taxes and service. Assume that hotels operate on the European Plan (EP, with no meal provided) unless we note that they use the Breakfast Plan (BP), Modified American Plan (MAP, with breakfast and dinner daily, known as "halb pension"), or Full American Plan (FAP, or "voll pension," with three meals a day). Higher prices (inquire when booking) prevail for any meal plans.

Timing

Depending on your interests, the Eastern Alps makes a good destination at various times of year. Snowy conditions can make driving a white-knuckle experience, but winter also brings extensive, superb skiing throughout the region—often at a fraction of the cost of the more famous resorts in Tirol. In summer, the craggy mountain peaks and lush meadows provide challenge and joy to hikers, while spelunkers head into the bowels of the behemoths. Placid lakes and meandering mountain

8

Striking Gold The biggest vacation hit in the Eastern Alps may be a golden opportunity: gold-washing at Alten Pocher, a 16th-century–style Goldgräberdorf (gold-mining town) built upon historic gold mines in the Fleiss valley. The Hohe Tauern was considered one of the most important gold-mining regions of its day, and gold was mined near Heiligenblut from the 14th century until the turn of the 20th century. Many caves were created through grueling labor by thousands of miners over this period, under the most arduous conditions (of course, the owners of the mines themselves lived comfortable and rich lives). Alten Pocher, 10 minutes from Heiligenblut and over 1,800 m (5,906 ft) above sea level, showcases the lives of the miners who dug for gold here for so many centuries; don't forget to visit the Freilichtmuseum (open-air museum), where you can gain insight into their living conditions. If you get struck by gold fever, you can try panning for gold in the Fleiss stream under expert supervision—and perhaps go home a little richer. (At the very least, those who try will get a coin as a souvenir.)

Highway to Heaven The National Park Hohe Tauern is one of the most varied and unspoiled landscapes on the globe—high alpine meadows, deep evergreen woods, endless spiraling rock cliffs, and glacial ice fields—and, at 1,786 square km (690 square mi), the largest national park of central Europe. To help you see the Hohe Tauern's myriad splendors is the unique and world-renowned Großglockner Hochalpenstraße, one of the most spectacular sightseeing roads in the Alps. This 48-km (30-mi) engineering masterpiece was opened in 1935. More than 3,000 workers were needed to build its road and tunnels, which twist and turn their way up to the 4,138-km (2,571-mi) high Edelweißspitze ("Edelweiss point"—and indeed you can smell the fragrant blossoms while navigating the twisty turns). Approximately 1.5 million people come to traverse the scenic road every year between May and October, stopping at the many information stations, trails, and viewpoints along the way. The Großglockner Hochalpenstraße will bring you directly to Heiligenblut, an alpine vision on its own, and an ideal starting point for activities like hiking, climbing, and glacier excursions.

streams attract anglers for some of the best fishing to be found in the country.

TO LIENZ, UP THE DEFEREGGENTAL & BACK

Take Route 86 south out of Villach, through Warmbad Villach, and then Route 83 to Arnoldstein, about 10 km (6 mi) away. You're in the Gail River valley here, with the magnificent Karawanken mountains rising in Yugoslavia on your left. Just beyond Arnoldstein, turn right onto Route 111, marked for Hermagor. On the way up, the views will now be on the right, the dramatic Gailtal Alps in the background as you head west.

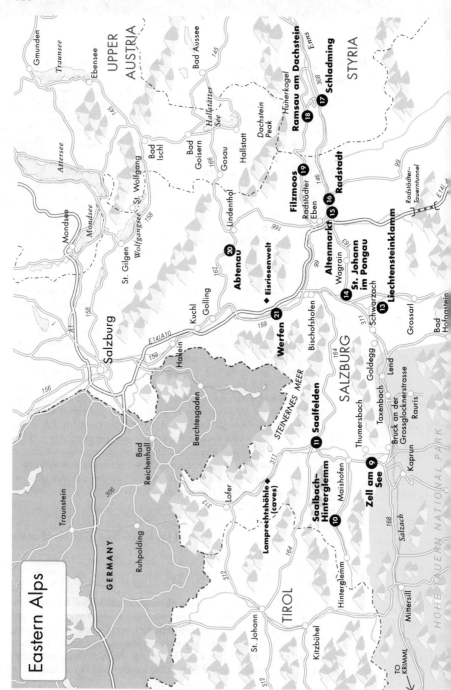

Eastern Alps

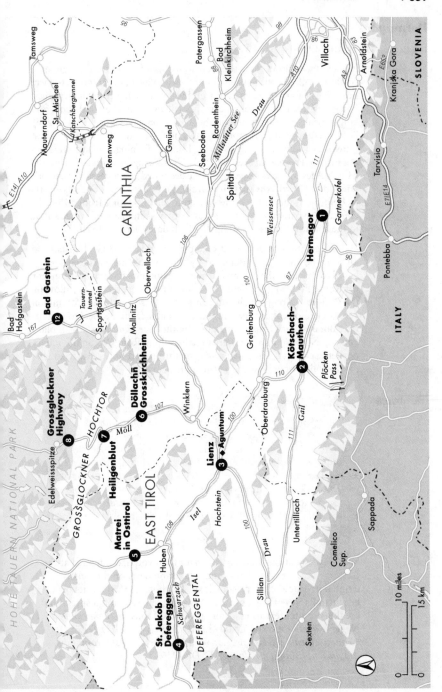

Hermagor

❶ *46 km (29 mi) west of Villach.*

The swift Gail flows along the southwest edge of Carinthia through small scattered villages with ancient churches and aged, often wooden, farm houses. The narrow valley is peacefully soft, with many old linden trees, but its fir-treed slopes rise steeply, particularly on the south side, and craggy peaks peer from behind them. The main town in the Gail valley is Hermagor, situated approximately in its center. Hermagor is best known as a summer resort, offering hiking, climbing, and swimming in the nearby Pressegger See, but it also has skiing in winter. During the Middle Ages, villagers believed that the decorated keystones in Hermagor's late-Gothic **Pfarrkirche** (parish church) symbolized Jesus Christ's efforts to hold the framework of the church together. Dating from 1484, the church is also notable for its intricately carved and painted winged altar in the south Wolkenstein Chapel, which dates back to 1510.

Did the creation of the world take place in this area? Geologists from all over the world are fascinated by the possible answers that are believed to lie within the nearby Gartnerkogel mountain south of Hermagor off Route 90. Amateur sleuths can join in the experience by following the **Geo-Trail**, along which you can gather fossils and trace 50 million years of geological history. Maps are available from the local tourist office. Botanists are equally intrigued by the blue *Wulfenia,* which blankets the Nassfeld mountain area farther along Route 90 on the Italian border each June. The flower, which is protected under Austrian law, can be found only here and in the Himalayas.

> **en route** From Hermagor, both Route 87, running northwest to Greifenburg, and Route 111 up to the adjoining villages of Kötschach and Mauthen offer gorgeous views, and the distances to Lienz on both are about 55 km (35 mi). If you choose Route 87, you can turn right shortly before
★ Greifenburg for a detour to the blue-green **Weissensee,** a relatively undeveloped narrow lake 11 km (7 mi) long, tucked in between high mountain ridges, where there are excellent fishing and boating and, in winter, ice skating and cross-country skiing. Then at Greifenburg turn west onto Route 100 up the Drau River valley toward Lienz. Or, from Kötschach, drive north on Route 110 to reach Oberdrauburg, then west onto Route 100.

You may stay at the Weissensee longer than you had intended at the ☒ **Alpenhof,** a true wellness and relaxation oasis on the mostly uninhabited side of the pristine lake. The hotel ($$$$) has its own beach and acres of meadow, a rather complete spa, and a sprawling breakfast buffet featuring locally produced foods. ✉ *Panoramaweg 1 Naggl, Kärnten A-9762* ☎ *04713/2107–0* 🖶 *04713/2107–15* 🌐 *www.alpenhof-weissensee.at* ↪ *35 rooms* ⚭ *Restaurant, lake, spa, beach, fishing; no a/c* ▭ *AE, DC, MC, V.*

Kötschach–Mauthen

② *25 km (16 mi) west of Hermagor.*

Most sightseers travel to Kötschach and Mauthen, its twin across Route 111, to enjoy the natural beauty the area has to offer and to pay a call on the Kellerwand, one of Austria's top restaurants. The year-round resort is a good base for excursions via the Plöcken Pass over the border into Italy or up the Lesach Valley through the Austrian (Lienzer) Dolomites. The early frescoes and unusual decorated arched ceiling that adorn Kötschach–Mauthen's **Pfarrkirche** (parish church), which dates from 1527, make it worth a stop, too.

Where to Stay & Eat

★ **$$$–$$$$** ✕⛺ **Kellerwand.** Elegant tables in a quiet, luxurious atmosphere highlight the superb quality of the food, an uncommonly imaginative treatment of area specialties, including outstanding delicate pasta dishes and roast lamb or venison. Frau Sonnleitner, the owner and head chef, is one of the most celebrated chefs in Austria. The unpretentious residence includes a small hotel, where rooms with tile floors and luxury suites are attractively decorated in a country style. ⊠ *Mauthen 24, A-9640 Mauthen* ☎ *04715/269–0* 🖷 *04715/269–16* ⊕ *www.sissy-sonnleitner.at* ⇄ *12 rooms, 6 suites* ⚶ *Restaurant, in-room safes, minibars, sauna, bar; no a/c* ▤ *AE, DC, MC, V* ⊘ *Closed mid-Apr. and 2 wks in Dec. Restaurant closed Mon. and Tues.* ⫟⊙⫟ *BP, MAP.*

$$ ✕⛺ **Naturabenteuer Hotel Post.** This interesting house of eccentric design, with odd balconies and a triangular garden, is in the center of town. Rooms are attractively decorated, and in summer, excursions, climbing, rafting, and fishing are offered. ⊠ *Hauptplatz 66, A-9640 Kötschach–Mauthen* ☎ *04715/221–0* 🖷 *04715/222–59* ⇄ *24 rooms* ⚶ *Restaurant, café, some in-room safes, minibars, pool, gym, sauna, fishing, bar, Internet; no a/c* ▤ *MC, V* ⊘ *Closed late Oct.–mid-Apr.* ⫟⊙⫟ *BP, MAP.*

> **en route** The scenic Route 110 north over the Gailberg will bring you, after about 14 km (9 mi) and some dramatic twists and turns, to Route 100 at Oberdrauburg. From here to Lienz (20 km [12 mi]), the highway follows the Drau River valley, with splendid views up into the Kreuzeck mountain range on your right. The Romans recognized the strategic importance of the region and in about AD 50 established **Aguntum** here to protect the important trade route against possible attack by native tribes. About 4 km (2½ mi) before you reach Lienz, you'll come to the excavations to the right of the road. You can explore the site, where archaeologists have been unearthing remains of this ancient settlement, quite freely.

Lienz

③ *34 km (21 mi) northwest of Kötschach–Mauthen.*

Tucked in at the confluence of the Drau and Isel rivers, with the Dolomites a dramatic backdrop to the south, Lienz, a summer and winter resort, is now the capital of the region. The awe-inspiring peaks rising around the town might make your first impression one of human insignificance in the face of overwhelming power and glory. Such feelings of reverence may account for the number of notable churches in Lienz; at least five are worth a visit, particularly the **St. Andrä Pfarrkirche** (parish church) on Patriadorferstrasse, which you can reach by walking up Muchar Gasse and Schweizergasse or by following the Rechter Iselweg along the river. A Romanesque lion decorates the doorway, attesting to the church's early roots. The present-day Gothic edifice was completed in 1457, while the interior is Baroque, from the winged high altar to the vividly colored ceiling fresco (1761). Note the ornate marble tombstones of the noble Görz family.

Three blocks from St. Andrä—cross the Pfarrbrücke into Beda Weber-Gasse and turn left into Patriadorferstrasse—you'll find the **War Memorial Chapel**, designed in 1926 by Clemens Holzmeister, the architect responsible for Salzburg's Festspielhaus and Felsenreitschule (the festival theaters). The wall paintings are by Albin Egger-Lienz (1868–1926), who is renowned for his ability to portray human strength and weakness and who is also buried here. Close to the center of town, the **Franciscan Church** on the Muchargasse was originally a Carmelite cloister, founded in 1349 by the Countess Euphemia of Görz. The church was taken over by the Franciscans in 1785 and restored in 1947–48. A Gothic pietà from about 1400 adorns the left side altar at the back; the wall frescoes are from the 15th century.

A wooden statue dedicated to St. Wolfgang can be found on the Schweizergasse in the 1243 **Dominican Church,** which was subsequently rebuilt in late-Gothic style. **St. Michael's** on Michaeler Platz on the north side of the Isel was completed in 1530, but the north tower, with its onion dome, dates only from 1713. Note the fancy ceiling ornamentation, the 1683 high altar, and the gravestones. The Rococo **St. Joseph's,** by the Spitalsbrücke, was badly damaged in 1945 and rebuilt in 1957. **St. Antonius** on the Hauptplatz dates from the 16th century. The restored 16th-century **Lieburg Palace** on the Hauptplatz, with two towers, now houses provincial government offices.

A massive tower looms over **Schloss Bruck,** a battlemented residential castle that dates from 1280 and now serves as the city museum. The remarkably well-preserved castle also has a Romanesque chapel with a late 15th-century ceiling and wall frescoes. Works by Egger-Lienz and Franz Defregger (1835–1921), another Tirolean painter, are displayed here, along with Celtic and Roman relics from nearby excavations. ⊠ *Iseltaler Strasse* ☎ *04852/62580–83* ⊡ *€2* ⊘ *Mid-May–Nov., daily 10–6.*

Where to Stay & Eat

★ $$$ ×⊡ **Traube.** In summer, the striped awnings of this central hotel shade the cafés on the street and balcony. A note of elegance is struck, thanks to a mix of older furniture and antiques in the spacious, comfortable rooms. The historic hotel has its own fishing waters and a rooftop swimming pool with wonderful views of the surrounding mountains. The Italian restaurant's food is not quite up to the scenery, but take the recommendations and you won't be unhappy. ✉ *Hauptplatz 14, A-9900* ☎ *04852/ 64444* ⊟ *04852/64184* ⇨ *51 rooms* ⚭ *Restaurant, café, indoor pool, sauna, fishing, bar, Internet; no a/c* ⊟ *AE, DC, MC, V* ⎮⊙⎮ *BP, MAP.*

★ **$$** ✕⎯ **Parkhotel Tristachersee.** A little more than 4 km (2½ mi) southeast of Lienz (take the road via Amlach marked to Tristachersee) is a small lake hidden away up a hill. It's a magical setting for this diminutive country hotel, whose rooms have dark paneled walls and lots of fabrics. A lakeside terrace provides opportunity for relaxation, and an excellent restaurant (open only to guests) ladles out regional cuisine, including fresh fish from the hotel's own ponds. Try the grilled slices of Zander (pike-perch) with homemade noodles and lightly braised tomatoes. ✉ *Tristachersee 1, A-9900* ☎ *04852/67666* ⊟ *04852/67699* ⊕ *www. parkhotel-tristachersee.at* ⇨ *40 rooms, 7 suites* ⚭ *Restaurant, indoor pool, lake, sauna, bar; no a/c* ⊟ *DC, MC, V* ⊙ *Closed Apr. and Nov.–mid-Dec.* ⎮⊙⎮ *BP, MAP.*

¢ ✕⎯ **Gasthof Goldener Stern.** If you are watching your budget but would like to stay in historic surroundings, then this is the place to go: the "Golden Star" was built around 1400. The interiors are done in simple peasant style—nothing fancy, but everything cozy. Some rooms in the newer annex have balconies. There's no restaurant, but coffee and homemade cake in the afternoon will add to the coziness. ✉ *Schweizergasse 40, A-9900* ☎⊟ *04852/62192* ⇨ *20 rooms* ⊟ *No credit cards* ⎮⊙⎮ *BP.*

Sports & the Outdoors

HIKING Lienz and its surrounding area have miles of marked trails, and detailed maps, available from the tourist office, show mountain lodges where you can spend the night and other facilities. Trails in Tirol are designated as easy, moderate, or difficult. Just before Schloss Bruck there is a chairlift that rises nearly to the crest of the 6,685-foot **Hochstein** mountain, from which you get a splendid panoramic view over Lienz and to the east. You'll have to hike the last kilometer (⅗ mi) to reach the very top.

If you want to learn to climb, contact Leo Baumgartner at the **Alpinschule Lienz** (✉ Gaimberg, A-9900 ☎ 04852/68770).

WHITE-WATER Stretches of the **Isel River** from Matrei down to Lienz are raftable from
RAFTING May to mid-October. The Drau, which always has enough water, is used for easy rides or beginners. Hard-core rafters will enjoy the Schwarzach in the Defereggental, known as "East Tirol's toughest river." For outfitters, check with a tourist office, or contact the **Osttiroler Kajak Club** (☎ 04852/61159) in Lienz. Several companies offer rafting tours at prices beginning around €25 per person and with a minimum of five people. White-water outfitters include Dieter Messner at **Kids and Family Rafting** (✉ Ainet 41, A-9900 Ainet ☎ 04853/5231). **Osttirol Adventures** (✉ Rechter Drauweg 1B–Dolomitenbad, A-9951 Ainet ☎ 04853/ 200–30 ⊕ www.osttirol-adventures.at) can help you with canyoning and paragliding.

St. Jakob in Defereggen

❹ *43 km (27 mi) northwest of Lienz.*

Few American tourists venture into the Defereggen mountain range, although its craggy slopes are sprinkled with unspoiled villages. The small resort of St. Jakob in Defereggen is one of the most charming in East Tirol. Sports enthusiasts flock to the area for hiking, climbing, rafting, and fishing in summer and skiing in winter. There are also sulfur baths at nearby St. Leonhard and a waterfall at Mariahilf. To reach St. Jakob from Lienz, head northwest on Route 108, following the Isel Valley, and turn left at the village of Huben, about 19 km (12 mi) out of Lienz, onto a scenic side roadway that takes you up the valley, the Defereggental. St. Jakob is 23 km (14 mi) from Huben. The right-hand side of the Defereggental constitutes the beginning of **Hohe Tauern National Park,** an area of mountains that touches on three states (Salzburg, Carinthia, and Tirol) and includes the Grossglockner group. The more hardy traveler may want to spend a few days hiking and lodging at any one of several refuges, where one is sometimes treated to very rustic, homemade victuals (cheeses and hams). The national park has several offices; the closest to Lienz is in **Matrei** (⊠ Nationalparkverwaltung Tirol, Rauterplatz 1, A-9971 Matrei in Osttirol ☎ 04875/5161–0 📠 04875/5161–20 ⊕ www.hohetauern.at).

Where to Stay & Eat

$$–$$$ ✕🏨 **Alpenhof.** A large chalet set against a velvet-green hillside is an ideal starting point for summer hiking and for skiing. From the outside it is completely out of style with the modest houses of the Defereggental, but the rooms are comfortable, with flower-decked balconies, and the hotel pays particular attention to families with children. The restaurant showcases regional dishes; ask for recommendations. ⊠ *Innerrotte 35, A-9963* ☎ *04873/5351–0* 📠 *04873/5351–500* ⊕ *www.alpenhof-defereggental. at* ➳ *85 rooms* ⚐ *Restaurant, in-room safes, minibars, indoor pool, sauna, bar, nightclub, children's programs (ages 3–7); no a/c* ⊟ *AE, DC, MC, V* ☯ *Closed May and mid-Oct.–mid-Dec.* ❍ *BP, MAP.*

¢ 🏨 **Farmhouses.** If you fall in love with the Hohe Tauern mountains (which happens instantly for the most part) and decide you may want to stay for a while, ask at any tourist office about booking rooms at a farmhouse. Some even offer meals. It's a wonderful way to get close to the land itself. Prices range from about €15 to €20 per person per day. The little brochure "Urlaub am Bergbauernhof" will whet your appetite, and you may consider moving to Osttirol at once, for good. For more information, contact **Osttirol Werbung** (⊠ Albin-Egger Strasse, A-9900 Lienz ☎ 04852/65333–2 ⊕ www.osttirol.com).

Matrei in Osttirol

❺ *31 km (19 mi) northeast of St. Jakob in Defereggen.*

Because of its strategic location on one of the easier north–south routes over the Alps, Matrei in Osttirol has a long history to look back on, including Celtic and then Roman periods. Every year on the eve of St.

Nicholas's Day (December 6), fantastically dressed characters with furs and bells storm through town in an old tradition called *Klaubaufgehen,* a way to frighten off bad spirits. The **Church of St. Alban** in town is definitely worth entering for its rich interior. The real treasure, however, is the Romanesque **Church of St. Nicholas,** which is on the other side of the Isel at the beginning of the Virgen Valley. It contains some simple carvings, such as the 15th-century statue of St. Nicholas, and its late-13th-century frescoes of biblical scenes elevate it to a high work of art. Remarkably well-preserved 14th-century frescoes decorate the outside walls. Just north of Matrei, standing on a daunting rock, is **Schloss Weissenstein,** a 12th-century castle that underwent substantial rebuilding in the 1800s and is now privately owned.

Where to Stay & Eat

★ $$–$$$ ✕⊡ **Rauter.** With an ultramodern facade, clean lines, and slick surfaces, this fashionably contemporary house offers elegant comfort in stark contrast to the usual rustic Alpine style. Here, too, are many diversions and the best restaurant in East Tirol. The fish comes from the hotel's own waters, the lamb from the nearby mountains, and the house bakery provisions the café. A hotel bus brings you to and from hiking areas in summer, and ski slopes in winter. Fishing is available for those staying three days or longer, and there is horseback riding nearby. ⊠ *Rauterplatz 3, A-9971* ☎ *04875/6611* 🖷 *04875/6613* ⊕ *www.hotel-rauter.at* ⬩ *50 rooms* ⚬ *Restaurant, café, indoor-outdoor pools, gym, sauna, fishing, bar; no a/c* ⊟ *AE, DC, MC, V* ⊘ *Closed Nov.–mid-Dec.* ¶⚬ *BP, MAP.*

★ ¢   ⊡ **Alpengasthof Tauernhaus.** There's quiet comfort in this simple rustic Gasthof about 14 km (9 mi) up the Tauern Valley at the base of the Felbertauern pass. The hotel began as a rest house, founded in 1207 by the archbishops of Salzburg. It is a good starting point for hiking and skiing. ⊠ *A-9971* ☎ *04875/8811* 🖷 *04875/8812* ⊕ *www.matreiertauernhaus.at* ⬩ *41 rooms, 21 with full bath, 12 with shower* ⚬ *Restaurant, sauna; no a/c* ⊟ *No credit cards* ⊘ *Closed Nov.* ¶⚬ *BP.*

ACROSS THE GROSSGLOCKNER PASS

This is the excursion over the longest and most spectacular highway through the Alps, the Grossglockner High Alpine Highway, an engineering achievement of the first magnitude. There is a thrill every hundred yards along this scenic route, but your first will be sighting Heiligenblut, one of Austria's prettiest towns, at the foot of the Grossglockner. To explore this region, winter travelers have no choice but to drive north out of Lienz on Route 108, arriving in Mittersill in Salzburg Province via the 5-km (3-mi) Felbertauern toll tunnel (€10 one-way, €15 day pass) under the Tauern mountains, and taking Route 168 east to Zell am See. But if the road is open, go north over the Grossglockner Highway. (The trip can be done by car or bus.) Leave Lienz via Route 107, but stop on the way up the hill outside Iselsberg–Stronach for a great panoramic view over the city. As you go over the ridge, you'll be entering Carinthia again. At Winklern the road follows the Möll River valley, and after about 11 km (7 mi) you'll come to Döllach–Grosskirchheim.

Döllach–Grosskirchheim

❻ *28 km (17 mi) northeast of Lienz.*

The **Gartl Waterfall** is a short stroll from the center of town—in summer, you can safely walk through the spray to feel the water's power and refresh yourself on a warm day.

Where to Stay & Eat

$$ ╳☒ **Schlosswirt.** Rooms range from somewhat spartan to elegant in this appealing chalet hotel at the base of the mountains on the fringe of the Grossglockner. In season you can climb, hike, ski, and ride horseback in the gorgeous "hidden valley" of the Graden brook. The hotel has its own fishing streams and lake, and it organizes alpine programs for guests. The restaurant has slipped since it started serving tour groups but is still worth a try; ask for recommendations. ☒ *A-9843* ☎ *04825/211–0 or 04825/411–0* 🖷 *04825/211–165* 🛏 *25 rooms* ♨ *Restaurant, tennis court, lake, sauna, steam room, fishing, horseback riding; no a/c* ☐ *AE, MC, V* ☺ *Closed Nov. and 3 wks in Apr.* ¶◯| *BP, MAP.*

Heiligenblut

❼ *10 km (6 mi) north of Döllach–Grosskirchheim.*

Fodor'sChoice
★

Some say the best time to experience this little slice of Alpine nirvana is after a leisurely dinner at one of the many Gasthöfe, gazing out at the starry firmament over the Hohe Tauern range. Others relish standing around an early morning thaw-out fire used by hikers setting out to conquer the mighty foothills of the Grossglockner peaks, the highest in Austria. This small town nestled in a valley is known for its picturesque church set against an equally picturesque mountain backdrop (there are 40 peaks over 3,000 meters, or 10,000 feet, here), but it's the famed mountain-climbing school and climbing and skiing possibilities that draw flocks of all-out active types.

According to local legend, St. Briccius, after obtaining a vial of the blood of Jesus, was buried by an avalanche, but when his body was recovered, the tiny vial was miraculously found hidden within one of the saint's open wounds. The town gets its name, Heiligenblut (Holy Blood), from this miraculous event. Today the relic is housed in the Sakramenthäuschen, the chapel of the small but beautiful Gothic **Church of St. Vincent.** Completed in 1490 after more than a century of construction under the toughest conditions, the church is marked by its soaring belfry tower. Sublimely, the sharply pointed spire finds an impressive echo in the conical peak of the Grossglockner. St. Vincent's contains a beautifully carved late-Gothic double altar nearly 36 feet high, and the Coronation of Mary is depicted in the altar wings, richly carved by Wolfgang Hasslinger in 1520. The region's most important altarpiece, it imparts a feeling of quiet power in this spare, high church. The church also has a noble crypt and graveyard, the latter sheltering graves of those lost in climbing the surrounding mountains.

You can get to Heiligenblut by bus from Lienz or Zell am See (note that some buses stop in the tiny hamlet of Winklern, directly below the town). During the winter, buses run from Heiligenblut to nearby ski runs. Heiligenblut loves tourists, and special deals are usually offered, ranging from bargain cards issued to visitors staying more than three days to cut-rate, one-day ski passes.

Where to Stay & Eat

$$$–$$$$ ⤬▦ **Glocknerhof.** This dark-wood chalet in the center of the village fits perfectly into the surroundings. Close to climbing in summer and skiing in winter, the hotel has its own fishing streams. Tour groups stop here on the way over the Grossglockner Highway, and the restaurant is quite good. It serves its own trout and other mountain-stream fish; ask if there is *Gams* (local chamois) on the menu. ✉ *Hof 6, A-9844* ☎ *04824/2244* 🖷 *04824/2244–66* ⊕ *www.glockner.co.at* ⇌ *52 rooms* ♨ *Restaurant, in-room safes, indoor pool, sauna, fishing, bar, children's programs (ages 3–7); no a/c* ▭ *MC, V* ☉ *Closed mid-May–mid-June, Oct., and Nov.* |◎| *BP, MAP.*

$$$$ ▦ **Heiligenblut.** This family-friendly hotel a short distance from the town center consists of an older house with apartments, and a newer house, wherein lie the hotel rooms and restaurant. All quarters have balconies, and you may request either a view of the mountains or of the Aldstadt (Old Town). Meals are served buffet style, which is practical for families. ✉ *Winkl 46, A-9844* ☎ *04824/4111* 🖷 *04824/4111–88* ⊕ *www.hotel-heiligenblut.at* ⇌ *125 rooms* ♨ *Restaurant, in-room safes, tennis courts, indoor pool, gym, massage, sauna, Ping-Pong, bar, baby-sitting, Internet; no a/c* ▭ *AE, DC, MC, V* ☉ *Closed Easter–May and Sept.–mid-Dec.* |◎| *BP, MAP.*

★ $$–$$$ ▦ **Hotel Lärchenhof.** This charming hotel is a true *Panoramagasthof*— a guest house with spectacular views of the surrounding Alpine scenery from room balconies festooned with flowers in summer. The chalet-style building is perched on a mountain slope and surrounded by lush forest, so it's easy to feel you've left civilization behind. Rooms are comfortably appointed with pastel fabrics and sturdy wood furniture. ✉ *Hof 70, A-9844* ☎ *04824/2262* 🖷 *04824/2262–45* ⊕ *www.ski-heiligenblut.at* ⇌ *23 rooms* ♨ *Restaurant, sauna, bar; no a/c* ▭ *AE, DC, MC, V* |◎| *BP, MAP.*

$$ ▦ **Senger.** Weathered wood and flowered balconies highlight this old farmhouse chalet, which has been cleverly enlarged while keeping its original rustic appeal. The rooms and romantic apartments, featuring lots of pillows and country prints, continue the attractive rural theme. It's a bit outside the center of town. ✉ *Heiligenblut 23, A-9844* ☎ *04824/2215* 🖷 *04824/2215–9* ⇌ *14 rooms, 8 apartments* ♨ *Restaurant, gym, sauna, bar; no a/c* ▭ *No credit cards* ☉ *Closed 1 wk after Easter–June and mid-Oct.–mid-Dec.* |◎| *BP, MAP.*

Sports & the Outdoors

DIGGING FOR GOLD From mid-June through September, you can pan for gold in the streams around Heiligenblut. Buy a ticket for an excursion in the town at the **Tourist Office** (☎ *04824/2001–21*). The price (€12) includes the necessary equipment and a permit to take home your finds.

This is a hiker's El Dorado, with (in summer) more than 240 km (150 mi) of marked pathways and trails in all directions. There are relatively easy hikes to the Naturlehrweg Gössnitzfall–Kachlmoor (1½ hrs), Wirtsbauer–Alm (2 hrs), and the Jungfernsprung (2 hrs), which arrives atop a 152-meter (500-foot) stone cliff above the Mölltal. Enjoyable group or private **guided tours** are available. They cost anywhere from €5 to join a short group tour to €120 per person per day for a private tour lasting from one to three days. The **National Park Programs Office** (☎ 04825/616114 or 04824/2700) has all the information.

Grossglockner Highway

❽ *Grossglockner Highway is 46 km (29 mi) long.*

This is the excursion over the longest and most spectacular highway through the Alps, officially named the Grossglockner High Alpine Highway (107)—the Grossglocknerstrasse. There is a bit of mystery about this road: before it was built, there had been no passage anywhere between the Brenner Pass and the Radstädter Tauern Pass (more than 160 km [100 mi] apart) leading over these high mountains, nor was it on record that there had ever before been a regularly used route across the barrier at this point. Yet when the engineers who built the High Alpine Highway were blasting for the Hochtor tunnel, through which it passes at one point, they found, deep in the bowels of a mountain, a Roman statuette of, appropriately, Hercules.

You can traverse the Grossglockner Highway by bus or private car. From Heiligenblut the climb begins up the Carinthian side of the Grossglockner. A €26 toll here allows you to use the highway as much as you like on the same day. There's also a ticket for €35 good for any thirty consecutive days. The peak itself—at 12,470 feet the highest point in Austria—is off to the west. You can get somewhat closer than the main road takes you by following the highly scenic but steep Gletscherstrasse westward up to the Gletscherbahn on the Franz-Josef-Plateau, where you'll be rewarded with absolutely breathtaking views of the Grossglockner peak and surrounding Alps, of the vast glacier in the valley below, and, on a clear day, even into Italy.

The Grossglockner road twists and turns as it struggles to the 8,370-foot Hochtor. At this point you've crossed into Salzburg Province. The road was completed in 1935, after five years of labor by 3,200 workers. You're now on Edelweiss-Strasse. A stop at the **Edelweissspitze** yields an unbelievable view out over East Tirol, Carinthia, and Salzburg, including 19 glaciers and 37 peaks over the 9,600-foot mark. The rare white edelweiss—the Trapps sang its praises in *The Sound of Music*—grows here. Though the species is protected, don't worry about the plants you get as souvenirs; they are cultivated for this purpose. However, it is strictly forbidden to pick a wild edelweiss (and several other plant species), should you happen to come across one. Be sure to stop in at the visitor center and the Alpine museum. An excellent short film (in English) tells the story of the area, and computer-driven dioramas show how animals survive the extreme climatic changes atop the mountain range. ⊠ *Grossglockner Hwy., Km 26* ☎ *0662/873673 road information* ⊕ *www.grossglockner.at* 🎫 *Free* ☉ *Early May–late Oct., daily 9–5.*

Zell am See

★ ❾ *8 km (5 mi) northwest of the Grossglockner.*

After the toll station on the north side of the Grossglockner peak, the highway finally exhausts its hairpin turns (more than 30) and continues to Bruck an der Grossglocknerstrasse. From here it's only about 8 km (5 mi) west on Route S11 and then north on Route 311 to Zell am See. This lovely lakeside town got its name from the monks' cells of a monastery founded here in about AD 790.

In the town center, visit the 17th-century Renaissance **Schloss Rosenberg,** now the town hall. The **Kastnerturm,** built around 1300, was originally a fortified tower for an abbey and then a granary. It now houses the city museum, with an eclectic collection of old furnishings and handicrafts, open May–October, weekdays 1:30–5:30. Unusually fine statues of St. George and St. Florian can be found on the west wall of the splendid Romanesque **St. Hippolyte Pfarrkirche** (parish church), built in 1217. The tower came about two centuries later, and the church itself was beautifully renovated in 1975.

Several locations offer up stunning vistas of the town and its environs. On ground level, take a boat ride to the village of **Thumersbach,** on the opposite shore, for a wonderful reflected view of Zell am See. For a bird's-eye view, a cable car leads virtually from the center of Zell am See up to the **Schmittenhöhe** for a 180-degree panorama that takes in the peaks of the Glockner and Tauern granite ranges to the south and west and the very different limestone ranges to the north. This sweep will impress upon you the geology of Austria as no written description ever could. In addition, there are four other cable-car trips up this mountain, offering some of the most spectacular vistas of the Kitzbühel Alps.

Ⓒ The romantic narrow-gauge **Pinzgauer Railroad** winds its way under steam power on a two-hour trip through the Pinzgau, following the Salzach River valley westward 54 km (34 mi) to Krimml. Nearby are the famous Krimmler waterfalls, with a 1,300-foot drop, which you can see from an observation platform or explore close at hand if you can manage a hike of about three and a half to four hours. Be sure to take a raincoat and sneakers. ☎ *06542/17000* 🎫 *Round-trip €19.70* ☉ *Trains depart July 4–Sept. 19, Tues., Thurs., and weekends at 9:15 AM.*

Where to Stay & Eat

$$$$ ✕🏨 **Grand Hotel Zell am See.** In the style of the great turn-of-the-century resort hotels, this palatial lake house is, as its name implies, probably the grandest place to stay in Zell. It stands on its own peninsula, is decorated with mansard roofs and whipped-cream stuccowork, and serves up some fine dining. Most of the accommodations are small apartments, some with fireplaces; the best are those farthest out on the small peninsula. ⊠ *Esplanade 4, A-5700* ☎ *06542/788* 🖶 *06542/788–305* ⊕ *www.grandhotel-zellamsee.at* 🛏 *111 rooms* 🍴 *2 restaurants, in-room safes, kitchenettes,*

*minibars, indoor pool, lake, sauna, boating, squash, bar, children's pro-
grams (ages 3–12); no a/c* ☰ *AE, DC, MC, V* ⏻◯⏻ *BP, MAP.*

★ **$$$$** ✕▦ **Salzburgerhof.** Sophisticated travelers often describe this impressive
family-managed chalet, not far from the lake and the ski lift, as the town's
foremost hotel, where comfort and personal service rule. Each of the
attractive rooms and suites has a flower-bedecked balcony. The restaurant is truly excellent; try the *Tafelspitz* (boiled beef) or rack of lamb in
an herb pastry crust. The pleasant garden is used for barbecues and
evenings of folkloric entertainment. Golfers get a 30% discount at the
local club. ✉ *Auerspergstrasse 11, A-5700* ☎ *06542/765–0* 🖷 *06542/
76566* ⊕ *www.salzburgerhof.at* ⤴ *36 rooms, 24 suites* ⚲ *Restaurant,
in-room safes, minibars, indoor pool, lake, gym, sauna, spa, bar; no a/c*
☰ *AE, DC, MC, V* ⊙ *Closed Nov.* ⏻◯⏻ *BP, MAP.*

★ **$$$$** ✕▦ **Schloss Prielau.** With its turreted towers and striped shutters, this
castle looks as if it stepped out of a fairy tale. The elegantly furnished
rooms, decorated with sumptuous fabrics and traditional carved-wood
furniture, are a bit dim because of the narrow, old-fashioned windows.
But the service will make you feel as if you are the newest member of
royalty to take up residence here. The restaurant serves classic Austrian
dishes like schnitzel but with a lighter, more refined touch than you find
in most other establishments. ✉ *Hofmannsthalstrasse, A-5700* ☎ *06542/
72911–0* 🖷 *06542/72911–11* ⊕ *www.schloss-prielau.com* ⤴ *12 rooms*
⚲ *Restaurant, minibars, lake, sauna, bar; no a/c* ☰ *AE, DC, MC, V*
⊙ *Closed May* ⏻◯⏻ *BP, MAP.*

$–$$ ✕▦ **St. Hubertushof.** On the opposite side of the lake from town, this sprawl-
ing hotel complex offers a great view across the water. Wood paneling
and antlers over the fireplace in the lounge add to its rural feel. Golfers
get a 30% discount at the local course. The restaurant offers both international and local dishes, and the dance bar draws a regular crowd.
✉ *Seeuferstrasse 7, A-5705 Thumersbach* ☎ *06542/767* 🖷 *06542/767–
71* ⊕ *www.zellamsee.at/hubertushof* ⤴ *112 rooms* ⚲ *Restaurant, café,
sauna, bar; no a/c* ☰ *AE, DC, MC, V* ⊙ *Closed Nov.* ⏻◯⏻ *BP, MAP.*

Nightlife & the Arts

The emphasis in Zell is more on drinking than on dancing, but the scene
does change periodically. One of the "in" places is the **Crazy Daisy**
(☎ 06542/76359), a dance pub near the Zell am See tourist office. Also
near the tourist office and popular is the pub **Sugarshack** (☎06542/43059).
A mature crowd gathers at the **Wunderbar** (☎06542/73059), in the Grand
hotel (⇨ Where to Stay & Eat, *above*). Check out the action in the cellar of the **Sporthotel Lebzelter** (☎ 06542/766). Excellent cocktails and
sophisticated music are the draw at **B17** (☎ 06542/47424).

Sports & the Outdoors

BICYCLING The area around Zell am See is ideal for bicycling. If you left your wheels
at home, you can rent some at **Sport Achleitner** (☎06542/73581) for €10
per day for a city bike or €18 for a mountain bike. Renting by the week
is cheaper. From April to October, bike tours run from south of Zell am
See up to St. Johann and Salzburg via the Tauern cycle route. Check with
Austria Radreisen (✉Joseph-Haydn-Strasse 8, A-4780 Schärding ☎07712/
5511–0 🖷 07712/4811).

FISHING The lake's tranquil waters offer fine fishing, and many hotels in the area have packages for avid anglers. Boats are for hire at the **Strandbad** (☎ 0664/2068506).

SKIING Together with nearby Kaprun, Zell am See offers good skiing for beginners to experts, along with a wide spectrum of terrain. Towering over Zell am See, the Schmittenhöhe has tree-lined runs that will feel familiar to Colorado and New England skiers. The nearby Kitzsteinhorn mountain (3,200 meters, or 10,499 feet), famous throughout Austria, offers year-round glacier skiing and was the first glacier ski area in Austria. Together these mountains offer 57 lifts, with 130 km (80 mi) of prepared slopes. In addition, there are more than 200 km (124 mi) of cross-country trails and 8 ski schools. For full information on skiing facilities, contact the **local tourist office** (✉ Brucker Bundesstrasse, A-5700 Zell am See ☎ 06542/770-0 🖷 06542/72032 ⊕ www.zell.at).

WATER SPORTS Boating—from paddleboating to sailing—and swimming are excellent on the uncrowded Zeller See. Since powerboats are restricted on many Austrian lakes, you won't find much waterskiing, but there is a waterskiing school, **Wasserskischule Thumersbach** (✉ Strandbad, Thumersbach ☎ 06542/72355), on the lake.

Saalbach–Hinterglemm

🔟 *17 km (9 mi) northwest of Zell am See.*

Noted skiing headliners Saalbach and its neighbor Hinterglemm are part of an area comprising also Kaprun and Zell am See, that becomes a ski circus in winter. A clever layout of lifts and trails enables you to ski slopes without duplication and still get back to your starting point. When the snow melts, the region offers sensational hiking; both towns offer a full panoply of sports. Saalbach and Hinterglemm have each banned cars from its village center. You can drive to your hotel to unload baggage; watch carefully for signs or ask for specific directions—the routes are convoluted and confusing. Take the **Kohlmais cable car** north out of Saalbach to the top of the ridge for a superb 360-degree view of the surrounding mountain ranges.

To get to Saalbach–Hinterglemm from Zell am See, continue north on Route 311 to Maishofen, where the Glemm Valley opens to the west; then continue westward for about 9 km (5½ mi). For those traveling by train or bus, head first to Zell am See for transfers up the valley.

Where to Stay & Eat

★ ¢–$ ✕ **Iglsbergerhof.** This utterly unpretentious family-run Gasthof serves up some of the best authentic regional specialties in the area. Start with beef bouillon with *Pinzgauer Käspressknödel* (cheese dumplings), then have *Speckknödel* (bread dumpling with bacon chunks) with sauerkraut, and finish with a delicious *Pinzgauer Bauernkrapfen* (filled doughnut). ✉ *Vorderglemm 340, Saalbach* ☎ 06541/6491 ▭ *MC, V* ⊘ *Closed Apr. and Nov. No lunch Wed.*

$$$$ 🏨 **Saalbach Hof.** This family-run chalet complex in the center of town is identified by a rustic bell tower and overflowing pots of red geraniums against weathered dark wood. Warm paneling and a large fireplace

welcome you; the rooms are spacious and comfortable. Golfers get a 30% discount on greens fees at Zell am See courses, and every guest gets one free tennis hour daily on the hotel's own court. ✉ *Dorfplatz 27, A-5753* ☎ *06541/7111–0* 🖷 *06541/7111–42* 🌐 *www.saalbacherhof.at* *88 rooms* *3 restaurants, golf privileges, tennis court, pool, sauna, bar, nightclub* 💳 *MC, V* ⏲ *Closed mid-Apr.–May and mid-Oct.–early Dec.* 🍽 *BP, MAP.*

$$$–$$$$ **Glemmtalerhof.** This massive chalet is surprisingly intimate inside, with pleasant paneled rooms, some in Alpine style, most with balconies. It is mainly a winter resort, but there's still plenty to do in summer. Golfers get a 30% discount on greens fees at Zell am See courses. ✉ *Dorfstrasse 150, A-5754 Hinterglemm* ☎ *06541/7135* 🖷 *06541/7135–63* 🌐 *www.glemmtalerhof.at* *62 rooms, 20 apartments* *2 restaurants, café, pool, gym, sauna, horseback riding, 2 bars, nightclub, children's programs (ages 3–7); no a/c* 💳 *AE, DC, MC, V* ⏲ *Closed Apr.–mid-May and Nov.* 🍽 *BP, MAP.*

Sports & the Outdoors

SKIING In addition to offering tobogganing, sleigh riding, and curling, Saalbach and Hinterglemm have some of the finest skiing in Land Salzburg and possibly the finest interconnected lift system in Austria. There are 55 lifts, numerous cross-country ski trails, and, for ski potatoes, races and competitions are often run on the Saalbach–Hinterglemm Slalom. The most popular expert run is on the Zwölferkogel mountain (a cable car takes you there from the center of Saalbach–Hinterglemm), where, on high, a restaurant offers fine dining. This is an intermediate skier's paradise, especially the north side of the mountain. Numerous ski schools provide the area with more than 200 instructors. For more information on skiing facilities, contact the **Saalbach Hinterglemm Tourism Association** (✉ A-5753 Saalbach–Hinterglemm ☎ 06541/6800–68 🖷 06541/680069 🌐 www.saalbach-hinterglemm.com).

Nightlife

BARS Saalbach–Hinterglemm has a number of places that crowd up quickly as the slopes are vacated. The tourist office has a list of bars and discos. For après-ski, try the **Hinterhagalm** (☎ 06541/7212). The scene is pretty and cool at the **Spitzbub** (☎ 06541/6279). You can boogie down to the disco in the **Hotel Kristall** (☎ 06541/6662). Try the Alpenhotel's **Arena Club** (☎ 06541/6666–0) for lively action. Local bands regale patrons of the **Neuhaus Taverne** (☎ 06541/7151). There's usually a scene at the **Glemmerkeller** (☎ 06541/7135) in the Hotel Glemmtalerhof. Popular with many is the **Pinzgauer Stüberl** (☎ 06541/6346–37) in Hotel Wolf in Hinterglemm. The Londoner in the **Hotel Knappenhof** (☎ 06541/6497) in Hinterglemm offers disco or live music in winter. Among **bars,** Stamperl, Zum Turm, and Kuhstall in Saalbach, and Bla-Bla, Harley Bar, Pfiff, and Rudi's Kneipe in Hinterglemm are current favorites.

Saalfelden

⓫ *25 km (15 mi) northeast of Saalbach–Hinterglemm.*

Saalfelden nestles at the foot of the **Steinernes Meer** (Sea of Stone), the formidable ridge that divides Austria from Germany. The town, farther up Route 311 from Saalbach–Hinterglemm, is a climber's dream, but only for those who are experienced and who can tackle such challenges as the 2,941-meter (9,649-feet) Hochkönig. At the edge of the Steinernes Meer, signs lead you to a late-Gothic **cave chapel**, containing a winged altarpiece near a stone pulpit and hermit's cell. Saalfelden is a main stop on the Innsbruck–Salzburg train route.

Sights in town include a 19th-century Romanesque Pfarrkirche (parish church) with a late-Gothic winged altar (1539); the nearby 14th-century Farmach Castle, which is now a retirement home; and the 13th-century Lichtenberg Castle, which is now privately owned. For many, the most interesting attraction is the **Ritzen Castle** museum, where the Christmas manger collection of artisan Xandl Schläffer as well as exhibits on minerals, native handicrafts, and local history are on view. *€3.30 ⊙ Mid-June–mid-Sept., daily 10–noon and 2–5; mid-Sept.–mid-June, Wed. and weekends 2–4.*

Very enjoyable is the 1½-km (1-mi) **summer toboggan run.** With 63 curves and three tunnels, it is the longest such run in Europe. Take the chairlift up the Huggenberg southwest of Saalfelden on the road to Zell. Other well-marked attractions in the area include the **Vorderkaserklamm gorge.** The **Hirschbichl pass** was a strategic route where several battles were fought during the Napoleonic Wars.

off the beaten path

LAMPRECHTSHÖLE – About 14 km (8 mi) northwest of Saalfelden on Route 311 heading toward Lofer, you come to Weissbach, whose claim to fame is a system of caves totaling about 35 km (19 mi). An old legend has it that a treasure is buried here, but no one has ever found it, though not for lack of trying. *06582/8343 €3.20 ⊙ May–mid-Oct., daily 8–6; mid-Oct.–Dec., daily 10–5.*

Where to Stay & Eat

★ **$$** ✕ **Schatzbichl.** The reputation of this simple Gasthaus slightly east of Saalfelden draws guests from near and far. The pine-paneled interior is bright and cheerful, as is the usually overworked staff. Regional dishes are simply prepared and presented; try the garlic soup, lamb chops, or any of the fish offered. ⊠ *Ramseiden 82* 🕾 *06582/73281* 🖷 *06582/73281-4* ⌕ *Reservations essential* ⊟ *AE, MC, V* ⊙ *Closed Tues. and Apr. and Nov.*

$$$–$$$$ ✕🖾 **Gasthof Hindenburg.** This 500-year-old inn in the center of town provides modern comfort while retaining historic touches. Room colors are warm and inviting, complementing the wood flooring and the combination of antique and modern furnishings. Some suites have a duplex layout. In summer the garden restaurant is particularly inviting. ⊠ *Bahnhofstrasse 6, A-5760* 🕾 *06582/793-0* 🖷 *06582/793-78* ⊕ *www.hotel-hindenburg.at* ⌕ *38 rooms, 6 apartments* ⌕ *4 restaurants, in-room safes, minibars, sauna, spa, steam room, bar; no a/c* ⊟ *AE, DC, MC, V* ⍥ *BP, MAP.*

$$$–$$$$ ✕🖾 **Hotel Gut Brandlhof.** This sprawling ranch, about 5 km (3 mi) outside town, is perfect for an active vacation. The vast complex provides all manner of sports facilities, including the 18-hole, par-72 Saalfelden golf course, which belongs to the hotel. The comfortable rooms are done in Alpine-country style. In the wood-paneled restaurant, a *Kachelofen* (tile stove) radiates warmth; the Austrian cuisine is first-class, with an eye to healthy meals, fresh salads, and seasonal specialties. ⊠ *Hohlwegen 4, A-5760* ☎ *06582/7800–0* 🖷 *06582/7800–598* ⊕ *www.brandlhof. com* 🛏 *150 rooms* ⚅ *Restaurant, in-room safes, minibars, 18-hole golf course, tennis court, indoor-outdoor pools, gym, sauna, fishing, bowling, horseback riding, squash, 2 bars, children's programs (ages 3–7); no a/c* ☰ *AE, DC* ⑩ *BP, MAP.*

¢ 🏨 **Pension Klinglerhof.** This is just one of several modest bed-and-breakfasts in Saalfelden, where things are simple, comfortable, and inexpensive, and the service is all by owners (the Hölzls in this case). The Klinglerhof is quiet, right near the golf course, the cross-country ski trails, and the lifts. ⊠ *Schinking 1, A-5760* ☎ *06584/7713* 🖷 *06584/7713–4* ✐ *klinglerhof@gmx.at* ☰ *No credit cards.*

Sports & the Outdoors

BICYCLING The valley leading to Saalfelden is a great place for seeing sights on two wheels. You can rent a bike at the **railroad station** (☎ 06582/2344–0). **Bikeworld Leogang** (⊠ Glemmerstrasse 21 ☎ 6542/80480–25 ⊕ www. bikeworld.at) is the rather pretentious name for the region's expansive mountain-biking development, an infrastructure that includes special downhill courses, guided tours, a rental and service center, and, most interestingly, a lift ticket allowing you to take your bike on any of the lifts in the area's massive ski-lift system (in summer, of course).

HIKING From Saalfelden, you can head off through the magnificent Saalach Valley on any of five, five- or six-day self-guided expeditions called **"Hiking Without Luggage."** Your bags are transported, your choice of accommodation is prebooked, and guidebooks are available in English. The exhilaration can't be described in words. Information is available from Saalfelden's **Pinzgau regional tourist office** (⊠ Lofererstrasse 3 A-5760 ☎ 06582/74017 🖷 06582/74017–4).

MOUNTAIN SPAS & ALPINE RAMBLES

Glacier-covered Alps, hot springs, luxurious hotels, and tranquil lakes are the enticing combinations this Austrian region serves up superlatively. Gold and silver mined from the mountains were the source of many local fortunes; today, glittering gold jewelry finds many buyers in the shops of Bad Gastein's Empress Elisabeth Promenade. To set off on this trip, head south from Salzburg on the A10 and take the Bischofshofen exit toward St. Johann im Pongau, which gets you to Route 311 and, 17 km (11 mi) later, the Route 167 junction. From Zell am See, head east on Route 311 to pass Bruck again, continue through Taxenbach to Lend, and turn south at the intersection of Route 167.

Bad Gastein

⑫ *54 km (34 mi) southeast of Zell am See.*

Though it traces its roots all the way back to the 15th century, this resort, one of Europe's leading spas, gained renown only in the 19th century, when VIPs from emperors on down to impecunious philosophers flocked to the area to "take the cure." Today Bad Gastein retains much of its time-burnished allure. The stunning setting—a mountain torrent, the Gasteiner Ache, rushes through the unusual town—adds to the attraction. Most attempts at rejuvenating this turn-of-the-last-century jewel have met with failure, and everyone can be thankful for it. The old buildings still dominate the townscape, giving it a wonderful feeling of solidity and charm. The baths themselves, however, are state-of-the-art, as evidenced by the massive **Felsentherme Gastein** (spa complex) and the nearby **Thermalkurhaus** (treatment complex). The most unusual spa is the "healing mine" in **Böckstein,** near the Empress Elisabeth Promenade; it's an abandoned gold mine with very special air. For complete information on the town's main spas, contact the Bad Gastein tourist office (➪ The Eastern Alps A to Z, *below*).

A very special tradition in Bad Gastein is the old heathen *Perchtenlaufen* processions in January of every fourth year (the next is scheduled for 2010): people wearing big masks and making lots of noise chase the winter away, bringing good blessings for the new year.

Bad Gastein is serviced by many rail lines, with many expresses running from Salzberg and Klagenfurt. You can also reach the town by bus from Salzburg.

Where to Stay & Eat

$$$$ ✕⌨ **Grüner Baum.** You're out of the center of town here, in a relaxing, friendly hotel village set amid meadows and woodlands. The guest list in this hotel has included Austria's Empress Elisabeth and Saudi King Saud. Five separate houses have comfortable rustic, wood-paneled rooms, giving the complex a feeling of intimacy and personality. Children are well looked after. The elegant restaurant has an excellent reputation. ⊠ *Kötschach-Mauthental, A-5640* ☎ *06434/2516–0* 🖨 *06434/2516–25* ⊕ *www.grunerbaum.com* ➴ *80 rooms* ♻ *Restaurant, in-room safes, minibars, tennis court, indoor-outdoor pools, gym, sauna, bar, children's programs (ages 3–7); no a/c* ⊟ *AE, DC, MC, V* ⊗ *Closed Nov.* ¶⊘| *BP, MAP.*

★ **$$$$** ✕⌨ **Hotel Weismayr.** This grand old hotel in the middle of town is without a doubt the top address in Bad Gastein—a 77-room palace with a reputation for luxury and service going all the way back to 1832. Everything is done here to make sure your stay will be pleasant, even healthy: it's a typical spa hotel with all the applications local nature can offer. The expansive dining rooms in Biedermeier style are the setting for luxurious meals including many seasonal dishes (asparagus in May and June, game in autumn), but the menu also reflects the fact that you are at a spa and health club (fresh salads, vegetarian dishes). ⊠ *Kaiser-Franz-Josef-Strasse 6, A-5640* ☎ *06434/2594–0* 🖨 *06434/2594–14* ⊕ *www.weismayr.com* ➴ *77 rooms* ♻ *Restaurant, in-room safes, minibars, gym, spa, piano bar; no a/c* ⊟ *AE, DC, MC, V* ¶⊘| *BP, MAP.*

$$–$$$ ⌨ **Elisabethpark.** The dining and drawing rooms and music bars go on and on in this elegant hotel, which manages to marry the modern and the old school. The stateliness is underscored by Oriental carpets, marble, and crystal chandeliers. Rooms, with period furnishings, are particularly comfortable, and service has a pleasantly personal touch. The majestic waterfall—symbol of Bad Gastein—is adjacent to the hotel. ⊠ *A-5640* ☎ *06434/2551–0* 🖷 *06434/2551–10* ⊕ *www.arcotel.cc* 🛏 *120 rooms ⏥ Restaurant, café, indoor pool, gym, sauna, spa, bar, children's programs (ages 2–12 in summer, 3–12 in winter)* ☰ *AE, DC, MC, V* ⊙ *Closed mid-Apr.–mid-June and Sept.–mid-Dec.* ❙❙ *BP, MAP.*

$$ 🏨 **Alpenblick.** Perched high above the town like an eagle's nest, this old-fashioned chalet with a sweeping view of the valley is an ideal base for skiers and hikers. Not particularly modern, but nevertheless well kept, the staff provides you with congenial service, a lovely garden with heated outdoor pool, and breathtaking views. ⊠ *A-5640* ☎ *06434/ 2062–0* 🖷 *06434/2062–58* ⊕ *www.alpenblick-gastein.at* 🛏 *40 ⏥ Restaurant, bar, pool, playground; no a/c* ☰ *AE, DC, MC, V* ⊙ *Closed Nov.–mid-Dec.* ❙❙ *BP, MAP.*

Nightlife & the Arts

The **Grand Hotel de l'Europe casino** (⊠ Kaiser-Franz-Josef-Strasse 14 ☎ 06434/2465 🖷 06434/2465–25) has baccarat, blackjack, roulette, and slot machines. A passport is required. The casino is open mid-July–September and December 25–March, daily 7 PM–2 AM. Keep an eye out also for concerts, especially at the **Kongresshaus** in the middle of town (New Year's concerts are held here, for example).

Sports & the Outdoors

As a good spa town, Bad Gastein will keep guests entertained with all sorts of events from snowboarding competitions to dog-sleigh races. You will not be bored.

HANG GLIDING Flinging yourself off high places with a few sails is ideal in the Alps. You'll find a hang gliding school and a **rental company** at the cable car in Dorfgastein, 16 km (10 mi) north of Bad Gastein. Contact the **tourist office** (☎ 06432/6455–50) there for details.

SKIING Although not as well known to outsiders as other resorts, the Gastein ski area is popular with Austrians. The slopes of the four areas—Dorfgastein, Bad Hofgastein, Bad Gastein, and Sportgastein—are not well connected, so you'll often have to use the free shuttle bus and do some hoofing in your ski boots. Runs are mostly intermediate, with limited advanced and beginner slopes. The other ski run near Bad Gastein is the Graukogel peak, which also offers a restaurant and great Alpine hikes. For information, contact the **Tourist office** (⊠ Kaiser-Franz-Josef-Strasse 1, A-5640 Bad Gastein ☎ 06432/3393–560 🖷 06432/3393–537 ⊕ www. badgastein.at), or surf the interactive Web site (www.skigastein.com).

Liechtensteinklamm

★ ⑬ *38 km (24 mi) north of Bad Gastein.*

Traveling from Bad Gastein along Route 311, turn east toward Schwarzach in Pongau, where the road heads north, to find, between Schwarzach and St. Johann, the **Liechtensteinklamm,** the deepest (1,000 feet), narrowest (12½ feet), and most spectacular gorge in the Eastern Alps. At its far end is a 200-foot waterfall. A tour on a wooden walkway crisscrossing the gorge takes about one hour. ☎ *06412/8572* 🖃 *€3.50* ☉ *Early May–Oct., daily 9–4.*

St. Johann im Pongau

★ ⑭ *43 km (27 mi) north of Bad Gastein.*

St. Johann has developed into a full-fledged year-round resort. The area is favored by cross-country and intermediate downhill skiers, as the gentle slopes provide an almost endless variety of runs. The huge, twin-spired Pfarrkirche (parish church), built in 1861 in neo-Gothic style, is known locally as the **Pongau Domkirche** (cathedral)—a mammoth structure that rises quite majestically out of the townscape.

Every four years during the first week of January, the people of St. Johann, like the Bad Gasteiners, celebrate Pongauer Perchtenlauf, which can be poetically translated to mean "away with winter's ghost." Taking to the streets, they ring huge cowbells and wear weird masks and costumes to drive away evil spirits. The next celebration will be in the year 2009; check with the tourist office for the exact date. St. Johann is on the rail lines connecting Munich, Klagenfurt, and Salzburg.

Where to Stay & Eat

$$ ✕🖫 **Sporthotel Alpenland.** This centrally placed hotel has a somewhat more commercial approach to innkeeping than do the family-run chalets, but you get an attractive room, efficient service, and plenty of facilities. Three restaurants offer pizza, international, or Austrian cuisine. 🖂 *Hans-Kappacher-Strasse 7, A-5600* ☎ *06412/7021–0* 🖷 *06412/7021–51* ⊕ *www.alpenland.at* 🛏 *137 rooms* ⚭ *3 restaurants, tennis court, indoor pool, gym, sauna, 2 bars, dance club; no a/c* ▤ *AE, DC, MC, V* �🍽 *BP, MAP.*

Sports & the Outdoors

SKIING Linked by buses and 80 km (50 mi) of ski runs with other towns in the Pongau Valley, St. Johann remains the ski capital of the region called **Amadé,** which showcases more than 200 lifts and more than 860 km (534 mi) of well-groomed slopes. St. Johann alone has 14 ski lifts plus several cable-car ascents. Along with other Pongau valley runs, the town offers a Drei-Täler-Skischaukel (three-valley) pass. Contact **Tourismusverband St. Johann** (🖂 Alpendorf, A-5600 St. Johann ☎ 06412/6036 🖷 06412/6036–74 ⊕ www.sanktjohann.com).

Altenmarkt

⑮ *22 km (14 mi) east of St. Johann im Pongau.*

You cross over to Altenmarkt by leaving St. Johann im Pongau on Route 163 heading east across Wagrain and Reitdorf. Altenmarkt is small, but the **Church of St. Mary** contains the *Schöne Madonna,* an outstanding statue of the Virgin Mary that dates from before 1384. Nearby streams make the town a prime fishing site in summer, and skiing takes the spotlight during the winter months. The ski mountain here is part of the extensive Amadé ski region, so a lift ticket gives you access to 860 km (534 mi) of mostly interconnected runs.

Where to Stay & Eat

★ **$$-$$$** ✕⊡ **Lebzelter.** Luxury permeates this central hotel on Marktplatz. The excellent, window-filled country restaurant has a wide reputation: from steaks to fish to vegetarian meals, the emphasis is on traditional fare. ⊠ *Marktplatz 79, A-5541* ☎ *06452/6911* 🖷 *06452/7823* ⊕ *www. lebzelter.com* ⥂ *29 rooms* ⚭ *Restaurant, minibars, gym, sauna, bar; no a/c* ▤ *AE, DC, MC, V* ⊗ *Closed Oct.* ¶❍¶ *BP, MAP.*

$$ ✕⊡ **Schartner.** Although close to the center of Altenmarkt, this hotel may make you feel that you are at a country inn, thanks to its large garden and the adjacent meadow. Summer visitors will especially enjoy taking their leisurely breakfast or evening meal in the outdoor *Gastgarten*. The family-run inn also features a noteworthy restaurant serving fish specialties, Highland beef, and vegetarian entrées. ⊠ *Hauptstrasse 35, A-5541* ☎ *06452/5469* 🖷 *06452/5469–27* ⊕ *www.hotel-schartner.at* ⥂ *16 rooms, 14 suites* ⚭ *Restaurant, sauna, steam room, bar, playground; no a/c* ▤ *No credit cards* ¶❍¶ *BP, MAP.*

$-$$ ✕⊡ **Markterwirt.** This traditional house in the center of town dates back 900 years. The personal style of the family that runs it is reflected in the charming country decor of the comfortable rooms. A little "hunting lodge" directly on the lake, with several cozy apartments, makes for a romantic getaway. The main dining room and the informal *Stube* are good, and the bar offers the tastiest pizza in town. ⊠ *Marktplatz 4, A-5541* ☎ *06452/5420* 🖷 *06452/5420–31* ⊕ *www.markterwirt.at* ⥂ *28 rooms* ⚭ *Restaurant, café, lake, sauna, fishing; no a/c* ▤ *MC, V* ⊗ *Closed Nov.* ¶❍¶ *BP, MAP.*

Radstadt

⑯ *4 km (2½ mi) east of Altenmarkt.*

Despite wars and fires, the walled town of Radstadt still retains its 12th-century character. Standing guard over a key north–south route, Radstadt was once granted the right to warehouse goods and to trade in iron, wine, and salt, but the town's present prosperity is due to tourism: the area is growing in popularity as a skiing destination and has been a longtime lure for hikers in summer. Radstadt's north and west walls, dating from 1534, are well preserved, as are three of the towers that mark the corners of the Old Town. Most of the buildings around the square are also from the 16th century. The late-Romanesque **Pfarrkirche** (parish church), north of the square, dominates the town, but reconstructions over the ages have destroyed much of its original character. The interior contains several Baroque altars. To get to Radstadt, motorists usually take the A10 from Salzburg, about a one-hour drive. Trains and buses, too, connect Salzburg with Radstadt (occasionally with a transfer at Bischofshofen).

Where to Stay & Eat

$$ ✕⊡ **Sporthotel Radstadt.** This rambling, chalet-style resort set on a huge, sunny meadow right out of "The Sound of Music" is a great base whatever the season. In summer, the emphasis is on water, and the sport is fishing; the hotel has rights on 16 km (10 mi) of the Enns River. Huge outdoor pools and a water slide offer great fun for children. Don't shy away in winter, either: the slopes are nearby, and the spa is one of the nicest in town. The restaurant (for hotel guests only) specializes in trout and other local favorites. ⊠ *Schlossstrasse 45, A-5550* ☎ *06452/5590–0* 🖨 *06452/5590–28* ⊕ *www.sporthotel-radstadt.com* ⇝ *10 rooms, 18 apartments* ⚬ *Restaurant, in-room safes, some minibars, 3 indoor and outdoor pools, sauna, fishing; no a/c* ☰ *MC, V* ⊙ *Closed mid-Apr.–May and mid-Oct.–mid-Dec.* ⧈ *BP, MAP.*

Sports & the Outdoors

CROSS-COUNTRY SKIING   *Langlaufen,* or cross-country skiing, is wildly popular with many Europeans, and some resort areas such as Radstadt cater to these ski specialists. Sure, it takes a great deal of energy when the going is not all downhill, but gliding along through silent, snow-covered pine forests on "skinny" skis offers natural beauty and tranquility as its own rewards. Besides maintaining a 180 km (112 mi) groomed trail system, Radstadt hosts annually the Internationale Tauernlauf, a cross-country ski race that attracts over 1,000 participants each year.

Schladming

⑰ *20 km (13 mi) east of Radstadt.*

In the 14th and 15th centuries, Schladming was a thriving silver-mining town; then in 1525 the town was burned in an uprising by miners and farmers. Most of what you see today dates from 1526, when reconstruction began, but traces of the earlier town wall and the old miners' houses stand as testament to the town's imposing earlier wealth. Dominating the skyline is the Romanesque tower of the **St. Achaz Pfarrkirche,** or parish church.

Schladming is popular as a year-round resort. This is an area where sport is taken seriously; not only does it attract the world's best skiers, but it also gives beginners ample scope. In summer the area becomes a mountain biker mecca and hosts an annual world cup downhill race. In happy contrast to fashionable resorts in Tirol and Vorarlberg, Schladming and its surrounding areas (Radstadt, Ramsau am Dachstein, and Filzmoos) are reasonably priced. To get to Schladming from Radstadt, take scenic Route 320 east along the Enns River valley for about 20 km (13 mi) over the provincial border into Styria at Mandling, or if time is of the essence, take the A10 Autobahn to the Altenmark exit and follow the signs. The town is also accessible by rail via the Salzburg–Graz line.

Where to Stay & Eat

★ $$–$$$ ✕⊞ **Alte Post.** This traditional house in the center of town dates from 1618 and is notable for its particularly attractive *Stube* and the older rooms with vaulted ceilings. Guest rooms are cozy and comfortable. The restaurants offer good regional and Austrian cuisine in an appropriately genuine atmosphere. It's the place to sit outside in summer, watch people go by, and enjoy solid Austrian cooking, cholesterol and all. Golf arrangements can be made for the nearby Dachstein-Tauern club. ⊠ *Hauptplatz 10, A-8970* ☎ *03687/22571* 🖨 *03687/22571–8* ⊕ *www. alte-post.at* ⇝ *40 rooms* ⚬ *2 restaurants, minibars, golf privileges, tennis court, hair salon, spa, bar; no a/c* ☰ *AE, DC, MC, V* ⧈ *BP, MAP.*

Sports & the Outdoors

FISHING From May to mid-September you can cast a fly for trout in the nearby rivers and lakes. Contact **Gasthof Tetter** (✉ Untertal ☎ 03687/61130).

GOLF Schladming-Haus (Haus is a little village incorporated into Schladming) has an Alpine setting that's reason enough to play the 18-hole, par-71 course at the **Golf & Country Club Dachstein-Tauern.** ☎ 03686/2630–0 🖷 03686/2630–15 ◷ May–Oct.

SKIING Although not well known to North Americans, Schladming and neighboring Ramsau am Dachstein make up one of Austria's most popular downhill and cross-country ski destinations. There are a total of nine mountains to ski on, with more than 226 km (140 mi) of downhill runs, navigated by 95 modern lifts. Free ski buses connect the more remote mountains in the region, but you'll have plenty of skiing without having to leave the slopes. The main ski runs here are on the Hochwurzen and Planai peaks, both offering cable cars, chairlifts, and expert downhill runs. Another lure is the bustling après-ski scene. For details, contact the **Regionalverband Dachstein-Tauern office** (✉ Ramsauerstrasse 756, A-8970 Schladming ☎ 03687/2331–0 🖷 03687/23232 ⊕ www.dachstein-tauern.at).

Ramsau am Dachstein

⓲ *6 km (4 mi) north of Schladming.*

Heading north out of Schladming, you take a narrow, winding road that offers increasingly spectacular views of the Enns Valley and ends in a broad, sun-bathed valley at the foot of the mighty Dachstein range. About 4½ km (3 mi) west of Ramsau, a small toll road (€7 per car) forks off to the north onto the Dachstein itself, a majestic craggy outcrop of almost 3,500 meters (9,826 feet). Take the impressive 10-minute **Dachstein cable-car ride** to the top of the Alps; a round-trip (without skis) costs €23. A phone call to 03687/81241 will tell you in German what the weather's like up there. To the north lie the lakes of the Salzkammergut; to the west, the Tennen mountain range. South and east lie the lower Tauern mountains. You can hike over to the Dachstein peak if you're wearing proper hiking boots. In summer, the south cliff at Hunerkogel is a favorite "jumping-off spot" for paragliders. To get to Ramsau without a car, take a bus from Schladming.

Where to Stay & Eat

$$$ ✕🏨 **Pehab-Kirchenwirt.** *Kirchenwirt* means "inn next to the church," and that's exactly where this rustic hotel is. It's been family-run for the past 200 years. Many of the comfortable rooms have balconies; those in the back have the best mountain view. You're close to hiking trails in summer and the hotel-operated ski lift and ski runs in winter. Hotel guests have use of the nearby indoor pool, which has a sauna and solarium. The restaurant serves good Styrian specialties. ✉ A-8972 ☎ 03687/81732 🖷 03687/81655 ⊕ *www.pehab.at* ⇆ *40 rooms, 5 apartments △ Restaurant, café, indoor pool, Weinstuben; no a/c* ▤ *AE, MC* ◷ *Closed Nov. and 1 month after Easter* ⅋ *BP, MAP.*

★ **$$$** 🏠 **Peter Rosegger.** This rustic chalet in a quiet area on the forest's edge is decorated with homey mementos—framed letters and embroidered mottoes—of the Styrian novelist after whom it is named. This is the place to stay when you've come for climbing, as Fritz Walcher heads the Alpine school. Rooms are country comfortable, and the restaurant (hotel guests only) is one of the best in the area, with such local specialties as house-smoked trout, Styrian corned pork, and stuffed breast of veal. ⊠ *A-8972* ☎ *03687/81223–0* 🖷 *03687/81223–8* 🛏 *13 rooms* ⚙ *Restaurant, gym, sauna; no a/c* ▭ *No credit cards* ⊗ *Closed mid-Apr.–May and Nov.–mid-Dec.* ⊺◯∣ *BP, MAP.*

Sports & the Outdoors

HIKING   If you're interested in learning to climb in the difficult Dachstein area, contact **Alpinschule Dachstein** (⊠ Ramsau am Dachstein 233, A-8972 ☎ 03687/81223–0). The **Bergführer Büro Ramsau am Dachstein** (⊠ A-8972 ☎ 3687/81287 ⊕ www.bergsteigerschule.net) is a long-established resource for mountain-climbers.

SKIING   The famous **Dachstein Glacier** can be skied year-round, although summer snow conditions require considerable expertise. The altitude, however, guarantees good snow conditions late into the winter season. A lift ticket also gives you access to the larger Sportregion Schladming-Ramsau/Dachstein. The Gletscherbahn Ramsau (glacier cable-car), completed in 1969, is a remarkable technical achievement. A fully suspended steel cable carries up to 70 persons a distance of more than 2,000 meters (6,600 feet) in about 10 minutes to the top of the Dachstein glacier, 2,700 meters (8,900 feet) high. For details on skiing facilities, contact the **Tourismusverband** (⊠ A-8972 Ramsau am Dachstein ☎ 03687/818–33 🖷 03687/81085 ⊕ www.ramsau.com).

Shopping

In the nearby village of Rössing, Richard Steiner's **Lodenwalker** (☎ 03687/81930) has been turning out that highly practical feltlike fabric made from loden since 1434. Here you can find various colors and textures at reasonable prices. It's open weekdays.

Filzmoos

★ ⑲ *14 km (9 mi) west of Ramsau am Dachstein.*

Filzmoos, one of the most romantic villages in Austria, is still a well-kept secret. Though skiing in the nearby Dachstein mountains is excellent, the not-terribly-expensive winter resort has yet to be discovered by foreign tourists. During the summer months, meandering mountain streams and myriad lakes attract anglers eager for trout, while hikers come to challenge the craggy peaks. Filzmoos calls itself a balloon village, not only for the International Hot Air Balloon Week every January, but because it relies heavily on hot-air balloons to show its guests the region. To get up, up, and away, contact **Büro Dachstein-Tauern-Ballons** (☎ 03687/80863). For general information, contact the **Tourist Office Filzmoos** (☎ 06453/8235 ⊕ www.filzmoos.at).

Where to Stay & Eat

$$$–$$$$ ✕🏨 **Hubertus.** Every last detail—from romantic furnishings to modern
Fodor'sChoice conveniences—is done to perfection at this highly personal hotel in the
★ center of town. Fishing enthusiasts have 20 km (12 mi) of mountain
streams and two small lakes at their disposal. The restaurant is the best
in the area, if not all of alpine Austria: chef Johanna Maier's way with
trout (which you might have caught yourself) is exquisite, but don't over-
look the game, roast poultry, or veal sweetbreads. Finish with
Topfenknödel (cream cheese dumpling), a house specialty. Frau Maier
offers cooking courses several times each month—call or check the Web
site for dates. ⊠ *Am Dorfplatz 1, A-5532* 🕾 *06453/8204* 🖷 *06453/
82046* 🌐 *www.hotelhubertus.at* ↪ *17 rooms* ⚲ *Restaurant, café, pool,
sauna, fishing, bar; no a/c* ☰ *AE, MC* ⊘ *Closed mid-Apr.–mid-May and
mid-Oct.–mid-Dec.* �𝍖 *BP.*

$ 🏨 **Alpenkrone.** From the balconies of this chalet complex above the town
center, you'll have a great view of the surrounding mountains. Rooms
are simple and in "Laura Ashley" style, as might be expected from the
British owner, who provides friendly management and four-star com-
fort at three-star prices, even when the customary half board is consid-
ered. ⊠ *Filzmoos 133, A-5532* 🕾 *06453/8280-0* 🖷 *06453/8280-48*
🌐 *www.alpenkrone.com* ↪ *51 rooms* ⚲ *Restaurant, indoor pool, gym,
sauna, bar; no a/c* ☰ *MC, V* ⊘ *Closed Easter–mid-May and mid-
Oct.–mid-Dec.* �𝍖 *BP, MAP.*

┌─────────┐
│ en route │ From Filzmoos, rejoin Route 99/E14 again at Eben im Pongau. Here
└─────────┘ you can take the A10 autobahn north to Salzburg, if you're in a hurry.
But if you have time for more majestic scenery and an interesting
detour, continue about 4 km (2½ mi) north on Route 99/E14, and turn
north on Route 166, the **Salzburger Dolomitenstrasse** (Salzburg
Dolomites Highway), for a 43-km (27-mi) swing around the Tennen
mountains. Be careful, though, to catch the left turn onto Route 162
at Lindenthal; it will be marked to Golling. Head for Abtenau.

Abtenau

⓴ *44 km (28 mi) northwest of Filzmoos.*

Abtenau is a charming little town with a pretty old village square flanked
by colorful burghers' houses and the 14th-century **St. Blasius Church,** which
has late-Gothic frescoes and a Baroque high altar. A **museum** of local
history, which documents primarily the life of local farmers, has been
set up south of town in the Arlerhof, an ancient house built in 1325.
It's open June–mid-September, Tuesday, Thursday, and Sunday 2–5.
Nearby, nature has arranged its own museum, the Trickl and Dachser
waterfalls, with the nearby cave known as the "cold cellar" (der Kalte
Keller), where beer used to be stored.

Where to Stay & Eat

$–$$ ✕🏨 **Post.** This older, central hotel, decorated in rustic style with natural wood, has comfortable rooms with up-to-date facilities. Trans-
portation is available right at the door: the Windhofer family also runs

the town's taxi and excursion service. The restaurant is good; try the rump steak Tirol or any of the other beef dishes. ✉ *Markt 39, A-5441* ☎ *06243/2209–0* 📠 *06243/3353* 🌐 *www.hotel-post-abtenau.at* *56 rooms* *Restaurant, café, indoor pool, sauna; no a/c* 💳 *No credit cards* ⏲ *Closed Apr. and Nov.–mid-Dec.* 🍽 *BP, MAP.*

$$$ **Moisl.** This group of typical Alpine chalet–style houses in the center of town, with flower-laden balconies and overhanging eaves, dates back to 1764, but its services and facilities are absolutely up to date. Rooms are done in country decor. Evening entertainment includes candlelit dinner and wine and grill parties. ✉ *Markt 26, A-5441* ☎ *06243/22100* 📠 *06243/2210–612* 🌐 *www.hotelmoisl.at* *75 rooms* *Restaurant, café, in-room safes, minibars, tennis court, indoor pool, sauna, bowling, bar; no a/c* 💳 *MC, V* ⏲ *Closed Apr. and mid-Oct.–mid-Dec.* 🍽 *BP, MAP.*

Sports & the Outdoors

WHITE-WATER RAFTING

From May to the middle of October, you can raft the Salzach and Lammer rivers. The Lammer, with its "Hell's Run," is particularly wild. Runs begin at about €35 per person. For details: **Alpin Sports** (☎ 06243/3088 📠 06243/30884 🌐 www.alpinsports.at). **David Zwilling Resort** (☎ 06243/3069–0 📠 06243/3069–17 🌐 www.zwilling-resort.at), a standout among Abtenau's several active clubs, can also help you to experience paragliding, mountaineering, and many other adventure sports.

Werfen

21 *41 km (26 mi) from Abtenau.*

Fodor's Choice ★

The small town of Werfen, adorned with 16th-century buildings and a lovely Baroque church, belies its importance, for it actually is the base for exploring three extraordinary attractions: the largest and most fabulous ice caverns in the world; one of Austria's most spectacular castles; and a four-star culinary delight, Obauer. The riches of Werfen, in other words, place it on a par with many larger, more highly touted Austrian cities.

★ From miles away, you can see **Burg Hohenwerfen,** one of the most formidable fortresses of Europe (it was never taken in battle), which dates from 1077. Though fires, reconstructions, and renovations have altered the appearance of the imposing fortress, it still maintains its medieval grandeur. Hewn out of the rock on which it stands, the castle was called by Maximilian I a "plume of heraldry radiant against the sky." Inside, it has black-timber beamed state rooms and an enormous frescoed Knights' Hall. It even has a torture chamber. Eagles, falcons, and other birds of prey swoop dramatically above the castle grounds, adding considerably to the medieval feel. The castle harbors Austria's first museum of falconry, and the birds of prey are rigorously trained. Special shows with music, falconry, and performers in period costume are held at least twice a month; call ahead for dates and times. ☎ *06468/7603* 📠 *06468/7603–4* 🌐 *www.salzburg-burgen.at* *€9.50 for admission, tour, and birds-of-prey performance* ⏲ *Oct. and Nov., daily 9:30–4:30; May, June, and Sept., daily 9–5; July and Aug., daily 9–6; Apr., Tues.–Sun. 9:30–4:30. Birds-of-prey performance daily at 11 and 3.*

off the beaten path

EISRIESENWELT – The "World of the Ice Giants," just southwest of Abtenau, houses the largest known complex of ice caves, domes, galleries, and halls in Europe. It extends for some 42 km (26 mi) and contains a fantastic collection of frozen waterfalls and natural statuesque formations. Drive to the rest house, about halfway up the hill, and be prepared for some seriously scenic vistas. Then walk 15 minutes to the cable car, which takes you to a point about 15 minutes on foot from the cave, where you can take a 1¼-hour guided tour. You can also take a bus to the cable car from the Werfen **railroad station** (☎ 06468/5293), but be sure to leave at least an hour before the start of the next scheduled cave trip. The entire adventure takes about half a day. And remember, no matter how warm it is outside, it's below freezing inside, so bundle up, and wear appropriate shoes. ☎ *06468/ 5291 or 06468/5248 ☒ €16, including cable car ⊙ Tours May–Oct., daily 9:30–3:30 hourly; July–Aug., daily 9:30–4:30 hourly.*

Where to Stay & Eat

$$$$ ✕ **Obauer.** Among Austria's top dining spots, Obauer is presided over
Fodor'sChoice by the brothers Karl and Rudolf, who share chef-de-cuisine responsi-
★ bilities. Thanks to their flair, this has become a culinary shrine, especially for Salzburgers. Trout Strudel, or sole with peaches, green beans, and nutmeg, or stuffed duck (anyone for a garnish of mugwort?)—any of these specialties might top the nightly bill of fare. Regional delights, such as Pongau lamb, are deftly mixed with newer-than-now nouvelle garnishes, many inspired by the far-flung travels of the brotherly duo. Obauer is also a *Landgasthaus* (country inn); although the exterior is sweetly traditional, inside are 10 minimalist guest rooms flaunting coved ceilings, moderne-hued velvets, stark steel vases, and high-tech bathrooms—all resolutely anti-gemütlich in style. ☒ *Markt 46 ☎ 06468/ 5212–0 ☒ 06468/5212–12 ⊕ www.obauer.com ⚌ Reservations essential ▤ AE ⊙ Closed 2 (varying) days per wk.*

$ ▦ **Hotel-Garni Erzherzog Eugen.** You can't miss this hot-pink Gasthaus with window boxes trailing garlands of geraniums. It's smack in the middle of town. Though the decor is basic and a bit bland—traditional white lace curtains and nondescript furniture—the staff extends a warm and hospitable welcome. The lodging is under the same management as the nearby Obauer (see *above*). ☒ *Markt 38, A-5450 ☎ 06468/5210–0 ▤ 06468/7552–3 ⇲ 12 rooms ⚐ Bar; no a/c ▤ MC, V ◎ BP, MAP.*

EASTERN ALPS A TO Z

To research prices, get advice from other travelers, and book travel arrangements, visit www.fodors.com.

AIR TRAVEL

The busiest airport in the Eastern Alps region is in Carinthia at Klagenfurt, 50 km (31 mi) east of Villach, served by Austrian Airlines, Lufthansa, and Ryanair. The Salzburg airport is larger and offers even more connections. Both have frequent connections to other Austrian cities and points in Europe, including London and Birmingham, England, but neither has scheduled overseas direct flights.

BUS TRAVEL

As is typical throughout Austria, where trains don't go, the post office and railway buses do, though some side routes are less frequently covered. Coordinating your schedule with that of the buses is not as difficult as it sounds. The Austrian travel offices are helpful in this regard, or bus information is available in Villach and in Salzburg. You can take a post office bus from the Zell am See rail station up and over the mountains to the glacier at Kaiser-Franz-Josefs-Höhe, a 2½-hour trip, or from the Lienz rail station via Heiligenblut to the glacier, about two hours on this route. Buses run from early June to mid-October.

🚍 Bus Information **Post.Bus AG Information** ☎ 01/711-01 general information, 04242/ 44410 or 04242/2020-4041 in Villach, 0662/167 or 0622/872150 in Salzburg. **Lienz rail station** ☎ 04852/67067. **Zell am See rail station** ☎ 06542/2295.

CAR TRAVEL

If you're coming from northern Italy, you can get to Villach on the E55/ A13 in Italy, which becomes the A2 and then the A10; from Klagenfurt, farther east in Carinthia, taking the A2 autobahn is quickest. The fastest route from Salzburg is the A10 autobahn, but you will have to take two tunnels into account at a total cost of €10.20 (Tauern- and Katschbergtunnel). In summer on certain weekends (when the German federal states have their official vacations), the A10 southbound can become one very long parking lot, with hour-long waits before the tunnels. Taking the normal road over the passes, although long, is a very attractive option, but you will not be the only person who thought of it. If coming from abroad, don't forget to buy the autobahn *vignette* (sticker) for Austria (⇨ Driving *in* Smart Travel Tips A to Z).

ROAD CONDITIONS A car is by far the preferred means of seeing this area; the roads are good, and you can stop to picnic or just to marvel at the scenery. Be aware that the Grossglockner High Alpine Highway is closed from the first heavy snow (mid-November or possibly earlier) to mid-May or early June. Though many of the other high mountain roads are kept open in winter, driving them is nevertheless tricky, and you may even need chains. Keep in mind the cost of driving these roads as well: tunnels, passes, and panoramic roads often have tolls.

TOURS

Bus tours from Salzburg include the Grossglockner Highway (⇨ Salzburg A to Z *in* Chapter 5).

TRAIN TRAVEL

Villach and Salzburg are both served by frequent rail service from Vienna. Villach is also connected to Italy and Salzburg, which in turn is well connected to Germany. For train information, try one of the stations listed below. In addition, the larger train stations have a travel agent, who usually speaks good English.

You can reach most of the towns in the Eastern Alps by train, but the Grossglockner and Dachstein mountains are reachable in a practical sense only by road. If you do travel by rail, you can go from Villach to Hermagor, to Lienz, and northward (north of Spittal an der Drau) via Mallnitz and Bad Gastein to the main line at Schwarzach. There you can cut back westward to Zell am See or continue onward to Bischofshofen, connecting there via Radstadt to Schladming, or staying on the main line north to Salzburg.

🚆 Train Information **Klagenfurt** ☎ 0463/1717. **Salzburg Hauptbahnhof** ☎ 0662/1717. **Villach** ☎ 04242/1717.

VISITOR INFORMATION

For information about Carinthia, contact Kärntner Tourismus. The central tourist board for East Tirol is Osttirol Information. For information about Salzburg Province, contact Salzburger Land Tourismus. The main tourist bureau for Styria is Steiermark Information.

Many individual towns have their own *Fremdenverkehrsamt* (tourist office); they are listed below by town name.

🚆 Tourist Information **Infobüro Abtenau** ✉ Markt 34, A-5441 ☎ 06243/4040-0 🖷 06243/4040-40. **Altenmarkt-Zauchensee** ✉ Sportplatzstrasse 486, A-5541 ☎ 06452/ 5511 🖷 06452/6066. **Bad Gastein, Kur & Touristikbüro** ✉ Kaiser-Franz-Josef-Strasse 27, A-5640 ☎ 06434/2531-0 🖷 06434/2531-37. **Döllach–Grosskirchheim** ✉ Döllach 47, A-9843 ☎ 04825/521-21 🖷 04825/522-30. **Filmoos** ✉ Filzmoos 50, A-5532 ☎ 06453/8235 🖷 06453/8685. **Grossglockner Hochalpenstrasse** ✉ Rainerstrasse 2, A-5020 Salzburg ☎ 0662/873673-0 🖷 0662/873673-13 ⊕ www.grossglockner.at. **Heiligenblut** ✉ Hof 4, A-9844 ☎ 04824/2001-21 🖷 04824/2001-43. **Hermagor** ✉ Gösseringlände 7, A-9620 ☎ 04282/2043-0 🖷 04282/2043-50. **Kärntner Tourismus** ✉ Casinoplatz 1, A-9220 Velden ☎ 0463/3000 🖷 04274/52100-50. **Kötschach-Mauthen** ✉ Kötschach-Mauthen 390, A-9640 ☎ 04715/8516 🖷 04715/8513-30. **Lienz** ✉ Europaplatz 1, A-9900 ☎ 04852/65265 🖷 04852/65265-2. **Matrei in Osttirol** ✉ Rauterplatz 1, A-9971 ☎ 04875/6527 🖷 04875/6527-40. **Osttirol Information** ✉ Wilhelm-Greil-Strasse 17, A-6010 Innsbruck ☎ 0512/7272 🖷 0512/5320-174 ⊕ www. tirol.at. **Radstadt** ✉ Stadtplatz 17, A-5550 ☎ 06452/7472 🖷 06452/6702. **Ramsau am Dachstein** ✉ Kulm 40, A-8972 ☎ 03687/81833 🖷 03687/81085. **Saalbach-Hinterglemm** ✉ Saalbach-Hinterglemm 550, A-5753 ☎ 06541/680068 🖷 06541/680069. **Saalfelden** ✉ Bahnhofstrasse 10, A-5760 ☎ 06582/72513 🖷 06582/75398. **St. Jakob in Defereggen** ✉ Unterrotte 75A, A-9963 ☎ 04873/63600 🖷 04873/6360-60. **St. Johann im Pongau** ✉ Ing. Ludwig Pech Strasse 1, A-5600 ☎ 06412/6036 🖷 06412/6036-74. **Salzburger Land Tourismus** ✉ Wiener Bundesstrasse 23, Postfach 1, A-5300 Hallwang bei Salzburg ☎ 0662/6688-0 🖷 0662/6688-66. **Schladming** ✉ Erzherzog-Johann-Strasse 213, A-8970 ☎ 03687/22268 🖷 03687/24138. **Steiermark Information** ✉ St. Peter-Hauptstrasse 243, A-8042 Graz ☎ 0316/400-30 🖷 0316/4003-30 ⊕ www.steiermark.com. **Werfen** ✉ Markt 24 A-5450 ☎ 06468/5388 🖷 06468/7562. **Zell am See** ✉ Brucker Bundesstrasse 3, A-5700 ☎ 06542/770-0 🖷 06542/72032.

INNSBRUCK & TIROL

9

MAKE THE "GOLDEN ROOF"
your first stop in historic Innsbruck ⇨*p.398*

LINE UP FOR THE SKI SAFARI
at Kitzbühel's 91-mile downhill trail ⇨*p.421*

PICK UP A SHINY BAUBLE OR TWO
at crystal-giant Swarovski ⇨*p.412*

HEAR TOP ALPINE YODELERS
at the May Gauderfest ⇨*p.414*

ENJOY HEAVENLY VIEWS GRATIS
dining at above-it-all Lichtblick ⇨*p.403*

CONJURE UP PAST PLEASURES
while at Kufstein's 1504 "Lustschloss" ⇨*p.418*

DON'T MISS "HANNIBAL"'S ICE SHOW
staged atop a high glacier ⇨*p.427*

MORPH FROM BEGINNER BUNNY TO STAR
at St. Anton's famed ski school ⇨*p.430*

Updated by
Lee Hogan

TIROL IS SO DIFFERENT from the rest of Austria that you might think you've crossed a border, and in a way you have. The frontier between the provinces of Salzburg and Tirol is defined by mountains; four passes routed over them are what makes traffic possible. The faster trains cut across Germany rather than agonizing through the Austrian Alps. To the west, Tirol is separated from neighboring Vorarlberg by the Arlberg Range.

As small, relatively, as the province is, the *idea* of Tirol remains huge— it is virtually the shop window of Austria. Its very name conjures up visions of chains of never-ending snowcapped mountains; remote, winding Alpine valleys; rushing mountain torrents; and spectacular glaciers that rise out of the depths like brilliant, icy diamonds. In winter you'll find masses of deep, sparkling powder snow; unrivaled skiing and tobogganing, and bizarre winter carnivals with grotesquely masked mummers. Come summer, you can enjoy breathtaking picture-postcard Alpine scenery, cool mountain lakes, and rambles through forests. Throughout the year there are yodeling and zither music, villagers in lederhosen and broad-brimmed feathered hats, and, of course, the sounds of those distinctive cowbells.

As if the sheer physical splendor of Tirol weren't enough, the region can look back on a history filled with romance. Up to the beginning of the 16th century, Tirol was a powerful state in its own right, under a long line of counts and dukes, including personages of such varying fortunes as Friedl the Penniless and his son Sigmund the Wealthy. (On the whole, Tyrolean rulers were more often wealthy than penniless.) The province reached the zenith of its power under Emperor Maximilian I (1459–1519), when Innsbruck was the seat of the Holy Roman Empire. Maximilian's tomb in Innsbruck gives ample evidence of this onetime far-reaching glory. Over the centuries, the Tyroleans became fiercely nationalistic. In 1809–10 Andreas Hofer led bands of local patriots against Napoléon in an effort to break free from Bavaria and rejoin Austria. After three successful battles, including the Battle of Bergisel just outside Innsbruck, Hofer lost the fourth attempt against combined French and Bavarian forces, was executed in Mantua, and became a national hero.

Today Tirol looks to Vienna for political support in its perpetual dispute with Italy over the South Tirol, a large and prosperous wine-growing region that was ceded to Italy after World War I. Many Austrian Tyroleans still own property in South Tirol and consider it very much a part of their homeland. Yet even Austria's Tirol is physically divided: East Tirol, a small enclave of remarkable natural magnificence wedged between the provinces of Salzburg and Carinthia, belongs to Tirol, but it can be reached only through Italy or the province of Salzburg.

And what about the Tyroleans themselves? Like most other mountain peoples, the Tyroleans are very proud and independent—so much so that for many centuries the natives of one narrow valley fastness had little communication with their "foreign" neighbors in the next valley. (It's still possible to find short, dark, and slender residents in one valley and

Tirol has wonders abounding: the Holy Roman Empire splendors of Innsbruck, Hansel-and-Gretel villages, majestic mountain peaks, masked Carnival revelers, and much, much more. Brush off your best lederhosen and set out to shop for cuckoo clocks; then try out your vibrato on some *Jodeln* (yodeling), true Tyrolean singing. Then head for the great ski resorts—St. Anton, Kitzbühel, and Innsbruck—where *Sport und Spiel* are always in high gear.

9

Numbers in the text correspond to numbers in the margin and on the Innsbruck, Eastern Tirol, and Western Tirol maps.

If you have 3 days

Head straight to the heart of Tirol to the provincial capital of ☒ **Innsbruck** ❶–⓬ the city is conveniently situated for access to Tirol, for it lies almost exactly in the center of the province on the Inn River. Even if you have already settled on a resort for your holiday, you should spend at least a day in the capital first to check out the beautiful buildings built by the Emperor Maximilian I—from the **Goldenes Dachl** ❶ to the **Hofburg** ❺—and by Austria's Empress Maria Theresa, who gave her name to the principal street of the town, the Maria-Theresien-Strasse; any sightseeing in Innsbruck begins on this street, which runs through the heart of the city from north to south and is the main shopping center. Far from being exhausting to explore, Innsbruck is only a half-hour walk from one end of the Old Town to the other. The next day, let the funicular whisk you up the **Hungerburg** for the breathtaking views of Innsbruck below. You can take a leisurely hike along the mountain trail and see the flora and fauna at the Alpine zoo. Alternatively, take the Sightseer bus to the observation deck and restaurant atop the **Bergisel** ⓬ ski jump, which has a superb view of Innsbruck and the Nordkette mountains to the North. After returning to lower ground, set out on your final day to visit **Schloss Ambras,** with its impressive collections of medieval curiosities—pack a picnic and stay for a concert if you're traveling during the summer season. More ambitious travelers should consider a quick day trip to the seriously scenic **Stubaital Valley,** one of the showpieces of the Tirol—via the narrow-gauge electric Stubaitalbahn.

If you have 5 days

Begin your Tyrolean sojourn with two days in attraction-studded ☒ **Innsbruck** ❶–⓬—but don't forget to experience your first taste of the region's grand Alpine landscape by fitting in some quick excursions to the outlying **Hungerburg** peak, **Schloss Ambras,** or the **Swarovski Crystal World** in nearby Wattens. On Day 3, start off with a train ride from Innsbruck's main station to **Seefeld,** a charming Alpine resort. Wind your way up—and, at times, through—the mountain on your way to the Seefeld plateau. Splurge on a horse-drawn carriage ride around the lake, go for a round of golf, or in winter, work out on the world-class cross-country ski trails. On the fourth day, spend time exploring castle ruins, Baroque churches, and yet more spectacular scenery in **Imst** ㉕ and **Landeck** ㉙. For the peak experience of your trip—literally—head to the slopes on your final day at **St. Anton am Arlberg** ㉚. Keep in mind that modern highways can get you to your destination quickly, but often the most beautiful scenic views lie on off-the-beaten-track roads: ask your hotel concierge for advice on finding the best beauty spots. If you prefer staying closer to Innsbruck on your last day, ride the old-fashioned trolley (Tram 6 departs hourly from the main train station or the Bergisel tram station) to **Igls**, situated on a sunny plateau south of Innsbruck overlooking the valley. The village used to be an exclusive spa resort and is still home to many of the area's wealthiest.

If you have

7 days

🗺 **Innsbruck** ❶–⓬ makes a good base for discovering the entire region but is well worth two days of exploring on its own. After seeing the riches of the Old Town of the imperial city and its neighboring attractions, the **Hungerburg** peak and **Schloss Ambras,** set out on the morning of the third day to see how the Habsburgs amassed their vast wealth. Visit the mint at **Hall in Tirol** ⓭ and the silver mines at **Schwaz** ⓮. Then spend the night overlooking the pristine 🗺 **Achensee** ⓯. On your fourth day, head south following the Ziller River with stops along the way in **Zell am Ziller** ⓰ and **Mayrhofen** ⓱. From there you can head east to climb the impressive Kreuzjoch mountain in nearby 🗺 **Gerlos** ⓲. On the fifth day, challenge the slopes at either of the world-famous resorts of 🗺 **St. Johann in Tirol** ㉒ or **Kitzbühel** ㉓—two towns that have become almost more fashionable as warm-weather destinations than as skiing meccas. On Day 6, visit Emperor Maximilian's pleasure palace in 🗺 **Kufstein** ㉑. On your final day, visit the medieval glass-making town of **Rattenberg** ⓴. Then cross the Inn River and venture beyond **Kramsach** to beautiful Lake Zireiner before making your way back to Innsbruck. A side trip through nearby Albachtal to picturesque **Alpbach** ⓳ is great if time permits.

---

blond, blue-eyed, strapping giants in the next.) But Tirol can also be very cosmopolitan, as any visitor to Innsbruck will attest. The city is Tirol's treasure house—historically, culturally, and commercially. It's also sited smack dab in the center of the Tyrolean region and makes a convenient base from which to explore. Even if you are staying at an area resort, spend a day or two in Innsbruck first: it will give you a clearer perspective on the rest of the region.

Exploring Innsbruck & Tirol

Innsbruck makes a good introduction and starting point for exploring Tirol, but Tirol's gorgeous geography precludes the convenient loop tour from the capital city. You must go into the valleys to discover the hundreds of charming villages and hotels, and a certain amount of backtracking is necessary. We've outlined four tours over familiar routes, touching on the best of the towns and suggesting side trips and some pleasures that are off the beaten track. "Around the Lower Inn Valley" will take you east of Innsbruck through the lower Inn Valley, then south into the Ziller Valley, with detours to the Achensee and to Gerlos. "From Jenbach to Kitzbühel," also east of Innsbruck, continues up the Inn Valley to Kufstein on the German border and to the ski resorts of St. Johann and Kitzbühel. "West from Innsbruck to Imst, the Ötz & Paznaun Valleys" explores the Inn Valley west of Innsbruck to Imst, then goes south up the Ötz Valley and to Ischgl in the Paznaun. "Landeck, Upper Inn Valley & St. Anton" heads west from Imst, takes in Landeck and the upper Inn Valley, ending with St. Anton and the Arlberg. Whether you mix or match these tours or do them all, they'll allow you to discover a cross section of Tirol's highlights: the old and the new, glossy resorts, medieval castles, and, always, that extraordinary scenery.

About the Restaurants & Hotels

Tyrolean restaurants range from grand-hotel dining salons to little Tyrolean *Wirtshäser,* rustic restaurants where you can enjoy hearty local specialties like *Tiroler Gröstl* (a skillet dish made of beef, potatoes, and onions), *Knödel* (dumpling) soup, or *Schweinsbraten* (roast pork with sauerkraut), while sitting on highly polished wooden seats (rather hard ones!). In Innsbruck, urban, modern-styled eateries are the trend lately. Also, don't forget to enjoy some of the fine Innsbruck coffeehouses, famous for their scrumptious cakes and cappuccino. Outside of Innsbruck, some of the best eateries are those in hotels and resorts, which usually serve meals on the early side.

For one reason or another, travelers do not stay very long in Innsbruck itself. The rival attractions of the magnificent countryside, the lure of the mountains, and countless Alpine valleys perhaps prove too strong—in any case, Innsbruck hotels report the average stay is usually two to three days in summer, and one week in winter, so there is a fast turnover and, most always, a room to be had. Even so, if you travel during the high season (July–August) or in the winter, it's best to book in advance. If you're driving, you may want to ask in advance about parking, since some hotels have free, on-site spots, while others offer parking only a short distance away. Hotel rates vary widely by season, with the off-peak periods being March–May and September–November. Some travelers opt to set up their base not in Innsbruck but *overlooking* it, on the Hungerburg Plateau to the north, or in one of the nearby villages perched on the slopes to the south. In any case, the official **Innsbruck Reservation Center,** online at ⊕www.innsbruck-reservierung.at or ⊕www.ski-innsbruck.at, proffers a one-stop booking source for Innsbruck and the surrounding villages, as well as a trove of visitor information.

Room rates include taxes and service and, except in the most expensive hotels, almost always breakfast and one other meal. *Halb pension* (half board), as this plan is called, is de rigueur in most lodgings and usually is the best deal. However, most will offer a breakfast buffet–only rate if requested. Most hotels offer in-room phones and TV (some feature satellite or cable programming). A few hotels still do not take credit cards. If you're out for savings, it's a good idea to find lodgings in small towns nearby rather than in the resorts themselves; local tourist offices may be able to help you get situated, possibly even with accommodations in pensions (simple hotels) or *Bauernhöfe* (quaint farmhouses). Note that the $$$$ ranked hotels in the posh resort towns of Kitzbühel, St. Anton, and Seefeld have room rates higher than our price-chart norm; their rooms can occasionally top off as high as €400.

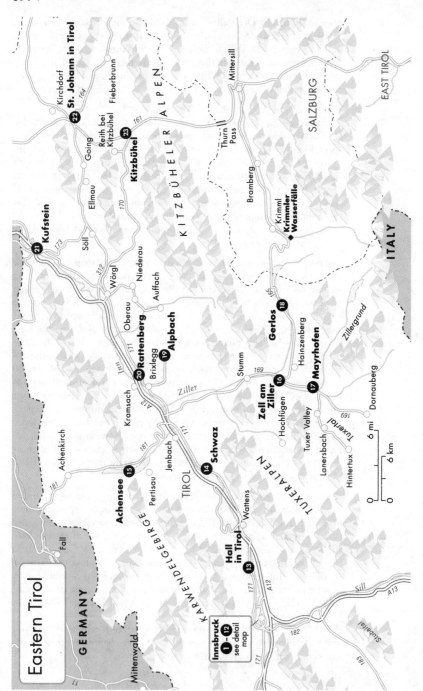

Eastern Tirol

9

Hiking Heaven Tirol has a good share of the more than 50,000 km (35,000 mi) of well-maintained mountain paths that thread the country. Hiking is one of the best ways to experience the truly awesome Alpine scenery, whether you just want to take a leisurely stroll around one of the crystalline lakes mirroring the towering mountains or trek your way to the top of one of the mighty peaks. Mountain-climbing is a highly organized sport in Tirol, a province that contains some of the greatest challenges to lovers of the sport: the Kaisergebirge (base: Kufstein), the Zillertaler and Tuxer Alps (base: Mayrhofen), the Wettersteingebirge and Karwendel ranges (base: Seefeld), the Nordkette range (base: Innsbruck), and the Ötz Valley. The instructors at the Alpine School Innsbruck are the best people to contact if you want to make arrangements for a mountain-climbing holiday or if you wish to attend a mountain-climbing school; if you already know how, contact the Österreichischer Alpenverein in Innsbruck.

Skiing Downhill was practically invented in Tirol, which came to the forefront as a prime tourist destination because of the excellence of its skiing. Modern ski techniques were developed here, thanks to the legendary skiing master Hannes Schneider, who took the Norwegian art of cross-country skiing and adapted it to downhill running. No matter where your trip takes you, world-class—and often gut-scrambling—skiing is available, from the glamour of Kitzbühel in the east to the imposing peaks of St. Anton am Arlberg in the west.

Close to the Arlberg Pass is **St. Anton,** which, at 4,300 feet, proudly claims one of the finest ski schools in the world. The specialty at St. Anton is piste skiing—enormously long runs studded with moguls (and few trees), some so steep and challenging that the sport is almost the equal of mountain climbing. In fact, this is the only place in Austria where you can heli-ski. It was here in the 1920s that Hannes Schneider started the school that was to become the model for all others. A short bus ride to the top of the pass brings you to **St. Christoph,** at 5,800 feet. Many excellent tours, served by the Galzip cable railway, start here, but the *Skihaserl,* or ski bunny, would do well to stay down at St. Anton where there are gentler—and kinder—nursery-level slopes. If you care to mingle with royalty on the lifts, then the close-by, posh winter-only villages of **Zürs** and **Lech,** on the Vorarlberg side of the Pass, are for you.

Farther along the Inn is the Ötz Valley. From the Ötztal station you can go by bus to **Sölden,** a resort at 4,500 feet that has become as well known for its party scene as for its superb skiing. The up-and-comer of Austrian ski resorts is **Ischgl,** in the Paznaun Valley bordering on Switzerland, where good snow is assured by more than 120 mi of runs above 2,000 feet, and where young snowboarders are as numerous as skiers. Long, wide runs resembling those in Colorado go as far as the Swiss border. Not far from Innsbruck is **Seefeld,** at 3,870 feet, long popular with cross-country skiers for its miles of meticulously groomed tracks. At the farther end of Tirol lies **Kitzbühel,** chic and *charmant,* perhaps most famous for its "Ski Safari," a system of ski lifts and trails, some floodlit at night, that allows skiers to ski for weeks without retracing their steps. The best time for skiing around **Innsbruck** is January to April.

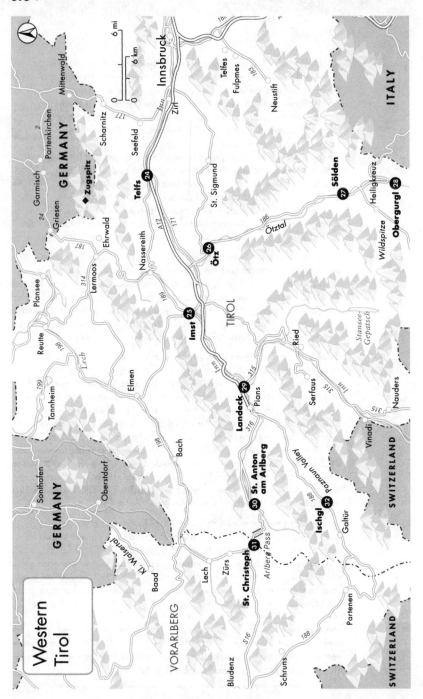

Western Tirol

WHAT IT COSTS In euros					
	$$$$	$$$	$$	$	¢
RESTAURANTS	over €22	€18–€22	€13–€17	€7–€12	under €7
HOTELS	over €175	€135–€175	€100–€135	€70–€100	under €70

Restaurant prices are per person for a main course at dinner. Hotel prices are for a standard double room in high season, including taxes and service. Assume that hotels operate on the European Plan (EP, with no meal provided) unless we note that they use the Breakfast Plan (BP), Modified American Plan (MAP, with breakfast and dinner daily, known as "halb pension"), or Full American Plan (FAP, or "voll pension," with three meals a day). Higher prices (inquire when booking) prevail for any meal plans.

Timing

The physical geography of the Tirol makes it an especially ideal place in which to enjoy the outdoor life year-round. Ski-crazy travelers descend on the resorts during the winter months; in the summer, when the mountains are awash with wildflowers, camping tents spring up like mushrooms in the valleys as hikers, spelunkers, mountain bikers, and climbers take advantage of the palatial peaks. The annual Tyrolean calendar is packed with special events: the famous Schemenlaufen, a procession of carved wooden masks, held in February in Imst; the Fasching balls, which reach their peak at the end of February the Hahnenkamm ski race and curling competition held in winter in Kitzbühel; the world-famous Gauderfest at Zell am Ziller during the first weekend in May; the castle concerts and music and dance festivals in summer, primarily in Kufstein and Innsbruck; and the many village harvest festivals in the fall throughout Tirol. For a rundown of Tirol's cultural venues and events, visit ⊕ www.culture.tirol.at.

INNSBRUCK

★ *190 km (118 mi) southwest of Salzburg, 471 km (304 mi) southwest of Vienna, 146 km (91 mi) south of Munich.*

The capital of Tirol is one of the most beautiful towns of its size anywhere in the world, owing much of its charm and fame to its unique location. To the north, the steep, sheer sides of the Alps rise, literally from the edge of the city, like a shimmering blue-and-white wall—an impressive backdrop for the mellowed green domes and red roofs of the Baroque town tucked below. To the south, the peaks of the Tuxer and Stubai ranges undulate in the hazy purple distance.

Innsbruck has been an important crossroads for hundreds of years. When it was chartered in 1239, it was already a key point on the north–south highways between Germany and Italy and the east–west axis tying eastern Austria and the lands beyond to Switzerland. Today Innsbruck is the transit point for road and rail traffic between the bordering countries.

The charming Old World aspect of Innsbruck has remained virtually intact, and includes ample evidence of its Baroque lineage. The skyline encircling the center suffers somewhat from high-rises, but the heart, the **Altstadt**, or Old City, remains much as it was 400 years ago. The protective vaulted arcades along main thoroughfares, the tiny passageways giving way to noble squares, and the ornate restored houses all contribute to an unforgettable picture.

Squeezed by the mountains and sharing the valley with the Inn River (Innsbruck means "bridge over the Inn"), the city is compact and very easy to explore on foot. Reminders of three historic figures abound: the local hero Andreas Hofer, whose band of patriots challenged Napoléon in 1809; Emperor Maximilian I (1459–1519); and Empress Maria Theresa (1717–80), the last two of whom were responsible for much of the city's architecture. Maximilian ruled the Holy Roman Empire from Innsbruck, and Maria Theresa, who was particularly fond of the city, spent a substantial amount of time here.

Pick up a free Club Innsbruck card at your hotel for no-charge use of ski buses and reduced-charge ski-lift passes. For big savings, buy the **all-inclusive Innsbruck Card,** which gives you free admission to all museums, mountain cable cars, the Alpenzoo, and Schloss Ambras, plus free bus and tram transportation, including bus service to nearby **Hall in Tirol** (⇨ Around the Lower Inn Valley). The card now includes unlimited ride-hopping onboard the big red **Sightseer** bus, which whisks you in air-conditioned comfort to all of the major sights, and even provides recorded commentary in English and five other languages. Cards are good for 24, 48, and 72 hours at €21, €26, and €31, respectively, and are available at the tourist office, on cable cars, and in larger museums.

❶
FodorsChoice
★
Any walking tour of Innsbruck should start at the **Goldenes Dachl** (Golden Roof), which made famous the late-Gothic mansion whose balcony it covers. In fact, the roof is capped with 2,600 gilded copper tiles, and its refurbishment is said to have taken 14 kilograms (nearly 31 pounds) of gold. Legend has it that the house was built in the 1400s for Duke Friedrich (otherwise known as Friedl the Penniless), and that the indignant duke had the original roof covered with gold to counter the rumor that he was poor. In truth, the 15th-century house was owned by Maximilian I, who added a balcony in 1501 as a sort of "royal box" for watching street performances in the square below. The structure was altered and expanded at the beginning of the 18th century, and now only the loggia and the alcove are identifiable as original. Maximilian is pictured in the two central sculpted panels on the balcony. In the one on the left, he is with his first and second wives, Maria of Burgundy and Bianca Maria Sforza of Milan; on the right, he is pictured with an adviser and a court jester. The magnificent coats of arms representing Austria, Hungary, Burgundy, Milan, the Holy Roman Empire, Styria, Tirol, and royal Germany are copies. You can see the originals (and up close, too) in the Ferdinandeum. The Golden Roof building houses the **Maximilianeum,** a small museum which headlines memorabilia and paintings from the life of Emperor Maximilian I. The short video presentation about Maximilian is worth a look. ⊠ *Herzog-Friedrich-Strasse 15* ☎ *0512/5811–11* 🖳 *€3.60* ☉ *May–Sept., daily 10–6.*

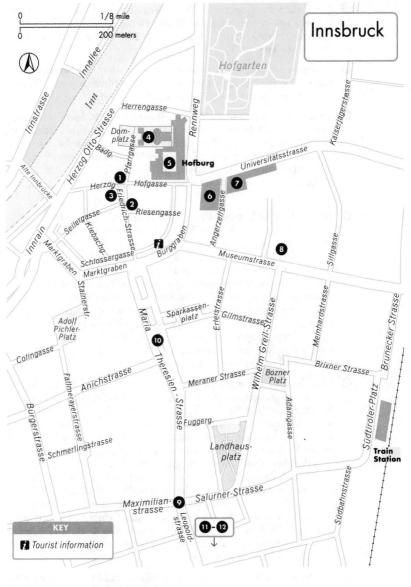

Innsbruck

Annasäule **10**

Bergisel **12**

Domkirche zu
St. Jakob **4**

Ferdinandeum **8**

Goldenes Dachl **1**

Grassmayr Bell
Foundry **11**

Helbling House **3**

Hofburg **5**

Hofkirche **6**

Stadtturm **2**

Tiroler
Volkskunstmuseum **7**

Triumphpforte **9**

2 Down the street from the Goldenes Dachl is the **Stadtturm**, a 15th-century city tower, with a steep climb of 148 steps to the top. ⊠ *Herzog-Friedrich-Strasse 21* ☎ *0512/5615–00* 💶 *€2.50* ⊙ *Oct.–June, daily 10–5; July–Sept., daily 10–8.*

3 Facing the Stadtturm is the dramatic blue-and-white **Helbling House**, originally a Gothic building (1560) to which the obvious, ornate Rococo decoration was added in 1730. ⊠ *Herzog-Friedrich-Strasse 10.*

4 The main attraction of the Baroque **Domkirche zu St. Jakob** is the high-altar painting of the Madonna by Lucas Cranach the Elder, dating from about 1530. The cathedral was built in 1722. Amidst the ornate Baroque interior, look in the north aisle for a 1620 monument honoring Archduke Maximilian III. ⊠ *Domplatz 6* ☎ *0512/5839–02* 💶 *Free* ⊙ *Oct.–May, daily 7:30–6:30; May–Sept., daily 7:30–7:30 except during worship.*

★ **5** One of the most historic attractions of Innsbruck is the **Hofburg**, or imperial palace, which Maximilian I commissioned in the 15th century. (The booklet in English available at the ticket office will tell you more interesting tidbits about the palace than the tour guide.) Center stage is the **Giant's Hall**—designated a marvel of the 18th century as soon as it was topped off with its magnificent trompe l'oeil ceiling, painted by Franz Anton Maulpertsch in 1775. The Rococo decoration and the portraits of Habsburg ancestors in the ornate white-and-gold great reception hall were added in the 18th century by Maria Theresa; look for the portrait of "Primal" (primrose)—to use the childhood nickname of the empress's daughter, Marie-Antoinette. ⊠ *Rennweg 1* ☎ *0512/587186* 💶 *€5.45* ⊙ *Hourly tours daily 9–5.*

6 Close by the Hofburg is the **Hofkirche** (Court Church), built as a mausoleum for Maximilian I (although he is actually buried in Wiener Neustadt, south of Vienna). The emperor's ornate black marble tomb is surrounded by 24 marble reliefs depicting his accomplishments, as well as 28 larger-than-life-size statues of his ancestors, including the legendary King Arthur of England. Andreas Hofer is also buried here. Don't miss the 16th-century **Silver Chapel**, up the stairs opposite the entrance, with its elaborate altar and silver Madonna. The chapel was built in 1578 to be the tomb of Archduke Ferdinand II and his wife, Philippine Welser, the daughter of a rich and powerful merchant family. Visit the chapel for picture-taking in the morning; the blinding afternoon sun comes in directly behind the altar. ⊠ *Universitätsstrasse 2* ☎ *0512/584302* ⊕ *www.hofkirche.at* 💶 *€3, combined ticket with Tiroler Volkskunstmuseum €5* ⊙ *Mon.–Sat. 9–5.*

7 The **Tiroler Volkskunstmuseum** (Tyrolean Folk Art Museum), in the same complex as the Hofkirche, exhibits Christmas crèches, costumes, rustic furniture, and entire rooms from old farmhouses and inns, decorated in styles ranging from Gothic to Rococo. Displays are somewhat static, and the information cards are in German. The small Christmas Manger Museum, on the other hand, is fascinating. ⊠ *Universitätsstrasse 2* ☎ *0512/584302* ⊕ *www.tiroler-volkskunstmuseum.at* 💶 *€5* ⊙ *Mon.–Sat. 9–5, Sun. 9–noon and 1–5.*

❽ The **Ferdinandeum** (Tyrolean State Museum Ferdinandeum) houses Austria's largest collection of Gothic art, 19th- and 20th-century paintings, and medieval arms, along with special exhibitions. The museum benefits from a total renovation completed in 2003. Here you'll find the original coats of arms from the Goldenes Dachl balcony. Chamber music concerts are offered throughout the year. ✉ *Museumstrasse 15* ☎ *0512/ 59489* 💶 *€8* 🕙 *June–Sept., daily 10–6; Oct.–May, Tues.–Sun. 10–6* ⊕ *www.tiroler-landesmuseum.at.*

❾ The **Triumphpforte,** or Triumphal Arch, was built in 1765 to commemorate both the marriage of emperor-to-be Leopold II (then Duke of Tuscany) and the death of Emperor Franz I, husband of Empress Maria Theresa. One side clearly represents celebration, and the other, tragedy. ✉ *Salurner-Strasse.*

❿ The **Annasäule,** or St. Anne's Column, erected in 1706, commemorates the withdrawal of Bavarian forces in the war of the Spanish Succession on St. Anne's Day (July 26) in 1703. From here is a classic view of Innsbruck's Altstadt (Old City), with the glorious Nordkette mountain range in the background. ✉ *Maria-Theresien-Strasse.*

⓫ A visit to the 400-year-old **Grassmayr Bell Foundry** contains a surprisingly fascinating little museum, and will give you an idea of how bells are cast and tuned. Guided tours in English can be arranged. Take Bus J, K, or S south to Grassmayrstrasse. ✉ *Leopoldstrasse 53* ☎ *0512/ 59416–37* 💶 *€4* 🕙 *Jan.–Apr., Oct., and Nov., weekdays 9–5; May–Sept. and Dec., Mon.–Sat. 9–5.*

⓬ The ski jumping stadium **Bergisel** now towers over Innsbruck as never before with a gloriously modern, concrete-and-glass observation deck and restaurant designed by world-celebrated architect Zaha Hadid. It's easy to reach using the **Sightseer** bus from Innsbruck. Parking a car will cost you €3.20 for 90 minutes. ✉ *Bergiselweg 3* ☎ *0512/589259* ⊕ *www.bergisel.info* 💶 *€7.90; free with Innsbruck Card* 🕙 *Daily 9:30–5; restaurant 9–5.*

Three Excursions

Hungerburg

🕑 From just east of the old town center, the Hungerburg Funicular carries you to the Hungerburg Plateau, and then via the Nordkettenbahn Cableway upwards to the top of the mountains for a commanding view of Innsbruck. Take the **Sightseer** bus, Streetcar 1, or Bus C to the **base station** (✉ Rennweg 41 ☎ 0512/293344). From here take the funicular up to the Hungerburg station (2,800 feet), then a two-stage cable car to Seegrube at 6,250 feet and onward to Hafelekar at the dizzying height of 7,500 feet. The round-trip to Hungerburg costs €4.30; the round-trip to Hafelekar is €21.80, or is free with the Innsbruck Card. At all three stops are breathtaking views over the Tyrolean Alps and Innsbruck.

🕑 The **Alpenzoo,** a short walk from the Hungerburg station, has an unusual collection of Alpine birds and animals, including endangered species. The zoo alone is worth the trip up the Hungerburg; if you buy your ticket for the zoo at the base station, the trip up and back is free. ⊠ *Weiherburggasse 37A* ☎ *0512/292323* ⊕ *www.alpenzoo.at* ☜ *€7, children €3.50; free with Innsbruck Card* ⊙ *Sept.–May, daily 9–5; June–Aug., daily 9–6.*

Schloss Ambras

When Archduke Ferdinand II wanted to marry a commoner for love, the court grudgingly allowed it, but the couple was forced to live outside the city limits. Ferdinand revamped a 10th-century castle for the bride, Philippine Welser, which was completed in 1556 and was every bit as deluxe as what he had been accustomed to in town. Amidst acres of gardens and woodland, it is an inviting castle with cheery red-and-white shutters on its many windows, and is, curiously, home to an odd-ball collection of armaments. The upper castle now houses rooms of noble portraits and the lower section has the collection of weaponry and armor. Be sure to inspect Philippine's sunken bath, a luxury for its time. Look around the grounds as well to see the fencing field and a small cemetery containing samples of earth from 18 battlefields around the world. The castle is 3 km (2 mi) southeast of the city. To reach it without a car, take Tram 3 or 6 to Ambras (a short walk to the Castle) or Route 1 on the **Sightseer** from Maria-Theresien-Strasse. ⊠ *Schloss Strasse 20* ☎ *0512/348446* ⊕ *www.khm.at/ambras* ☜ *€8; free with Innsbruck Card* ⊙ *Daily 10–5.*

The Stubaital Valley

The delightful little Stubai Valley, less than 40 km (25 mi) long, is one of the showpieces of the Tirol, with no fewer than 80 glistening glaciers and more than 40 towering peaks. If you just want to look, you can see the whole Stubaital in a full day's excursion from Innsbruck. The narrow-gauge electric **Stubaitalbahn** (departure from the center of Innsbruck on Maria-Theresien-Strasse and in front of the main rail station, as well as from the station just below the Bergisel ski jump) goes as far as Fulpmes, partway up the valley. You can take the bus as far as Ranalt and back to Fulpmes, to see more of the valley, then return on the quaint rail line. Buses leave from Gate 1 of the **Autobusbahnhof** (⊠ Stubaitalbahn ☎ 0512/5307–102), just behind the rail station at Südtiroler Platz, about every hour.

Where to Eat

$$$$ ✕ **Europastüberl.** This elegant yet comfortable dining room in Innsbruck's top hotel, the Europa Tyrol, envelopes you in charming Tyrolean surroundings while offering regional specialties, particularly wild local game, an impressive wine list, and an attentive waitstaff. Carved wooden alcoves harbor intimate tables dressed with white linens and candles. ⊠ *Brixner Strasse 6* ☎ *0512/5931* ⊕ *www.europatyrol.com* ⌖ *Reservations essential* ☰ *AE, DC, MC, V.*

★ $$$–$$$$ ✕ **Schwarzer Adler.** This intimate, romantic restaurant on the ground floor of the Schwarzer Adler hotel has leaded-glass windows and rustic Tyrolean embellishments—and in summer, dining on the rooftop terrace—offering the perfect backdrop for a memorable meal. The innovative cooks present a new menu every couple of months, often based on seasonal specialties and favorites, such as asparagus in spring or wild game in the fall. The fish and Tyrolean offerings are likewise outstanding. It's a bit off the beaten track, but worth the effort it takes to get there. ⊠ *Kaiserjägerstrasse 2* ☏ *0512/587109* 🖶 *0512/561697* ⊕ *www. deradler.com* ⊟ *AE, DC, MC, V* ⊘ *Closed Sun.*

$$$ ✕ **Goldener Adler.** A true rarity, this restaurant in Innsbruck's most famous hotel is as popular with Austrians as it is with travelers. The liveliest crowds favor the Batzenhäusl on the arcaded ground-floor level. Start with an Adler-Royal—a glass of *Sekt* (Austrian sparkling wine) with a dash of blackberry liqueur—while perusing the menu, which showcases a modern slant on traditional dishes. Pork medallions are topped with ham and Gorgonzola, and the *Tiroler Zopfbraten* (veal steak strips with a creamy herb sauce) is accompanied by spinach dumplings and carrots. ⊠ *Herzog-Friedrich-Strasse 6* ☏ *0512/5711–11* ⚔ *Reservations essential* ⊟ *AE, DC, MC, V.*

$$-$$$ ✕ **Lichtblick.** "Seventh heaven" not only describes this little restaurant's
Fodor'sChoice location atop the seventh floor of the chic **Rathausgalerie**, but also the
★ dining experience. The all-around glass architecture of Lichtblick ("bright spot") provides you with sensational views of the Altstadt (Old City), and the kitchen, led by Andreas Zeindinger, offers wonderfully creative, captivating dishes made from fresh, local ingredients. The menu changes often and the desserts are especially good. ⊠ *Rathaus Gallery, 7th floor* ☏ *0512/566550* ⊕ *www.restaurant-lichtblick.at* ⚔ *Reservations essential* ⊟ *AE, DC, MC, V* ⊘ *Closed Sun.*

★ **$$-$$$** ✕ **Ottoburg.** This ancient Altstadt landmark conveys an abundance of historical charm. It's fun just to explore the rabbit warren of paneled rustic rooms upstairs in this red-and-white-shuttered house built in 1494. Several of the bay-window alcoves have great views toward the Goldenes Dachl square, while others overlook the Inn river. The *Gaststube* downstairs is less intimate but offers lower-cost selections. Try the trout if it's on the menu, but the chicken and duck dishes are also excellent. ⊠ *Herzog-Friedrich-Strasse 1* ☏ *0512/584338* ⊟ *AE, DC, MC, V* ⊘ *Closed Mon.*

$$-$$$ ✕ **Weisses Rössl.** In the authentically rustic rooms upstairs, an array of antlers and a private art gallery add to the Austrianness of it all. This is the right place for solid local standards, like *Tiroler Gröstl*, a tasty hash treatment, and Wiener Schnitzel (veal cutlet), both of which taste even better on the outside terrace in summer. ⊠ *Kiebachgasse 8* ☏ *0512/ 583057* ⊟ *AE, MC, V* ⊘ *Closed Sun., early Nov., mid-Apr.*

★ **$-$$$** ✕ **Café Sacher.** The Café Sacher's celebrated Sachertorte can now be savored in Innsbruck, in a turn-of-the-last-century, plushy atmosphere reflecting the original Sacher in Vienna. This oh-so-Austrian chocolate layer cake is not the only draw—coffee and sweets are scrumptious, and the full menu includes Eduard Sacher's original recipes for *Tafelspitz* (prime boiled beef) and *Backhendl "Anna Sacher"* (Viennese fried chicken). This is a good choice following a show at the nearby Kongresshaus or Tiroler Landestheater, but expect higher than average prices. In the summer, the garden courtyard is yet another temptation. ⊠ *Rennweg 1* ☏ *0512/ 565626* ⊕ *http://cafes.sacher.com* ⊟ *AE, DC, MC, V.*

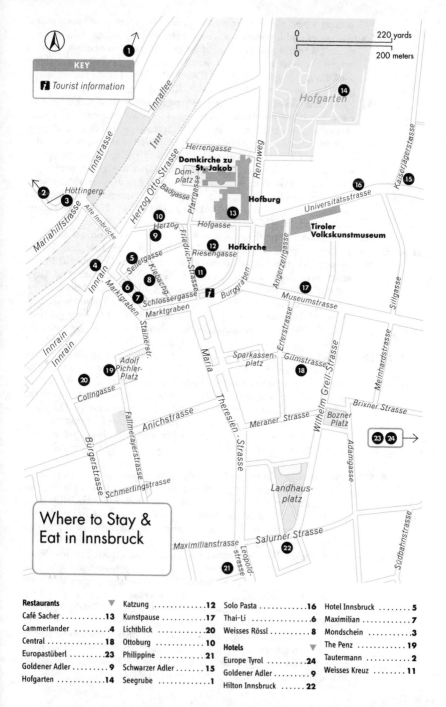

KEY

🇮 *Tourist information*

220 yards

200 meters

Hofgarten

Innallee

Innstrasse

Inn

Herrengasse

Rennweg

Domkirche zu St. Jakob

Dom-platz

Pfarrgasse

Höttingerg.

Mariahilfstrasse

Alte Innbrücke

Herzog Otto-Strasse

Badgasse

Hofburg

Tiroler Volkskunstmuseum

Universitätsstrasse

Kaiserjägerstrasse

Hofgasse

Herzog

Friedrich-Strasse

Riesengasse

Hofkirche

Angerzellgasse

Seilergasse

Kiebachg.

Schlossergasse

Burggraben

Museumstrasse

Sillgasse

Innrain

Marktgraben

Marktgraben

Stainerstr.

Maria

Adolf Pichler-Platz

Sparkassen-platz

Gilmstrasse

Erlerstrasse

Wilhelm Greil-Strasse

Meinhardstrasse

Colingasse

Innrain

Anichstrasse

Theresien - Strasse

Meraner Strasse

Bozner Platz

Brixner Strasse

Adamgasse

Bürgerstrasse

Faltmeyerstrasse

Schmerlingstrasse

Landhaus-platz

Where to Stay & Eat in Innsbruck

Maximilianstrasse

Leopold-strasse

Salurner Strasse

Südbahnstrasse

Restaurants ▼

Café Sacher **13**
Cammerlander **4**
Central **18**
Europastüberl **23**
Goldener Adler **9**
Hofgarten **14**

Katzung **12**
Kunstpause **17**
Lichtblick **20**
Ottoburg **10**
Philippine **21**
Schwarzer Adler **15**
Seegrube **1**

Solo Pasta **16**
Thai-Li **6**
Weisses Rössl **8**

Hotels ▼

Europe Tyrol **24**
Goldener Adler **9**
Hilton Innsbruck **22**

Hotel Innsbruck **5**
Maximilian **7**
Mondschein **3**
The Penz **19**
Tautermann **2**
Weisses Kreuz **11**

$ ✕ **Cammerlander.** This large, multi-level café–bar is the only Altstadt (Old City) restaurant positioned directly alongside the Inn River, and is popular with locals and tourists alike for its multi-faceted character and diverse menu offerings. Enjoy the large, covered terrace for breakfast or lunch, or ask for a table on the glass-enclosed balcony, with a fine view of the Inn. You may have to order *Apfelstrudel* for dessert, as portions are not overly generous. ⊠ *Innrain 2* ☎ *0512/586398* ⊕ *www. cammerlander.at.*

$ ✕ **Philippine.** The food here is not exclusively vegetarian (fish is also offered), but with so many tempting non-meat choices it's hard not to "go veggie." You might start with polenta topped with Gorgonzola and ruby-red tomatoes and then go on to cannelloni stuffed with potatoes and smoked tofu, or pumpkin risotto with pumpkin seeds, ginger, and Parmesan. Portions are substantial. The restaurant is light and cheerful, and tables are candlelit at night. ⊠ *Müllerstrasse and Templstrasse* ☎ *0512/589157* ⊟ *MC, V.*

¢–$ ✕ **Central.** Since 1878, this large, traditional, Viennese-style café has been *the* place to relax over a coffee. Newspapers and magazines are available, as is a variety of food and pastries. On Sunday night enjoy your cappuccino with live piano accompaniment. ⊠ *Gilmstrasse 5, in the Central Hotel* ☎ *0512/5920–0* ⊟ *AE, DC, MC, V* ⊗ *Closed Nov.*

¢–$ ✕ **Hofgarten.** This is *the* summer gathering place in Innsbruck, perhaps because it is so pleasant to eat and drink outdoors amidst the beauty of the city's ancient and splendid Hofgarten park. Whether enjoying a beer and light meal on a sunny afternoon, or celebrating with friends after a show at the nearby Landestheater, this is a fine place for having fun. ⊠ *Rennweg 6a* ☎ *0512/588871* ⊟ *AE, DC, MC, V.*

$ ✕ **Seegrube.** If your plans include a Friday night stay in Innsbruck and the weather is clear, try to book a table at this restaurant in the Seegrube cableway station. The mostly Tyrolean cuisine is good, and the view of the lights of Innsbruck twinkling below is unparalleled. ⊠ *Höhenstrasse 145* ☎ *0512/293375* ⚔ *Reservations essential* ⊟ *MC, V* ⊗ *Closed Sat.–Thurs. No lunch Fri.*

¢–$ ✕ **Kunstpause.** Within the **Ferdinandeum** (➪ Innsbruck, *above*), the "Art pause" offers breakfast, light meals, and a wine bar in elegant but relaxed surroundings. ⊠ *Museumstrasse 15* ☎ *512/572020* ⌨ *512/5884064* ⊕ *www.kunstpause.at* ⊟ *AE, DC, MC, V.*

¢–$ ✕ **Solo Pasta.** Modern and chic, Innsbruck's urban pasta boutique nevertheless offers Old World Italian epicure. The owner's Italian heritage is evident in the fresh, ample portions of authentic Italian dishes presented alongside a spacious wine list, enjoyed either with a meal or in the adjoining Solo Vino bar. ⊠ *Universitätsstrasse 15b* ☎ *0512/587206* ⊟ *AE, DC, MC, V.*

¢–$ ✕ **Thai-Li.** This intimate, authentic Thai cookery has quietly fashioned a reputation as one of the finest, yet most affordable dining spots in the Old Town. Thai-Li is short on elbow room, but long on excellent Thai food presented with elegance and efficiency. The owners have opened a new Thai-Li restaurant (Thai-Li Ba) in the trendy **Rathaus Gallery** (➪ Shopping, *below*), where the food is equally good but service is often slow. ⊠ *Marktgraben 3* ☎ *0512/562813* ⊟ *AE, DC, MC, V* ⊗ *Closed Mon.*

¢ ✕ **Katzung.** This bright, contemporary *Kaffee* house, a few steps from the Golden Roof, offers a dizzying array of coffee specialties and, for the kids, divine ice cream. ⊠ *Riesengasse 13* ☎ *0512/582347.*

Where to Stay

★ $$$$ ✕🏠 **Europa Tyrol.** This grand hotel adjacent to the train station has provided lodging to the celebrated and wealthy since its opening in 1869, and has lost none of its warmth and charm in the decades since. Bavarian King Ludwig II is reported to have called it "the most desirable place in Innsbruck to celebrate a festival." Rooms are richly appointed, modern, and comfortable, and the staff provides personal, attentive service. Ask for a tour of the splendid "Barocksaal," a meeting room built in 1883 by Ludwig II's own architect and, thankfully, untouched by the extensive bombing the hotel sustained during WWII. ⊠ *Südtirolerplatz 2, A-6020* ☎ *0512/5931* 🖷 *0512/58700* ⊕ *www.europatyrol.com* ➯ *110 rooms, 10 suites* ♨ *Sauna, Internet, business services, meeting rooms* ▭ *AE, DC, MC, V* ⍩ *BP, MAP.*

$$$–$$$$ 🏠 **Hilton Innsbruck.** This modern high-rise close to the city center looks out of place but offers contemporary comfort in friendly Scandinavian style. The rooms are simply furnished and efficiently modern. Look for Scandinavian specialties in the restaurants; the City Lunch Buffet is justifiably popular. High rollers take note: the hotel has an in-house casino. ⊠ *Salurner Strasse 15, A-6010* ☎ *0512/5935–0* 🖷 *0512/5935–220* ⊕ *www.hilton.com* ➯ *172 rooms* ♨ *2 restaurants, minibars, indoor pool, sauna, bar, casino, Internet, free parking* ▭ *AE, DC, MC, V* ⍩ *BP, MAP.*

$$$–$$$$ 🏠 **The Penz.** The Penz hotel is Innsbruck's newest top address. Although within the Altstadt (Old City), it is centuries away if measured by its ultramodern, glittering, light-and-glass architecture. The rooms are small but elegant. Ensconced in the chic Rathausgalerie shopping galleria, the rooftop American Bar makes a fine gathering spot, complete with panoramic vistas of the Old City and the Alps. ⊠ *Adolf-Pichler-Platz* ☎ *0512/5657–0* ⊕ *www.the-penz.com* ➯ *96 rooms* ♨ *Restaurant, bar, Internet, parking (fee)* ▭ *AE, DC, MC, V* ⍩ *BP, MAP.*

$$$ 🏠 **Hotel Innsbruck.** Modern is the mood here, from the tastefully understated lobby to the efficiently functional guest rooms with their accents of polished wood. The hotel and its cheerful restaurant rank among Innsbruck's finest. From some rooms you'll get gorgeous views of the Altstadt (Old City), and, from those on the river side, of the Nordkette mountains directly behind. ⊠ *Innrain 3, A-6020* ☎ *0512/59868–0* 🖷 *0512/572280* ⊕ *www.hotelinnsbruck.com* ➯ *111 rooms* ♨ *Restaurant, indoor pool, sauna, free parking; no a/c* ▭ *AE, DC, MC, V* ⍩ *BP, MAP.*

★ $$–$$$ 🏠 **Goldener Adler.** There may be grander, more luxurious, better-appointed, quieter hotels in and around Innsbruck—but even so, none of them could replace the beloved Goldener Adler, or Golden Eagle. Over the centuries the hotel has welcomed nearly every king, emperor, duke, or poet who passed through Innsbruck. Gustav III of Sweden (hero of Verdi's opera *A Masked Ball*), Metternich, Ludwig I, Goethe, Heine, and Paganini, who etched his name on the window of his room, all stayed here. Centrally placed in the very heart of Old Innsbruck, the hotel is just across the street from the Goldenes Dachl. The outside of the hotel looks suitably ancient, with low arches at street level and typical Tyrolean decoration higher up. Inside, the passages and stairs twist romantically, but beware: readers have complained about closetlike rooms on the upper floors. ✉ *Herzog-Friedrich-Strasse 6, A-6020* ☎ *0512/586334* 📠 *0512/584409* ⊕ *www.goldeneradler.com* ⟿ *35 rooms* ♿ *2 restaurants, in-room safes, minibars; no a/c* ▤ *AE, DC, MC, V* ℹ️ *BP, MAP.*

$$-$$$ 🛏 **Mondschein.** Behind the modest exterior and smallish lobby you'll find a fully modernized hotel, now part of the Best Western chain. Rooms are furnished in rich blue and gold tones, and those facing the Inn River offer excellent views of the Altstadt (Old City). ✉ *Mariahilfstrasse 6, A-6010* ☎ *0512/22784* 📠 *0512/22784-90* ⊕ *www.mondschein.at* ⟿ *35 rooms* ♿ *Restaurant, in-room safes, minibars, bar, meeting room, free parking; no a/c* ▤ *AE, DC, MC, V* ℹ️ *BP.*

$$ 🛏 **Maximilian.** Only steps from the free ski-bus stop, the comfortable guest rooms in this small family-run hotel are furnished in warm, Tyrolean woods and crisp white linens. The hotel's Old Town location couldn't be better, and the breakfast buffet provides excellent nourishment for a day on the ski piste. ✉ *Marktgraben 7–9, A-6020* ☎ *0512/59967* 📠 *0512/577450* ⊕ *www.hotel-maximilian.com* ⟿ *43 rooms* ♿ *Restaurant; no a/c* ℹ️ *BP.*

$ 🛏 **Tautermann.** This red-shuttered house within walking distance of the city's center has been successfully turned into a friendly, family-run hotel with rooms in natural woods and white. Some upper rooms on the west side have bay windows with gorgeous views of the imposing Hungerburg mountain. Bus A from the main station to Höttinger Kirchenplatz gets you close to the door. ✉ *Stamserfeld 5, at Höttingergasse, A-6020* ☎ *0512/281572* 📠 *0512/281572-10* ⊕ *www.hotel-tautermann.at* ⟿ *28 rooms* ♿ *Free parking; no a/c* ▤ *AE, DC, MC, V* ℹ️ *BP.*

★ ¢–$ 🛏 **Weisses Kreuz.** At first encounter you may fall in love with this hotel, set over stone arcades in the heart of the Altstadt (Old City). It has seen massive renovations since the first Gasthof stood on this site in 1465, and the rooms are simple but comfortable, with mainly rustic furniture and lots of light wood. The service is friendly and accommodating, and there are special rooms on the ground floor in which you can keep your skis. ✉ *Herzog-Friedrich-Strasse 31, A-6020* ☎ *0512/59479* 📠 *0512/59479-90* ✉ *hotel.weisses.kreuz@eunet.at* ⟿ *39 rooms* ♿ *2 restaurants; no a/c* ▤ *AE, MC, V* ℹ️ *BP, MAP.*

Nightlife & the Arts

The Arts

Internationaler Tanzsommer Innsbruck (✉ Burggraben 3, A-6021 ☎ 0512/561–561 ⊕ www.tanzsommer.at) brings the world's premiere dance companies to Innsbruck between mid-June and mid-July. The Alvin Ailey Dance Theater, Russia's Boris Eifmann Ballet, and China's Cloud Gate Dance Theater are some of the groups that have recently performed. Tickets are available online or through the tourist office, or contact the festival. The **Festwochen der Alten Musik** (Festival of Early Music;

✉ Burggraben 3, A-6021 ☏ 0512/5710–32 🖶 0512/5631–42) is a good reason to visit Innsbruck between late July and late August, as the annual festival highlights music from the 14th to 18th centuries, performed by many of Europe's finest musicians in such dramatic settings as Innsbruck's beautiful Schloss Ambras and the Hofkirche. Contact the Innsbruck Tourist office or the festival. And during the summer there are frequent brass-band (Musikkapelle) concerts in the Old Town. It's said that Tirol has more bandleaders than mayors. Folklore shows at the **Messehalle** and other spots around the city showcase authentic Tyrolean folk dancing, yodeling, and zither music. The tourist office and hotels have details.

Concerts take place in the modern Saal Tirol of the **Kongresshaus** (✉ Rennweg 3 ☏ 0512/5936–0). Innsbruck's principal theater is the **Tiroler Landestheater** (✉ Rennweg 2 ☏ 0512/52074–4). Both operas and operettas are presented in the main hall, usually starting at 7:30; plays in the Kammerspiele start at 8. Obtain tickets at the box office or at the main tourist office.

Nightlife

The jazzy **casino** adjacent to the Hilton Innsbruck offers blackjack, baccarat, roulette, and plenty of slot machines, as well as a bar and a good restaurant. You must present your passport to enter the casino. ✉ *Salurner Strasse 15* ☏ *0512/587040–0* 💲 *€21, exchangeable for €25 worth of chips; admission free for those not playing* 🕙 *Daily 3 PM–3 AM.*

A popular spot is **Arcos** (✉ Leopoldstrasse 1 ☏ 0512/582423), next to the arch. The beautiful people gather at **Novembar** (✉ Univeritätsstrasse 1 ☏ 0512/566544 ⊕ www.novembar.at). When the weather is fine, the rooftop **Segafredo Sky Bar** (✉ Univeritätsstrasse 15 ☏ 0512/574910) is the place to be. The tiny **Piano Bar** (✉ Herzog-Friedrich-Strasse 5 ☏ 0512/571010) exudes Old World charm and has occasional live music.

Currently, the basement **Blue Chip disco** (✉ Wilhelm-Greil-Strasse 17 ☏ 0512/565050) is the leading hot spot. The upstairs **Jimmy's bar** (✉ Wilhelm-Greil-Strasse 19 ☏ 0512/570473) is also wildly popular. If it's a pint of Guinness you're longing for, seek out **Limerick Bill's Irish Pub** (✉ Maria-Theresien-Strasse 9 ☏ 0512/582011) with authentic Irish ambience.

Along the nightclub circuit, start first at **Filou** (✉ Stiftgasse 12 ☏ 0512/580256), where in summer you can sit in an attractive garden until 10 PM, when things move indoors for the sake of neighborhood peace and quiet. **Lady O** (✉ Brunecker Strasse 2 ☏ 0512/578574) is the traditional striptease nightclub; you can see a teaser program on the ground floor at 9 PM for a €2 admission charge, but the first drink costs €10.50.

Sports & the Outdoors

Golf

Golf Course Sperberegg (☏ 0512/377165) in Lans, about 9 km (5½ mi) outside the city, is a 9-hole, par-66 course. It is open April–November. **Golfplatz Rinn** (☏ 05223/78177) in Rinn, about 12 km (7½ mi) away, has 18 holes, with a par 71, and offers a sweeping panorama of the Inn Valley. The course is open April–October. Both courses charge greens fees of about €40 on weekdays, €45 on weekends, and discounts are offered at Rinn with the Club Innsbruck card. Several hotels—Europa-Tyrol in Innsbruck, Sporthotel Igls and Gesundheitszentrum Lanserhof at Lans, and the Geisler at Rinn—have special golfing arrangements.

Health & Fitness Clubs

To buff up for the slopes in Innsbruck, try **City Fitness** (⊠ Hunoldstrasse 5 ☎ 0512/365696 ⊕ www.injoy-innsbruck.at). For a centrally located, women-only fitness facility there is **Fame** (⊠ Bürgerstrasse 2 ☎ 0512/ 5671–71), which proffers extensive aerobics schedules.

Hiking

Both easy paths and extreme slopes await hikers and climbers. From June to October, holders of the Club Innsbruck card (free from your hotel) can take free, daily, guided mountain hikes. The tourist office has a special hiking brochure. If you want to learn to climb, look to the **Alpine School Innsbruck** (⊠ Natters, In der Stille 1 ☎ 0512/546000–0 ⊕ www. asi.at). If you're already an experienced *Kletterer* (rock climber), check in with the **Österreichischer Alpenverein** (⊠ Wilhelm-Greil-Strasse 15 ☎ 0512/59547–0).

Horseback Riding

Horseback riding can be arranged through **Reitclub Innsbruck** (⊠ Langer Weg ☎ 0512/347174).

Skiing

In winter, check with the **Tourist Office Innsbruck** (☎ 0512/59850) for information on snow conditions and transportation to the main ski areas, which include the Axamer Lizum, Patscherkofel, Seegrube-Nordpark, Glungezer, Schlick 2000, and Stubai Glacier. You'll find a variety of terrains and challenges in Innsbruck, from the beginner slopes of the Glungezer to the good intermediate skiing of the Axamer Lizum and Patscherkofel and the steep runs and off-piste skiing of Seegrube. Your Club Innsbruck membership card (free with an overnight stay in any Innsbruck hotel) will get you free transportation to the areas and reductions on a number of ski lifts. A Super Ski Pass covers all the ski areas of Innsbruck, the Stubai Glacier, Kitzbühel, and St. Anton, with 520 km (290 mi) of runs, 210 lifts, and all transfers. The Gletscher Ski Pass includes Innsbruck and the Stubai Glacier. If you're a summer skier (and can handle the altitude), there's year-round skiing on the Stubai Glacier, about 40 km (25 mi) from Innsbruck via the free ski shuttle bus (ask at your hotel). You can book all your skiing needs, including lift tickets, equipment rentals, and ski lessons, with the **Schischule Innsbruck** (☎ 0512/ 582310) or through the tourist office. Hotels have details on winter ski kindergartens. A good bet for ski or snowboard rentals is **Snowboard Börse** (⊠ Leopoldstrasse 4 ☎ 0512/581742–0), tucked into an alley just south of the Triumphpforte.

Swimming

Around Innsbruck there are plenty of lakes, but in town you have little choice other than pools, indoors and out. To swim under the sun with a panoramic view of the mountains, try the **Freischwimmbad Tivoli** (⊠ Purtschellerstrasse 1 ☎ 0512/342344). If the weather goes south, try the turn-of-the-20th-century indoor **Hallenbad Amraser Strasse** (⊠ Amraser Strasse 3 ☎ 0512/342585). **Hallenbad Höttinger Au** (⊠ Fürstenweg 12 ☎ 0512/282339) is a popular indoor facility.

Tennis

Innsbruck has an abundance of courts, although they tend to be scattered and booked up well ahead. Your hotel or the tourist office can help.

Austrian tennis pro Barbara Schett might be spotted on-court at the **Allround Tennis Center** (⊠ Wiesengasse 16 ☎ 0512/360110). Reserve a court at the **Tennisclub IEV** (⊠ Reichenauer Strasse 144 ☎ 0512/346229), where your Club Innsbruck card will get you a reduction.

Shopping

The best shops are along the arcaded Herzog-Friedrich-Strasse in the heart of the Altstadt, or Old City along its extension, Maria-Theresien-Strasse; and the adjoining streets Meraner Strasse and Anichstrasse. Innsbruck is *the* place to buy native Tyrolean clothing, particularly lederhosen (traditional brushed leather shorts and knickers) and loden (sturdy combed-wool jackets and vests). Look also for cut crystal and wood carvings; locally handmade, delicate silver-filigree pins make fine gifts.

For sheer holiday delight, nothing tops the traditional **Christmas Market,** open from November 23 to December 28 and featuring numerous dealers selling wooden and glass handicrafts, Christmas tree decorations, candles, and Tyrolean toys and loden costumes. The market stalls are set up around the giant, illuminated Christmas tree just next to the Goldenes Dachl (Golden Roof) museum at Herzog-Friedrich-Strasse 15, in the heart of the Altstadt (Old City).

Rathausgalerie (⊠ Maria-Theresien-Strasse, Anichstrasse, or Adolf-Pichler-Platz) is Innsbruck's swish, centrally located, and glass-roofed indoor mall, address to luxury boutiques and famous names known worldwide, where you can not only shop, but also eat and drink, in style. **Galerie Thomas Flora** (⊠ Herzog-Friedrich-Strasse 5 ☎ 0512/577402) sells graphics by the droll Tyrolean artist Paul Flora; there's much to smile at here, and maybe even to take home. **Rudolf Boschi** (⊠ Kiebachgasse 8 ☎ 0512/589224) turns out reproductions of old pewterware, using the original molds when possible. Among other wares, he has locally produced, hand-decorated beer mugs with pewter lids. The dazzling **Swarovski Crystal Gallery** (⊠ Herzog-Friedrich-Strasse 39 ☎ 0512/573100) features almost everything from the world-renowned crystal maker, whose headquarters is in nearby Wattens, east of Innsbruck. **Tiroler Heimatwerk** (⊠ Meraner Strasse 2–4 ☎ 0512/582320) is the first place to look for local mementos and souvenirs of good quality. The extremely attractive shop carries textiles and finished clothing, ceramics, carved wooden chests, and some furniture, but don't expect to bargain shop here. You can also have clothing made to order. **Lodenhaus Hubertus** (⊠ Sparkassenplatz 3 ☎ 0512/585092) is an outstanding source of dirndls, those attractive country costumes for women, with white blouse, dark skirt, and colorful apron. It also has children's clothing.

Igls

5 km (3 mi) south of Innsbruck

Perched on a sunny plateau ascending to the famed Brenner Pass to the south of Innsbruck, Igls is one of the several lovely holiday villages minutes away from Innsbruck's city center. Here you'll find the charm and quiet of a small Austrian village with easy access to Innsbruck and its attractions. Igls is close to the area's golf courses and **Schloss Ambras**, and is the best starting point for hiking or skiing the Patscherkofel mountain, whose conical shape towers volcano-like over the village. Trams and buses run hourly between Innsbruck and Igls; take Tram 6, which arrives in Igls via Lans and Schloss Ambras, from either the main train station or the **Bergisel** tram station. The **Igls tourist office** (☎ 0512/377101 ⊕ www.innsbruck-tourismus.com/igls) is a large, free-standing building in the village center.

Where to Stay

$$$–$$$$ 🏨 **Sporthotel Igls.** With its large, crackling fireplaces, elegant parlors, winter garden, and piano bar, this central Best Western hotel will make you feel right at home. The rooms and the lobby are spacious, warm and inviting. ⊠ A-6080 ☎ 0512/377241 🖷 0512/378679 ⊕ www.sporthotel-igls.com 🛏 80 rooms ⚒ Restaurant, indoor pool, gym, sauna, bar, meeting rooms; no a/c ☰ AE, MC, V ¶○¶ BP, MAP.

¢   🏨 **Bon-Alpina.** Nothing fancy here, but this thrifty, family-run hotel in the heart of Igls is directly on the ski slope. The staff is friendly, and the bus to Innsbruck stops outside the door. ⊠ Hilberstrasse 8, A-6080 ☎ 0512/377219 🖷 0512/37760010 ⊕ www.innsbruck-hotels.at 🛏 97 rooms ⚒ Restaurant, pizzeria, indoor-outdoor pool, sauna, bar; no a/c ☰ AE, MC, V ⊙ Closed Nov–mid-Dec. ¶○¶ BP, MAP.

AROUND THE LOWER INN VALLEY

Northeast of Innsbruck the Inn River valley broadens out and courses right through Tirol toward Kufstein and the German border. Route 171 along the valley is a much more pleasant route than the parallel autobahn. Often overlooked by travelers zipping between Innsbruck and Salzburg on the autobahn, this region is nonetheless worth a visit for the well-preserved old towns of Hall and Schwaz and for a trip into the beautiful Zillertal (Ziller Valley), dotted with ski areas and popular as a year-round resort area. Many of the Tirol's finest folk musicians come from this valley, so if you go, ask about live music programs. In summer, a day at the crystal-blue Achensee should be on your program.

Hall in Tirol

⑬ *9 km (5½ mi) east of Innsbruck.*

Hall in Tirol is an old city founded by salt miners. Narrow lanes running east–west, interrupted by a few short cross alleys, make up the old part of the town. Stop and look around; from the main road, you cannot get a proper perspective of the fine old buildings. The **Rathaus,** built in the mid-15th century, has ornately carved councillors' rooms and beautifully worked craftsmanship. The 17th-century **monastery church** is the oldest Renaissance ecclesiastical building in Tirol. The famed **mint tower,** symbol of the town, was moved to Hall from Meran, and the first coins were struck here in 1477. Legend has it that Duke Sigmund the Wealthy, son of Friedl the Penniless, got his nickname by tossing handfuls of Hall-minted coins to the populace wherever he went. The Inntal (Inn Valley) gave its name to the coin, known as the *Taler*, from which came the word "dollar."

Where to Stay & Eat

¢ ✕ **Aniser.** This ancient little restaurant just inside the Altstadt (Old City) wall is madly popular with locals for its colossal schnitzels (so big you can't see the plates on which they're served) at tiny prices. The traditional Austrian offerings are all freshly prepared, and if you're searching for the fries, they're usually hiding under the schnitzel. The owners thoughtfully leave a roll of aluminum foil on the table, since so many patrons are forced to take home leftovers. ⊠ *Schlossergasse 15* ☎ *05223/ 57314* ▤ *No credit cards.*

$$ ✕▥ **Hotel Restaurant Heiligkreuz.** Perched on a hillside shrouded with trees, the Hotel Restaurant Heiligkreuz is an intimate home away from home. Dark-wood paneling and comfortable overstuffed furniture decorate the hotel. Rooms are equally elegant and welcoming, as is the friendly staff. The restaurant offers light takes on Austrian cuisine, as well as traditional rib-sticking classics such as *G'röstl*, a concoction of eggs, bacon, and potatoes guaranteed to satisfy the heartiest of appetites. ⊠ *Reimmichlstrasse 18, A-6060* ☎ *05223/57114* ▤ *05223/571145* ⊕ *www. holycross.at* ⤳ *35 rooms* ⌂ *Restaurant, in-room safes, cable TV, bar, Internet, meeting room; no a/c* ▤ *AE, MC, V* ⑪ *MAP.*

Shopping

Traveling east between Hall in Tirol and Schwaz, you'll pass the home of the Swarovski cut-crystal empire, in Wattens. Stop at the **Swarovski Crystal World Shop** to browse and perhaps buy some of the famous— and now some of the chicest—crystal and glassware, or if you have more time, explore **Crystal World,** an eclectic but fascinating multimedia gallery that has become one of Tirol's most popular attractions, featuring the works of 15 or more artists including Salvador Dali, Brian Eno, André Heller, and Andy Warhol. ⊠ *Kristallweltenstrasse 1* ☎ *05224/51080–0* ⊕ *www.swarovski-crystalworld.com* 🎫 *€8* ☉ *Daily 9–6.*

Schwaz

⑭ *16 km (10 mi) northeast of Hall in Tirol.*

The Habsburg emperors in the 15th and 16th centuries owed much of their wealth to the silver and copper extracted from the mines here by the Fugger family, bankers and traders who emigrated from Augsburg. First mentioned in the 10th century and incorporated as a town in the 12th century, Schwaz, on the south bank of the Inn, evolved into a rich and important mining center. The mines of the **Silberbergwerk Schwaz**—dug deep under the towering Tuxer Alps—may have provided the impetus behind the establishment of the mint in nearby Hall. ⊠ *Alte Landstrasse 3a* ☎ *05242/72372-0* ⊕ *www.silberbergwerk.at* ☑ *€15* ⊙ *May–Oct., daily 8:30–5; Nov.–Apr., daily 9:30–4.*

The 15th- and 16th-century houses built during those prosperous times still stand, and the marketplace has kept its atmosphere. Look at the vast **parish church,** the largest Gothic hall-church in Tirol. The church was expanded in 1490 and divided into two parts (once they were separated by a wooden wall): the southern chancel for the miners and the northern, or "Prince's Chancel," for the upper classes.

Another outstanding monument from the 15th and 16th centuries in Schwaz is the treasure-filled **Franciscan Church** (Franziskanerkirche), founded in the early 16th century by emperor Maximilian I. This may well be the mendicant order's most beautiful church in the Alpine region.

A fascinating addition to Schwaz is the **Haus der Völker,** a museum dedicated to ethnography. Displays include ancient Asian sculptures as well as African art. ⊠ *Christoph-Anton-Mayr-Weg 7* ☎ *05242/66090* 🖷 *05242/66091* ⊕ *www.hausdervoelker.com* ☑ *€5.10* ⊙ *Daily 10–6.*

en route   **Jenbach,** 8 km (5 mi) north of Schwaz, across the river, is notable mainly as a rail and highway junction; from here Route 169 follows the Ziller Valley (Zillertal) south, past the Gerlos Valley (Route 165) and the Tuxer mountain range to Mayrhofen. The Achensee lies on the plateau to the north, fed by the Achen river rising high in the mountains beyond, on the German border. Both regions have become immensely popular with tourists.

Achensee

⑮ *25 km (17 mi) north of Schwaz, 17 km (12 mi) from Jenbach.*

From Jenbach, many travelers head to the Achensee. If you're driving, take Route 181; the initial stretch involves challenging hairpin turns and a steep climb, but the views over the Inn Valley are exquisite.

To get from Jenbach to the Achensee, you could drive or take a bus, but the most adventuresome and romantic way to reach the Achensee is on the steam-powered train, the **Achenseebahn** (☎ 05244/62243 ⊕ www.achenseebahn.at), built in 1889 as Tirol's first mountain cog railway. The line does its 1,300-foot climb in a nearly straight line more than 7 km (4½ mi) to the lower end of the Achensee (Seespitz). Once at the lower end of the Achensee (Seespitz) you can get a lake steamer operated by **Achensee Schiffahrt** (☎ 05243/5253 ⊕ www.achenseebahn.at) on to Maurach/Buchau and, at the north end of the lake, Achenkirch. From Jenbach, a round-trip train/steamer excursion takes about four and a half hours. Trains and ships run on a regular schedule between June and September.

The Achen Valley has fine skiing in winter, but the Achensee in summer, with water sports and excellent fishing, is the main attraction. It is the largest and most beautiful lake in Tirol—10 km (6 mi) long—with the great mountains of the Karwendel and Rofan ranges rising from its blue-green waters. The lake steamer connects the villages strung along its length.

Where to Stay

$$$ 🏨 **Posthotel Achenkirch Resort & Spa.** This comfortable Alpine chalet is also a wellness hotel, providing every convenience for taking care of fitness, weight loss, and exercise. Horseback riders will find mounts ranging from Lipizzaners (the largest private herd in Europe) to Shetland ponies. Rooms are in typical Tyrolean country style. ⊠ *Achenkirch, A-6215* ☎ *05246/6522–0* 🖷 *05246/6522–468* ⊕ *www.posthotel.at* 📞 *165 rooms* ⟂ *Restaurant, in-room safes, minibars, tennis court, indoor-outdoor pools, gym, sauna, horseback riding, squash, beer garden; no a/c* ☰ *MC, V* 🍴 *BP, MAP.*

Zell am Ziller

⑯ *25 km (16 mi) southeast of Jenbach.*

Fodor'sChoice ★ The main town of the Zillertal—the biggest and most famous of the many beautiful Alpine valleys of the Tirol—is noted for its traditional 500-year-old **Gauderfest,** held on the first weekend in May, when thousands of tourists from far and wide pack the little market town of Zell am Ziller for the colorful skits, music, and singing—and great quantities of *Gauderbier,* a strong brew run up for the occasion. You can hear some of the country's best singing by the valley residents and listen to expert harp and zither playing, for which the valley is famous throughout Austria. Tradition runs strong here: witness the Perchtenlaufen, processions of colorfully masked well-wishers going the neighborhood rounds on January 5, or the annual Almabtrieb during the last September and first October days, when the cows are hung with wreaths and bells and, amid celebrations, herded back from the high Alpine pastures into the lower fields and barns. This is a typical Tyrolean country town, with Alpine lodges and a round-domed pink village church (note the Baroque painting of the Holy Trinity); in winter it's a center for skiing and sports. Contact the local **tourist board** (☎ 05282/2281 🖷 05282/228180).

Where to Stay & Eat

★ $$ ✕🏨 **Bräu.** The core of this thick-walled, five-story, frescoed building in the center of town dates from the 16th century; subsequent renovations have brought it quite up to date. The rooms are decorated in warm Alpine style, in beiges, greens, and browns. The hotel can arrange fishing trips. The three-room restaurant complex serves fine food, with emphasis on fish and game. Reserve for the *Bräustübl,* and enjoy the house beer; the house brewery is also the source of the *Gauderbier.* ⊠ *Dorfplatz 1, A-6280* ☎ *05282/2313* 🖷 *05282/2313–17* ⊕ *www.tiscover.at/hotel-braeu* 📞 *41 rooms* ⟂ *Restaurant, café, sauna, steam room, bar; no a/c* ☰ *No credit cards* ⊘ *Closed Apr. and mid-Oct.–mid-Dec.* 🍴 *BP, MAP.*

Mayrhofen

⑰ *10 km (6 mi) south of Zell am Ziller.*

Down the road you'll come to Mayrhofen, end of the line for the narrow-gauge railway. This is the valley's main tourist base and the favorite summer resort for British and Dutch visitors for many years. Mayrhofen is the starting point for summer hiking into the highly scenic valleys that branch off to the southeast, south, and southwest and for excursions into the Ziller glacier areas, at heights of 9,750 feet and more. Hiking maps and guide information are available from the **tourist office** (☎ 05285/67600).

At Mayrhofen the valley splits into three *Täler* (valleys): the Zillergrund, Stilluptal, and Zemmgrund—prime examples of picture-postcard Alpine areas, swept at the top with glittering, pale-blue glaciers.

Where to Stay & Eat

¢–$ ✕**Wirtshaus zum Griena.** The restaurant tucked into this 400-year-old farmhouse is about a 10-minute drive north of Mayrhofen. The route is not simple, but everybody knows Griena's—ask at your hotel for directions. Once you get there, you'll find yourself in rustic surroundings glowing in natural-wood paneling. Such local favorites as beer soup, potatocheese specialties, and schnitzel are tempting. The beer is local and excellent, but the wines somewhat disappointing. ✉ *Dorfhaus 768* ☎ *05285/62778* ☱ *MC, V* ☉ *Closed June–early July and Nov.–early Dec.*

★ $$$$ ✕▦ **Elisabeth.** This newish house in Tyrolean style radiates elegance without being too formal. The same is true of the well-decorated, luxurious bedrooms, some with ceramic stoves and beautiful wood-carved walls and ceilings. Each room has a balcony overlooking the mountains, and a few have Jacuzzis set in windowed alcoves offering stunning views, plus fireplaces and canopied beds. The hotel has a loyal following, so book ahead. Every Saturday evening there is a huge Tyrolean buffet and live music. ✉ *Einfahrt Mitte 432, A-6290* ☎ *05285/6767* ☱ *05285/6767–67* ⊕ *www.elisabethhotel.com* ➭ *32 rooms* ☖ *Café, pizzeria, indoor pool, gym, sauna, bar; no a/c* ☱ *MC, V* ❜⦿ *BP, MAP.*

$$–$$$ ▦ **Kramerwirt.** Here's the center of the action in Mayrhofen, where the crowd gathers. The welcoming warmth of natural wood in the lobby and in the Kröll Stube (a small, rustic dining room) is accented by the Tyrolean antiques. Still family-run, this hostelry has been around for centuries, and the comfortable rooms will make you feel at home. ✉ *Am Marienbrunnen 346, A-6290* ☎ *05285/6700* ☱ *05285/6700–502* ⊕ *www.tiscover.at/kramerwirt* ➭ *85 rooms* ☖ *Restaurant, in-room safes, sauna, bar; no a/c* ☱ *MC, V* ☉ *Closed Nov.* ❜⦿ *BP, MAP.*

Sports & the Outdoors

CLIMBING For the adventuresome, Peter Habeler at the **Alpinschule u. Schischule Mount Everest** (✉ Hauptstrasse 458 ☎ 05285/62829 ☱ 05285/64260) gives instruction in ice climbing.

Action Club Zillertal (☎ 05285/62977) is the contact for adventure sports like canyoning, rafting, and mountain biking.

en route Hainzenberg, 6 km (4 mi) south of Zell am Ziller, was once a gold-mining town. If passing through, stop at the **Maria Rast pilgrimage church,** built in 1739 by the prospectors, to see its stuccoes and fine ceiling paintings. Don't look for the western transept wing of the church; it slid down the precipice in 1910.

Gerlos

⑱ *18 km (10 mi) east of Zell am Ziller.*

The sensationally scenic Route 165 climbs east out of Zell am Ziller up to Gerlos, a less glitzy but still splendid choice for a summer or winter holiday, with the 8,300-foot Kreuzjoch mountain looming in the background. Scheduled buses make the run up from Zell am Ziller. The Gerlos ski slopes are varied, and in summer the same slopes offer excellent hiking.

Where to Stay

$$$$ ⊞ **Gaspingerhof.** The three Alpine chalets that make up this family-run, rustically furnished complex in the center of town are connected by underground passages. Rooms are done in the bright local custom, with natural woods and colorful fabrics. ⊠ *A-6281* ☎ *05284/5216* 🖷 *05284/ 533549* ⊕ *www.gaspingerhof.at* 🖛 *73 rooms* ⚲ *Restaurant, in-room safes, indoor pool, sauna; no a/c* ☰ *MC, V* ⊙ *Closed mid-Apr.–mid-May and mid-Oct.–early Dec.* ⦿ *BP, MAP.*

¢–$ ⊞ **Almhof.** In typical Tyrolean style, this Alpine inn about 2 km (1 mi) out of the center offers a friendly reception area and comfortable rooms. ⊠ *A-6281 Gerlos–Gmünd* ☎ *05284/5323–0* 🖷 *05284/5323–23* 🖛 *45 rooms* ⚲ *Restaurant, tennis court, indoor pool, gym, sauna; no a/c* ☰ *MC, V* ⊙ *Closed May–early June and Oct.–mid-Dec.* ⦿ *BP, MAP.*

en route Beyond Gerlos, the highway climbs the 5,300-foot Gerlos Pass and plunges into the province of Salzburg in a series of double-back hairpins close to the dramatic 1,300-foot **Krimmler Wasserfälle** (waterfalls). You can complete the circuit back into Tirol by continuing east to Mittersill and cutting north to Kitzbühel via the Thurn Pass.

ON THE ROAD TO KITZBÜHEL

In many ways the area between Jenbach and Kitzbühel, north of the Kitzbüheler Alps and south of the German border, is a distillation of all things Tyrolean: perfectly maintained ancient farmhouses with balconies overflowing with flowers; people who still wear the traditional lederhosen and dirndls as their everyday attire; Alpine villages and medieval castles; and wonderfully "kitschy" winter resorts like Kitzbühel and St. Johann. Other delightful destinations here include Kufstein, with its brooding Festung Kufstein (Festung is German for fortress) and a bevy of warm-water lakes in its vicinity, and Rattenberg, with its glass workshops founded by Sudeten German refugees from the Czech Republic. Everywhere the people are welcoming and the scenery is beautiful.

Alpbach

⑲ *24 km (15 mi) east of Jenbach.*

From Highway 171 at the town of Brixlegg, a small side road runs up a valley to the unspoiled picture-book village of Alpbach. The town takes the international spotlight once a year in August, when world leaders of government and industry gather to discuss global issues at the European Forum.

Where to Stay & Eat

★ **$$–$$$** ✕❐ **Böglerhof.** Much of the original character has been preserved in this beautifully restored 14th-century double chalet, with its heavily beamed ceilings and old stonework. The rooms are attractively decorated in Tyrolean style. The excellent restaurant, with its small *Stuben* (side rooms), is known for such Austrian specialties as cabbage soup and fillet points in light garlic sauce. ✉ *A-6236* ☎ *05336/5227* 🖷 *05336/5227–402* ⊕ *www.boeglerhof.com* ⇨ *50 rooms* ⚘ *Restaurant, tennis court, indoor pool, outdoor pool, gym, sauna, bar, Internet; no a/c* ⊟ *MC, V* ☉ *Closed mid-Apr.–mid-May and late Oct.–mid-Dec.* ⍥ *BP, MAP.*

$$$$ ❐ **Alpbacher Hof.** The massive fireplace sets the keynote in the public rooms of this newly refurbished typical chalet hotel, and the welcoming feeling carries over to the bedrooms. The encompassing view of the valley is yours to enjoy from the large, common terrace. ✉ *A-6236* ☎ *05336/5237* 🖷 *05336/5237–200* ⇨ *55 rooms* ⚘ *Restaurant, café, indoor pool, sauna, bar; no a/c* ⊟ *V* ☉ *Closed mid-Apr.–mid-May and late Oct.–mid-Dec.* ⍥ *BP, MAP.*

Sports & the Outdoors

Sport Ossi (✉ Wittberg 105, A-6233 Kramsach ☎ 05337/63300 🖷 05337/ 64967 ⊕ www.sport-ossi.at) is the area's best contact for rafting, kayaking, rock climbing, and mountain biking.

Rattenberg

⑳ *14 km (9 mi) northeast of Jenbach.*

This medieval town, perhaps the smallest in Austria, was once famous for its silver mines. When the mines were exhausted, Rattenberg lapsed into a deep sleep lasting for centuries. You might think you're back in the Middle Ages as you ramble the narrow old streets full of relics of its past; the town has remained remarkably unchanged for centuries. Today Rattenburg is known for its glass and crystal artists, whose shops are mostly along Südtirolerstrasse. Local legend has it that the ruins of Emperor Maximilian's massive castle, which looms above the town, are haunted by ghosts from a bygone era.

Where to Eat

★ **$** ✕ **Hacker.** People come from miles around to sample the scrumptious pastries and excellent coffee in this traditional café, which has been a coffeehouse since 1774. You can also choose from a variety of ice-cream sundaes. Service is especially friendly, and in summer tables are set outside. ✉ *Südtirolerstrasse 46, A-6240* ☎ *05337/62322* ⊟ *No credit cards* ☉ *Closed Nov.*

Shopping

If you're looking for something special and different, go to **Helga Danek** (✉ Inngasse 60 ☎ 05337/63113 ⊕ www.rattenberg.at) for beautiful painted glass. There is always a sale section available.

Across the river from Rattenberg lies Kramsach, a glass-production center since the 17th century. At the **glassworks school** (☎ 05337/62623) you can watch craftsmen etching, engraving, and painting. Call ahead to arrange a visit.

en route

From Kramsach, follow the road on past Breitenbach toward the **Reintaler Seen** (Rein valley lakes) to the **Museum Tyrolean Bauernhöfe,** where over a dozen complete Tyrolean farmhouses and barns, most dating back to at least the 18th century, have been brought here, restored, and displayed in an idyllic setting. The museum and nearby lakes, perhaps the most beautiful (and warmest) in Tirol, are perfectly suited for exploring on a summer afternoon. ☎ 05337/62636 ⊕ www.museum-tb.at €5.50 ⊙ Apr. 3–Oct. 31, daily 9–6.

Kufstein

㉑ 26 km (16 mi) from Rattenberg.

Kufstein marks the border with Germany. The town was captured from Bavaria in 1504 by Emperor Maximilian I, who added it to the Habsburg domains. Kufstein is dominated by a magnificent fortress right out ★ of a Dürer etching, **Festung Kufstein,** originally built as a "castle for contemplation" in 1200. But Maximilian decided it was better suited for merrymaking and expanded and strengthened it in 1504, rechristening it *Lustschloss,* or "pleasure palace." The considerably renovated fortress contains a small **museum,** a panoramic windowed funicular (cable car), and an organ concert daily at noon, showcasing the famed "Heroes' Organ" (said to burst into sound when a national hero dies). With sumptuous rooms and terraced gardens, Festung Kufstein ranks among the finest of the 1,001 Tyrolean castles. The town of Kufstein itself has some beautiful medieval-period streets. ☎ 05372/602360 ⊕ www.festung. kufstein.at €7.99 includes guided tour ⊙ Nov.–mid-Mar., daily 10–4; mid-Mar.–Oct., daily 9–5.

The center of town harbors a remarkable concentration of art nouveau buildings, both public and private. The **Burgher's Tower** houses the Heldenorgel, the world's largest outdoor organ, with 26 registers and 1,800 pipes. The instrument is played year-round daily at noon and in summer at noon and 6 PM.

Where to Stay & Eat

★ **$$–$$$** ✕🏠 **Best Western Alpenrose.** On the edge of town in green surroundings, this rustic house welcomes you immediately with its friendly lobby, which seems to continue the outdoors; the feeling of relaxed comfort carries over into the attractive bedrooms as well. The elegant restaurant is the best in the area; the *Tafelspitz* (boiled beef) and fish, game, and goose in season are particularly recommended, as is the orange souf-

flé. ⊠ *Weissachstrasse 47, A-6330* ☎ *05372/62122* ⊟ *05372/62122–7*
⊕ *www.bestwestern.com* ⌁ *19 rooms* ᴧ *Restaurant, in-room safes, mini-bars, bar; no a/c* ⊟ *AE, DC, MC, V* ☉ *Closed 1 wk before and 1 wk after Easter* ⦿*⊧ BP, MAP.*

Shopping
Kufstein is home to the world-famous **Riedel glass works** (☎ 05372/64896–0); a visit to the factory may be possible. Otherwise you can buy pieces at the **factory outlet** (⊠ Weissachstrasse 28–34 ☎ 05372/64896–0), which is open weekdays 9–noon and 1–6, Saturday 9–noon.

en route   At Wörgl most travelers begin to head east toward the great resorts of St. Johann and Kitzbühel, described below. Route 312 takes you to St. Johann, the noted vacation center, about 30 km (19 mi) away. You can do the circuit of St. Johann and its more famous neighbor, Kitzbühel, by taking Route 161 for 10 km (6 mi) between the two resorts and returning to Wörgl via Route 170.

Going, Ellmau & Söll

10 km (6 mi) to 20 km (13 mi) south of Kufstein.

The villages of Going, Ellmau, and Söll have developed into attractive small winter and summer resorts. Their altitudes (and their snow) are about the same as those in Kitzbühel and St. Johann, but prices are lower, although rising as their popularity grows. Some of the region's finest restaurants and hotels are found around these villages.

The **Goinger Handwerks-Kunstmarkt,** an arts-and-crafts fair, is held one Friday each month from June through September. You can sample local specialties such as *Kässpätzle* (a noodle skillet dish with cheese and onions) and *Prügeltorte* (chocolate layer cake), along with locally distilled schnapps. Farmers and their families demonstrate crafts and skills handed down through the centuries, and if you are there at 8 PM you can hear the Going Musikkapelle (brass band) perform. For details on the Going fair, contact the town's **tourist office** (☎ 05358/2438).

Where to Stay & Eat

$$$$ ✕ **Schindlhaus.** Original variations on Austrian dishes are served up in a modern setting at this restaurant. Try the lightly braised fillet of venison with red cabbage or one of the fish specialties, served with a delicate sauce. The gemütlich atmosphere and friendly staff provide the perfect finishing touches. ⊠ *Dorf 134, Söll* ☎ *05333/5161* ⊟ *DC, MC, V* ☉ *Closed Mon., Tues. in summer.*

$$$ ✕ **Gasthof Restaurant Lanzenhof.** This festive *Tiroler Wirtshaus,* or traditional Tyrolean guest house, serves impeccable traditional Tyrolean *Schlutzkrapfeln* (ravioli stuffed with cheese, potatoes, and spinach) and lamb chops, among other options, with roast pork a particular favorite for many diners. ⊠ *Dorf 23, A-6353 Going* ☎ *05358/2428* ⊟ *05358/3592* ⊟ *V* ☉ *Closed Sun. and Apr. and Nov.*

$$$$ ✕⊡ **Der Bär.** Within walking distance of the village center, The Bear is known throughout Austria as one of the foremost country inns. Elegant but relaxed comfort pervades in every respect, attractive bedrooms in Tyrolean style included. The kitchen does best with local dishes, such as roast lamb or game. The wine list also has an extensive choice of Austrian, French, and Italian vintages. ⊠ *Kirchbichl 9, A-6352 Ellmau* ☎ *05358/2395* 🖷 *05358/2395–56* ⊕ *www.hotelbaer.com* ⇗ *45 rooms* ♨ *Restaurant, in-room safes, minibars, indoor-outdoor pools, gym, sauna; no a/c, no smoking* ☰ *AE, MC, V* ☉ *Closed mid-Mar.–May and early Nov.–mid-Dec.*

$$$$ 🏨 **Stanglwirt.** A 300-year-old coaching inn forms the core of this large health-and-fitness complex, which is also a popular mealtime stop for tour buses, and a noted location for spotting celebrities. Rooms in the newer section are spacious; some are studios with old-fashioned ceramic stoves, in keeping with the Tyrolean decor. Guests can ride, swim, hunt, ski in season, or play tennis and squash. The tennis school is one of the best in Austria. This hotel is a great favorite with Germans. Children will enjoy the "kiddies' farm." ⊠ *Sonnseite 50, A-6353 Going* ☎ *05358/2000* 🖷 *05358/2000–31* ⊕ *www.stanglwirt.com* ⇗ *62 rooms, 6 apartments* ♨ *Restaurant, minibars, tennis courts, indoor-outdoor pools, gym, sauna, horseback riding, squash; no a/c* ☰ *AE, DC, MC, V* ⧖ *BP, MAP.*

St. Johann in Tirol

㉒ *32 km (24 mi) southeast of Kufstein, 14 km (9 mi) northeast of Kitzbühel.*

For years St. Johann lived in the shadow of Kitzbühel, but today the town, with its colorfully painted houses, has developed a personality of its own, and for better or worse is equally mobbed winter and summer. The facilities are similar, but prices are still lower, although climbing. (The dark horses here could be Kirchdorf, 4 km [2½ mi] north of St. Johann, where costs appear to be holding, or Fieberbrunn, 12 km [7 mi] east on Route 164.) While in St. Johann, don't miss the magnificently decorated Baroque **parish church** or the Gothic **Spitalskirche,** with its fine late-medieval stained glass, just west of town in Weitau.

Where to Stay & Eat

★ **$$$–$$$$** ✕🏨 **Das Bräu.** A great place to stop on Highway 312 between Salzburg and Innsbruck is Das Bräu (25 km [15 mi] northeast of St. Johann in Tirol), in the village of Lofer (actually in Salzburg Province). There are two restaurants: one for casual dining or for a clearly more elegant meal. In the "rural" restaurant—with red gingham tablecloths and cowbells, harnesses, and stirrups hanging from the wooden beams— dishes include locally caught fish, fried chicken, and lamb. If you are going upscale, you'll be offered delights such as Fogosh filet in pepper sauce with potato straw or cream cheese parfait with strawberry pulp. The desserts are scrumptious beyond belief. If you don't feel like driving on, you can stay overnight in one of the 28 pleasant bedrooms upstairs. ⊠ *Hauptstrasse 28, Lofer* ☎ *06588/82070* 🖷 *06588/820771* ✍ *dasbraeu@aon.at* ☰ *AE, DC, MC, V.*

$$–$$$ ✕🏨 **Post.** The painted stucco facade identifies this traditional hotel in the center of town. Natural woods and reds carry over from the public spaces and restaurant into the guest rooms. ⊠ *Speckbacherstrasse 1, A-*

6380 ☎ 05352/62230 🖷 05352/62230–3 ⊕ *www.hotel-post.tv* ⇨ *46 rooms* ⟁ *Restaurant, café; no a/c* ▤ *AE, DC, MC, V* ⊗ *Closed Apr. and Nov.* ⎜◎⎜ *BP, MAP.*

$$$$ 🏠 **Stanglwirt.** A 300-year-old coaching inn forms the core of this large health-and-fitness complex in the small village of Going. The resort is a popular mealtime stop for tour buses en route to St. Johann in Tirol, and a noted location for spotting celebrities. Rooms in the newer section are spacious; some are studios with old-fashioned ceramic stoves, in keeping with the Tyrolean decor. Guests can ride, swim, hunt, ski in season, or play tennis and squash. The tennis school is one of the best in Austria. Children will enjoy the "kiddies' farm." ✉ *Sonnseite 50, A-6353 Going* ☎ *05358/2000* 🖷 *05358/2000–31* ⊕ *www.stanglwirt. com* ⇨ *62 rooms, 6 apartments* ⟁ *Restaurant, minibars, tennis courts, 2 indoor-outdoor pools, gym, sauna, horseback riding, squash; no a/c* ▤ *AE, DC, MC, V* ⎜◎⎜ *BP, MAP.*

$$ 🏠 **Alpenapartment Europa.** This apartment-hotel adjacent to a recreation center (where guests can pay extra for swimming, sauna, and tennis facilities) is attractively furnished in Baroque and regional decor; many rooms have Tyrolean four-posters. Exhausted skiers can delight in knowing that breakfast is served until 11 AM. ✉ *Achenallee 18, A-6380* ☎ *05352/62285–0* 🖷 *05532/62285–5* ⇨ *16 apartments* ⟁ *Kitchenettes* ▤ *No credit cards* ⎜◎⎜ *EP.*

Kitzbühel

❷❸ *20 km (12 mi) south of St. Johann, 71 km (44 mi) northeast of Gerlos.*

Kitzbühel is indisputably one of Austria's most fashionable winter resorts, although the town is now staking a claim on its summer season as well. "Kitz" offers warm-season visitors a hefty program of hiking, cycling, and golf, along with outdoor concerts and theater, and a pro tennis tournament in July. As for skiing, the famous Ski Safari (previously known for decades as the Ski Circus)—a carefully planned, clever combination of lifts, cable railways, and runs that lets you ski for more than 145 km (91 mi) without having to exert yourself climbing a single foot—originally put this town on the map. Today Kitzbühel is in perpetual motion, and is always packed December through February, notably at the end of January for the famed **Hahnenkam** downhill ski race. But at any time during the season there's plenty to do, from sleigh rides to fancy-dress balls.

Built in the 16th century with proceeds from copper and silver mining, Kitzbühel itself is scenic enough. Among its pleasures are its churches, such as **St. Andrew's parish church** (1435–1506), which has a lavishly rococo chapel, the Rosakapelle, and the marvelously ornate tomb (1520) of the Kupferschmid family. The **Church of St. Catherine,** built about 1350, houses a Gothic winged altar dating from 1515.

In summer, you'll be offered a free guest card for substantial reductions on various activities (some of which are then free, like the hiking program), such as tennis, riding, and golf. The best swimming is in the nearby Schwarzsee. To see Alpine flowers in their native habitat, take the (new) cable car up the Kitzbüheler Horn to the **Alpine Flower Garden Kitzbühel** at 6,500 feet; cars leave continuously.

Where to Stay & Eat

$$$$ ✕ **Wirtshaus Unterberger Stuben.** In this former residence done up in typical Tyrolean fashion with beige and red decor, you may have to reserve weeks ahead to get a table in winter; the place is usually booked solid. The international cuisine is good if not always a match for the prices, offering such temptations as creamed pumpkin soup and stuffed oxtail. ⊠ *Wehrgasse 2* ☎ *05356/66127–0* ⊞ *05356/66127–6* ⚠ *Reservations essential* ⊟ *No credit cards* ⊙ *Closed early June and Nov. No lunch weekends.*

¢–$ ✕**Praxmair.** Après-ski can't begin early enough for the casually chic crowds who pile into this famous pastry shop–café, known for its Florentines and *Krapfen,* which are something like jelly doughnuts, and available throughout Austria in January and February. ⊠ *Vorderstadt 17* ☎*05356/ 62646* ⊟ *AE, DC, MC, V* ⊙ *Closed Apr. and Nov.*

$$$$ ✕⊡ **Romantik Hotel Tennerhof.** Adored by everyone from the Duke of Windsor to Kirk Douglas, this alpine Shangri-la set in a huge garden near the golf course. Inside the hilltop mountain inn you'll find all is both rustic and glamorous, with gold chandeliers hung over country cupboards and silken sofas next to shuttered windows. The guest rooms are done in Tyrolean country furnishings, all different, some with ceramic stoves, and most with balconies. The staff is exceptionally warm and accommodating, and you'll find this is the kind of place you want to settle into for days. Families love the special supervised children's room. The elegant restaurant (reservations essential), under the direction of chef Thomas Ritzer, is one of the best in Austria. Ritzer's cuisine is based on classic Austrian cooking with a light Mediterranean–Asian accent. The *Lieblingsmenü der "Hausherren"* (owner's favorite menu) includes a *Brennessel* (nettle) cream soup with sheep-cheese croutons, duck-liver tart with caramelized red-wine pears, fresh-caught local Zander fillet on basil risotto, a superb bouillabaisse, and a dreamy, creamy lemon soufflé. Vegetables and herbs come straight from the hotel garden. ⊠ *Griesenauweg 26, A-6370* ☎ *05356/63181* ⊞ *05356/63181–70* ⊕ *www.tennerhof. com* ↵ *40 rooms* ⚟ *Restaurant, in-room safes, minibars, indoor-outdoor pools, sauna, spa, Internet; no a/c* ⊟ *AE, DC, MC, V* ⊙ *Closed Apr.–mid-May and mid-Oct.–mid-Dec.* ⊠ *BP, MAP.*

FodorsChoice ★ (margin note for Romantik Hotel Tennerhof)

$$$$ ⊡ **Weisses Rössl.** The "White Horse" greets you with domed glass ceilings, a piano bar, and a revamped restaurant. The former garden has become a modern wellness facility with warmly intimate public salons. The spacious, comfortable guest rooms are adorned in light fir and complemented by modern amenities. Suites are available, as is the centuries-old wine cellar, now converted into a unique private dining room. Summer guests are offered free greens fees on area links. ⊠ *Bichlstrasse 5, A-6370* ☎ *05356/62541–0* ⊞ *05356/63472* ⊕ *www.weisses-roessl. com* ↵ *69 rooms* ⚟ *Restaurant, indoor pool, spa, bar; no a/c* ⊟ *AE, DC, MC, V* ⊠ *BP, MAP.*

$$–$$$ ⊡ **Golf-Hotel Rasmushof.** For a superb Alpine panorama and year-round proximity to outdoor activities, it's difficult to find a better address in Kitzbühel than the Rasmushof, situated directly on the 9-hole **Ras-**

mushof golf course, with a view of the famous Streif downhill ski run and only steps from the lift. The rooms are drenched in Tyrolean antiques, with finishes of barn wood and plush upholstered furnishings. Facilities are fully modern; large family suites are available. ⊠ *Ried Ecking 15, A-6370 Kitzbühel* ☎ *05356/65252* 🖷 *05356/65252–49* ⊕ *www. rasmushof.at* ⬧ *49 rooms, 4 suites* ⚑ *Restaurant, in-room safes, 9-hole golf course, tennis court, indoor pool, exercise equipment, sauna, steam room, Internet, meeting room; no a/c* ⊟ *AE, DC, MC, V* ⎮◉⎮ *BP, MAP.*

$$ 🏰 **Schloss Lebenberg.** A 16th-century castle on a hilltop outside town has been transformed into a wholly modern, owner-managed family hotel. The bedrooms are contemporary in flavor. ⊠ *Lebenbergstrasse 17, A-6370* ☎ *05356/6901* 🖷 *05356/64405* ⊕ *www.tiscover.com/schloss-lebenberg* ⬧ *109 rooms, 42 suites* ⚑ *Restaurant, in-room safes, indoor pool, gym, sauna, baby-sitting, airport shuttle; no a/c* ⊟ *AE, DC, MC, V* ⎮◉⎮ *BP, MAP.*

$–$$ 🏰 **Goldener Greif.** The original building dates from 1271; renovations in the 1950s gave the house a more contemporary but still traditional Tyrolean charm, emphasized by the magnificent vaulted lobby with open fireplaces and antiques. The rooms are warm and the hotel houses the Kitzbühel casino. ⊠ *Hinterstadt 24, A-6370* ☎ *05356/64311* 🖷 *05356/65001* ⊕ *www.hotel-goldener-greif.at* ⬧ *47 rooms* ⚑ *Restaurant, sauna, bar, casino; no a/c* ⊟ *AE, DC, MC, V* ⊘ *Closed Apr.–mid-June and Oct.–mid-Dec.* ⎮◉⎮ *BP, MAP.*

Nightlife & the Arts

Much activity centers on the **casino** in the Goldener Greif hotel, which abounds in baccarat, blackjack, roulette, and one-armed bandits. There are a restaurant and a bar, and no set closing time. A valid passport is needed to enter the casino. ⊠ *Hinterstadt 24* ☎ *05356/62300* 🎫 *Free* ⊘ *Daily from 7 PM.*

The **Tenne** has for generations been *the* evening spot in Kitz. It's partly because of its friendliness and capacity, as well as the music, but most of all it's because you can meet people here. ⊠ *Hotel zur Tenne* ☎ *05356/64444–0* 🖷 *05356/64803–56* ⊟ *AE, DC, MC, V* ⊘ *Daily.*

The disco crowd moves from place to place, but check out **Take Five** (⊠ Hinterstadt 22 ☎ 05356/71300–30), the town's hot spot. A top nightspot is **Ecco** (⊠ Hinterstadt 22 ☎ 05356/71300–20) which serves light food in an upscale setting. A favorite for many is **Jimmy's** (⊠ Vorderstadt 31 ☎ 05356/644–09). Established favorites include the **Stamperl bar and restaurant** (⊠ Franz-Reisch-Strasse 7 ☎ 05356/62555). The **Londoner** (⊠ Franz-Reisch-Strasse 4 ☎ 05356/71428) is a popular watering hole. The **Fünferl bar** (⊠ Franz-Reisch-Strasse 1 ☎ 05356/71300–5) in the Kitzbüheler Hof has many aficionados.

Sports & the Outdoors

GOLF With 18 courses within an hour's drive, Kitzbühel may properly lay claim to being the "golf center of the Alps." The Golf Alpin Pass offers special deals for 3 or 5 greens fees; available at select hotels, golf clubs, or the tourist office. Go to ⊕ www.golf-alpin.at or ⊕ www.kitzbuehel-golf. com. Golf privileges can be arranged between the Kitzbühel courses and any of the town's top-ranked hotels.

Golf Eichenheim (☎ 05356/66615), an 18-hole, PGA-rated fairway, is the area's newest course, and offers impressive views of the grand Kitzbuhel Alps. **Golfclub Kitzbühel** (☎ 05356/63007), 9 holes, par-36, is open April–October. **Golf-Club Kitzbühel-Schwarzsee** (☎ 05356/71645), 18 holes, par-72, is open April–October. **Rasmushof Golf Club** (☎ 05356/65252–0), 9 holes, is situated in the finish area of the legendary "Streif" downhill run, and is the closest course to the town center.

WEST FROM INNSBRUCK

The upper Inn Valley, from Innsbruck stretching down to the Swiss border, is beautiful countryside, particularly the narrow valleys that branch off to the south. Most visitors take Route 171 west from Innsbruck along the banks of the Inn, rather than the autobahn, which hugs the cliffs along the way. This is a region of family-run farms perched on mountainsides and steep granite peaks flanking narrow valleys leading to some of Austria's finest ski areas.

Telfs

㉔ *32 km (20 mi) southeast of Reutte.*

Mythical masked figures invade the streets of Telfs every five years just before Lent, when the town hosts its traditional Carnival celebration of **Schleicherlaufen**. In Telfs, this well-attended event dates back to the 16th century. Some of the grotesque masks can be seen in the local museum.

Where to Stay

$$$$ 🏨 **Interalpen Tyrol.** This resort, outside town at 3,900 feet up the slopes, is simply huge, from the lobby, with its vast expanse of carpet, to the modern rooms. But the lobby's crackling fire is welcoming, and it's a far quieter, more relaxing spot than you might guess from a first impression. ⊠ A-6410 ☎ 05262/606 🖷 05262/606–190 ⊕ www.interalpen. com ⇄ 300 rooms ⌕ Restaurant, in-room safes, minibars, tennis courts, indoor pool, gym, sauna, spa; no a/c ⊟ AE, DC, MC, V ⊗ Closed Apr.–early May and Nov.–mid-Dec. ⟐ BP, MAP.

$ 🏨 **Tirolerhof.** You're within a couple of blocks of the center of town in this comfortable, balconied, family-run hotel, convenient also to nearby pools and tennis and squash courts. The restaurant offers standard regional fare. ⊠ Bahnhofstrasse 28, A-6410 ☎ 05262/62237 🖷 05262/62237–9 ⊕ www.der-tirolerhof.at ⇄ 37 rooms ⌕ Restaurant; no a/c ⊟ MC, V ⊗ Closed 3 wks around Easter ⟐ BP, MAP.

en route Driving west from Innsbruck or north up the mountain from Telfs you arrive at **Seefeld**, perched on a sunny plateau at 1,200 meters (3,937 feet), only a few kilometers from the German border. As you travel, the views looking back into the Inn Valley are spectacular, and the mountains surrounding the vacation village are grand. In summer, Seefeld does service as a base for climbers and hikers in the pristine Karwendel mountain preserve, and in winter attracts hordes of cross-country ski fans and downhill skiers alike.

Imst

25 *35 km (22 mi) west of Telfs.*

Imst, a popular summer resort lying a half mile or so back from the Inn River and the railway line, makes an excellent base from which to explore the Paznaun Valley and the upper Inn Valley, leading into Switzerland and Italy.

Here the **Schemenlaufen,** a masked procession depicting the struggle between good and evil, usually takes place in February. Many of the magnificently carved masks worn by the mummers—especially those of the fearsome witches—are very old and qualify as works of art. The event is scheduled every four years and will next occur in the year 2008. The tradition is ancient, and as in Telfs you can see many of the 100-year-old carved masks in the local **museum** (⊠ Strelenegasse 6); check with the tourist office for opening times. A great feature of these rustic carnivals is the ringing of cowbells of all shapes, sizes, and tones, and the resulting noise is quite deafening when the procession hits its stride. Don't overlook the 15th-century frescoed **parish church** in the upper part of Imst.

Where to Stay & Eat

★ **$$–$$$** ✕▥ **Post.** Set in the center of town next to a large park, this 16th-century former castle paints a picture of romance with onion-dome towers. The friendly interior is furnished with antiques, and the modern bedrooms are cheerful. The restaurant is recommended, particularly for its game courses. ⊠ *E.-Wallnöfer-Platz 3, A-6460* ☎ *05412/66555* 🖷 *05412/266519–55* ⊕ *www.romantikhotels.de/imst* ⤶ *35 rooms* ⌂ *Restaurant, indoor pool; no a/c* ▤ *DC, MC, V* ⊗ *Closed Nov.–Jan.* ⋈ *BP, MAP.*

$$ ▥ **Linserhof.** This double-chalet hotel is outside town, set in a lush Alpine meadow at the base of a wooded hillside. The attractive rooms are in rustic Tyrolean decor, with much natural wood; those on the south side with balconies are preferable. ⊠ *A-6460 Imst/Teilwiesen* ☎ *05412/66415* 🖷 *05412/66415–133* ⤶ *42 rooms, 20 apartments* ⌂ *Restaurant, tennis court, indoor pool, lake, gym, sauna, bicycles, bar, convention center; no a/c* ▤ *AE, DC, MC, V* ⋈ *BP, MAP.*

¢–$ ▥ **Zum Hirschen.** This comfortable *Gasthof-Pension,* close to the center of town, pays particular attention to families with children. ⊠ *Th.-Walsch-Strasse 3, A-6460* ☎ *05412/6901–0* 🖷 *05412/69017* ⤶ *70 rooms* ⌂ *Restaurant, sauna, bar; no a/c* ▤ *AE, DC, MC, V* ⊗ *Closed early–mid-Dec.* ⋈ *BP, MAP.*

en route The Ötz Valley climbs in a series of six great natural steps for nearly 42 km (26 mi) from the Inn River to the glaciers around Obergurgl, 6,200 feet above sea level. The entire span offers stunning scenery, with the most dramatic part beginning around Sölden, where the final rise begins to the 8,100-foot pass over the Timmel Alps and across the Italian border into South Tirol. It was in this area that Ötzi, the Iceman mummy, was discovered in 1992. The body, which is more than 5,000 years old, was found by Austrians who were unaware they had crossed the Italian border. Ötzi is now in the possession of Italy, who at first wanted nothing to do with him, thinking he was a 20th-century murder victim. To reach the valley, turn south off Route 171 onto Route 186.

Ötz

26 *21 km (12 mi) southeast of Imst, 23 km (14 mi) southwest of Telfs.*

Gothic houses with colorful fresco decorations grace this typically Tyrolean mountain village. The parish church of **St. George and St. Nicholas,** whose tower was once a charnel house, sits on a rock promontory above the village. The small St. Michael's Chapel also has a splendid altar dating from 1683.

Where to Stay

$$ ▦ **Drei Mohren.** You can't miss the roof of this inn, with its wonderful collection of odd towers and onion domes. The interior is less exotic, with elegantly paneled, comfortable rooms; most have balconies. The restaurant, offering standard local fare, is intended primarily for hotel guests and is tastefully decorated with old etchings. ⊠ *Hauptstrasse 54, A-6433* ☎ *05252/6301* 🖷 *05252/2464* 🖉 *hotel.3mohren@telering.at* 🖙 *22 rooms* ♻ *Restaurant, tennis court; no a/c* ☰ *AE, DC, MC, V* ✆ *Closed Nov.–mid-Dec.* ❘⊘❘ *BP, MAP.*

Sölden

27 *28 km (18 mi) south of Ötz.*

Sölden's newest addition to its already massive lift network is the "Black Blade," which carries eight at a time over 3,000 meters (9,800 feet) to the Rettenbach glacier, completing the only lift system in Austria to boast skiing on three mountains more than 3,000 meters high. The view from any of the three peaks provides a panoramic 360° view of the mountains. Sölden's reputation as a wild, aprés-ski party town is well-deserved, meaning that if you are searching for a tranquil, romantic ski holiday, or have small children, you may want to try the village of **Hochsölden**— on the slopes above town, where things are quieter—or search elsewhere. For information on Sölden's skiing facilities, contact the **Tourismusverband Sölden** (⊠ Ötztal Arena, A-6450 ☎ 05254/510–0 🖷 05254/3131 ⊕ www.soelden.com).

Where to Stay & Eat

$$$$ ✕▦ **Central.** Huge arches and heavy wooden timbers accent the antique furniture and set the mood in this massive, riverside hotel where the prominent are said to gather. The bedrooms are spacious and luxuriously furnished. Half board is standard. The intimate Ötztaler Stube restaurant is the best in town; sample the fillet of venison, and don't overlook the excellent desserts. ⊠ *Hochsölden Hof 418, A-6450* ☎ *05254/2260–0* 🖷 *05254/2260–511* 🖙 *92 rooms* ♻ *Restaurant, indoor pool, sauna; no a/c* ☰ *DC, MC, V* ✆ *Closed June–mid-July* ❘⊘❘ *BP, MAP.*

HANNIBAL ON ICE

HANNIBAL BARCA, *The Carthaginian general who, over 2,200 years ago, strode boldly from his homeland in northern Africa to lead his fierce troops against the mighty Roman Empire in the Second Punic War, is most often remembered for his daring and risky crossing of the Alps from the north to attack the Romans in Italy.*

He began the crossing with 60,000 men and 37 elephants, reputedly losing more than 15,000 of those men and most of the elephants along the treacherous route. However, he was able to recruit new soldiers along the way, and the general and his troops inflicted horrific defeats on the Romans for 16 years in Italy. The crossing is remembered as one of the most brilliant ideas in military history.

As the years passed, however, support for the war effort abated; supplies and reinforcements from Carthage dried up, while Rome rebuilt its war machine to previously unknown strengths. When Hannibal and his troops arrived at the city of Rome, he uncharacteristically hesitated for several days before attacking, allowing the Romans to successfully defend the city.

The failed attack sent Hannibal's men packing. Carthage was then besieged by the Romans on all sides, and Hannibal was forced to defend his homeland. At the decisive battle at Zama (present-day Makhtar, Tunisia), the general's troops were scattered and destroyed by the mightier Roman forces; Hannibal surrendered, but skillfully negotiated a peace treaty that left him in command of the government of Carthage, where he doggedly renewed his ambition of conflict with Rome.

Taking note of his desires, the Romans drove him from Carthage, and the general, now a fugitive, was forced to sell his military skills to the highest bidder.

Hannibal continued to fight alongside various anti-Roman armies before eventually being defeated in battle in northern Asia Minor. Rather than be taken alive, he committed suicide by poison.

The exact route of Hannibal's fascinating Alps crossing is unknown, but this hasn't stopped the town of Sölden and director Hubert Lepka from claiming the story as their own. Lepka's annual show, **"Hannibal—Journey Across the Alps"** (☎ 05254/508 🖷 05254/508–120 ⊕ www.karthago.tv ✉ €27, €33 with round-trip transfer from Sölden to Rettenbach Glacier), recreating the general's heroics, is usually staged in mid-April (check the Web site for the exact date) on the Rettenbach Glacier 3,000 meters (10,000 feet) above Sölden, where "Carthage"—a pyramid, a mountain of ice, a palace—rises out of snow and light.

Upon this unique glacier stage, the story of Hannibal unfolds over 6 square km (2½ square mi) in a blaze of high-tech, Hollywood theatrical excess. The play itself is comprises 10 scenes, and the story is told in narrative fashion before thousands of (warmly-clad) spectators. Snow cats serve as elephants, roaring their way over crevices and powdery fields. Night skiers, as African storm troopers, swish into battle. The evening sky is filled with helicopters, airplanes, and parachute jumpers.

All the while, lasers, lights, fireworks, and music fill the glacial air with excitement. The extravaganza comes to a grand finale with the Battle of Zama, where Hannibal suffered his historic defeat in 202 BC.

$$$–$$$$ Liebe Sonne. You'll be right next to the chairlift to Hochsölden if you stay in this sprawling, rustic complex. The paneled rooms are cozy. Half board is required. ⊠ *Rainstadl 85, A-6450* ☎ *05254/2203–0* 🖷 *05254/2423* ⊕ *www.sonnenhotels.at* 📞 *59 rooms* ⚒ *Restaurant, indoor pool, gym, sauna, spa, bar; no a/c* 🖃 *AE, MC, V* ⊙ *Closed May and June* 🍴 *BP, MAP.*

Nightlife

The nightlife here varies from non-existent to wild, depending on the season. In winter the more than 85 bars, discos, pubs, and eateries are packed, and many nightspots have live bands, but expect cover charges of around €5.

The most popular music bar is **Bierhimml** (☎ 05254/50120), with a never-ending selection of beers and decent food. **Fire & Ice** (☎ 05254/2203) keeps the dance floor pumped until 2 in the morning. Don't pass up the whimsical **Bla-Bla** aprés-ski bar (☎ 05254/2646), the town's most renowned see-and-be-seen watering hole.

Sports & the Outdoors

CLIMBING The nearby Ventertal valley burrows still farther into the Ötztal Alps, ending in the tiny village of Vent, a popular resort center. In summer, the village is transformed into a base for serious mountain climbers experienced in ice and rock climbing, who want to attempt the formidable **Wildspitze** (12,450 feet) or other, even more difficult neighboring peaks. Hiring a professional local guide is strongly advised. To reach Vent from Sölden, turn off at the road marked to Heiligenkreuz.

RAFTING **Vacancia Outdoor Tirol** (⊠ Hauptstrasse 438 ☎ 05254/3100 ⊕ www.vacancia.at) can provide you with what you need to enjoy the area's wild water, including guided rafting trips, and offers special outdoor adventures for kids. In winter, you can secure skiing gear, lessons and, again, children's programs.

Obergurgl

 11 km (7 mi) south of Sölden.

Austria's highest village, tiny Obergurgl gained its reputation not only for superb winter sports but also as the place where the Swiss physicist Auguste Piccard landed his famous stratospheric balloon in 1931. In winter, a vast expanse of snow and ice shimmers all around you, and the great peaks and glaciers of the Ötztal Alps appear deceptively close all year. A high Alpine road takes you from Obergurgl to the hotel settlement at **Hochgurgl,** another excellent skiing spot, and farther up to the Timmelsjoch Pass (closed in winter) through magnificent mountain scenery. Since 1988 Hochgurgl has also been accessible by cable car, bridging the two ski areas. From Hochgurgl, a three-stage chairlift brings you into an area of year-round skiing. For details on Obergurgl's skiing facilities, contact the **Tourismusverband Obergurgl/Hochgurgl** (⊠ A-6456 Ötztal ☎ 05256/6466 🖷 05256/6353 ⊕ www.obergurgl.com). In summer, also ask at the tourist office about hiking and river-rafting possibilities.

Where to Stay

★ **$$$$** 🏠 **Edelweiss und Gurgl.** Traditionally, this relaxed, family-run hotel is *the* place to stay, and it's right at the ski lift. The cheery, spacious rooms in this massive house have attractive natural-wood touches. ✉ *A-6456* ☎ *05256/6223* ⊕ *www.edelweiss-gurgl.com* ✒ *100 rooms ⚄ 2 restaurants, indoor pool, sauna, bar, meeting room; no a/c* ▤ *AE, DC, MC, V* ⊘ *Closed May–mid-June and Oct.–Nov.* ⚭ *BP, MAP.*

★ **$$$–$$$$** 🏠 **Bellevue.** This friendly Alpine chalet lives up to its name in every respect: is there another "Bellevue" among the probable thousands in the world with a vista to equal the one here? You can ski right out the front door. Rooms are cozy, but half board is required. ✉ *A-6456* ☎ *05256/6228* ⊕ *www.austria-bellevue.com* ✒ *26 rooms ⚄ Restaurant, some minibars, indoor pool, gym, sauna; no a/c* ▤ *MC, V* ⊘ *Closed May and Oct.* ⚭ *BP, MAP.*

LANDECK, UPPER INN VALLEY & ST. ANTON

Landeck

㉙ *24 km (15 mi) southwest of Imst.*

On Route 171 west, Landeck is a popular place in summer and a good base from which to explore the Paznaun Valley and the upper Inn Valley, leading into Switzerland and Italy. Landeck also serves well in winter as a less-expensive base for skiing the nearby world-class slopes at St. Anton or Ischgl. Landeck is known for an ancient and awe-inspiring rite that takes place on **"Cheese Sunday,"** the Sunday following Ash Wednesday. At dawn the young men set out to climb to the top of the great rocky crags that overshadow and hem in the Altstadt (Old City) on three sides. As dusk falls, they light huge bonfires that can be seen for miles around and then set fire to great disks of pinewood dipped in tar, which they roll ablaze down to the valley below. The sight of scores of these fiery wheels bounding down the steep slopes toward town is a fearsome spectacle worthy of Ezekiel.

The 13th-century **Burg Landeck castle** dominates from its position above the town. Climb up and catch the superb views from this vantage point. Also note the 16th-century winged altar in the 15th-century Gothic **parish church of the Assumption.** Downhill and, increasingly, cross-country skiing can be found in Landeck and throughout the Upper Inn Valley. Equipment is available for rent, though the selection and quality will vary from place to place.

Where to Stay

$ 🏠 **Schrofenstein.** Directly in the middle of town, this older house still shows its original beamed ceilings and marble floors in the public areas. The rooms, in contrast, are comfortably modern while those overlooking the river are preferable. ✉ *Malser Strasse 31, A-6500* ☎ *05442/62395* ⊕ *www.schrofenstein.at* ✒ *60 rooms ⚄ Restaurant, convention center; no a/c* ▤ *AE, DC, MC, V* ⊘ *Closed mid–late Apr. and Nov.–mid-Dec.* ⚭ *BP, MAP.*

$ ⌧ **Schwarzer Adler.** Virtually in the shadow of the town castle, this traditional, family-run hotel offers solid comfort in typical Tyrolean style, with red checks and light wood. ⌧ *Malser Strasse 8, A-6500* ☎ *05442/62316* 🖶 *05442/62316–50* ✉ *office@schwarzeradler.at* ⇥ *32 rooms* ♨ *Restaurant; no a/c* ⊟ *No credit cards* ⊘ *Closed Nov.–mid-Dec.* ❑ *BP, MAP.*

Sports & the Outdoors

HIKING   Would-be climbers can take lessons by contacting Hugo Walter at the **Bergsteigerschule Piz Buin-Silvretta** (⌧ *A-6563* Galtür ☎ 05443/8565).

St. Anton am Arlberg

★ ⑳ *22 km (15 mi) west of Landeck.*

Tucked between the entrance to the Arlberg Tunnel and the railway, St. Anton swarms with visitors at the height of the season. The wealthy, the prominent, including, occasionally, the royal, appear regularly to see and be seen—some even to enjoy the winter sports. Their presence boosts prices into the very-expensive-to-outrageous category, but if you shop around you can find accommodations outside the center of the action at a bearable price. St. Anton is a particularly lovely town in summer—which has also become a fashionable season.

Modern skiing techniques were created and nurtured in St. Anton. In 1921, Hannes Schneider (1890–1955), an unknown young ski instructor with innovative ideas, set up a ski school to teach his new technique, at the invitation of the just-founded Kandahar Ski Club. This "Arlberg School" method, developed by Schneider in the '20s and '30s, laid down the basic principles since followed by all skiing courses the world over. St. Anton's remains one of the world's leading ski schools. Thanks to an amazing system of cable cars, double chairlift, and interconnected T-bars, St. Anton can access skiers to the Arlberg's region's enormous 300-odd km (200-odd mi) of marked runs. If you decide to take to the slopes, remember that skiing remains serious business in St. Anton: many slopes are so steep you'll be sharing them with mountain climbers.

Where to Stay & Eat

$$$$ ✕⌧ **Brunnenhof.** In the homey intimacy of an old farmhouse in nearby St. Jakob is one of the best restaurants in the area. From the excellent Tyrolean and international menu you might choose a mushroom, garlic, or cheese soup and follow it with roast rack of lamb in an herb crust. The wine list is good. The 10-room hotel offers cozy comfort at moderate prices from December to April and from June to September. ⌧ *St. Jakober Dorfstrasse 53, A-6580* ☎ *05446/2293* 🖶 *05446/2293–5* ⊕ *www.arlberg.com/brunnenhof* ♨ *Restaurant, airport shuttle; no a/c* ⊟ *MC, V* ⊘ *Closed May–June and Oct.–Nov.* ❑ *BP, MAP.*

★ $$$–$$$$ ⌧ **Schwarzer Adler.** The beautifully frescoed facade of this 430-year-old inn in the center of town creates the right setting for the open fireplaces, Tyrolean antiques, and colorful Oriental carpets within. Rooms are tastefully furnished in Alpine style and fully equipped. An annex across the street has somewhat less elegant (but cheaper) rooms. ⌧ *A-6580* ☎ *05446/2244–0* 🖶 *05446/2244–62* ⊕ *www.schwarzeradler.com*

🛏 *63 rooms ᗢ Restaurant, café, in-room safes, pool, gym, dance club, baby-sitting, Internet; no a/c ⊟AE, DC, MC, V ☉ Closed mid-Apr.–May and Oct.–Nov.* ⬚| BP, MAP.

$$$–$$$$ ⌨ **Anton.** If you have simply had enough of quaint Tyrolean hotels and *Bierstube*, then this centrally located, modern, wood-and-glass house is for you. Built in 2000, the concept is spartan and casual, almost Asian in simplicity. The fully furnished apartment concept—many rooms can be connected or separated—allows the hotel to provide accommodations for almost any size group or family. In the evening, live "house music" DJs turn the café into an après-ski hangout light years away from the usual "beer and wurst" scene. Book in advance, since the hotel has a loyal following. ⊠ *Kandaharweg 4, A-6580* ☎ *05446/2408* 🖷 *05446/2408-19* ⊕ *www.anton-aparthotel.com ᗢ Café, sauna, bar; no a/c* ⊟ *AE, DC, MC, V* ⬚| *BP.*

Nightlife & the Arts

For some visitors to St. Anton, the show, not the snow, is the thing. Nobody complains about a lack of action!

Check out these popular après-ski spots: **Bar Kandahar** (⊠ Sporthotel St. Anton ☎ 05446/30260); the **Postkeller cellar disco** (⊠ Hotel Neue Post ☎ 05446/2213–274); and the **terrace of the Hotel Alte Post** (⊠ Hotel Alte Post ☎ 05446/2553), which hops in early spring. In Moos, Gunnar Munthe's **Krazy Kanguruh** (☎ 05446/2633) with its cellar disco is a favorite gathering spot; it opens at 3:30 PM. Some of the best, original, local Alpine drinking and dining can be found at **Rodelalm** (☎ 0699/10858855) and **Sennhütte** (☎ 05446/2048).

Sports & the Outdoors

SKIING The *Skihaserl*, or ski bunny, as the beginner is called, usually joins a class on St. Anton's good "nursery" slopes, where he or she will have plenty of often very distinguished company. The **Skischule Arlberg** (☎ 05446/3411 🖷 05446/2306 ⊕ www.skischool-arlberg.com) here is excellent and is considered by some to be the Harvard of ski schools. Once past the Skihaserl stage, skiers go higher in the Arlberg mountains to the superlative runs from the top of the Galzig and the 9,100-foot Valluga above it. Check with your hotel or ski-lift ticket offices about an **Arlberg Skipass**, which is good on cable cars and lifts in St. Anton and St. Christoph on the Tirol side and on those in Zürs, Lech, Oberlech, and Stuben in Vorarlberg—85 in all. For complete details on St. Anton's skiing facilities, contact the town's **tourist office** (☎ 05446/22690 🖷 05446/2532 ⊕ www.stantonamarlberg.com).

St. Christoph

🛈 *2 km (1 mi) west of St. Anton am Arlberg.*

A hospice to care for imperiled travelers stranded by the snows on the pass was founded in what is now St. Christoph as early as the 15th century. Today the snow is what attracts visitors to the area. Even the Austrian government has gotten in on the act, holding its exacting courses for aspiring ski instructors here. While St. Christoph hasn't the same social cachet as St. Anton, the skiing facilities are precisely the same (and even closer at hand). If you take your skiing seriously and are willing to forgo the high life as too distracting or too expensive, you may find winter sports per se more fun at St. Christoph.

Where to Stay & Eat

★ $$$$ **Arlberg Hospiz.** This huge pink building re-creates much of the legendary ancient hospice that stood here until a fire in the 1950s. Carved-wood paneling and rich Oriental carpets abound. The rooms are luxurious in the extreme; service is attentive but not obtrusive. The associated Hospizalm restaurant has earned a reputation for creative cooking: you might be offered cream of lobster or oyster soup, veal or venison, or fish dishes. The wine list is outstanding. ✉ *A-6580 St. Christoph am Arlberg* ☎ *05446/2611* 📠 *05446/3545* 🌐 *www.hospiz.com* *102 rooms* *Restaurant, in-room safes, some minibars, indoor pool, gym, sauna, bar, dance club, baby-sitting; no a/c* 💳 *AE, DC, MC, V* ⏲ *Closed May and Oct.–Nov.* *BP, MAP.*

Ischgl

32 *67 km (42 mi) southeast of St. Christoph.*

Ischgl, the largest town in the Paznaun Valley, has become as renowned for its party scene as for its excellent skiing, particularly in the small Fimber Valley to the south, and in summer it is a popular high-altitude health resort. You can get to the 7,500-foot Idalpe via the 4-km-long (2½-mi-long) Silvretta cable-car run. The enchanting Paznaun Valley follows the course of the Trisanna River for more than 40 km (25 mi). The valley runs into the heart of the Blue Silvretta mountains, named for the shimmering ice-blue effect created by the great peaks and glaciers. They are dominated by the Fluchthorn (10,462 feet), at the head of the valley near Galtür.

Slightly higher up the valley is **Galtür,** the best-known resort in the Paznaun, equally popular as a winter-sports area, a summer resort, and a base for mountain climbing. Although Galtür is a starting point for practiced mountaineers, many of the climbs up the Blue Silvretta are very easy and lead to the half dozen mountain huts belonging to the Alpenverein. Galtür and the Silvretta region inspired Ernest Hemingway's novella *Alpine Idyll*; the author spent the winter of 1925 here, and the town still remembers him.

Alpinaurium. Following an avalanche of catastrophic proportion which took dozens of lives and destroyed many centuries-old homes and guest houses, the community of Galtür undertook a massive building project resulting in the Alpinarium, which is at once a memoriam, museum, conference center, café, indoor climbing hall, library, and most significantly a 345-meter-long (1,132-foot-long) wall built of steel and concrete designed to prevent such an accident from occurring again. ✉ *Hauptstrasse 29c, A-6563* ☎ *05443/20000* 🌐 *www.alpinarium.at* ⏲ *Tues.–Sun. 10–6.*

Where to Stay

$$$$ **Post.** The oldest part of this traditional hotel dates back 200 years. Seemingly the center of activity in this lively resort, the Post plies you

with Tyrolean charm, attractive rooms that include minibars and safes, and a recommendable restaurant offering many different cuisines. The hotel bar is a busy nightspot, so you might want to request a room toward the back of the hotel. ☒ *A-6561* ☎ *05444/5232* 🖷 *05444/5617–33* ⊕ *www.post-ischgl.at* ➷ *83 rooms* ⚘ *Restaurant, in-room safes, minibars, pool, spa, bar, Internet; no a/c* ⊟ *AE, DC, MC, V* ⵦ *BP, MAP.*

$$$$ ⊞ **Trofana Royal.** The Trofana is a luxe hotel situated right next to the Silvretta cable car. A timeless elegance carries through from the massive lobby to the four unique dining rooms and plushy guest quarters. You may want to take the optional half board, thanks to the renowned restaurant, where chef Martin Sieberer delights in a synthesis of haute cuisine and Tyrolean tradition. The wine list is outstanding. ☒ *A-6561* ☎ *05444/600* 🖷 *05444/600–90* ⊕ *www.trofana.at* ➷ *82 rooms* ⚘ *Restaurant, in-room safes, minibars, spa, bar, baby-sitting; no a/c* ⊟*AE, DC, MC, V* ⵦ *BP, MAP.*

$$$ ⊞ **Christine.** This modern, sunshiny little house puts you in the heart of Ischgl and a few steps from the ski slopes. Most rooms look out toward Silvretta mountain. ☒ *A-6561* ☎ *05444/5346* 🖷 *05444/5346-46* ⊕ *www.tiscover.at/christine.ischgl* ➷ *33 rooms* ⚘ *In-room safes, minibars, bar; no a/c* ⊟ *No credit cards* ⵦ *BP.*

Nightlife & the Arts

Ischgl has such a rousing nightlife that, during the ski season, it would be difficult not to find the après-ski and nightlife action. Popular après-ski destinations include the rustically themed **Kuhstall** (☒ Sporthotel Silvretta ☎ 05444/5223). Among the many nightlife possibilities in Ischgl, start with the **Tenne** (☒ Hotel Trofana ☎ 05444/601).

INNSBRUCK & TIROL A TO Z

To research prices, get advice from other travelers, and book travel arrangements, visit www.fodors.com.

AIRPORTS & TRANSFERS

Innsbruck Flughafen, the airport 3 km (2 mi) west of Innsbruck, is served principally by Austrian Airlines and Air Alps.

🎿 Airport Information **Innsbruck Flughafen** ☎ 0512/22525 flight information ⊕ www.innsbruck-airport.com.

TRANSFERS Buses (Line F) to the main train station in Innsbruck take about 20 minutes. Get your ticket from the bus driver; it costs €1.60. Taxis should take no more than 10 minutes into town, and the fare is about €10–€12. Transfer services operated by Connect and Four Seasons Travel run to and from the *Zentralbereich* at Munich airport. Service to and from Innsbruck and Munich is on demand; make arrangements in advance, or when arriving in Munich, go directly to the shuttle operator's counter, allowing 2½ hours for travel. One-way fare is €34, round-trip €64 reservations are recommended. A similar service is offered by Connect, which also provides shuttle service to the Salzburg airport.

🎿 Shuttles **Connect** ☒ Grabenweg 67b ☎ 0512/343533 ⊕ www.tirolconnect.com. **Four Seasons Travel** ☒ Müllerstrasse 14 ☎ 0512/584157 🖷 0512/585767 ⊕ www.airport-transfer.com.

BUS TRAVEL

Innsbruck is connected by bus to other parts of Tirol, and the Innsbruck Hauptbahnhof terminal is beside the train station.

In Tirol, as throughout Austria, where the train doesn't go, the post office or railway bus does, and except in the most remote areas buses are frequent enough that you can get around. But bus travel requires time and planning. In summer, tour-bus operators run many sightseeing trips through Tirol that often include East and South Tirol. Check with your travel agent or the nearest tourist office.

The bus is the most convenient way to reach the six major ski areas outside the city. A Club Innsbruck pass (free from the tourist office or your hotel if you spend one night or more) gives you free transportation to the ski areas; many hotels provide shuttle service to the special ski bus stop. These are not the regular city buses, but special, deluxe ski buses that leave from the Landestheater on Rennweg, across from the Hofburg. Check with your hotel or the tourist offices for schedules.

🚌 Bus Information **Innsbruck Hauptbahnhof** ⊠ Südtiroler Platz ☎ 0512/1717 or 0512/585155.

For inter-city bus schedules and fares contact **Postbus AG** ⊠ Rossaugasse 10, Innsbruck ☎ 04379/444–0 ⊕ www.postbus.at/tirol.

CAR RENTAL

🚌 Major Agencies **Avis** ⊠ Tourist Center, Salurner Strasse 15 ☎ 0512/571754 🖨 0512/577149. **Budget** ⊠ Michael-Gaismayr-Strasse 7 ☎ 0512/588468 🖨 0512/584580. **Europcar** ⊠ Salurner Strasse 8 ☎ 0512/582060 🖨 0512/582107.

CAR TRAVEL

To get to Innsbruck, exit from the east–west autobahn (Route A12/E60) or from the Brenner autobahn (Route A13/E45) running south to Italy. Driving is the best way to see the rest of Tirol, since it allows you to wander off the main routes at your pleasure or to stop and admire the view. Roads are good, but a detailed highway map is recommended. Curiously, most of the road signs in Austria name the upcoming cities and towns, but not the distances to reach them.

The autobahns are fastest, but for scenery you're best off on the byways. One important exception is the 1¼-km (1-mi) Europa Bridge on the Brenner autobahn running south into Italy, although if you follow the parallel route from Patsch to Pfons, you'll have the views without the traffic. Roads with particularly attractive scenery are marked on highway maps with a parallel green line. To drive on Austria's autobahn, a *vignette,* or sticker, is required, for sale at almost all service stations. A 10-day sticker costs €7.60, a 60-day €21.88.

PARKING Since the Innsbruck Old City is a pedestrian zone and much of the rest of the downtown area is paid parking only, it's best to leave your car in a central garage unless your hotel has parking. Private cars are not allowed on many of the Altstadt streets, and parking anywhere near the center in Innsbruck requires vouchers, which you buy from blue coin-operated dispensers found around parking areas. Each half hour normally costs €0.50–€1. Maximum parking time is 1½ hours. Large blue P signs direct you to parking garages. The bus is about as convenient as a car for reaching the ski areas if you are going to have to cope with chains and other complications of winter driving.

EMERGENCIES

Several pharmacies stay open late in Innsbruck on a rotational basis. The newspaper will give their names, addresses, and phone numbers. Ask your hotel for help.

🛈 Emergency services **Ambulance** ☎ 144. **Police** ☎ 133.

LODGING

HOSTELS Call for information on youth hostels. The booklet "Children's Hotels" (in English, available from the Tyrolean tourist office) lists Tyrolean hotels that cater particularly to families with children.

🛈 Organizations **Jugend Herberge** ☎ 0512/346179 or 0512/346180.

RESERVING A ROOM If you arrive in Innsbruck without a hotel room, check with the Innsbruck Reservations Office, located in the main tourist office in the Old City, or inside the main train station. The downtown office is open weekdays 10–7 and Saturday 8–noon, and the train station branch is open daily 9–6.

🛈 **Innsbruck Reservation** ✉ Burggraben 3 ☎ 0512/562000-0 🖶 0512/562000-220 ⊕ www.innsbruck.info.

MONEY MATTERS

CURRENCY EXCHANGE In addition to banks (open weekdays 7:45–12:30 and 2:15–4) and post offices, you can change money in Innsbruck at the main train station (the office is open daily 7:30–12:30, 12:45–6, and 6:30–8:15) and the city tourist information office. But compare rates; a post office or bank is probably the best option. Cash machines can be found at almost all banks.

TOURS

BUS TOURS The Ferrari-red **Sightseer** bus, a service of the Innsbruck Tourist Office, is the best way to see the sights of Innsbruck without walking, and features a recorded commentary (heard through the provided headphones) in several languages including English. There are two routes, both beginning from Maria-Theresien-Strasse in the Altstadt (Old City), but you can catch the bus from any of the nine marked stops, and jump off and on the bus whenever you like. The air-conditioned luxury bus is free with your Innsbruck Card, or buy your ticket from the driver or at the tourist office.

WALKING TOURS Guided walking tours of the Aldstadt (Old City) daily at 11 and 2 highlight historic personalities and some offbeat features associated with Innsbruck. Your hotel or one of the tourist offices will have tickets and details.

TAXIS

In Innsbruck, taxis are not much faster than walking, particularly along the one-way streets and in the Old City. Basic fare is €3.78 for the first 1½ km (1 mi). Call to order a radio cab.

🛈 Taxi Companies **Funktaxi** ☎ 0512/5311.

TRAIN TRAVEL

Direct trains serve Innsbruck from Munich, Vienna, Rome, and Zürich, and all arrive at the railroad station *Innbruck Hauptbahnhof* at Südtiroler Platz. A new station was erected in 2004, outfitted with restaurants, cafés, a supermarket, and even a post office.

The railroad follows nearly all the main routes in Tirol, with highways and tracks sharing the same narrow valleys. Some of the most fascinating and memorable side trips can be made by rail: two narrow-gauge lines steam out of Jenbach, for example, one up to the Achensee, the other down to Mayrhofen in the Zillertal. From Innsbruck, the narrow-gauge Stubaitalbahn runs south to Telfes and Fulpmes.

The main railway line of Tirol runs east–west, entering Tirol via the Griessen Pass, then heading on to St. Johann and Kitzbühel before wandering over to Wörgl and onward to Jenbach, Hall in Tirol, and Innsbruck. From Innsbruck on, the line follows the Inn Valley to Landeck, then to St. Anton, where it plunges into an 11-km (7-mi) tunnel under the Arlberg range, emerging at Langen in Vorarlberg. From Innsbruck, a line runs north into Germany to Garmish-Partenkirchen and onward back into Austria, to Ehrwald and Reutte in Tirol and beyond, into Germany again. A line from Innsbruck to the south goes over the dramatic Brenner Pass (4,465 feet) into Italy.

🚊 Train Information **ÖBB–Österreichisches Bundesbahn** ☎ 0512/1717 information and reservations ⊕ www.oebb.at.

TRANSPORTATION AROUND INNSBRUCK & TIROL

In Innsbruck, most bus and streetcar routes begin or end at Maria-Theresien-Strasse, nearby Bozner Platz, or the main train station (Hauptbahnhof). You can get single tickets costing €1.60 on the bus or streetcar. Multiple-ride tickets bought in advance at most tobacconists (*Tabak-Trafik*), the IVB (transportation services) office, or the tourist office are cheaper; a block of four tickets is €5.10. A 24-hour ticket good for the city costs €3.20; other 24-hour network tickets cover areas outside the immediate city. You can transfer to another line with the same ticket as long as you continue in more or less the same direction in a single journey. A weekly ticket costs €10.70. For information, check with the tourist office.

Horse-drawn cabs, still a feature of Innsbruck life, can be hired at the stand in front of the Landestheater. Set the price before you head off; a half-hour ride will cost around €25.

🚊 **IVB Kundencenter** ✉ Stainerstrasse 2 ☎ 0512/5307500 ⊕ www.ivb.at.

TRAVEL AGENCIES

American Express is open weekdays 9–5:30, Sat. 9–noon.

🚊 Local Agent Referrals **American Express** ✉ Brixnerstrasse 3 ☎ 0512/582491-0 🖷 0512/573385. **Verkehrsbüro** ✉ Buxnerstrasse 2 ☎ 0512/52079-0 🖷 0512/52079-85.

VISITOR INFORMATION

Innsbruck's main tourist office is open daily 8–6. Tirol's provincial tourist bureau, the Tirol Werbung, is naturally also in Innsbruck. The Österreichischer Alpenverein is the place to go for information on Alpine huts and mountaineering advice. It's open weekdays 8:30–6, Saturday 9–noon.

Many small-town tourist offices have no specific street address and are accommodated in the town hall. Address letters to the Fremdenverkehrsamt (tourist office) and include the postal code of the town. On the Internet, information is available from the Web site of the Austrian National Tourist Board or from Tirol Werbung.

▓ Tourist Information **Austrian National Tourist Board** ⊕ www.tiscover.com/tirol. **Achensee** ✉ A-6215 ☎ 05246/5300 🖶 05246/5333. **Gerlos** ✉ A-6281 ☎ 05284/5244-0 🖶 05284/5244-24. **Imst** ✉ Johannesplatz 4, A-6460 ☎ 05412/6910-0 🖶 05412/6910-8. **Innsbruck Main Tourist Office** ✉ Burggraben 3 A-6021 ☎ 0512/59850 🖶 0512/59850-7 ⊕ www.tiscover.com/innsbruck-tourismus. **Ischgl** ✉ A-6561 ☎ 05444/52660 🖶 05444/5636. **Jenbach** ✉ Achenseestrasse 37, A-6200 ☎ 05244/63901 🖶 05244/63552. **Kitzbühel** ✉ Hinterstadt 18, A-6370 ☎ 05356/62155 🖶 05356/62307. **Kufstein** ✉ Unterer Stadtplatz 8, A-6330 ☎ 05372/62207 🖶 05372/61455. **Landeck** ✉ Malserstrasse 10, A-6500 ☎ 05442/62344 🖶 05442/67830. **Mayrhofen** ✉ Dursterstrassse 225, A-6290 ☎ 05285/6760 🖶 05285/6760-33. **Obergurgl/Hochgurgl** ✉ Hauptstrasse 108, A-6456 ☎ 05256/6466 🖶 05256/6353. **Österreichischer Alpenverein** ✉ Wilhelm-Greil-Strasse 15 ☎ 0512/59547-34 🖶 0512/575528. **Rattenberg** ✉ Klostergasse 94, A-6240 ☎ 05337/63321 🖶 05337/65417. **St. Anton am Arlberg** ✉ Dorfstrasse 67, A-6580 ☎ 05446/2269-0 🖶 05446/2532. **St. Johann in Tirol** ✉ Poststrasse 2, A-6380 ☎ 05352/63335-0 🖶 05352/65200. **Schwaz** ✉ Franz-Josef-Strasse 26, A-6130 ☎ 05242/63240 🖶 05242/65630. **Sölden/Ötztal** ✉ Rettenbach 288, A-6450 ☎ 05254/2212-0 🖶 05254/3131. **Tirol Werbung** ✉ Maria-Theresien-Strasse 55, A-6010 ☎ 0512/7272 🖶 0512/7272-7 ⊕ www.tirol.at. **Zell im Zillertall** ✉ Dorfplatz 3a, A-6280 ☎ 05282/2281 🖶 05282/2281-80.

VORARLBERG

10

SEE DIVAS AND TENORS EMOTE
on a floating stage at Bregenz Festspiele ⇨*p.448*

CATCH TOP APRÈS-SKI VIEWS
from the terrace at Schruns-Tschagguns ⇨*p.456*

SEND MAIL HOME
from Feldkirch's writers' retreat ⇨*p.452*

SAVOR EVERY NOTE
of the elegant Schubertiade Festival ⇨*p.450*

BRING YOUR OWN SKI EXPERT
to the posh enclave of Zürs ⇨*p.457*

LOG SIGHTINGS OF ALPINE PEAKS
from the Pfänderbahn cable car ⇨*p.445*

ENJOY HOT/COOL NIGHTLIFE ACTION
at the popular ski town of Lech ⇨*p.460*

Updated by
Lee Hogan

LIKE STUDYING THE OCEAN IN A SINGLE DROP OF WATER, it is said you can know everything about Austria just by going to the Vorarlberg. This postage stamp–size province seems to contain the country in miniature— it features a sampling of the best of everything the country has to offer. Music devotees descend every summer on Vorarlberg for its elegant Schubertiade—held in Schwarzenberg and Bezau—and on Bregenz for its famed lakeside music festival. Nature lovers head to the Bregenzerwald—a wide area of dense forests, charming valleys, and lush meadows dotted with thick clusters of red, white, and yellow Alpine flowers—a region that remains decidedly private and unostentatiously beautiful. Literature buffs come to see the sun set in the village of Schruns, where Hemingway spent several winters writing *The Sun Also Rises*. And merrymakers like to throng Lech and Zürs, two top ski resorts where the fragrances of hot chocolate and *Pfefferminztee* mingle with the aromas of expensive perfumes trailed by the jet set.

Tiny Vorarlberg covers an area of less than 1,000 square mi and is the smallest (with the exception of Vienna) of Austria's federal states. As its name implies, the state lies "before the Arlberg"—that massive range of Alps, the watershed of Europe, mecca of winter sports—and forms the western tip of Austria. Until the tunnel was cut through, the Arlberg was passable only in summer; in winter Vorarlberg was effectively cut off from the rest of the country. And while Austrians from the east may go skiing or vacation in neighboring Tirol, and may consider themselves to be well traveled, many never make it to Vorarlberg over the course of their lives. The Viennese semi-affectionately refer to Vorarlberg as the "Ländle," or "Little Province."

Nowhere else in Austria will you find such devoted adherence to old customs as in the villages and towns of the Vorarlberg. You'll see folk costumes worn on the street, and your chances are good of running into a local celebration at any time of year. The province has much in common with its neighbor, Switzerland. Not only are the dialects similar, but the terrain flows across the border with continuity. Both peoples are descended from the same ancient Germanic tribes that flourished in the 3rd century BC, and both have the same characteristics of thrift, hard work, and a deep-rooted instinct for democracy and independence. In fact, after the collapse of the Habsburg monarchy following World War I, Vorarlberg came very close to becoming a part of Switzerland. In 1919, 80% of the populace voted in favor of negotiating with the Swiss to join the confederation, but the St. Germain peace conference put an end to such ideas, and Vorarlberg remained Austrian.

Exploring Vorarlberg

This chapter divides Vorarlberg into three sections. Our first exploring tour takes you through Bregenz, the region's historic capital. Then head out to the glorious countryside, taking in the legendary Bregenzerwald to Bludenz, following the Ill Valley to Feldkirch, and heading north again to Bregenz. Here you can relax while enjoying the beautiful, if somewhat hair-raising, country roads as you pass through mountain ham-

10

"What God has put asunder by mountain, let no man join by tunnel" is an old Vorarlberg saying. However, once the Arlberg Tunnel linked this westernmost province to the rest of Austria, the secret was out: Vorarlberg—nicknamed the Ländle, the "Little Province"—was really first cousin to Switzerland's ski country, albeit measurably cheaper and somewhat less efficient. The world at large discovered ski slopes that rival those of Austria's neutral neighbor, plus gorgeous Lake Constance and the lush forests of the Bregenzerwald. In colder months, a winter wonderland is the main lure—especially at Lech and Zürs, where skiing is almost as important as being seen.

Numbers in the text correspond to numbers in the margin and on the Vorarlberg map.

If you have 2 days

If you only have a weekend to visit Vorarlberg, head to the capital of ⊞ **Bregenz** ❶ on the shore of the Bodensee (Lake Constance). Spend a day wandering around the lakeshore and the lovely, romantic remains of the once-fortified medieval town. The next day take a boat ride into neighboring Switzerland or Germany. Around the lake are extensive hiking and biking trails for those who'd rather see the sights under their own steam.

If you have 5 days

Visit the resorts in the Arlberg and the Montafon Valley, which have attracted such notables as Ernest Hemingway and the late Princess Diana. Start your trip in ⊞ **Schruns** ❿, visiting Hemingway's haunts. Now you're ready for the Arlberg resorts. On your second day, head up north for **Stuben** ⓬, the hometown of skiing pioneer Hannes Schneider, moving on for your next overnight in ⊞ **Zürs** ⓭. After a little hobnobbing with film stars and royalty, spend your final two overnights in Vorarlberg's most famous ski resort, ⊞ **Lech** ⓮.

If you have 7 days

If you have more time in Vorarlberg, begin by exploring the natural marvels of the **Bregenzerwald** and the history-rich sights of ⊞ **Bregenz** ❶. After two overnights in Bregenz, you can venture off the beaten track on your third day by stopping for discount shopping in Egg on your way to the picturesque town of **Schwarzenberg** ❷, home of the **Schubertiade** (Schubertiade; ⇨ Nightlife & the Arts, *Schwarzenberg*. Then on your fourth day head to ⊞ **Bezau** ❸ to savor the incomparable beauty of the surrounding forests and mountains with a hike into the hills. That afternoon, visit breathtaking **Damüls** ❹, where flowers blanket the hillsides during the summer and great skiing welcomes visitors in winter. Head for ⊞ **Bludenz** ❺ to explore one of the five magical valleys surrounding the town. The fifth day, follow the Ill Valley to the medieval town of ⊞ **Feldkirch** ❻, and spend two days meandering through its narrow, winding streets, admiring the burgher homes and castle from an earlier age, when lords and ladies peopled the province. Make a stop in **Hohenems** ❼ on your last day for a visit to the local Jewish Museum and **Dornbirn** ❽, famous for its textiles, on your way back to the capital.

lets reeking with Old World charm, few having been discovered by the guidebooks. The last excursion takes in the Arlberg ski resorts.

About the Restaurants & Hotels

The gastronomic scene of Austria's westernmost province is as varied as its landscape: first-rate gourmet restaurants, traditional inns, rustic local taverns, as well as international chains and ethnic cuisine are all part of the mix. In small towns throughout the region, restaurants are often the dining rooms of country inns, and there are plenty of these. Most restaurants housed in hotels and resorts will be closed in the off-season, usually November and April. In ski season, breakfast is typically served early enough so that guests can hit the slopes, and dinner early enough for the tired-out to get to bed and rest up for the next day.

Vorarlberg has loads of accommodation options, from local farmhouses where you share chores to ski chalets high on the slopes of the Western Alps—to even a converted castle-hotel perched above the Bodensee. In the most famous ski resorts in Vorarlberg, hotel rates in season are often well above the range of our chart. For those on the lookout for savings, tourist offices can usually help lead you to more moderate lodgings in private houses. In some towns, such as Bregenz, summer is the high season, particularly during the Bregenzer Festspiele (Bregenz Music Festival) and may put the establishment into the next-higher price category.

Room rates include taxes and service and almost always breakfast, except in the most expensive hotels, and one other meal. Half board, as this plan is called, is de rigueur in most lodgings. However, most will offer a breakfast buffet–only rate if requested. Most hotels offer in-room phones and TV (some feature satellite or cable programming). Summer prices are often as much as 50% lower than during the ski season.

WHAT IT COSTS In euros					
	$$$$	**$$$**	**$$**	**$**	**¢**
LECH/ZURS					
RESTAURANTS	over €28	€23–€28	€17–€22	€10–€16	under €10
HOTELS	over €270	€170–€270	€120–€170	€80–€120	under €80
OTHER TOWNS					
RESTAURANTS	over €22	€18–€22	€13–€17	€7–€12	under €7
HOTELS	over €175	€135–€175	€100–€135	€70–€100	under €70

Restaurant prices are per person for a main course at dinner. Hotel prices are for a standard double room in high season, including taxes and service. Assume that hotels operate on the European Plan (EP, with no meal provided) unless we note that they use the Breakfast Plan (BP), Modified American Plan (MAP, with breakfast and dinner daily, known as "halb pension"), or Full American Plan (FAP, or "voll pension," with three meals a day). Higher prices (inquire when booking) prevail for any meal plans.

The Sound—and Sights—of Music

Festival fever in the Vorarlberg every summer summons the faithful to some of the finest concerts in Austria. Grand opera is offered lakeside at the Bregenzer Festspiele (Bregenz Summer Music Festival), while elegant recitals of the Schubertiade take place in neighboring villages Schwarzenberg and Bezau. The Bregenz festival is famed for its floating stage—in actuality a group of man-made islands mounted on pilings. There is also an indoor theater to accommodate the festivities. At the famed Schubertiade concerts, Schubert and *Lieder* lovers come to hear fine musicians offer homage to the great Biedermeier-era composer, as well as works by Brahms, Mozart, Beethoven, and other composers in May, June, August, and September.

On the Menu

Vorarlberg long ago shed its culinary incivility, an image built around simple farm fare like *Kaspätzle*, a filling dish of bite-size noodles smothered in cheese. Today, Vorarlberg's cuisine is as good and varied as any in neighboring Tirol and the rest of Austria—albeit lighter—and is often associated with Swiss gastronomy, from which many of its elements originated. Fresh ingredients from the region's farms, lakes, and forests are the norm, with an emphasis on dairy products from the cows that graze the mountains and meadows of the region. Be sure to try a slab of *Vorarlberg Alpine* from one of the huge rounds, or any of the 30 other varieties of cheese produced at local farms. Cheese is also added to soups and noodle dishes and fried in fritters. Fresh *Egli* (as perch is called here), trout, and whitefish are caught in the waters of Lake Constance and in the surrounding lakes and streams. Fish—fried, broiled, and steamed—appear regularly on restaurant menus throughout Vorarlberg.

Skiing

One of the main attractions of a stay in Vorarlberg is the world-class skiing available in Austria's Western Alps. After all, modern ski techniques were developed in Vorarlberg by local Hannes Schneider, who founded the first ski school in Arlberg in the 1920s. From intimate, rustic resorts to the glamour of Lech and Zürs, the province has slopes to suit all tastes and levels, and fewer crowds than in the rest of the country.

Timing

Vorarlberg has something to offer visitors in every season. If you're in the province during warm weather, make sure to stop in Bregenz when the city comes to life with the Bregenzer Festspiele (Bregenz Music Festival). Boat excursions to Switzerland and Germany are also a must. History buffs will enjoy the sights in Bregenz, Bludenz, and especially Feldkirch. And sports enthusiasts will love the wealth of hiking, biking, sailing, and fishing that is available around the region. Of course, if you travel to Vorarlberg during the winter months, then step into your bindings and head to the slopes.

BREGENZ

❶ *150 km (90 mi) west of Innsbruck, 660 km (409 mi) west of Vienna, 120 km (75 mi) east of Zürich, 193 km (120 mi) southwest of Munich.*

Lying along the southeastern shore of the Bodensee (Lake Constance) with the majestic Pfänder as its backdrop, Bregenz is where Vorarlbergers themselves come to make merry, especially in summer. Along the lakeside beach and public pool, cabanas and candy floss lure starched collars to let loose, while nearby an enormous floating stage is the site for performances of grand opera and orchestral works (Verdi, Rimski-Korsakov, Strauss, and Gershwin are just some of the composers who have been featured) under the stars. Bregenz is the capital of Vorarlberg and has been the seat of the provincial government since 1819. The upper town has maintained a charming Old World character, but the lower part of the city fronting the lake's edge is fairly unimpressive. Unfortunately, the waterfront is cut off by railroad tracks, though there is a strip of pedestrian walkway that hugs the shoreline.

Fodor'sChoice
★
Bregenz is pleasant at any time of year, but the best time to visit is during the **Bregenzer Festspiele** (Bregenz Music Festival; ⇨ Nightlife and the Arts, *below*). Acclaimed artists from around the world perform operas, operettas, and musical comedies on the festival's floating stage, part of the Festspiel und Kongresshaus (Festival Hall and Congress Center) complex. In front of the stage, the orchestra pit is built on a jetty, while the audience of 6,800 is safely accommodated on the 30-tier amphitheater built on dry land—a unique and memorable setting you are sure to enjoy. Reserve your tickets in advance, as performances sell out early.

The lake itself is a prime attraction, with boat trips available to nearby Switzerland and Germany. Don't forget to bring along your passport. The **Bodensee White Fleet** ferries offer several trip options. You can travel to the "flower isle" of Mainau or make a crossing to Konstanz, Germany, with stops at Lindau, Friedrichshafen, and Meersburg. The longest round-trip excursion is the Drei-Länder Rundfahrt, which includes stops in Germany and Switzerland. The ferries have different operating schedules, but most run only in the summer months. The Mainau excursion is the exception, running from May to mid-September. ⊠ *Bodenseeschiffahrt Ticket Office, Seestrasse 4* ☎ *05574/42868* 🖷 *05574/93000–520* ⊕ *www.bsb-online.com.*

Most of the important sights of Bregenz can be seen in the course of a walk of about two hours. The town's neoclassical main **Post Office** (⊠ Seestrasse 5) was built in 1893 by Viennese architect Friedrich Setz. Because of the marshy conditions, the post office is built on wood pilings to prevent it from sinking. Behind the post office, the **Nepomuk-Kapelle** (⊠ Kaspar Moosbrugger Platz), or Nepomuk Chapel, was built in 1757 to serve the city's fishermen and sailors. Today the town's Hungarian community celebrates mass here. To the right of the Nepomuk-Kapelle along Kornmarktstrasse is the **Gasthof Kornmesser,** built in 1720 and a gorgeous example of a Baroque town house. Just after the alley simply marked THEATER along Kornmarktstrasse you'll reach the **Theater am Ko-**

rnmarkt, originally constructed in 1838, when Bregenz was still an important commercial port, as a grain storehouse; in 1954 the granary was converted into a 700-seat theater.

Next door to the Theater am Kornmarkt is the **Landesmuseum** (Provincial Museum), where relics from Brigantium, the Roman administrative city that once stood where Bregenz is today, are housed. Gothic and Romanesque ecclesiastical works are also on display in this turn-of-the-20th-century building. ⊠ *Kornmarktplatz 1* ☎ *05574/46050* 🎫 *€2* ☉ *Sept.–June, Tues.–Sun. 9–noon and 2–5; July and Aug., daily 9–5.*

Vorarlberg now has its own modern art museum, the **Kunsthaus.** Designed by Swiss architect Peter Zumthor, the steel-and-concrete building, shingled in etched-glass panels, creates a feeling of space and light. Note the innovative feature of 8-foot openings between each story, which allows sunlight to enter the translucent glass through the ceiling. This marvel of design bathes each gallery in natural light in spite of concrete walls. ⊠ *Karl-Tizian-Platz, A–6900* ☎ *05574/485940* 🖷 *05574/485948* ⊕ *www.kunsthaus-bregenz.at* 🎫 *€6* ☉ *Tues.–Sun. 10–6, Thurs. 10–9.*

Originally used as a grain warehouse when it was built in 1685, the **Rathaus,** on Rathausgasse, was turned over to the city in 1720. The ornate facade and tower were added to the city hall in 1898. Next door to the Rathaus is the **Seekapelle** (Lake Chapel), topped with an onion dome. The chapel was put up over the graves of a band of Swiss whose 1408 attempt to incorporate Bregenz into Switzerland was defeated. Behind the Seekapelle is the traditional **Gösser Braugaststätte** (⊠ Anton-Schneider-Gasse 1). This might be just the moment for a cool beer, a cup of coffee, or the daily vegetarian special. Try to get a table in the Zirbenstüble, with its beautifully carved wood-paneled walls and ceiling.

☾ From Deuringstrasse, which borders on Anton-Schneider-Gasse, take a left on Belrupstrasse to reach the **Pfänderbahn** cable car, which takes you up to the 3,460-foot peak overlooking the city. You can see four countries—and almost 240 Alpine peaks—from here, and the restaurant is open June–mid-September. Children will enjoy a 30-minute circular hike to a small outdoor zoo, with deer, Alpine goats, and wild boar. Admission is free. An added attraction is the **Adlerwarte** (☎ 0663/053040 or 0664/053040 🎫 €4.10), where eagles and other birds of prey demonstrate their prowess in free flight May–September at 11 and 2:30. ☎ *05574/42160* 🎫 *Round-trip €8 Oct. 14–Mar. 21, €9.50 Apr. 1–Oct. 31* ☉ *Dec.–mid-Nov., daily 9–7; service on hr and ½ hr.*

Off of Belrupstrasse, the **Herz-Jesu Kirche** (Sacred Heart Church) was built in 1908 in brick Gothic style. The stained-glass windows by Martin Hausle are especially bright and colorful. Go left from Belrupstrasse onto Maurachgasse. Walking up Maurachgasse, you'll reach the **Stadtsteig** guarding the entrance to the Old City, which bears the emblem of a Celtic-Roman equine goddess (the original is now housed in the Landesmuseum; ⇨ *above*). Inside the gate are the coats of arms of the dukes of Bregenz and the dukes of Montfort, the latter crest now the Vorarlberg provincial emblem.

Next to the Stadtsteig, explore the interior of the tiny **Martinskirche** (✉ Martinsplatz) for its fine 14th-century frescoes. The **Martinsturm** (✉ Martinsgasse 3b) boasts the largest onion dome in Central Europe. The tower (1599–1602) has become a symbol of Bregenz and was the first Baroque construction on Lake Constance; it is closed on Monday from October to April. Remains of the ancient **city wall** are to the right of the tower on Martinsgasse. The coats of arms of several noble Bregenz families can still be seen on the house standing next to the wall's remains.

Angle on along Martinsgasse to Graf-Wilhelm-Strasse and the brightly shuttered **Altes Rathaus** (Old City Hall). The ornate half-timber construction was completed in 1622. Behind the Altes Rathaus on Eponastrasse stands the former **Gesellenspital** (Journeymen's Hospital); remnants of a fresco still visible on its wall depict St. Christopher, St. Peter, and a kneeling abbot. At the bottom of Eponastrasse is **Ehreguta Square,** named for the legendary woman who saved Bregenz during the Appenzell War of 1407–09. Ehreguta was a maid who overheard the enemy planning an invasion of Bregenz. Discovered listening at the door, she was warned that she would be killed if she breathed a word to anybody. Torn between protecting the city and saving her own life, she decided to tell all to the fire blazing in the kitchen one night, but spoke loud enough for others to overhear and take action to save Bregenz. The **Montfortbrunnen** (fountain) in the center of Ehreguta Square is the scene of a ritual washing of wallets and change purses, when carnival jesters clean out their empty pockets and spin tales about the events of the previous year. The fountain honors the minnesinger Hugo von Montfort, who was born in the city in 1357. The small parallel streets running uphill from Ehreguta Square roughly outline the boundaries of the town in the Middle Ages. Hidden around the corner of the building at the beginning of Georgen-Schilde-Strasse are the **Meissnerstiege** (Meissner steps), named after a local poet, that lead from the Old City to the **parish church of St. Gallus.** At the bottom of the steps, follow Schlossbergstrasse up the hill to the church, which combines Romanesque, Gothic, and rococo elements. The interior is decorated simply with pastel coloring instead of the usual excessive gilding. Empress Maria Theresa donated the money for the high altarpiece. You'll notice the monarch's features on one of the shepherdesses depicted there. From the hill outside the church there is a wonderful view of the southwestern wall of the Old City, including the **Beckenturm,** the 16th-century tower once used as a prison and named after bakers imprisoned there for baking rolls that were too skimpy for the town fathers. The **Künstlerhaus Thurn und Taxis** (✉ Gallusstrasse 8) was owned by the princely Thurn und Taxis family until 1915. The building, erected in 1848, now contains a modern gallery. The **Thurn und Taxispark** contains rare trees and plants from around the world.

🅒 Children and parents alike will enjoy a ride on the **Hohentwiel** (☎ 05574/ 48983–0 information 🖷 05574/42467–86 ⊕ www.greber.cc), a restored old-time paddle-wheel steamship that cruises Lake Constance out of Hard, 8 km (5 mi) southwest of Bregenz. Lunch and dinner cruises are offered, but check ahead, since sailings are scheduled irregularly from May to October.

Where to Stay & Eat

$$$–$$$$ ✕ **Wirtshaus am See.** This half-timbered house with a gabled roof is right on the shore of Lake Constance, next to the floating stage used for the Bregenz Festival. The menu has the usual Austrian favorites from schnitzel to *Zwiebelrostbraten* (a skirt steak topped with crispy fried onions), fresh fish, and a worthy wine list. The main attraction here is the spectacular lake view. You can watch the world go by from the restaurant's extensive outdoor terrace. ⊠ *Seepromenade 2* ☎ *05574/42210* 🖷 *05574/42210–4* ⊕ *www.wirtshausamsee.at* 🖃 *MC, V* ☉ *Closed Jan. and Feb.*

$$–$$$ ✕ **Ilge-Weinstube.** This cozy, intimate *Keller* (cellar) is Old Bregenz at its best. Rustic decor in the basement of a 300-year-old house close to the oldest section of town draws the youngish "in" crowd. The atmosphere alone makes the Ilge-Weinstube worth a visit. ⊠ *Maurachgasse 6* ☎ *05574/43609* 🖃 *AE, DC, MC, V* ☉ *Closed Mon.*

★ $$ ✕ **Gasthof Goldener Hirsch.** Allegedly the oldest tavern in Bregenz and close to the Old City, this rustic restaurant offers delicious traditional fare and drink in lively surroundings. The ambitious chef occasionally highlights certain foods, as during the oft-repeated Noodle Week, when diners can choose from a special menu offering a mouthwatering selection of pasta dishes. Particularly good are the spicy spaghetti in a tomato, onion, bacon, and red pepper sauce, or spinach tagliatelle with grilled turkey in a tomato cream sauce with Gorgonzola gratiné. ⊠ *Kirchstrasse 8* ☎ *05574/42815* 🖃 *AE, DC, MC, V* ☉ *Closed Tues. and 2 wks in Sept.*

$ ✕ **Café Götze.** Locals frequent this small, unpretentious café because it's known to have the best pastries in town. The location halfway between the waterfront and the Old City is convenient. ⊠ *Kaiserstrasse 9* ☎ *05574/44523* ☉ *Closed Sun. and Oct. and Nov.*

★ $$$$ ✕▥ **Deuring-Schlössle.** This 400-year-old castle with its Baroque tower has inspired paintings by Turner and Schiele. Rooms are tastefully furnished and have polished wood floors and lovely wainscoting. The owner, who is also the chef of the hotel's highly regarded restaurant, offers gourmet cooking classes on request. Specialties include beautifully presented pike-perch on a bed of pumpkin puree with baby asparagus. If you want a blow-out meal in a lovely, romantic setting, this is the place to go. But be prepared for inflated prices, small portions, and inattentive service. ⊠ *Ehregutaplatz 4, A–6900* ☎ *05574/47800* 🖷 *05574/47800–80* ◄⊃ *13 rooms* ⚑ *Restaurant; no a/c* 🖃 *AE, DC, MC, V.*

$$$–$$$$ ▥ **Schwärzler.** This city hotel atop a green oasis on the edge of town beams with traditional hospitality and sports a cozy restaurant and large, modern rooms. It's only a 15-minute walk to the center of town, but if you'd rather not hoof it, the bus stops right in front. ⊠ *Landstrasse 9, A–6900* ☎ *05574/4990* 🖷 *05574/47575* ⊕ *www.s-hotels.com* ◄⊃ *75 rooms* ⚑ *Indoor pool, sauna, steam room, bicycles, free parking* ¶◯ *BP.*

$$–$$$ ▥ **Weisses Kreuz.** This traditional, family-run, turn-of-the-century house has been renovated with care and charm and is now a Best Western hotel. The location on the edge of the pedestrian zone is central, and the staff is particularly friendly. The rooms are comfortable and modern; those overlooking the private park out back are quieter. ⊠ *Römerstrasse 5, A–6900* ☎ *05574/4988–0* 🖷 *05574/4988–67* ⊕ *www.bestwestern. com* ➴ *44 rooms* ⟳ *Restaurant, in-room safes, minibars, bar, Internet; no a/c* ⊟ *AE, DC, MC, V* ⊙ *Closed Christmas–mid-Jan.* ⍾⊙⏽ *BP.*

Nightlife & the Arts

The cultural year starts with the **Bregenzer Frühling,** the spring music and dance festival that runs from March to May. Information and tickets are available through the **tourist office** (⊠ Bahnhofstrasse 14, A–6900 ☎ 05574/4959) in Bregenz. The big cultural event in Bregenz

Fodor'sChoice is the **Bregenzer Festspiele** (Bregenz Music Festival; ⬠ Box 311, A–6901
★ ☎ 05574/4076 🖷 05574/407400 ⊕ www.bregenzerfestspiele.com), held mid-July to late August. For information and tickets, contact the festival office. Tickets are also available at the Bregenz tourist office. In the event of rain, the concert performance is moved indoors to the massive Festival Hall and Congress Center adjacent to the floating stage (it can accommodate at least 1,800 of the 6,800 seats usually available for performances on the floating lake stage). Travel and performance packages are available through **Bodensee-Alpinrhein Tourism** (⊠ A–6900, Bregenz ☎ 05574/434430 🖷 05574/43443–4 ⊕ www. bodensee-alpenrhein.at).

The **casino** (⊠ Platz der Wiener Symphoniker, A–6900 ☎ 05574/ 45127–0) is the site of much activity. The house opens at 3 PM. Bring your passport.

Outdoor concerts are held during the summer months in the horseshoe-shape **Music Pavilion** at the end of the promenade on the lake.

Sports & the Outdoors

Bicycling

It is possible to cycle around Lake Constance in two to four days, traveling all the while on well marked and maintained paths (don't forget your passport). If this sounds too strenuous, parts of the route can be covered by boat. Rental bikes can be hired at local sports shops, or at the train stations in Bregenz or Feldkirch; the tourist office can provide you with maps and details. Another cycling path, popular with families, follows the Rhine—a 70-km (43-mi) stretch from Bregenz south to Bludenz. Parts of the route are possible by train.

Skiing

Skiers head for the **Pfänder** mountain, in Bregenz's backyard, which has a cable tramway and two drag lifts. The views are stunning from atop the peak, stretching as far as the Black Forest and the Swiss Alps. The **runs** (☎ 05572/4216–0 ⊕ www.pfaender.at) are closed during the second and third weeks of November.

Water Sports

With the vast lake at its doorstep, Bregenz offers a variety of water sports, from swimming to fishing to windsurfing. You can even learn to sail, although a minimum of two weeks is required for a full course at **Segelschule Lochau.** ✎ *Box 7, Alte Fähre* ☎ *05574/52247.*

THROUGH THE BREGENZERWALD TO BLUDENZ & FELDKIRCH

Directly behind Bregenz lies the **Bregenzerwald** (Bregenz Forest), a beautiful area studded with densely wooded highlands, sweeping valleys, and lush meadows radiant with wildflowers in summer, all set against a fabulous backdrop of majestic, towering Alps. As you go along, you come across one village after another with *au*—a term originally used to designated meadows where cows were allowed to graze—in its name: as such areas developed, names were given to the meadows in which settlements were established. Here you can see the Vorarlbergers as they really are. In the little villages you can spot women still wearing the handsome, stiffly starched folk dress of their ancestors. On festive occasions the girls wear a golden headdress shaped like a small crown, and married women a black or white pointed cap. Men's costume is worn by musicians in the local bands—which play traditional marches, polkas, and waltzes, and which seem to include nearly everyone—with the shape of the cap and the color of various parts of the clothing differing from town to town. Secure in their mountains and still, to a great extent, feeling no call to mix with the outside world, Bregenzerwalders have remained true to the habits of their forebears. One of those habits is cheese making, which, in the last two decades has undergone a magnificent revival. Regional farmers now produce over 30 varieties of *Käse*—from Emmental to beer cheese, Tilsit to red-wine cheese, and *Bergkäse* (mountain cheese) in dozens of varieties. Look for discreet *KäseStrasse* signs along the road, pointing you toward the region's elite cheese makers, or for the word *Sennerei*, which means Alpine dairy (⊕ www.kaesestrasse.at).

To reach the Bregenzerwald, travelers can take one of the daily buses that leave Bregenz or Dornbirn hourly on the main line from Feldkirch to Lindau in Germany—there are no train routes servicing the area. By car, leave Bregenz headed south on Route 190; then make a sharp left after crossing the river on a road marked to Wolfurt and Schwarzach. About 21 km (13 mi) farther, at Alberschwende you'll come to Route 200; follow the signs for **Egg,** where you should note the old country houses before heading on to Schwarzenberg. If you haven't bought your Alpine hat before you get to Egg, go to the **Capo hat and cap factory outlet** (✉ Melisau 1130 ☎ 05512/2381-0). It's open weekdays 9–noon and 1–5, and sells fashionable headgear as well as Alpine styles.

Schwarzenberg

★ ❷ *31 km (19 mi) southeast of Bregenz.*

One of the region's most colorful villages is Schwarzenberg. The artist Angelika Kauffmann (1741–1807), who spent most of her life in England and Italy, considered this her real home. Even though she became one of the most renowned female artists of the 18th century, few people in Austria east of the Arlberg mountains knew of her until her picture appeared on an issue of Austrian currency a few years ago. You can see several of her larger works in the Baroque village church, including a painting of the 12 apostles she did at age 16 and an altar painting of the Annunciation from about 1800 (the Landesmuseum in Bregenz has her portrait of the Duke of Wellington).

The Schwarzenberg **Heimatmuseum** has a room dedicated to Angelika Kauffmann. ⊠ *Brand 34* ☎ *05512/4249* ⌷ *€2.50* ☉ *May–Oct., Tues., Thurs., and Sat. 2–4; in winter by appointment.*

Nightlife & the Arts

FodorśChoice Schwarzenberg is home to the annual **Schubertiade** (⊠ Villa Rosenthal,
★ Schweizer Strasse 1, A–6845 ☎ 05576/72091 ⌷ 05576/75450 ⊕ www. schubertiade.at), a small but elegant music festival devoted to Franz Schubert and his circle. Everyone from Vladimir Ashkenazy to Dietrich Fischer-Dieskau has performed here, starring along with members of the Vienna Philharmonic and Vienna Symphony. For the 2005 season, concerts will also be held in the nearby (and gorgeous) town of Bezau.

Bezau

★ ❸ *4 km (2½ mi) south of Schwarzenberg, 35 km (23 mi) east of Bregenz.*

Stunningly idyllic is the only way to describe this enchanting village snuggled under a mountain range and surrounded by meadows so green they look like astroturf. According to local legend, Bezau's district hall was built on tall columns and accessible only by ladder. Once the councillors were gathered inside, the ladder would be removed, and not replaced until they came to a decision. The **Heimatmuseum**, slightly south of the center, contains exhibits, including local folk costumes, on the town's interesting past. ⊠ *Ellenbogen 181* ☎ *05514/2559* ⌷ *€2.50* ☉ *June–Sept., Tues., Thurs., and Sat. 3:30–5:30, Wed. 10–noon; Nov.–May, Tues. 2–3.*

⟲ At the **Bregenzerwald Museumsbahn,** visitors can see all that is left of the onetime narrow-gauge railroad that ran from Bregenz to Bezau and was abandoned in 1980. The museum has managed to preserve more than 6 km (almost 4 mi) of track to Bersbuch, beyond Schwarzenberg, and runs diesel and steam excursions. ⊠ *Bahnhof 147* ☎ *05513/6192* ⌷ *05513/ 6192–4* ⌷ *Round-trip by steam €7, by diesel €5.50* ☉ *June–mid-Oct., weekends at 11, 2, and 4; hours vary in Nov. and Dec.*

As for the arts, Bezau's Post Hotel has a high-tech, very striking tennis court that makes for an interesting summer setting for a number of the concerts held by the **Schubertiade,** the festival based in Schwartzenberg (*see above*).

Where to Stay

★ **$$$** ⊡ **Gasthof Gams.** Dating from the 17th century, this friendly house in the center of town offers every comfort and is a great base for exploring. The rooms have an attractive country-rustic decor, and the hotel welcomes families. ⊠*Platz 44, A–6870* ☎*05514/2220* 🖷*05514/2220–24* ⊕*www. hotel-gams.at* ⇥ *35 rooms, 5 suites* ♨ *Restaurant, tennis court, pool, gym, sauna, bar; no a/c* ⊟ *MC, V* ⊗ *Closed Nov.–mid-Dec.*

Sports & the Outdoors

SKIING Bezau has four regular trails for cross-country skiers and one lift that takes downhill skiers up to the 5,300-foot Baumgartenhöhe. This small area is part of the Bregenzerwald Ski Region. A regional pass (the "3 Valley Superpass") gives you access to 135 lifts in Bregenzerwald, Grosses Walsertal, and Lechtal in Tirol, encompassing 282 km (160 mi) of prepared slopes (see Damüls).

Damüls

④ *14 km (9 mi) south of Bezau, 59 km (37 mi) southeast of Bregenz.*

If you turn right onto Route 193 at Au, you'll be on the way to Damüls— the road is narrow, with a 14% gradient at one point, but when you reach the town you'll agree the climb was worth it. You're at 4,640 feet, the top of the Bregenzerwald. This is great skiing country in winter; for information on facilities, contact the **Bregenzerwald tourism office** (📮 Postfach 29, A–6863 Egg ☎ 05512/2365 🖷 05512/3010 ⊕ www. bregenzerwald.at). There are enough slopes and lifts, and the crowds are generally elsewhere. In summer the area is knee-deep in wildflowers, but don't pick them; it's against the law. Check the frescoes in the **parish church,** which date from 1490, just after the church was built, but were rediscovered under later plaster only about 40 years ago.

en route The **Grosswalsertal** (Great Walliser Valley) is extremely scenic. As you start the descent from Damüls heading toward Bludenz along Route 193, look across at the St. Gerold Monastery to your right. After reaching Blons, however, be sure to keep your eyes on the road: It's full of hairpin turns.

Bludenz

⑤ *22 km (13 mi) southwest of Damüls, 60 km (37 mi) south of Bregenz.*

Bludenz rests at the junction of five mountain valleys, sheltered in part by the Muttersberg peak, nicknamed "the Sun Balcony." The Old City's narrow streets are tightly packed with 17th-century houses and relics of the ancient town defenses, while the mountains present ski lifts, good slopes, and hiking trails. People here are pleased when you ask for a hot chocolate instead of coffee: Bludenz is a major chocolate-producing center, as you may detect if the wind is coming from the direction of the factories. The town, adorned with houses and pergolas that seem more Italian than Austrian, is a major transportation crossroads, serviced by frequent bus and train routes.

The **Milka Lädele** is the ideal place to stock up on the sweet stuff at bargain prices. ⊠ *Fohrenburgstrasse 1* ⊗ *Weekdays 9 AM–11:30 AM and 1:30–4:30.*

Where to Stay

$–$$ 🏨 **Schlosshotel Dörflinger.** Perched on a hill above the castle and overlooking the town, this modern hotel with balconies offers splendid views of the Rätikon mountain range to the south, on the Swiss border; ask for a room in front above the café terrace. The house's pseudo-rustic decor continues into the guest rooms, whose clean lines and modern furnishings are, in fact, quite attractive. ⊠ *Schlossplatz 5, A–6700* ☎ *05552/63016–0* 🖶 *05552/63016–8* ⌗ *42 rooms* ♨ *Restaurant, café, miniature golf; no a/c* 🖃 *AE, DC, MC, V* ⏐Ⓞ⏐ *BP.*

Feldkirch

❻ *33 km (22 mi) southwest of Bregenz.*

Feldkirch is Vorarlberg's oldest town, with parts dating from the Middle Ages that contribute greatly to the town's romantic character. Picturesque arcades line the narrow main street, and wrought-iron oriels festoon some of the quainter town houses. Marvelous towers and onion domes top some of the buildings, watched over by an assembly of imposing stone blockhouses, which compose the Schattenburg castle complex just above the town.

A number of luminaries have spent time in Feldkirch. James Joyce stopped for several months en route from Italy to Switzerland, saying later that he formed the basis for *Ulysses* here and that he gathered material for *Finnegan's Wake.* There is a plaque honoring him at the train station, where he spent hours every day observing people and trains for his writing. As a promising student, Sir Arthur Conan Doyle attended the Jesuit boarding school, Stella Matutina, which is now the Provincial Conservatory of Music. He wrote two short stories for the local newspaper, which are stored in the archives. And Thomas Mann used the same boarding school as a setting in *The Magic Mountain.*

An easy walk around the center of Feldkirch will take you to most of the town's highlights. The center of town is **St. Nicholas Cathedral,** on Domplatz. A mystical light in this church, built in 1478, comes through the stained-glass windows. From the cathedral, walk toward the river, past the district government offices (once a Jesuit monastery) and the bishop's palace, a block back of Herrengasse, to the **Katzenturm** (literally, "cats' tower"; figuratively, "the clergy"), reconstructed by Emperor Maximilian I. This is the most prominent remnant of the town's fortifications and now holds the 7½-ton town bell. Down the Hirschgraben, pass the Chur gate, is the **Frauenkirche** (Church of Our Lady), originally dedicated to St. Sebastian in 1473. Down Montfortgasse you'll find the **Wasserturm** (water tower) and the **Diebsturm** (thieves' tower) standing guard over the Schillerstrasse bridge. Wander down Vorstadt to the **Pulverturm** (powder tower) and across to the **Mühlenturm** (mill tower), which contrasts greatly with the modern Leonhardsplatz. Turning left from the Mühlenturm, you'll find the St. Johann Church (1218) and, behind it, the **market square** (market days Tuesday and Saturday). The square is the site of the annual wine festival during the second week of July. Across the pedestrian zone is Liechtenstein Palace, once the administrative center. Adjacent to the Liechtenstein Palace is the **Rathaus** of 1493, with its frescoes and paneled rooms.

Overlooking Feldkirch, in the Neustadt, is the 12th-century **Schattenburg,** a massive castle that now houses a restaurant and a museum devoted to the decorative arts and armor. Arcades climb up the hill to frame the castle in an intriguing vista. ⊠ *Burggasse 1, A–6800* ☎ *05522/71982* 🎫 *€3* ☉ *Dec.–Oct., Tues.–Sun. 9–noon and 1–5.*

Where to Stay & Eat

$$$ ✕ **Gasthof Lingg.** Since 1878 this family-run inn has been known for delicious meals. Seasonal specialties, such as wild game, venison, and asparagus, are featured. The building, near the Katzenturm in the Old City, is notable for the murals on the facade, which the Lingg family commissioned in 1888. ⊠ *Am Marktplatz A–6800* ☎ *05522/72062–0* 🖶 *05522/72062–6* ⊕ *www.lingg.at* ⊟ *AE, DC, MC, V* ☉ *Closed Mon. and 2 wks in Aug. No dinner Sun.*

$–$$ ✕ **Schäfle.** A bit outside the (Old City) in a neighborhood called *Altenstadt,* this Gasthaus offers atmosphere and food more typical of that in the countryside. The tables are elegantly set, and you can expect such regional fare as schnitzel, beef fillet, or perch from Lake Constance, all served with delicate sauces and a fine touch. When weather permits, request a table in the charming garden. ⊠ *Naflastrasse 3* ☎ *05522/72203–0* ⊕ *www.vol.at/schaefle* ⊟ *AE, DC, MC, V* ☉ *Closed Sun. and mid-Dec.–mid-Jan. No lunch Mon.*

$$–$$$ ✕🏠 **Central Löwen.** The rooms are large and comfortable but lacking a bit in the charm department. However, the hotel staff is friendly and outgoing. ⊠ *Schlossgraben 13, A–6800* ☎ *05522/72070–0* 🖶 *05522/72070–5* 🛏 *68 rooms* ⚘ *Restaurant, sauna, steam room; no a/c* ⊟ *DC, MC, V.*

★ **$** 🏠 **Alpenrose.** This charming old burghers' house in the center of the Old City has been renovated outside and in and offers unusually personal service. Rooms are tastefully done in period furnishings. ⊠ *Rosengasse 6, A–6800* ☎ *05522/72175* 🖶 *05522/72175–5* 🛏 *24 rooms* ⊟ *AE, DC, MC, V.*

Hohenems

★ ❼ *9 km (5½ mi) northeast of Feldkirch, 24 km (15 mi) southwest of Bregenz.*

"The antiquity of Hohenems is so apparent, so forceful, it looms like a presence, a mysterious knight, armored cap-a-pie, visor lowered," observed James Reynolds in his 1956 book *Panorama of Austria.* Hohenems is a town dominated by castles, both ruined (the 12th-century Alt-Ems citadel atop the Schlossberg) and ravishing, especially the Schloss Glopper and the castle of Prince-Archbishop Marcus Sittikus von Hohenems, with its elegantly ornate Rittersaal. Empress Elisabeth of Austria used to stay in this castle toward the end of her tragically shortened life and, in fact, used the title of Countess Hohenems when she traveled "anonymously" around the world. The **Pfarrkirche** (parish church), dedicated to St. Carlo Borromeo and rebuilt in 1797, has a noted painted altar-piece of the Coronation of the Virgin.

In 1617 a decree was signed that welcomed Jews to Hohenems and allowed them to live and work in peace. For the next 300 years a large Jewish community thrived here, but by 1938 fewer than 20 Jews remained. The **Jüdisches Museum** (Jewish Museum), housed in the Villa Heimann-Rosenthal, has a large library, as well as photographs and historical documents on display. ⊠ *Schweizerstrasse 5, A–6845* ☎ *05576/73989* ⊕ *www.jm-hohenems.at* ⊠ *€5* ⊗ *Tues.–Sun. 10–5.*

Dornbirn

❽ *4 km (2½ mi) northeast of Hohenems, 13 km (8 mi) southwest of Bregenz.*

Dornbirn, the industrial center of Vorarlberg, is known as the "city of textiles." The annual Dornbirn Fair, held in early September to tie in with the Bregenz Music Festival, shows a range of goods and technologies, but textiles are especially featured.

Where to Stay & Eat

★ **$$$** ✕ **Rotes Haus.** The "red" in the name of this 1639 gabled wood house in the center of town refers to bull's blood, originally used as pigment for the facade, which is still basically red, with decorative panels. Traditional cuisine—lamb, game, and fish are on the menu—is served here in a charming series of small rooms. ⊠ *Marktplatz 13* ☎ *05572/31555* 🖷 *05572/31625* ☐ *AE, DC, MC, V* ⊗ *No lunch Sun.*

$$–$$$ ▨ **Martinspark.** This hotel in the very heart of Dornbirn is a functional fantasy of art and ultra-modern architecture. The bright and warm rooms use local wood, tile, and contemporary artwork generously, making the Martinspark a memorable stay. ⊠ *Mozartstrasse 2, A–6850* ☎ *05572/3760* 🖷 *05572/3760–376* ⊕ *www.martinspark.at* ⇄ *98 rooms* ⚮ *Restaurant, hair salon, sauna, bar, meeting rooms* ☐ *AE, DC, MC, V* ▯⨀▯ *BP.*

THE ARLBERG & MONTAFON RESORTS

The Western Alps are a haven for those who love the great outdoors. It's also a region that provides getaway space and privacy—Ernest Hemingway came to Schruns to write *The Sun Also Rises.* In the spring, summer, and fall, travelers delight in riding, tennis, swimming, and, of course, hiking the Montafon Valley, which is dominated by the "Matterhorn of Austria," the Zimba peak, and is probably the most attractive of Vorarlberg's many tourist-frequented valleys. When the first snowflakes begin to fall, skiers head to the hills to take advantage of the Arlberg mountain range, the highest in the Lechtal Alps. If you want to avoid the crowds that can clog Austria's other resorts, keep in mind that Lech and Zürs are resorts where the seeing is almost as important as the skiing. If you're traveling by train, Langen is the stop closest to the ski resorts; Route S16/316 takes you by car from Bludenz to Langen and beyond to Route 198 heading north.

Brand

⊙ *70 km (43 mi) south of Bregenz.*

Since it was first settled by Swiss exiles centuries ago, the lush and beautiful Brand Valley has attracted many travelers interested in visiting the enormous glaciers and one of the largest lakes in the Alps, located near the town. Today, Brand is known as a health resort and a winter-sports center. Its hotels lie at the foot of the Scesaplana mountain group (which marks the Swiss border and is the highest range in the Rätikon). There are no rail lines to Brand, so the best way to reach the resort is to take the train to Bludenz and then the bus from there to Brand.

If you are fond of hiking, you can climb by easy stages along the forest paths without much exertion to the famous glacier lake, the **Lünersee**. In winter the skiing is excellent, and there is a modern chairlift up the Niggenkopf (5,500 feet) to take you up to the finest ski slopes in just a few minutes. Anyone interested in geology should pay a visit to the tiny village chapel, known as the **"trowel stone" chapel**, built of local rock that can be cut into shape quite easily with an ordinary saw. When exposed to the air, the masonry then shrinks slightly and hardens and becomes rather brittle.

Where to Stay & Eat

$$$–$$$$ ✕🏨 **Sporthotel Beck.** The Beck family runs this sports hotel in the shadow of the nearby mountains. Rooms are comfortably furnished and light-filled and have flower-bedecked balconies that look out over spectacular views. The hotel's restaurant features classic Austrian fare like schnitzel, but also lighter dishes for those watching their waistlines. Sports enthusiasts will like the myriad of activities available in the hotel as well as the great mountain-climbing nearby. ⊠ *A–6708* ☎ *05559/306–0* 📠 *05559/306–70* 🛏 *Restaurant, driving range, pool, gym, massage, horseback riding, children's programs (ages 10 and up); no a/c* ▤ *AE, DC, MC, V.*

$$$ ✕🏨 **Hotel Scesaplana.** This family-run hotel is ideally situated at the end of the Brandnertal valley—surrounded by the towering mountains and glaciers of the Rätikon region and steps from the Brand ski lift. A variety of pampering options plus sports facilities assure that you won't get bored. Take half-board with breakfast and champagne-bar, organic foods, afternoon snacks, and dinner buffet. ⊠ *A–6708* ☎ *05559/221* 📠 *05559/221* ⊕ *www.s-hotels.at* 🛏 *61 rooms* 🛏 *Restaurant, golf privileges, 6 tennis courts, indoor pool, hot tub, massage, sauna, 2 bars, meeting rooms* ▤ *AE, DC, MC, V* ☉ *Closed mid-Oct.–mid-Dec.*

Sports & the Outdoors

HIKING From a leisurely stroll to serious mountain trekking, Brand has hiking galore. The most noted trail runs from Brand via Innertal and the Schattenlagant-Alpe to the lower end of the Lünersee. Inquire at the local tourist office for maps.

SKIING The Brandnertal offers 50 km (31 mi) of groomed ski runs served by eight chairlifts. It is part of the Alpenregion Bludenz, which also includes

Klostertal, Grosses Walsertal, Brandnertal, and Walgau. Rental equipment is available. For details on facilities, contact **Alpenregion Bludenz** (✉ Rathausgasse 12, A–6700 Bludenz ☎ 05552/30227 🖶 05552/30227–3 ⊕ www.alpenregion.at). The area immediately around the Brandnertal features ski passes good for 1 to 16 days, with rates for adults, children, and senior citizens varying according to season. The Brandnertal encompasses some 14 lifts and 42 km (25 mi) of prepared runs.

Schruns-Tschagguns

10 km (6 mi) northeast of Brand, 60 km (39 mi) south of Bregenz.

Author Ernest Hemingway spent many winters at the Schruns–Tschagguns skiing area in the Montafon Valley. Today neither of the towns—sited across the Ill River from each other—is as fashionable as the resorts on the Arlberg, but the views over the Ferwall Alps to the east and the mighty Rätikon on the western side of the valley are unsurpassed anywhere in Austria. In winter, the powdery snow provides wonderful skiing. Thanks to an integrated system of ski passes and lifts, the Montafon Valley is considered a "ski stadium" by skiers in the know. They love to head for Hochjoch-Zamang—the main peak at **Schruns**—to have lunch on the spectacularly sited sun terrace of the Kapell restaurant. Then it's on to Grabs-Golm over the river in **Tschagguns.** Others prefer the Silvretta-Nova run at Gaschurn and St. Gallenkirch. In summer, the heights are given over to climbers and hikers, the mountain streams to trout fishermen, and the lowlands to tennis players.

Where to Stay & Eat

$$$$ ✕▥ **Löwen.** This central hotel looks huge, but inside, the country style works well, and the rustic dark-wood exterior is carried over elegantly into the modern rooms with balconies. The hotel is set in the center of a grassy garden platform, which forms a greenbelt around the main building and serves as a roof for the ground-floor pool and restaurants. The excellent Edelweiss restaurant, with its graceful table settings (candlelit at night), serves regional specialties done with flair. ✉ *Silvrettastrasse 8, A–6780* ☎ *05556/7141* 🖶 *05556/73553* ⊕ *www.loewen-hotel.com* ⇝ *85 rooms* ♨ *4 restaurants, indoor pool, gym, sauna, bar, dance club* ▤ *AE, DC, MC, V* ⊗ *Closed mid-Apr.–mid-May and mid-Oct.–mid-Dec.*

$$$–$$$$ ✕▥ **Montafoner Hof.** This cozy hotel in Tschagguns is perfect for families. The management is warm and friendly and makes guests feel at home. The hotel is also known for its popular restaurant, which features delicious, traditional Austrian cooking. ✉ *Kreuzgasse 9, A–6774 Tschagguns* ☎ *05556/7100–0* 🖶 *05556/7100–6* ⊕ *www.montafonerhof.at* ⇝ *48 rooms* ♨ *Restaurant, in-room safes, minibars, indoor–outdoor pool, sauna, Internet; no a/c* ▤ *No credit cards.*

★ $ ▥ **Alpenhof Messmer.** Set on a lush green hillside slightly out of the center of town, this oversize double chalet welcomes you with fireplaces and comfortable rustic furnishings. Most of the imaginatively decorated rooms have balconies with a view over the town. The family management is particularly friendly and helpful, and the same goes for the restaurant staff. ✉ *Grappaweg 6, A–6780* ☎ *05556/72664–0* 🖶 *05556/76156* ⊕ *www.hotel-alpenhof-messmer.at* ⇝ *35 rooms* ♨ *Restaurant,* *indoor pool, gym, sauna, bar; no a/c ⊟ No credit cards ⊘ Closed mid-Apr.–mid-May and mid-Nov.–mid-Dec.*

Sports & the Outdoors

FISHING The local mountain streams and rivers are full of fish. Licenses are available; ask the regional tourist office in Bregenz for detailed information on seasons and locations.

SKIING Schruns is one of the skiing centers of the Montafon region, which also includes the Bartholomäberg, Gargellen, Gaschurn-Partenen, St. Gallenkirch/Gortipohl, Silbertal, and Vandans ski areas. They are accessible with a Montafon Ski Pass and together have 65 lifts and 208 km (129 mi) of groomed runs. Ski passes are valid for 3 to 14 days or 21 days, with rates for adults, children, and senior citizens varying according to season. Rental equipment is available. For details contact **Montafon Tourism** (✉ Montafonerstrasse 21, A–6780 Schruns ☎ 05556/722530 🖷 05556/74856 ⊕ www.montafon.at).

Stuben

⑫ *38 km (23 mi) northeast of Schruns, 29 km (23 mi) east of Bludenz.*

Traveling through the Montafon via Route 316, you'll come to the village of Stuben, hometown of that pioneer of Alpine ski techniques, Hannes Schneider. From December to the end of April, the magnificent skiing, at 4,600 feet, makes Stuben popular among serious skiers willing to forgo the stylish resorts such as Lech just up the road. Stuben has skiing links with St. Anton, Lech, and Zürs. The village is poised right above the Arlberg Tunnel, so you can't—appearance to the contrary on maps—arrive there via rail from Innsbruck or Bregenz. You must detrain at Langen am Arlberg and then take a bus on to Stuben. For information on its skiing facilities contact the **Arlberg region tourist office** (🕮 Postfach 54, A–6764 Lech ☎ 05583/2161-0 🖷 05583/3155 ⊕ www.lech.at).

Where to Stay & Eat

$$–$$$ ✕🖭 **Hotel Mondschein.** A welcoming exterior, accented with pink geraniums in flower boxes and dark green shutters, greets visitors as they come down the street from the town church. Inside this traditional Alpine country house, dating back to 1739, the greeting is almost as warm as the fires blazing in the hotel's hearths, while the pricey restaurant prides itself on its fish selections. Unlike other Stuben hostelries, this one is right in the center of town. Depending on the season, rates include half board. ✉ A–6762 ☎ 05582/511 or 05582/721 🖷 05582/736 ⊕ www.mondschein.com ➱ 25 rooms ☖ Restaurant, indoor pool, health club, baby-sitting; no a/c ⊟ MC, V ⊘ Closed May and mid-Sept.–mid-Dec.

Zürs

⑬ *13 km (8 mi) north of Stuben, 90 km (56 mi) southeast of Bregenz.*

The chosen resort of the rich and fashionable on this side of the Arlberg, Zürs is little more than a collection of large hotels. Perched at 5,600 feet, it is strictly a winter-sports community; when the season is over, the hotels close. But Zürs is more exclusive than Lech and certainly more so than Gstaad or St. Moritz in Switzerland—this is the place where wealthy emirs bring their private ski instructors. Zürs is also the place where the first ski lift in Austria was constructed in 1937. Full board is required in most hotels, so there are relatively few "public" restaurants in town and little chance to dine around. But the hotel dining rooms are elegant; in many, jacket and tie are de rigueur in the evening.

Where to Stay & Eat

$$$$ 🏨 **Lorünser.** The hospitable elegance of this hotel draws royalty, including Princess Caroline of Monaco and Queen Beatrix of the Netherlands. Carved ceiling beams, open fireplaces, and attractive accessories create a welcoming reception. Rustic wood is used to good effect in the stylish guest rooms. Prices include half board. ⊠ *A–6763* ☎ *05583/ 2254–0* 🖨 *05583/2254–44* 🛏 *74 rooms* ⚹ *Restaurant, gym, sauna, bar; no a/c* ⊟ *MC, V* ⊙ *Closed mid-Apr.–early Dec.*

★ $$$$ 🏨 **Zürserhof.** When celebrities seek privacy, they head here. This world-famous hostelry at the north end of town comprises five of the most luxurious and expensive chalets in the world (prices can top $800 a day with board). Many of the elegant accommodations are spacious apartments or suites with fireplaces; newer ones have Roman baths. The family-run house has nevertheless managed to preserve a certain intimacy. Prices include half board. ⊠ *A–6763* ☎ *05583/2513–0* 🖨 *05583/3165* ⊕ *www.zuerserhof.at* 🛏 *97 rooms* ⚹ *Restaurant, driving range, tennis court, indoor pool, gym, hair salon, sauna, bar, dance club* ⊟ *No credit cards* ⊙ *Closed mid-Apr.–Nov.*

$$$–$$$$ ✕🏨 **Sporthotel Edelweiss.** This 19th-century house has received an agreeable face-lift, including the guest rooms, giving it a colorful, contemporary interior. The Zürserl disco is *the* place in the evening. The restaurant, Chesa Verde (reservations essential), is the best in town, offering fresh fish, game, and other regional standards. Prices include half board. ⊠ *A–6763* ☎ *05583/2662* 🖨 *05583/3533* ⊕ *www.edelweiss. net* 🛏 *66 rooms, 5 apartments* ⚹ *Restaurant, gym, sauna, dance club* ⊟ *V* ⊙ *Closed mid-Apr.–Nov.*

Sports & the Outdoors

SKIING   There are three main lifts: east of Zürs, take the chairlift to Hexenboden (7,600 feet) or the cable-car to Trittkopf (7,800 feet), with a restaurant and sun terrace; to the west, a lift takes you to Seekopf (7,000 feet), where there is another restaurant. This mountain often gets huge snowfalls. Skiers need to be particularly aware of avalanche conditions, so check with the tourist office or your hotel before you hit the slopes.

Lech

⑭ *4 km (2½ mi) north of Zürs, 90 km (56 mi) southeast of Bregenz.*

Fodor'sChoice
   ★   Just up the road from the Zürs resort, Lech is a full-fledged community—which some argue detracts from its fashionableness. But there are more hotels in Lech, better tourist facilities, bigger ski schools, more shops, and more nightlife, with prices nearly as high as those in neighboring Zürs. Zürs has the advantage of altitude, but Lech is a less artificial and very pretty Alpine village. And Lech is a favorite winter vacation spot

for Queen Beatrix of the Netherlands and also the Belgian royal family. Be sure to check with the hotel of your choice about meal arrangements; some hotels recommend that you take half board, which is usually a good deal. You can't get to Lech via rail; take the train to Langen am Arlberg station stop, then transfer to a bus for the 15-minute ride to town.

Where to Stay & Eat

★ $$$–$$$$ ✕ **Brunnenhof.** This cozy dinner restaurant in the hotel of the same name, slightly north of the town center, can back up its self-proclaimed title: "Gourmet-Hotel." The menu has offered such innovative dishes as anglerfish with curry, onion, and black noodles, and fillet of beef with artichoke sauce. The wine list includes selections from Austria, France, Italy, Spain, Australia, and California. Be sure to reserve well in advance, for this is one of the best restaurants in town and is regularly full. ⊠ *House 146* ☎ *05583/2349* 🖶 *05583/2349–59* ⊕ *www.brunnenhof. com* ⚐ *Reservations essential* ☰ *MC, V* ⊗ *Closed Sun. and mid-Apr.–mid-Dec.*

★ $$$$ ✕🏨 **Gasthof Post.** A *gemütlich* atmosphere dominates in this blue-shuttered chalet hotel, with murals, flower boxes, and a wood-paneled interior. The à la carte restaurant is the best in town; try the medaillon of lamb or grilled salmon, and save space for one of the outstanding desserts. ⊠ *Dorf 11, A–6764* ☎ *05583/2206–0* 🖶 *05583/2206–23* ⊕ *www.postlech.com* ⇆ *40 rooms* ⚐ *Restaurant, indoor pool, sauna, bar; no a/c* ☰ *AE, MC, V* ⊗ *Closed May–mid-June, Oct., and Nov.*

$$$$ ✕🏨 **Krone.** Directly across the street from two of the main lifts, this family-managed hotel grew out of a 250-year-old house. The adaptations and modernization have not affected the general ambience of comfort and well-being reflected in the beamed ceilings, tile stoves, and Oriental carpets. The restaurant, one of the town's three best, is noted for its game and regional specialties; try the fillet of whitefish on cucumber or the rack of lamb. ⊠ *House 13, A–6764* ☎ *05583/2551* 🖶 *05583/2551–81* ⊕ *www.kronelech.at* ⇆ *56 rooms* ⚐ *Restaurant, indoor pool, gym, sauna, bar, dance club; no a/c* ☰ *V* ⊗ *Closed mid-Apr.–mid-June, Oct., and Nov.*

★ $$$–$$$$ ✕🏨 **Montana.** An outgoing expatriate Alsatian runs this easygoing hotel in Oberlech, in the pedestrian zone just above the town. He has installed a *Vinothek* (wine shop), where tastings are held and wine is sold by the glass or bottle. The bright interior colors contrast well with the weathered wood; the rooms are friendly and snug. The ski slopes are just outside the door. The restaurant, Zur Kanne, has French overtones and is remarkable for its attention to detail, both in the kitchen and in the table settings. Dishes range from lobster hash to beef fillet gratiné. ⊠ *House 279, A–6764* ☎ *05583/2460* 🖶 *05583/2460–38* ⊕ *www. montanaoberlech.com* ⇆ *42 rooms* ⚐ *Restaurant, in-room safes, indoor pool, sauna, bar, wineshop* ☰ *MC, V* ⊗ *Closed May–Nov.*

$ 🏨 **Aurelio.** This hillside chalet fairly close to the center of town is not far from the lower station of two of the lifts, one of which runs in summer as well. The hotel is family-run and friendly; the rooms are cheerful and cozy. ⊠ *NR 130, A–6764* ☎ *05583/2214* 🖶 *05583/3456* ⊕ *www.aurelio.at* ⇆ *17 rooms, 2 apartments* ⚐ *Restaurant, bar, chil-*

dren's programs (ages 3–7); no a/c ▣ *MC, V* ☉ *Closed Apr.–mid-June, Oct., and Nov.* ⦿ *BP.*

Nightlife & the Arts

Lech is known almost as much for après-ski and nightlife as for the snow and the slopes. Ask at the tourist office about the "in" spots, as the crowd tends to move around. Prices vary from place to place, but in general a mixed drink will cost €8–€9.

You can join the snacks-and-drinks crowd as early as 11 AM at the outdoor and famed **Umbrella** bar (☎ 05583/3232) at the Petersboden Sport Hotel at Oberlech. Activity continues at the late afternoon **tea dance** (☎ 05583/2202) at the Tannbergerhof.

The bar at the **Goldener Berg** (☎ 05583/2205) is usually a hot après-ski spot. The bar in the **Burg** (☎ 05583/2291) hotel in Oberlech features live music most nights. Among the popular places for a mid-evening drink (starting at 9:30) are **Pfefferkorndl** (☎ 05583/2525–429) in the Pfefferkörn Hotel. The **Krone Bar** in the Krone hotel (*see* Where to Stay & Eat, *above*) opens at 9 PM and goes on until 2 or 3 AM.

Sports & the Outdoors

SKIING Lech is linked with Oberlech and Zürs with more than 30 ski lifts, all accessed by the regional ski pass, which allows skiers to take in the entire region, including Lech, Oberlech, Zürs, Stuben, St. Christoph, and St. Anton. You can ski right from Zürs to Lech. In addition, there is a vast network of cross-country trails. For complete information on skiing facilities contact the **Lech-Zürs Tourist Office** (⌂ Postfach 54, A–6764 Lech ☎ 05583/2161–0 🖷 05583/3155 ⊕ www.lech-zuers.at).

VORARLBERG A TO Z

To research prices, get advice from other travelers, and book travel arrangements, visit www.fodors.com.

AIR TRAVEL

CARRIERS Austrian Airlines flies from Vienna into St.Gallen/Altenrhein on Lake Constance in Switzerland. A direct bus service takes passengers free of charge to and from the airport and Bregenz, Dornbirn, and Lustenau. Intersky flies from Vienna, Berlin, and Cologne into Friedrichshafen in Germany.

🖪 Airlines & Contacts **Austrian Airlines** ☎ 01/7007–36911 in Vienna, 05574/48800 in Vorarlberg 🖷 01/7007–6915 in Vienna, 05574/48800–8 in Vorarlberg ⊕ www.austrianair. com. **Intersky** ☎ 490/7541–28401 in Friedrichshafen, Germany ⊕ www.intersky.biz.

AIRPORTS

Bregenz's closest intercontinental airport is in Zürich, 120 km (75 mi) away. Munich's airport is 185 km (115 mi) away, and Innsbruck, which serves several European cities, is 200 km (124 mi) from Bregenz. Several trains a day serve Bregenz from the Zürich Kloten airport.

🖪 Airport Information **Zürich Kloten Airport** ☎ 041/81622 ⊕ www.zurich-airport.com.

TRANSFERS In winter a bus leaves the Zürich airport Friday, Saturday, and Sunday several times each day for resorts in the Arlberg and Montafon regions. You can book the transfer through Swiss International or Arlberg Express.

🚐 Taxis & Shuttles **Arlberg Express** ☎ 05583/2000 ⊕ www.arlbergexpress.com. **Swiss International** ⊕ www.swiss.com.

BOAT & FERRY TRAVEL
From May to October, passenger ships of the Austrian railroad's Bodensee White Fleet connect Bregenz with Lindau, Friedrichshafen, Meersburg, and Konstanz on the German side of the lake. The Eurailpass and Austrian rail passes are valid on these ships. You must bring your passport.

🚢 Boat & Ferry Information **Bodensee White Fleet** ☎ 05574/42868 🖷 05574/93000−520 ⊕ www.bsb-online.com.

BUS TRAVEL
Post office, railway, and private bus services connect all the towns and villages not served by train (which includes most of the Bregenzerwald), using vehicles with snow chains when necessary in winter. Even so, some of the highest roads become impassable for a few hours.

CAR RENTAL
At Avis, cars are available only with a reservation.

🚗 Major Agencies **Avis** ✉ ÖBB train stations ☎ 0512/571754. **Hertz** ✉ Schwefel 44, Dornbirn ☎ 05572/27706 🖷 05572/31878.

CAR TRAVEL
From Germany, the autobahn (Route A14/E17) takes you into Bregenz; roads from Switzerland lead to Lustenau and Hohenems; from Liechtenstein, Route 16 (Route 191 in Austria) goes to Feldkirch; and Routes A12/E60 from eastern Austria and 315 from Italy meet at Landeck to become Route 316/E60, then head westward through the Arlberg auto tunnel (toll €9). Alternatively, your car (and you) can get to Vorarlberg on the car train that runs to Feldkirch from Vienna, Graz, or Villach.

ROAD CONDITIONS A car is the most flexible way of getting about in Vorarlberg, but the roads can be treacherous in winter. Cars are not allowed on some mountain roads in the Arlberg without chains, which you can rent from a number of service stations.

EMERGENCIES
🚨 Emergency services **Ambulance** ☎ 144. **Fire department** ☎ 122. **Police** ☎ 133.

TAXIS
Taxis start at about €4, so taking one even a short distance can be expensive. Call to order a radio cab.

🚕 Taxi Companies **City Taxi** ☎ 05574/65400 or 05574/42222.

TRAIN TRAVEL
The main rail line connecting with Vienna and Innsbruck enters Vorarlberg at Langen after coming through the Arlberg Tunnel. Both the *Arlberg*

and *Orient Express* trains follow this route, which then swings through Bludenz to Feldkirch. There the line splits, with the *Arlberg* going south into Liechtenstein and Switzerland, the other branch heading through Dornbirn to Bregenz and on to Lindau in Germany.

The railroads connect the main centers of Vorarlberg remarkably well; besides the lines described above, the Montafon electric (with occasional steam) rail line runs parallel to the highway from Bludenz southeast to Schruns.

📶 Train Information **ÖBB–Österreichisches Bundesbahn** ☎ 05/1717 ⊕ www.oebb.at.

TRANSPORTATION AROUND VORARLBERG
A Bodensee-Pass includes the Swiss and German as well as the Austrian lake steamers, all at half price, plus area trains, buses, and cable-car lifts. The pass comes in 7- and 15-day variations. The Network Vorarlberg ticket makes public transport economical, with passes good for a day, a week, or a month. You can choose tickets for regions of various sizes, from a single urban area to the entire Vorarlberg network. The Family 1-day Runabout is a real bargain, and valid for an entire family regardless of size; the Vorarlberg information offices in Bregenz and Vienna have details.

VISITOR INFORMATION
The headquarters for tourist information about Vorarlberg is based in Bregenz. There is a branch office in Vienna. Other regional tourist offices (called either Tourismusbüro, Verkehrsverein, or Fremdenverkehrsamt) are located throughout the province using the contact information listed below by town name.

📶 Tourist Information **Vorarlberg tourism information** ✉ Bahnhofstrasse 14, A-6900 Bregenz ☎ 05574/42525-0 🖶 05574/42525-5 ⊕ www.vorarlberg-tourism.at ✉ Tuchlauben 18, A-1010 Vienna ☎ 01/535-7890 🖶 01/535-7893. **Bezau** ✉ Platz 39, A-6870 ☎ 05514/2295 🖶 05514/3129. **Bludenz** ✉ Werdenberger Strasse 42, A-6700 ☎ 05552/62170 🖶 05552/67597. **Bregenz** ✉ Bahnhofstrasse 14, A-6900 ☎ 05574/43443-0 🖶 05574/43443-4 ⊕ www.bodensee-alpenrhein.at. **Bregenzerwald** ✉ A-6863 Egg ☎ 05512/2365 🖶 05512/3010 ⊕ www.bregenzerwald.at. **Damüls** ✉ A-6884 ☎ 05510/6200 🖶 05510/549 ⊕ www.damuels.at. **Feldkirch** ✉ Herrengasse 12, A-6800 ☎ 05522/73467 🖶 05522/79867. **Hohenems** ☎ 5576/42780 🖶 5576/76800 ⊕ www.hohenems.at. **Lech** ✉ A-6764 ☎ 05583/2161-0 🖶 05583/3155 ⊕ www.lech.at. **Montafon Valley** ✉ Montafoner Strasse 21, A-6780 Schruns ☎ 05556/72253-0 🖶 05556/74856 ⊕ www.montafon.at. **Zürs** ✉ A-6763 ☎ 05583/2245 🖶 05583/2982 ⊕ www.zuers.at.

UNDERSTANDING AUSTRIA

DO I HEAR A WALTZ?

POWDER-PERFECT SKIING

AUSTRIA AT A GLANCE

BOOKS AND MOVIES

CHRONOLOGY

WORDS AND PHRASES

MENU GUIDE

DO I HEAR A WALTZ?

N OFT-TOLD STORY CONCERNS an airline pilot whose pre-landing announcement advised, "Ladies and gentlemen, we are on the final approach to Vienna Airport. Please make sure your seat belts are fastened, please refrain from smoking until you are outside the terminal, and please set your watches back one hundred years." Apocryphal or not, the pilot's observation suggests the allure of a country where visitors can sense something of what Europe was like before the pulse of the 20th century quickened to a beat that would have dizzied our great-grandmothers. Today's Austria—and in particular its capital, Vienna—reminds many of a formerly fat man who is now at least as gaunt as most people but still allows himself a lot of room and expects doors to open wide when he goes through them. After losing two world wars and surviving amputation, annexation, and occupation, a nation that once ruled Europe now endures as a somewhat balkanized republic but endures as one of the most popular tourist meccas in the world.

Julie Andrews may wish it wasn't so, but *The Sound of Music* hangs on as one of the most beloved films of all time and, in recent years, the annual New Year's Day Musikverein concerts televised from Vienna have attracted millions of equally devoted fans. Jaded New Yorkers are lining up for a taste of gemütlich-tinged elegance at superchef David Bouley's Danube restaurant and Ronald Lauder's Neue Galerie of Austrian art on upper Fifth Avenue's Museum Mile. The year of 2003 saw the 100th anniversary of Wiener Werkstätte, whose decorative arts masterworks by Adolf Loos, Otto Wagner, Josef Hoffman, and Koloman Moser enchant collectors and connoisseurs everywhere. And with the 2006 Mozart Year, we will all be touched by the magic of the Mozart baton. These and other manifestations remind us of the large—and apparently growing—public still entranced by the champagne-splashed whirl of once-Imperial Austria. But despite the spell cast by Austria's never-never land, with its castles, turrets, swords, gold-braid, ravishing Secession School art, and clouds of whipped cream, the stop-press news is that this dowager of Old Europe is ready to straighten up and fly right, once again to lead the vanguard. Museums of contemporary art are opening across the country; Vienna's *beisl*-bistros are getting trumped by the nouvelle novelties whipped up at Vienna hotspots (click your heels three times for Tyrolean eagle garnished with three caviars); and cities everywhere are rumbling with architectural activity, from Vienna's massively renovated MuseumsQuartier to Salzburg's eye-knocking Museum fur Moderner Kunst, newly risen on the site of the fusty Café Winkler, where Julie "do-re-mi"-'d with the von Trapp brood. In many ways, it appears that Austria is taking a Giant Step Forward, virtually leapfrogging from yesterday to tomorrow.

In some sense, we should not be surprised, for Austria has always been "modern." In the purely geographic sense, the country only dates from 1918, the year in which the great and polyglot Austro-Hungarian Monarchy of the Habsburgs came to an end. Before that date, many of its millions had no consciousness of belonging to a race of "Austrians." They were simply the German-speaking peoples of the many-tongued Austro-Hungarian empire, which once reached from the black pine woods of Eastern Poland to the blue shores of the Adriatic. Those were the great times and many Austrians today just can't forget their exalted past. So, is it any wonder that History has given the Austrians a strong feeling for tradition?

Indeed, the most important clue to the Austrians is their love of the Baroque—not, of course, just its 18th-century architectural technicalities, but its spirit. When you understand this, you will not longer be a stranger in Austria. The *Barock* was the style taken up in painting, sculpture, and decoration to celebrate the Austrians' emergence from a century of tribulation—the woeful 17th-century, when the Viennese had battled invading Turks and the plague. Conquering both, the people embraced this new, flamboyant, bejeweled, and emotional import from Italy and went to town creating gilded saints and cherubs, gilt columns, painted heavens on ceilings, joyous patinated domes. From this theater, from this dream, the spirit of Austria has never really departed.

You can enter this dream at certain moments, such as those Sunday mornings from September to June when—if you've reserved months in advance—you can hear (but not see) those "voices from heaven," the Vienna Boys' Choir, sing mass in the marble-and-velvet royal chapel of the Hofburg. Lads of 8 to 13 in sailor suits, they peal out angelic notes from the topmost gallery, and you might catch a glimpse of them after mass as you cut across the Renaissance courtyard for the 10:45 performance of the Lipizzaner stallions in the Spanish Riding School around the corner. Beneath crystal chandeliers in a lofty white hall, expert riders in brown uniforms with gold buttons and black hats with gold braid put these aristocrats of the equine world through their classic paces to the minuets of Mozart and the waltzes of Strauss.

Music, like wine, takes its flavor from the soil and the season in which it grows, and the roots of Mozart's and Strauss's melodies were nourished by moments in history in which an aging civilization had reached peaks of mellowness. Nowhere but in Austria could they have composed their melodious messages, for they are Austria—her quiet lakes, her laughing streams and rushing rivers, her verdant forests, her sumptuous Baroque palaces. Somehow in Austria, everything seems to come back to music, and at nearly every bend in the road, you can see where masterpieces were committed to paper, whether it be Mozart's "Magic Flute" Cottage in Salzburg, Beethoven's Pasqualati House (where he wrote much of *Fidelio*), or the apartment of Johann Strauss the Younger on the Praterstrasse, in whose salon he composed his greatest waltzes, including "The Beautiful Blue Danube."

It is thanks to the Strausses, father and son, that the Viennese traditionally live in two countries. One is on the map. The other is the imaginary region where wine flows, love triumphs, and everything is silk-lined. This is the land of the waltz. This region of the Viennese mind is not just a shallow, sybaritic fantasy. Like Viennese music itself, it embodies a substantial premise. At its surprising best—in such creations as "Tales from the Vienna Woods" or the "Emperor's Waltz"—the waltz is perhaps the closest description of happiness ever attained in any art. Paradoxically, the music is not merry. A haze of wistfulness lies over the sunniest tunes, and their sweetness sometimes touches on melancholy. Though the dance is a swirling embrace, the music countermands sensual abandonment. It insists on grace; it remains pensive in the midst of pleasure.

In Vienna and Salzburg, there was a lot of pleasure to be had. For centuries, the Habsburg rulers maintained a tradition of fostering the arts. The implicit tenet was that beauty begets pleasure, and pleasure begets contentment. These two great imperial cities owe their splendor to the enduring assumption that civic beauty is the key to civic tranquillity. Under these conditions, the whole of Austria came to be pervaded by a certain musicality—an innate, casual feeling for form and harmony. It was evident in the visual charm of the Austrian Baroque that left its mark on Austria's main cities. But a feeling for the Baroque and its later, lighter variants was by no means confined to the leading architects employed in the design of palaces. It filtered down to the humblest mason molding garlanded cherubs above the gate of an ordinary house. It guided the hand of the cabinetmaker who filled the house with the playful curves of rococo and Biedermeier furniture. In such an ambience, the ear, too, became attuned to the refinements and delights of form, and therefore much of Austria became a natural breeding ground for musicians. A contemporary chronicler, Eduard Bauernfeld, observes that "every hole is full of musicians who play for the people. Nobody wants to eat his *Bratl* at the inn if he can't have table music to go with it." Mozart, in fact, began by composing "table music" to soothe the stomach of his first employer, Prince-Archbishop Hieronymus von Colloredo of Salzburg. No feast or celebration was complete without a special overture composed for the occasion. More than 60 piano factories flourished in 19th-century Vienna, which numbered a mere 250,000 inhabitants, and next to good looks and a dowry, musical talent was considered a girl's chief asset. Every Sunday, churches resounded with the musical settings of the Mass—"operas for the angels," as Mozart called them. Performed by choirs and orchestras of remarkable proficiency, these compositions often made divine services into public concerts.

Clearly, no other city has ever been so suffused by an art as Vienna was by music. What other nations say with words, the Austrians say with music. In Paris or London, music was regarded as entertainment. Not so in Vienna. Here it was a personal necessity, an indispensable part of everyday life, shared alike by countesses as well as shopkeepers and janitors. In the crowds who thronged to hear performances of Beethoven symphonies, Haydn oratorios, or Mozart operas, burghers and artisans easily joined princes of the realm. Conversely, in the little rustic *heurige* wine taverns tucked among the hillsides of the Vienna Woods, members of the nobility mixed quite casually with lesser folk to dance to the sweet and giddy folk tunes of the region. In many sense, music created an instant democracy of manners, and class barriers melted in the balmy atmosphere of relaxed hedonism. Is it any wonder that poets and musicians have always felt at home in Austria? The land pulses with the heartbeat of humanity. Mozart and Strauss were just two of the composers who felt that pulse and shaped it into special music that lifted Austria from its moorings on the map and fixed it to the souls of people everywhere.

Austrian skiing is a fairy tale. Strip away the ski history and the tourist-brochure hype, and it's still a fairy tale. Austria has the same high, treeless bowls and slopes that make skiing all over the Alps so different from skiing in North America, plus something extra—the loveliest mountain villages in Europe. Classic Austrian ski villages look, and feel, like an art director's fantasy of Alpine charm.

It's hard for American skiers who haven't skied in the Alps to imagine the sheer size and scale of Alpine ski resorts, where many individual ski areas are linked together with a common ski pass and a spiderweb network of lifts, spanning and connecting different valleys and multiple mountains. These large, interconnected ski domains add a new dimension to skiing—that of exploration. To take full advantage of the promise of so much snowy terrain, American skiers should consider hiring a ski-instructor/guide for a day or two. Private instructors are much less expensive in Austria than in the United States, and the upper levels of Austrian ski-school classes are more about guiding than actual teaching.

Another surprise for the American skier in Austria will be the degree to which the entire country seems to embrace skiing (and winter sports in general, including cross-country skiing and, more recently, snowboarding). Skiing is deeply woven into the daily patterns of winter life in the Austrian countryside. A far greater percentage of the population skis than in the United States. In Austria skiing isn't just another sport, it's the national sport. Ski racers are national heroes; the sports pages of Austrian newspapers award ski competitions banner headlines. Winter, Austria, and skiing are virtually synonymous.

Packages, Discounts, and Information

Your best source for information about Austrian ski vacations and resorts is the **Austrian National Tourist Office** (✉ 500 5th Ave., Suite 2009, New York, NY, 10110, ☎ 212/944–6880, 🖷 212/730–4568, ⊕ www.anto.com). They are well-connected to stateside tour operators providing ski and vacation packages to Austria, and will be happy to send you all sorts of maps and brochures about Austrian ski regions. Contacting the tourist bureaus at individual resorts for this kind of information is a much slower process. But all of Austria's Alpine resorts do have tourist bureau–central reservation services that can make hotel reservations for you (see the addresses and phone numbers for individual resorts, below), and most have websites offering packages which can be booked directly through the internet.

Skiing is neither more nor less expensive in the Alps—and in Austria—than in the States. Some costs, like those for lift tickets, are muchlower; others, like those for fine meals, are higher. Some resorts, like Kitzbühel, are very posh indeed, but there are almost always budget alternatives nearby (neighboring ski villages with more modest prices that are nonetheless connected by lifts to the same large ski domain). Some airlines offer all-inclusive air-lodging-skiing packages to many Austrian resorts. (One of the easiest ways to reach the great resorts of the Vorarlberg and the Tirol is to fly to Munich, then take a short and convenient bus transfer south into the Austrian Alps.)

The Austrian ski season typically runs from late November to April, depending on local snow conditions. Areas with glacier skiing are a better bet in dry snow years. A number of these very high glacier locations offer summer and autumn skiing. But summer ski zones are rather small; the real magic of Austrian skiing involves snow-frosted villages and endless slopes. More and more ski areas, including all the major resorts, now have snow-making machines in case Mother Nature is not cooperating.

Austrians take their snow reports very seriously. In winter, one television channel is devoted exclusively to broadcasting images of snow conditions, captured by remote-control cameras, at ski areas across the country. Americans can check snow conditions by calling the **Austrian National Tourist Office** in New York and listening to its very accurate "snow-phone" survey of all major Austrian resorts (☏ 212/944–6880, ext. 993).

Favorite Destinations

There are so many choices when it comes to Austrian skiing that you're not going to see it all, and ski it all, in one lifetime. Ski areas dot the map of Austria like spots on a Dalmatian. Foreign ski enthusiasts and newcomers to Austrian slopes would do well to focus first on the biggest ski regions of the Arlberg, Tirol, and Land Salzburg. These mega-ski regions showcase what makes Alpine skiing so special: an astonishing variety of slopes and lifts that allows the visitor to ski, day after day, often from one village to the next, without ever repeating a lift or a piste. True, there are many tiny and delightful ski villages in Austria, real discoveries for adventurous skiers, but it makes more sense to sample the feast of a major Skigebiet (interconnected ski region, and sometimes called a ski arena) first. Here, to get you started, are some of the finest.

The Arlberg

This is a capital of Austrian skiing: a double constellation of ski-resort towns—Zürs, Lech, and Oberlech, in the Vorarlberg; and, just across the Arlberg

Pass to the east and thus technically in the Tirol, St. Anton, St. Christoph, and Stuben. These classic Arlberg resorts are interconnected by ski lifts and trails and share more than 260 km (160 mi) of groomed slopes (and limitless off-piste possibilities), 83 ski lifts, snowboard parks, carving areas and permanent race courses and, significantly, a common ski pass.

A skier in **St. Anton,** where Hannes Schneider started the first real ski school, can feel like a character out of a 1930s Luis Trenker ski film: from enjoying Jaeger tea after skiing to dinner at the Post Hotel. Neighboring **St. Christoph** is a spartan resort for skiing purists, a handful of handsome hotels lost in a sea of white, high above timberline, and the permanent home of the Austrian National Ski School's training and certification courses. Several valleys farther west, the plaster walls of many of Lech's hotels are painted with folk art and poetry.

The pièce de résistance of Arlberg skiing is the all-day round-trip, on skis, from Zürs to Lech, Oberlech, and back. This ski epic starts with a 5-km (3-mi) off-piste run from the Madloch down to Zug and ends, late in the afternoon, many lifts and many thousands of vertical feet later, high on the opposite side of Zürs, swinging down the slopes of the Trittkopf.

Visitor Information

Lech: (✉ Verkehrsbüro A–6764 Lech ☏05583/2161–0 📠05583/3155 ⊕www.lech-zuers.at). **St. Anton:** (✉ Verkehrsbüro A–6580 St. Anton am Arlberg ☏ 05446/22690 📠 05446/253215 ⊕ www.stantonamarlberg.com).

The Tirol/Innsbruck

The Tirol is really the heart of Austrian skiing—about a third of all Austrian ski resorts are found in this province. After St. Anton and the Arlberg, **Kitzbühel,** in the heart of the Tirol, is Austria's best-known ski destination and although not as exclusive as Lech or Zürs, certainly one of Austria's most elegant. "Kitz" is picture-perfect and posh—all medieval cobbled streets, wrought-iron signs, and candles flickering in the windows of charming restaurants.

But *Achtung!* Kitzbühel's ski slopes are rather low in altitude, and the snow there is sometimes not as good as at higher resorts. Check the snow depth before a trip here. Fortunately, the area served by the Kitzbühel Safari Pass includes nearby Pass Thurn, a much higher ski area that should have adequate snow even in dry years. New in 2004, you can "fly" between the slopes of Kitzbühel, Pass Thurn, Jochberg, and Kirchberg on one of the longest, most spectacular cable car systems in the world, which means you never have to leave the slopes to ski all the area pistes. A common pass lets you access 63 lifts serving 157 km (97 mi) of groomed slopes—the most celebrated of which is the Hahnenkamm, the course for Europe's toughest downhill race. Deep-snow enthusiasts will gravitate to the ungroomed slopes of the Schwarzkogel.

In high season, if you want to enjoy the chic atmosphere of Kitz, ski all the celebrated pistes of the Kitzbüheler Ski Safari, and avoid high-end prices, consider staying just down the Brixen Valley in neighboring **Kirchberg**. But if you must be where the action is, with a little looking around you'll find accommodations in all price ranges in Kitzbühel itself.

For an altogether different sort of ski vacation, especially for mixed groups of skiers and nonskiers, consider staying in downtown **Innsbruck** and making day trips to the six ski areas of Olympia Ski world Innsbruck. Innsbruck has twice hosted the winter Olympics and boasts a stunning collection of medium-size ski areas with grand views: Seegrube-Nordpark, Patscherkofel, Glungezer, Schlick 2000, Stubaier Gletscher, and especially Axamer-Lizum. Year-round skiing is possible on the Stubaier Gletscher, at the upper end of the spectacular Stubai Valley.

In ever-increasing numbers, skiiers are attracted by the excellent snow conditions and après-ski nightlife of **Ischgl**, in the Paznaun (Valley) southwest of Innsbruck, and not far from better-known St. Anton. Although it's not as chic as Kitz or St. Anton, skiiers and snowboarders are drawn to Ischgl and neighboring resorts **Galtur** and **Kappl** by the 265 km (165 mi) of groomed slopes and 67 lifts found here. It is even possible to ski from Ischgl into the village of Samnaun, Switzerland, for some duty-free shopping, before hopping the impressive double-decker Pendlebahn back into Austria.

No tour of Austria's finest ski areas would be complete without a look into the Ötz Valley, particularly **Sölden**, the valley's premier resort, and one of the best, most au courant all-round resorts in Austria. While not so well-known to Americans, Sölden has excellent snow conditions, due to its three superbly developed three thousand meter (10,000 ft.) mountains, known as the "Big 3." State-of-the-art mountain railways (holding a capacity of 66,000 persons per hour) guarantee ultimate skiing fun without lift lines. The wide variety of 147 km ski runs and modern snow-making machines guarantee good skiing, and the Aqua Dome, a grandiose new spa facility, ensures relief for your tired muscles.

A favorite Austrian Skigebiet has to be the **Zillertal**, just south and east of Innsbruck. Almost unknown to American skiers, there are 10 different ski areas, strung like pearls up the long Ziller Valley, culminating in the Tux Glacier at the very top (a popular summer-skiing site, too). Mayerhofen, a pretty town full of painted buildings halfway up the Zillertal, is a perfect base for skiing the whole valley. The Ahorn, right above Mayerhofen, is one of the smallest ski areas in this large valley, but it has the finest children's ski school I've ever seen. The Zillertal ski pass includes efficient bus and train transportation up and down the valley from one ski area to

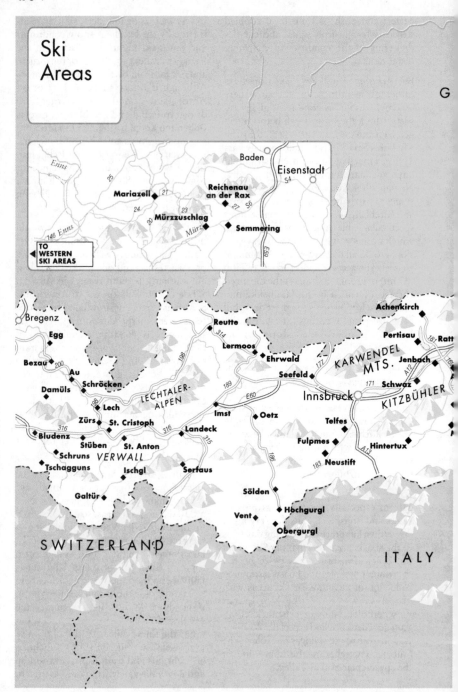

Ski Areas

G

Enns

Baden

Eisenstadt

S4

Mariazell

21

Reichenau
an der Rax

24   23   27   S6

20

Mürzzuschlag

Semmering

Mürz

146 Enns

TO
WESTERN
SKI AREAS

Bregenz

Egg

Reutte

314

Achenkirch

Pertisau   18   Ratt

Lermoos

Bezau   200

Au

Schröcken

Ehrwald

KARWENDEL
MTS.

Jenbach

A12

Damüls

LECHTALER-
ALPEN

198

Seefeld

177

171   Schwaz

Lech

189   E60

Innsbruck

KITZBÜHLER

Zürs   St. Cristoph

Imst

Oetz

Telfes

Bludenz   316

Stüben   St. Anton

316

Landeck

315

Fulpmes

Hintertux

Schruns

VERWALL

186

Neustift   A13

Tschagguns

Ischgl

Serfaus

183

Galtür

Sölden

Vent   Hochgurgl

SWITZERLAND

Obergurgl

ITALY

GERMANY

Inn

Salzburg

SEE INSET FOR
EASTERN
SKI AREAS

Gmunden

E55-60

158

Salzach

St. Gilgen

St. Wolfgang

145

Bad Ischl

Bad
Aussee

169

Abtenau

166

145

162

Hallstatt

Obertraun

Kufstein

Kirchdorf

312

311

Filzmoos

Ramsau

E45/60
A12

Wörgl

312

St. Johann

Kitzbühel

Saalfelden

Radstadt

146

Niederau

170

St.
Johann

Schladming

Rattenberg

Inn

Oberau
Auffach

161

Saalbach
Hinterglemm

Zell
am See

Altenmarkt

NIEDERE TAUERN

Alpbach ALPEN

165

168

Zell am
Ziller

Mittersill

Salzach

Gerlos

Krimml

Kaprun

Bad
Hofgastein

E55

88

167

Mayrhofen

HOHE   TAUERN

Matrei

107

Badgastein

Heiligenblut

Grossglockner

99

GURKTALERALPEN

Döllach

106

108

St. Jakob

Lienz

98

100

100

Spittal
an der Drau

88

Bad
Kleinkirchheim

Drau

Y

Gail

the next. The common Ziller Valley ski pass lets you ski 400 km (240 mi) of groomed slopes and use 140 lifts.

Visitor Information

Innsbruck: (☒ Tourismusverband, Burggraben 3 A–6020 ☎ 0512/59850 🖷 0512/59850–7 ⊕ www.tiscover.com/innsbruck ⊕ www.innsbruck.info). **Ischgl:** (☒ Tourist Office A–6561 ☎ 05444/5266–0 🖷 05444/5636 ⊕ www.ischgl.com). **Kitzbühel:** (☒ Tourismusverband, Hinterstadt 18 A–6370 ☎ 05356/2155 🖷 05356/2307 ⊕ www.kitzbuehel.com). **Sölden/Ötztal Arena:** (☒ Tourist Office A–6450, Sölden ☎ 05444/5266–0 🖷 05444/5636 ⊕ www.soelden.com). **Zillertal:** (☒ Tourismusverband A–6280 Zell im Zillertal ☎ 05254/5100 🖷 05254/510520 ⊕ www.tiscover.com/zell). **Mayrhofen:** (☒ Tourismusverband A–6290 Mayrhofen ☎ 05285/6760 🖷 05285/6760–33 ⊕ www.mayrhofen.com).

Salzburg

Farther east, in the province of Salzburg, there are also a number of stunning integrated ski regions. Despite its grandiose name, the **Europa-Sportregion** is only a grouping together of two—splendid—ski resorts, Kaprun and Zell am See. The skier population here comes from all across Europe, and the large number of British and Scandinavian skiers guarantees that Americans without a word of German will feel at home. Zell am See, a lakeside village, sits beneath the Schmittenhöhe, a wide mountain served by 25 ski lifts, known for its long runs. A few miles away, the village of Kaprun lies under the 10,509-ft Kitzsteinhorn peak, and its glacier skiing makes a winter vacation here very "snow safe." (This is also a major summer-skiing location.) Kaprun has only 16 ski lifts, but they climb quite high.

The **Gasteiner Tal** (Gastein Valley) is the place to combine skiing and spa vacationing. Badgastein and neighboring Bad Hofgastein are better known to Americans for their luxurious thermal and mineral baths. But their ski slopes, linked with

those of Grossarl in the next valley over, comprise a beautiful and rather large ski region. Accommodations range from luxury hotels—Badgastein has a distinctly chichi reputation—to traditional Alpine farmhouses. The Gasteiner Tal and nearby Grossarl together offer 44 ski lifts serving 201 km (124 mi) of groomed slopes.

The slopes of **Saalbach-Hinterglemm,** linked with nearby Leogang, are not particularly steep or difficult, but this is a beautifully integrated ski offering with 200 km (120 mi) of groomed pistes and more than 70 lifts, one of which, the Schattbergbahn, is said to be the largest cable car in Austria. It's a good choice for long, aesthetic intermediate ski runs.

The **Salzburger Sportwelt Amadé** Skigebiet drapes over three large valleys and a number of smaller ones. Resorts like Wagrain, Filzmoos, St. Johann im Pongau, Kleinarl, and Radstadt have never been written up in American ski magazines, which invariably stick with the big names like St. Anton and Kitz, but this ski region nonetheless links more than 320 km (200 mi) of groomed slopes with 120 lifts. Lower altitudes make this a recommended destination only in good snow years.

Visitor Information

Europa-Sportregion: (☒ Kurverwaltung, Brucker Bundesstrasse 1a A–5700 Zell am See ☎ 06542/7700 🖷 06542/72032 ⊕ www.europa-sport-region.com). **Gastein Valley:** (☒ Gasteinertal Tourist Office, Tauernplatz 1, A–5630 Bad Hofgastein ☎ 06432/3393 🖷 06432/3393–120 ⊕ www.gastein.at). **Saalbach-Hinterglemm:** (☒ Tourist Office, Glemmtalerlandesstrasse 550, A–5753 Saalbach ☎ 06541/6800–68 🖷 06541/6800–69 ⊕ www.saalbach.com). **St. Johann:** (☒ Tourismusverband A–5600 ☎ 06412/6036 🖷 06412/6036–74 ⊕ www.salzburg.com/stjohann-tourismus).

Styria

The mountains tend to become lower and the snow conditions less certain as one travels east in the Austrian Alps, so it makes sense for American skiers to concentrate on the more westerly ski destinations. One possible exception is in Styria, the **Dachstein-Tauren Region.** Here the Dachstein Glacier offers a bonus of high-altitude snow. Nine separate villages share a common pass that gives access to 78 lifts, serving 140 km (87 mi) of groomed slopes above the wide Enns river valley. But Dachstein slopes are not as interconnected as those in many other Austrian ski regions and you tend to wind up spending each skiing day above just one of the region's villages: Schladming, Rohrmoos-Unter-tal, Pichl, Haus im Ennstal, Aich-Assach, Pruggern, Gröbming, Mitterberg, and Ramsau am Dachstein. Cross-country skiing is as popular as downhill skiing in this valley with an amazing 240 km (152 mi) of prepared cross-country trails.

Visitor Information

Ramsau am Dachstein: (✉ Tourismusverband A–8972 ☎ 3687/81833 🖷 3687/81085 ⊕ www.ramsau.com). **Schladming:** (✉ Sportregion Schladming, Coburgstrasse 52 A–8970 ☎ 3687/22268 🖷 3687/24138 ⊕ www.schladming-rohrmoos.com).

— Lito Tejada-Flores

AUSTRIA AT A GLANCE

Fast Facts

Capital: Vienna
National anthem: *Land der Berge, Land am Strome (Land of Mountains, Land on the River)*
Type of government: Federal republic
Administrative divisions: Nine states
Independence: 1156 (from Bavaria)
Constitution: 1920; revised 1929, reinstated 1945
Legal system: Civil law system with Roman law origin; judicial review of legislative acts by the Constitutional Court; separate administrative and civil/penal supreme courts
Suffrage: 18 years of age; universal; compulsory for presidential elections
Legislature: Bicameral Federal Assembly consists of Federal Council (62 members; members represent each of the states on the basis of population, but with each state having at least three representatives; members serve a five- or six-year term) and the National Council (183 seats; members elected by direct popular vote to serve four-year terms)
Population: 8.2 million
Population density: 99 people per square km (257 people per square mi)
Median age: Female 41.2, male 38.8
Life expectancy: Female 81.9, male 76
Infant mortality rate: 4.7 deaths per 1,000 live births
Literacy: 98%
Language: German (official nationwide), Slovene (official in Carinthia), Croatian (official in Burgenland), Hungarian (official in Burgenland)
Ethnic groups: German 89%; other 9%; indigenous minorities (includes Croatians, Slovenes, Hungarians, Czechs, Slovaks, Roma) 2%
Religion: Roman Catholic 74%; other 17%; Protestant 5%; Muslim 4%

Geography & Environment

Land area: 82,444 square km (31,832 square mi)
Terrain: Steep Alps in the west and south; mostly flat along the eastern and northern borders; at the crossroads of central Europe with many easily traversable Alpine passes and valleys
Natural resources: Antimony, coal, copper, graphite, hydropower, iron ore, lignite, magnesite, natural gas, oil, salt, timber, tungsten, uranium, zinc
Natural hazards: Avalanches, earthquakes, landslides
Environmental issues: Forest degradation caused by air and soil pollution; soil pollution results from the use of agricultural chemicals; air pollution results from emissions by coal- and oil-fired power stations and industrial plants and from trucks transiting Austria between northern and southern Europe

Economy

Currency: Euro
Exchange rate: 0.82 EUR
GDP: $245.5 billion
Inflation: 1.7%
Unemployment: 4.3%
Work force: 4.3 million; services 67%; industry and crafts 29%; agriculture and forestry 4%
Debt: $15.5 billion

Major industries: Chemicals, communications equipment, construction, food, lumber and wood processing, machinery, paper and paperboard, vehicles and parts, tourism

Agricultural products: Cattle, dairy products, fruit, grains, lumber, pigs, potatoes, poultry, sugar beets, wine

Exports: $83.5 million

Major export products: Chemicals, foodstuffs, iron and steel, machinery and equipment, metal goods, motor vehicles and parts, paper and paperboard, textiles

Export partners: Germany 31.5%; Italy 9.3%; Switzerland 5.4%;

US 4.9%; UK 4.9%; France 4.7%; Hungary 4.3%

Imports: $81.6 billion

Major import products: Chemicals, foodstuffs, machinery and equipment, metal goods, motor vehicles, oil and oil products

Import partners: Germany 42.6%; Italy 6.6%; Hungary 5.1%; Switzerland 4.8%; Netherlands 4.4%

Who could deny that our Austria is richer than any other country? As the saying goes: "We have money like manure."

— Franz Grillparzer

Political Climate

Austria has been moving to the right in recent years. After three decades of social-democratic governments, political battles have centered on which parties belong in the ruling right-wing coalition, with reactionary politicians garnering enough support to create a stir. Austria has long been one of the most developed and self-sufficient nations, so its entry into the EU has been a prickly one. Inside its borders, pension and healthcare reform as well as lower taxes and unemployment form the boilerplate of the debate.

Did You Know?

• The Vienna Staatsoper, the venue of many of the world's most famous musical performances, is the site of the world's longest round of applause. For one hour and 30 minutes and 101 curtain calls, an Austrian crowd applauded Placido Domingo for his performance in Othello in 1991.

• Austria recycles around 80% of its glass products, second only to Switzerland with 91%.

• Austria has the most organically farmed land of any nation. An estimated 10% of the land is farmed without chemically formulated fertilizers, growth stimulants, antibiotics, or pesticides. It's also considered to be nearly self-sufficient in terms of food production

• The Alps take up three-fourths of Austria.

• Though almost nine-tenths of Austria's people are of Germanic origin, the nation has received almost 2 million refugees since 1945. About 300,000 of Austria's workforce are now foreign laborers.

BOOKS & MOVIES

Books

Gordon Brook-Shepherd's *The Austrians: A Thousand-Year Odyssey* traces the history of Austria through the postwar years. The 2,000-year history of Vienna is detailed in *The Viennese: Splendor, Twilight and Exile,* by Paul Hofmann. Alan Palmer's *Twilight of the Hapsburgs* covers the years of Emperor Franz Josef's life (1830–1916). For an intriguing portrait of Vienna in the months before and after the murder-suicide of Crown Prince Rudolf and his teenage mistress, read Frederic Morton's *A Nervous Splendor: Vienna 1888/1889. In the Shadow of Death: Living Outside the Gates of Mauthausen,* by Gordon J. Horwitz, explores what life was like for the townspeople living near Austria's largest concentration camp. How much did they know about the horrors going on inside? What did they think? What did they do? *The World of Yesterday,* Stefan Zweig's haunting memoir, begins in what Zweig calls the "Golden Age of Security," the period that was shattered by the First World War. Zweig witnesses the rise of anti-Semitism, which causes him to flee Austria in the 1930s. Austria has produced many great composers. Recommended as background reading are Maynard Solomon's *Mozart: A Life* and Richard Rickett's *Music and Musicians in Vienna.* *Wittgenstein's Vienna,* by Allan Janik and Stephen Toulmin, tells the story of the brilliant young philosopher and his city in the waning days of the Austro-Hungarian Empire. In *Sigmund Freud,* Richard Wollheim provides a concise analysis of the man and his theories. Robert Musil's most famous work, the sprawling, unfinished, modernist novel *The Man Without Qualities,* is set in Vienna on the eve of World War I. John Irving's first novel, *Setting Free the Bears,* follows two university students as they conspire to liberate the animals at the Vienna Zoo. As for fiction, the leading figure these days is Elfriede Jelinek, whose novels include *The Piano Teacher, Lust, Women as Lovers,* and *Wonderful Times.* She explores the undercurrents of Viennese life in these startling works, including a heavy dose of sadomasochism.

Movies

Vienna and Austria have served as settings for a number of fine films. In *'38: Vienna Before the Fall* (1986), nominated for an Oscar for Best Foreign Language Film, a Gentile and a Jew fall in love just before the Nazi takeover. Postwar Vienna is the backdrop for Graham Greene's suspense classic *The Third Man* (1949), with direction by Carol Reed and zither music by Anton Karas. Ethan Hawke and Julie Delpy are strangers in Richard Linklater's *Before Sunrise* (1995); they meet on a train and impulsively decide to spend Hawke's last hours in Europe together by wandering through Vienna. *Brother of Sleep* (1995), about a musical genius who is unhappy in love, was filmed in Vorarlberg and was nominated for a Golden Globe for Best Foreign Language Film. The young Dr. Freud (Montgomery Clift) battles with the Viennese medical establishment for acceptance of his beliefs in John Huston's *Freud* (1962). In *The Seven Percent Solution* (1976), a cocaine-addicted Sherlock Holmes (Nicol Williamson) and his sidekick, Dr. Watson (Robert Duvall), team up with Sigmund Freud (Alan Arkin) to rescue a beautiful woman in peril (Vanessa Redgrave). Omar Sharif, Ava Gardner, James Mason, and Catherine Deneuve star in *Mayerling* (1968), an account of the murder-suicide of Crown Prince Rudolf and his mistress Marie Vetsera. Rodgers and Hammerstein's *The Sound of Music* (1965) was filmed in Salzburg and the Lake District; it won Oscars for Best Director (Robert Wise) and Best Picture and has become an integral part of tourist promotion for Salzburg.

— Keith Besonen

CHRONOLOGY

ca. 800 BC   Celts move into Danube Valley.

ca. 100 BC   Earliest fortresses set up at Vindobona, now the inner city of Vienna. Roman legions, and Roman civilization, advance to Danube. Carnuntum (near Petronell, east of Vienna) is established about 30 years later as a provincial capital.

AD 180   Emperor Marcus Aurelius dies at Vindobona. Other Roman settlements include Juvavum (Salzburg) and Valdidena (Innsbruck).

ca. 400–700   Danube Valley is the crossing ground for successive waves of barbarian invaders. Era of the events of the Nibelung saga, written down circa 1100.

ca. 700   Christian bishop established at Salzburg; conversion of pagan tribes begins.

791–99   Charlemagne, king of the Franks, conquers territory now known as Austria.

800   Pope Leo III crowns Charlemagne Emperor of the West.

ca. 800–900   Invasion of Magyars; they eventually settle along the Danube.

962   Pope John XII crowns Otto the Great, of Germany, emperor of the Holy Roman Empire, constituting the eastern portion of Charlemagne's realm. Neither holy, nor Roman, nor an empire, this confederation continued until 1806.

The House of Babenberg

976   Otto II confers the eastern province of the Reich—i.e., Österreich, or Austria—upon the margrave Leopold of Babenberg.

1095–1136   Reign of Leopold III, later canonized and declared patron saint of Austria.

1156   Austria becomes a duchy. Duke Heinrich II makes Vienna his capital, building a palace in Am Hof.

1192   Leopold V imprisons King Richard the Lion-Hearted of England, who is on his way back from a crusade. Parts of Vienna and several town walls, particularly Wiener Neustadt, south of Vienna, are later built with the ransom money.

The House of Habsburg

1273   Rudolf of Habsburg in Switzerland is chosen duke by the electors of the Rhine; his family rules for 640 years.

1282   Habsburgs absorb the land of Austria.

1365   University of Vienna founded.

1496   Maximilian's son, Philip, marries Juana of Castile and Aragon, daughter of Ferdinand and Isabella of Spain.

1519 Death of Maximilian; his grandson, Charles I of Spain, inherits Austria, Burgundy, and the Netherlands; he is elected Holy Roman Emperor as Charles V.

1521 Charles V divides his realm with his brother Ferdinand, who becomes archduke of Austria and the first Habsburg to live in the Hofburg in Vienna.

1529 Turks lay siege to Vienna.

1556 Charles V abdicates; Ferdinand becomes Holy Roman Emperor. A Catholic with many Protestant subjects, he negotiates the Peace of Augsburg, which preserves a truce between the Catholic and Protestant states of his realm until 1618.

1618–48 Thirty Years' War begins as a religious dispute but becomes a dynastic struggle between Habsburgs and Bourbons, fought on German soil by non-Germans. The Peace of Westphalia, 1648, gives Austria no new territory and reestablishes the religious deadlock of the Peace of Augsburg.

1683 Turks besiege Vienna; are routed by combined forces of Emperor Leopold I, the duke of Lorraine, and King Jan Sobieski of Poland. By 1699, armies led by Prince Eugene of Savoy drive the Turks east and south, doubling the area of Habsburg lands. The Turkish legacy: a gold crescent and a sack of coffee beans; Vienna's coffeehouses open for business.

1740 Last male Habsburg, Charles VI, dies; succession of his daughter Maria Theresa leads to attack on the Habsburg dominions; long-term rivalry between Austria and Prussia begins.

1740–80 Reign of Maria Theresa, a golden age, when young Mozart entertains at Schönbrunn Palace and Haydn and Gluck establish Vienna as a musical mecca. Fundamental reforms modernize the Austrian monarchy.

1780–90 Reign of Maria Theresa's son Joseph II, who continues her liberalizing tendencies by freeing the serfs and reforming the Church. Her daughter, Marie Antoinette, has other problems.

1806 Napoléon forces Emperor Franz II to abdicate, and the Holy Roman Empire is no more; Franz is retitled emperor of Austria and rules until 1835.

1814–15 The Congress of Vienna defines post-Napoleonic Europe; Austria's Prince Metternich (who had arranged the marriage between Napoléon and Franz II's daughter Marie Louise) gains territory and power.

1815–48 Rise of nationalism threatens Austrian Empire; as chief minister, Metternich represses liberal and national movements with censorship, secret police, force.

1848 Revolutions throughout Europe, including Budapest, Prague, Vienna; Emperor Ferdinand I abdicates in favor of his 18-year-old nephew Franz Josef. Under his personal rule (lasting until 1916), national and liberal movements are thwarted.

1856–90 Modern Vienna is created and much of the medieval city torn down; the "waltz kings," Johann Strauss, father and son, dominate popular music. Sigmund Freud (1856–1939) begins his research on the human psyche in Vienna. By 1900, artistic movements include the Secession and Expressionism.

1866 Bismarck's Prussia defeats Austria in a seven-week war, fatally weakening Austria's position among the German states.

1867 In response to Hungarian clamor for national recognition, the Ausgleich, or compromise, creates the dual monarchy of Austria-Hungary with two parliaments and one monarch.

1889 Franz Josef's only son, Rudolf, dies mysteriously in an apparent suicide pact with his young mistress, Baroness Marie Vetsera.

1898 Empress Elisabeth is murdered in Geneva by an anarchist.

1914 June 28: Archduke Franz Ferdinand, nephew and heir of Franz Josef, is assassinated by a Serbian terrorist at Sarajevo in Bosnia–Herzegovina. By August 4, Europe is at war: Germany and Austria-Hungary versus Russia, France, and Britain.

1916 Death of Franz Josef.

The Republic

1918 End of World War I; collapse of Austria-Hungary. Emperor Karl I resigns; Republic of Austria is carved out of Habsburg crown lands, while nation-states of the empire declare autonomy. Kept afloat by loans from the League of Nations, Austria adjusts to its new role with difficulty. Culturally it continues to flourish: Arnold Schoenberg's 12-tone scale recasts musical expression, while the Vienna Circle redefines philosophy.

1934 Dollfuss suppresses the socialists and creates a one-party state; later in the year he is assassinated by Nazis. His successor, Kurt von Schuschnigg, attempts to accommodate Hitler.

1938 Anschluss: Hitler occupies Austria without resistance.

1945 Austria, postwar, is divided into four zones of occupation by the Allies; free elections are held.

1955 Signing of the Austrian State Treaty officially ends the occupation. Austria declares itself "perpetually" neutral.

1989 Austria becomes the first destination for waves of Eastern European emigrants as the borders are opened.

1990 Austria applies for membership in the European Union.

1999 Spearheaded by Jörg Haider, the anti-immigration and extremist Freedom Party was admitted to Austria's national cabinet, setting the government on a collision course with fellow members of the European Union, who subsequently issued economic and political sanctions against Austria.

2002   The Austrian government was in full upheaval. The status of the ÖVP coalition as the leading party in power was in doubt, with the SPÖ party coming to the fore. The leaders of the Freedom Party resigned because of differences with Jörg Haider, who, in the September elections, became head of this party again, only to back down from taking over the leadership. Happily, the launch of euro notes and coins continues to be a tremendous success in Austria.

2004   Elfriede Jelinek wins the Nobel Prize for Literature, confirming her status as one of Austria's most important and controversial cultural figures. Her novels deal with sexual violence and oppression and right-wing extremism. After years of friction with the government, her plays are once again performed in her homeland. The revered and respected president of Austria, Dr. Thomas Klestil, died of heart failure just days before his second 4-year term expired in July. He is replaced by Dr. Heinz Fischer, a prominent member of the Socialist Pary, who was elected in April. Pope John Paul II beatifies the last Austrian emperor, Karl I, who was against fighting in WWI. And Austria's most famous export since Mozart, Arnold Schwarzenegger, completes his first year as governor of California.

WORDS AND PHRASES

Austrian German is not entirely the same as the German spoken in Germany. Several food names are different, as well as a few basic phrases.

Umlauts have no similar sound in English. An ä is pronounced as "eh." An äu or eu is pronounced as "oy". An ö is pronounced by making your lips like an "O" while trying to say "E" and a ü is pronounced by making your lips like a "U" and trying to say "E".

Consonants are pronounced as follows:

CH is like a hard H, almost like a soft clearing of the throat.

J is pronounced as Y.

Rs are rolled.

ß, which is written "ss" in this book, is pronouced as double S.

S is pronounced as Z.

V is pronounced as F.

W is pronounced as V.

Z is pronounced as TS.

An asterisk (*) denotes common usage in Austria.

English	German	Pronunciation

Basics

English	German	Pronunciation
Yes/no	Ja/nein	yah/nine
Please	Bitte	**bit**-uh
May I?	Darf ich?	darf isch?
Thank you (very much)	Danke (vielen Dank)	**dahn**-kuh (**fee**-len dahnk)
You're welcome	Bitte, gern geschehen	**bit**-uh, gairn ge**shay**-un
Excuse me	Entschuldigen Sie	ent-**shool**-di-gen zee
What? (What did you say?)	Wie, bitte?	vee, **bit**-uh?
Can you tell me?	Können Sie mir sagen?	kunnen zee meer **sah**-gen?
Do you know ____?	Wissen Sie ____?	**viss**-en zee
I'm sorry	Es tut mir leid.	es toot meer lite
Good day	Guten Tag	**goo**-ten tahk
Goodbye	Auf Wiedersehen	owf **vee**-der-zane
Good morning	Guten Morgen	**goo**-ten **mor**-gen
Good evening	Guten Abend	**goo**-ten **ah**-bend
Good night	Gute Nacht	**goo**-tuh nahkt
Mr./Mrs.	Herr/Frau	hair/frow

Miss	Fräulein	**froy**-line
Pleased to meet you	Sehr erfreut.	zair air-**froyt**
How are you?	Wie geht es Ihnen?	vee **gate** es **ee**-nen?
Very well, thanks.	Sehr gut, danke.	sair goot, **dahn**-kuh
And you?	Und Ihnen?	oont **ee**-nen?
Hi!	*Servus!	**sair**-voos

Days of the Week

Sunday	Sonntag	**zohn**-tahk
Monday	Montag	**moan**-tahk
Tuesday	Dienstag	**deens**-tahk
Wednesday	Mittwoch	**mitt**-voak
Thursday	Donnerstag	**doe**-ners-tahk
Friday	Freitag	**fry**-tahk
Saturday	Samstag	**zahm**-stahk

Useful Phrases

Do you speak English?	Sprechen Sie Englisch?	**shprek**-hun zee **eng**-glisch?
I don't speak German.	Ich spreche kein Deutsch.	isch **shprek**-uh kine doych
Please speak slowly.	Bitte sprechen Sie langsam.	**bit**-uh **shprek**-en zee **lahng**-zahm
I don't understand	Ich verstehe nicht	isch fair-**shtay**-uh nicht
I understand	Ich verstehe	isch fair-**shtay**-uh
I don't know	Ich weiss nicht	isch vice nicht
Excuse me/sorry	Entschuldigen Sie	ent-**shool**-di-gen zee
I am American/ British	Ich bin Ameri-kaner(in)/Eng-länder(in)	isch bin a-mer-i-**kahn**-er(in)/**eng**-len-der(in)
What is your name?	Wie heissen Sie?	vee **high**-sen zee
My name is . . .	ich heiße . . .	isch **high**-suh
What time is it?	Wieviel Uhr ist es? *Wie spät ist es?	**vee**-feel oor ist es **vee** shpate ist es
It is one, two, three . . . o'clock.	Es ist ein, zwei, drei . . . Uhr.	es ist ine, tsvy, dry . . . oor
Yes, please/	Ja, bitte/	yah **bi**-tuh/
No, thank you	Nein, danke	**nine** dahng-kuh
How?	Wie?	vee

When?	Wann? (as conjunction, als)	vahn (ahls)
This/next week	Diese/nächste Woche	**dee**-zuh/**nehks**-tuh **vo**-kuh
This/next year	Dieses/nächstes Jahr	**dee**-zuz/ **nehks**-tuhs yahr
Yesterday/today/ tomorrow	Gestern/heute/ morgen	**geh**-stern/ **hoy**-tuh/**mor**-gen
This morning/ afternoon	Heute morgen/ nachmittag	**hoy**-tuh **mor**-gen/ **nahk**-mit-tahk
Tonight	Heute Nacht	**hoy**-tuh nahkt
What is it?	Was ist es?	**vahss** ist es
Why?	Warum?	vah-**rum**
Who/whom?	Wer/wen?	vair/vehn
Who is it?	Wer ist da?	vair ist dah
I'd like to have . . .	Ich hätte gerne . . .	isch **het**-uh gairn
a room	ein Zimmer	ine **tsim**-er
the key	den Schlüssel	den **shluh**-sul
a newspaper	eine Zeitung	i-nuh **tsy**-toong
a stamp	eine Briefmarke	i-nuh **breef**-mark-uh
a map	eine Karte	i-nuh **cart**-uh
I'd like to buy . . .	ich möchte . . . kaufen	isch **merhk**-tuh **cow**-fen
cigarettes	Zigaretten	tzig-ah-**ret**-ten
I'd like to exchange . . .	Ich möchte . . . wechseln	isch **merhk**-tuh . . . **vex**-eln/
dollars to schillings	Dollars in Schillinge	dohl-lars in **shil**-ling-uh
pounds to schillings	Pfunde in Schillinge	pfoonde in **shil**-ling-uh
How much is it?	Wieviel kostet das?	**vee**-feel **cost**-et dahss?
It's expensive/ cheap	Es ist teuer/billig	es ist **toy**-uh/**bill**-ig
A little/a lot	ein wenig/sehr	ine **vay**-nig/zair
More/less	mehr/weniger	mair/**vay**-nig-er
Enough/too much/ too little	genug/zuviel/ zu wenig	geh-**noog**/tsoo-**feel**/ tsoo **vay**-nig
I am ill/sick	Ich bin krank	isch bin krahnk
I need . . .	Ich brauche . . .	isch **brow**-khuh
a doctor	einen Arzt	I-nen artst
the police	die Polizei	dee po-lee-**tsai**
help	Hilfe	**hilf**-uh

Fire!	Feuer!	**foy**-er
Caution/Look out!	Achtung!/Vorsicht!	**ahk**-tung/**for**-zicht
Is this bus/train/ subway going to . . . ?	Fährt dieser Bus/ dieser Zug/ diese U-Bahn nach . . . ?	fayrt **deez**er buhs/ **deez**-er tsook/ **deez**-uh **oo**-bahn nahk . . .
Where is . . .	Wo ist . . .	**vo** ist
the train station?	der Bahnhof?	dare **bahn**-hof
the subway station?	die U-Bahn- Station?	dee **oo**-bahn- **staht**-sion
the bus stop?	die Bushaltestelle?	dee **booss**-hahlt-uh- **shtel**-uh
the airport?	der Flugplatz? *der Flughafen?	dare **floog**-plats dare **floog**-hafen
the hospital?	das Krankenhaus?	dahs **krahnk**-en- house
the elevator?	der Aufzug?	dare **owf**-tsoog
the telephone?	das Telefon?	dahs te-le-**fone**
the rest room?	die Toilette?	dee twah-**let**-uh
open/closed	offen/geschlossen	**off**-en/ge-**schloss**-en
left/right	links/rechts	links/**recktz**
straight ahead	geradeaus	geh-**rah**-day-owws
is it near/far?	ist es in der Nähe/ist es weit?	ist es in dare **nay**-uh? ist es vite?

MENU GUIDE

English	German
Entrées	Hauptspeisen
Homemade	Hausgemacht
Lunch	Mittagsessen
Dinner	Abendessen
Dessert	Nachspeisen
At your choice	Önach Wahl
Soup of the day	Tagessuppe
Appetizers	Vorspeisen

Breakfast

Bread	Brot
Butter	Butter
Eggs	Eier
Hot	Heiss
Cold	Kalt
Caffeine-free coffee	Café Hag
Jam	Marmelade
Milk	Milch
Juice	Saft
Bacon	Speck
Lemon	Zitrone
Sugar	Zucker

Soups

Stew	Eintopf
Goulash soup	Gulaschsuppe
Chicken soup	Hühnersuppe
Potato soup	Kartoffelsuppe
Liver dumpling soup	Leberknödelsuppe
Onion soup	Zwiebelsuppe

Fish and Seafood

Trout	Forelle
Prawns	Garnele
Halibut	Heilbutt
Lobster	Hummer
Crab	Krabbe
Salmon	Lachs
Squid	Tintenfisch
Tuna	Thunfisch
Turbot	Steinbutt

Meats

Veal	Kalb
Lamb	Lamm
Beef	Rindfleisch
Pork	Schwein

Game and Poultry

Duck	Ente
Pheasant	Fasan
Goose	Gans
Chicken	Hühner
Rabbit	Kaninchen
Venison	Reh
Turkey	Truthahn
Quail	Wachtel

Vegetables and Side Dishes

Red cabbage	Rotkraut
Cauliflower	Karfiol
Beans	Bohnen
Button mushrooms	Champignons
Peas	Erbsen
Cucumber	Gurke
Cabbage	Kohl
Lettuce	Blattsalat
Potatoes	Kartoffeln
Dumplings	Knödel
French fries	Pommes frites

Fruits

Apple	Apfel
Orange	Orangen
Apricot	Marillen
Blueberry	Heidelbeere
Strawberry	Erdbeere
Raspberry	Himbeere
Cherry	Kirsche
Cranberry	Preiselbeere
Grapes	Trauben
Pear	Birne
Peach	Pfirsich

Desserts

Cheese	Käse
Crepes	Palatschinken
Soufflé	Auflauf
Ice cream	Eis
Cake	Torte

Drinks

Tap water	Leitungswasser
With/without water	Mit/ohne wasser
Straight	Pur
Non-alcoholic	Alkoholfrei
A large/small dark beer	Ein Krügel/Seidel Dunkles
A large/small light beer	Ein Krügel/Seidel Helles
Draft beer	Vom Fass
Sparkling wine	Sekt
White wine	Weisswein
Red wine	Rotwein
Wine with mineral water	Gespritz

INDEX

A

A. E. Köchert (shop, Vienna), 121
Abteilung für Vor-und Frühgeschichte (Archaeological Museum; Graz), 177
Abtenau, 384–385
Achensee, 392, 413–414
Achensee Schiffahrt, 413
Achenseebahn, 413
Addresses, F34–F35. ⇨ Also under specific cities and regions.
Aenea (Maria Wörth) ✕▥, 342
Aguntum, 363
Aiola (Graz) ✕, 176
Air travel, F35–F36. ⇨ Also specific cities and regions.
Airports, F36. ⇨ Also specific cities and regions.
Akademie der bildenen Künste (Academy of Fine Arts; Vienna), 56, 57
Akademietheater (Vienna), 111
Albertina Museum (Vienna), 3, 51, 52
Alpbach, F20, 392, 417
Alpenhof Messmer (Schruns-Tschagguns) ▥ 456–457
Alpenhotel Gösing (Mariazell) ✕▥, 187
Alpenrose (Feldkirch) ▥, 453
Alpenzoo (Hungerberg), 401–402
Alpinaurium (Galtür), 432
Alpine Flower Garden Kitzbühel, 422
Alps. ⇨ Eastern Alps
Alt Wein ✕, 79–80
Altaussee, 297, 298, 323–324
Alte Galerie (Graz), 175
Alte Post (Krems) ▥, 208
Alte Post (Schladming) ✕▥, 381
Altenmarkt, 357, 379–380
Alter Dom (Linz), 217, 218
Alter Markt (Salzburg), 244, 249
Alter Platz (Klagenfurt), 334
Altes Rathaus (Bregenz), 446
Altes Rathaus (Linz), 217, 218

Altes Rathaus (Vienna), 22, 23
Alt-Österreich (shop; Vienna), 120
Altstadt (Innsbruck), 398
Altstadt (Vienna) ▥, 14, 99–100
Altstadt (Salzburg), 244, 246, 248-249, 251–254, 256–259
Altstadt Radisson SAS (Salzburg) ▥, 278
Am Förthof (Krems) ✕▥, 208
Am Hof (Vienna), 22, 23
Am Steinhof Church (Vienna), 57
Annasäule (St. Anna's Column; Innsbruck), 401
Arcadia (shop; Vienna), 121
Arlbert Hospiz (St. Christoph) ✕▥, 432
Ars Electronica Museum, 217, 218
Artner Weinbau (winery), 147
Augarten (Graz) ▥, 179
Augustinerkeller (winery), 83
Augustinerbräu (Salzburg), 277
Augustinerkirche (Vienna), 34, 35
Austrian Open-Air Museum (Stübing bei Graz), 182
Austrian Riviera, F16
Autobusbahnhof (Stubaital Valley), 402

B

Bad Aussee, F16, F21, 297, 298, 321–322
Bad Blumau ✕▥, 169
Bad Gastein, F17, 357, 376–378
Bad Hall, 228
Bad Ischl, F16, F19, 297, 298, 309–312
Baden, 133, 138–140
Badener Puppen und Spielzeugmuseum (Doll and Toy Museum; Baden), 214
Bärenschützklamm (gorge; Mixnitz), 183, 185
Bärnbach, 182–183
Basilika St. Laurenz (Enns), 230
Baumgartenberg, 200, 214
Beckenturm (Bregenz), 446

Beethoven Haus (Baden), 139
Beethoven's Heiligenstadt residence (Vienna) 9
Bellevue (Obergurgl) ▥, 429
Belvedere Palace (Vienna), F12, 3, 56, 57–58
Bergisel (ski jump), 391, 401
Bergkirche (Eisenstadt), 162–163
Bernstein, 165, 167
Best Western Alpenrose (Kufstein) ✕▥, 418–419
Bezau, 441, 450–451
Bibliotheca Mozartiana (Salzburg), 265
Bier Museum (Laa an der Thaya), 143
Bike travel, F36–F37. ⇨ Also specific cities and regions.
Bischofshof (Linz), 215, 218
Bistro 151 (Klagenfurt) ✕, 336–337
Blaue Gans (Salzburg) ✕, 271
Bludenz, 441, 451–452
Blumau, 169
Blutgasse District (Vienna), 51, 52
Boat and ferry travel, F37. ⇨ Also specific cities and regions.
Böckstein, 377
Bodensee White Fleet, 444
Böglerhof (Alpbach) ✕▥, 417
Bohème (Vienna), 78
Bohemian Court Chancery (Vienna), 22, 23
Books and Movies, 476
Börse (Stock Exchange; Vienna), 48
Brahms Museum (Mürzzuschlag), 188
Brand, 455–456
Bräu (Zell am Ziller) ✕▥, 414
Bräugasthof (Hallstatt) ✕▥, 320
Bregenz, F19, 441, 444–449
Bregenz Music Festival, F17
Bregenzer Festspiele, 444, 448
Bregenzerwald, F17, 441, 449
Bregenzerwald Museumsbahn, 450
Bristol (Salzburg) ▥, 280

British Bookshop (Vienna), *118*

Bruck an der Mur, *151, 185*

Brunnenhof (Lech) ✕, *459*

Burg (Graz), *173, 174*

Burg (Wiener Neustadt), *191*

Burg Bernstein 🏨, *166, 167*

Burg Forchtenstein, *165*

Burg Güssing, *166, 167*

Burg Hohenwerfen, *385*

Burg Kreuzenstein, *204–205*

Burg Landeck castle, *429*

Burg Landskron (Bruck an der Mur), *185*

Burg Liechtenstein (Mödling), *137*

Burg Schlaining, *166*

Burgtheater (Vienna), *111*

Burgenland, *F14*

Bürgeralpe (Mariazell), *187*

Burggarten (Vienna), *34, 35*

Burgher's Tower (Kufstein), *418*

Burgmuseum (Salzburg), *262*

Burgtheater (National Theater; Vienna), *41, 42*

Büro Dachstein-Tauern-Ballons, *383*

Büro Die Schlösserstrasse, *166*

Bus travel, *F37.* ⇨ *Also* specific cities and regions.

Business hours, *F37–F38*

C

Café Central (Vienna) ✕, *22, 24, 87*

Café Hawelka, *F12, 88*

Café Mozart, *88–89*

Café Museum, *89*

Café Sacher (Innsbruck) ✕, *403*

Café Society, *7*

Café Tomaselli (Salzburg) ✕, *276*

Café Zauner (Bad Ischl) ✕, *311*

Cameras and photography, *F38*

Capo, *449*

Car rental and travel, *F38–F41.* ⇨ *Also* specific cities and regions.

Carinthia, *F16–F17, 327–354*
children, activities for, 334, 336, 350, 351
Gurktal Region, 345–352
itineraries, 331
Klagenfurt and the southern lakes, 332, 334, 336–344
outdoor activities and sports, 354
price categories, 332
transportation, 353, 354
visitor information, 354

Carinthischer Sommer (Summer Festival), *348*

Carnuntum, *133, 146–147*

Carolino Augusteum Mueseum (Salzburg), *255*

Casinos, *139, 378*

Castle Hinterhaus (Spitz), *212*

Castle of Greifenstein, *236*

Castle of Klam (Baumgartenberg), *214*

Castle Road, *166*

Cave chapel (Saalfelden), *375*

Cheese Sunday (seasonal event; Landeck), *429*

Children, *F41–F42*
Christkindlmärte, F23

Christmas Eve service, *F23*

Church of St. Alban (Matrei in Osttirol), *367*

Church of St. Barbara (Bärnbach), *182*

Church of St. Catherine (Kizbühel), *421*

Church of St. George (Wiener Neustadt), *191–192*

Church of St. Mary (Altenmarkt), *379*

Church of St. Nicholas (Matrei in Osttirol), *367*

Church of St. Peter-an-der-Sperr (Wiener Neustadt), *191*

Church of St. Vincent (Heiligenblut), *368*

Climate, *F22*

Club U im Otto-Wagner-Café (disco, Vienna), *112*

Coburg (Vienna) ✕, *72*

Computers, *F42*

Consumer protection, *F42*

Copa Kagrana, *49*

Corpus Christi holiday, *F24*

Cortisen am See (St. Wolfgang) 🏨, *308*

Credit card abbreviations, *F10*

Customs and duties, *F42–F44*

D

Dachstein cable-car ride (Ramsau am Dachstein), *382*

Dachstein Ice Caves, *F16, 297, 320–321*

Damüls, *441, 451*

Danube Valley, *F14–F15, 197–239*
children, attractions for, 218
emergencies, 238
excursions from Linz, 226–230
itineraries, F18, 199–200
Linz, 214–226
North Bank of, 200, 204–206, 208–214
outdoor activities and sports, 238
price categories, 200
South Bank of, 230–236
tours, 238–239
transportation, 237–238,239
travel agencies, 239
visitor information, 239

Das Bräu (St. Johann in Tirol) ✕🏨, *420*

Das Triest (Vienna), *97*

Daxlueg (Salzburg), *275*

Demel (pastry shop; Vienna), *30*

Deuring-Schlössle (Bregenz) ✕🏨, *447*

Deutsch-Griffen, *349*

Deutschordenskloster (concert room; Vienna), *108*

Die Weisse (Salzburg), *275*

Dietheater Wien (dance venue; Vienna), *105*

Dining, *F44–F45* ⇨ *Also* specific cities and regions.

Disabilities and accessibility, *F45–F46*

Discounts and deals, *F39*

DO & CO Stephansplatz (Vienna) ✕, *74*

Döllach-Grosskirchheim, *357, 368*

Dom (Gurk), *349*

Dom St. Rupert (Salzburg), *243, 246, 249, 251*

Dominican Church (Lienz), *364*

Dominican monastery (Friesach), *350–351*

Dominikanerkirche (Vienna), *12*

Domkirche (Graz), *173, 174*

Domkirche (Klagenfurt), *334*

Domkirche zu St. Jakob (Innsbruck), *400*

Dornbirn, *441, 454*

Dorotheum (Vienna), *29, 30, 119*

Drei Mohren (Linz) 🏨, *223*

Dreifaltigkeitskirche
(Salzburg), 261–262
Dürnstein, F14, 199,
209–211

E

Easter Festival, F24
Eastern Alps, F16–F17,
356–388
children, attractions for, 371,
375
Grossglockner Pass, 367–376
itineraries, 357
Lienz and Defereggental, 359,
362–367
Mountain spas and alpine
rambles, 376–386
price categories, 358
tours, 388
transportation, 386–388
visitor information, 388
Eastern Austria, F14–F15,
150–195
children, attractions for, 167,
175–176, 182, 186, 189–190
emergencies, 193
Graz and environs, 169–183
itineraries, 151
Land of Castles, 155–157
outdoor activities and sports,
153, 193–194
price categories, 155
Styria to Vienna, 183–192
tours, 194
transportation, 192–193,
194–195
travel agencies, 195
visitor information, 195
Ebensee, 313
Edelweiss und Gurgl
(Obergurgl) ⊡ 429
Edelweissspitze, 370–371
Egg, 449
Egg am Faaker See, 331,
344
Egon Schiele Museum (Tulln),
234–235
Ehreguta Square (Bregenz),
446
**Eisenbahnmuseum Das
Heizhaus** (Strasshof),
144–145
Eisenstadt, F14, 151,
161–164
Eiserner Brunnen (Bruck an
der Mur), 185
Eisriesenwelt (ice caves), 357,
386
Electricity, F44

Elisabeth (Mayrhofen) ✕⊡ ,
415
Elizabeth Chapel (Puchberg
am Schneeberg), 190
Ellmau, 419–420
Embassies, F46. ⇨ Also
specific cities and regions.
Emergencies, F46
in Danube Valley, 238
in Eastern Austria, 193
in Innsbruck and Tirol, 435
in Salzburg, 290–291
in Salzkammergut, 325
in Vienna and environs, 124,
148
in Voralberg, 461
**English-language and local
media**, F46–F47
Enns, 230–231
Ephesus Museum (Vienna),
34, 35
Ernst Triebaumer (winery),
160
Esplanade (Bad Ischl), 309
Ethnological Museum
(Vienna), 39
Etiquette and behavior, F47
Europa Tyrol (Innsbruck)
✕⊡ , 406

F

Fasching (carnival), F24
Feldkirch, 441, 452–453
Feldkirchen (Carinthia), 331,
348–349
Felsenmuseum (Stone
Museum; Bernstein), 165
Felsentherme Gastein (spa
complex), 377
Ferdinandeum (Tyrolean
State Museum; Innsbruck),
401
Festival KlangBogen, 108
Festivals and seasonal events,
F23–F24
Festsaal (concert hall;
Vienna), 108
Festspielhaus (Salzburg), 248,
251–252
Festung Kufstein, 418
Festungsbahn (funicular
railway; Salzburg), 262
Festwochen der Alten Musik
(Innsbruck), 407–408
Figarohaus (Vienna), F13, 4,
51, 53
Filmmuseum (Vienna), 106
Filzmoos, F17, 357,
383–384

Finanzministerium (Vienna),
51, 53
Fischerkirche (Rust), 160
Flex (disco; Vienna), 112
Floh (Tullin) ✕ , 235
Florianer Bahn, 226
Forchtenstein, 164–165
Fortress Hohensalzburg
(Salzburg), F15, 243, 259,
262
Franciscan Church (Lienz),
364
Franciscan Church (Schwaz),
413
Franziskanerkirche
(Salzburg), 243, 248, 252
Frauenkirche (Women's
Church; Feldkirch), 452
Frauenkirchen, 158
Freihaus district (Vienna), 49
Freud House (Vienna), 41, 42
Freyung (Vienna), 22, 24–25
Friedrichstor (Freidrich
Gate), 220
Friesach, 331, 350–351
Fürberg (St. Gilgen) ⊡ , 306
Fuschl, 298, 304–305

G

Gaisberg, 267
Gallery Christine Koenig
(Vienna), 106
Gallery Georg Kargl (Vienna),
106
Gallery Julius Hummel
(Vienna), 106
Galtür, 432
Gartl Waterfall, 368
Gasthaus Drachenwand
(Mondsee), 303–304
Gasthaus Erwin Schwarz
(Weissenkirchen), 211
Gasthof Gams (Bezau) ⊡ ,
450–451
Gasthof Hohlwegwirt
(Salzburg) ✕ , 278
Gasthof Kornmesser
(Bregenz), 444
Gasthof Ladner (Grundlsee)
✕⊡ , 322
Gasthof Moser
(Kremsmünster) 227–228
Gasthof Post (Lech) ✕⊡ ,
459
Gasthof zur Dankbarkeit
(Podersdorf) ✕ , 158
Gauderfest, 414
Gay and lesbian travel, F47
Geo-Trail (Hermagor), 362

Gerlos, *392, 416*
Gersberg Alm (Salzburg) 🏨,
282
Gesellenspital (Journeymen's
Hospital; Bregenz), *446*
Getreidegasse (Salzburg),
243, 249, 252–253
Gisela (steamship; Gmunden),
313
Glockenspiel (Salzburg), *246,
253*
Glockenspielplatz (Graz),
171–173, 174
Glockenturm (Graz), *176*
Glödnitz, *349*
Gloriette (Vienna), *63–64*
Gmoa Keller (Vienna) ✕,
80
Gmunden, *298, 312–315*
Goggau, *349*
Going, *F20, 419–420*
Goinger Handwerks-
Kunstmarkt, *419*
Goldener Adler (Innsbruck)
🏨, *406–407*
Goldener Hirsch (Salzburg)
🏨, *278–279*
Goldenes Dachl (Innsbruck),
F17, 391, 398
Göllersdorf, *141–142*
Gosau am Dachstein, *F16,
F21, 297, 298, 316–317*
Gösser Braugaststätte, *445*
Göttweig, *199, 234*
Gnadenkapelle (Chapel of
Miracles; Mariazell), *186*
Graben (Vienna), *29, 30–31*
Grand Hotel Sauerhof (Baden)
✕🏨, *139*
Grand Hotel Wiesler (Graz)
✕🏨, *178–179*
Grassmayr Bell Foundry, *401*
Graz, *F14, 151*
Greifenstein, *235–236*
Greifvogelwarte Riegersburg
(Birds-of-Prey Keep), *168*
Grein, *200, 214*
Griechenbeisl (Vienna) ✕,
12, 13, 74
Grosse Aula (Salzburg), *255*
Grosses Festspielhaus
(Salzburg), *285*
Grossglockner Highway,
F16–F17, 357, 370–371
Grosswalsertal (Great
Walliser Valley; Damüls),
451
Grünberg, *313*
Grundlsee, *328*

Gumpoldskirchen, *F13–F14,
133, 138*
Gurk, *F16, 331, 349–350*
Gurktaler Museumbahn, *350*
Güssing, *167–168*

H

Hacker (Rattenberg) ✕,
417
Hainzenberg, *416*
Haitzendorf, *199, 205–206*
Halbturn, *158–159*
Hall in Tirol, *392, 411–412*
Hallein, *267–268*
Hallstatt, *F15, F19–F20, 297,
298, 318–320*
Hauptplatz (Friesach), *350*
Hauptplatz (Graz), *171,
174–175*
Hauptplatz (Wiener
Neustadt), *191*
Haus der Musik (Museum
of Music), *51, 53*
Haus der Völker (museum;
Schwaz), *413*
Haus für Mozart (Salzburg),
285–286
Haydn Festival, *164*
Haydn House, *9*
Haydn Museum (Eisenstadt),
163
Health, *F47–F48*
Heiligenblut, *F17, F20, 357,
368–370*
Heiligen Kreuz (Linz), *217,
218*
Heiligenkreuz, *133, 140–141*
Heiligenkreuz (Holy Cross
Church; Villach), *345*
Heiligenkreuzerhof (Vienna),
12, 13
Heimatmuseum (Bad Ausee),
321
Heimatmuseum (Bezau), *450*
Heimatmuseum (Mariazell),
186
Heimatmuseum (Oberndorf),
268
Heimatmuseum (Puchberg am
Schneeberg), *190*
Heimatmuseum
(Schwarzenberg), *450*
Helbling House, *400*
Heldenplatz (Hofburg Palace;
Vienna), *34, 35, 37*
Hellbrunn Castle, *F15*
Helmut Lang (shop; Vienna),
122
Hemetsberger, 318

Herberstein Palace (Graz),
173, 175
Hermagor, *357, 362*
Herz-Jesu Kirche (Sacred Heart
Church; Bregenz), *445*
Hettwer Bastion (Salzburg),
262
Heurigen (wine taverns),
7–8, 83–86
Himmelpfortgasse (Vienna),
51, 54
Hirschbichl pass, *375*
Historical excavation
(Hallstatt), *319*
Hochgurgl, *428*
Hochosterwitz Castle, *F16,
331, 351–352*
Hofbibliothek (Vienna), *3, 34,
37*
Hofburg (Imperial Palace;
Innsbruck), *391, 400*
Hofburg (Imperial Palace;
Vienna), *F12, 3, 33–40*
Hofburgkapelle, *34, 37*
Hofkeller (Graz) ✕, *178*
Hofkirche (Innsbruck), *F17,
400*
Hofpavillon (Vienna), *63, 64*
Hohe Tauern National Park
(St. Jakob in Defereggen),
366
Hohe Wand (High Wall;
Puchberg am Schneeberg),
190
Hohenems, *441, 453–454*
Hohensalzburg, *F15*
Hohentwiel (steamship;
Bregenz), *446–447*
Hoher Markt (Vienna), *12, 13*
Holidays, *F48*
Höllental, *188*
Hotel Gasthof zur Post (St.
Gilgen) ✕🏨, *305–306*
Hotel Koller (Gosau am
Dachstein) ✕🏨, *317*
Hotel Lärchenhof
(Heiligenblut) 🏨, *369*
Hotel Panhans (Semmering)
✕🏨, *189*
Hotel Post (Villach) ✕🏨, *346*
Hotel Tauern National Park,
366
Hotel Weismayr (Bad Gastein)
✕🏨, *377*
Hotels. ⇨ *Also* specific cities
and regions.
*price categories, 91, 134, 155,
200, 245, 300, 332, 358,
397, 442*

Hubertus (Filzmoos) ✕⌷, 384
Hubertushof (Velden) ✕⌷, 343
Hundertwasserhaus (public housing; Vienna), F13, 4, 16
Hungerburg, 391, 392

I

Igls, 391, 411
Iglsbergerhof (Saalbach-Hinterglemm) ✕, 273
Imperial (Vienna) ⌷, 94
Imst, 391, 424
In der Burg (Vienna), 34, 37
Innsbruck and Tirol, F17, 390–437
  children, attractions for, 401–402
  emergencies, 435
  excursions from, 401–402
  itineraries, F19, 391–392
  Landeck, Upper Inn Valley, and St. Anton, 429–433
  Lower Inn Valley, 411–416
  money matters, 435
  outdoor activities and sports, 408–410
  nightlife and the arts, 407–408
  price categories, 397
  Road to Kitzbühel, 416–424
  shopping, 410–411
  tours, 435
  transportation, 433–435, 436
  travel agencies, 436–437
  visitor information, 436
  West from Innsbruck, 424–426, 428–429
Insurance, F39
International Chamber Music Festival (Lockenhaus), 167
International Theater (Vienna), 111
Internationaler Tanzsommer Innsbruck, 407
Ischgl, 432–433
Itineraries, F18–F21

J

Jagdmuseum (Hunting Museum; Graz), 176–177
Jenbach, 413
Jewish Museum (Vienna), 29, 31
Johann Strauss the Younger, 9
Josefsplatz (Vienna), 34, 38
Joseph Haydn's house, 9

Judenplatz Museum (Vienna), 22, 25
Jüdisches Museum (Jewish Museum; Hohenems), 454
Julius Meinl am Graben (Vienna) ✕, 70–71
Justizpalast (Central Law Courts; Vienna), 48

K

Kahlenbergerdorf, 236
Kaiserappartements, 34, 38
Kaiserball, F23
Kaisergruft (Imperial Burial Vault; Vienna), 4, 51, 54
Kaiserliches Hofmobiliendepot (Imperial Furniture Museum), 41, 50
Kaiservilla (Bad Ischl), 309–310
Kammeroper (Vienna), F23, 110–111
Kammerspiele (theater; Vienna), 111
Kapuzinerberg Hill (Salzburg), 261, 262–263
Kapuzinerkloster (Salzburg), 262–263
Karikaturmuseum (Krems), 206
Karlskirche (Vienna), F12, 54, 59
Karlsplatz (Vienna), 56, 59–60
Karmelitenkloster (Linz), 217, 218
Karnerhof (Egg am Faaker See) ✕⌷, 344
Kärntnerstrasse (Vienna), 51, 54
KäseStrasse, 449
Kastnerturm (Zell am See), 371
Katzenturm (Feldkirch), 452
Kellerwand (Kötshach-Mauthen) ✕⌷, 363
Keltenmuseum (Hallein), 268
Kepler Haus (Linz), 217, 219
Kirche Am Hof (Vienna), 22, 25
Kitzbühel, F17, F20, 392, 395, 421–434
Klagenfurt, F16, F21, 331, 332, 334, 336–339
Kleines Festspielhaus (Salzburg), 255
Klopeinersee, 336
Klosterneuburg, 199, 200, 236

Kober (shop; Vienna), 121
Kohlmais cable car (Saalbach-Hinterglemm), 373
Kohlmarkt (Vienna), 30, 31
Kollegienkirche (Salzburg), 248, 253
Koloman-Wallisch-Platz (Bruck an der Mur), 185
Konzerthaus (concert salon; Vienna), 107
Korneuburg, 199, 2204–205
Kornmesserhaus (Bruck an der Mur), 185
Korso (Vienna) ✕, 72
König von Ungarn (Vienna) ⌷, 97
Kötschach-Mauthen, 357, 363
Kramsach, 392
Krems, F14, 199, 206, 208
Kremsmünster, 199, 227–228
Kremsmünstererhaus (Linz), 215, 219
Kriminal Museum (Vienna), 16
Krimmler Wasserfälle (waterfalls), 416
Krimpelstätter (Salzburg), 276
Krinzinger Gallery (Vienna), 106
Krumpendorf, 331, 339
Kufstein, 392, 418–419
Kugelhof (Salzburg) ✕, 275–276
Kummer (Vienna) ⌷, 98
Kunsthaus (Bregenz), 445
Kunsthaus (Graz), 173, 175
Kunsthaus Wien (Vienna), 16
Kunsthistorisches Museum (Museum of Fine Art; Vienna), F12, 3, 41, 42–43, 48
Künstlerhaus (Vienna), 59–60
Künstlerhaus Thurn und Taxis (Bregenz), 446
Kurpark (Baden), 139

L

Laa an der Thaya, 143–144
Lake District. ⇨ Salzkammergut
Lake Neusiedl, F14, 151, 156
Lamprechtshöhle (caves), 357, 375
Landeck, 391, 429–430
Landesmuseum (Bregenz), 445
Landesmuseum (Eisenstadt), 163

Landesmuseum Joanneum (Graz), 171, 175
Landestheater (Salzburg), 247, 287
Landeszeughaus (Graz), 171, 175–176
Landhaus (Graz), 171, 176
Landhaus (Klagenfurt), 334
Landhaus (Linz), 215, 219
Landhaus Bacher (Mautern) ✕▨, 233–234
Landhaus zu Appesbach (St. Wolfgang) ✕▨, 307–308
Landschloss (Gmunden), 313
Landskron, 345
Language, F48
Le Méridien (Vienna) ▨, 94
Lebzelter (Altenmarkt) ✕▨, 380
Lech, F17, 441, 458–460
Lehár's Villa (museum; Bad Ischl), 311
Lentos (Linz), 217, 219
Lichtblick (Innsbruck) ✕, 403
Lieburg Palace (Lienz), 364
Liechtenstein Museum, 41, 43–44
Liechtensteinklamm, 357, 378–379
Lienz, F17, 357, 363–365
Linz, F15, F17, F18, 199, 200, 214–230
Linz Castle, 215, 220
Lipizzaner Museum, 34, 38
Lipizzaner Stud Farm (Piber), 182
Lobmeyr (shop; Vienna), 119
Lockenhaus, 166
Loden-Plankl (shop; Vienna), 118
Lodging, F48–F50. ⇨ Also specific cities and regions.
Loibnerhof (Dürnstein) ✕, 210
Looshaus (Vienna), 29, 31
Loser Mountain, 323
Luegg House (Graz), 174
Lünersee, F17, 455
Lurgrotte (cave; Peggau), 183

M
M. Kunst, Genuss (Krems) ✕, 206, 208
Mail and shipping, F50
Mailberger Hof (Vienna) ▨, 98
Marchegg, 133, 145–146

Maria am Gestade (church; Vienna), 12, 16–17
Maria Gail, 344
Maria Himmelfahrt (church; Weissenkirchen), 211
Maria Loretto (Klagenfurt) ✕, 337
Maria Rast pilgrimage church (Hainzenberg), 416
Maria Taferl, 213–214
Maria Taferl Basilica, 213
Maria Wörth, F16, 331, 341–342
Mariazell, 151, 186–187
Mariazeller Basilica, 186
Mariazellerbahn (narrow-gauge rail line; Mariazell), 186–187
Marionettentheater (Salzburg), F15, 247, 261, 263–264, 287
Martinskirche (Bregenz), 446
Martinsturm (Bregenz), 446
Matrei in Osttirol, 357, 366–367
Mautern, 200, 233–234
Mauthausen, 231
Mauthausen Konzentrationslager (concentration camp), 231
Mayer am Pfarrplatz (winery), 84
Mayerling, F13, 133, 140
Mayrhofen, 392, 415–416
Meal plans, F11, F48
Melk Abbey, F14, 199, 231–233
Melker skeller (winery), 83
Menu guide, 485–487
Michaelerkirche (Hallstatt), 318–319
Michaelerkirche (Mondsee), 302
Michaelerplatz (Vienna), 29, 31–32
Midsummer Night, F24
Milka Lädele (shop), 451
Mines (Altaussee), 323
Minimundus park, 334
Minorite cloister (Tulln), 235
Minoritenkirche (Linz), 215, 219
Minoritenkirche (Stein), 209
Minoritenkirche (Vienna), 22, 25
Mint tower (Hall in Tirol), 412
Mirabell Gardens (Salzburg), F15, 261, 263–264

Mirabell Palace (Salzburg), 261, 264, 286
Mixnitz, 183, 185
Mödling, 133, 136–137
Monastery (Ossiach), 347
Monastery church (Hall in Tirol), 412
Monatsschlösschen, 268
Mönchsberg elevator (Salzburg), 248, 253
Mondsee, F21, 297–298, 302
Money matters, F50–F52
Montana (Lech) ✕▨, 459
Montfortbrunnen fountain (Bregenz), 446
Mörbisch, 161
Mörwald (Haitzendorf) ✕▨, 205–206
Mörwald im Ambassador (Vienna) ✕, 71
Mozart, Wolfgang Amadeus, 19, 266
Mozart Audio and Video Museum, 264
Mozart Haus (Linz), 215, 219–220
Mozart Week, 247
Mozart Wohnhaus (Salzburg), 261, 264–265
Mozart Year, 109
Mozarteum, 261, 265
Mozart-Gedenksstätte St. Gilgen, 305
Mozartplatz (Salzburg), 243, 246, 253–254
Mozart's birthday, F23, 255
Mozarts Geburtshaus (Salzburg), F15, 243, 249, 254
MS Landskron, 345
Münzensammlung (Numismatic Museum; Graz), 177
Murinsel (Graz), 173
Mürzzuschlag, 187–188
Museum Carnuntium, 146
Museum der Moderne Kunst (Salzburg), 253
Museum der Moderner (Salzburg), 244, 249, 254, 256, 257
Museum der Stadt Ischl, 310
Museum für Angewandte Kunst (MAK; Museum of Applied Arts; Vienna), 12, 17
Museum Industrielle Arbeitswelt (Industrial Museum; Steyr), 229

Museum Tyrolean Bauernhöfe (farmhouse museum), *418*
MuseumsQuartier (MQ), *F13, 3, 41, 44, 46–47*
Museumtramway, *186*
Musical Instruments Collection, *34, 38*
Musical Summer/KlangBogen, *F24*
Musikverein (Vienna), *30, 60, 107*

N

Naschmarkt (Vienna), *4, 56, 60, 115*
National Library, *F12*
Naturhistorisches Museum (Natural History Museum; Vienna), *41, 47, 48*
Naturpark Raab-Örsg-Goricko (Güssing), *167*
Nepomuk-Kapelle (Bregenz), *444*
Neue Burg (Hofburg Palace; Vienna), *34, 38–39*
Neue Galerie (Graz), *175*
Neuer Dom (Linz), *215, 217, 220*
Neuer Markt (Vienna), *51*
Neues Haas-Haus (Vienna), *29, 32*
Neukloster Church (Wiener Neustadt), *191*
Neusiedl am See, *156–157*
Nibelungenau, *213*
Nonnberg Convent (Salzburg), *244, 259, 265*
Nordico (Linz), *217, 220*
Nussdorferstrasse 54, *9*

O

Obergurgl, *F17, 429–429*
Oberndorf, *268*
Open-Air Theater (Graz), *176*
Opera House (Vienna), *51, 55*
Opernball, *F24*
Ossiach, *331, 347–348*
Österreichischer Bundestheaterkassen (State Theater Booking Office), *105*
Österreichisches Barockmuseum (Austrian Museum of Baroque Art; Vienna), *58*
Österreichisches Galerie (Austrian Gallery; Vienna), *57*

Österreichisches Jüdisches Museum (Eisenstadt), *163*
Otto Wagner Houses, *56, 60–61*
Otto Wagner Stadtbahn Pavillions, *60*
Ötz, *426*
Outdoor activities and sports, *F54–F55.* ⇨ *Also* specific cities and regions.

P

Packing for the trip, *F52–F53*
Palais Coburg (Vienna) 🏨, *94–95*
Palais Daum-Kinsky (Vienna), *22, 26*
Palais Ferstel (Vienna), *22, 25–26*
Palais Harrach (Vienna), *22, 26*
Palais Khuenburg (Graz), *173, 176*
Palais Porcia (Klagenfurt) 🏨, *338*
Palais Schwarzenberg (Vienna) 🏨, *95*
Palmenhaus (tropical greenhouse; Vienna), *63, 64*
Palmenhaus (Vienna), *76*
Panoramhotel Wagner (Semmering) 🏨, *189*
Parish church (Baumgartenberg), *214*
Parish church (Bruck an der Mur), *185*
Parish church (Hermagor), *362*
Parish church (Hohenems), *453–454*
Parish church (Imst), *425*
Parish church (Kötschach-Mauthen), *363*
Parish church (Maria Wörth), *342*
Parish church (Radstadt), *380*
Parish church (St. Johann in Tirol), *429*
Parish church (St. Veit an der Glan), *352*
Parish church (Schwaz), *413*
Parish church (Spitz), *212*
Parish church of St. Gallus (Bregenz), *446*
Parish church of St. Hippolyte (Zell am See), *371*
Parish church of the Assumption (Landeck), *429*

Parkhotel Tristachersee (Lienz) ✕🏨, *365*
Parlament (Vienna), *41, 47, 48*
Pasqualatihaus (Vienna), *F13, 4, 22, 26*
Passports and visas, *F53*
Paysdorf, *133, 144*
Peggau, *183*
Pension Nossek (Vienna) 🏨, *101–102*
Pension Pertschy (Vienna) 🏨, *100–101*
Pension Wild (Vienna) 🏨, *104*
Perchtoldsdorf, *133, 136*
Peter Rosegger (Ramsau am Dachstein) 🏨, *383*
Petersfriedhof (Salzburg), *243, 258*
Peterskirche (Vienna), *29–30, 32*
Pfänderbahn cable car, *445*
Pfarrkirche. ⇨ Parish church.
Pfefferschiff (Salzburg) ✕, *270*
Pferdeschwemme (Salzburg), *243, 248, 256*
Photography museum (Bad Ischl), *310*
Piber, *182*
Pilgrimage church (Frauenkirchen), *158*
Pillar to the Holy Trinity (Linz), *215, 220*
Pinzgauer railroad (Zell am See), *371*
Podersdorf, *157–158*
Pongau Cathedral, *379*
Pörtschach, *331, 339–341*
Post (Imst) ✕🏨, *425*
Post Office (Bregenz), *444*
Pöstlingberg (Linz), *221*
Postsparkasse (Post Office Savings Bank; Vienna), *12, 17*
Prater (park; Vienna), *17–18*
Praterstrasse 54, *9*
Price categories
 for *Cartinthia, 332*
 for *Danube Valley, 200*
 for dining, *67, 134, 155, 200, 245, 300, 332, 358, 397, 442*
 for *Eastern Alps, 358*
 for *Eastern Austria, 155*
 for *Innsbruck and Tirol, 397*
 for lodging, *91, 134, 155, 200, 245, 300, 332, 358, 397, 442*

for *Salzburg,* 245
for *Salzkammergut,* 300
for *Vienna and environs,* 67, 91, 134
for *Vorarlberg,* 442
Prunkräume (State Apartments; Graz), 176
Puchberg am Schneeberg, 151, 189–191
Puchberg cog-wheel steam train, 189–190
Pukelsheim (St. Viet an der Glan) ✕, 352
Puppen und Spielzeug Museum (Doll and Toy Museum; Baden), 22, 26
Purbach, 159
Pyramidenkogel, 336

R

Radisson (Vienna) ⌶, 98
Radstadt, 357, 380–381
Rahofer (Steyr) ✕, 229
Raimundtheater (Vienna), 110
Rainersmuseum (Salzburg), 262
Ramsau am Dachstein, 357, 382–383
Rathaus (Bregenz), 445
Rathaus (Bruck an der Mur), 185
Rathaus (Feldkirch), 452
Rathaus (Graz), 174–175
Rathaus (Hall in Tirol), 412
Rathaus (St. Veit an der Glan), 352
Rathaus (Salzburg), 256
Rathaus (Vienna), 41, 47, 48
Rathaus (Wiener Neustadt), 191
Rathaus Wine & Design (Vienna) ⌶, 101
Rathauskeller (Rust), 160
Rattenberg, F20, 392, 417–418
Rauchhaus (farmhouse; Mondsee), 302
Rauter (Matrei in Osttirol) ✕⌶, 367
Raxbahn (cable car; Semmering), 188
Reckturm (Salzburg), 262
Reckturm (Wiener Neustadt), 191
Regina (Vienna) ⌶, 101
Reinthaler (Vienna) ✕, 81
Reinthaler Seen (Rein valley lakes), 418

Reptilian Zoo (Klagenfurt), 336
Residenz (Salzburg), 243, 246, 256–257, 286
Residenzgalerie (Salzburg), 256–257
Restaurant Weiler (Laa an der Thaya) ✕, 143–144
Restaurants. ⇨ *Also* specific cities and regions.
price categories, 67, 91, 134, 200, 245, 300, 332, 358, 397, 442
Retz, , 142–143
Retzer Erlebniskeller, 143
Richard Löwenherz (Dürnstein) ✕⌶, 210
Richard the Lion-Hearted Castle (Dürnstein), 209–210
Richterhöhe, 244
Riegersburg, 168
Ringstrasse (Vienna), F12, 40–51
Ritzen Castle (museum; Saafelden), 375
Robert Musil Museum (Klagenfurt), 336
Rohrau, 146
Romantik Hotel Tennerhof (Kitzbühel) ✕⌶, 422
Römersteinbruch (outdoor opera venue), 161
Römischer Kaiser (Vienna) ⌶, 99
Ronacher (theater, Vienna), 110
Rosenkranzkirche (Rosary church), 342
Rotes Haus (Dornbirn) ✕, 454
Ruben's Palais (Vienna) ✕, 73
Rupertinum (Salzburg), 248, 257
Ruprechtskirche (Vienna), 12, 18
Russian War Memorial (Vienna), 61
Rust, 151, 159–161

S

Saalbach-Hinterglemm, 357, 373–374
Saalfelden, 357, 374–376
Sacher (Vienna) ⌶, 95–96
Sacher Salzburg ⌶, 14, 279
St. Achaz parish church (Schladming), 381

St. Andrä Pfarrkirche (Lienz), 364
St. Andrew's parish church (Kitzbühel), 421
St. Anton am Arlberg, 391, 395, 430–431
St. Antonius (church; Lienz), 364
St. Blasius parish church (Abtenau), 384
St. Christoph, F17, 395, 431–432
St. Egyd (Klagenfurt), 334
St. Florian Abbey, 199, 226–227
St. George and St. Nicholas (parish church; Ötz), 426
St. George's Chapel (Salzburg), 262
St. Gilgen, 298, 305–306
St. Hubertushof (Zell am See) ✕⌶, 372
St. Jacob (Villach), 345
St. Jakob in Defereggen, 357, 366
St. Johann am Imberg (Salzburg), 262
St. Johann im Pongau, F17, 379
St. Johann in Tirol, 392, 420–421
St. Joseph's (church; Lienz), 364
St. Laurence parish church (Ybbs an der Donau), 231
St. Michael's church (Lienz), 364
St. Nicholas cathedral (Feldkirch), 452
St. Nicholas parish church (Stein), 209
St. Nikolaus (Bad Ischl), 310
St. Othmar Gothic parish church (Mödling), 137
St. Peter's Cemetery (Salzburg), 248, 258
St. Sebastian's Cemetery (Salzburg), 243, 258, 261, 265, 267
St. Stephen's Cathedral, 51–55
St. Veit an der Glan, F16, 331, 352
St. Wolfgang, F15, F19, 298, 306–309
Salamander diesel train, 190

Salzburg, *F15, 18, 241–293*
Altstadt, 246, 248–249,
251–254, 256–259
children, attractions for, 258,
263–264, 268–269
dining, 270–271, 274–277
consulates, 290
emergencies, 290–291
excursions from, 267–269
Fortress and New Town, 259,
261–265, 267
itineraries, F18, 243–244
lodging, 277–285
money matters, 291
nightlife and the arts, 285–288
price categories, 245
shopping, 288–289
tours, 291–292
transportation, 289–290, 291,
292–293
travel agencies, 293
visitor information, 293
Salzburg Festival, *F24, 247,*
285, 287
Salzburg Marionette Theater,
F15, 247
Salzburg Museum, *246,*
257–258
Salzburger Dolomitenstrasse
(Salzburg Dolomites
Highway), *384*
Salzburger Festspiele
(summer festival), *F24,*
247, 285, 287
Salzburger Festungskonzerte,
286–287
Salzburger Schlosskonzerte,
286
Salzburgerhof (Zell am See)
✕⊡, *372*
Salzkammergut (the Lake
District), *F15–F16,*
F20–F21, 18, 295–327
emergencies, 323
Gosau, Hallstatt, and Bad
Aussee, 316–324
itineraries, F18, 297–298
outdoor activities and sports,
325–326
price categories, 300
St. Wolfgang and Bad Ischl,
300, 302–315
tours, 326
transportation, 324–325, 326
visitor information, 326–327
Sammlung Essl
(Klosterneuburg), *236*
Sandwirth (Klagenfurt) ✕⊡,
337–338

Schafberg, *307*
Schallaburg, *233*
Schattenburg (Feldkirch), *453*
Schatzbichl (Saalfelden) ✕,
375
Schatzkammer (Imperial
Treasury; Vienna), *3, 34,*
39
Schaubergwerk (salt mines;
Hallstatt), *319*
Schemenlaufen (seasonal
event; Imst), *425*
Schickh (Göttweig) ✕, *234*
Schladming, *F17, 381–382*
Schleicherlaufen (Carnival
celebration; Telfs), *424*
Schloss Ambras, *391, 392,*
411
Schloss Artstetten (Maria
Taferl), *213*
Schloss Bruck (Lienz), *364*
Schloss Café (Linz) ✕, *222*
Schloss Dürnstein
✕⊡ *210–211*
Schloss Eggenberg (Graz),
173, 176–177
Schloss Esterházy
(Eisenstadt), *162*
Schloss Frohnburg (Hallein),
269
Schloss Fuschl ✕⊡, *304–305*
Schloss Grafenegg, *199, 205*
Schloss Halbturn, *158–159*
Schloss Hartberg, *166*
Schloss Hellbrunn, *F15,*
268–269
Schloss Herberstein, *166*
Schloss Kremsegg, *227*
Schloss Laxenburg, *133, 137*
Schloss Leonstain (Pörtschach)
✕⊡, *340–341*
Schloss Leopoldskron, *F15,*
269
Schloss Mönchstein (Salzburg)
⊡, *279–280*
Schloss Mondsee ✕⊡,
302–303
Schloss Niederweiden, *146*
Schloss Obermayerhofen
(Blumau) ✕⊡, *169*
Schloss Orth, *F16, 313*
Schloss Petersburg, *351*
Schloss Pöckstein, *350*
Schloss Prielau (Zell am See)
✕⊡, *372*
Schloss Riegersburg, *168*
Schloss Rohrau, *146–147*
Schloss Rosenberg, *371*
Schloss St. Veit, *352*

Schloss Schallaburg, *233*
Schloss Schönborn, *142*
Schloss Schönbühel and der
Donau, *233*
Schloss Seefels (Pötschach)
✕⊡, *340*
Schloss Stubenberg, *166*
Schloss Weikersdorf (Baden)
✕⊡, *139–140*
Schloss Weissenstein, 367
Schlossberg (Graz), *173, 176*
Schlossbergbahn (funicular
railway; Graz), *176*
Schlosshof, *145–146*
Schlosshotel Feyregg (Bad
Hall) ⊡, *228*
Schlossmuseum Linz, *215,*
220
Schlosstheater Schönbrunn
(concert salon; Vienna),
108, 111
Schmetterlinghaus (butterfly
house; Vienna), *34–35*
Schmittenhöhe, *371*
Schneeberghof (Puchberg am
Schneeberg) ✕⊡, *190–191*
Schönbrunn Palace (Vienna),
F12, 3, 63, 65
Schönbrunn Schlosspark
(Palace Park; Vienna), *66*
Schönbühel an der Donau,
233
Schönlaterngasse (Vienna),
12, 18
Schottenhof, *26–27*
Schottenkirche, *22, 27*
Schreiberhaus (winery), *85*
Schruns-Tschagguns, *441,*
456–457
Schubert Festival in
Hohenems, *F17*
Schubertiade (festival;
Schwarzenberg), *441,*
450
Schwarzenberg, *449–450*
Schwarzenberg Palace
(Vienna), *61*
Schwarzenbergplatz (Vienna),
56, 61
Schwarzer Adler (Innsbruck)
✕, *402–403*
Schwarzer Adler (St. Anton
am Arlberg) ⊡, *430–431*
Schwaz, *392, 412–413*
Schweizertor (Vienna), *34,*
39
Secession Building (museum;
Vienna), *4, 56, 61–62*
Seebad, *160*